SIR WILLIAM LAIRD CLOWES was born in 1865 and made his reputation as naval correspondent of *The Times* between 1890 and 1895. He was a member of the Navy League and involved in the agitation for greater naval resources, and his anonymous articles which appeared in the *Daily Graphic* in 1893 undoubtedly influenced the naval Estimates.

He wrote and compiled this seven-volume history of the Royal Navy between 1897 and 1903, involving a number of distinguished contemporary writers to assist him. From America he employed Captain Mahan, author of *The Influence of Sea Power upon History*, and Theodore Roosevelt who covered the history of the war with the United States. Sir Clements Markham, President of the Royal Geographical Society, dealt with the history of voyages and discoveries, and H W Wilson, author of *Battleships in Action*, described many of the minor naval operations.

Vice-Admiral Cuthbert, Baron Collingwood.

From the painting by Henry Howard, R.A. in Greenwich Hospital.

The Royal Navy

A History

From the Earliest Times to the Present

By

Wm. Laird Clowes

Fellow of King's College, London ; Gold Medallist U.S. Naval Institute ;
Hon. Member of the Royal United Service Institution

Assisted by

Sir Clements Markham, K.C.B., P.R.G.S.
Captain A. T. Mahan, U.S.N.
Mr. H. W. Wilson
Col. Theodore Roosevelt, Governor of New York
etc.

Vol. V.

Chatham Publishing

LONDON

PUBLISHER'S NOTE
In the original edition the four photogravure plates and
twelve full-page illustrations faced the text pages as
listed on pages xvii–xviii. In this edition these
illustrations are collected at the back of the book
after page 567, in the order in which they
appeared in the first edition.

Published in 1997 by
Chatham Publishing,
1 & 2 Faulkner's Alley, Cowcross Street,
London EC1M 6DD

Chatham Publishing is an imprint of
Gerald Duckworth and Co Ltd

First published in 1900 by
Sampson Low, Marston and Company

ISBN 1 86176 014 0

A catalogue record for this book is available from the British Library

Printed and bound in Great Britain by Biddles Ltd, Guildford, Surrey

INTRODUCTION TO VOLUME V.

THE present volume contains the record of the whole of the great naval struggle with the empire of the first Napoleon, from the beginning of the renewed war in 1803, when, indeed, Napoleon had not yet assumed the imperial dignity, up to the summer of 1815, when the peace of Europe was secured by the deportation of the wonderful Corsican to St. Helena. I had hoped also to include in the volume the history of the war between Great Britain and the United States of America, 1812–1815; but, owing to the considerable length to which it necessarily extends, I have found myself unable to do so without swelling this section of the book to extravagant proportions. Governor Roosevelt's account of the American War, therefore, will occupy the first place in the next and final volume of the work. Nor do I much regret that I am not now able to include it, seeing that the contents of the present volume are already, so far as they go, complete in themselves, and that, although the two were waged simultaneously, our wars with France and with America in the early years of the nineteenth century had little or no connection one with the other, and were of fundamentally different origin and character.

I am personally responsible for the whole of the instalment of the History now given to the reader. It was originally arranged that my friend, Mr. H. W. Wilson, should contribute the record of the minor operations of the war of 1803–15; and he actually wrote so much of it as brought the story up to nearly the close of the year 1810; but he was unable to revise what he had written, or to complete the account; and that task, in consequence, remained for me. I much regret that pressure of other engagements should have thus deprived me of his co-operation.

The central episode of the present volume is, of course, the ever memorable campaign of Trafalgar, with, as subsidiary, but very closely related incidents, the blockade of Brest, the watching of Toulon, the victories of Calder and Strachan, and the assembly and proceedings of the Invasion Flotilla. After Trafalgar, although other actions were fought in almost every quarter of the field of hostilities, the naval part of the war languished. The nature of its conclusion could be plainly foreseen by all; and not even the later adherence of Russia and Denmark to the cause of the Emperor was then capable of materially influencing the result. Trafalgar determined the 'sea war in our favour; and the issue of the land war, although that issue was delayed for ten years, was, I believe, never for a moment in doubt after the day when Great Britain had so convincingly vindicated her claim to be considered mistress of the seas.

In view, therefore, of the enormous importance, both to Great Britain and to the world at large, of the victory of October 21st, 1805, I desire to call special attention to some of the peculiar circumstances which gave us that victory. In the interests alike of our island security and of our imperial development, it is imperative that we should be under no misapprehensions on such a subject. It is certainly not desirable that we should hastily assume, as I fear too many of us do, that Trafalgar is a success which we can at any moment duplicate, should need arise. It is assuredly not reasonable that we should merely look upon it, as many of us do, as a not very surprising demonstration of the superiority of British foresight, strategy, seamanship, tactics, physique, and bravery. Yet I do not hesitate to say that most of us habitually misinterpret our great naval victories, and the victory of Trafalgar in particular; and that, so long as we continue to misinterpret them, our naval position is a false and dangerous one.

Let us not, for example, continue to cherish the incorrect belief that Englishmen are, or were, braver than Frenchmen or Spaniards; and that we owe our naval successes to that cause. The truth is that no bravery could have exceeded the bravery of the Frenchmen and Spaniards who fought at Trafalgar. Many of their ships, ere they surrendered, had lost nearly half their complements; and the nature and amount of the punishment which our enemies sustained, before submitting, would do credit to the most gallant and determined fighters who ever existed. We, of a surety, showed no finer devotion. Again, we have no right to claim that the foresight and strategy of the Admiralty were sounder than the foresight and strategy of Napoleon. The Admiralty did not so manage as to place a fleet of superior force at the disposal of Nelson for the critical battle. Napoleon, on the contrary, although his difficulties were fully as serious as ours were, did manage to place at the disposal of Villeneuve a force numerically superior to the force of Nelson. Nor is that all. If Napoleon's plans and directions had been loyally and intelligently carried out by his lieutenants, the Franco-Spanish force on October 21st would have been very much more numerically superior than it was to our own. As I have said elsewhere :—

"If Napoleon had succeeded in carrying out the naval combinations which he ordered, and if his admirals had invariably obeyed him, it is probable that the allies might have found themselves in such overwhelming force, on the occasion of the decisive battle, that not even Nelson could have saved Britain from defeat. One of Napoleon's schemes for the invasion of England contemplated the concentration at the mouth of the Channel of fifty sail of the line ; another scheme contemplated the concentration there of at least fifty-six sail, and, in certain contingencies, of about seventy-one. If either of these schemes had been carried out with precision, or if, in March, 1805, Ganteaume had dared to leave Brest with twenty-one sail of the line, and had fallen upon Cornwallis, who had then with him only about sixteen ; or if Salcedo, instead of remaining inactive at Cartagena, had joined Villeneuve when the latter was off the port on April 6th, 1805 ; or if, after his return from the West Indies and his action with Calder, Villeneuve had not put in to Vigo and Ferrol, thence proceeding to Cadiz, instead of to Brest and the Channel, as Napoleon had directed—then the victory of Trafalgar might have been humanly impossible, and the plans of invasion might have been carried forward. If Villeneuve had been active and energetic, he might have put to sea from Ferrol on August 2nd with twenty-nine sail, and caught Calder outside with only nine. Cornwallis, usually a most accomplished strategist, made the mistake, at the very crisis of the campaign, of separating the Channel Fleet, and of leaving himself, with only seventeen sail, between Villeneuve's twenty-seven or twenty-eight ships on the one hand, and Ganteaume's twenty-one on the other. Even on the very eve of the battle, Villeneuve might have left Cadiz, and crushed or driven off Collingwood before the arrival of Nelson." [1]

Neither, then, to superior foresight and strategy, nor to superior bravery, do we, I think, owe the surprising result of Trafalgar. Do we owe it to tactics ? I suspect not ; for Nelson's tactics came as no surprise to the enemy, Villeneuve himself having divined beforehand with fair accuracy what was to be his opponent's method of attack, and having, apparently, made plans to meet it. Moreover, after the battle had been once fairly joined, tactics played very little part in it. Each captain, on the British side at least, was left to fight as he deemed best, subject only to the general

[1] 'The Navy and the Empire.'

rules which had been laid down for him by the Commander-in-Chief. As for the question of physique, it is notorious that when, in the war of 1803–15, it came to hand-to-hand fighting, a Frenchman was generally no bad match for an Englishman.

And yet, in spite of all, Trafalgar ranks as a British victory, and as the greatest and most pregnant success that has ever been won upon the seas. In addition, it ranks as a striking exception to the law that, in fleet actions, victory usually inclines to the side of the " bigger battalions."

But, some may say, surely that law, if there be a law of the sort, does not apply with much consistency to the experiences of the British Navy. On that point, also, strange misconceptions prevail. Most of our great victories have been gained by superiority of numbers. With superiority of numbers we gained the battles of the Kentish Knock, of Portland, of Lowestoft, of Barfleur, of Vigo Bay, of Cape Passaro, of Finisterre (Hawke's), of Lagos, of Quiberon Bay, of Cape St. Vincent (Rodney's), of Martinique, of Lorient, of Camperdown, of November 3rd, 1805 (Strachan's), and of San Domingo, as well as many other actions ; and in engagements to which we have been parties, and in which victory has not inclined to the side of the bigger battalions, we have been almost as often the vanquished as the victors. We cannot, for instance, be said to have beaten the Dutch in any one of the three very hard-fought battles of 1673 ;[1] yet on each occasion we had on our side the superiority of force. And, as late as 1801, the French, with inferior forces, caused us to miscarry in Algeciras Bay. It is true that, with numerically inferior forces, we beat the Dutch, off Scheveningen, in 1653, and in the mouth of the Thames in 1666 ; but, from that time forward, there seems not to have been any case of our defeating a superior enemy in a fleet action until 1794. Even on " The Glorious First of June," the forces on each side were so nearly equal that the difference between the two lines of battle was a matter of about thirty guns only in an action in which upwards of four thousand guns were engaged.

Then came the day of Nelson. With numerically inferior forces we were victorious at St. Vincent (1797), at the Nile, and at

---

[1] In these actions, De Ruijter's genius and influence served the Netherlands just as Nelson's genius and influence served Great Britain in 1805. Moreover, there was the same kind of jealousy and friction between the English and their French allies in 1673 as there was between the French and their Spanish allies at the time of Trafalgar.

Trafalgar. What had previously been a very exceptional issue for an action, became almost the rule when Nelson was a participator. It can have been no mere accidental coincidence; and I think that we are bound to accept as a fact that, especially after his reputation had been well established, Nelson's presence with a British fleet was worth half-a-dozen battleships. It was also worth something more. I need not here try to point out exactly why Nelson was of such remarkable value to his country. Most people will be content to take it that he was a genius, with extraordinary power of influencing and inspiring those under him; that he had a marvellous and contagious devotion both to his country and to his splendid profession; and that he was withal the most brilliant sea-warrior in all history. Therein lies the solution of part of the problem of Trafalgar. Nelson was the British leader. But because we found a Nelson in the hour of our need at the beginning of the nineteenth century, we are not entitled to hope that Nelsons will always be ready to our hand when miracles are called for at sea. There is but one Nelson in history. It may well chance that there will never be another; and, in the meanwhile, we remain face to face with the general law—to which, save under Nelson, there have been so few exceptions, and those as often against us as in our favour—that in fleet actions victory inclines to the bigger battalions. The lesson, therefore, is that Great Britain, instead of relying upon any supposed superiority of her sons, and instead of trusting to find a Nelson when he is needed, should take care always to have the bigger battalions on her side. With the bigger battalions, and with officers and men as good as those of any other nations, she may count on holding her own.

At Trafalgar, I repeat, Nelson was the great controlling factor. But I cannot believe that Nelson's presence in command is alone enough to account for the extraordinary issue of the battle of Trafalgar. We must go further to discover the whole of the explanation of what occurred. We must take into account the general excellence of the gunnery of Nelson's fleet; and the fact that, on the British side, all engaged were animated by common aspirations and allegiance, whereas our foes were of two nationalities, temporarily brought together by political schemers, yet destined to be bitterly and genuinely hostile to one another within a brief three years of the day of the action. When we are in the humour for pluming ourselves upon our past glories, we are apt to forget that, even before October, 1805, public opinion in the Peninsula had begun to object to the French alliance ; that the Spanish authorities already betrayed an unwillingness to supply stores to the vessels of the French fleet ; that Villeneuve, by his weakness and irresolution, had lost much of the confidence of his own people ; that the allied chiefs were jealous of one another ; and that, when the combined fleets quitted Cadiz, the Spaniards went out protesting that they were not ready. We are apt to forget also that, at least according to the views of one of the most competent of modern naval critics, Villeneuve's subordinates disobeyed him and were false to him during the battle.

I quote the following admirable passages from the well-known work [1] of Captain E. Chevalier, of the French Navy :—

" In the engagement of October 21st, 1805, known in history as the battle of Trafalgar, the English fought us, at every point, with superior forces. During several hours, twenty-three vessels only, of the thirty-three which formed the combined fleet, were in action. Would it have been possible, by some skilful combination, or by suitably given orders, if not to confound the plans of the English Admiral, at least to mitigate their effects ? It would appear that there was nothing to prevent the ten leading vessels [2] from taking part in the fight. Such being the case, to whom are we to attribute the inaction of our van ? At 12.10 P.M., the *Royal Sovereign* passed through the line astern of the *Santa Ana.* A little later, the *Bucentaure* and the *Santisima Trinidad* opened fire on the *Victory.* At that time it was impossible to be under any misapprehension concerning the mode of attack adopted by the enemy. At 12.30, just as the *Victory* passed under the stern of the *Bucentaure,* Admiral Villeneuve ordered every ship which was not engaged to get into action. It must be supposed that Rear-Admiral Dumanoir Le Pelley did not consider this signal to be addressed to the vessels which he commanded, seeing that he made no movement in response. By not making a fresh signal directing the van to get instantly into action, Admiral Villeneuve appeared to approve the conduct of his lieutenant. The latter, by intimating at one o'clock that the van had no opponents to engage, demonstrated his unwillingness to take the initiative in any measure which should have for its object modification of the formation of the fleet. Instead of acting, he asked for orders. Vice-Admiral Villeneuve did not give him any, or, rather, he gave him them too late. It was 1.50 when the *Bucentaure* signalled to the van to get into action and to put about together. By that time the centre was no longer offering any serious resistance to the enemy. It was, therefore, too late. Undoubtedly it is the business of a commander-in-chief to direct the movements of his fleet, so long as he can make signals. Admiral Villeneuve, in consequence, may be reasonably held responsible for the inaction of the ten ships ahead of the *Santisima Trinidad.* But this is not equivalent to saying that the conduct of Admiral Dumanoir should meet with approbation. On the contrary, it is well to look more narrowly into the nature of the responsibility which rested upon him. What, in fact, are we to make of the behaviour of a commander of the van who, when the fate of the action was in the balance, waited so long for orders which he knew to be urgently

---

[1] ' Histoire de la Marine Française sous le Consulat et l'Empire,' 223.

[2] *I.e.,* the nine ships originally ahead of the *Santisima Trinidad* and the *Intrépide.*—W. L. C.

needed, since he himself asked for them ? Moreover, ought he not to have recollected that Villeneuve, in his instructions dated December 20th, 1804, had said, ' Any captain who is not in action will not be in his station ; and the signal that recalls him to his duty will be a stain upon his character ' ? He certainly knew that the van was not in its station, seeing that he signalled that it had no enemy to engage. Rear-Admiral Dumanoir, consequently, committed a serious error in not, on his own responsibility, leading the division which he commanded to the assistance of the *Bucentaure*, as soon as that vessel had been surrounded. The calm alone, he declared in one of his dispatches, prevented the van from putting about earlier than it did. Up to the moment, so he wrote in a second dispatch, when the Admiral signalled to the van to put about together, the calm had rendered such an evolution impossible. It seems difficult to admit that explanation. The fourteen vessels which followed the *Royal Sovereign*, and the ten in the wake of the *Victory*, found enough wind to bring them up to the scene of action. The twelfth ship of the northern column, the *Africa*, which had become separated from the English fleet during the night, was able to pass to windward of the entire van, and to join the vessels which were engaging the *Santisima Trinidad*. How is it that, while the English found the thing possible, we did not find it so ?

"It would appear that fatality clung to the movements of our van. When, after having been too long inactive, it did turn towards the scene of the fighting, it split up. As a compact force, it might have done something ; as a divided one, it actually invited the blows of the foe. If Rear-Admiral Dumanoir had been followed by the whole of the van, there is room for belief that he might have fallen upon the ships which surrounded the *Bucentaure* and the *Santisima Trinidad*. Ten vessels which had been scarcely engaged appearing at the centre of action would not, probably, have changed the issue of the day, but certainly they would have inflicted serious losses on the enemy. We lost the *San Agustin*, the *Neptuno*, and the *Intrépide*, over an attempt in that direction. It will be recollected that those three ships were captured separately. The two last covered themselves with glory ; but it is to be regretted that gallant officers like Captains Valdès and Infernet did not understand the necessity for the vessels of the van to remain together. And such a result could be secured only by following Rear-Admiral Dumanoir. As for the *Héros*, *Rayo*, and *San Francisco d'Asis*, their conduct was the more blameworthy in that they did not fight. They made for the rear, avoiding such vessels as they met with. ' I had good right,' wrote the commander of the van, 'to complain in my dispatch of having been followed in the *Formidable* by three ships only. The *Intrépide*, while putting about in answer to the signal, fell on board the *Mont Blanc*, and tore out that ship's fore-mast. She then, together with four other ships, kept away, running with the wind on the quarter to join the allied vessels to leeward ; but, as she sailed very badly, it was not long ere she was overhauled by the enemy ; and it was then that she made that splendid defence of which Captain Infernet is entitled to feel proud. As for the *Neptuno*, Captain Valdès, she was leader of the fleet, and was to windward. After having put about, she remained to windward, kept away, came to the wind again, and manœuvred with the greatest lack of decision. At length, but very late in the day, she made up her mind to follow me. I was well past the Admiral when she fell into my wake. Up to that moment she had kept her luff, having never drawn as close to the enemy as we did.' With only four ships, Dumanoir, as we have seen, did not dare to bear up towards the foe.

"The attitude of the commander of the van was severely condemned in Paris. Upon returning to France, Rear-Admiral Dumanoir, seeing himself in disgrace, asked for an inquiry. Some years elapsed ere that satisfaction was accorded him. However, on September 13th, 1809, nearly four years, that is to say, after the battle of Trafalgar, the government did agree to submit the examination of his behaviour to a court of inquiry. This court, composed of Vice-Admirals Bougainville, who was a Senator, Rosily, and Thevenard, and M. de Fleurieu, also a Senator and a retired captain in the navy, was directed to answer the four questions following: 'Did Rear-Admiral Dumanoir act in accordance with the signals, and with the dictates of duty and honour? Did Rear-Admiral Dumanoir do his best to relieve the centre of the fleet, and especially the flagship of the commander-in-chief? Did Rear-Admiral Dumanoir attack the enemy systematically, and did he get so closely into action as to take as intimate a share in the action as he could take? Did Rear-Admiral Dumanoir quit the scene of action when he was in a condition to fight?' The court of inquiry unanimously decided: 1. That Rear-Admiral Dumanoir had acted in accordance with the signals, and with the dictates of duty and honour; 2. That he had done what the wind and the circumstances had allowed him towards succouring the commander-in-chief; 3. That he had fought, at as close quarters as was possible, such vessels as he had fallen in with as far as the centre of the line; 4. In short, that he had personally quitted the scene of action only when thereto obliged by the damage of all sorts which his ship had sustained, and particularly by the impossibility of manœuvring to which she was reduced by the condition of her masts. Two very important questions seem to have been overlooked by the Minister. Ought Rear-Admiral Dumanoir, ere proceeding to the assistance of the centre, to have waited for the signal which was made by Admiral Villeneuve at 1.50 P.M.? If, on the other hand, it was his duty, as soon as the *Bucentaure* was surrounded—that is, at one o'clock—to lead the van into action, was he in a position to declare that it had been then impossible for him to manœuvre? These were the two points upon which it would have been desirable to learn the opinion of the court, not by implication, but with preciseness.

"We do not find any documents which show clearly the nature of the command exercised by Admiral Gravina when the combined fleet left Cadiz. In his correspondence with the Minister, before putting to sea, Admiral Villeneuve does not mention the squadron of observation. This makes its appearance for the first time in the dispatch written after the battle of October 21st. There is room for supposing that Admiral Gravina had the supreme command of the reserve squadron. As a matter of fact, we find that this squadron was kept on the right of the fleet on the 20th. It retained that position during the evening of the same day, although the combined fleet, at Admiral Villeneuve's orders, had formed line of battle on the starboard tack. Finally, on the 21st, at eight in the morning, it took station at the head of the line, but only after having received an order to that effect from Admiral Gravina. Admiral Decrès, after all the dispatches relating to the battle had reached him, wrote: 'The squadron of observation, commanded by Admiral Gravina, instead of making its way to the points where events called for its presence, placed itself in the rear, and rendered none of those contingent services for which it had been specially designed. It made no movement, allowed itself to be attacked, and fled in detail.' How could the Minister have employed language such as this if he had not been convinced that Vice-Admiral Gravina exercised an independent command over the squadron of observation? Moreover, the court of inquiry which met in 1809 to examine into the conduct of Rear-Admiral Dumanoir, blamed the behaviour of Vice-Admiral Gravina. 'When,' said the court of inquiry, 'the combined fleet went about together, the squadron of Gravina was naturally to windward, and it would have maintained that position if, without any signal from Admiral Villeneuve to the squadron of observation, it had not ranged itself in the line in response to a signal made by M. Gravina.' Elsewhere it declared that 'the squadron of Gravina, which was a squadron of observation, ought to have kept its station to the windward of the line, where it would have covered the centre, instead of moving to the rear to prolong the line, without having been signalled to do so.' The court of inquiry would not have had any opinion to express upon that point if it had not been established that Admiral Gravina had the immediate and personal direction of the squadron of observation. On this hypothesis, it is hard to understand why the squadron did not remain to windward of the fleet. Why, too, having placed himself in the rear, did not Vice-Admiral Gravina, when he saw the evolution of the English method of attack, lead back the squadron of observation to windward of the line of battle? Certainly the signal, made to the rear at 11.30, to keep its luff, so as to be in a position to cover the centre of the fleet, shows what was Villeneuve's opinion. The chief-of-staff, Commander de Prigny, says in his report : 'At 11.30, the breeze being light, a signal was made to the squadron of observation (Gravina), which was then in the rear, and which was bearing away to take station in the wake of the fleet, to keep its luff in order to proceed to reinforce the centre of the line against the attack of the enemy, who was bearing down on it in two columns, as is set forth in Admiral Villeneuve's dispatch.' It is evident that just blame may be given to Admiral Gravina for his behaviour on October 21st."

Although, in short, we won Trafalgar with inferior forces, we happened to have exceptional circumstances in our favour—circumstances which are very unlikely to favour us in an equal degree on any future occasion. Only if we take steps to make ourselves numerically superior to our enemies, and, at the same time, see to it that our ships, our guns, and above all, our officers and men, are as good as theirs, shall we have any reasonable right to count upon being able to retain the dominion of the seas.

In the preparation of materials for the present volume I have been so fortunate as to be assisted by most of those who have aided me in my work on those volumes which have preceded it. As before, I beg to tender them my best thanks. Acknowledgment is also due for the kind voluntary help afforded me by numerous friends, and even by unknown correspondents, who have written from all parts of the world, and especially from America. For their courtesy in procuring information on doubtful points, for lending subjects for the illustrations, or for answering inquiries which, I fear, may have caused them considerable trouble, I am particularly indebted to the late Lord Vernon, Mrs. Nelson Ward, Professor Johan Fogh, of the University of Copenhagen, the Rev. A. G. Kealy, R.N., Captain Prince Louis of Battenberg, R.N., Lady Hoste, Mrs. Crawford, Mr. R. B. Marston, Mr. F. G. O. Brace, Mr. F. Broad Bissell, and, above all, to the First Lord of the Admiralty and other Admiralty officials, to all of whom I am most grateful. Owing to my continuous ill-health, and to my enforced long absences from England in consequence, the co-operation of those more fortunately placed has been unusually valuable, and my demands upon the good offices of such people have been correspondingly numerous ; yet the kindness of my friends has generally exceeded both my requests and my expectations.

W. L. C.

Davos am Platz, *July*, 1900.

ERRATUM.

P. 160.   *For* Galloway, *read* Gallaway.

CONTENTS.

VOLUME V.

—◦◦—

CHAPTER XXXVIII.

CHAPTER XXXIX.

CHAPTER XL.

PUBLISHER'S NOTE
The photogravure plates and twelve full-page illustrations listed below
appear in this edition at the back of the book, after page 567.

LIST OF ILLUSTRATIONS.

VOLUME V.

—◆—

PHOTOGRAVURE PLATES.

FULL-PAGE ILLUSTRATIONS.

ILLUSTRATIONS IN THE TEXT.

NAVAL HISTORY

CHAPTER XXXVIII.

CIVIL HISTORY OF THE ROYAL NAVY, 1803–1815.

Importance of the period—Deterioration of the Navy after Trafalgar—Wholesome teachings of the American War—Sequence of administrative officers—Corruption —The Commission of Inquiry—St. Vincent's excessive zeal—Ill-judged economies —Impeachment of Melville—The Commission of Revision—Malpractices in connection with prize-money—Naval expenditure—Seamen and Royal Marines voted —Increased numbers of officers—Material strength of the Navy—The French "establishment" for ships of war—Confusion in measurement—Improvements in naval architecture—Solid bows—Diagonal timbering—Circular sterns—Teak built ships—Iron knees—Cut-down 74's—Cut-down 60's—Ill-considered new models— Some typical ships of the period—New types of guns—Lighting and buoying the coasts—Chronometers—Logs—Lifeboats—Increased complements—Bad crews— Causes of the deterioration of the personnel—Life on the lower deck—Good and bad officers—Ill-treatment of newly joined men—Routine of a line-of-battle ship— Introduction of rum and cocoa—Bullying midshipmen—A French female prisoner —External painting of ships—Immorality on shipboard—Defrauding the revenue —Punishments—Flogging round the fleet—Flogging at the gangway—Running the gauntlet—Starting—Gagging—Abuse of punishment—The death penalty— Prolonged commissions and deferred payment of wages—Increase of pay— Admirals of the Red—The Royal Naval Asylum—Extension of the Order of the Bath—Unsatisfactory regulations connected with it—Foreign spies in British ships — Sub-Lieutenants — Naval uniform — The pig-tail—The Royal Marine Artillery—The Woolwich Division of Marines—The Berlin Decrees and their consequences—The effect of the war on British trade.

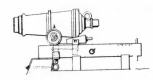

CONGREVE MOUNTING FOR 12-PR.
CARRONADE.

[*From Ch. Dupin.*]

THE twelve eventful years which witnessed the battle of Trafalgar, the war of 1812, and the fall of Napoleon, form the most interesting and important period that is open to the student of the history of the British Navy. Firstly, it was a period of extraordinary triumphs. It saw the exhaustion, by the steady force of sea-power, of the greatest military organisation that the world has ever known; and it exhibited the influence of

B

sea-power under two distinct aspects. At Trafalgar, amid the roar of guns and with the terrible impressiveness that belongs to the critical moments of the world's story, the flower of the navies of France and Spain was destroyed. After Trafalgar, more quietly yet not less surely, what remained of the colonies, the commerce, the wealth and the resources of Great Britain's allied foes was slowly taken from them, until they were rendered so weak by the steady denial to them of any use of the sea, that even the small army of Great Britain was able to take a decisive share in the annihilation of the military horde which, for years, had terrorised Europe.

Secondly, it was a period of great reforms. St. Vincent had already reformed naval discipline, and had given his country a maritime fighting force such as she had never previously possessed. The beginning of the period saw him endeavouring to effect equally radical reforms in the administration of the service; and, although he failed for the moment, and fell from office, his honesty and energy bore fruit quickly in the impeachment of Lord Melville and the consequent exposure of the manifold abuses of the Navy Board, and, at a later date, in the reorganisation by Sir James Graham of the entire administrative system.

Thirdly, it was a period of peculiar danger In the war of the French Revolution, from 1793 to 1802, Great Britain, it ought to be candidly admitted, had been seldom called upon to meet foes who were quite worthy of her steel. The French had lost most of their best officers, and were, to a large extent, led by new men who had neither experience nor ability for command. The Spaniards were untaught, ill-disciplined and devoid of seaman-ship. And although, in the earlier years of the war with the Empire, from 1803 to 1815, both French and Spaniards were more formidable opponents than they had been in the previous period, the British Navy, thanks largely to St. Vincent, had made still more marked advances in efficiency, and remained as superior as ever to its enemies. The experiences of Trafalgar, indeed, bred, it must be feared, in British minds more self-satisfaction and more self-confidence than the event, splendid and unrivalled though it was, altogether justified, and the experiences of the six or seven years after Trafalgar served only to confirm the old-fashioned risky creed that a Briton was as good as any two other men, and certainly better than any two Frenchmen or any three Spaniards. There can be little doubt that, thus in a degree despising the enemy, the British naval administration became less careful than in the past, the British naval officer grew less attentive, and the British seaman deteriorated. Nor was contempt of the enemy the only cause of the falling-off. The decline was not very marked, nor, as regards officers and men, was it at all universal. But there are many indications that a distinct decline had fairly set in long before the year 1812. Then there came into the field a new foe. He was young, he was inexperienced, he was poor. Britain realised all those facts, and prepared to treat him as if he also might be safely despised. She forgot, however, that her new enemy was of her own blood ; and she did not then know that the old blood in the new land had lost none of its old virtue, and, like all the blood of the stock, would be stimulated rather than weakened by the prospect of a really serious struggle. And so there came the American War, with its early defeats and its various disappointments. It brought the lesson which Great Britain needed after her unexampled course of success. The combat was glorious for the United States, although, in spite of the American victories, the campaign was, upon the whole, favourable to the mother country. It was salutary for Great Britain, although it cost her some shame and vast expense ; for it left her, when at length a general peace blessed the world, with truer notions than she would have otherwise entertained of the conditions upon which, if she wished to preserve it, she must be prepared to defend her dominion of the sea. The history, therefore, both civil and military, of the Navy during the years 1803–1815 deserves, and must receive, somewhat fuller consideration than that of the service during any previous era.

The succession of the principal administrative officers, in continuation of the lists given in earlier chapters, was as follows :—

FIRST LORD OF THE ADMIRALTY.

John, Earl St. Vincent, K.B., Admiral.
May 15, 1804. Henry, Viscount Melville.
May 2, 1805. Charles, Lord Barham, Admiral.
Feb. 10, 1806. Rt. Hon. Charles Grey, M.P. (Earl Grey, 1807).
Sept. 29, 1806. Rt. Hon. Thomas Grenville, M.P.
Apr. 6, 1807. Henry, Lord Mulgrave.
May 4, 1810. Rt. Hon. Charles Yorke, M.P.
Mar. 25, 1812. Robert, Viscount Melville (till 1827).

SECRETARIES OF THE ADMIRALTY.

First Secretary.

Evan Nepean (Bart., 1804).
Jan. 21, 1804. William Marsden.
June 24, 1807. Hon. H. W. W. Pole.
Oct.   8, 1809. John Wilson Croker, M.P.
(later, Rt. Hon.), till
1830.

Second Secretary.

William Marsden.
Jan. 21, 1804. Benjamin Tucker.
May 22, 1804. John Barrow.
Feb. 10, 1806. Benjamin Tucker.
Apr.   9, 1807. John Barrow (Bart., 1835).

TREASURER OF THE NAVY.

Rt. Hon. Charles Bragge.
June   3, 1803. Rt. Hon. George Tierney.
May 29, 1804. Rt. Hon. George Canning.
Feb. 22, 1806. Rt. Hon. Richard Brinsley
Sheridan, M.P.
Apr. 15, 1807. Rt. Hon. George Rose,
M.P.

CONTROLLER OF THE NAVY.

Sir Andrew Snape Ham-
ond (1), Bart., Capt.,
R.N.
Feb. 19, 1806. Henry Nicholls, Capt., R.N.
June 7, 1806. Sir   Thomas   Boulden
Thompson, Bart., Capt.,
R.N.(Rear-Adm., 1809;
Vice-Adm., 1814), till
1816.

DEPUTY CONTROLLER OF THE NAVY.

Henry Duncan (1), Capt.,
R.N.
June   7, 1806. Sir Robert Barlow, Kt.,
Capt., R.N.
Nov. 18, 1808. Sir Francis John Hart-
well, Bart., Capt., R.N.
July 30, 1814. William   Shield,   Capt.,
R.N.

SURVEYORS OF THE NAVY.

Sir William Rule (till
1813).
June   7, 1806. Sir Henry Peake, Kt.
(till 1822).
May 26, 1813. Joseph Tucker (till 1831).
May 26, 1813. Sir Robert Seppings, Kt.
(till 1832).

COMMISSIONERS WITHOUT SPECIAL FUNCTIONS.

Aug.   8, 1803. Osborne Markham.
Feb. 11, 1804. Hon. Henry Legge.
May 22, 1805. Hon. Edward Bouverie.

May 22, 1805. John Deas Thomson.
June   7, 1806. Thomas Hamilton.
Sept. 22, 1808. Isaac Schomberg, Capt.,
R.N.
Nov. 18, 1808. Robert Gambier Middle-
ton, Capt., R.N.
May 26, 1813. Hon. Edward Stewart.
Aug. 11, 1813. William   Shield,   Capt.,
R.N.
Apr. 27, 1814. Percy Fraser, Capt., R.N..

CHAIRMAN OF THE COMMISSIONERS OF VICTUALLING.

(In Jan. 1800). John Marsh.
Mar. 1809.   John Clarke Searle, Capt.,
R.N.

COMMISSIONERS AT H.M. DOCKYARDS, ETC.

Chatham.

Charles Hope (1), Capt.,
R.N.
Nov. 18, 1808. Sir Robert Barlow, Kt.,
Capt., R.N. (K.C.B.,
1820).

Portsmouth.

Sir Charles Saxton, Bart.,
Capt., R.N.
July 22, 1806. Hon. George Grey (1),
Capt., R.N. (Bart.,
1814 ; K.C.B., 1820).

Plymouth.

Robert   Fanshawe   (1),
Capt., R.N. (till 1815).

Sheerness.

Isaac Coffin, Capt., R.N.
(Rear-Adm. and Bart.,
1804).
Apr. 24, 1804. Hon. George Grey (1),
Capt., R.N.
Feb. 24, 1807. William Brown (1), Capt.,
R.N.(Rear-Adm., 1811).

Aug. 9, 1811. William Granville Lobb, Capt., R.N.

July 30, 1814. Hon. Courtenay Boyle Capt., R.N. (till 1822).

Gibraltar, etc.

Sir Alexander John Ball, Bart., Capt., R.N.

May 5, 1803. William Albany Otway, Capt., R.N.

July 10, 1805. Robert Gambier Middleton, Capt., R.N.

Nov. 18, 1808. William Granville Lobb, Capt., R.N.

Sept. 9, 1811. Percy Fraser, Capt., R.N.

Dec. 4, 1813. Isaac Wolley, Capt., R.N. (till Jan. 9th, 1818).

Malta.

Dec. 18, 1805. William Brown (1), Capt., R.N.

July 22, 1806. William Granville Lobb, Capt., R.N.

May 25, 1808. Percy Fraser, Capt., R.N.

Sept. 9, 1811. Joseph Larcom, Capt., R.N.

Halifax, Nova Scotia.

John Nicholson Inglefield, Capt., R.N.

Sept. 9, 1811. Hon. Philip Wodehouse, Capt., R.N. (till Aug. 12th, 1819).

CHAIRMAN OF THE COMMISSIONERS FOR THE TRANSPORT SERVICE.

Sir Rupert George, Kt., Capt., R.N. (Bart., 1809).

This Board was discontinued, March 26, 1817, and its business was placed in charge of the Navy Board.

HYDROGRAPHER.

Alexander Dalrymple.

May 28, 1808. Thomas Hurd, Capt., R.N. (till 1823).

Before the beginning of the war with revolutionary France, in 1793, the ties between the civil departments of the Navy and the Board of Admiralty had become strained; and, as a result, the Admiralty, by an Order in Council of January 12th, 1792, had been directed to institute an inquiry into the working of each department. But although it had been quickly seen that corruption and malpractice were rampant, little progress had been made with the investigations, ere the breaking out of hostilities rendered further scrutiny for the time difficult if not impossible. The machine, bad though it was, could not in such days of stress be effectively mended without risk of bringing it to a temporary standstill. Things, therefore, were allowed to go on as before; but the unsatisfactory condition of affairs was never lost sight of by the party of reform ;[1] and in 1801, Lord St. Vincent, who, in 1797, had written,[2] " You may rest assured the civil branch of the Navy is rotten to the very core," assumed the office of First Lord, with both the design and the authority to do his best towards the cleansing of the Augean stables. Yet even St. Vincent, keen as he was in the cause of honesty and efficiency, could not begin his work at once. " Nothing but a radical sweep in the dockyards," he wrote at the time of

[1] In 1798, for example, the Finance Committee represented that an inquiry was urgent.

[2] St. Vincent to Spencer, Aug. 27th, 1797.

his entry upon his duties, " can cure the enormous evils and corruptions in them, and this cannot be attempted till we have peace."

Peace came at length, and then, in pursuance of an Act of 43 Geo. III., Royal Commissioners were appointed in 1803 " for inquiring into irregularities, frauds, and abuses practised in the naval departments, and in the business of prize agency." Between 1803 and 1806, inclusive, they presented no fewer than fourteen reports upon various branches and aspects of the subject submitted to them ; and these, says Admiral Sir R. Vesey Hamilton [1]—

" exposed a mass of iniquity and corruption almost incredible. They discovered a lack of controlling power in the Navy Board that laid open the way to vast peculation and fraud. Accounts, both of cash and stores, remained uncleared for years, and it was reported to Parliament that, at the end of 1805, the outstanding imprests amounted to upwards of eleven millions sterling."

St. Vincent's determination to effect reform, and his unyielding advocacy of a purer system, were not easily forgiven him by his political and service enemies. Still less were they forgiven him by the large army of people who had profited under the old system, and many of whom he had caused to suffer for their dishonesty. Inspired, it must be feared, more by the baffled peculators than by any sincere conviction, Pitt attempted in March, 1804,[2] to fix upon the great seaman himself the responsibility for the abominable state of things that had been found to exist. The charge could not be made good. St. Vincent was not, of course, responsible. Yet, in his anxiety to benefit his country and the service which he loved, he had undoubtedly on several occasions gone to unwise lengths ; and his stern inflexibility raised up for him so many enemies that, when the Addington Ministry fell, he went from office followed by a storm of virulent abuse such as has rarely been showered upon an upright man. He had failed, it would seem, to adequately grasp the fact that the roots of corruption extended to high places as well as to low ones. He had made the mistake of supposing that all men of rank and high office were as honest as himself ; and, directly or indirectly, it was these men who thwarted him, and who would, had they been able, have ruined him.

After Earl St. Vincent's well-meant, but ill-thought-out attempts to lessen the terrible corruption which prevailed throughout the

[1] 'Naval Administration,' p. 15.   [2] Ho. of Comms., Mar. 15th.

service, economy, in certain directions, began to be carried to pernicious lengths.

> " Economy in medicines was particularly enforced. Blue ointment and pills, being requisite only for complaints that might be avoided, were issued in minimum quantity ; so that, for the cure of seamen so disordered, the Captain or Surgeon had to purchase those essential medicines, which were the more imperatively necessary in consequence of an order that no such complaint should be received in the hospitals. Even a more barbarous order than this was enforced : that in consequence of the expense of lint for washing wounds, sponges should be substituted, which, from becoming infected by application to tainted sores, cost the lives of some and the limbs of many. I was myself on a survey at the hospital of Plymouth Dock (now called Devonport) when, I think, seven persons appeared among the objects to be surveyed, who had lost limbs from this cause."[1]

The reports, however, produced in many ways a salutary effect. A First Lord, Henry, Lord Melville, who, at an earlier stage of his career, had twice held the office of Treasurer of the Navy in days when corruption was at its worst, was impeached before the House of Lords in April, 1806; and although, after a trial lasting for fifteen days, he secured an acquittal, the evidence showed very conclusively that he was morally responsible for many malpractices which had been causes of scandal, and that he had repeatedly acted in opposition to laws and regulations which he had himself been instrumental in making.[2] The Navy Board, moreover, was formally reproved[3] by the Admiralty ; and Commissioners for revising and digesting the civil affairs of his Majesty's Navy were appointed, and, between 1806 and 1809 inclusive, produced thirteen reports, many of the recommendations embodied in which became the subject of various Orders in Council issued in 1809. During the period under review, however, the full radical reform did not come, and the sweeping measures advocated by St. Vincent were not adopted. Here and there evils were purged, and improvements were made ; but the ancient machinery, with its clumsiness, its wastefulness, and much of its foulness, remained until Sir James Graham became First Lord of the Admiralty in 1830, and set about the work of something like complete reconstruction. St. Vincent's part in the work must not, however, be forgotten. It is, in fact, to the man who first gave real discipline to the fleet that we owe the beneficial Act of 2 Will. IV., c. 40.

---

[1] Dundonald, ' Observats. on Nav. Affairs,' 18.

[2] ' Reports . . . in relation to the Proceedings upon the Impeachment . . . ' 1806.

[3] ' Letter and Minute of Censure from the Lords of the Admiralty to the Navy Board,' 1805.

Corruption was nowhere more glaring than in connection with the Admiralty Courts and the award of prize-money. Captain William Stanhope Badcock recounts that he was so unfortunate as to lose every penny of the prize-money to which he became entitled during the French war, owing to bankruptcy, in different parts of the world, of four agents to whom he had entrusted his prize affairs.

" These honest people," he says, " have an easy way of getting rid of money committed to their charge. A ship brings captured vessels into harbour. On board comes Mr. A., B., C., or D., with a smirking face and soft tongue, making low bows, hoping he may have the honour—being an accredited agent under a bond for £20,000—to transact the affairs of H.M. ship. Officers generally being strangers in the port, and having orders frequently to proceed to sea again in forty-eight hours after completing water and provisions, have no time to look after, or make inquiries about, stability of prize-agents, and therefore trust the concerns to the first that comes. . . . The prizes in the meanwhile are sold by the agent. Now what does he generally do with the money ? Why, speculates with it on his own account. . . . If he fails, the prize-agent breaks, and off he starts, paying perhaps not a shilling in the pound." [1]

Of course, there remained the bond for £20,000 ; but out of that there would have to be paid huge law costs ; and the balance, divided among, perhaps, the five or six thousand officers and men in a fleet of moderate size, would be scarcely worth having.

As for the extraordinary corruption prevailing in the Admiralty Courts abroad, the extortionate nature of their fees, and the manner in which prize-money was swallowed up by them, even when there was no bankruptcy on the part of the prize-agents, one has but to read Chapter XXXI. of Dundonald's ' Autobiography of a Seaman.' At Malta, Dundonald found that one Jackson, who held the office of Marshal of the Court, did his Marshal's work by deputy, in order that he might also hold the office of Proctor, and might, as Proctor, charge for attending upon himself as Marshal. This person also made various illegal perquisites ; and, until Dundonald exposed them, the local malpractices were facilitated by the fact that the table of Court fees, instead of being hung up, as directed by the Act, in the Court itself, were wafered behind the door of the Judge's private water-closet.

The expenditure upon the Navy, and the number of seamen and Royal Marines voted during each of the years 1803–1815 were :—

[1] Lovell, ' Personal Narr.,' p. 82.

EXPENDITURE ON THE NAVY, 1803–1815,

as voted by Parliament; with the authorised number of Seamen and
Royal Marines for each year.

Year.	"Extra."	"Ordinary."	—	No. of Seamen and Marines.	Total Naval Supplies Granted.
	£	£			£
1803	901,140	1,488,238	2 mos. 4 mos. 7 mos.	50,000 60,000 100,000	10,211,378
1804	948,520	1,345,670	..	100,000	12,350,606
1805	1,553,690	1,394,940	..	120,000	15,035,630
1806	1,980,830	1,435,353	..	120,000	18,864,341
1807	2,134,903	1,557,934	1 mo. 12 mos.	120,000 130,000	17,400,337
1808	2,351,188	1,142,959	..	130,000	18,087,547
1809	2,296,030	1,408,437	..	130,000	19,578,467
1810	1,841,107	1,511,075	..	145,000	18,975,120
1811	2,046,200	1,578,113	..	145,000	19,822,000
1812	1,696,621	1,447,125	..	145,000	19,305,759
1813	2,822,031	1,700,135	..	140,000	20,096,709
1814	2,086,274	1,730,840	7 mos. 6 mos.	117,400 90,000	19,312,070
1815	2,116,710	2,278,929	3 mos. 10 mos.	70,000 90,000	19,032,700[1]

[1] Including £2,000,000 towards paying off the Navy Debt.

The number of Royal Marines fluctuated as follows during the
period. In 1803 it rose from 12,000 to 22,400; in 1804 it was
22,000; in 1805, 30,000; in 1806, 29,000; in 1807 it rose from
29,000 to 31,400; in 1808 it was 31,400; in 1809, 31,400; in 1810,
31,400; in 1811, 31,400; in 1812, 31,400; in 1813, 31,400; in 1814
it was reduced from 31,400 to 16,000; and in 1815, after having
stood at 15,000 for the first three lunar months of the year, it rose
again to 20,000 for the last ten months.

In view of the subsequent block of promotion caused by the
enormous entries of officers during the war, and of the difficulties
which were experienced in providing for those officers for whom

—	1803	1804	1805	1806	1807	1808	1809	1810	1811	1812	1813	1814	1815
Admirals [1]	45	41	50	55	52	48	46	49	65	62	64	65	70
Vice-Admirals [1]	36	32	36	50	57	55	59	61	60	65	69	68	73
Rear-Admirals [1]	51	50	63	56	50	58	71	60	56	60	68	76	76
Captains . .	668	673	639	617	693	700	689	725	753	777	802	798	824
Commanders .	413	409	422	416	502	501	543	608	558	566	602	628	762
Lieutenants .	2480	2457	2472	2437	2728	2912	3036	3114	3071	3163	3268	3285	3211
Masters . .	529	541	556	541	429	549	491	501	544	567	629	674	666

[1] The names, and dates of commissions, etc., of these, will be found in the Appendices.

there were no hopes of employment after the general peace of 1815, it is useful to show, as is shown in the foregoing table, the increase in the active list of Flag-officers, Captains, Commanders, Lieutenants, and Masters in the period under consideration.

The active sea-going material of the Navy, exclusive of harbour vessels and inefficient or non-fighting ships, underwent almost as notable an increase as the number of officers, and may be thus tabulated :—

THE ACTIVE LIST OF THE SHIPS OF THE ROYAL NAVY, 1803–1815.[1]

Class.	1803	1804	1805	1806	1807	1808	1809	1810	1811	1812	1813	1814	1815
First-rates . .	6	6	7	7	6	6	6	6	7	7	7	7	8
Second-rates . .	15	15	14	15	15	11	12	11	12	10	9	8	7
Third-rates . .	90	94	95	98	102	109	109	107	105	103	108	103	94
Total of the line	111	115	116	120	123	126	127	124	124	120	124	118	109
Fourth-rates . .	11	10	13	13	10	10	8	7	6	5	3	10	9
Fifth-rates . .	102	106	114	125	138	141	144	146	139	137	123	134	126
Sixth-rates . .	22	22	25	26	29	32	28	24	20	18	19	29	42
Sloops	78	91	121	131	172	191	251	246	225	209	214	212	185
Bombs. . . .	10	17	17	15	12	10	10	8	5	7	6	8	9
Fireships . . .	2	2	1	..	..	..	..	..	..	..	..	..	..
Brigs, cutters, etc.	52	60	127	160	173	163	160	144	138	127	121	126	74
Grand total . .	388	423	534	590	657	673	728	699	657	623	610	637	554

The total tonnage of the vessels enumerated above was, in 1803, 356,400 ; in 1805, the year of Trafalgar, 407,814 ; in 1807, 465,647 ; in 1809, 501,596 ; in 1811, 479,986 ; in 1813, 460,396 ; and in 1815, 446,720.

It may be mentioned here, although, perhaps, it is not of very great importance, that most of the French-built men-of-war which were captured by Great Britain between 1793 and 1815 had been constructed according to an "establishment" prescribed by an ordinance of 1786. English writers on the naval architecture of the period have, almost without exception, committed the error of assuming the French foot, or *pied du roi*, to have been equal to the English foot of 12 inches, whereas it was, in fact, 6·57 per cent. longer. In translating, therefore, these writers, omitting to allow for the difference, have ascribed to French vessels dimensions and

---

[1] Chiefly from the Appendices in James. These, however, have been checked by reference to Steel, and the official lists, and to the 'Naval Chronicle.'

tonnage which, according to the accepted formulæ, are inconsistent one with the other. In short, the dimensions given are usually not great enough to account for the alleged tonnage. The same writers have also, in some instances, committed the further error of giving the dimensions of the frames only, instead of the outside measurements ; and thus the discrepancy has been magnified. It may be useful, therefore, to give, reduced to British feet and inches, the dimensions for the principal classes of ships as fixed by the French establishment of 1786,—an establishment which, with but little modification, remained in vogue in France until fifteen or twenty years after the fall of the First Empire. These were as follows :—

—	120-gun[1] ship.		110-gun ship.		80-gun[2] ship.		74-gun[3] ship.		64-gun ship.		40-gun[4] frigate (18-pr.)		Frigate (12-pr.)		20-gun[5] corvette.		"Aviso"	
	Ft.	ins.	Ft.	ins.	Ft.	ins.	Ft.	ins.	Ft.	ins.	Ft.	ins.	Ft.	ins.	Ft.	ins.	Ft.	ins.
Length : Lower deck . .	208	10	197	1	191 10 to 196 1		181	2	166	3	153	6	144	10	119	4	85	2
Extreme outside breadth .	55	1	54	6	52	4	48	9	45	0	40	0	37	10	31	0	25	0
Draught, forward . . .	24	2	23	6	22		21	2	20	0	16	2¼	14	7	12	6	10	8
Draught, aft	26	8	26	3	24	0	22	11	21	0	17	0¼	16	4	14	2	12	3
Height of lowest ports above water-line. . .	5	8	5	4	5	10	5	10	5	4	6	4½	6	4½	..		..	
Tons. Load displacement	5246		4910		3825		3248		2300		1479		1162		546		266	

[1] E.g., *Commerce de Marseille.*   [2] E.g., *Canopus*, ex *Franklin.*   [3] E.g., *Tigre, Pompée.*
[4] E.g., *Renommée, Loire.*   [5] E.g., *Babet, Danaé, Bonne Citoyenne.*

It has not been deemed necessary, for the purposes of this work, to systematically examine into the absolute correctness or otherwise of the dimensions of French prizes as set forth in such works as those of Charnock, Fincham, and James, or in the dispatches of the captors ; nor, indeed, are the facts requisite for the making of such an examination always forthcoming. What has been written will, however, indicate to those who are specially interested in the question the most probable source of any small discrepancies and inconsistencies which may be observed in the published statistics. Further information should be sought for in the works of French authors, especially in those of the late Admiral Pâris.[1]

One of the greatest improvements in naval architecture during the period under review was the general substitution of the round

[1] See also ' U.S. Mag.,' Dec. 1886.

solid bow for the old-fashioned beak-head. The improvement
originated as follows. Mr. Robert Seppings,[1] the well-known
naval architect, when master-builder at Chatham, received instructions to reduce the *Namur* from a 90 to a 74-gun ship. It
having occurred to him that by not removing the solid bow on the
second deck in order to build up instead of it the flimsy fabric called
the beak-head, he would not only leave additional strength to that
part of the ship's frame, but would also afford some protection to
the crew against raking fire from ahead, he suffered the *Namur's*
circular bow to remain. The advantages of the innovation struck
everyone who saw the vessel when she was finished as a 74 in 1804;
and it was subsequently ordered that all new ships built for the
Navy should be constructed with round bows. Mr. Seppings also
introduced two other improvements of scarcely inferior importance.
One was the use of diagonal instead of rectangular timbering. The
system was first tried in 1800 upon the *Glenmore*, 32; and in 1805
it was applied at Chatham to the *Kent*, 74, in order to give additional
strength to that ship. It was afterwards applied, in a partial degree,
to the *Warspite*, 74, and then, completely, to the *Tremendous*, 74,[2] the
principle being carried out even in the building of the decks. The
Tremendous was found to be so thorough a success that the diagonal
system quickly became generally employed in the repairing as well
as in the building of ships for the Navy. The *Howe*,[3] launched on
March 28th, 1815, was the first vessel laid down and built in accordance with the new practice. Seppings's third great improvement
was the substitution of rounded, or "circular," for square sterns in
ships. These gave greatly increased strength, enlarged the stern
battery, diminished the risk of being pooped, and did away with the
projecting quarter-galleries which had been found greatly to obstruct
a ship's progress when she was sailing on a wind.[4] By an order of
June 13th, 1817, it was directed that all new ships, down to fifth-
rates inclusive, were to be built with rounded sterns, and that old
vessels brought forward for extensive repairs were to have rounded
sterns built into them if the timbers of the old square sterns proved
to be defective. An improvement not due to Mr. Seppings was the
occasional adoption of teak for the construction the hulls of

---

[1] Later Sir Robert Seppings, one of the Surveyors of the Navy.
[2] When she was rebuilt.
[3] Of 2619 tons, and 120 guns. She was built at Chatham.
[4] For a full account of these improvements, *see* Mr. J. Knowles's appendix on the
subject in 'Elements of Naval Architecture.'

H.M. ships. The country had already benefited by the services of teak-built Indiamen which had been presented to, or bought into, the Navy; but the first ship built of teak for the Navy was the *Salsette*,[1] 36, which was launched at Bombay in 1805.

The introduction of iron instead of wooden knees in the construction of men-of-war, deserves notice as a very considerable improvement. It was due to Mr. T. Roberts, master shipwright, of Pembroke Yard, and was generally adopted from about the year 1808.

The numerous successes of American cruisers, and the proved effectiveness of the American 44-gun frigates during the early part of the war of 1812–15, led to much feverish activity and to several ill-considered innovations in the British dockyards. Three of the smaller 74's[2] were cut down fore and aft to the clamps of the quarter-deck and forecastle, and were armed and manned as follows :—

Main-deck	.	.	.
Upper deck	.	.	.

Main-deck . . . 28 long 32-prs. ⎫
Upper deck . . . 28 carr. 42-prs. ⎬ 495 men and boys.
2 long 12-prs. ⎭

58 guns.

At about the same time two vessels of a new class,[3] styled " frigates with spar-decks," but being in reality two-deckers, were built of pitch-pine, with very light scantling, and were thus armed and manned :—

Main, or " upper " deck . 30 long 24-prs. ⎫
Upper, or " spar " deck . 26 carr. 42-prs. ⎬ 480 men and boys.
4 long 24-prs. ⎭

60 guns.

Another 60-gun " frigate " was produced by cutting down the *Akbar*, a teak-built Indiaman,[4] which in still later days became the 44-gun frigate *Cornwallis*.[5] But these " frigates," being all two-deckers, might without shame have been avoided by the American

---

[1] Called, for a short time, the *Pitt*.

[2] *Goliath, Majestic,* and *Saturn*.

[3] *Leander*, 1572 tons, from designs by Sir William Rule: *Newcastle*, 1556, from designs by M. L. C. Barrallier, who was then Rule's assistant, and who was later chief constructor at Toulon. The *Java*, originally designed as a 52-gun frigate, was altered, while on the stocks, to a 60 of the *Leander* class.

[4] Purchased in 1801.

[5] Used for some years as a troopship.

44's; and, if one of them had taken an American 44, she would have gained no great glory by the exploit.   Of regular frigates, five were built from the draught, slightly modified, of the *Endymion*.   Of these, the *Forth*, *Liffey*, and *Severn*, were of fir, and the *Glasgow* and *Liverpool*, of pitch-pine.   They carried :—

Main-deck . . .	28 long 24-prs.	}
Quarter-deck and forecastle	20 carr. 32-prs.	} 350 men and boys.
	2 long 9-prs.	}

50 guns.

BRIG'S 12-PR. CARRONADE OF THE TIME OF THE AMERICAN WAR OF 1812–1815.

(From a drawing by E. W. Cooke, R.A.)

Numerous other frigates, chiefly of the old 18-pounder classes, were also hastily and cheaply built of red and yellow pine, some of them being given medium 24's instead of long 18's.   It was deemed necessary, moreover, for the purpose of meeting the Americans, to build not only special frigates but special sloops as well.   The Americans had in the *Peacock*, *Wasp*, and *Frolic* vessels of about 540 British tons, carrying one hundred and seventy-five men and boys, and mounting twenty carronade 32-pounders and two long 18-pounders, though rated merely as 18-gun sloops. To oppose this class, as many as eighteen vessels, to be hurriedly built of fir, were foolishly ordered, a reduced and modified *Bonne Citoyenne*[1] being taken as the model. These craft measured only 115 feet 6 inches on the main-deck, with a beam of 29 feet 8 inches, and were of but 455 tons. When they had been supplied with twenty carronade 32-pounders, and two long 9-pounders, it was found that the batteries were hopelessly overcrowded; and the 9-pounders had to be returned to the shore. The sloops then went to sea with their twenty carronades and a complement of only one hundred and thirty-five men and boys. It soon appeared that they had been so wretchedly designed that the tillers could not be worked while the stern carronades were pointing through their ports. Short-sightedness and hurry inspired the Admiralty at that critical period; and scarcely a ship that was built or altered for the particular purpose of fighting the cruisers of the United States ever fulfilled the expectations of those who had been responsible for her.

Models of many of the most typical vessels which were added to the Navy during the period under review are to be seen at Greenwich. Among them are whole or half-block models of the following ships:—

Name.	Length of Gun-deck.		Beam.		Depth in Hold.		Tons.	Men.	Guns.	When and where Built, or how Acquired, etc.
	Ft.	In.	Ft.	In.	Ft.	In.				
Caledonia	205	0	54	6	23	2	2,616	875	120	Launched 1808, at Devonport. Designed by Sir W. Rule.
Hercules	176	1	48	4¼	21	0	1,750	590	80	Launched 1815, at Chatham. Designed by Surveyor's Dept.
Bulwark	181	10	49	3	20	7	1,940	590	74	Launched 1807, at Portsmouth. Designed by Sir W. Rule.
Java	171	11½	44	1	14	3	1,458	480	60	Launched 1815, at Devonport. Designed by Surveyor's Dept.
President	173	3	44	4	13	11	1,533	..	50	Taken 1815, from the Americans.
Chesapeake	151	0	40	11	13	9	1,135	315	48	Taken 1813, from the Americans.
Lively	154	1	39	6	13	6	1,076	284	46	Launched 1804, at Woolwich. Designed by Sir W. Rule.
Euryalus	145	2	38	2½	13	3	946	264	42	Launched 1803, by Adams, Bucklershard. Designed by Sir W. Rule.
Lacedemonian	150	4	40	0½	12	9½	1,073	..	38	Launched 1812, at Portsmouth. Built after the French *Hébé*, taken in 1782.
Barbados	140	0	36	7	16	0	800	195	36	Ex-*Brave*. Taken from the French, 1804.
Eden	108	6	30	8	9	0	451	150	28	Launched 1804, by Courtney, Chester. Designed by Sir W. Rule.
Andromeda	129	7	36	5⅜	11	0	812	195	24	Ex-*Hannibal*. Taken 1812, from the Americans.
Florida	119	5½	32	0	14	2	539	135	20	Ex-*Frolic*. Taken 1814, from the Americans.
Epervier	95	1	28	6	8	9½	315	121	16	Taken 1803, from the French.
Cadmus	90	3	24	6	11	0	237	76	10	Launched 1808, by Dudman, Deptford. Designed by H. Peake.

[1] *Bonne Citoyenne*, 120 ft. 1 in. long on main-deck; 30 ft. 11 in. broad; 511 tons; 135 men. American *Frolic*, 119 ft. 6 in. long on main-deck; 32 ft. broad; 540 tons; 22 guns; 175 men. It will be seen, therefore, that, even before the reduction, the *Bonne Citoyenne* class was inferior to the *Frolic*.

More than once, during the French wars, the inconvenience of having in a single ship guns of three or four different calibres, with, of course, different-sized and non-interchangeable carriages, shot, sponges, utensils, etc., was felt; and more than once proposals were made to remedy it.   But nothing practical was done until certain inventors, notably Congreve, Texier de Norbec, Bourdé, Blomefield, Thévenard, and Gover, thought of applying to naval ordnance further modifications of those principles which had resulted, several years earlier, in the production of the carronade.   It was then realised that although a ship could not properly carry upon her upper or middle deck the same weight of guns as upon her lower deck, it might be desirable to make the difference of weight dependent not, as had been the case up to that time, upon differences of calibre, but upon differences in the length and weight of guns of the same calibre. The long gun already existed; so did the carronade.   When the several inventors who have been named appeared with various medium guns which were found to be more or less excellent weapons, the solution of the problem became easy.   In the period now under consideration only medium 24-pounders[1] seem to have found their way into favour; and, naturally, any extensive re-armament of the Navy was rendered difficult, especially in war-time, by considerations of cost and of the capacities of the foundries. Yet, at the end of 1806, several British two-deckers were, in deference to the trend of service opinion on the subject, re-armed throughout with guns of one calibre, namely, long 24-pounders, medium (Gover) 24-pounders, and 24-pounder carronades; so that, as James says, " the ships, being old and weak, had much less weight to carry, with only a slight diminution in their broadside force." [2]   The lengths and weights, with carriages, of the three guns were :—

	Long 24-pr.		Medium 24-pr.		24-pr. carr.	
	ft	in.	ft.	in.	ft.	in.
Length . .	9	6	6	6	3	8

	cwt.	qrs.	cwt.	qrs.	cwt.	qrs.
Weight . .	58	3	39	0	19	0

Thus the differences between the old and new armaments and broadside weights of the re-armed 74's were as follows :—

---

[1] Of the Gover, Congreve, and Blomefield types.   The first and third differed little from each other in appearance ; the second had a muzzle like that of a carronade.

[2] James (1837), iv. 279.

	Guns.	Weight of guns and carriages.	Broadside weight of metal
Old { Lower deck . . 28 long 32-prs. Main-deck . . 28 long 18-prs. Quarter-deck . . 6 long 12-prs. and F'castle . . 12 carr. 32-prs. }		181 cwt.	928 lbs.
New { Lower deck . . 28 long 24-prs. Main-deck . . 28 Gover 24-prs. Quarter-deck . . 4 Gover 24-prs. and F'castle . . 14 carr. 24-prs. }		157 cwt.	888 lbs.

But, although the innovation was satisfactory, little further progress was made in the same direction until after the peace.

During the period under review continuous progress was made in the lighting and buoying of the coasts. The Bell Rock lighthouse, now the oldest rock lighthouse tower in Great Britain, was begun in 1807 and completed in 1811; and the lighting of the Goodwin Sands, begun in 1795 by the mooring of the North Sand Head lightship, a model of which is still preserved at Trinity House, was improved in 1809, when the Gull lightship was first put in position. It may be mentioned here that the South Sand Head lightship dates only from 1832, and the East Goodwin lightship from as late as 1874.

Some of the greatest improvements in the chronometer are due to Earnshaw, who was born in 1749, and died in 1814. He invented the spring detent escapement, and the compensation balance, both of which are still used. Massey's mechanical log, the first of its kind, and the ancestor of the modern " Cherub," was invented in 1808. It was not, however, much employed. Of far greater practical value was Greathead's lifeboat, which dates from 1789, and which, in 1802, received the patronage of Trinity House, and a substantial reward from Parliament. From that time it rapidly grew in favour.

The earliest lessons of the war with the United States in 1812–15 taught, or seemed to teach, that the complements of British frigates were, upon the whole, too small. The established complements, therefore, which, since 1804, had been increased, reduced, and again slightly increased, were, by an order of January, 1813, fixed as follows: the 24-pounder 40-gun frigate, 350; the large 38-gun frigate, 320; the 18-pounder 36-gun frigate, 284; the 18-pounder 32-gun frigate, 270; and the 18-gun quarter-decked ship-rigged sloop, 135 men and boys. But naval opinion appeared to incline to the belief that the increase might, with advantage, have been carried even further, and that the complements included far too great a proportion of boys. A more dangerous mistake committed by the administration during the war was that of sending to sea against the Americans quantity rather than quality of ships and men. Many of the ships commissioned were old or weak ; many of the complements were raw or otherwise unsatisfactory. Had only the best ships of their respective classes, and only the pick of the seamen, been despatched to American waters, where Great Britain had to meet the most capable naval foe she had ever encountered, the results of some of the earlier actions of the war might, perhaps, have been different. The inferior ships and men would still have been good enough to hold in check the demoralised and exhausted cruisers of France. To say this is not to excuse British defeats nor to minimise American successes. The prime element of all naval strategy and tactics is the putting of superior force where it can be most effectively employed. The Americans did not underrate their enemy, and, both in the council-room and afloat, did all they could to beat him. The British began by underrating their enemy, and by dreaming of dealing with him as they had so often dealt with an ill-disciplined Frenchman or an incompetent Spaniard. It is therefore childish to cry out, as many a British writer has cried out, that British ships were often beaten simply and solely because they were in one way or another overmatched. That is not the reason. The reason is that Washington, though possessed of fewer resources, looked further and thought deeper than London did.

Concerning the nature and causes of the deterioration of the personnel of the Navy between the time of Trafalgar and the outbreak of the war with the United States, there are many hints to be found in the pages of Lord Dundonald's ' Observations on Naval Affairs ' (1847). Take, for example, the following from among the numerous resolutions which were brought forward by his lordship in the House of Commons on July 5th, 1813 :—

" That it is an indisputable fact that long and unlimited confinement to a ship, as well as to any other particular spot, and especially when accompanied with the diet necessarily that of ships of war, and a deprivation of the usual recreations of man, seldom fails to produce a rapid decay of the physical powers, the natural parent, in such cases, of despondency of mind.

" That the duration of the term of service in His Majesty's Navy is absolutely without any limitation; and that there is no mode provided for by law for the fair and impartial discharge of men therefrom ; and that, according to the present practice, decay, disease, incurable wounds, or death can alone procure the release of any seaman of whatever age or whatever length of service.

" That seamen who have become wholly unfit for active service are, in place of being discharged and rewarded according to their merits and their sufferings, transferred to ships on harbour duty,[1] where they are placed under officers wholly unacquainted with their character and former conduct, who have no other means to estimate them but on the scale of their remaining activity and bodily strength; where there is no distinction made between the former petty officers and the common seamen, between youth and age; and where those worn-out and wounded seamen who have spent the best part of their lives, or have lost their health, in the service of their country, have to perform a duty more laborious than that of the convict felons in the dockyards, and with this remarkable distinction, that the labours of the latter have a known termination.

" That though the seamen thus transferred and thus employed have all been invalided, they are permitted to re-enter ships of war on actual service; and that such is the nature of the harbour duty that many, in order to escape from it, do so re-enter, there being no limitation as to the number of times of their being invalided, or that of their re-entering.

" That to obtain a discharge from the Navy by purchase, the sum of £80 sterling is required by the Admiralty, which, together with other expenses, amounts to twenty times the original bounty, and is equal to all that a seaman can save, with the most rigid economy, during the average period in which he is capable of service; that this sum is demanded alike from men of all ages, and of all lengths of servitude, from those pensioned for wounds, and also from those invalided for harbour duty; thus converting the funds of Greenwich and the reward of former services into a means of recruiting the Navy."[2]

Dundonald also attributes some part of the deterioration of naval efficiency to the undue prominence which, about the year 1806, began to be assigned to what is still vulgarly called in the service " spit and polish." Too much importance was attached to the " brightening of brass heads, of bitts, and capstan hoops," and too little to the condition of the ship as a pure fighting machine.[3]

" It will, perhaps, hardly be credited hereafter that there was at that time no regular system of exercise [in gunnery] established by authority in the British Navy, but that each ship had its own particular plan and method, varying, of course, according to the experience and degree of information possessed by the Captain, as well as to the degree of importance which he attached to the subject."[4]

It had not begun to be realised, save by a few, that gunnery was the great determining factor in naval warfare, and that good gunnery could be secured only by constant practice. British seamen had seldom, indeed, had opportunities of learning what good gunnery was.

" Even in the later periods of Napoleon's reign, when he had certainly effected considerable improvements in his marine, the state of practical gunnery was still so

---

[1] This practice was established in 1803.

[2] 'Observations on Naval Affairs,' 130, 131.

[3] *Ibid.*, p. 6.

[4] 'Remarks on the Conduct of the Naval Administration of Great Britain since 1815.' By a Flag Officer. 3rd ed., 1847, p. 52.

wretched that we have seen ships fully officered, superbly equipped, and strongly manned, playing batteries of twenty or thirty heavy guns against our vessels, crowded with men, without more effect than might easily have been produced by one or two well-directed pieces ; and we have seen some cases in which heavy frigates have used powerful batteries against our vessels for a considerable time without producing any effect at all." [1]

For an account of life on the lower deck of a British man-of-war at the time of Trafalgar there is perhaps no better authority than a rare little book [2] which, although it appears not to have been published until 1836, was written by a man who had served as a seaman in the *Revenge* from May, 1805, until the end of 1811, during which period that ship was commanded by Captain Robert Moorsom, the Hon. Charles Elphinstone Fleeming, Sir John Gore (2), the Hon. Charles Paget, M.P., Aelxander Robert Kerr, and others.

The writer was no captious and unreasonable grumbler. Summarising his conclusions as to the naval service in his day, he says : " There is, indeed, no profession that can vie with it ; and a British seaman has a right to be proud, for he is incomparable when placed alongside those of any other nation." Yet his revelations, the truth of which is entirely borne out by other evidence which might be cited, show that, especially with what was the normal type of Captain in command, the line-of-battle ship of the early years of the century was often a hell upon earth. There were, of course, many officers who knew how to make themselves beloved as well as respected by their ship's companies ; but, says Jack—

" out of a fleet of nine sail of the line I was with, there were only two Captains thus distinguished. They kept order on board without resorting to the frequent and unnecessary call upon the Boatswain and his cat, adopted by the other seven ; and what was the consequence ? Those two ships beat us in reefing and furling ; for they were not in fear and dread, well knowing they would not be punished without a real and just cause. Those men would have stormed a battery, or have engaged an enemy at sea, with more vigour and effect than the other seven ; for the crews of those seven felt themselves so degraded at being wantonly and unmanly beaten about, that their spirits were partly broken."

The writer joined the Navy voluntarily ; yet his early treatment half inclined him to regret the step which he had taken.

[1] 'Remarks on the Conduct of the Naval Administration of Great Britain since 1815,' p. 55.

[2] 'Nautical Economy ; or Forecastle Recollections of Events during the last War. Dedicated to the brave Tars of Old England by a Sailor, politely called by the Officers of the Navy Jack Nasty-Face.' Published by William Robinson, 9 Staining Lane. N.D. pp. xvi. + 124, 8vo. Internal evidence shows the author's ship to have been the *Revenge*, though he does not mention her by name.

" After having," he says, " been examined by the doctor, and reported sea-worthy, I was ordered down to the hold, where I remained all night (9th May, 1805) with my companions in wretchedness, and the rats running over us in numbers. When released, we were ordered into the Admiral's tender, which was to convey us to the Nore. Here we were called over by name, nearly two hundred, including a number of the ' Lord Mayor's Men,' a term given to those who enter to relieve themselves from public disgrace, and who are sent on board by any of the City magistrates for a street frolic or night charge. These poor fellows have a sad time of it, as they are the derision of the old and more experienced and hardened sailors, who generally cut the tails from their coats, and otherwise abuse and ridicule them. Upon getting on board this vessel, we were ordered down in the hold, and the gratings put over us ; as well as a guard of Marines placed round the hatchway, with their muskets loaded and fixed bayonets, as though we had been culprits of the first degree, or capital convicts. In this place we spent the day and following night huddled together ; for there was not room to sit or stand separate ; indeed, we were in a pitiable plight, for numbers of them were sea-sick, some retching, others were smoking, whilst many were so overcome by the stench, that they fainted for want of air. As soon as the officer on deck understood that the men below were overcome with foul air, he ordered the hatches to be taken off, when daylight broke in upon us ; and a wretched appearance we cut, for scarcely any of us were free from filth and vermin."

At the Nore the men were sent to the receiving ships, where they were supplied with slops, the cost of which was subsequently stopped out of their pay, and whence they were presently distributed among those sea-going vessels whose complements were deficient. Jack complains that in the receiving ships the transient visitors were systematically plundered by the regular crews ; but he seems to have been quickly drafted to the *Revenge,* and to have then sailed in her to join the Channel Fleet. He gives the following account of the routine on board : —

" Our crew were divided into two watches, starboard and larboard. When one was on deck the other was below : for instance, the starboard watch would come on at eight o'clock at night, which is called eight bells ; at half-past is called one bell, and so on ; every half-hour is a bell, as the hour-glass is turned, and the messenger sent to strike the bell, which is generally affixed near the fore-hatchway.[1] It now becomes the duty of the officer on deck to see that the log-line is run out, to ascertain how many knots the ship goes an hour, which is entered in the log-book, with any other occurrence which may take place during the watch. At twelve o'clock, or eight bells in the first watch, the Boatswain's Mate calls out lustily, ' Larboard watch, a-hoy.' This is called the middle watch, and when on deck, the other watch go below to their hammocks, till eight bells, which is four o'clock in the morning. They then come on deck again, pull off their shoes and stockings, turn up their trowsers to above their knees, and commence ' holy-stoning ' the deck, as it is termed (for Jack is sometimes a little impious in the way of his sayings). Here the men suffer from being obliged to kneel down on the wetted deck, and a gravelly sort of sand strewed over it. To perform this work they kneel with their bare knees, rubbing the deck with a stone and the sand, the grit of which is often very injurious. In this manner the watch continues till about four bells, or six o'clock ; they then begin to wash and swab the decks till seven bells, and at

---

[1] It is now generally near the quarter-deck hatchway.

eight bells the Boatswain's Mate pipes to breakfast. This meal usually consists of burgoo, made of coarse oatmeal and water; others will have Scotch coffee, which is burnt bread boiled in some water, and sweetened with sugar. This is generally cooked in a hook-pot in the galley, where there is a range. Nearly all the crew have one of these pots, a spoon, and a knife; for these things are indispensable; there are also basins, plates, etc., which are kept in each mess, which generally consists of eight persons, whose berth is between two of the guns on the lower deck, where there is a board placed, which swings with the rolling of the ship, and answers for a table. . . . At half-past eight o'clock, or one bell in the forenoon watch, the larboard watch goes on deck, and the starboard remains below. Here again the 'holy-stones,' or 'hand-bibles,' as they are called by the crew, are used, and sometimes iron scrapers. After the lower deck has been wetted with swabs, these scrapers are used to take the rough dirt off. Whilst this is going on, the cooks from each mess are employed in cleaning the utensils and preparing for dinner; at the same time the watch are working the ship, and doing what is wanting to be done on deck.

"About eleven o'clock, or six bells, when any of the men are in irons, or on the black list, the boatswain or mate are ordered to call all hands; the culprits are then brought forward by the Master-at-Arms, who is a warrant-officer, and acts the part of Jack Ketch when required; he likewise has the prisoners in his custody, until they are put in irons, under any charge. All hands being now mustered, the Captain orders the man to strip; he is then seized to a grating by the wrists and knees; his crime is then mentioned, and the prisoner may plead; but, in nineteen cases out of twenty, he is flogged for the most trifling offence or neglect, such as not hearing the watch called at night, not doing anything properly on deck or aloft which he might happen to be sent to do, when, perhaps, he has been doing the best he could, and, at the same time, ignorant of having done wrong, until he is pounced on, and put in irons. So much for legal process. After punishment, the Boatswain's Mate pipes to dinner, it being eight bells, or twelve o'clock; and this is the pleasantest part of the day, as at one bell the piper is called to play 'Nancy Dawson,' or some other lively tune, a well-known signal that the grog [1] is ready to be served out. It is the duty of the cook from each mess to fetch and serve it out to his messmates, of which every man and boy is allowed a pint, that is, one gill of rum and three of water, to which is added lemon acid, sweetened with sugar. Here I must remark that the cook comes in for the perquisites of office, by reserving to himself an extra portion of grog, which is called the over-plus, and generally comes to the double of a man's allowance. Thus the cook can take upon himself to be the man of consequence, for he has the opportunity of inviting a friend to partake of a glass, or of paying any little debt he may have contracted. It may not be known to everyone that it is grog which pays debts, and not money, in a man-of-war. Notwithstanding the cook's apparently pre-eminent situation, yet, on some occasions, he is subject to censure or punishment by his messmates, for not attending to the dinner properly, or suffering the utensils of his department to be in a dirty condition. Justice, in these cases, is awarded by packing a jury of cooks from the different messes, for it falls to the lot of each man in a mess to act as cook in his turn. The mode or precept by which this jury is summoned is by hoisting a mess swab or beating a tin dish between decks forward. . . . At two bells in the afternoon, or one o'clock, the starboard watch goes on

---

[1] "Will it be believed that, until the peace of 1802, French merchants had a contract for supplying the British Navy with French brandy, while our West Indian merchants knew not what to do with their rum and cocoa! At last John Bull awoke from his dream, and it struck him that soldiers and sailors liked rum just as well as brandy, and that, by giving them cocoa for breakfast, it would not only assist the West Indian merchants, but give general satisfaction throughout the fleet."—Lovell, 'Personal Narrative,' p. 21.

deck, and remains working the ship, pointing the ropes, or doing any duty that may be required, until the eight bells strike, when the Boatswain's Mate pipes to supper. This consists of half a pint of wine, or a pint of grog, to each man, with biscuit, and cheese or butter. At the one bell, or half-past four, which is called one bell in 'the first dog-watch,' the larboard watch comes on duty, and remains until six o'clock, when that is relieved by the starboard watch, which is called the 'second dog-watch,' which lasts till eight o'clock. To explain this, it must be observed that these four hours, from four to eight o'clock, are divided into two watches, with a view of making the other watches come regular and alternate. . . . By this regular system of duty, I became inured to the roughness and hardships of a sailor's life. I had made up my mind to be obedient, however irksome to my feelings, and, our ship being on the Channel Station, I soon began to pick up a knowledge of seamanship."

The *Revenge* presently joined the blockading squadron before Cadiz, witnessed Nelson's arrival to take command, and shared in the battle of Trafalgar. Of the moments before going into action, Jack says :—

"During this time each ship was making the usual preparations, such as breaking away the Captain's and officers' cabins, and sending all the lumber below ; the doctors, parson,[1] purser, and loblolly men were also busy, getting the medicine chests and bandages out, and sails prepared for the wounded to be placed on, that they might be dressed in rotation, as they were taken down to the after cockpit."

Jack goes on to describe the incidents of the engagement so far as he observed them. When everything was over, all hands were called to splice the main-brace ; and then general efforts were made to get the crippled ship into serviceable condition again as soon as possible. Two incidents of the fight, as noted by the writer, are sufficiently suggestive or curious to deserve mention here.

"We had a Midshipman on board our ship of a wickedly mischievous disposition, whose sole delight was to insult the feelings of the seamen, and furnish pretexts to get these punished. His conduct made every man's life miserable that happened to be under his orders. He was a youth not more than twelve or thirteen years of age ;[2] but I have often seen him get on the carriage of a gun, call a man to him, and kick him about the thighs and body, and with his fist would beat him about the head ; and these,

---

[1] Naval Chaplains, until after the close of the long wars, were still very often discredits to their cloth. "Our old parson was a 'rum' subject. After trying all other mess places he got old Pipes, the Boatswain, to take him into his. They agreed very well for a little while ; but, one unfortunate day, the evil genius of poor old Fritz prevailed, for Pipes, coming down rather unexpectedly to his cabin in the fore cockpit to get a glass of grog, having got wet when the hands were turned up reefing topsails, found the parson helping himself rather too freely out of his liquor-case. This was a crime Mr. Boatswain could not put up with. A breach immediately ensued, and an instant dismissal from his berth took place, with the exclamation of, 'The parson is such a black ; I cannot allow him to mess with me any longer.' After this occurrence the Captain interfered, and he again messed in his proper place with the officers in the ward-room."—Lovell, 'Personal Narrative,' p. 38.

[2] His name might be given here, but is withheld in deference to his family.

although prime seamen, at the same time dared not murmur. It was ordained, however, by Providence, that his reign of terror and severity should not last; for, during the engagement, he was killed on the quarter-deck by a grape shot, his body greatly mutilated, his entrails being driven and scattered against the larboard side; nor were there any lamentations for his fate."

The other incident is of a more agreeable character. From a burning French ship a number of people were rescued.

" Among those," says Jack, " who were thus preserved from a watery grave [1] was a young Frenchwoman, who was brought on board our ship in a state of complete nakedness. Although it was in the heat of the battle, yet she received every assistance which at that time was in our power; and her distress of mind was soothed as well as we could, until the officers got to their chests, from whence they supplied her with needles and thread, to convert sheets into chemises, and curtains from their cots to make somewhat of a gown, and other garments, so that by degrees she was made as comfortable as circumstances would admit; for we all tried who would be most kind to her."

She was a married woman who had been unable to bring herself to quit her husband when the latter had been ordered to sea; and, having disguised herself as a man, she had entered herself on board her husband's ship, and done duty at his side during the engagement until he had fallen. In her consequent grief she betrayed the secret of her sex. Upon her ship catching fire, she was "lowered into the ocean by a rope from the taffrail, the lead of which was melting at the time, and, whilst letting her down, some of it dropped, and burnt the back of her neck." Upon the arrival of the *Revenge* at Gibraltar, the woman, overflowing with gratitude, was put into a cartel for conveyance to a Spanish port.

Up to the beginning of the nineteenth century, ships of the Royal Navy were usually painted with blue upper works, bright yellow sides, and broad black strakes at the waterline; and the interior surfaces were generally red. Nelson, influenced by various considerations, put the ships of his fleets into a new uniform. He caused the hulls to be painted black, with a yellow strake along each tier of ports, but with black port-lids. This method of painting, known as double yellow, or chequer-painting, distinguished all, or very nearly all, the British ships which fought at Trafalgar, and was soon afterwards adopted as the regular uniform for British men-of-war, white being eventually, however, substituted for yellow as the colour of the strakes. The fact of being a chequer-sided ship, or "one of Nelson's chequer-players," brought no small glory

---

[1] She had been picked up by a boat belonging to the *Pickle*.

to the *Revenge*, when, having refitted at Gibraltar, she returned to Portsmouth ; and " Jack " records that enormous dissatisfaction was caused among the crew by one of the first acts of the Captain [1] who there superseded Captain Moorsom. The new commander painted out the chequers, and substituted for them a single stripe or strake. A little later, upon Captain Sir John Gore (2)[2] hoisting his pennant in her, the *Revenge* was again, " Nelsonified," to the great joy of her ship's company.

H.M.S. " VICTORY," 100, QUITTING CHATHAM DOCKYARD, APRIL 18TH, 1803.

(*From a pencil sketch made on the spot by John Constable, R.A., and kindly lent for reproduction by Mr. C. Constable. The sketch represents the ship as she was at Trafalgar.*)

About the external painting of foreign men-of-war at the time of Trafalgar, Captain William Stanhope Lovell,[3] who took part in

[1] Hon. Charles Elphinstone Fleeming, " whose name was a terror to every ship's company he commanded, and was cursed from stem to stern in the British Navy.' ' Naut. Econ.'

[2] Who had served repeatedly with Nelson, and was a very good officer.

[3] This officer, whose original name was W. S. Badcock, was born in 1788, became a Commander in 1812, and was posted in 1815. He retired as a Captain in 1846, and died, a retired Vice-Admiral, in 1859.

the action in the *Neptune,* gives some interesting particulars. Speaking of the ships of the allies, he says :—

" Some of them were painted like ourselves—with double yellow sides ; some with a single red or yellow streak ; others all black ; and the noble *Santisima Trinidad,* with four distinct lines of red, with a white ribbon between them. . . . The *Santa Ana* . . . was painted all black. . . . It was remarked by (Nelson) that the enemy had the iron hoops round their masts painted black. Orders were issued by signal to whitewash those of his fleet, that, in the event of all the ensigns being shot away, his ships might be distinguished by their white masts and hoops." [1]

Several references have already been made to the morality of the Navy, and especially of the lower-deck ; but it is necessary to return to the subject, in order that the conditions of service life on ship-board during the most glorious period of British history may be properly understood. Speaking of his next return to Spithead, " Jack " writes :—

" After having moored our ship, swarms of boats came round us : some were what are generally termed bomb-boats,[2] but are really nothing but floating chandler's shops ; and a great many of them were freighted with cargoes of ladies, a sight that was truly gratifying, and a great treat ; for our crew, consisting of six hundred and upwards, nearly all young men, had seen but one woman on board for eighteen months ; and that was the daughter of one of the Spanish chiefs, who made no stay on board, but went on shore again immediately. So soon as these boats were allowed to come alongside, the seamen flocked down pretty quick, one after the other, and brought their choice up, so that, in the course of the afternoon, we had about four hundred and fifty on board. Of all the human race, these poor young creatures are the most pitiable : the ill-usage and degradation they are driven to submit to are indescribable ; but from habit they become callous, indifferent as to delicacy of speech and behaviour, and so totally lost to all sense of shame that they seem to retain no quality which properly belongs to woman but the shape and name. . . . On the arrival of any man-of-war in port, these girls flock down to the shore, where boats are always ready ; and here may be witnessed a scene somewhat similar to the trafficking for slaves in the West Indies. As they approach a boat, old Charon, with painter in hand, before they step on board, surveys them from stem to stern with the eyes of a bargaining Jew ; and carefully culls out the best looking, and the most dashingly dressed ; and, in making up his complement for a load, it often happens that he refuses to take some of them, observing (very politely), and usually with some vulgar oath, to one that she is ' too old ' ; to another that she is ' too ugly ' ; and that he shall not be able ' to sell them ' ; and he'll be d——d if he has any notion of having his trouble for nothing. The only apology that can be made for the savage conduct of these unfeeling brutes is, that they run a chance of not being permitted to carry a cargo alongside, unless it makes a good show-off ; for it has been often known that, on approaching a ship, the officer in command has so far forgot himself as to order the waterman to push off—that he should not bring such a cargo of d——d ugly devils on board, and that he would not allow any of his men to have them. . . . Here the waterman is a loser, for he takes them conditionally : that is, if they are made choice of, or what he calls ' sold,' he receives three shillings each ; and if

---

[1] ' Personal Narr. of Events from 1799 to 1815,' 2nd ed., 1879, p. 46.

[2] More commonly " bumboats." From " bum," the buttocks, on account of their clumsiness (Donald) ; or, perhaps, from " boom," such boats being allowed to lie at the booms of anchored ships.

not, then no pay: he has his labour for his pains: at least, these were the terms at
Portsmouth and Plymouth in war-time. . . . A boat usually carries about ten of these
poor creatures at a time, and will often bring off three cargoes of these ladies in a day;
so that, if he is fortunate in his 'sales,' as he calls them, he will make nearly five
pounds by his three trips. . . . It may seem strange to many persons that seamen
before the mast should be allowed to have these ladies on board, while the officers must
not, on pain of being tried by a court-martial for disobedience of orders, the Admiralty
having made a regulation to that effect. The reason of this is, that the seamen are not
allowed to go ashore, but the officers are." [1]

On occasions such as that described, drunkenness as well as
immorality ruled upon the lower-deck; and, for many years afterwards the same kind of pandemonium was frequently suffered to
prevail in ships lying at Spithead and in Plymouth Sound. As
late as 1834, on board the *Pique*, 36, Captain the Hon. Henry John
Rous,[2] an unfortunate woman, one of a number who had been
brought off to the ship by boatmen from Portsmouth, went aloft
when drunk, and, falling from a yard to the deck, was killed.[3] Nor
did the vicious practice of suffering a certain number of men—
generally petty officers—to carry their wives to sea with them
cease until after the expiration of the period now under review.
Lord St. Vincent discouraged it; Nelson and Collingwood stead-
fastly opposed it; but weak or indifferent Captains still permitted it.
Officers also often took their wives with them to sea;[4] and Captains
did so sometimes, until well after the middle of the nineteenth
century, and, indeed, after an order expressly forbidding it had
been issued. "Jack's" reminiscences throw no light upon this
question; but they suggest that many of the naval officers of his
time, especially after the failure of the expedition to Walcheren,
were deeply implicated in defrauding the revenue.

"On board the different ships," says "Jack," "there were numerous packages
which had been shipped at Flushing: and no doubt but they were intended to be
smuggled into England, from the secret manner and the different stratagems used in the
getting of them afterwards on shore. The bread-room of our ship was crowded with
them, directed for different officers holding high rank both in army and navy: and may

---

[1] 'Naut. Econ.,' 56. *See also* 'Statement of Certain Immoral Practices prevailing
in His Majesty's Navy,' 1822.

[2] Died an Admiral (ret.), June 19, 1877. He was the well-known racing man.

[3] Letter from Mr. James Francis Ballard Wainwright, Midshipman, H.M.S. *Pique*:
in Auth.'s Coll. Mr. Wainwright died a Rear-Admiral, in April, 1872.

[4] *See* 'The Post-Captain,' and the novels of Marryat, Mr. Scott, Chamier, etc.
Vice-Adm. George Losack was married on board his ship the *Jupiter*, 50, on the Cape
Station. Marshall, 'Roy. Nav. Biog.,' i. 380. And Admiral John Ayscough, who died
as lately as 1864, was born on board H.M.S. *Swan*, which his father commanded, while
she was actually in action with an enemy's vessel. O'Byrne, 'Nav. Biog. Dict.,' 30.

have been intended as presents, or for their own use; but they did not pay the duty. These packages consisted of sets of Hamburg china and table services, down for beds, spirits, and various other articles of foreign produce. Not being able to land all these goods at once without detection, we contrived it at different intervals, safely thus got rid of some of them by different conveyances; and then we became 'Channel gropers' again; and, whilst on this duty, we landed the balance of our secret cargo at Weymouth and Plymouth, as we were frequently running into those ports. Whilst on the Cherbourg blockading station, it often occurred that we were in chase of vessels, supposing them to be smugglers, and, at the same time, we were meditating how to get rid of the bulk of our bread-room stowage, which did not intend to pay any duty."

Upon the subject of punishment " Jack " says much that is of interest.

" The extent to which cruelty was carried on under the name of discipline, on board many ships during the late war, is not generally known; nor will a British public believe that any body of men would submit to such marks of degradation as they were compelled to undergo. It was partially known at Somerset House[1] by the different ships' logs; but the real crime, if any, was not, it is believed, therein set down; for there it all came under the head of ' disobedience,' or under a peculiar article of war which runs as follows: ' All crimes not capital shall be punished according to the customs and manners used at sea.' This article shelters the Captains in the Navy in resorting to almost any mode of punishment they may think proper. . . . Whilst lying at Spithead, in the year 1809 or 1810, four impressed seamen attempted to make their escape from a frigate then lying there: one of their shipmates, a Dutchman to whom they had entrusted the secret, betrayed their intention, and informed the commanding officer of their designs. They were tried by a court-martial, and sentenced to receive three hundred[2] lashes each, through the fleet. On the first day after the trial that the weather was moderate enough to permit, the signal was made for a boat from each ship, with a guard of Marines, to attend the punishment. The man is placed in a launch, *i.e.*, the largest ship's boat, under the care of the Master-at-Arms and a doctor. There is a capstan bar rigged fore and aft, to which this poor fellow is lashed by his wrists; and for fear of hurting him—humane creatures—there is a stocking put over each, to prevent him from tearing the flesh off in his agonies. When all is ready, the prisoner is stript and seized to the capstan bar. Punishment commences by the officer, after reading the sentence of the court-martial, ordering the Boatswain's Mates to do their duty. The cat-o'-nine tails is applied to the bare back, and at about every six lashes a fresh Boatswain's Mate is ordered to relieve the executioner of this duty, until the prisoner has received, perhaps, twenty-five lashes. He is then cast loose, and, allowed to sit down with a blanket rolled round him, is conveyed to the next ship, escorted by this vast number of armed boats, accompanied by that doleful music, ' The Rogue's March.' In this manner he is conveyed from ship to ship, receiving alongside of each a similar number of stripes with the cat, until the sentence is completed. It often, nay generally, happens that nature is unable to sustain it, and the poor fellow faints and sinks under it, although every kind method is made use of to enable him to bear it, by pouring wine down his throat. The doctor will then feel his pulse, and often pronounces that the man is unable to bear more. He is then taken, most usually insensible, to what is termed the ' sick bay '; and, if he recovers, he is told he will have

---

[1] Where were the offices of the Civil Departments of the Navy.

[2] As many as 500 lashes were sometimes awarded. The Boatswains' Mates were drilled to flog effectively, by being made to practise on a cask, under the superintendence of the Boatswain.

to receive the remainder of his punishment. When there are many ships in the fleet at the time of the court-martial, this ceremony, if the prisoner can sustain it, will last nearly half the day.

"On the blanket being taken from his back, and he supported or lifted to be lashed to the capstan bar after he has been alongside of several ships, his back resembles so much putrified liver, and every stroke of the cat brings away the congealed blood; and the Boatswain's Mates are looked at with the eye of a hawk to see they do their duty, and clear the cat's tails after every stroke, the blood at the time streaming through their fingers: and in this manner are men in the Navy punished for different offences, more particularly impressed men who attempt to make their escape."

It could at least be said on behalf of such a terrible punishment as flogging round the fleet that it was never inflicted save in pursuance of the sentence of a court-martial, and that individual tyranny or caprice was powerless to order it. But other punishments, almost equally savage, could be, and commonly were, dealt out to the men at the irresponsible will of a superior; and it is notorious that very often no record of them was ever set down, although a report of all punishments was directed to be made.

"Jack" describes several of these punishments. The most common was flogging at the gangway or on the quarter-deck.

"The Captain orders this punishment for anything that himself or any of his officers may consider a crime. The prisoner is made to strip to the waist; he is then seized by his wrists and knees to a grating or ladder; the Boatswain's Mate is then ordered to cut him with the cat-o'-nine tails; and after six or twelve lashes are given another Boatswain's Mate is called to continue the exercise: and so they go on, until the Captain gives the word to stop. From one to five dozen lashes are given, according to the Captain's whim; but the general number is three dozen; and this number the Captain has power to give every day, if he has any bad feeling for an individual; and a tyrant of a Captain will frequently tell the Boatswain's Mate to lay it on harder, or that he should be flogged next himself. This punishment is . . . inflicted without trial by court-martial, at the discretion of the Captain. It is not so in the army."

Of "running the gauntlet," a punishment inflicted for petty theft, "Jack" says:—

"The criminal is placed with his naked back in a large tub, wherein a seat has been fixed; this tub is secured on a grating, and is drawn round the deck by the boys, the Master-at-Arms, with his drawn sword, pointing to the prisoner's breast. The cavalcade starts from the break of the quarter-deck, after the Boatswain has given the prisoner a dozen lashes, and the ship's crew are ranged round the deck in two rows, so that the prisoner passes between them, and each man is provided with a three yarn nettle; that is, three rope yarns tightly laid together and knotted. With this each man must cut him, or be thought implicated in the theft. Six Boatswain's Mates give him half-a-dozen each as he passes round the decks, so that he receives four dozen lashes from the Boatswain and his Mates with a cat-o'-nine tails, and six hundred cuts with the three yarn nettle from the crew of a line of battleship, that being the average number of men before the mast in war time. This punishment is inflicted by the Captain's orders, without the formal inquiry by a court-martial."

Another punishment, known as "starting," seems to have been more generally abused than any.

"This may be carried," says "Jack," "to a great extent of torture, as every Boatswain's Mate carries a rope's end in his pocket: it is part of their equipment; and, when ordered to start the men by any of the officers, they must not be found wanting of that appendage. The man is ordered to pull off his jacket, and sometimes his waistcoat, if he has one on at the time: the Boatswain's Mate then commences beating him, and continues to do so until he is ordered to stop, or unless his arm is tired, and then another Boatswain's Mate is called to go on with the ceremony. Some of those men's backs have often been so bad from the effects of the 'starting system,' that they have not been able to bear their jackets on for several days; and as this punishment is inflicted without tying the man up, he will naturally endeavour to ward off or escape as many of the blows as possible, and in doing so he frequently gets a serious cut in the face or head. This punishment is so common that no minute is made of it even in the logbook; and but few men in war time can escape the above mode of punishment, particularly in those ships whose Captains give that power to their inferior officers."

The punishment of "gagging" was—

"inflicted at the time of the offence being committed, which is generally for a seaman's daring to make a reply to his superior. The man is placed in a sitting position, with both his legs in irons, and his hands secured behind him; his mouth is then forced open, and an iron bolt put across, well secured behind his head. A sentinel is placed over him with his drawn bayonet, and in this situation he remains until the Captain may think proper to release him, or until he is nearly exhausted.

"To go through all the different modes of punishment resorted to in the British Navy would," continues "Jack," "be impossible, as almost every Captain, when appointed to a fresh ship, adopts new customs, with different ways to punish: and I have heard the Captain say, when a man has been brought to the gangway to be flogged, and he has pleaded hard, by honestly stating that he did not know he was doing wrong, as it had been the customary order of the former Captain: and what was the reply of this furious and unreasonable officer? It was this: 'It was not my order, and I will flog every man of you, but I will break you in to my ways'; and he nearly kept his word, for within a short period of this time upwards of three hundred men had been flogged or started, and this too whilst we were blockading an enemy's port. It is generally supposed that no man could be punished without having been guilty of some serious offence; but that is not always the case, for nineteen out of twenty men that are punished suffer without being conscious that they have violated any law; and in many instances they are the most expert and able seamen. For instance, the fore, main, and mizen-top men are selected from the crew as the most sprightly and attentive to their duty; and yet those men are more frequently punished, and are always in dread when aloft lest they should be found fault with for not being quick enough, for punishment is sure to follow, and, sure enough, their conjectures are generally too true; for they are not only flogged, but their grog is stopped, or compelled to drink six or eight water grog for a certain length of time. How many of those valuable seamen perished during the late war. When aloft, and trembling from fear, how many have actually fell from the yards and lost their lives, either on the decks or overboard; and how many hundreds have run away, and, by disguising themselves, got over to America, leaving behind, perhaps, two or three years' hard-earned pay and prize-money. In this manner, together with those killed in battle, our ship was three times manned in a little less than seven years; for our complement of men was upwards of six hundred, and we had on our ship's books, within that period, twenty-one hundred. Many of these men had purser's names, that is fictitious ones, to avoid detection in case they saw an opportunity to run away."

Under the Articles of War, death remained the punishment for such offences as refusal of obedience on the ground that wages remained unpaid, uttering mutinous words, sleeping on watch, striking a superior officer, and neglect in steering a ship : but death, of course, could only be legally inflicted in pursuance of the sentence of a court-martial. Death was, nevertheless, not infrequently caused by the brutalities of tyrannical officers. The minutes of courts-martial reveal, comparatively speaking, a considerable number of examples in point. As for the legal sentence, it was inflicted freely. "Jack" mentions that while at Lisbon in 1811 he witnessed the hanging of two Marines who had been found guilty of having thrown overboard an officer who had upon various occasions treated them with cruelty.

Inordinately long commissions, and the established practice of paying the seamen nothing until the ships themselves were paid off, were among other legitimate grievances of the lower deck until long after the conclusion of the French wars. Speaking in his place in Parliament in 1811, Lord Dundonald, then Lord Cochrane, said that—

" an increase of pay to the seamen in the Navy would be of little advantage to them, so long as the present system continued. He had in his hands a list of ships of war in the East Indies. The *Centurion* had been there eleven years. The *Rattlesnake*, fourteen years, came home the other day with only one man of the first crew. The *Fox*, frigate, under the command of his brother, had been there fifteen years; the *Sceptre* eight years ; the *Albatross* twelve, etc. Not one farthing of pay had been given all that period to all those men. He had made a calculation on the *Fox*, frigate, and, supposing only one hundred of the men returned, there would be due to the crew £25,000, not including the officers. What became of these sums all the while ? The interest ought to be accounted for to Government or to the seamen themselves. The *Wilhelmina* had been ten years, the *Russell* seven years, the *Drake* six years. . . . The seamen, from the want of their pay, had no means of getting many necessaries of the utmost consequence to their health and comfort." [1]

On April 25th, 1806, on the motion of Mr. Grey, afterwards Lord Howick, an increase of pay was granted to the officers and men of the Navy. Ordinary seamen were given an addition of 6*d*. a week ; able seamen, an addition of 1*s*. a week ; petty officers, an addition of from 5*s*. to 9*s*. 6*d*. a month ; and Masters' Mates and some other warrant officers, an addition of 6*s*. a month. The pay of

[1] Dundonald, ' Autobiog. of a Seaman,' ii. 182.

Masters and Surgeons was not increased; but Chaplains were made eligible to hold the additional appointment of Schoolmaster, which would better their pay by £20 a year. The daily pay of the commissioned officers was increased by the following sums : Admiral of the Fleet, 10s. ; Admiral, 7s. ; Vice-Admiral, 5s. ; Rear-Admiral, 3s. 6d. ; Captain, 4s. ; and Lieutenant, 1s. The various additions involved an increase of £288,366 in the estimates. At the same time something was done for the pensioners. The funds of the Chest at Chatham, which, in conjunction with those of Greenwich Hospital, had borne the cost of providing for the aged, infirm, and wounded, were admitted to be inadequate; and it was decided to increase them by a grant of one shilling in the pound from all prize-money. This was designed to admit of the gradual increment in certain cases of the allowance to out-pensioners from £7 a year to 1s. a day (£18 5s. a year).

On November 9th, 1805, it was announced that " His Majesty having been pleased to order the rank of Admirals of the Red to be restored to His Majesty's Navy," certain flag-officers were that day promoted accordingly. It is not known who was responsible for the terms of the notice; but it should be pointed out that they are historically incorrect. The rank of Admiral of the Red had never previously existed in England. Up to the middle of the eighteenth century, when there was but one flag-officer of each rank and colour—nine flag-officers in all—the senior of them was called, not Admiral of the Red, but Admiral of the Fleet; and until 1805 the Admiral of the Fleet, for the time being, was, in effect, the Admiral of the Red. The innovation really created an entirely new rank between that of Admiral of the Fleet and that of Admiral of the White. An impression seems to have prevailed that at some remote date the rank had existed, and had been abolished in consequence of a holder of it having been captured by the enemy; but there is no foundation for this belief.

In 1809 the Royal Naval Asylum, which had been for some years in existence under the management of the Patriotic Fund, of Lloyd's, and which, in 1829, was merged in Greenwich Hospital School, was provided with a regular and fixed establishment, in pursuance of recommendations made by the Commissioners of the Asylum in accordance with directions conveyed to them by a royal warrant of July 25th, 1805. The number of children to be admitted was limited to one thousand, being seven hundred boys and three hundred girls, legitimate sons and daughters of warrant and petty officers and seamen of the Royal Navy, and non-commissioned officers and men of the Royal Marines; and the officers were to consist of a Governor, who was to be of post-rank at least, a Lieutenant and Secretary, who was to be a Commander or Lieutenant, R.N., a clerk, an auditor, a chaplain, a steward, a surgeon, a quarter-master of instruction, sergeant-assistants, a drummer, a matron, and assistant-matron and schoolmistress, one reading mistress, one knitting mistress and sempstress, a nurse to each ward, infirmary nurses, a cook, a laundress, and a sergeant-porter. All officers, as far as possible, were to be persons who had served in the Navy or Royal Marines, or, if women, widows or other relatives of persons who had so served.

The conclusion, or, rather, what was believed to be the conclusion, of the long wars with France, was celebrated, on January 2nd, 1815, by an extension of the Order of the Bath—

"to the end that those officers who have had the opportunity of distinguishing themselves by eminent services during the late war may share in the honours of the said Order, and that their names may be delivered down to remote posterity, accompanied by the marks of distinction which they have so nobly earned."

The Order had previously consisted of one class only, that of Knights of the Bath; and it may be said without exaggeration that no similar distinction had ever, upon the whole, been more deservedly bestowed or more highly valued than that of K.B.[1] It was the hall-mark of military competency and success. Under the new rules, the Order was to consist of three classes, *i.e.*, Knights Grand Crosses (G.C.B.), limited to seventy-two, of whom twelve might be persons eminent in civil or diplomatic life; Knights Commanders (K.C.B.), limited to one hundred and eighty, exclusive of ten foreigners holding British commissions; and Companions of the Bath (C.B.). The old K.B.'s were to become G.C.B.'s; and the remaining two classes were to be altogether new. The qualifications for a Companion were thus somewhat unsatisfactorily defined :—

"No officer shall be nominated a Companion of the said most honourable Order, unless he shall have received, or shall hereafter receive, a medal or other badge of honour, or shall have been especially mentioned by name in dispatches, published in the *London Gazette*, as having distinguished himself by his valour and conduct in

---

[1] For this reason, officers who, prior to 1815, had the rank of K.B., are described throughout this history as K.B.'s, although in 1815 they became, of course, G.C.B.'s.

action against his Majesty's enemies, since the commencement of the war in 1803, or shall hereafter be named in dispatches, published in the *London Gazette*, as having distinguished himself."

For, as James points out, it might, as indeed it sometimes did happen, that dispatches, received by the Admiralty and recording the distinguished behaviour of an officer in action, were never, owing to neglect or other reasons, published in the *London Gazette* at all. Again, as far as the Navy was concerned, the enlarged Order could be conferred on no officers below the rank of Post-Captain. So that, to take one case by way of example, had Commander William Manners, who, in 1814, fought one of the most gallant actions on record with an American man-of-war of immensely superior force, survived and returned to England, he would have been precluded by two equally ridiculous considerations from receiving a C.B. Firstly, the account of his most splendid action did not figure in the *London Gazette* ; [1] secondly, Manners was but a Commander. That Manners's ship was taken by the enemy would, it must be feared, have supplied the authorities with an additional reason for withholding any reward; for when, many years later, it was tardily decided to issue medals to all who had been engaged in certain actions of the long war, the list of actions selected was restricted to actions which had resulted successfully. The medal was not granted to men who had stood up to the last against overwhelming forces, and whose defeat had been as glorious as any victory.

In the history of the time there are fewer references than might be expected to the utilisation of spies ; yet foreigners did obtain entrance to the British service; and it may be that, on the other hand, Englishmen occasionally managed to get a temporary footing on board ships belonging to the enemy. Captain William Stanhope Badcock, when acting-Lieutenant of the *Melpomene*, in 1806, had the misfortune to be taken prisoner by the French off Leghorn. With him and his boat's crew was a supposed Russian midshipman, who, for some time previously, had been serving in the frigate. Says Badcock :—

" The young Russian . . . afterwards turned out to be a Frenchman, sent into our service by Bonaparte, through Russian influence, with some of their own youngsters,

---

[1] Nor does any account, strange to say, find a place in Brenton's History, though Brenton, being himself a naval officer, should have found special pride in chronicling so magnificent an addition to the glorious records of the service.

and passed off on our Government as a Russian. All that I can say is that he was a clever, smart lad. I met him in Paris in 1318 (*lieutenant de vaisseau*), when he laughed at the trick that had been played, and told me several more Russian midshipmen in our service were young Frenchmen. This was done by some of the Emperor Alexander's official servants, when it was the policy of Russia, after the fatal battle of Austerlitz, in December, 1805, to endeavour to please Napoleon." [1]

In December, 1804, it was announced that "a new class of officers, to be called Sub-Lieutenants, are to be appointed, selected from Midshipmen who have served their time. They are to receive half-pay." [2] The innovation, due to the initiative of Earl St. Vincent, did not, however, take root in the Navy, and the new rank quickly languished and disappeared, not to be revived until half a century later.

The uniform of executive officers remained until 1812 as it had been settled in 1795; but on January 22nd, 1805, a uniform was established for medical officers; and on June 29th, 1807, uniforms were also established for Masters and for Pursers. In 1812 the white facings of the period anterior to 1795 were temporarily re-introduced; and an alteration was made in the uniform button, which Mates and Midshipmen, as well as their superiors, were directed to wear. The new button bore a crown above the anchor on it. Commanders as well as Captains were at the same time allowed to wear two epaulettes, those of the Commanders being plain, those of Captains of less than three years' standing bearing a silver anchor, and those of Captains of three years' standing and upwards having a silver crown above a silver anchor. The Lieutenants were given a single epaulette, to be worn on the right shoulder. There was no further change until 1825.

Still there was no uniform for seamen, although there was a customary dress, consisting of white trousers, a blue jacket, and a tarpaulin hat. These clothes could be drawn, with others, from the purser's stores. In most ships, however, any decent clothes were allowed to be worn. Straw hats became common from about 1802; petticoats, which had been common at sea since the days of Elizabeth, were occasionally worn until 1820, and perhaps later. They were of either tarpaulin or canvas, and reached to the knee. Purser's slops were, of course, of a recognised pattern; and Captains had power to make any man who was ragged draw them, provided that the value did not exceed two months' pay. Some Captains, however, elected to supply part of their ship's companies—especially their

---

[1] 'Personal Narrative,' p. 71.   [2] *Nav. Chron.*, 1804, ii. 510.

own boat's crews—with a uniform of their own designing, made at their own cost; and, when they did so, the dresses were sometimes both expensive and excentric. The pigtail remained on the lower-deck for some time after it had disappeared from the quarter-deck, where, as early as 1805, it had begun to be the exception rather than the rule, particularly among young officers. The men, as has, indeed, always been their habit, were excessively fond of making decorative additions to their new clothes, if they were permitted to do so; and pipings of silk or canvas in the seams of jackets, braid trimmings, rows of bright buttons, and gaudy hat ribbons, with or without a name or motto on them, were much in favour at, and in the ten years subsequent to, the time of Trafalgar. Lower-deck dandies also wore black neckties, and white socks or stockings, and had their trousers cut particularly tight round the hips and particularly loose round the ankles.

The month of August, 1804, saw the establishment of the Royal Marine Artillery. Three companies of artillery, one for each of the then existing divisions, were ordered to be formed for service afloat, the officers and men to receive additional pay. But the officers of the new corps were not then separated from the general Marine list, nor were they promoted except in turn with the others. Moreover, on attaining the rank of Major, they lost their appointments in the artillery.

By an Admiralty Warrant of August 15th, 1805, a fourth division of Royal Marines was established. The older divisions had their headquarters at Chatham, Portsmouth, and Plymouth respectively. The new division had its seat at Woolwich. During Lord Mulgrave's administration additional second Colonels-Commandant were appointed to each of these, every division thenceforward having two; and forage allowance for one horse was granted to Lieutenant-Colonels, Majors, and Adjutants.

On November 21st, 1806, provoked by Great Britain's well-proved superiority at sea, and by the single-minded manner in which she used her sea-power for the confusion of his plans, Napoleon issued the famous Berlin Decrees, which, like the decrees which he subsequently issued from Milan and from the Tuileries, were intended to destroy Britain by destroying her commerce. The important articles of the Berlin Decrees were as follows:—

1. The British Islands are declared to be in a state of blockade.
2. All commerce and all correspondence with the British Isles are prohibited.

3. The letters or packets which are addressed to England or to Englishmen, or which are written in the English language, shall not be forwarded by the posts, and shall be seized.

4. Every individual who is an English subject, no matter what his condition, who may be found in the countries occupied by our troops, or those of our allies, shall be made prisoner of war.

5. Every warehouse, every commodity, every article of property, no matter of what sort, belonging to an English subject, shall be declared good prize.

6. The trade in English commodities is prohibited; and every article which belongs to England, or is the produce of her manufactures and colonies, is declared good prize.

7. One half of the proceeds of the confiscation of the articles, property, and goods, declared good prize by the preceding articles, will be employed to indemnify the merchants for the losses which they suffer by the seizure of trading vessels by English cruisers.

8. No ship which comes direct from England or the English colonies, or has been there after the publication of the present decree, shall be admitted into any harbour.

9. Every ship which trades with a false declaration in contravention of the above principles, shall be seized, and the ship and cargo confiscated as if they were English property.

As the influence of Napoleon increased upon the Continent, so did the boycott, which was thus established, spread; but it is upon the whole astonishing how little harm was directly done to Great Britain by the decrees. British goods, thanks to 'the activity of smugglers, still found their way to France and to all parts of Europe, in spite of Napoleon; and, while the Continent had to pay very heavily for them, the British producers and manufacturers managed to retain many of their markets. But, as a reply to the Emperor's decrees, Great Britain was obliged, by various Orders in Council, to prohibit all trade by neutrals with France, unless the vessels carrying on such trade should first enter a British port and there pay a stipulated duty on her cargo. And the effect of the Decrees on the one hand, and of the Orders on the other, was to so greatly injure and irritate neutrals, as to be in a very large measure responsible for the outbreak, in 1812, of war between Great Britain, the most powerful of the maritime belligerents, and the United States, the most interested of the neutral nations. Over and over again it was prophesied in Parliament and elsewhere that, by annoying America, the Orders would hurt Great Britain more than they hurt France; but the British Government stood firm and enforced the retaliatory measures even after the United States, in 1809, passed an Act prohibiting all intercourse either with France or with Great Britain, pending revocation, modification, or non-enforcement of the objectionable edicts. It is true that, in 1809, a treaty for reviving amity and commerce between the United

States and Great Britain was actually signed ; but the proceedings of Mr. Erskine, who, as British Minister at Washington, had signed it, were disavowed by the Government in London ; and the tension was allowed steadily to increase, until, at the beginning of 1812, it became abundantly evident that if the situation were suffered to grow any worse, war must promptly result. Early in the session of that year a motion was made for the repeal of the obnoxious Orders in Council, and it was purposed to address the Regent, praying him to suspend or annul them ; but, on the strength of Lord Castlereagh's intimation that a conciliatory proposition was about to be made to America, the motion was withdrawn. Accordingly, there appeared in the *Gazette* a declaration revoking the Orders in Council, so far as they applied to United States' vessels, but adding that if, after the notification of the revocation to the government at Washington, the Americans did not also revoke their interdicts against British commerce, the British revocation should be null and void. Unhappily the concession was made too late. Ere America knew of it, the two countries were already actually at war.

In spite of the stress of continuous hostilities, trade prospered enormously between 1803 and 1815. In 1803, British trade was represented by the following figures [1] :—

	Imports.	Exports.
Great Britain . . .	£21,646,968	£22,252,101
Ireland	5,275,650	4,629,086

In 1815 the figures were [2] :—

Great Britain . . .	£35,987,582	£44,053,455
Ireland	7,245,043	6,558,103

There was thus, during the war, an increase in the imports of £16,310,007, and in the exports of £23,730,371.

---

[1] 'Commons' Journals,' lix., App. 584 and 608.
[2] *Ib.*, lxxi., App. 801 ; lxx., App. 709.

APPENDIX TO CHAPTER XXXVIII.

LIST OF FLAG-OFFICERS PROMOTED FROM THE RESUMPTION OF THE WAR IN 1803 TO THE GENERAL PEACE IN 1815.

(In continuation of the List in Vol. IV., pp. 192–195.)

Name and Titles	Born	Post-Captain	Rear-Admiral			Vice-Admiral			Admiral			Admiral of the Fleet	Died
			Blue	White	Red	Blue	White	Red	Blue	White	Red		
Thomas Drury	20-1-1755	21-3-1782		23-4-1804	9-11-1805	28-4-1808		31-7-1810	4-6-1814	19-7-1821	22-7-1830		5-9-1832
Albemarle Bertie (Bart. 1812, K.C.B. 1815)	20-1-1755	21-3-1782		23-4-1804	9-11-1805	28-4-1808		31-7-1810	4-6-1814	19-7-1821			1824
William, Earl of Northesk (K.B. 1805)	10-4-1756	7-4-1782		23-4-1804	9-11-1805	28-4-1808		31-7-1810	4-6-1814	19-7-1821	22-7-1830		28-5-1831
James Vashon	1742	12-4-1782		23-4-1804	9-11-1805	28-4-1808		31-7-1810	4-6-1814	19-7-1821			20-10-1827
Sir William Henry Douglas (1), Bart.		15-4-1782		23-4-1804	9-11-1805	28-4-1808							5-1809
Thomas Wells (1)		30-4-1782		23-4-1804	9-11-1805	28-4-1808		31-7-1810					31-10-1811
Sir Edward Pellew, Bart. (Viscount Exmouth, 1814, K.C.B. 1815)	19-4-1757	31-5-1782		23-4-1804	9-11-1805	28-4-1808		31-7-1810	4-6-1814	19-7-1821	22-7-1830		23-1-1833
Isaac Coffin (Bart. 1804)	16-5-1759	13-6-1782	23-4-1804	9-11-1805	28-4-1808	25-10-1809	31-7-1810	12-8-1812	12-8-1819	27-5-1825	22-7-1830		23-7-1839
John Aylmer (1)		28-6-1782	23-4-1804	9-11-1805	28-4-1808	25-10-1809	31-7-1810	12-8-1812	12-8-1819	27-5-1825	22-7-1830		4-1841
Samuel Osborn		6-7-1782	23-4-1804	9-11-1805	28-4-1808	25-10-1809	31-7-1810	12-8-1812					10-10-1816
Richard Boger		6-7-1782	23-4-1804	9-11-1805	28-4-1808	25-10-1809	31-7-1810	12-8-1812	12-8-1819				1822
Jonathan Faulknor (2)		12-8-1782	23-4-1804	9-11-1805	28-4-1808								1809
John Child Purvis (1)		1-9-1782	23-4-1804	9-11-1805	28-4-1808	25-10-1809	31-7-1810	12-8-1812	12-8-1819	27-5-1825			
Theophilus Jones	1745	4-9-1782	23-4-1804	9-11-1805	28-4-1808	25-10-1809	31-7-1810	12-8-1812	12-8-1819	27-5-1825			1835
William Domett (K.C.B. 1815)	1754	9-9-1782	23-4-1804	9-11-1805	28-4-1808	25-10-1809	31-7-1810	12-8-1812	12-8-1819	27-5-1825			1828
William Wolseley		14-9-1782	23-4-1804	9-11-1805	28-4-1808	25-10-1809	31-7-1810	4-12-1813	12-8-1819	27-5-1825	10-1-1837		1842
John Manley (1)	1759	9-10-1782	23-4-1804	9-11-1805	28-4-1808	25-10-1809	31-7-1810	4-12-1813	12-8-1819	27-5-1825			
George Murray (3) (K.C.B. 1815)	1759	12-10-1782	23-4-1804	9-11-1805	28-4-1808	25-10-1809	31-7-1810	4-12-1813					28-2-1819
John Sutton (K.C.B. 1815)		28-11-1782	23-4-1804	9-11-1805	28-4-1808	25-10-1809	31-7-1810	4-12-1813	12-8-1819	27-5-1825			
Robert Murray		15-12-1782	23-4-1804	9-11-1805	28-4-1808	25-10-1809	31-7-1810	4-12-1813	12-8-1819	27-5-1825			1834
Hon. Alexander Forester Inglis Cochrane (K.B. 1806)[1]	22-4-1758	17-12-1782	23-4-1804	9-11-1805	28-4-1808	25-10-1809	31-7-1810	4-12-1813	12-8-1819	27-5-1825			29-6-1832
Sir Thomas Troubridge, Bart.	1758	1-1-1783	23-4-1804	9-11-1805	28-4-1808								D 2-3-1807
John Markham		3-1-1783	23-4-1804	9-11-1805	28-4-1808	25-10-1809	31-7-1810	4-12-1813	12-8-1819	27-5-1825			1827
Charles Stirling (1)[2]	28-4-1760	15-1-1783	23-4-1804	9-11-1805	28-4-1808	31-7-1810	1-8-1811	4-6-1814	12-8-1819	27-5-1825			7-11-1833
Henry d'Esterre Darby (K.C.B. 1820)		15-1-1783	23-4-1804	9-11-1805	28-4-1808	31-7-1810	1-8-1811	4-6-1814	12-8-1819				1823
Edward Bowater		16-1-1783	23-4-1804	9-11-1805	28-4-1808	31-7-1810	1-8-1811	4-6-1814	12-8-1819	27-5-1825			8-9-1834
George Palmer	1755	18-1-1783	23-4-1804	9-11-1805	28-4-1808	31-7-1810	1-8-1811	4-6-1814	12-8-1819	27-5-1825			6-3-1811
William O'Brien Drury		18-1-1783	23-4-1804	9-11-1805	28-4-1808	31-7-1810	1-8-1811	4-6-1814					12-7-1816
Thomas Louis (Bart. 1806)	1753	20-1-1783	23-4-1804	9-11-1805									17-5-1807
John M'Dougal	1758	20-1-1783	23-4-1804	9-11-1805	28-4-1808	31-7-1810	12-8-1812	4-6-1814					21-12-1814
James Alms (2)	1749	20-1-1783	9-11-1805		28-4-1808	31-7-1810	12-8-1812	4-6-1814	12-8-1819				1816
Eliab Harvey (K.C.B. 1815, G.C.B. 1825)		21-1-1783	9-11-1805		28-4-1808	31-7-1810	12-8-1812	4-6-1814	12-8-1819	27-5-1825			1830
John Peyton		27-1-1783	9-11-1805		28-4-1808								2-8-1809
Sir Edmund Nagle, Kt. (K.C.B. 1815)		27-1-1783	9-11-1805		28-4-1808	31-7-1810	12-8-1812	4-6-1814	12-8-1819	27-5-1825			1830
John Wells (K.C.B. 1820, G.C.B. 1834)	1763	1-3-1783		28-4-1808	25-10-1809	31-7-1810	12-8-1812	4-6-1814	19-7-1821	22-7-1830	10-1-1837		19-11-1841

[1] Prefixed Inglis to his family name of Cochrane, 1815.

[2] Sentenced by C.-M. of 9-5-1814 to remain on half-pay, and to be included in no further promotion.

LIST OF FLAG-OFFICERS—*continued.*

Name and Titles	Born	Post Captain	Rear-Admiral Blue	Rear-Admiral White	Rear-Admiral Red	Vice-Admiral Blue	Vice-Admiral White	Vice-Admiral Red	Admiral Blue	Admiral White	Admiral Red	Admiral of the Fleet	Died
Richard Grindall (K.C.B. 1815), G.C.B.)		13-3-1783	9-11-1805	28-4-1808	25-10-1809	31-7-1810	12-8-1812	4-6-1814					23-5-1820
George Martin (2) (K.C.B. 1815, G.C.B. 1821, G.C.M.G. 1836).	1763	17-3-1783	9-11-1805	28-4-1808	25-10-1809	31-7-1810	12-8-1812	4-6-1814	19-7-1821	22-7-1830	10-1-1837	9-11-1846	28-7-1847
Sir Alexander John Ball, Bart.	1757	20-3-1783	9-11-1805	28-4-1808									20-10-1809
Sir Richard John Strachan, Bart. (K.B. 1806)	27-10-1760	26-4-1783	9-11-1805	28-4-1808	25-10-1809	31-7-1810	12-8-1812	4-6-1814	19-7-1821				
Sir William Sidney Smith, Kt. (K.C.B. 1815, G.C.B. 1838)	21-6-1764	7-5-1783	9-11-1805	28-4-1808	25-10-1809	31-7-1810	12-8-1812	4-6-1814	19-7-1821	22-7-1830	10-1-1837		26-5-1840
Thomas Sotheby		11-6-1783	9-11-1805	28-4-1808	25-10-1809	31-7-1810	12-8-1812	4-6-1814	19-7-1821				
Edward O'Bryen (1)		15-6-1783	9-11-1805	28-4-1808	25-10-1809	31-7-1810	12-8-1812	4-6-1814					18-12-1808
Nathan Brunton	1751	6-8-1783	9-11-1805	28-4-1808	25-10-1809	31-7-1810		4-6-1814					19-11-1814
William Hancock Kelly	1746	8-8-1783	9-11-1805	28-4-1808	25-10-1809	31-7-1810	4-12-1813	4-6-1814					2-5-1811
John Schank		15-8-1783	9-11-1805	28-4-1808	25-10-1809	31-7-1810	4-12-1813	4-6-1814					22-2-1824
Hon. Michael de Courcy (1)	1764	6-9-1783	9-11-1805	28-4-1808	25-10-1809	31-7-1810			19-7-1821				21-2-1813
William Bentinck		15-9-1783	9-11-1805	28-4-1808		31-7-1810		4-6-1814	19-7-1821				1810
Paul Minchin		18-12-1783	9-11-1805	28-4-1808		31-7-1810		4-6-1814					18-9-1816
Philip d'Auvergne, Prince de Bouillon	22-11-1754	22-1-1784	9-11-1805	28-4-1808		31-7-1810	4-12-1813						1819
John Hunter	9-1738	15-12-1786	2-10-1807	28-4-1808	31-7-1810	1-8-1811	4-12-1813						
Francis Pender		1-12-1787	2-10-1807	28-4-1808	31-7-1810	1-8-1811	4-6-1814	4-6-1814					30-7-1815
William Albany Otway	1756	1-12-1787	2-10-1807	28-4-1808	31-7-1810	1-8-1811	4-6-1814	4-6-1814					9-2-1812
George Lumsdaine		1-12-1787	2-10-1807	28-4-1808	31-7-1810	1-8-1811	4-6-1814	12-8-1819					24-12-1814
Sir Samuel Hood (2), (K.B. 1801, Bart. 1809)	11-1762	24-5-1788	2-10-1807	28-4-1808	31-7-1810	1-8-1811	4-6-1814	12-8-1819					
Henry Nicholls (K.C.B. 1820)		1-12-1788	6-10-1807	28-4-1808	31-7-1810	1-8-1811	4-6-1814	12-8-1819	27-5-1825				1829
Herbert Sawyer (2), (K.C.B. 1815)		3-2-1789	2-10-1807	28-4-1808	31-7-1810	1-8-1811	4-6-1814	12-8-1819	27-5-1825	22-7-1830			13-11-1833
Davidge Gould (K.C.B. 1815, G.C.B. 1833)	1758	25-3-1789	2-10-1807	25-10-1809	31-7-1810	1-8-1811	4-6-1814	12-8-1819	27-5-1825	22-7-1830	10-1-1837		23-4-1847
Richard Goodwin Keats (K.B. 1808)		24-6-1789	2-10-1807	25-10-1809	31-7-1810	12-8-1812	4-6-1814	12-8-1819	27-5-1825				5-4-1834
Robert Devereux Fancourt		2-12-1789	28-4-1808	25-10-1809	31-7-1810	12-8-1812	4-6-1814	12-8-1819					1824
Edward Buller (Bart. 1808)		19-7-1790	28-4-1808	25-10-1809	31-7-1810	12-8-1812	4-6-1814	12-8-1819	27-5-1825	22-7-1830			
Hon. Robert Stopford (K.C.B. 1815, G.C.B. 1831, G.C.M.G. 1837)	5-2-1768	12-8-1790	28-4-1808	25-10-1809	31-7-1810	12-8-1812	4-6-1814	12-8-1819	27-5-1825	22-7-1830	10-1-1837		26-6-1847
Mark Robinson (2)	1754	21-9-1790	28-4-1808	25-10-1809	31-7-1810	12-8-1812	4-6-1814	12-8-1819					21-2-1831
Thomas Revell Shivers		21-9-1790	28-4-1808	25-10-1809	31-7-1810	12-8-1812	4-6-1814	12-8-1819					
Charles Cobb		21-9-1790	28-4-1808	25-10-1809	31-7-1810	12-8-1812	4-6-1814	12-8-1819					24-2-1818
Francis Pickmore	1758	21-9-1790	28-4-1808	25-10-1809	31-7-1810	12-8-1812	4-6-1814	12-8-1819	27-5-1825				16-2-1814
John Stephens Hall		21-9-1790	28-4-1808	25-10-1809	31-7-1810	12-8-1812	4-6-1814	12-8-1819		27-5-1825			18-2-1827
John Dilkes		21-9-1790	28-4-1808	25-10-1809	31-7-1810	12-8-1812	4-6-1814	12-8-1819					1815
William Lechmere		21-9-1790	28-4-1808	25-10-1809	31-7-1810	12-8-1812	4-6-1814	12-8-1819	27-5-1825				
Thomas Foley (3) (K.C.B. 1815, G.C.B. 1820)	1756	21-9-1790	28-4-1808		31-7-1810	12-8-1812	4-6-1814	12-8-1819	27-5-1825	22-7-1830			9-1-1833
Charles Tyler (1) (K.C.B. 1815)	1764	21-9-1790	28-4-1808		31-7-1810	4-12-1813	4-6-1814	19-7-1821	27-5-1825	22-7-1830			28-9-1835
Robert Carthew Reynolds		24-9-1790	28-4-1808		31-7-1810	4-12-1813	4-6-1814						D 24-12-1811
Robert Watson		25-10-1790	28-4-1808	31-7-1810	31-7-1810	4-12-1813	4-6-1814						
Hon. Alan Hyde Gardiner (Lord Gardiner, 1809, K.C.B. 1815)	6-2-1770	12-11-1790	28-4-1808	31-7-1810	1-8-1811	4-12-1813	4-6-1814						27-12-1815

Name	Born	Captain	Rear-Admiral			Vice-Admiral			Admiral				Died
Manley Dixon (K.C.B. 1819)	1760	22-11-1790	28-4-1808	31-7-1810	1-8-1811	4-12-1813	4-6-1814	19-7-1821	27-5-1825	22-7-1830		—	8-2-1837
George Lossack		22-11-1790	28-4-1808	31-7-1810	1-8-1811	4-12-1813	4-6-1814	19-7-1821	27-5-1825	22-7-1830	10-1-1837	—	
William Mitchell (K.C.B. 1815)	1746	22-11-1790	28-4-1808	31-7-1810	1-8-1811	4-12-1813	4-6-1814					—	7-3-1816
George Hart	1752	22-11-1790	28-4-1808	31-7-1810	1-8-1811							—	28-4-1812
Thomas Bertie (2) (Kt. 1813)[1]	3-7-1758	22-11-1790	28-4-1808	31-7-1810	1-8-1811	4-12-1813	4-6-1814	19-7-1821	27-5-1825	22-7-1830	10-1-1837	—	
Rowley Bulteel		22-11-1790	28-4-1808	31-7-1810	1-8-1811	4-12-1813	4-6-1814	19-7-1821	27-5-1825	22-7-1830	10-1-1837	—	
William Luke		22-11-1790	28-4-1808	31-7-1810	1-8-1811	4-12-1813	4-6-1814	19-7-1821	27-5-1825	22-7-1830	10-1-1837	—	
Isaac George Manley	1756	22-11-1790	28-4-1808	31-7-1810	1-8-1811	4-12-1813	4-6-1814	19-7-1821	27-5-1825	22-7-1830		—	1837
John Osborn		22-11-1790	28-4-1808	31-7-1810	1-8-1811	4-12-1813	4-6-1814	19-7-1821	27-5-1825	22-7-1830	10-1-1837	—	
Edmund Crawley		22-11-1790	28-4-1808	31-7-1810	1-8-1811	4-12-1813	4-6-1814	19-7-1821	27-5-1825	22-7-1830		—	1834
Charles Boyles	1756	22-11-1790	28-4-1808	31-7-1810	1-8-1811	4-12-1813	4-6-1814					—	9-11-1816
Sir Thomas Williams (4), Kt. (K.C.B. 1815)	1762	22-11-1790	25-10-1809	1-8-1811	12-8-1812	4-6-1814	12-8-1819	19-7-1821	27-5-1825	22-7-1830	10-1-1837	—	10-10-1841
Thomas Hamilton	1754	22-11-1790	25-10-1809	1-8-1811	12-8-1812	4-6-1814						—	26-6-1815
Sir Thomas Boulden Thompson, Bart. (K.C.B. 1815, G.C.B. 1822)[2]	28-2-1766	22-11-1790	25-10-1809	1-8-1811	12-8-1812	4-6-1814	12-8-1819	19-7-1821	27-5-1825			—	3-3-1828
George Countess		22-11-1790	25-10-1809	1-8-1811								—	1811
John Laugharne		22-11-1790	25-10-1809	1-8-1811	12-8-1812	4-6-1814	12-8-1819	19-7-1821	27-5-1825	22-7-1830	10-1-1837	—	
William Hargood (1) (K.C.B. 1815)	1759	22-11-1790	31-7-1810	12-8-1812	4-12-1813	4-6-1814	12-8-1819	19-7-1821	27-5-1825	22-7-1830	10-1-1837	—	12-12-1839
George Gregory		22-11-1790	31-7-1810	12-8-1812	4-12-1813							—	24-1-1814
John Ferrier		22-11-1790	31-7-1810	12-8-1812	4-12-1813	4-6-1814	12-8-1819	19-7-1821	27-5-1825	22-7-1830		—	27-1-1836
Richard Incledon Bury[3]	6-1760	22-11-1790	31-7-1810	12-8-1812	4-12-1813	4-6-1814	12-8-1819	19-7-1821	27-5-1825	22-7-1830	10-1-1837	—	
Robert Moorsom (K.C.B. 1816)	25-5-1767	22-11-1790	31-7-1810	12-8-1812	4-12-1813	4-6-1814	12-8-1819	19-7-1821	27-5-1825	22-7-1830		—	1835
Sir Charles Hamilton, Bart. (K.C.B. 1833)	21-5-1765	22-11-1790	31-7-1810	12-8-1812	4-12-1813	4-6-1814	12-8-1819	19-7-1821	27-5-1825	22-7-1830	23-11-1841	—	14-9-1849
Hon. Henry Curzon	1763	22-11-1790	31-7-1810	12-8-1812	4-12-1813	4-6-1814	12-8-1819	19-7-1821	27-5-1825	22-7-1830	10-1-1837	—	2-5-1846
William Bligh	2-4-1764	22-11-1790	31-7-1810	12-8-1812	4-12-1813	4-6-1814						—	12-12-1817
Lawrence William Halsted (K.C.B. 1816, G.C.B. 1837)		31-5-1791	31-7-1810	12-8-1812	4-12-1813	4-6-1814	12-8-1819	19-7-1821	27-5-1825	22-7-1830	10-1-1837	—	22-4-1841
Edward Oliver Osborn	1764	1-10-1791	31-7-1810	12-8-1812	4-12-1813	4-6-1814	12-8-1819	19-7-1821	27-5-1825	22-7-1830	10-1-1837	—	
Sir Harry Burrard Neale, Bart. (K.C.B. 1815, G.C.B. 1822)[4]	6-6-1768	1-2-1793	31-7-1810	12-8-1812	4-12-1813	4-6-1814	12-8-1819	19-7-1821	27-5-1825	22-7-1830	10-1-1837	—	7-2-1840
Sir Joseph Sydney Yorke, Kt. (K.C.B. 1815)	25-10-1766	4-2-1793	31-7-1810	12-8-1812	4-12-1813	4-6-1814	12-8-1819	19-7-1821	27-5-1825	22-7-1830		—	5-5-1831
Hon. Arthur Kaye Legge (K.C.B. 1815)		6-2-1793	31-7-1810	12-8-1812	4-12-1813	4-6-1814	12-8-1819	19-7-1821	27-5-1825	22-7-1830		—	12-5-1835
Francis Fayerman		24-4-1793	31-7-1810	12-8-1812	4-12-1813	4-6-1814	12-8-1819	19-7-1821	27-5-1825	22-7-1830	10-1-1837	—	
George, Earl of Galloway	24-3-1768	30-4-1793	31-7-1810	12-8-1812	4-12-1813	4-6-1814	12-8-1819	19-7-1821	27-5-1825	22-7-1830		—	27-3-1834
Thomas Francis Fremantle (K.C.B. 1815)	1765	16-5-1793	12-8-1812	4-12-1813	4-6-1814	12-8-1819						—	19-12-1819
Sir Robert Barlow, Kt. (K.C.B. 1820)[5]	25-12-1757	24-5-1793	12-8-1812	4-12-1813	4-6-1814	12-8-1819	19-7-1821	27-5-1825	22-7-1830	12-11-1840	23-11-1841	—	11-6-1843
Sir Francis Laforey, Bart. (K.C.B. 1815)	31-12-1767	5-6-1793	12-8-1812	4-12-1813	4-6-1814	12-8-1819	19-7-1821	27-5-1825	22-7-1830			—	1835
Philip Charles Durham (K.C.B. 1815, G.C.B. 1830)[6]	7-1765	24-6-1793	12-8-1812	4-12-1813	4-6-1814	12-8-1819	19-7-1821	27-5-1825	22-7-1830	10-1-1837	23-11-1841	—	2-4-1845
Israel Pellew (K.C.B. 1815)	25-8-1758	25-6-1793	12-8-1812	4-12-1813	4-6-1814	12-8-1819	19-7-1821	27-5-1825	22-7-1830			—	2-8-1832
Alexander Fraser (1)	1751	1-7-1793	12-8-1812	4-12-1813	4-6-1814	12-8-1819	19-7-1821	27-5-1825	22-7-1830	10-1-1837	23-11-1841	—	
Benjamin Hallowell (K.C.B. 1815, G.C.B. 1831)[7]	1760	30-8-1793	4-6-1814	12-8-1819	19-7-1821	27-5-1825	22-7-1830					—	2-9-1834
George Johnstone Hope (K.C.B. 1815)[8]	6-7-1767	13-9-1793	4-6-1814									—	2-5-1818

1 Originally Thomas Hoar. Assumed name of Bertie, 1788.
2 Originally Thomas Boulden. Assumed name of Thompson, 1785.
3 Originally Richard Incledon. Assumed name of Bury about 1802.
4 Originally Harry Burrard. Assumed name of Neale, 1795.

5 Superannuated Captain, 31-7-1810; superannuated Rear-Adm. 24-1-1823: restored to active list, 1840.
6 Assumed, in or after 1817, name of P. C. Calderwood Henderson Durham.
7 Assumed name of B. Hallowell Carew, 1828.
8 Originally George Hope.

List of Flag-Officers—*continued.*

Name and Titles	Born	Post Captain	Rear-Admiral			Vice-Admiral			Admiral			Admiral of the Fleet	Died
			Blue	White	Red	Blue	White	Red	Blue	White	Red		
Lord Amelius Beauclerk (K.C.B. 1815, G.C.B. 1835)	1771	16-9-1793	1-8-1811	12-8-1812	4-6-1814	12-8-1819	19-7-1821	27-5-1825	22-7-1830	10-1-1837	23-11-1841		10-12-1846
William Taylor		24-9-1793	1-8-1811	12-8-1812	4-6-1814	12-8-1819	19-7-1821	27-5-1825	22-7-1830	10-1-1837	23-11-1841		1842
James Nicholl Morris (K.C.B. 1815)		7-10-1793	1-8-1811	12-8-1812	4-6-1814	12-8-1819	19-7-1821	27-5-1825					1830
George Burdon (1)		28-10-1793	1-8-1811	12-8-1812	4-6-1814								1814
William Brown (1)		29-10-1793	1-8-1811	12-8-1812	4-6-1814								
Thomas Byam Martin (K.C.B. 1815, G.C.B. 1830)	1773	5-11-1793	1-8-1811	12-8-1812	4-6-1814	12-8-1819	19-7-1821	27-5-1825	22-7-1830	10-1-1837	23-11-1841	13-10-1849	21-10-1854
John Lawford (K.C.B. 1833)	1756	1-12-1793	1-8-1811	4-12-1813	4-6-1814	12-8-1819	19-7-1821	27-5-1825	22-7-1830	10-1-1837	23-11-1841		22-12-1842
Frank Sotheron	1766	11-12-1793	1-8-1811	4-12-1813	4-6-1814	12-8-1819	19-7-1821	27-5-1825	22-7-1830	10-1-1837			7-2-1839
Thomas Wolley		19-12-1793	1-8-1811	4-12-1813	4-6-1814	12-8-1819	27-5-1825	22-7-1830					
William Johnstone Hope (K.C.B. 1815, G.C.B. 1825)[1]	16-8-1766	9-1-1794	12-8-1812	4-12-1813	4-6-1814	12-8-1819	27-5-1825	22-7-1830					2-5-1831
Lord Henry Paulet (K.C.B. 1815)	31-3-1767	9-1-1794	12-8-1812	4-12-1813	4-6-1814	12-8-1819	27-5-1825	22-7-1830					28-11-1832
Charles William Paterson	1756	20-1-1794	12-8-1812	4-12-1813	4-6-1814	12-8-1819	27-5-1825	22-7-1830	10-1-1837				10-3-1841
George Cockburn (K.C.B. 1815, G.C.B. 1818, P.C. 1827)	1772	20-2-1794	12-8-1812	4-12-1813	4-6-1814	12-8-1819	27-5-1825	22-7-1830	10-1-1837	23-11-1841		1-7-1851	1853
Thomas Surridge		1-3-1794	12-8-1812	4-12-1813	4-6-1814	12-8-1819	27-5-1825	22-7-1830					
Samuel Hood Linzee		8-3-1794	12-8-1812		4-6-1814	12-8-1819	27-5-1825	22-7-1830					
James Carpenter	1759	25-3-1794	12-8-1812		4-6-1814	12-8-1819	27-5-1825	22-7-1830	10-1-1837	23-11-1841			16-3-1845
Robert Barton		2-4-1794	12-8-1812	4-6-1814		19-7-1821	27-5-1825	22-7-1830					
Graham Moore (K.C.B. 1815, G.C.M.G. 1832, G.C.B. 1836)		2-4-1794	12-8-1812	4-6-1814		19-7-1821	27-5-1825	22-7-1830	10-1-1837	23-11-1841			25-11-1843
Matthew Henry Scott	10-12-1759	4-4-1794	12-8-1812	4-6-1814		19-7-1821	27-5-1825	22-7-1830					31-10-1836
Joseph Hanwell	1765	5-4-1794	12-8-1812	4-6-1814		19-7-1821	27-5-1825	22-7-1830	10-1-1837				1839
Henry William Bayntun (K.C.B. 1815)		4-5-1794	12-8-1812	4-6-1814		19-7-1821	27-5-1825	22-7-1830	10-1-1837				15-12-1840
Hon. Francis Farington Gardner	21-6-1773	6-5-1794	12-8-1812	4-6-1814		19-7-1821							1821
Sir Richard King (2), Bart. (K.C.B. 1815)	28-11-1774	14-5-1794	12-8-1812	4-6-1814		19-7-1821	27-5-1825	22-7-1830					4-8-1834
Edward Griffith (K.C.B. 1831)[2]	1767	21-5-1794	12-8-1812	4-6-1814		19-7-1821	27-5-1825	22-7-1830					9-11-1832
Edward James Foote (K.C.B. 1831)	1767	7-6-1794	12-8-1812	4-6-1814		19-7-1821	27-5-1825	22-7-1830					23-7-1833
Richard Lee (K.C.B. 1815)	1765	7-6-1794	12-8-1812	4-6-1814		19-7-1821	27-5-1825	22-7-1830	10-1-1837				1837
William Bradley (1)[3]		23-6-1794	12-8-1812	4-6-1814		19-7-1821	27-5-1825	22-7-1830					
William Pierrepont	1766	4-8-1794	12-8-1812										7-8-1813
Peter Halkett (Bart. 1837)	1765	13-8-1794	4-12-1813	4-6-1814		19-7-1821	27-5-1825	22-7-1830	10-1-1837				10-1839
Philip Wilkinson[4]	8-1-1764	15-8-1794	4-12-1813	4-6-1814		19-7-1821	27-5-1825						9-1827
William Shield[5]		5-9-1794	4-12-1813	4-6-1814		19-7-1821	27-5-1825	22-7-1830	10-1-1837	23-11-1841			1846
Hon. Charles Elphinstone Fleeming[6] (K.C.B. 1816)	20-6-1759	7-10-1794	4-12-1813	4-6-1814		19-7-1821	27-5-1825	22-7-1830	10-1-1837				30-10-1840
Charles Vinicombe Penrose (K.C.B. 1815)		7-10-1794	4-12-1813	4-6-1814		19-7-1821	27-5-1825	22-7-1830	12-11-1840	23-11-1841	9-11-1846		
William Hotham (2) (K.C.B. 1840, G.C.B. 1840)	2-1772	7-10-1794	4-12-1813	4-6-1814		19-7-1821	27-5-1825	22-7-1830	10-1-1837	23-11-1841	9-11-1846		31-5-1848
George Hopewell Stephens (K.C.B. 1815)		11-10-1794	4-12-1813	4-6-1814									25-12-1819
Pulteney Malcolm (K.C.B. 1815, G.C.M.G. 1829, G.C.B. 1833)	20-2-1768	22-10-1794	4-12-1813	4-6-1814		19-7-1821	27-5-1825	22-7-1830	10-1-1837				20-7-1838
William Nowell (1)		24-10-1794	4-12-1813	4-6-1814		19-7-1821	27-5-1825	22-7-1830					

Name	Born	Post-Captain	Flag-officer promotion dates (in order)	Died
James Bissett	—	24-10-1794	4-12-1813; 4-6-1814; 12-8-1819; 27-5-1825; 22-7-1830	21-8-1836
John Clements	—	24-10-1794	4-12-1813; 4-6-1814; 12-8-1819; 27-5-1825; 22-7-1830	17-2-1837
Sir John Gore (2), Kt. (K.C.B. 1815)	1772	12-11-1794	4-12-1813; 4-6-1814; 12-8-1819; 27-5-1825; 22-7-1830	19-4-1833
John Harvey (2) (K.C.B. 1833)	—	16-12-1794	4-12-1813; 4-6-1814; 12-8-1819; 27-5-1825; 22-7-1830	21-9-1815
Hon. Henry Hotham (K.C.B. 1815; G.C.B. 1833)	19-2-1777	13-1-1795	4-6-1814; 12-8-1819; 27-5-1825; 22-7-1830	11-9-1820
George Burlton (K.C.B. 1815)	—	16-3-1795	4-6-1814; 12-8-1819; 27-5-1825	10-1-1842
Charles Dudley Pater	—	16-3-1795	4-6-1814; 12-8-1819	—
Sir Home Riggs Popham, Kt. (K.C.B. 1815)	1762	4-4-1795	4-6-1814; 12-9-1819	—
Sir Josias Rowley, Bart. (K.C.B. 1815; G.C.M.G. 1834, G.C.B. 1840)	1765	6-4-1795	4-6-1814; 12-8-1819; 27-5-1825; 22-7-1830; 10-1-1837	28-4-1851
Edward Codrington (K.C.B. 1815; G.C.M.G. 1827, G.C.B. 1833)	1770	6-4-1795	4-6-1814; 12-8-1819; 27-5-1825; 22-7-1830; 10-1-1837; 23-11-1841	24-12-1847
George Parker (K.C.B. 1833)	1767	6-4-1795	4-6-1814; 12-8-1819; 27-5-1825; 22-7-1830; 10-1-1837; 23-11-1841; 9-11-1846	14-2-1834
Robert Plampin	—	7-4-1795	4-6-1814; 12-8-1819; 19-7-1821; 27-5-1825; 22-7-1830; 10-1-1837; 23-11-1841; 9-11-1846	1856
Frederick Watkins[7]	—	21-4-1795	4-6-1814; 12-8-1819; 19-7-1821; 27-5-1825; 22-7-1830; 12-11-1840; 23-11-1841; 10-12-1846	21-12-1832
Edward Leveson Gower	8-5-1776	26-4-1795	12-8-1819; 19-7-1821; 27-5-1825; 22-7-1830; 12-11-1840; 23-11-1841; 10-12-1846	25-7-1847
Hon. Henry Blackwood (Bart. 1814; K.C.B. 1819)	28-12-1770	1-6-1795	12-8-1819; 19-7-1821; 27-5-1825; 22-7-1830; 10-1-1837; 28-6-1838; 23-11-1841	18-6-1831
John Erskine Douglas	—	2-6-1795	12-8-1819; 19-7-1821; 27-5-1825; 22-7-1830; 10-1-1837	30-9-1840
George Byng (2), Viscount Torrington	5-1-1768	10-6-1795	12-8-1819; 19-7-1821; 27-5-1825; 22-7-1830; 10-1-1837; 23-11-1841; 10-12-1846	2-10-1844
Ross Donnelly (K.C.B. 1837)	1763	18-6-1795	12-8-1819; 19-7-1821; 27-5-1825; 22-7-1830; 10-1-1837; 28-6-1838	23-10-1818
Sir John Poo Beresford, Bart. (K.C.B. 1819)	1760	24-6-1795	12-8-1819; 19-7-1821; 27-5-1825; 22-7-1830; 10-1-1837; 28-6-1838	1835
Henry Lidgbird Ball	—	25-6-1795	12-8-1819; 27-5-1825; 22-7-1830; 10-1-1837	1857
Thomas Eyles	—	9-7-1795	12-8-1819; 19-7-1821; 27-5-1825; 22-7-1830	10-10-1845
Thomas Le Marchant Gosselin[8]	7-5-1765	13-7-1795	12-8-1819; 19-7-1821; 27-5-1825; 22-7-1830; 10-1-1837; 23-11-1841	29-9-1814
Charles Rowley (K.C.B. 1815, G.C.B. 1840)	16-12-1770	23-7-1795	12-8-1819; 19-7-1821; 27-5-1825; 22-7-1830; 10-1-1837; 23-11-1841; 24-4-1847	18-11-1839
Thomas Rogers	—	1-8-1795	12-8-1819; 27-5-1825; 22-7-1830; 10-1-1837	1835
Samuel James Ballard	—	10-8-1795	12-8-1819; 27-5-1825; 22-7-1830; 10-1-1837	5-5-1845
Robert Rolles	—	10-8-1795	12-8-1819; 27-5-1825; 22-7-1830; 10-1-1837	1814
Walter Locke	1764	12-8-1795	12-8-1819; 27-5-1825; 22-7-1830; 10-1-1837	11-11-1819
David Milne (K.C.B. 1816, G.C.B. 1840)	25-5-1763	22-9-1795	12-8-1819; 27-5-1825; 22-7-1830; 10-1-1837	12-5-1846
George Dundas	—	2-10-1795	12-8-1819; 27-5-1825	22-1-1837
James Young (2)	—	3-10-1795	12-8-1819; 27-5-1825	26-12-1814
James Macnamara (2)	—	5-10-1795	12-8-1819	1833
Donald Campbell (1)	—	6-10-1795	12-8-1819; [21-8-1827]	27-1-1833
Robert Waller Otway (1) (K.C.B. 1826, G.C.B. 1845)	4-1772	26-10-1795	12-8-1819; 27-5-1825; 22-7-1830; 10-1-1837; 23-11-1841	1841
Richard Dacres[9]	9-1761	30-10-1795	12-8-1819; 27-5-1825; 22-7-1830; 10-1-1837	
Thomas Western	16-5-1761	31-10-1795	12-8-1819; 27-5-1825; 22-7-1830; 10-1-1837	
John William Spranger	1768	12-11-1795	12-8-1819; 27-5-1825	
William Lukin[10]	1761	24-11-1795	12-8-1819; [5-7-1827]; 22-7-1830	1833
Shuldham Peard[11]	1761	28-11-1795	12-8-1819; 27-5-1825; 22-7-1830	27-1-1833
Edward Fellowes	1771	7-12-1795	12-8-1819; 27-5-1825; 22-7-1830	1841

1 Originally William Hope.

2 Assumed name of E. G. Colpoys, 1821.

3 Removed from the list, 1814.

4 Assumed name of Phillip Stephens, 1820.

5 Comm. of the Navy, 1807; Depty.-Controller, 1814; Comm. at Plymouth, 1815-29; retd. Rear-Adm., 1829; restored to active list, 1840.

6 Originally Charles Elphinstone. Assumed name of Fleeming 'on death of his grand-mother.

7 Superannuated Rear-Adm., 11-6-1814; restored to active list, 1840.

8 This officer, though long at the top of the flag-list, was never promoted to be Adm. of the Fleet, as vacancies occurred.

9 Superannuated Rear-Adm., 29-3-1817; restored to active list, 1827.

10 Assumed name of William Windham, 1824.

11 Superannuated Rear-Adm., 5-7-1814; restored to active list, 1827.

CHAPTER XXXIX.

MAJOR OPERATIONS OF THE ROYAL NAVY, 1803–1815.

Causes of the renewal of the war—Commanders-in-Chief, 1803—Naval strength of France—Expedition to Pondicherry—Cornwallis begins his blockade of Brest—The Home station—The Invasion Flotilla—Owen off Blanc Nez—Mundy off Le Hâvre—Owen off Dieppe and St. Valery-en-Caux—Operations off Granville—Jackson and Honyman off Calais—Nelson appointed to the Mediterranean—Observation of Toulon—Agincourt Sound — Reduction of St. Lucia, Tobago, Demerara, Essequibo and Berbice—Loring at Cape François—French evacuation of Hayti—The East Indies—Cruise of Linois—Cornwallis off Brest in 1804—The Invasion Flotilla—British coast defences—Williams off Gravelines—Capture of Wesley Wright—Action with Ver Huell—Oliver at Le Hâvre—Skirmish off Etaples—Owen off Vimereux—The "catamaran"—Abortive attack on shipping at Boulogne—Henniker at Gris Nez—Loss of the *Conflict*—The catamaran discredited—The Mediterranean in 1804—The *Amazon* off Toulon—Bragadoccio of Latouche-Tréville—Origin of the Trafalgar campaign—Projects of French naval concentration—Death of Latouche-Tréville—Difficulties of blockade—Appointment of Villeneuve—Revised French projects—Spain joins France—Nelson's lack of frigates—Seizure of the *Surinam*—Bligh's ill success at Curaçoa—Surrender of Surinam—Capture and recapture of Gorée—Franco-Spanish convention of 1805—Strength of the opposed navies—Cochrane off Ferrol—Orde off Cadiz—Orde's jealousy of Nelson — The Admiralty's neglect of Nelson — Beginning of the Trafalgar campaign—Escape of Villeneuve from Toulon—Nelson searches to the eastward—Villeneuve's cruise—He returns to Toulon—Missiessy escapes from Rochefort—His instructions—Nelson resumes the observation of Toulon—French projects again modified—Situation of the rival forces in March, 1805—Napoleon's instructions to avoid a fleet action—Villeneuve again escapes from Toulon—Causes of Nelson's delay in following to the westward—Flight of Orde from off Cadiz—Nelson in chase of the French—Disposition of the British Navy—The Brest fleet overawed by Gardner—Villeneuve at Martinique—Nelson follows to the West Indies—He sacrifices to the safety of a convoy—His plan of action—Nelson at Barbados—He has news of Villeneuve—The French reduce the Diamond Rock—Ganteaume fails to meet Villeneuve—Villeneuve returns to Europe with Nelson at his heels—Nelson learns that the enemy has sought shelter in port, and hauls down his flag—British dispositions during Nelson's absence—Prompt action of Lord Barham—Calder reinforced off Ferrol—Calder's action with the allies under Villeneuve—Villeneuve enters Corunna—Cornwallis's strategical mistake—Villeneuve's remissness—He enters Vigo Bay—He proceeds to Ferrol—He seeks in vain for Allemand from Rochefort—The allies enter Cadiz—Fury of Napoleon—Villeneuve's supersession determined on—Cornwallis drives Ganteaume back to Brest—Collingwood reinforced off Cadiz—Napoleon abandons his plans of invading England—He decides to send his fleet to the Mediterranean—Nelson resumes command — Villeneuve's eagerness to escape supersession by distinguishing himself—Nelson's anxieties—His plan of action—He has to weaken his force—The allies leave Cadiz for the Mediterranean—The battle of Trafalgar—Nelson's glorious death—Other officers killed and wounded—Results of the action—Collingwood omits to anchor the fleet—Fate of the prizes—Nelson's funeral—His character—Honours to his relatives—Honours to the victors—Fate of Villeneuve—Strachan defeats Dumanoir Le Pelley—Effects of the Trafalgar campaign—Concentration of the Invasion Flotilla—Honyman off Boulogne—Adam off Fécamp—Loss of the *Plumper* and *Teazer*—Ver Huell's voyage southward—Bromley and Hamelin off St. Valery—Constitution of the Invasion Flotilla in 1805—Cruise of Missiessy—His proceedings in the West Indies—He relieves San Domingo and returns to France—Sortie of Leissègues and Willaumez from Brest—Warren and Strachan pursue—Brisbane warns Duckworth—Duckworth's excessive caution and its results—Duckworth defeats Leissègues off San Domingo—Exploits of Willaumez — Insubordination of Jérôme Bonaparte — Return of Willaumez — Cornwallis strikes his flag—Collingwood off Cadiz—Escape of the French frigates from Cadiz—Austria and Prussia treat with France—French action against Naples—Sidney Smith at Gaeta and Capri—British invasion of Calabria—Hoste at Cotrone—Popham takes the Cape of Good Hope—Capture of the *Volontaire*—Popham's expedition to the River Plate—Capture and recapture of Buenos Aires—Capture of Maldonado—Trial of Popham—British aid to the Northern Powers in 1807—Chetham at Danzig—The French navy at the peace of Tilsit—Demand for the Danish fleet—Gambier's expedition to the Baltic—Capture of the *Frederikscoarn*—Bombardment and capture of Copenhagen—Russell takes Helgoland—French intrigues with Turkey—Louis sent to the Dardanelles—The British ambassador leaves Constantinople—Duckworth reinforces Louis and takes command—Loss of the *Ajax*—Passage of the Dardanelles—Sidney Smith destroys a Turkish squadron—Duckworth's lack of decision—Useless negotiations—Retreat of the fleet from Constantinople—Huge Turkish shot—Duckworth refuses to re-enter the strait—Expedition to Egypt—Surrender of Alexandria—Russian action against Turkey — Portugal unwillingly joins France — Sidney Smith blockades the Tagus—Dom João abandons Portugal for Brazil—Sidney Smith blockades Seniavine in the Tagus—Madeira taken—Stirling supersedes Popham in the Plate—Montevideo taken—Operations against Buenos Aires—Withdrawal of the expedition—Punishment of Whitelocke—Brisbane captures Curaçoa—Denmark loses St. Thomas and St. Croix—Expedition to Java—French naval activity in 1808—Escape of Allemand from Rochefort—He enters Toulon—Ganteaume leaves Toulon for the eastward—Collingwood suffers him to return to Toulon—Final evacuation of Calabria—Collingwood and the Spanish patriots—Surrender of the French squadron at Cadiz—Spain and Portugal act with Great Britain—Wellesley to the Peninsula—Surrender of the Russian squadron in the Tagus—Expedition to the Baltic—Surrender and burning of the *Sewolod*—Operations at Nyborg—Capture of Marie Galante—Capture of Désirade—Repulse at St. Martin—Willaumez leaves Brest—Stopford and Jurien—Willaumez blockaded in Aix Road—Gambier assumes the blockade—Preparation of fireships—Cochrane summoned—Allemand supersedes Willaumez—Cochrane attacks Allemand's squadron—Destruction of French ships—Mismanagemeut of the affair—Trial of Gambier—Treatment of the French captains—Reduction of Anholt—The French in the Schelde—Expedition to the Schelde—Operations in Walcheren—Siege of Flushing—British mismanagement—Passage of the forts—Fall of Flushing—Collapse of the expedition—Baudin relieves Barcelona—Baudin's second sortie—Hallowell in Rosas Bay—Successes in the Ionian Islands—Capture of Sénégal, Martinique, and Cayenne—Gallantry of Yeo—Death of Collingwood—Capture of Sta. Maura—Allemand supersedes Ganteaume at Toulon—Skirmishes off the port—Capture of Guadeloupe, St. Martin, St. Eustatius and Saba—Reduction of Amboyna—Capture of Banda—Mauritius taken—Inactivity of the great French fleets—Pellew and Emeriau off Toulon—Reduction of Java—Naval impotence of France

—Russia deserts Napoleon—Allemand cruises from Lorient—Pellew off Toulon—
Murat deserts Napoleon—Pellew and Cosmao-Kerjulien—Hoste captures Cattaro
—Other operations in the Adriatic—Passage of the Adour—Penrose in the Gironde
—First restoration of Louis XVIII.—Napoleon taken to Elba—Events of the
Hundred Days—Napoleon deported to St. Helena—Capture of the *Melpomène*—
Operations in the West Indies—Conditions of the Peace of Paris—Great Britain's
gains—The Navy's share in the results secured for Europe and civilisation.

NAVAL HALFPENNY TOKEN OF 1812, COMMEMORA-
TIVE OF NELSON.

(From an original lent by H.S.H. Captain Prince Louis of
Battenberg, G.C.B., R.N.)

IT has been said that, under the provisions of the Treaty of Amiens, the islands of Malta, Gozo, and Comino were to be returned to the Order of St. John of Jerusalem, which had held them previous to the war of 1793–1802, and that the troops of Great Britain were to evacuate the islands within three months of the exchange of ratifications. It has also been said that the republic of the Ionian Islands was acknowledged, and that Egypt and the other territories of the Sultan were restored to the *status quo ante bellum*. It had been arranged by the treaty that the independence of Malta should be guaranteed by Great Britain, France, Austria, Russia, and Spain ; but when, moved thereto by French influences, Russia put herself forward as the special protector of the island; when, moreover, it became evident that Napoleon still had designs against the Ionian Republic and Egypt; [1] and when warlike preparations on a large scale began in all the ports of France, Great Britain very wisely objected to evacuate the Maltese islands. The immediate result was that Napoleon very rudely informed Lord Whitworth, the British Ambassador in Paris, of his intention to regard as a *casus belli* a refusal to deliver up Malta. The interview in which he conveyed this intimation was a public one; and the First Consul's manner was so insulting that the Ambassador might well have quitted Paris instantly ; but he remained, and eventually presented Napoleon with an ultimatum proposing that Great Britain should retain Malta for ten years. France's reply was that the island must be ceded to Russia ; and with that reply Lord Whitworth left Paris.

[1] Sebastiani's report.

When he reached London, it was felt that, in view of the attitude of the First Consul, further negotiation was useless, and that prompt action was most desirable. On May 16th, 1803, therefore, Great Britain authorised the issue of letters of marque and general reprisals,[1] and on May 18th she formally declared war against

SIR JOHN BARROW, BART.
Secretary of the Admiralty, 1804–1845.
(*From the picture by Jackson, painted in* 1824.)

France. It is now clear that the declaration must have somewhat surprised Napoleon, who had expected that he would succeed in postponing the outbreak of hostilities until the autumn.[2] Such is, very briefly, an outline of the causes which led to what was practically a renewal of the old war.

The British officers holding command of the chief stations during the year 1803 were:—

---

[1] Vessels of the Batavian Republic, then in effect a part of France, were at the same time ordered to be detained.

[2] Instruct. au Gén. Decaen, Feb. 1803; in Dumas, 'Précis des Evén. Milit.,' xi. 189.

Portsmouth . . . .   Admiral Mark Milbanke.
                     Admiral Lord Gardner, *from Mar.* 16*th.*
Plymouth . . . .   Admiral Sir Thomas Pasley.
                     Admiral Lord Keith, *from Mar.* 11*th.*[1]
                     Admiral George Montagu, *from May* 26*th.*
                     Admiral Sir John Colpoys, *from June* 8*th.*
Channel. . . . .   Admiral the Hon. Wm. Cornwallis.
Mediterranean . . . R.-Adm. Sir Richard Hussey Bickerton.
                     V.-Adm. Lord Nelson, *from May* 16*th.*
Downs . . . . .   Admiral Lord Keith.
North America . . . V.-Adm. Sir Andrew Mitchell (1).
East Indies. . . .   V.-Adm. Peter Rainier (1).
Jamaica . . . .   R.-Adm. Sir John Thomas Duckworth.
Leeward Islands . . Commod. Sir Samuel Hood (2).

That war was inevitable had been plainly foreseen in England for many months; and the King, addressing Parliament on March 8th, did not scruple to use language which indicated that he was prepared to face it. France, likewise, realised early in the year that Great Britain would not purchase peace at the price of concessions; though so speedy an outbreak was hardly expected. In March orders were given for the equipment at Flushing of an "escadre du Nord," for the construction in all the ports of the lower Schelde, Weser, and Elbe of great numbers of gun-vessels and flat-bottomed boats, and for the accumulation of vast quantities of naval stores. The total French line-of-battle force which, immediately after the issue of these orders, was ready, or in process of being made ready for sea, was :—

	At sea.	Ready for sea.	Nearly ready.	Building or ordered.	Total.
	10[1]	..	..	..	10
Brest	..	6	12	3	21
Lorient	..	..	3	2	5
Rochefort . . .	..	..	3	3	6
St. Malo . . .	..	..	..	1	1
Flushing, etc. . .	..	..	..	5[2]	5
Ostend	..	..	..	1[2]	1
Nantes	..	..	..	2[2]	2
Bordeaux. . . .	..	..	..	1[2]	1
Toulon	..	7	2	5	14
Marseilles . . .	..	..	..	1[2]	1
Genoa.	..	..	..	1	1
	10	13	20	25	68[3]

[1] *Viz.*, nine at, or coming from, San Domingo, and one proceeding to the East Indies with Decaen, the *Marengo.*
[2] These ten ships (74's) were to form the "escadre du Nord."
[3] James makes the total 66 only, but he omits two vessels building at Toulon.

In addition, about seven ships of the line of the Batavian Navy were serviceable.

[1] Declined the post and went to the Downs.

In March, also, General Decaen, supplied with full instructions to guide him in the event of an outbreak of war, sailed from Brest for India with the *Marengo*, 74, the frigates *Atalante*, *Sémillante*, and *Belle-Poule*, and the transports *Marie Françoise* and *Côte d'Or*, conveying about 1350 troops ostensibly destined to take possession of Pondicherry, which was to be returned to France under the third article of the Treaty of Amiens.

As early as the evening of May 17th, Admiral the Hon. William Cornwallis left Cawsand Bay with ten sail of the line and some frigates, and with his flag in the *Dreadnought*, 98,[1] to cruise off Ushant and to watch Brest. Smaller squadrons were sent a little later to cruise, one to the southward of Brest, one in the Irish Channel, and one in the North Sea, while about twenty additional ships of the line were being brought forward at Portsmouth and Devonport for commission at the earliest possible moment. Cornwallis watched, or blockaded Brest, without experiencing much relief from the monotony of the service, until December 25th, when a very violent south-west gale obliged him to return to his ports. In the meantime, of the nine French sail of the line which had been at San Domingo, two had already reached Rochefort, five had taken refuge in Ferrol, and one, the *Aigle*, 74, had put into Cadiz. All these vessels were presently watched by adequate British forces. There was thus no opportunity in 1803 for any meeting of great fleets in the Atlantic. Indeed, the only active operations of importance on the western coasts of the Continent were such as were provoked by the collection in various ports from Ostend to Granville of gunboats and other craft suited for forming the nucleus of an invasion flotilla. British cruisers were stationed before all these ports, and not only did the enemy seldom venture out for exercise or other purposes without being attacked, but also he was frequently annoyed when still lying at his moorings in supposed safety. Some of these affairs deserve to be recorded.

In the morning of June 14th, the *Immortalité*, 36, Captain Edward William Campbell Rich Owen, *Cruiser*, 18, Commander John Hancock (1), and *Jalouse*, 18, Commander Christopher Strachey, chased on shore under batteries near Cape Blanc Nez the French gun-vessels *Inabordable*, 4, and *Commode*, 4. When the tide permitted, the *Cruiser* and *Jalouse* stood in, and, anchoring with springs on their cables, engaged and silenced the batteries, after

---

[1] He shifted it on July 9th to the *Ville de Paris*, 112.

which the boats of the squadron boarded and brought off both vessels, losing only one person wounded.[1]

On August 1st, having prevented a French armed lugger, the *Favori*, 4, from entering Le Hâvre, and forced her to haul close to the beach near the mouth of the Touque, Captain George Mundy, of the *Hydra*, 38, sent his boats under Lieutenant Francis M'Mahon Tracy and Midshipmen John Barclay and George French, to cut her out or destroy her. As they approached she was abandoned by her people, who, however, joined some troops and took station behind the sandbanks to cover her with their muskets. But in spite of their fire, the *Favori* was carried off, the British losing no more than one man killed.[2]

On September 14th, at 8 A.M., the *Immortalité*, 36, Captain Edward William Campbell Rich Owen, *Perseus*, bomb, Commander John Melhuish, and *Explosion*, bomb, Commander Robert Paul, ventured to bombard the Dieppe batteries and seventeen vessels, chiefly building, that lay in the port. They continued the fire until about 11.30 A.M., setting fire to the town in three places ; and then, proceeding to St. Valery-en-Caux, where six other vessels were constructing, and off which place they arrived at 3 P.M., threw shells into the place for an hour. It is doubtful whether very much damage was done, but Captain Owen's loss was slight—one missing and five wounded.[3]

In the evening of September 13th, the *Cerberus*, 32, Rear-Admiral Sir James Saumarez, Captain William Selby, with the sloops *Charwell*, Commander Philip Dumaresq, and *Kite*, Commander Philip Pipon (1), the *Eling*, 14, schooner, Lieutenant William Archbold, and the *Carteret*, cutter, anchored quite close in front of the town of Granville, to await the hourly-expected arrival of the bombs *Sulphur*, Commander Donald M'Leod, and *Terror*, Commander George Nicholas Hardinge, with the co-operation of which it was intended to endeavour to destroy some of the numerous gunboats lying within the pier, and to damage the port. The *Terror* appeared towards midnight ; but, as she grounded in the darkness at low water, she was not able to get into her assigned station until 2 A.M. on the 14th. She then shelled the gun-vessels and batteries for upwards of three hours, but was recalled towards daybreak,.

---

[1] Owen to Montagu, June 14th.

[2] Mundy to Saumarez, Aug. 1st.

[3] Owen to Keith, Sept. 14th.

and reanchored out of gunshot, with a loss of two men slightly
wounded. Soon afterwards, the *Sulphur* joined; but little could
be done that evening, as the tide prevented even the small craft
from getting sufficiently close. On the morning of the 15th, however, all the ships were able to station themselves to good advantage;
and from 5 A.M. to 10.30 A.M. they maintained a hot fire, though
it is not certain that they produced very much effect. They were
then obliged, by the state of the tide, to withdraw; and although
they had been opposed by twenty-two gun-vessels, besides the
batteries on shore, they suffered no loss and very little damage.
After weighing, however, the *Cerberus* grounded on a shoal. Nine
gunboats, thereupon, hauled out and began to annoy her; but they
were at length compelled to retire; and at the end of three hours
the *Cerberus* was refloated.[1]

On the night of September 27th a division of small craft, under
Commander Samuel Jackson, of the *Autumn*, 16, bombarded Calais
for several hours, apparently inflicting some damage, but receiving
none. The British vessels were then driven off by a north-easterly
gale;[2] and on the following day, taking advantage of their absence,
numerous French gunboats left Calais for Boulogne, and made the
passage in safety although they were chased and fired at by the
Leda, 36, Captain Robert Honyman. On September 29th, twenty-
five other gunboats attempted to follow the first detachment. The
Leda drove two ashore, where they were bilged; but the rest
reached their destination, making, with those already there, a
flotilla of fifty-five sail.[3] On October 31st, while working in
towards the shore near Etaples, Captain Honyman, who had
with him the sloops *Lark* and *Harpy*, saw a gun-brig and six
schooners and sloops coming out of port and making for Boulogne.
He ordered the *Lark* and *Harpy* to chase; but ere they could
get up with the enemy, the hired cutter *Admiral Mitchell*, 12,
Lieutenant Alexander Shippard, being already off Boulogne, intervened to such good effect that, although she had to contend
with a land battery at Le Portel as well as with the vessels,
she succeeded, after an engagement of two hours and a half, in
driving ashore the gun-brig and one of the sloops. The *Admiral
Mitchell* was a good deal cut about aloft, had a carronade dis-

---

[1] Saumarez to Nepean, Sept. 15th.
[2] Jackson to Montagu, Sept. 28th.
[3] Honyman to Keith, Sept. 29th.

mounted, and had several shot in her hull; but she had only five men wounded.[1]

At the time of the renewal of the war there were in the Mediterranean ten British sail of the line under Rear-Admiral Sir Richard Hussey Bickerton, Bart. (W.). That force, though sufficient, perhaps, for the observation of Toulon, where but eight or ten ships were ready for sea,[2] might, it was felt, soon become unequal to the task of controlling waters, nearly all the coasts of which were either

ADMIRAL SIR RICHARD HUSSEY BICKERTON, BART.

(From Ridley's engraving after T. Maynard's drawing of a picture painted in Malta, ca. 1803.)

under the dominion of, or more or less obedient to Napoleon. It was not easy at once to send from England any large reinforcements up the Strait; but it was possible to dispatch thither an officer whose

---

[1] Honyman to Keith, Oct. 31st: Shippard to Honyman, Oct. 31st.

[2] Afloat were the *Formidable*, 80, *Indomptable*, 80, *Atlas*, 74, *Berwick*, 74, *Intrépide*, 74, *Mont Blanc*, 74, and *Scipion*, 74. In dock were the *Annibal*, 74, and *Swiftsure*, 74; and on the stocks were the *Bucentaure*, 80, *Neptune*, 80, *Borée*, 74, *Pluton*, 74, and *Phaëton*, 74. The fleet was commanded by Vice-Admiral René Madeleine de Latouche-Tréville.

mere presence, it was well known, would be equivalent to the
addition of one or two ships of the line to the fleet. Vice-
Admiral Lord Nelson, therefore, was offered and accepted the chief
command in the Mediterranean. On May 18th he hoisted his flag
in the *Victory*, 100, at Portsmouth, and at 5 P.M. on the 20th he
left Spithead[1] accompanied by the *Amphion*, 32, Captain Thomas
Masterman Hardy. His orders were to repair to Admiral the Hon.
William Cornwallis, off Brest, and, if that officer required assistance,
to leave the *Victory* with him and to proceed in the *Amphion*. On
the 22nd and 23rd Nelson sought in vain for Cornwallis on and near
the rendezvous off Ushant, for the British fleet had been blown from
its station. Unwilling to delay further, the Vice-Admiral shifted his
flag to the *Amphion*, and at 8 P.M. on the 23rd made sail in her with
a fair wind, leaving the *Victory*, Captain Samuel Sutton, to follow in
case her services should not be needed in the Channel. Within two
days of the departure of the *Amphion*, Sutton fell in with Cornwallis,
who permitted him to continue his voyage; and on May 28th, in
lat. 45° 40′ N., long. 6° 10′ W., the *Victory* was so fortunate as to
capture the *Embuscade*, 32,[2] homeward bound from Cape François
to Rochefort.[3] She reached Gibraltar on June 12th, sailed again on
the 15th, anchored at Valetta on July 9th, quitted the port on the
11th, and rejoined Nelson off Cape Sicié at 4 P.M. on July 30th.

In the meantime, the Vice-Admiral, in the *Amphion*, reached
Gibraltar on June 3rd, sailed again early on June 4th, and anchored
on June 15th at Valetta. Thence, on the 17th he proceeded to
Naples, where he anchored on the 25th, expecting to find Bickerton.
The Rear-Admiral, however, had sailed on the 4th for Toulon,
whither the *Amphion* followed him, and where he found him on
July 8th, with eight ships of the line. Nelson, confident that Cornwallis would not detain the *Victory*, kept his flag flying in the frigate
until the evening of July 30th, when he shifted it to the three-
decker, taking with him Hardy, whose place in the *Amphion* was
transferred to Captain Sutton. The force then immediately with
the Commander-in-Chief consisted of the following ships, five

---

[1] "Such was the anxiety of Lord Nelson to embark that yesterday, to everyone
who spoke to him of his sailing, he said, 'I cannot before to-morrow, and that's an
age.' This morning, about ten o'clock, his Lordship went off in a heavy shower of
rain, and sailed with a northerly wind." Portsmouth report, May 20th, in *Nav. Chron.*,
June, 1803.

[2] The ex-British frigate *Ambuscade*. She was only partially gunned and manned.

[3] Sutton to Nepean, June 12th.

other sail of the line being at the time detached on various
services :—

Ships.	Guns.	Commanders.
Victory	100	Vice-Adm. Lord Nelson, K.B. Capt. George Murray (3), Capt. of the Fleet. Capt. Thomas Masterman Hardy.
Gibraltar	80	Capt. George Frederick Ryves (1).
Belleisle	74	Capt. John Whitby.
Donegal	74	Capt. Sir Richard John Strachan, Bart.
Renown	74	Capt. John Chambers White.
Monmouth	64	Capt. George Hart.
Active	38	Captain Richard Hussey Moubray.
Phœbe	36	Capt. Hon. Thomas Bladen Capell.
Amphion	32	Capt. Samuel Sutton.

In the early part of August the fleet before Toulon was joined by
the *Canopus*, 80, Rear-Admiral George Campbell, Captain John
Conn, and *Triumph*, 74, Captain Sir Robert Barlow, from England,
and by the *Kent*, 74, Rear-Admiral Sir Richard Hussey Bickerton,
Bart., Captain Edward O'Bryen (1), and *Superb*, 74, Captain Richard
Goodwin Keats, from elsewhere on the station ; but Nelson kept only
six ships of the line, besides frigates, with him, detaching the rest.
Latouche-Tréville, nevertheless, made no effort to leave port, nor
did any Spanish fleet from Barcelona or elsewhere endeavour, as
Nelson at one time thought it would, to join the French in Toulon.

   In 1802, Captain George Frederick Ryves (1), then of the
Agincourt, 64, had found and surveyed a well-sheltered and otherwise very admirable anchorage among the Maddalena Islands, off
the north coast of Sardinia. It is formed by an indented bay[1] on the
larger island, and is protected on the north by Maddalena, Spargi,
Caprera, and St. Stefano. Its capabilities having been made
known to the Commander-in-Chief, and, the fleet being in want of
water, Nelson, on October 24th, quitted his station off Cape Sicié,
and made for the anchorage, which he ultimately named Agincourt
Sound. He left the frigates *Seahorse* and *Narcissus* to watch the
enemy's port; and they remained cruising before it, and quite undisturbed, until the Vice-Admiral returned on November 23rd.[2]   On
the following day he was joined by the *Excellent*, 74, Captain Frank
Sotheron, from England. The work of blockade, owing to the
persistence of heavy N.W. and N.E. gales, and the bad state of

---

[1] The Gulf of Arsachena.
[2] He had left Agincourt Sound on Nov. 9th, but was delayed by bad weather.

many of the ships, was rendered extremely trying ; but Nelson found some relief by stationing himself off Cape St. Sebastian instead of off Cape Sicié—a change which he made upon receiving intelligence which induced him to suppose that no interference was to be apprehended from the side of Spain. In the second week of December, however, he was obliged to take shelter in Palma Bay, whence on December 21st he went again to Agincourt Sound. There he remained until after the close of the year, trusting to Captain Ross

VICE-ADMIRAL SIR SAMUEL HOOD (2), BART., K.B.
(From a drawing by W. Evans, after a picture by Sir Wm. Beechey, R.A.)

Donnelly, who, in the *Narcissus*, with one or two other frigates in company, continued off Toulon, to send him timely news of any important movement on the part of the French.

The outbreak of war saw, as usual, almost immediate extension of the over-sea possessions of Great Britain. On June 21st, 1803, Commodore Samuel Hood (2), in the *Centaur*, 74, Captain Bendall Robert Littlehales, with the *Courageux*, 74, Captain Benjamin

Hallowell, and several smaller vessels, carrying troops under Lieut.-
General Grinfield, anchored in Choc Bay, St. Lucia, at 11 A.M.
Before 5 P.M. the troops were disembarked under the direction of
Captain Hallowell; half an hour later the French outposts were
driven in and the town of Castries was taken; and at 4 A.M. on the
22nd the fortress of Morne Fortunée, which had refused overnight
to surrender, was stormed and carried, with a loss to the assailants
of twenty killed and one hundred and ten wounded.[1] St. Lucia
having been thus easily reduced, the *Centaur*, with some small craft
and troops, sailed on June 25th for Tobago, and on the 31st arrived
off the island. The troops were instantly put ashore without loss,
and by 4.30 A.M. on the following day General Berthier, the commandant, capitulated.[2] Between that time and the end of September
the Dutch colonies of Demerara, Essequibo and Berbice were also
captured. No lives were lost in acquiring them, and at Demerara
the Batavian corvette *Hippomenes*, 14, was taken.[3]

On the Jamaica station British co-operation at sea soon enabled
the negroes of San Domingo to oust the French from all those parts
of the island which had previously been French, except Cape
François, where General Rochambeau commanded, and Mole St.
Nicolas, which was held by General Noailles. Cape François,
besides being invested by the blacks, was closely blockaded by a
small squadron under Commodore John Loring;[4] and on November 17th, Rochambeau offered to evacuate the place on certain
conditions. As, however, these were not accepted by Loring, the
French general made terms with Dessalines, the negro commander.
The agreement was that the French should evacuate the Cape and
its dependencies, and, within ten days from November 20th, should
be allowed to retire to France on board the ships then in port.
Rochambeau accordingly embarked, but Loring gave him no loop-
hole of escape; and on November 30th, when the specified limit of
time had expired, and the French were still in harbour, the blacks
began preparations for sinking their vessels with red-hot shot.
Loring thereupon sent in Captain John Bligh (2), of the *Theseus*,

---

[1] Hood to Nepean, June 22nd.

[2] Hood's disp. of July 1st.

[3] Disp. of Sept. 27th, enclosing disp. of Capt. Loftus Otway Bland, of *Heureux*, of
Sept. 26th. In these operations the ships engaged were *Centaur*, *Courageux*, *Argo*,
Ulysses, *Chichester*, *Hornet*, *Heureux*, *Emerald*, *Osprey*, *Venus*, *Port Mahon*, *Cyane*,
Brilliant, and *Netley*. Hood was made a K.B. for his services.

[4] Loring to Duckworth, June 9th.

and Captain Barré, under a flag of truce ; and, in virtue of an arrangement then come to, Dessalines agreed to suffer the French to put to sea, and the French consented, after discharging a broadside, *pro forma*, in reply to a shot fired across the bows of each, to haul down their colours, and surrendered to the British.   In pursuance of this convention, the *Surveillante*, 40, and several smaller craft, left harbour, struck, and were duly taken possession of.   As, however, the *Clorinde*, 40, came out, she grounded on the rocks[1] under Fort St. Joseph, beat off her rudder, and, after a few minutes, looked as if she must infallibly perish with all on board, including General Lapoype and several women and children—in all, about nine hundred souls.   Moreover, the negroes betrayed every intention of opening fire on her.   So utterly hopeless, indeed, appeared her situation that most of the officers in the British boats which had been assisting the exit of the French vessels, never thought of returning to attempt to save her.   But Lieutenant Nisbet Josiah Willoughby (act.), one of the most gallant officers who ever served under the British flag, happened to be in command of a launch belonging to the *Hercule*, 74,[2] and, upon his own responsibility, put back to try to preserve the unhappy French from the fate which threatened them.   Having taken precautions to prevent his launch from being swamped by the excited people who thronged the frigate's side, he boarded the *Clorinde* and persuaded her officers to waive the formality of waiting for a shot to be fired across their bows, and of returning a broadside, ere they surrendered.   Willoughby then hoisted the British flag on the frigate, and, proceeding on shore to General Dessalines, made that officer understand that the *Clorinde* was thenceforward a British man-of-war, and that although the French, being still at the mouth of the port, might not have strictly complied with the terms of the agreement, they must not be fired upon, seeing that they were prisoners under British protection. Obtaining assistance, both from the shore and from the squadron, Willoughby then began to attempt to get the frigate off the rocks ; and, thanks to his energy and ability,[3] as well as to a fall in the wind, he ultimately succeeded.   Both of the *Clorinde*, which was added to the navy as a 38-gun ship, and of Willoughby, there will be other occasions to speak.[4]

[1] Loring to Duckworth, Nov. 30th.
[2] Flag of Adm. Sir J. T. Duckworth.
[3] Disp. of R. Adm. J. T. Duckworth.   *Gazette*, 1804, 164, 166.
[4] Loring to Duckworth, Dec. 2nd : Duckworth to Nepean, Dec. 18th.

From Cape François, Commodore Loring went to St. Nicolas Mole; but General Noailles, upon being summoned, declined to consider the terms which were offered to him. For reasons which are not quite clear, he was not fully blockaded, almost the whole of the British squadron, with the prizes and prisoners, going on to Jamaica.[1] On the night following their departure, the French general and his garrison left the port in six small vessels, and in due time he, in a brig, arrived safely in Cuba.[2] Thus the French portion of San Domingo was finally handed over to the negro population. Part of the French garrison had previously escaped to the Spanish end of the island, and, under Generals Kerverseau and Ferrand, occupied the towns of San Domingo and Santiago; but those officers were never able to restore any semblance of French authority in Hayti; and one of the most important colonial expeditions upon which France ever embarked, resulted only, in spite of the care and expense which had been lavished on it, in the miserable sacrifice of twenty general officers and upwards of forty thousand men.[3]

The squadron[4] which conveyed General Decaen, as French governor-general, to India, was under the command of Rear-Admiral Linois, who had his flag in the *Marengo*, 74. It quitted Brest on March 6th, 1803, and, although it became separated on the way out, it re-assembled[5] in the road of Pondicherry on July 11th. The British authorities in the town had already been called upon to surrender the settlement in accordance with the Treaty of Amiens, but, owing to lack of orders, to informality in the application, or, perhaps, to a conviction that a renewal of war was imminent, they had declined to hand over their charge. In the meantime, also, a superior British force,[6] under Vice-Admiral Peter Rainier (1), had anchored on July 5th, partly in the road of Cuddalore, only about twenty miles from Pondicherry, and partly before Pondicherry itself; and, upon the arrival of Linois, Rainier concentrated his squadron and anchored the whole of it midway between Cuddalore and

---

[1] Duckworth to Nepean, Dec. 18th, where lack of provisions is alleged.

[2] The remaining five vessels were picked up by the *Pique*, which alone remained off St. Nicolas Mole.

[3] 'Vict. et Conq.,' xiv. 330.   [4] *See* p. 49, *antea.*

[5] With the exception of the transports, which arrived, the *Marie Françoise* on the 12th, and the *Côte d'Or* on the 13th.

[6] One 74, two 64's, one 50, one 44 *en flute,* three frigates and a sloop. Another sloop joined a few days later.

Pondicherry. Each party fully believed that war, if it had not already broken out, would begin almost immediately; and when, on the evening of July 12th, the French Rear-Admiral was joined by the brig *Bélier*, which had left Brest ten days later than the *Marengo*, and which probably apprised him of the tenour of King George's message to Parliament on March 8th,[1] Linois must have felt confident that the two countries were actually, by that time, again active enemies. The dispatches sent to him by the brig directed him to proceed at once to the Isle of France, there to make his ships ready, pending the receipt of orders to commence hostilities. Unfortunately he had already invited Vice-Admiral Rainier to breakfast with him on the morning of the 13th. Apprehensive lest the British Commander-in-Chief might know even more than he, and might detain the French squadron if it showed any disposition to move, Linois waived ceremony, and in the night silently slipped his cables, leaving some of his boats behind him. In the morning Rainier discovered that his host had flown; and, suspecting, for the moment, that news of the re-opening of the war had been received, he instantly detached the main part of his command to Madras. From the 13th to the 24th he himself remained at Pondicherry, while some of his cruisers carefully watched the two or three French vessels which appeared in the neighbourhood. On July 24th he too made for Madras; but not until September 3rd did the order for reprisals of May 16th reach him, and not until September 13th did he know of the formal beginning of hostilities. He does not appear to have then acted with much energy; for although Linois, who had reached the Isle of France on August 16th, and who had received later, by the *Berceau*, 20, news of the declaration of war, put to sea on October 8th, the British Vice-Admiral did not keep touch with the enemy, and seems to have been quite ignorant as to where he was or what he was aiming at. In point of fact, Linois, after having detached the *Atalante* to annoy the Portuguese at Muscat, proceeded to reinforce the garrisons of Réunion and Batavia. In the course of his cruise he took or destroyed a number of British merchantmen, and burnt some valuable warehouses at Sellabar. He reached Batavia in the second week of December, having sighted no British man-of-war since leaving the Isle of France.

The year 1804 witnessed great increase in the preparations which were being made in France for the invasion of Great

---

[1] This message reached Madras about July 5th.

Britain. Numerous new ships were laid down in the larger ports; and on the banks of almost every stream that communicated with the Atlantic the construction of gun-vessels, flat-bottomed boats, and prames was actively pressed forward.

It has been mentioned that Admiral the Hon. William Cornwallis had been driven, on December 25th, 1803, from his station off Brest. The weather moderating, he regained it, with thirteen ships of the line, on January 12th, 1804, and was presently joined by several other vessels. The blockade was thenceforward steadily maintained, although, by the end of April, the French had in the road seventeen sail of the line, including two three-deckers, ready for sea. Napoleon seems to have been greatly dissatisfied with the passive attitude of this considerable force, and, on May 1st, issued a set of directions which were intended not only to improve its efficiency, but also to make it a training school for a large number of French soldiers in the work usually done by marines. A few days later, the ships in the road were joined by two more sail of the line from the inner harbour, making nineteen in all; yet for more than two months longer the fleet made no effort to put to sea. On July 25th, with an E.N.E. wind and a dense fog to help them, five sail of the line and some frigates weighed and stood for the Passage du Raz; but, as soon as the weather cleared, they were observed by the British look-out vessels, and were promptly chased by the inshore squadron, then under Rear-Admiral Sir Thomas Graves (3), whereupon they hauled to the wind and worked back again. Thenceforward they remained quiet during the rest of the year, although it is now known that only unforeseen circumstances prevented the whole force, crowded with troops, from endeavouring to quit port in November, with the object of effecting a descent upon Ireland or Scotland.[1] In the meantime the effective Brest fleet had been brought up to twenty-three sail of the line; and Vice-Admiral Truguet, who had commanded it, but whose republican principles had not suffered him to acquiesce in Napoleon's assumption of the imperial dignity on May 14th, had been degraded, and superseded by Vice-Admiral Honoré Ganteaume.

---

[1] After disembarking about 35,000 men in Ireland or Scotland, Ganteaume was to have picked up off the Texel the ten ships of the " escadre du Nord," and a number of transports, and to have made for Boulogne, there to meet twenty sail of the line coming from Rochefort under Villeneuve. The combined force of fifty ships of the line was then to have covered the grand invasion of England. Napoleon's Instructs. to Vice-Adm. Decrès.

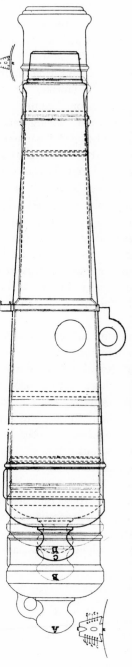

COMPARISON OF THE ORDINARY LONG AND SHORT 24-PRS. WITH THE CONGREVE AND THE SHORT BLOMEFIELD 24-PRS.

(*See* p. 16.)

A. Long 24-pr., length, 9 ft. 6 in.   C. Congreve 24-pr.
B. Short 24-pr.   D. Blomefield short 24-pr.

M. N. Congreve sights.

(*From Dupin.*)

The great invasion flotilla, upon the movements of which almost
the entire navy of France may be said to have been waiting,
numbered, when it reached its maximum force, no fewer than
2293 vessels, including 954 transports, upwards of 700 schooner,
brig, or lugger-rigged gun-vessels, chiefly armed either with three
long 24-pounders and one 8-inch mortar, or with one long
24-pounder and a field-gun ; a number of ship-rigged prames each
carrying twelve long 24-pounders, and having accommodation for
fifty horses, and about 400 schuyt-rigged " péniches." [1] Divisions
of these craft were assembled at Ostend, Dunquerque, Calais,
Ambleteuse, Vimereux, Boulogne, and Etaples, Boulogne being
the general headquarters of the whole and of the commander-in-
chief, Vice-Admiral Eustache Bruix, who, being in ill-health, was
given as his assistant Rear-Admiral Jean Raimond Lacrosse. [2] For
the purpose of accommodating and protecting the flotilla, many of
the ports named were either enlarged, or practically created, and
all were strongly defended by means of batteries. They were,
moreover, as they still are, naturally difficult of access to vessels
dependent only on sail power ; for they are faced by sandbanks and
washed by cross-tides.

On the British side of the Channel, corresponding preparations
were made, although it does not appear to have been the general
impression among the most distinguished naval officers [3] of the day
that, in the conditions which existed, any invasion was possible or
would be seriously attempted. Admiral Lord Keith, commanding
in the Downs, had under his orders cruisers which were instructed
to harass the French flotilla upon every occasion that offered ;
light flying squadrons watched various points on the French coast ;
numerous small gunboats were assembled at the Nore and at other
points between the Thames and Portsmouth ; old men-of-war were
armed with heavy carronades, and turned into floating batteries for
harbour defence ; a large army, of militia and volunteers as well as
of regulars, was kept on foot ; and, at very many points on the
coast, martello towers, most of which still remain, were erected,

---

[1] " *Péniche* est l'orthographe auriculaire française du mot *pinasse*, prononcé par
les Anglais. . . . C'était . . . un navire à rames et à voiles du genre des frégates de
la Méditerranée." Jal, ' Arch. Nav.,' I., 453. Did M. Jal know English ?

[2] The officer who had commanded the *Droits de l'Homme* on the occasion of
her loss.

[3] *See* Nelson's ' Disps.,' iv. 452 ; Pellew's speech, ' Parl. Debs.,' 15th March, 1804 ;
and Corr. of St. Vincent, 1804, *passim*.

gunned, and manned. As in the previous year, there were naturally frequent conflicts between British vessels and the French small craft belonging to the command of Bruix; and many of these deserve some mention here.

On the morning of February 20th, the hired cutter *Active* (2), 6, Lieutenant John Williams, being off Gravelines, sighted, close under the shore, sixteen sail of gunboats and transports which were apparently on their way from Ostend to Boulogne. Although the little British craft had a crew of only about thirty men and boys all told, she pluckily gave chase, and from 10.30 A.M. to 11 A.M. maintained a running fight with the flotilla. At the end of that time a transport, the *Jeune Isabelle*, struck; and, while she was being taken possession of, the remaining vessels ran under the shore batteries, whither they could not be followed.[1]

At daylight on May 8th, the *Vencejo*,[2] 18, Commander John Wesley Wright, found herself becalmed near the mouth of the Morbihan, and driven by the ebb close to the Teigneuse rock, off which, for safety, she had to drop anchor. The *Vencejo* was a quarterdecked and forecastled brig, mounting eighteen 18-pounder carronades, but pierced for twenty guns, and carrying fifty-one men and twenty-four boys. Although more formidable in appearance than in reality, she was of only 277 tons, and was scarcely a fair match for a couple of French gun-brigs. While, nevertheless, she was endeavouring, after she had weighed and warped into the channel, to sweep clear of the coast, she was approached from the mouth of the river by six brigs, each of three guns; six luggers, each of two guns; and five luggers, each of two guns; the total force arrayed against her being seventeen vessels, thirty-five guns (*i.e.*, six long 24-pounders, twenty-four long 18-pounders, and five 36-pounder carronades), and between 700 and 800 men, under Lieutenant Laurent Tourneur. The enemy rowed down within range, and at 8.30 A.M. they began to fire. By 9.30 A.M. they had so decreased their distance that Commander Wright swept his brig broadside on to them. For nearly two hours he engaged them within about a cable's length; but, having his rigging cut to pieces, his hull badly mauled, three of his guns disabled, two men killed, and twelve, including himself, wounded, and most of his armament temporarily put out of action by the fall of the booms, he at length ordered the colours to be

[1] Williams to Keith, Feb. 20th. [2] Wrongly called *Vincejo*.

struck.[1] Wright, carried prisoner to Paris, died in the Temple, on October 28th, 1805, in circumstances which strongly suggested foul play. Napoleon denied having used any violence whatsoever to the brave officer; but the true facts of the affair, some of which will be found very fully set forth in the *Naval Chronicle*,[2] are to this day involved in mystery. Wright, before his capture, had, in his ill-manned little craft, maintained his station almost continuously for three months, without a pilot, in the enemy's waters, and in presence of a largely superior force; had repeatedly chased into port more powerful vessels of the enemy; and had on one occasion

CAPTAIN JOHN WESLEY WRIGHT, R.N.

(*From T. Blood's engraving, after the portrait by Gaetano Calleja.*)

hauled his brig ashore on a French island only four miles from the mainland in order to repair her. It is satisfactory to be able to add that, before his untimely death, this active and gallant man heard of his advancement to post-rank.

Of the various light flying squadrons stationed off the enemy's coast, one, which especially watched Flushing, Hellevoetsluis, and Ostend, was under the orders of Commodore Sir William Sidney

[1] Wright to Marsden, May 14th.   [2] Vol. xxxv.

Smith, in the *Antelope*, 50. On May 15th, the inshore part of this squadron consisted of the *Cruiser*, 18, Commander John Hancock (1), and *Rattler*, 16, Commander Francis Mason. Another British force, which was cruising off Calais, could be communicated with by means of a line of four gun-brigs, which, under Lieutenant Patrick Manderston, of the *Minx*, was stationed between the two bodies. On the evening of the day in question, twenty-three gun-vessels were seen to haul out of Ostend harbour, and to anchor to the westward of the lighthouse. This induced Commander Hancock to make a signal to recall the four gun-brigs, which, he felt, would be of great help to him in case he should succeed in bringing the enemy to action, and to dispatch the hired armed cutter *Stag*, Lieutenant William Patfull, to Sir William Sidney Smith, who then lay in Schoneveld, with news of what was going forward. As darkness came on, Hancock got under way with his two sloops, and re-anchored within long range of the pier batteries, in order, if possible, to prevent the escape of the enemy. On the morning of the 16th, it was perceived that the four gun-brigs had either not seen or not understood the signal of recall, and the signal was again made. At 9.30 A.M. the *Rattler*, which lay somewhat to the eastward of the *Cruiser*, signalled, first five sail, and then a fleet, to the E.S.E. As subsequently appeared, the strangers were a Franco-Batavian flotilla which, under Rear-Admiral Carel Hendrik Ver Huell,[1] had quitted the Inner Wieling early that morning in order to enter Ostend; and they consisted of the two ship-rigged 12-gun prames, *Ville d'Anvers* and *Ville d'Aix*, nineteen schooners, and thirty-eight schuyts, mounting together upwards of one hundred long guns, besides carronades and mortars, and having on board about four thousand troops of the army of invasion. At 10 A.M., the *Cruiser* and *Rattler*, taking the earliest possible advantage of the tide, weighed and began to work towards the enemy. An hour later, the wind shifted to S.W., and, becoming favourable to the sloops, induced Ver Huell to bear up and put back towards Flushing. Sir William Sidney Smith, apprised of the movements of the foe, weighed from Schoneveld between 10 and 11 A.M. in the *Antelope*, 50, with the *Penelope*, 36, Captain William Robert Broughton, and the *Aimable*, 32, Captain William Bolton (1); and at about noon he sighted the two sloops. But Hancock and Mason, instead of waiting for him, pressed on; and at 1.30 P.M. the *Cruiser* overhauled, fired

[1] Later Minister of Marine, Marshal, and Graaf van Sevenaer.

at, and obliged to strike one of the rearmost schuyts. Ordering the
Rattler to take possession, she stood on after one of the prames.
In the meantime the wind had slightly shifted ; and Ver Huell,
perhaps a little ashamed of the part which he had been playing,
took advantage of it to stand back towards Ostend with the whole
of his force, except eight schuyts, which continued to make for the
Inner Wieling. At 1.45 P.M. the *Ville d'Anvers* was able to fire a
shot which passed over the *Cruiser.* A little later, a considerable
shift of wind caused both sloops to fall off their course, and to find
themselves nearly abreast of the leading prame, and upon the lee
beam of the flotilla. Thereupon the *Ville d'Anvers* and several
schooners and schuyts opened a heavy fire upon the sloops, which
presently fought their way into the midst of the enemy, in spite
of a storm of projectiles from the Blankenberghe batteries. In
a short time Hancock and Mason had driven ashore the *Ville
d'Anvers,* bearing Ver Huell's flag, and four of the schooners.

It was not until afterwards that any part of Sir William Sidney
Smith's force was able to take part. At 3.45 P.M. the *Aimable*
opened upon some schuyts which were close under Blankenberghe ;
and at about 4.30 P.M. the *Antelope* and *Penelope* also got into
action, and began to drive other schooners and schuyts ·ashore.
So the action went on until about 7.45 P.M., when Smith signalled
to cease firing, his ships having hardly any water under them.
The remnants of Ver Huell's flotilla, covered by the gun-vessels
which had hauled out of harbour on the previous evening, and
which were under Rear-Admiral Charles Magon, got into Ostend.
In this gallant action the *Cruiser* lost 1 killed and 4 wounded ; the
Rattler, 2 killed and 5 wounded ; and the *Aimable,* 7 killed (including a Master's Mate, and a Midshipman), and 14 wounded
(including Lieutenant William Mather).[1] The enemy admitted
a loss of 18 killed and 60 wounded. In the early morning of
May 17th the four gun-brigs, having joined, were sent in to
endeavour to destroy or bring off the grounded *Ville d'Anvers ;*
but she was so well covered by guns drawn up on the beach, and
by guns and mortars on the sandhills behind it, that, although they

---

[1] Smith's disp. (*Gazette,* 1804, 640) has been taken as implying that the *Antelope*
and consorts had an earlier and larger share in the affair than is attributed to them in
the text ; but the logs of the *Antelope* and *Aimable* conclusively show that the action
was fought as described above, and Ver Huell's report bears out the logs. (' Leven van
Ver Huell,' i. 216 *et seq.*)

fortunately suffered no loss, they were obliged to haul off.[1] On the
19th, assisted by the *Galgo*, 16, Commander Michael Dod, and the
Inspector, 16, Commander Edward James Mitchell, the gun-brigs
made another ineffectual effort. Ultimately the *Ville d'Anvers* and
five out of eight grounded schooners and schuyts were re-floated and
taken into the basin. Ver Huell was considered by the emperor to
have behaved very well, and was made an officer of the Legion of
Honour ; but neither Hancock nor Mason received any immediate
recognition,[2] although they both had certainly behaved with far
greater distinction.

At that time Le Hâvre was an important assembling depôt for
such vessels of the invasion flotilla as had been fitted out in the
Seine and its tributaries, ere they could be sent on to Boulogne.
On July 23rd, and again on August 1st, Captain Robert Dudley
Oliver, in the *Melpomène*, 38, with some sloops, bombs, and small
craft, bombarded and fired the town ; but it does not appear that
the French preparations were materially hindered thereby. On the
British side there was no loss.[3]

The British blockading divisions, though often driven off or
otherwise inconvenienced by bad weather, were occasionally able
to profit by it. On July 19th, for example, a strong N.N.E. wind
and heavy sea imperilled the safety of the French flotilla in Boulogne
road, and, in the evening, induced some of the leewardmost vessels
to weigh and work to windward, and others to run for Etaples.
In the road were left forty-five brigs and forty-three luggers.
About twenty-four miles to the westward lay the *Immortalité*, 36,
Captain Edward William Campbell Rich Owen, *Leda*, 38, Captain
Robert Honyman, and several small craft. Owen ordered the
Harpy, 18, Commander Edmund Heywood, and the brigs *Bloodhound*, Lieutenant Henry Richardson (2), and *Archer*, Lieutenant
John Price (3), to run in and open fire upon such vessels as were
attempting to stand off from the land. They were presently joined
by the *Autumn*, 16, Commander Samuel Jackson ; and for several
hours the enemy was annoyed in a desultory way. By daylight on
the 20th, only nineteen brigs and eight luggers remained in the
road, and, the weather continuing bad, these soon began to slip, and

---

[1] Smith to Keith, May 17th.

[2] John Hancock (1) was posted Jan. 22nd, 1806, and died a Rear-Adm. in 1839.
Francis Mason was also posted Jan. 22nd, 1806, and died a Vice-Adm. and K.C.B.
in 1853.

[3] *Gazette*, 1804, 898, 938 ; Oliver to Keith, July 24th, Aug. 2nd.

to run for Etaples or St. Valery-sur-Somme. The *Autumn* and her
consorts were then too far to leeward to interrupt them ; but, as
soon as the tide served, the *Immortalité* and *Leda* stood in close to
the town. How far the British fire had contributed to the result
is not known ; but it could be seen from the frigates that a brig,
a lugger, and several large boats were stranded westward of the
harbour, that three other brigs and a lugger were total wrecks on
the rocks near Le Portel, and that a brig and two luggers, anchored
close to the rocks, had signals of distress flying, and were in manifest
danger. Upwards of four hundred Frenchmen are known to have
perished on the occasion. Napoleon, who was present, " se montra
encore plus affligé que furieux." [1]

In August, 1804, a considerable British squadron, composed of
nearly twenty vessels, cruised off Boulogne under Rear-Admiral
Thomas Louis, in the *Leopard*, 50. Its main body usually lay
about ten miles to the north-west, while a division, under Captain
E. W. C. R. Owen, kept just out of shell-range of the shore
batteries. On August 25th, a division of gunboats, under Captain
Julien Le Ray, forming part of the one hundred and forty-six
vessels of the class then in the road, weighed, and, with a N.E.
wind, began working out towards Pointe Bombe, off which lay
the British gun-brig *Bruiser*, Lieutenant Thomas Smithies. The
Bruiser opened fire upon them, and the firing attracted the *Immortalité*, which, at 2.30 P.M., began to engage both the gun-vessels
and the batteries. She soon found, however, that she was too close
inshore, and eventually withdrew to a distance of about three miles.
Early on the following morning the brigs *Bloodhound*, Lieutenant
Henry Richardson (2), and *Archer*, Lieutenant John Price (3), got
into distant action with some luggers which were rounding Cape
Gris-Nez very near the shore ; and later in the day another division
of gunboats, under Captain Etienne Pévrieu, together with some
mortar vessels which had come from the Elbe, weighed and joined
Captain Le Ray, who was manœuvring between Ambleteuse and
Vimereux. The united force then numbered sixty brigs and more
than half as many luggers. It would appear that Bruix had ordered
it out of the road in hopes of inducing some of the British cruisers
either to run aground while in chase, or to venture into positions
where they could be crushed by the batteries. Be that as it
may, at 4 P.M. the *Immortalité*, with the *Harpy*, 18, Commander

[1] *Gazette*, 1804, 891. Owen to Louis, July 20th. ' Vict. et Conq.,' xvi. 138.

Edmund Heywood, *Adder*, gun-brig, Lieutenant George Wood,
and hired armed cutter *Constitution*, Lieutenant James Samuel
Aked Dennis (1), eventually joined by the *Bruiser*, Lieutenant
Thomas Smithies, approached the flotilla, and began to engage
it at 4.15 P.M., tacking and standing close in after the enemy;
whereupon the batteries opened heavily, and most of the craft
remaining in the roads weighed and proceeded to the assistance
of their friends.   At about 5 P.M. the *Constitution* was sunk by
a 13-inch shell which, falling on her deck, passed through her
bottom.   Her people were, however, all saved by the boats of
the squadron. A big shell also fell in the *Harpy*, but lodged in a
beam and failed to burst.   The *Immortalité* was twice struck in the
hull; but the whole British casualties seem to have been only one
killed and four wounded.   It was seen, however, that the batteries
effectually protected the enemy, and, after having compelled one
or two gunboats to beach themselves in order to avoid sinking,
Captain Owen drew off.   Desultory firing was renewed on the
27th and 28th, but no damage of importance was effected on
either side.[1]

The difficulty experienced in approaching the invasion flotilla, or
in persuading any considerable portion of it to venture beyond the
range of the French batteries, led to the adoption and employment
in the autumn of the year 1804 of a species of torpedo known as a
" catamaran."   It was composed of a lead-lined chest, measuring
about 21 feet long by 3 feet 3 inches broad, and having flat top and
bottom, and wedge-shaped ends.   Within were about forty barrels
of powder and various inflammables, some clockwork machinery,
and enough ballast to bring the deck of the contrivance to a level
with the surface of the water.   The outside of the whole was
caulked, covered with canvas, and well tarred.   The complete
machine weighed about two tons.   Upon the withdrawal of a peg,
the clockwork, after running for a given time, which might be
from six to ten minutes, would fire a pistol and explode the
charge.   The catamaran, which was supplied with a buoyed
grappling iron, designed to hook the machine on to an enemy's
cable, had to be towed to its destination; and this was the weak
point in the contrivance, seeing that provision was made for towing
it directly astern only, and not broad on the quarter or even a little

[1] Marshall, ii., 128–130; *Nav. Chron.*, xii., 247.

abaft the beam of the towing vessel, as was possible in the case of certain more modern torpedoes.[1]

Catamarans were first tried in October, 1804, when the presence of about one hundred and fifty French craft, moored in double line outside Boulogne Pier, seemed to promise a favourable opportunity for testing their effect. It was determined to send a number of fireships and catamarans against them. In the course of the morning of October 1st, Admiral Lord Keith, in the *Monarch*, 74, with three 64's, two 50's, and a number of frigates, sloops, bombs, brigs, and cutters, anchored about five miles from the flotilla. Later in the day, the flagship, three frigates, and some smaller vessels weighed and re-anchored just beyond gunshot of the enemy, who, under Rear-Admiral Lacrosse, in the prame *Ville de Mayence*, expected, and was fully prepared for an attack, his boats rowing guard, and his shore batteries being all alert. On the following day, at about 9.15 P.M., the fireships *Amity*, *Devonshire*, *Peggy*, and *Providence*, towed by armed launches, set out to attack, with a strong tide and fine breeze in their favour. The French opened fire as they approached, and sent forward some gunboats between which and the British launches some fighting ensued. Presently, however, having made ready and cast off their vessels, the launches withdrew, leaving the fireships to drift. The French in vain endeavoured to sink them. At 10.15 P.M. the *Providence* blew up between two of the enemy's gunboats, but did no harm beyond wounding a couple of men. At 10.35 P.M. the *Peggy* exploded after having passed through the French line. She wounded three persons. The *Devonshire* did not burst until about 1 A.M. on October 3rd. Like the *Providence*, she wounded two men only. As for the *Amity*, she blew up innocuously. At the same time four or five catamarans were employed, the last exploding at about 3.30 A.M. Only one seems to have done any damage, and that owing to a purely accidental circumstance. Some French soldiers and seamen, while chasing British boats in a " péniche " (No. 267), ran foul of one of the infernal machines, and was shattered to pieces, losing her commander and thirteen men. The attack, although it cost no British lives, must be regarded as a complete failure, seeing that the expenditure of four fireships and four or five catamarans caused a loss to the enemy of no more than fourteen killed and seven wounded, and did no material

---

[1] *E.g.*, the Harvey. The catamaran of 1804 recalls the " machine " of 1694 (*see* Vol. II., p. 476), and had about as brief a vogue in the Navy.

damage worth mentioning, beyond the destruction of a single
" péniche." [1] Nevertheless, from both sides of the Channel came
loud complaints that, by resorting to such methods of warfare, Great
Britain had returned to barbarism. The use of the catamaran was
no more barbarous than the use of the weapons then ordinarily
recognised ; but it was a premature and ill-considered step. The
machine had not been properly experimented with. As soon as
it was seen that Great Britain had begun to employ a device which,
it was possible, might prove more dangerous on the second than on
the first occasion, the French effectually protected their flotilla
from similar attempts by partially surrounding it with a very
elaborately constructed arrangement of booms and chain cables.

On October 8th, the look-outs in Jersey having detected a number
of French lugger-rigged gun-vessels going northward, close under
the Normandy coast, the *Albacore*, 18, Commander the Hon. Major
Jacob Henniker, slipped and went in search of the enemy. Towards
evening, she obliged five of the gun-vessels to anchor under a battery
to the southward of Gros-Nez. Henniker lay off until 10 A.M. on
the 9th, when, having a weather tide to help him, he stood in under
a heavy fire, anchored with springs on his cables near the gun-vessels
and only just outside the edge of the surf, and cannonaded the
enemy until all five luggers drove ashore with the waves breaking
over them. The *Albacore* was not able, unfortunately, to remain to
complete their destruction, for she dragged her anchor, and was
obliged to slip and haul off. She was somewhat cut about, but none
of her men were hit. [2]

At 4 P.M. on October 23rd, a division of two prames and eighteen
armed schuyts left Ostend for the westward, and was chased by the
Cruiser, 18, Commander John Hancock (1), the gun-brigs *Blazer*,
Lieutenant John Hinton, *Conflict,* Lieutenant Charles Cutts Ormsby,
Tigress, Lieutenant Edward Nathaniel Greensword, and *Escort*,
Lieutenant Joseph Gulstone Garland, and the hired armed cutters
Admiral Mitchell, Lieutenant Richard Williams (1a), and *Griffin*,
Lieutenant James Dillon. At 5.18 P.M. the headmost prame was
brought to action, and at 6.35 P.M. her fire was silenced ; but as the
tide was falling, darkness was increasing, the vessels were in very
shoal water, and the sands and currents were unfamiliar, the *Cruiser*

---

[1] Keith to Marsden, Oct. 3rd ; *Nav. Chron.*, xii., 329–331 : Chevalier, 117.

[2] Saumarez to Marsden, Oct. 13th ; Henniker to Saumarez, Oct. 17th ; d'Auvergne
to Saumarez, Oct. 10th.

hauled off and anchored. The *Conflict*, however, had grounded, and, when he found that he could not get her off, Lieutenant Ormsby, with his people, abandoned her, and pulled for the *Cruiser*. An attempt to bring her off was afterwards made by the *Admiral Mitchell* and *Griffin*, which were reinforced for the purpose ; but by that time the *Conflict*, high and dry, was in possession of the enemy, who were supported by field pieces and howitzers on shore ; and the British had to retire with a loss of three wounded, including Acting-Lieutenant Abraham Garland, of the *Cruiser*.[1]

On December 8th, an attempt was made, under the direction of Captain Sir Home Riggs Popham, of the *Antelope*, 50, to destroy Fort Rouge, a pile-built battery at the mouth of Calais harbour, by means of the fire-vessel *Susannah* and a couple of catamarans. The *Susannah* exploded, but did little harm ; one of the catamarans drifted clear of the fort, the other failed to blow up ; and on neither side was there any loss. From that time forward the catamaran fell into discredit. In its brief career, indeed, it never accomplished anything of importance, although considerable sums of money must have been spent upon it from first to last. Its use, however, marks an interesting step in the gradual evolution of the torpedo.[2]

In the Mediterranean, Lord Nelson, with the bulk of his fleet, remained at anchor in Agincourt Sound until after the beginning of the year 1804 ; but on January 4th, at which date Captain Ross Donnelly, of the *Narcissus*, still commanded the watching squadron off Toulon, the Vice-Admiral put to sea, leaving the *Amazon*, 38, Captain William Parker (2), with some small craft, as an assistance to the Sardinians, in case an invasion of their island should be attempted from Corsica. On the 9th, the *Superb*, 74, Captain Richard Goodwin Keats, was detached to Algier to settle some difficulties with the Dey ; on the 17th, to lend weight to his emissary's representations, Nelson showed himself off the African coast ; on the 18th, the *Superb* rejoined ; and on the 27th, the fleet re-anchored in Agincourt Sound, which the Commander-in-Chief deemed to be the best place wherein to await news from Toulon. On February 1st, the fleet put to sea again, and cruised near the French coast until the 8th, when it anchored off Caprera. It cruised once more from February 19th to March 25th, being joined on the 15th by the *Royal Sovereign*, 100, Captain Pulteney Malcolm, from England ; and on April 3rd, Nelson weighed yet again, and,

---

[1] Hancock to Keith, Oct. 24th ; Chevalier, 123.   [2] Popham to Keith, Dec. 10th.

passing between Elba and Cape Corso, stationed himself, on April
9th, off Capes Sicié and Cepet, to the southward of Toulon. In the
course of that afternoon the Cape Cepet batteries fired at the
Amazon, while she was engaged in taking possession of a prize
brig under the shore ; and three French frigates, ultimately followed
by four more ships, left Toulon as if to cut her off ; but, upon the
Donegal, 74, Captain Sir Richard John Strachan, and the *Active*,
38, Captain Richard Hussey Moubray, proceeding in support, the
French tacked and retired. On May 10th, the fleet was joined by
the *Leviathan*, 74, Captain Henry William Bayntun, and by three
bombs ; and on the 19th, it re-anchored in Agincourt Sound. On
the 14th, the *Gibraltar*, 80, Captain George Frederick Ryves (1),
rejoined from Naples ; and on the 19th, the fleet returned to its
station off Toulon, where, in the interim, the *Bucentaure*, 80, had
been launched, and had received the flag of Vice-Admiral Latouche-
Tréville. She lay ready for sea with seven other ships of the line,
and in the inner harbour were several more ships which were very
nearly ready.

On May 24th there occurred an affair which, at one moment,
seemed inclined to develop into a serious action. The main body
of the British fleet was out of sight in the offing ; and the *Canopus*,
80, Rear-Admiral George Campbell, Captain John Conn, *Donegal*,
74, Captain Sir Richard John Strachan, and *Amazon*, 38, Captain
William Parker (2), with a very slight S.W. breeze, were standing
on the port tack, eastward of Cape Cepet, in order to reconnoitre the
outer road, when, just before noon, a French ship of the line and
frigate were seen under sail close off the entrance to the harbour.
At 12.30 P.M. the British ships tacked in succession, being then
about three miles from the shore. No sooner had they begun to
put about than a number of gunboats swept out from under Cape
Cepet, and began a long-range fire at the *Amazon*. The *Canopus*,
firing a few of her lower-deck guns, stood on to the S.E. by E.
with a strengthening breeze which by that time blew from the
W.N.W. As soon as the heavy guns made themselves heard in
Toulon, two French ships of the line and two frigates, followed
at 2.30 P.M. by two more of the line, slipped and made sail to
assist their consorts outside. The leading French ship, a frigate,
being upon the weather quarter of the *Canopus*, presently opened
upon that vessel and the *Donegal*, which, of course, returned the
compliment ; but, having so superior a force in chase, Rear-Admiral

Campbell did not feel justified in encouraging an attack, and ordered his division to make sail. The pursuit was relinquished at 3.30 P.M., and at 9.30 P.M. the detachment rejoined the Commander-in-Chief.[1]

Another brush took place on June 14th. At that time, Lord Nelson, with the inshore or lee division of five ships of the line,[2] lay off Hyères, while Rear-Admiral Sir Richard Hussey Bickerton, with the weather division, also of five sail, cruised about sixty miles to seaward. In the course of the afternoon of June 13th, it was signalled to the Commander-in-Chief that two strange ships were under sail off the east end of Porquerolles, and the *Amazon*, 38, Captain William Parker (2), and *Phœbe*, 36, Captain the Hon. Thomas Bladen Capell, were ordered in chase. Not till noon on June 14th were the frigates able to get off the entrance of Grande Passe. They soon afterwards signalled that the strangers were frigates; and, it being known that there were batteries close at hand, Nelson ordered the *Excellent*, 74, Captain Frank Sotheron, to join the chase. By 5 P.M. the frigates *Incorruptible* and *Sirène*, with the *Furet*, 18, were seen at anchor under Porquerolles fort. At 5.30 P.M., one of the French batteries fired at the *Phœbe*; but the shot fell short. At 5.45 P.M., both frigates, cleared for action, anchored with springs on their cables just beyond reach of the guns in the northernmost battery; but immediately afterwards it was observed that the whole fleet in the outer road of Toulon was getting under way; whereupon the *Amazon* and *Phœbe* also weighed and stood to sea. At the same time the *Excellent* was recalled by signal; and she soon rejoined her division, which, since 4.30 P.M., had been making under all sail for Grande Passe, with the wind at W.S.W. Soon after 5 P.M., Nelson, perceiving M. Latouche-Tréville, with eight sail of the line and four frigates, coming out of Toulon, shortened sail, and hauled to the wind in line of battle on the starboard tack. "In the evening," says Nelson, "he stood under Cepet again; and, I believe I may call it, we chased him into Toulon the morning of the 15th."[3] Latouche-Tréville, on the other hand, most unwarrantably declared to his Government: "J'ai poursuivi jusqu'à la nuit: il courait au sud-est."[4] The truth

---

[1] *Nav. Chron.*, xii., 242, etc.: Chevalier, 112.

[2] *Victory, Canopus, Belleisle, Donegal*, and *Excellent*.

[3] Nelson to Acton, June 18th.

[4] Disp. of 26 Prairial, an 12: Chevalier, 113.

is that, having, by displaying his whole force of eight sail of the line, prevented his two frigates and a corvette from being cut off by a ship of the line and two frigates, M. Latouche-Tréville declined action with, and retired before Nelson, who had but five sail of the line. The British Commander-in-Chief was extremely angry at this misrepresentation, and, though he had a high opinion of the French vice-admiral's professional merit, could not thenceforward conceal his personal contempt for him. Latouche-Tréville's dispatch, which may well have been read in Paris as a declaration that the whole of the ten ships of the line forming the blockading fleet had fled before him, earned him promotion in the Legion of Honour to the rank of " grand officier de l'Empire," [1] and an appointment as Inspector of the Coasts of the Mediterranean.

The letter [2] in which Napoleon conveyed to M. Latouche-Tréville the news that he was to be thus rewarded is very important, since it contains the first draft of the directions for those movements which brought about the decisive campaign of Trafalgar. [3] Sixteen hundred picked troops were to be embarked in the line-of-battle ships, the complements of which were to be made up, if necessary, by putting corvettes out of commission and by sending press-gangs to Marseilles. The vice-admiral was further ordered, after endeavouring to deceive Nelson as to his destination, to put to sea, to pass the Strait of Gibraltar, to pick up a French ship lying in Cadiz, to give Ferrol and its blockading squadron a wide berth, and to make for Rochefort, off which he was to be joined by six sail of the line, including the new ship *Achille*. He would then, it was calculated, have with him sixteen sail of the line and eleven frigates. With them, either proceeding direct or doubling Ireland as circumstances might dictate, he was to appear off Boulogne. In the meantime, the French Brest fleet, of twenty-three sail of the line, full of troops, would divert the attention of Admiral the Hon. William Cornwallis, and oblige him to keep close to the port, so as to be in a position to intercept it. Off Boulogne, where it was hoped he would be sometime in September, Latouche-Tréville would receive additional instructions. Napoleon expected him, subject, of course, to the conditions being favourable, to sail from Toulon

---

[1] A style subsequently abolished in favour of Grand Cross.

[2] From Malmaison, July 2nd. ' Corr. de Nap.,' ix. 513.

[3] I say the "first draft"; but, in fact, a somewhat different scheme had been previously elaborated. ' Corr. de Nap.,' viii. 657; ix. 168.

about July 28th.[1] Latouche-Tréville did not live to carry out these directions ; for, ere he had an opportunity of escaping from Nelson's watchful eye, he died, on August 18th,[2] on board the *Bucentaure*, which still lay in Toulon.   Moreover, on August 2nd, finding that some divisions of the flotilla were not ready, Napoleon had written, postponing for several weeks the commencement of the strategic operations upon the issue of which his future depended to an extent greater than even he, in all probability, suspected.

For several days after July 11th, Nelson, troubled by the unseaworthy condition of many of his ships and by almost continuous heavy weather, experienced unusual difficulty in keeping his station ; and on the 19th, having been joined by the *Ambuscade*, frigate, and eight transports from England, he wore and stood for the Gulf of Palma, leaving the observation of Toulon to the *Belle-isle*, 74, Captain William Hargood (1), with the frigates *Niger* and *Fishguard*, the bomb *Acheron*, and a couple of transports.   On August 2nd, when these vessels, which had been driven off by renewed gales, were still out of sight of the shore, Rear-Admiral Dumanoir Le Pelley, with five sail of the line and six frigates, quitted port, to practise fleet tactics, or, more probably, to discover whether the blockade was still maintained.   He cruised off Toulon until the 5th, when Captain Hargood reappeared ; and on the 6th, although the French division had been promptly reinforced with an additional 80-gun ship from the port, it stood back into harbour.   When, on the 8th, Hargood reconnoitred, he found ten sail of the line, six frigates, and one brig lying in the road.   In the meantime Nelson had proceeded, for watering purposes, to a bay near Porto Torres in the island of Pulla.   He remained there from the 8th to the 10th, when he weighed and headed for his rendezvous ; but he was delayed by heavy weather.   On August 26th, he saw in Toulon road ten sail of the line and ten other ship-rigged vessels, and, in the inner harbour, fitting, a line-of-battle ship and a frigate.   His own force still included ten sail of the line only, for, though he had been joined by the *Conqueror*, *Spencer*, and *Tigre*, he had detached the *Gibraltar*, *Kent*, and *Triumph*.

To take the place of Latouche-Tréville, three flag-officers were eligible, Bruix, Rosily, and Villeneuve.[3]   Bruix already had com-

---

[1] " Let us only," adds this letter, " be masters of the Strait for six hours, and we shall be masters of the world."

[2] Some authorities say on Aug. 20th.   [3] Then in command at Rochefort.

mand of the invasion flotilla; yet, but for the bad state of his
health, he would probably have been transferred to Toulon. The
choice then lay between Rosily and Villeneuve; and, with some
misgiving, Napoleon selected the latter. The Emperor, it is certain,
did not consider that he had found a competent substitute for
Latouche-Tréville; for he almost immediately altered his plans for
the movements of the Toulon fleet.[1] In his instructions to Latouche-
Tréville he had given to that fleet the leading part in the projected strategical combination, and had left to the Brest fleet the
altogether subsidiary duty of keeping Cornwallis's attention fixed
upon it. According to new instructions, contained in a letter[2] of
September 29th to the Minister of Marine, Villeneuve, who was
supposed to have already assumed command, although, in fact, he
did not, in consequence of various delays, hoist his flag in the
Bucentaure until November 16th, was to quit the road of Toulon,
if possible before October 21st—ominous day!—having previously
received on board about 6500 troops under General Lauriston.

" The fleet, stated to consist of 11 ships of the line and 7 or 8 frigates, was to sail
out of the Mediterranean, call for the *Aigle* at Cadiz, detach two of its fastest sailers,
along with four frigates and two brigs, having on board 1800 troops, to relieve Sénégal,
retake Gorée, ravage the British settlements on the coast of Africa, and capture the
island of St. Helena, wanted as a dépôt for the French cruisers and their prizes in that
quarter of the globe; while, with 10 sail of the line and frigates, and the remainder of
the troops, Villeneuve was to steer for Cayenne. Having there taken on board the
celebrated General Victor Hugues, the French admiral was to proceed off Surinam, and
effect a junction with a squadron of 5 sail of the line and 4 frigates, under Rear-
Admiral Missiessy, M. Villeneuve's successor at Rochefort; who, it was supposed,
would already have fulfilled the first part of his mission. This was, with 3500 men
under General Legrange, to proceed to Martinique and Guadeloupe; and, after leaving
1000 men at each of those islands, to attempt, with the remaining 1500, the capture of
the island of Dominica, and, if possible, of St. Lucia. Having garrisoned the captured
islands, Rear-Admiral Missiessy was to proceed off Surinam, and await the arrival of
Admiral Villeneuve, who, with his forces now augmented to 15 sail of the line, 7 or 8
frigates, and full 5000 men, was to possess himself of Surinam and the other Dutch
colonies in this quarter. That done, the French admiral was to place under contribution all the British West India Islands, enter the different roadsteads, and capture or
burn the vessels lying there; leaving in the Antilles, purposely to harass British
commerce, the greater part of his corvettes, of which as many as possible were to quit
Toulon with the expedition. He was next to leave 1200 men with General Ferrand at
the city of San Domingo, raise the blockade of Ferrol, and, taking out the 5 ships in
that port, appear off Rochefort with 20 sail of the line. Here Vice-Admiral Villeneuve
would receive directions at what point he was to join Vice-Admiral Ganteaume and his
30 sail of the line,[3] in order to fulfil the ultimate object in view, the descent upon
England."[4]

---

[1] Chevalier, 114.   [2] 'Corr. de Nap.,' ix. 700.
[3] *I.e.*, the Brest fleet of 23 sail, *plus* 7 Dutch sail to be picked up by it in the Texel.
[4] This is the very correct summary given in James, iii. 240, 241.

As has been said, Villeneuve was expected to sail by October 21st. Missiessy was supposed to get to sea by November 1st; and Ganteaume, having heard of the departure of the other fleets, would, in that case, leave Brest before November 23rd. Ganteaume's duty, pending the reappearance of Villeneuve and Missiessy, would be to land in Ireland a corps under General Augereau, reach the neighbourhood of the Strait of Dover either by the Channel or by the north of Scotland, pick up the Dutch contingent from the Texel, and perhaps also Marmont's corps then assembled in Holland, and then act as the weather and the Emperor should dictate, to facilitate the project of invasion. It is necessary to describe these plans, although Villeneuve's delay prevented them from being punctually begun, and although, as will be seen, they were eventually much modified by various other circumstances, and especially by the addition, towards the end of 1804, of Spain to the list of the active allies of France and enemies of Great Britain.

It should be borne in mind that, ever since the Treaty of San Ildefonso, in 1796, Spain had been bound to furnish to France, upon demand, fifteen ships of the line as a reinforcement, and a body of troops. Bonaparte, after the renewal of war in 1803, would have preferred to accept an equivalent in money for the stipulated aid in ships and men, and to leave to Spain a nominal neutrality. When Spain objected that the specified conditions were onerous, the Emperor bluntly pointed out that his ally must pay the subsidy or declare war against Great Britain, or have war declared against her by France.[1] In the result, Spain agreed, on October 19th, 1803, to pay the subsidy. She was thereupon informed that Great Britain reserved to herself the right to regard the payment as a *casus belli,* should she choose at any time to do so;[2] and she was afterwards formally warned, first on January 24th, and again on February 18th, 1804, that unless Spanish naval preparations were suspended, war would ensue. But Spain had ceased to be her own master. Napoleon used her almost as if she were already his. The preparations in Spanish ports not only continued but increased; and at length the cabinet at Madrid was told that unless satisfactory explanations were given, the British ambassador would depart. Such was, in brief, the situation up to the moment when hostilities were suddenly, and without further warning, begun by orders of the British Govern-

---

[1] 'Corr. de Nap.,' viii. 580 *et seq.*: Chevalier, 125.
[2] 'Parl. Debs.,' 1805, iii. 70.

ment.[1] The particular course of action adopted was, perhaps, not
quite necessary ; nor was the force employed so great as it should
have been if, as ought to have been the case, it was desired to avoid
needless bloodshed ; but, after all has been said, it must be admitted
that Spain, ere she was struck, had received ample notice, and that
Great Britain had received more than ample provocation. Spain
formally declared war on December 12th, 1804.

Nelson went to his old anchorage in Agincourt Sound on
October 18th for wood, water, and provisions, and, having returned
at the beginning of November to his station before Toulon, there,
on November 14th, received intelligence of the attack upon the
Spanish treasure-frigates on October 5th. The new situation created
by this event obliged him to watch not only the French fleet in
Toulon, but also a Spanish squadron of five or six sail of the line,
lying in Cartagena ; and for all that duty his command, or at least
that part of it which exigencies allowed him to keep with him,
was hardly sufficient. The *Swiftsure* joined him on December 25th ;
but on the last day of the year, his fleet, owing to the absence
of the *Superb*, again consisted only of ten sail of the line, besides
two frigates and a bomb. With it he cruised S.E. of Cape San
Sebastian, while ready for sea in Toulon road were eleven sail
of the line and seven or eight frigates, with troops on board, waiting
an opportunity to begin the eventful cruise which was to terminate
at Trafalgar. Nelson's ships were nearly all much out of repair ;
they were often, nay, generally, short of stores ; and the command
was most inadequately supplied with frigates and small craft suitable
for service as scouts : but all these deficiencies were counterbalanced
by the fact that the fleet was the best officered and best manned
that had ever served Great Britain ; and thus, in spite of the
immense difficulties in the way, Nelson and his Captains succeeded
in watching, intimidating, and ultimately even beating, enemies
who ought to have been able to crush them.[2]

It will be recollected that, towards the conclusion of the war
of the French Revolution, the Dutch colony of Curaçoa had
capitulated, with a readiness little removed from eagerness, to the
British frigate *Néréide*, Captain Frederick Watkins. The Dutch
population had been actuated on that occasion by a very natural

---

[1] For particulars of the attack upon the Spanish treasure-ships, *see* next chapter.
[2] 'Nels. Disps.' Vols. v. and vi. are full of complaints of the material inefficiency
of the fleet.

desire to free itself from the tyranny of a large and rapacious force of French Republicans which occupied part of their island. At the beginning of the new war, when Curaçoa was once more Dutch, the situation was entirely different. The people, though still not entirely their own masters, had no causes of discontent so serious as to outweigh their loyalty. Yet the British officers on the Jamaica station failed to understand the changed condition of affairs. As soon as hostilities opened, Lieutenant (actg.) Michael Fitton, in the schooner *Gipsy*, 10, was sent from Jamaica to warn any British vessels that might be at Curaçoa of what had taken place. Mr. Fitton found in the harbour of St. Anne, the *Surinam*, 18, Commander (actg.) Robert Tucker, and, communicating the news, advised his brother officer to get under way as soon as possible. The *Gipsy*, which sailed immediately, was chased by two armed vessels of superior force. The *Surinam* was repairing, and her Commander did not, apparently, deem it necessary to make any special effort to leave the port. Instead, he busied himself in taking plans of the Dutch forts and batteries and in transmitting particulars [1] of them, and of the disposition of the inhabitants, to Rear-Admiral Sir John Thomas Duckworth, the Commander-in-Chief, and to Commodore Samuel Hood (2). Some of his dispatches falling into the hands of the Dutch, he and his ship were seized. [2] In spite, however, of this warning, Curaçoa was still officially regarded as a place which would quickly fall upon a small demonstration being made against it.

In December, 1803, Captain John Bligh (2), of the *Theseus*, 74, being then at Port Royal, Jamaica, received orders to proceed off the city of San Domingo, which was in French occupation, and, in conjunction with the *Vanguard*, 74, Captain James Walker (2), which was said to be already there, to blockade the port. He was at the same time verbally informed that he would be later directed to attack Curaçoa, but that the Commander-in-Chief did not wish him to risk the safety of the 74's by endeavouring to force the harbour of St. Anne. On December 19th, therefore, the *Theseus* sailed from Port Royal, and in due time arrived off San Domingo ;

---

[1] There is reason to believe that Tucker was much misled as to the force and temper of the garrison.

[2] James, iii. 283, gives an incorrect account of this incident. The story here given is from the proceedings of the court-martial, which acquitted Tucker, who, on the following March 21st, was promoted to be Commander.

but she neither found the *Vanguard* there, nor was joined by her subsequently. On January 15th, 1804, however, there arrived the *Hercule*, 74, Captain Richard Dalling Dunn, with orders to Bligh to take under his command the *Hercule* and *Vanguard*, together with the *Blanche*, 36, Captain Zachary Mudge, *Pique*, 36, Captain Charles Bayne Hodgson Ross, and *Gipsy*, 10, Lieutenant (actg.) Michael Fitton, and, proceeding in the *Theseus* to Curaçoa, to summon the island, to land men in case of refusal to surrender, but not " to hazard more than the object is worth."

With the two 74's—for the *Vanguard* was still missing—the two frigates, and the schooner, but with hardly any trustworthy information about the island, and with only two officers, Captain Ross and Lieutenant Fitton, who had ever sighted it, Bligh sailed, and, on January 30th, made the outlying island of Bonaire. Bearing up, he hove to on the following morning six miles to the eastward of St. Anne; and Captain Ross, going on board the *Gipsy*, at once went in with a summons. At 9.30 A.M. the *Gipsy* stood out of harbour, signalling that the terms had been rejected.

The mouth of the harbour is narrow; the batteries defending it mounted nearly one hundred guns; and within lay the *Hatslaar*, 36, and two French privateers. Leaving, therefore, the *Blanche* and *Pique* before the entrance, Bligh, with the rest of his force proceeded off a small cove which Lieutenant Fitton considered to be a suitable point for a disembarkation. As the ships withdrew from off the port they were fired at by Fort Amsterdam, which lies to the S.E. of the harbour's mouth; and at 11.30 A.M., when they were off the cove, they were fired at by Fort Piscadero, a work mounting ten 12-pounders. The fort was, however, soon reduced to comparative silence by the *Theseus*. In the meantime a landing party of 406 seamen and 199 Royal Marines had been prepared, under command of Captains Richard Dalling Dunn (*Hercule*) and William Bayne Hodgson Ross (*Pique*); Lieutenants Edward Henry a'Court and Richard Henry Muddle (*Theseus*); and John B. Hills, Nisbet Josiah Willoughby, and William Woolsey[1] (*Hercule*); and Lieutenants, R.M., Edward Nicolls, William Henry Craig, Earle Harwood, Bertrand Cahuac, and Samuel Perrot. At 1 P.M. a division of this force

---

[1] This officer took the place of Lieut. William Brathwaite, of the *Blanche*, who was incapacitated by his habitual drunkenness. James, iii. 285.

landed, stormed and carried Fort Piscadero, without loss, and then, losing only four or five in the operation, drove the Dutch from all the neighbouring positions. Thereupon the rest of the seamen and Royal Marines disembarked, and the *Gipsy* anchored in the cove. On February 1st and 2nd, some guns were landed and dragged with much difficulty to a spot whence they would command the west side of St. Anne; but this battery, which was placed under the orders of Lieutenant Willoughby, was not made effective until some loss had been caused by the fire from Fort Republiek, from another work, and from the privateers in port. Other guns were also landed and mounted elsewhere. On February 4th, and again on the 5th, skirmishes took place, resulting to the advantage of the British, but accompanied with regrettable loss. The loss in the batteries was also heavy and continuous, by sickness and, unhappily, by desertion,[1] as well as by the fire of the enemy. On the other hand, the Dutch received reinforcements. On February 23rd, therefore, Captain Bligh dispatched the *Gipsy* to inform Duckworth that he purposed to re-embark on March 4th, unless some favourable development should occur in the interim. No sooner had he done so than he had to allow the *Pique*, which had damaged her rudder, to bear up for Jamaica. Indeed, instead of the developments being favourable, they were so decidedly of the opposite character, that Bligh re-embarked his whole remaining force as early as February 25th, after having destroyed Fort Piscadero, and disabled such guns as it was found necessary to leave behind. The various operations, apart from the dysentery which ravaged the force, had involved a loss of eighteen killed and forty-two wounded, among the former being Midshipman Joseph Palmer, and, among the latter, three Lieutenants, R.M., Messrs. Harwood, Cahuac, and Perrot. It was an ill-considered expedition; yet it would probably have been successful, but for the failure of the *Vanguard* to co-operate in it. That failure must be attributed to the ineffective measures taken by Sir John Thomas Duckworth to apprise his Captains of what he expected of them; for, while Bligh was at Curaçoa, the *Vanguard* remained off the island, though not off the port, of San Domingo.

An expedition against Surinam had more satisfactory results. On April 25th, after a passage of twenty-two days from Barbados,

---

[1] About one-half the *Hercule's* Marines were Poles, who had unwisely been allowed to enter at San Domingo.

Commodore Samuel Hood (2) arrived off the Dutch island with the following force :—

SHIPS.	GUNS.	COMMANDERS.
Centaur	74	Commod. Samuel Hood (2). Capt. Murray Maxwell.
Pandour	44, en flûte.	Capt. John Nash.
Serapis	44, en flûte.	Com. Henry Waring.
Alligator	28, en flûte.	Com. Charles Richardson.
Hippomenes. . . .	18	Com Conway Shipley.
Drake	16	Com. William Ferris.
Unique, armed schooner	10	Lieut. George Rowley Brand.

And transports carrying about two thousand troops under Maj.-Genl. Sir Charles Green.

Off the mouth of the Surinam River was found the *Emerald*, 36, Captain James O'Bryen ; [1] and Commander Kenneth M'Kenzie, of the brig-sloop *Guachapin*,[2] though, owing to baffling winds and currents his vessel was obliged to remain about one hundred and fifty miles to leeward, presently joined with all her boats and most of her men. On the night of April 30th, about seven hundred men under Brig.-General Maitland, were landed in Warapee Creek under the direction of Commanders Shipley and M'Kenzie. On the following days Braam's Point was captured, after a battery on it had been silenced by the *Emerald*, *Pandour*, and *Drake* ; the Frederici battery and Leijden redoubt were stormed and carried by troops under Brig.-General Hughes, assisted by boats and seamen under Captain Maxwell, and Commanders Ferris and Richardson. Everything was then almost ready for attacking Fort Nieuw Amsterdam, where about eighty guns were mounted ; but on May 5th, before anything further could be done, the colony surrendered. With it were surrendered the Dutch men-of-war *Proserpine*, 32, *Pylades*, 18, a 10-gun schooner, and seven gunboats, together with several merchantmen which, under Captain Willem Otto Bloijs van Treslong, had been disposed to block the river. On neither side had there been any heavy loss. The British squadron had had but five killed, including Lieutenant James Edward Smith (*Centaur*) and Midshipman William Shuldham,

---

[1] Later Lord James O'Bryen, who died Admiral the Marquis of Thomond in 1855.

[2] *Guachapin* was the Anglicised form of *Guet-apens*, the name of a French small craft which had been lately captured and was used as tender to the British flagship on the station.

and eight wounded, including Lieutenants William King (1)[1] and Robert Henderson[1] (*Centaur*), and George Rowley Brand (*Unique*); and the army's casualties amounted only to three killed and thirteen wounded. The prisoners numbered upwards of two thousand; and two hundred and eighty-two guns of various sorts were captured.[2]

Little else of much importance happened during the year in America or Asia; but in Africa, Gorée, which had not been restored to France under the Treaty, was surrendered on January 18th by its commandant, Colonel Fraser, after a stubborn fight, to a much superior French force which, under Lieutenant Jean Michel Mahé, had crossed from Cayenne in the *Oncle Thomas*, 20, armed ship, *Renommée*, 14, *Oiseau*, 10, *Rosalie*, 2, *Vigie*, 2, and a schooner of unknown name. But the victors held the settlement for a short time only. On the morning of March 7th, the *Inconstant*, 36, Captain Edward Stirling Dickson, accompanied by a storeship and three transports, arrived off the place, and, seeing French colours hoisted, sent ashore Lieutenant Charles Pickford, in a cutter, to ascertain what had happened. Not receiving any news by 10 A.M., Captain Dickson manned and armed three boats, and sent them, under a Midshipman, Mr. Runciman, to cut out a vessel lying in the road. The duty was duly performed, although the heavy fire from the batteries sank a boat and wounded a man. From the prize the strength of the garrison was discovered. The *Inconstant* then stood to the westward to prevent supplies from being received from Sénégal; and, having been joined by a fourth transport, which furnished sufficient boats to complete the number needed to contain the troops which were to be disembarked, Captain Dickson prepared to effect a landing on the 8th. But when the morning dawned, the British colours were seen to be flying over the French. The garrison had, in fact, been induced to capitulate overnight to Lieutenant Pickford.[3]

Spain, it has been seen, had declared war against Great Britain on December 12th, 1804. The declaration was not received in London until January 7th, 1805; but, ere that, France had made preparations for utilising to the utmost the naval and military forces of her new ally. On January 4th, a secret convention between France and Spain was signed in Paris by Vice-Admiral Decrès,

---

[1] Made Commanders, June 21st, 1804.   [2] *Nav. Chron.*, xii. 80; De Jonge, v. 596.
[3] He was deservedly made a Commander on April 27th following.

for the one, and Vice-Admiral Don Federico Gravina for the other.

After recounting the forces at the disposal, by sea and land, of the French emperor,[1] the document goes on to declare that the King of Spain binds himself to commission, and supply with six months' provisions and four months' water, from 25 to 29 sail of the line, and to have them ready, with from 4000 to 5000 Spanish troops (to embark from Cadiz, together with 20,000 French troops), by, at the latest, March 30th, 1805. Of the sail of the line, Ferrol was to provide 7 or 8; Cadiz from 12 to 15; and Cartagena, 6. The Ferrol vessels were to act in combination with the 5 French sail of the line that lay in that port. Spain, as well as France, was to augment her active fleet by adding to it from time to time all ships of the line and frigates that might be constructed or fitted in her ports. Napoleon guaranteed the integrity of the king's dominions, and promised to do his best to procure the restoration to Spain of Trinidad, and of the treasure which had been captured in the Spanish frigates in October, 1804. Neither Power was to make a separate peace; and ratifications were to be exchanged within a month. Admiral Gravina, in a note, expressed his doubts as to whether Spain would be able in reasonable time to collect men and provisions for so large a fleet as she undertook to supply for the objects of the alliance.[2]

A reference to the statistical table given on p. 10 will show that, at the beginning of 1805, Great Britain had, nominally at her disposal for active service, one hundred and sixteen ships of the line. Of these, one hundred and five were actually in commission. Mr. James[3] is of opinion that, for various reasons, not more than eighty-three of these could be sent to sea, and that Bonaparte well knew that such was the case. It is probable that James somewhat understates the really available British force; but, even if this be so, it is clear that the Spanish arrangement added vastly to the possibilities of success of the great combinations upon which the Emperor had embarked. Before the arrangement, he had at his disposal, excluding the vessels of the Batavian navy, about forty-three ships of the line; after its conclusion, he had at least sixty-eight, and

---

[1] The summary is: In the Texel, 30,000 troops, with the necessary transports.

At Calais, Ostend, Dunquerque, Boulogne, and Le Hâvre, flotillas to embark 120,000 men and 25,000 horses.

At Rochefort, 6 sail of the line, and 4 frigates, having on board 4000 men.

At Brest, 21 sail of the line, besides frigates and transports, with 25,000 troops for embarkation.

At Toulon, 11 sail of the line, 8 frigates, and transports having cn board 9000 troops.

From the Brest fleet the *Océan* and some other ship appear to be excluded. In the Rochefort squadron is included the *Achille*, although she was only just ready for launching. The five ships of the line lying in Ferrol seem to be overlooked.

[2] 'Précis des Evénements,' xi. 215. The treaty was duly ratified on January 18th, 1805.

[3] James, iii. 298.

perhaps seventy, or even more ; and, with the Batavian ships, his numerical strength would be nearly, if not quite, equal to that of Great Britain.   In making estimates of military or naval force, one should, however, count brains rather than heads.   The British fleet was homogeneous, enthusiastic for a common cause, full of the prestige of victory, and very highly disciplined.   The allied fleets, on the contrary, were of three different nationalities, each jealous of the others, partly republican and partly monarchical, animated by diverse motives, oppressed by a long history of defeat, and, at least as regards the Spanish contingent, inexperienced and ill-trained. In addition, on one side were commanders like Nelson, Collingwood, Cornwallis, and Saumarez ; on the other, commanders like Bruix, Villeneuve, Gravina, Ganteaume, and Ver Huell.   Mere numerical equality in ships and men, in such circumstances, goes for very little. Indeed, where quality is deficient, mere quantity is often, in itself, a source of weakness.

In order to follow in a clear and consecutive manner the various movements which, beginning in the first months of the year, led up to the battle of Trafalgar on October 21st, 1805, it is necessary to temporarily abandon a plan which has hitherto been consistently pursued in these pages.   It has so far been my ordinary practice, when dealing with the major operations of the Navy in any given year, to describe the services of the British fleets, first on one station, then on another, and so on, until all stations upon which important events occurred have been glanced at in turn.   The far-reaching character of the greatest of all naval campaigns, that of 1805, and the sudden shiftings of scene, make it impossible to keep to the usual plan, and, at the same time, to present the drama as it should be presented.   It is purposed, therefore, in relating the central story of that *annus mirabilis*, to forget for the moment that there were then, as there are still, stations with definite limits and under different commanders-in-chief.   While Nelson was at sea on his final cruise, his personality ousted all other personalities from the field ; and his restless energy declined to admit any bounds to its activity.   When all the plot of the main drama shall have been told, and when the last and most brilliant progress of its hero shall have been followed from Agincourt Sound to Egypt, from Canopus to Cagliari, from Pulla to Barbados, from the West Indies to Spithead, and from Merton to the dim cockpit of the *Victory*, it will be seen that it is, indeed, genius of the highest type that needs half a world in order to have room for action. Then it will be time, seeing that the old bulkheads will be no longer in the way, to replace them, and to revert to the accustomed routine of the chronicle.

The last service of Nelson divides itself naturally into three separate, yet intimately connected episodes,—the cruise to the Levant, the chase to the West Indies and back, and the triumphant end of the whole work off Cape Trafalgar.

ADMIRAL SIR JOHN ORDE (1), BART.

(*From Ridley's engraving after the portrait by Romney.*)

By the beginning of the year 1805, the adhesion of Spain to the active enemies of Great Britain had already led to some new dispositions of the British forces. A squadron of seven sail of the line, under Rear-Admiral the Hon. Alexander Forester Inglis Cochrane, with his flag in the *Northumberland*, 74, watched Ferrol and Corunna, where lay, ready for sea, five French and seven Spanish sail of the line, besides three more Spanish ships which were still fitting. Another squadron, numbering sometimes five and sometimes six sail of the line, under Vice-Admiral Sir John Orde (1), in the *Glory*, 98, cruised off Cadiz, to watch one French and seven Spanish sail of the line which lay there ready for sea, with four other Spanish ships which were being made ready ; and Orde, in conjunction with Nelson, whose more special duty was to watch Toulon, had also to keep an eye upon six Spanish sail of the line which lay ready in Cartagena. Orde, it should be explained, was, in point of seniority, Nelson's superior officer, his commission as a Vice-Admiral dating from February 14th, 1799, while Nelson's dated only from January 1st, 1801. Yet Nelson was Commander-in-Chief in the Mediterranean, whereas Orde, who had aspired to that post, and who, being of a petty and jealous nature, had never forgiven his great junior for having received it, was only " commanding a squadron off Cape Finisterre." [1]

Nelson, as has been seen, cruised at the end of 1804 off Cape St. Sebastian. The immediate strategical objects which he had before him were, on the one hand, to prevent the junction of the eleven French ships of the line which lay in Toulon with the French and Spanish squadrons in Cartagena, Cadiz, and Ferrol, or with any of them ; and, on the other, to check any sally which the French at Toulon might attempt in the direction of Malta or of Egypt. As usual, the material supplied to him by the Admiralty was, on paper at least, quite inadequate to the work demanded of it. Many of the ships of the line required radical repairs ; his force was numerically inferior to that of his opponents ; and he had scarcely any frigates or small craft wherewith to obtain intelligence, or to communicate with distant points : but, as usual also, the personnel of his command was in the highest state of efficiency. Early in January he found it necessary to repair once more to his favourite anchorage ; and, detaching the *Active*, 38, Captain Richard Hussey Moubray, and the *Seahorse*, 38, Captain the Hon. Courtenay Boyle, to watch Toulon, he quitted his station on the 3rd, and, on the 11th, entered Agincourt Sound. There, on January 15th, he was rejoined by the *Superb*, 74, which had been engaged on diplomatic duty at Algier ; and there he remained until

---

[1] Nelson's feelings were hurt by Orde's appointment to this command ; for Nelson's station had previously extended as far as Cape Finisterre, including, of course, Cadiz. In spite of Orde's reputed enmity for Nelson, he was one of those chosen to support the pall at Nelson's funeral. He appears to have been an excitable and quarrelsome officer. He challenged Lord St. Vincent in 1799, and would have fought him, had not the police interfered.

January 19th, when, as will be shown presently, he was hurriedly summoned to sea.

Early in the afternoon of January 17th, Vice-Admiral Villeneuve, finding the coast apparently clear, and taking advantage of a good N.N.W. wind, left Toulon with eleven sail of the line, seven frigates, and two brigs, having on board three thousand five hundred troops under General Lauriston. By 5 P.M. his last ship was outside Cape Cepet: by 6.30 P.M. his leading vessels were sighted by the *Active* and *Seahorse*. He seemed to be bound southward; and the British frigates managed to keep part of his force in view until 2 A.M. on January 19th, when, still having reason to suppose that the French had designs to the southward, they crowded sail, and, by 1.50 P.M. on the same day, were able to signal to Nelson that the enemy was at sea. Nelson weighed at 4.30 P.M. The force with him, and the force which had left Toulon with Villeneuve, were as follows :—

BRITISH.			FRENCH.	
Ships.	Guns.	Commanders.	Ships.	Guns.
Victory . . .	100	Vice-Adm. Lord Nelson, K.B. (W.) Rear-Adm. George Murray (3) (B.). Capt. Thomas Masterman Hardy.	*Bucentaure* . .	80[1]
			Formidable . .	80[2]
			Neptune. . .	80
Royal Sovereign	100	Rear-Adm. Sir Richard H. Bickerton, Bt. (R.). Capt. John Stewart.	*Indomptable* .	80
			Annibal . .	74
			Mont Blanc .	74
Canopus . .	80	,, John Conn.	*Swiftsure* . .	74
Superb . .	74	,, Richard Goodwin Keats.	*Atlas* . . .	74
Spencer . . .	74	,, Hon. Robert Stopford.	*Intrépide* . .	74
Swiftsure . .	74	,, Mark Robinson (2).	*Scipion* . . .	74
Belleisle . .	74	,, William Hargood (1).	*Berwick*. . .	74
Conqueror . .	74	,, Israel Pellew.		
Tigre . . .	74	,, Benjamin Hallowell.	*Cornélie*. . .	40
Leviathan . .	74	,, Henry William Bayntun.	*Hortense* . .	40
Donegal . . .	74	,, Pulteney Malcolm.	*Incorruptible* .	38
			Rhin . . .	40
Active . . .	38	Capt. Richard Hussey Moubray.	*Sirène* . . .	36
Seahorse . .	38	,, Hon. Courtenay Boyle.	*Thémis* . . .	40
			Uranie . . .	40
			Furet . . .	18
			Naïade . . .	16

¹ Flag of Vice-Adm. P. C. J. B. S. Villeneuve.
² Flag of Rear-Adm. P. R. M. E. Dumanoir Le Pelley.

Proceeding in column of line ahead through the narrow passage between Biche and Sardinia, the British fleet obtained a clear offing by about 7 P.M., and Nelson then directed the *Seahorse* to round the southern end of Sardinia, look into San Pietro, and return immediately. At 8.30 P.M. he bore away along the island of Sardinia, and on the following morning he ordered the *Spencer* and *Leviathan*, his two best sailers, to act as a detached division, the *Spencer* to keep on the *Victory's* weather beam. During the afternoon of that day, January 20th, and during the whole night and succeeding day, the fleet encountered very strong S.S.W. and S.W. gales, and was, for the most part, under storm staysails. When, at 10 A.M. on the 22nd, the *Seahorse* rejoined, she reported

VICE-ADM. THE HON. SIR COURTENAY BOYLE, KT., K.C.H., F.R.S.

From the lithograph by Blood, after a family miniature painted about 1810, when Boyle was Commissioner of the Transport Board.

that on the afternoon of the 21st she had been chased by the *Cornélie*, 40, while standing towards Pulla Bay; but that, owing to the bad and thick weather, she had been unable to discover whether any ships lay either in that anchorage or in Cagliari, and that, for the same reason, she had lost sight of the French frigate. The *Seahorse*, this time in company with the *Active*, was sent back to Cagliari, but she found nothing there; nor did a message addressed to the authorities in that port elicit any news of the enemy.[1] Thereupon Nelson despatched the *Seahorse* to Naples, and ordered the *Active* to cruise for three days eastward of the island of Serpentina, and to communicate with any British ship that might be looking for the Commander-in-Chief. At noon on January 25th, Cape Carbonara, Sardinia, bore from the *Victory* N.N.E. ½ E. three and a half leagues; and on the 26th, the *Phœbe*, 36, Captain the Hon. Thomas Bladen Capell, joined, and reported having discovered at 4 P.M. on the 19th, off the west coast of Corsica, a disabled French ship of the line, recognised as the *Indomptable*, standing in for the land under courses only, with a strong W.N.W. wind, and having lost her topmasts. The *Phœbe* had passed within hail of the Frenchman, which seemed to be bound for Ajaccio, and had then borne up for Agincourt Sound, where she had expected to find Nelson. It was because she had first gone thither that she did not fall in with the fleet until the 26th.

Failing to gain any useful information, Nelson continued to the eastward, and, at 3 A.M. on the 29th, rounded Stromboli. He was anxious and uneasy. The enemy, he himself believed, had made for Egypt; but, though he continued to detach his three frigates in all directions as soon as they rejoined him, he could learn nothing. Nevertheless, he kept his ships night and day ready for action. Not a bulkhead was up in any of them. On February 4th, the *Canopus* sighted the Egyptian coast, and on the 7th the *Tigre* was sent into Alexandria; yet still nothing could be heard of the French. Upon being rejoined by the *Tigre* on the 8th, Nelson headed for Malta, and, by the 14th, was within three hundred miles of it. Not until after that date did he discover, by intelligence from Naples, what had become of the fleet of Villeneuve.

In the meantime he had explained as follows to the Admiralty the considerations which had induced him to go to Egypt[1]:—

" Feeling, as I do, that I am entirely responsible to my King and country for the whole of my conduct, I find no difficulty at this moment, when I am so unhappy at not finding the French fleet, nor having obtained the slightest information where they are, to lay before you the whole of the reasons which induced me to pursue the line of conduct I have done. I have consulted no man : therefore the whole blame of ignorance in forming my judgment must rest with me. I would allow no man to take from me an atom of my glory, had I fallen in with the French fleet; nor do I desire any man to partake of any of the responsibility. All is mine, right or wrong : therefore I shall now state my reasons, after seeing that Sardinia, Naples, and Sicily were safe, for

---

[1] Nelson to Melville, Feb. 14th; Clarke and M'Arthur, ii., 397.

believing that Egypt was the destination of the French fleet: and, at this moment of sorrow, I still feel that I have acted right. Firstly; the wind had blown from north-east to south-east for fourteen days before they sailed : therefore, they might, without difficulty, have gone to the westward. Secondly; they came out with gentle breezes at north-west and north-north-west. Had they been bound to Naples, the most natural thing for them to have done would have been for them to run along their own shore to the eastward, where they would have ports every 20 leagues of coast to take shelter in. Thirdly; they bore away in the evening of the 18th with a strong gale at north-west or north-north-west, steering south, or south by west. It blew so hard that the *Seahorse* went more than 13 knots an hour to get out of their way. Desirable as Sardinia is for them, they could get it without risking their fleet, although certainly not so quickly as by attacking Cagliari. However, I left nothing to chance in that respect, and therefore went off Cagliari. Having afterwards gone to Sicily, both to Palermo and Messina, and thereby given encouragement for a defence, and knowing all was safe at Naples, I had only the Morea and Egypt to look to, for although I knew one of the French ships was crippled, yet I considered the character of Bonaparte, and that the orders given by him on the banks of the Seine would not take into consideration wind or weather. Nor, indeed, could the accident of even three or four ships alter, in my opinion, a destination of importance: therefore such an accident did not weigh in my mind; and I went first to Morea and then to Egypt. The result of my inquiries at Coron and Alexandria confirms me in my former opinion; and therefore, my Lord, if my obstinacy or ignorance is so gross, I should be the first to recommend your superseding me. But, on the contrary, if, as I flatter myself, it should be found that my ideas of the probable destination of the French fleet were well founded, in the opinion of his Majesty's ministers, then I shall hope for the consolation of having my conduct approved by his Majesty; who will, I am sure, weigh my whole proceedings in the scale of justice."

What, then, had happened to Villeneuve? While crossing the Gulf of Lions, on the second day after leaving Toulon, he had fallen in with a violent gale, which had badly damaged several of his ships aloft, and which, on January 20th, had driven all save four of them back to port. The four exceptions were the *Indomptable* and the *Cornélie*, already mentioned, and the *Hortense* and *Incorruptible*. The *Cornélie* found shelter in Genoa, and returned to Toulon on January 22nd. The *Indomptable* returned on the 24th. The *Hortense* and *Incorruptible* did not rejoin for about nearly two months, and were fortunate in not encountering any serious enemy during that long period.

In the meantime, an effort had been made in another direction to further the development of Napoleon's general plan, as set forth in his letter of September 29th, 1804.[1] Rear-Admiral Missiessy, in pursuance of more detailed instructions which he had received in December, succeeded, on January 11th, 1805, in escaping from Rochefort during the temporary absence from the station of Rear-Admiral Sir Thomas Graves (3). His force consisted of the *Majestueux*, 120, *Lion*, 74, *Jemmapes*, 74, *Magnanime*, 74,

---

[1] *See* p. 77, *ante.*

Suffren, 74, *Gloire*, 40, *Armide*, 40, *Infatigable*, 40, *Actéon*, 16, *Lynx*, 16, and three thousand five hundred troops under General Joseph Lagrange, together with a quantity of stores and a park of artillery. He was sighted on the morning of the 12th by the schooner *Felix*, 12, Lieutenant Richard Bourne (2), of the blockading force; but Bourne was not able, until the 16th, to apprize Graves of what had happened; and then Graves was forced by a strong south-westerly gale to seek shelter in Quiberon Bay. On the 24th, Rear-Admiral the Hon. Alexander Forester Inglis Cochrane, with six sail of the squadron which had been watching Ferrol, went in pursuit, the place of his ships being presently taken by a detachment of equal force drawn from the fleet before Brest. Missiessy, though detained on the coast by adverse weather until the 25th, then proceeded undisturbed, his mission being, so far as can be gathered from the incomplete published correspondence [1] between Napoleon and his minister of marine, and from other sources, to disembark part of his military stores at Martinique and Guadeloupe, to make himself master of Dominica, and to ravage the weaker British colonies. If, within thirty-five days of his arrival in the West Indies, Villeneuve, with the Toulon fleet, should not appear, Missiessy was to set out for home, calling on his way at the city of San Domingo, and there leaving with General Ferrand such troops as he might have remaining on board. The rear-admiral's exploits will be recounted later. It is only necessary to say here that, since Villeneuve did not succeed in quitting the Mediterranean as early as had been hoped, Missiessy was ordered, by the *Palinure*, 16, which found him at Martinique, to accelerate his return, and that he re-anchored in Aix road on May 20th, 1805.

In the evening of February 27th, Nelson, weary and disappointed, anchored in Pulla road, Cagliari. On March 2nd he weighed, but, the weather being unfavourable, quickly re-anchored. On March 3rd, however, he weighed again, and, with a N.N.E. wind, stood to the westward. The wind shifting, however, to the N.W. and blowing strong, the fleet had to return; and not until March 12th was the Commander-in-Chief able to get sight of the heights of Faron, above Toulon. Late on the 15th, he resumed his winter station a little to the eastward of Cape San Sebastian. Thence he detached the *Leviathan*, 74, to show herself off Barcelona, in order to induce the belief that he was still on the

[1] There is a hiatus from Sept. 29th, 1804, to Ap. 14th, 1805.

Spanish coast;[1] and, working back to the eastward, he was himself off the west end of San Pietro on March 25th. Two days later he anchored in the Gulf of Palma, whither he had ordered his store-ships. On the 26th, he had been joined from England by Rear-Admiral Thomas Louis, in the *Ambuscade*, 32, Captain William Durban. At Palma Louis shifted his flag to the *Canopus*, 80, taking, in place of Captain John Conn, Captain Francis William Austen (1)[2] as his flag-captain. From March 27th until April 1st, Nelson lay refitting and provisioning in the Gulf of Palma. He then removed to Pulla road; and, on April 3rd, sailed to the west-ward, with a moderate N.E. breeze.

At Toulon, in the meanwhile, M. Villeneuve laid up the *In-corruptible*, which had been badly mauled in the action with the *Arrow*,[3] and, finding the *Annibal* unserviceable, turned over her ship's company to the new ship *Pluton*, 74. He also turned over the crew of the *Uranie*, which he decided to leave behind, to the *Hermione*, 40. When, therefore, he again put to sea, it was with eleven sail of the line, six frigates, and two brigs,[4] on board of which there were still the three thousand five hundred troops under General Lauriston.

By that time the details of Napoleon's great plan had been somewhat modified. The project of conquest in the Antilles by Missiessy had been abandoned; so also had that of the descent upon Ireland by Ganteaume and Augereau. The objects still to be aimed at were, firstly, a great concentration of naval force in the West Indies, or, at least, in some locality far away from France; secondly, the speedy return of the whole of that force to European waters; and, finally, the employment of that force to cover and protect the passage to England of the invasion flotilla. There had been delays and misunderstandings. It was confidently hoped that, owing to the forwardness of all the preparations, there would be no more of these; and it was therefore ordered that the various strategic movements which were designed to bring Great Britain to her knees were to begin in March; and Spain was specially warned to be ready to play her part at a moment's notice.

---

[1] The ruse was successful. Until April 1st Villeneuve believed Nelson to be off Barcelona.

[2] Capt. Austen had gone out as a passenger from England.

[3] For an account of this, see next chapter.

[4] Those in the table on p. 89, omitting the *Incorruptible*, and substituting the *Pluton* for the *Annibal*, and the *Hermione* for the *Uranie*.

The general situation, as it existed upon the eve of the commencement of these movements, did not much differ from the general situation of a few months earlier; but it may, with advantage, be briefly glanced at; and, for the sake of clearness, it may be thus summarised [1] :—

FRANCO-SPANISH.		BRITISH.	
PORT, ETC.	READY FOR SERVICE IN MARCH.	STATION.	READY FOR SERVICE IN MARCH.
THE TEXEL . .	9 ships of the line.[1] 80 transports. 25,000 troops.	THE DOWNS. .	11 sail of the line (Keith).
BOULOGNE, ETC.	950 transports. 1300 armed small craft. 130,000 troops.		
BREST . .	21 ships of the line (Ganteaume). Transports. 3600 troops (embarked).	THE CHANNEL .	About 17 sail of the line [2] (Cornwallis and others).
ROCHEFORT . .	2 ships of the line (Magon, and later Allemand).		
LORIENT . .	1 ship of the line.		
FERROL . . .	12 sail of the line [3] (Grandallana and Gourdon).	OFF FERROL .	8 ships of the line (Calder).
CADIZ . . .	7 sail of the line [4] (Gravina).	OFF CADIZ . .	6 ships of the line (Orde).
CARTAGENA . TOULON . .	6 sail of the line [1] (Salcedo). 11 sail of the line (Villeneuve). 3500 troops (embarked).	MEDITERRANEAN	12 ships of the line [5] (Nelson).

[1] Took no part in the campaign. [2] Increased, by April 1st, to 21. [3] Besides 3 not ready for sea. [4] Besides 8 or 9 not ready for sea. [5] Of which 1 was stationed at Naples.

In addition, the allies had 5, and Great Britain had 10 ships of the line in the West Indies; while Great Britain had about 9 ships of the line in the East Indies; and 2 British ships of the line were on their way from England to join Nelson in the Mediterranean. In the above summary, no mention is made of frigates.

Napoleon issued his detailed orders [2] to Villeneuve and Ganteaume on March 2nd. Villeneuve was to sail at the earliest possible date for Cadiz, and to be joined outside the port by the ships there ready. Thence he was to proceed to Martinique, and to wait forty days for Ganteaume. If the latter should not then appear, Villeneuve was to go to San Domingo, land troops, make for Santiago in the Canary

---

[1] The table is mainly based upon 'Nav. Chronicle,' xiii., 365 *et seq.*, and Steel's lists; corrected by reference to Adms.' Disps., and to James and Brenton.

[2] 'Corr. de Nap.,' x., 227, 232, 324, 447, etc. *See also* xi., 50.

Islands,[1] and there cruise for twenty days. " I prefer," wrote the
Emperor, "Martinique to all other places of rendezvous ; yet
Santiago is a better place than off Brest, the raising of the
blockade of which would involve some sort of action." Ganteaume,
who was to command in chief after the anticipated junction, was
to sail at the earliest possible moment, and to proceed to Ferrol,
destroying or driving off the blockading force which cruised there.
He was then to be joined by such French and Spanish ships as were
ready in the port, and to make the best of his way to Martinique,
there to meet Villeneuve, and, perhaps, Missiessy also. In case of
need he was to wait at least thirty days for Villeneuve. The united
force was to steer for the Channel ; and, it was intended, should
appear off Boulogne between June 10th and July 10th. If, by the
non-arrival of Villeneuve, or from any other cause, Ganteaume
should find himself with fewer than twenty-five ships of the line,
he was to go, not necessarily to the Channel, but, if he deemed it
best, to Ferrol, where he would be reinforced. When, on March
23rd, just as the great scheme was on the eve of being attempted,
Ganteaume reported that he was ready, that only fifteen British
ships were in the offing, and that, if he went out against them, he
was certain of victory, Napoleon's answer was : " A naval victory
at this time would produce no results. Keep a single object before
you. Fulfil your commission. Go to sea without fighting."

    Both the general orders and the specific instructions indicate
how completely the greatest military leader of modern times misunderstood the simplest elements of naval warfare. He was all for
evasion ; all for making his fleets vanish from the ken of the enemy,
and then drop, as it were, from the sky into the British Channel ; [2]
all for forgetting everything but the ulterior object ; all for not
risking a ship. If he had realised that, in order to effect his
ulterior object, no matter whether it was the invasion of England,
the seizure of Egypt, or the conquest of India, he must first reduce

----

    [1] A subsequent order erroneously named the Cape de Verdes as the rendezvous.
Santiago is a town in Tenerife, Canaries : São Thiago is an island of the Cape de
Verdes. Hence the confusion. Chevalier, 152. The mistake had the result of
delaying Villeneuve's return to Europe.
    [2] Spain pursued the same fatuous system in 1898. Cervera vanished, and dropped
into Santiago de Cuba. His strategy only led to his annihilation, and did not cost the
Americans a ship. Had he, on the other hand, sought his enemy at once, and fought
him, he might, at least, have done him some damage. He might even, catching him
unprepared or scattered, have beaten him ; though, looking to the state of the Spanish
navy, this is very unlikely indeed.

the British fleet to a condition of impotence, his plans might have ended differently. Who can say that, if Ganteaume had seized his most favourable opportunity, he might not have gone out and beaten Cornwallis's inferior force? Who can say that if Villeneuve, after leaving Toulon, had picked up the six ships from Cartagena and the seven from Cadiz, and had then, having frightened Orde away, turned to give battle to Nelson, he would have failed to crush him with twenty-four ships to eleven only? The British naval leaders of that day were giants; but they were not almighty; and it is well for the Britons of to-day and of to-morrow to remember that, although they triumphed in that decisive campaign of 1805, they owed their victory as much to the errors of the enemy as to the skill and bravery of themselves.

Nelson's withdrawal to the Gulf of Palma gave Villeneuve his opportunity. In the evening of March 29th, the entire French fleet quitted Toulon, and, on clearing Cape Cepet, steered S.S.W., with a pleasant breeze from the N.E. It had been expected that this breeze would increase, but instead, it veered on the morning of the 30th to N.N.W. and decreased considerably, so that little progress was made. In the afternoon of the 31st, Cape Sicié bearing north about thirty miles, the enemy was descried by the *Active*, 38, Captain Richard Hussey Moubray, and *Phœbe*, 36, Captain the Hon. Thomas Bladen Capell; and those frigates kept it in sight until nightfall, when the *Phœbe* bore up for Palma, while the *Active*, desirous of still watching the foe, stood upon a wind to the S.W., but, in the darkness, lost sight of the French. In the course of the morning of April 1st, Villeneuve learnt from a Ragusan vessel that five days earlier she had seen the British fleet to the southward of Sardinia; whereupon the French vice-admiral, who had previously supposed Nelson to be off Barcelona, and who had intended in consequence to pass eastward of the Balearic Islands, kept close in with the Spanish coast, and, on the 6th, appeared off Cartagena. Why Rear-Admiral Salcedo and his six ships did not join the French has never yet been satisfactorily explained. Villeneuve reported that they refused to do so, alleging that they had been ordered on another service. The Spanish ambassador in Paris declared, on the other hand, that Villeneuve declined their co-operation.[1] French historians for the most part incline to the belief that they were not ready.

---

[1] 'Précis des Ev.' xi., 236. Chevalier, 143, says that they had received no orders.

It has been said that Nelson left Pulla Bay on April 3rd, and steered to the westward. On the morning of the 4th, when he was a little to the westward of Toro, he saw through a drizzling rain the *Phœbe's* distance signal, which announced that the enemy was at sea. The Commander-in-Chief instantly despatched such cruisers as he had with him to search for the French ; and, lest Villeneuve should have preserved the southward course upon which the *Phœbe* had last seen him, the British lay to during the night. By the morning of the 4th they were about midway between Sardinia and the African coast. They remained in much the same position until the 7th, when, having received no fresh news, Nelson bore up for Palermo, with a view to being ready to act in case the French should have passed eastward of Corsica. For two days more he admitted the suspicion that the enemy might be bound for Egypt or the Levant. Then, still having heard nothing, he rid his mind of that idea ; [1] and on April 9th, being then off the west end of Sicily, he stood to the westward. The winds were chiefly W. and N.W. ; progress was very slow ; and the Commander-in-Chief, daily more and more convinced that the French had either left the Mediterranean or returned to Toulon, grew feverishly impatient. In the meanwhile he sent forward some light craft to Gibraltar and Lisbon. On the 16th, while beating up to round the southern point of Sardinia in order to get near Toulon, he was cheered by the news, obtained by the *Leviathan* from a neutral, that the enemy had been seen on the 7th off Cape de Gata. He soon afterwards learnt that Villeneuve had passed Gibraltar on the 8th. Thenceforward his plans were clear to him. " I have marked out for myself a decided line of conduct, and I shall follow it well up, although I have now before me a letter from the Physician of the Fleet, enforcing my return to England before the hot months. Therefore, notwithstanding I shall pursue the enemy to the East or West Indies if I know that to have been their destination, yet, if the Mediterranean Fleet joins the Channel, I shall request, with that order, permission to go ashore." [2] Not until April 30th did Nelson, kept back by adverse winds, sight Gibraltar. By that time he knew that Villeneuve had

---

[1] For some time afterwards, nevertheless, Napoleon tried his best to encourage or revive it. A fortnight later, he procured the insertion in a Dutch paper of a paragraph to the effect that the French had landed six thousand men in Egypt. In the meantime he knew nothing of Nelson's movements. In fact, he who tried to mislead was himself misled, for he wrote to Villeneuve that Nelson had gone to Alexandria.

[2] Nelson to Melville, Ap. 19th, 1805.

picked up reinforcements at Cadiz. The wind continued to blow strong from the W. or S. ; and, as it would not permit of the fleet passing the Strait, Nelson took it, on May 4th, to Mazari Bay, on the African coast, to water, sending the *Superb* at the same time to Tetuan for oxen, sheep, fruit and vegetables.

Villeneuve had gained a great start, and was by that time half-way across the Atlantic. On April 7th, with a fresh and favourable breeze, he had left Cartagena for the Strait ; at daylight on the 8th he had sighted Gibraltar ; at noon he had entered the Gut; and at 4 P.M. he had stood into Cadiz Bay, after frightening away Sir John Orde, who, apparently oblivious of the fact that his command held a place in the general strategical scheme, even after its work in blockading Cadiz had ceased, made the best of his way towards the Channel. Villeneuve anchored, and, having sent forward the *Hortense* to warn his friends, was quickly joined by the French *Aigle*, 74, *Torche*, corvette, and *Argus*, brig, and by the Spanish *Argonauta*, 80, *Firme*, 74, *Terrible*, 74, *América*, 64, *España*, 64, and a frigate, under Admiral Don Federico Gravina.[1] The *San Rafael*, 80, which also attempted to join him, grounded in going out, and was left to follow to the rendezvous at Martinique, as soon as she should be floated. Very early on April 9th, the combined fleet, consisting of seventeen sail of the line, seven frigates, and four smaller vessels, weighed and steered for the westward ; but Ville-neuve was almost immediately obliged to shorten sail in order to allow the Spaniards to keep up with him, and ere the evening, the wind shifted to W. The allies were, indeed, continually troubled with calms and head breezes for some days, and hindered also by the indifferent sailing of several vessels ; so that it was not till May 12th that any of their ships sighted Martinique.

It is now desirable for a moment to glance at the situation of affairs off the Atlantic coast of France, and, in particular, in and off Brest.

From the beginning of the year, Admiral the Hon. William Cornwallis maintained his station as before off Ushant. In the first week of January he had only eleven sail with him ; in the first week of February his force was augmented to sixteen, but was almost immediately reduced again to eleven sail by the detachment of Vice-Admiral Sir Robert Calder, with five ships, to watch Ferrol. A few weeks later, Cornwallis, who had most pertinaciously blockaded

---

[1] *Gaceta*, Ap. 13th.   Nap. to Decrès in ' Précis des Ev.,' xi. 229.

Brest for no less a period than twenty-two months, was driven by
the state of his health to return home.   He reached Spithead in the
Ville de Paris, 110, on March 20th, and, striking his flag, went
ashore.   Vice-Admiral Sir Charles Cotton, in the *San Josef*, 112,
was left in charge of the seventeen sail of the line off Ushant; but
on April 3rd, Admiral Lord Gardner, in the *Hibernia*, 110, assumed
the command.   The fleet, which then numbered twenty-one sail

ADMIRAL SIR ALAN GARDNER, LORD GARDNER, MAJOR-GENERAL OF MARINES.
(*From the engraving by Ridley, after a portrait which, in 1782, was in the possession of Mr. Dobree.*)

of the line, was driven from off the coast on April 11th; but part
of it regained its station on the 13th; and on the 14th, Gardner
ordered the *Warrior*, 74, Captain William Bligh, to look into the
port.   In the afternoon that ship rejoined, signalling that the French
were getting under way.   Gardner formed a line of battle in order
to be ready to receive them; but, although, on the 15th, the French
appeared off the Black Rocks, they returned to Brest after a few
hours spent in manœuvring.   Gardner had with him that day as

mány as twenty-four sail of the line ; and it seems probable that
such a display of force overawed Ganteaume, who had but twenty-
one.   Villeneuve, it will be remembered, had already sailed from
Toulon, and was by that time fairly on his way across the Atlantic ;
so that Ganteaume's retreat was even more unfortunate for Napoleon's plans than it was for Gardner's glory.   Indeed, the Emperor
was rapidly growing exasperated by Ganteaume's inaction.   " The
non-departure of Ganteaume annoys me greatly," he wrote on
April 21st; and, writing again on the 23rd to inform Decrès that
he had sent a messenger to Ganteaume with news that Nelson had
gone to look for Villeneuve in Egypt, he added : " God grant that
my courier shall not find him at Brest."   At length Napoleon
ordered that if Ganteaume failed to put to sea before May 20th, he
should remain where he lay.[1]   In the meantime he caused the
coasts of Bertheaume and Camaret bays to be hastily fortified, so
that Ganteaume might anchor in safety outside instead of inside
the Goulet, and so be better able to slip away at the first opportunity, either to the West Indies, or, if the long delay should have
rendered that plan useless, to reinforce Villeneuve in Ferrol.

Villeneuve anchored on May 14th in the harbour of Fort Royal
(or as it was then called, Fort de France), Martinique, with seventeen sail of the line, seven frigates, five smaller craft, including the
British *Cyane*, 18, which two of his frigates had picked up on the
previous day, and a storeship.   As the fleet passed the Diamond
Rock,[2] it had been briskly cannonaded from that natural fortress ;
and when, on the 16th, the *San Rafael*, 80, which had been left
behind at Cadiz,[3] approached the Rock, she also was fired at, though
she presently rejoined Villeneuve without having received any
important damage.

On May 5th, facilitated by a change of wind, Nelson weighed
from Mazari bay, and made sail to the westward, having in his
eagerness to be off, recalled the *Superb* from Tetuan ere she could
take on board the supplies which were being collected for her on the
beach ; but at 2 P.M. on the 7th, a failure of the breeze obliged him
to anchor, with part of his force, in Rosia Bay, Gibraltar.   That
afternoon Rear-Admiral Sir Richard Hussey Bickerton, who was to

[1] ' Précis des Ev.,' xi. 228–239.
[2] For an account of the occupation and defence of the Diamond Rock, *see* next
chapter.
[3] She had sailed thence on April 10th.

be left behind in charge of the Mediterranean station, shifted his
flag from the *Royal Sovereign*, 100, to the *Amfitrite*, 40, a frigate
which had been captured from the Spaniards by the *Donegal* on
November 25th, 1804. A little later, a fine easterly wind sprang up ;
and at 6 P.M. Nelson weighed and stood through the Strait. He
had, up to about that time, thought of looking first for the French
in the neighbourhood of the Scilly Isles, suspecting that they might
have designs upon Ireland ; but he was visited, while in the Strait,
by an old friend, Rear-Admiral Donald Campbell[1] of the Portuguese
navy, who supplied information which convinced the Commander-in-
Chief that Villeneuve had gone to the West Indies. To the West
Indies, therefore, Nelson determined to go also. On the 10th, he
anchored in Lagos bay, to see to the protection of some transports
which had been left there by Sir John Orde ; and at 9 A.M. on the
11th, having managed to fill up his ships with provisions for five
months, he once more weighed. Yet still, in spite of his burning
anxiety to follow the enemy, he waited for a short time off Cape
St. Vincent, in order to provide for the safety of a fleet of transports[2] which was expected from England on its way to the
Mediterranean. On the afternoon of the 12th, the transports
appeared, convoyed by the *Queen*, 98, Rear-Admiral John Knight
(2), Captain Francis Pender, and the *Dragon*, 74, Captain Edward
Griffith. Nelson knew that he was about to go in search of at
least eighteen sail of the line. It would have been but natural on
his part, had he been a less far-seeing and provident officer, to add
the *Queen* and the *Dragon* to his own poor force of eleven sail ; but
instead, conscious of the importance of the convoy, he actually
weakened himself by detaching the *Royal Sovereign*, 100, as some
additional protection for it. Such an action at such a critical time
is peculiarly eloquent of his greatness as a naval commander. Then,
having parted with Knight, he crowded sail to the westward with
the *Victory*, 100, *Canopus*, 80, *Superb*, 74, *Spencer*, 74, *Swiftsure*, 74,
Belleisle, 74, *Conqueror*, 74, *Tigre*, 74, *Leviathan*, 74, *Amazon*, 38,
Décade, 36, and *Amphion*, 32 ; ten line-of-battle ships and three
frigates, in chase of eighteen line-of-battle ships and seven frigates.
He had hopes of being joined at Barbados by six additional sail of

---

[1] Campbell's conduct reached the ears of the Spaniards, who, through their French
allies, made formal complaint about it ; and Campbell was, in consequence, removed
from the Portuguese active list. Clarke and M'Arthur, ii. 406.

[2] Carrying five thousand troops under Genl. Sir James Craig.

the line,[1] but he seems to have been prepared, with or without that reinforcement, to fight Villeneuve ; for, in the plan of attack which he is said to have drawn up while crossing the Atlantic, there is nothing to show that he counted upon having with him at the crucial moment a force nearly equal to that of his opponents. This plan, though it was not precisely carried out, and though it is, in places, awkwardly worded, and, indeed, a little obscure, is upon the whole so interesting and suggestive as to deserve transcription here :—[2]

"The business of an English commander-in-chief being first to bring an enemy's fleet to battle on the most advantageous terms to himself (I mean, that of laying his ships close on board those of the enemy as expeditiously as possible), and secondly, to continue them there without separating until the business is decided, I am sensible, beyond this object, it is not necessary I should say a word, being fully assured that the admirals and captains of the fleet I have the honour to command will, knowing my precise object—that of a close and decisive battle—supply any deficiency in my not making signals ; which may, if extended beyond these objects, either be misunderstood, or, if waited for, very probably from various causes be impossible for the commander-in-chief to make. Therefore it will only be requisite for me to state, in as few words as possible, the various modes by which it may be necessary for me to obtain my object, on which depends not only the honour and glory of our country, but possibly its safety, and, with it, that of all Europe, from French tyranny and oppression.

"If the two fleets are both willing to fight, but little manœuvring is necessary. The less the better. A day is soon lost in that business. Therefore I will only suppose that, the enemy's fleet being to leeward, standing close upon a wind on the starboard tack, and that I am nearly ahead of them, standing on the larboard tack ; of course I should weather them. The weather must be supposed to be moderate ; for, if it be a gale of wind, the manœuvring of both fleets is but of little avail, and probably no decisive action would take place with the whole fleet. Two modes present themselves ; one, to stand on just out of gunshot until the van ship of my line would be abreast of the centre ship of the enemy ; then make the signal to wear together ; then bear up ; engage with all our force the six or five van ships of the enemy, passing certainly, if

---

[1] *I.e.*, Cochrane's squadron, which had been detached from before Ferrol in chase of Missiessy in January, 1805.

[2] Villeneuve's plan of attack—for he, too, communicated one to his captains—may be fitly set alongside of Nelson's. The essential part of it is as follows :—

"I do not purpose to go in search of the enemy ; I even wish to avoid him in order to arrive at my destination ; but, if we should meet him, let there be no shameful manœuvring ; it would discourage our ships' companies, and bring about our defeat. If the enemy be to leeward of us, we, being masters of our movements, will form our order of battle, and bear down upon him together in line abreast. Each one of our ships will engage the one corresponding to her in the enemy's line, and must not hesitate to board her if the circumstances be favourable. . . . Every captain who is not under fire will not be in his proper station ; and a signal to recall him thither will be a dishonouring blot upon him. The frigates must equally take part in the action ; I do not want them for signalling purposes. They should select the point at which their co-operation may be useful, either to complete the discomfiture of an enemy's ship, or to aid a French ship that is too hotly pressed, and to help her, by towing or otherwise, as may be necessary." ' Vict. et Conq.,' xvi. 109.

opportunity offered, through their line. This would prevent their bearing up; and the action, from the known bravery and conduct of the admirals and captains, would certainly be decisive. The second or third rear ships of the enemy would act as they pleased; and our ships would give a good account of them, should they persist in mixing with our ships. The other mode would be, to stand under an easy but commanding sail directly for their headmost ship, so as to prevent the enemy from knowing whether I should pass to leeward or to windward of him. In that situation, I would make the signal to engage the enemy to leeward, and to cut through their fleet about the sixth ship from the van, passing very close. They being on a wind, you, going large, could cut their line when you please. The van ships of the enemy would, by the time our rear came abreast of the van ship, be severely cut up, and our van could not expect to escape damage. I would then have our rear ship, and every ship in succession, wear, continue the action with either the van ship or second ship, as it might appear most eligible from her crippled state; and, this mode pursued, I see nothing to prevent the capture of the five or six ships of the enemy's van. The two or three (?) ships of the enemy's rear must either bear up or wear; and, in either case, although they would be in a better plight probably than our two van ships (now in the rear), yet they would be separated and at a distance to leeward, so as to give our ships time to refit; and by that time, I believe, the battle would, from the judgment of the admirals and captains, be over with the rest of them. Signals, from these moments, are useless, when every man is disposed to do his duty. The great object is for us to support each other, and to keep close to the enemy, and to leeward of him. If the enemy are running away, then the only signals necessary will be to engage the enemy as arriving up with them, and the other ships to pass on for the second, third, etc.; giving, if possible, a close fire into the enemy in passing, taking care to give our ships engaged notice of your intention." [1]

In brief, the leading idea was to concentrate on part of the enemy; to paralyse and crush that part by engaging from leeward with a superiority of force, and, at the same time, to throw the other part into confusion; and then to deal as circumstances might dictate with the demoralised remnant. But Nelson, neither then nor at any other period of his career, was, quoting his own words, " one of those hot-brained people who fight at immense disadvantage without any adequate object." [2] He was prepared, if he saw the necessity, to fight eighteen or even twenty sail of the line with his ten; but, on the other hand, he was inclined, unless he saw a grave necessity for acting otherwise, or unless he was given an opportunity too tempting to be resisted, to merely hang on to the allies until he should find himself in a position to crush them decisively.

On May 15th, the fleet sighted Madeira. On May 29th, the *Amazon* was dispatched ahead to warn Rear-Admiral Cochrane at Barbados of Nelson's coming and of his need of reinforcements. On June 4th, the Commander-in-Chief, who on the previous day had received his first positive intelligence that the allies were in the

---

[1] Said to have been issued in May, 1805. Clarke and M'Arthur, ii. 427. Probably issued earlier.   [2] *Ib.* ii. 413.

West Indies, anchored in Carlisle Bay, Barbados, and, though he
found Cochrane there, had the disappointment of being joined by
two ships only of that officer's command. These were the *Northumberland*, 74, and *Spartiate*, 74.   The other four ships had been
detained at Jamaica by Rear-Admiral James Richard Dacres (1).
Misled by a baseless report that the enemy was bound for Tobago
and Trinidad, Nelson embarked two thousand troops under General
Myers, and, on the 5th, proceeded in the direction of the islands

VICE-ADMIRAL JAMES RICHARD DACRES (1).
(From Page's engraving, after the portrait by Bowyer.)

which were supposed to be threatened; but, on the 7th, when he
was in the Gulf of Paria, he discovered that he had been deceived;
and on the 9th, he succeeded in arriving off Grenada, where he
learnt that on the 6th the enemy had passed Dominica, steering
northward.

It was on the 9th also that Napoleon, writing from Milan,
betrayed his entire misapprehension, both of Nelson's strategical
sagacity, and of his determination and resource, by saying: "I

am nevertheless of opinion that Nelson is still in European waters. The most natural view is that he must have gone back to England to revictual, and to turn over his crews to other ships; for his vessels require docking, and his squadron may be supposed to be in very bad condition."

Early on June 13th, Nelson reached Antigua, and disembarked the troops; and later on the same day, leaving behind the *Northumberland*, Cochrane's flagship, but taking with him the *Spartiate*, 74, Captain Francis Laforey, he stood with his eleven sail of the line to the northward, "not absolutely," says James, "in pursuit of an enemy whose force he knew to consist of at least eighteen sail of the line, but in the hope, by a superior knowledge of tactics, to reach the shores of Europe before him." [1] It is correct to regard Nelson, at that time, as anxious, above all things, to gain and keep some kind of touch with the enemy; but it certainly is not just to suppose that the Vice-Admiral, who had declared "We won't part without a battle," [2] had any intention of merely getting home before Villeneuve. If only he could come up with his foe, he purposed never to leave hold of him until some fortuitous advantage or the receipt of reinforcements, or, in default of either, some adequate object to be gained, should justify an attack.

Villeneuve had reached Fort Royal, Martinique, on May 13th. He had been directed to occupy his leisure time—his forty days of prescribed waiting for Ganteaume—by doing as much harm as possible to the enemy; but he seems to have lain idle until May 29th, when he sent out the *Pluton*, 74, *Berwick*, 74, *Sirène*, 36, *Argus*, 16, *Fine*, armed schooner, and eleven gunboats, under Commodore Julien Marie Cosmao-Kerjulien, of the *Pluton*, with about three hundred and fifty troops on board, to attack the Diamond Rock, which lies about six miles to the S.E. of the entrance to Fort Royal bay. The squadron was not able to bear down upon the place until the morning of May 31st; and in consequence, Commander James Wilkes Maurice, who had held it since January, 1804, had time to make some necessary preparations. He abandoned the lower works, which he considered to be indefensible against such a force, and, at 8 A.M., when the enemy opened, returned his fire from a 24-pr. (Hood's battery), midway up the rock, and from two 18-prs. (Fort Diamond) on the summit. The bombardment con-

[1] James, iii. 334.   [2] Clarke and M'Arthur, ii. 413.

tinued from 8 A.M. on May 31st, to 4.30 P.M. on June 2nd, when
Maurice, having little powder and ball cartridges left, hoisted a flag
of truce.   Advantageous terms of surrender were quickly arranged ;
and the garrison, of one hundred and seven officers and men, was
presently taken off.   Maurice lost only two killed and one wounded.
The French lost certainly fifty, and probably seventy or more,
besides three of their gunboats.[1]   It is hardly needful to add that
when Commander Maurice stood his trial for the loss of his " sloop,"
he was not only honourably acquitted, but also highly complimented
upon his behaviour.

While the attack on the Diamond Rock was proceeding, the
Didon, 40, reached Villeneuve, on June 1st, from Guadeloupe,
bringing dispatches and fresh orders from Bonaparte, and reporting
that a reinforcement of two sail of the line from France had arrived
in the West Indies.   The *Didon* had left Lorient on May 2nd.
The two sail of the line referred to, the *Algésiras*, 74, and
Achille, 74, had left Rochefort under Rear-Admiral Magon on
May 1st, and had anchored on May 29th at Guadeloupe.   Bonaparte's new instructions were to the effect that the fleet should
seize St. Vincent, Antigua, Grenada, and perhaps Barbados ;[2]
and, having waited in the Antilles for thirty-five days in all after
the receipt of the dispatch, proceed direct to Ferrol, where, even if
Ganteaume should fail to join earlier, the Brest fleet would certainly
meet Villeneuve and Gravina.   On June 4th, therefore, the whole
of the allied fleet, except the *Santa Magdalena, Torche, Naïade*, and
Cyane, left Fort Royal, headed to the north, and was presently
joined by the two 74's from Guadeloupe.[3]   On June 6th, Villeneuve
lay to off that island and received on board additional troops.
Proceeding, he doubled Antigua on June 8th as if he really
intended to begin operations among the British West India
Islands ; but, hearing from an American schooner that there was
a British homeward-bound convoy in the N.N.E., he chased in
that quarter, and, ere nightfall, captured fifteen sail of merchantmen
which, with cargoes valued at £200,000, had left Antigua on the
7th.   The prizes were handed over to the charge of the *Sirène*,

---

[1] Maurice to Nelson, June 6th, 1805 : Maurice to Cochrane, June 19th, 1805. Both
printed in Marshall, Supp. Pt. I. 439, etc.   *See also* French account in ' Nav. Chron.,'
xv. 129, etc., and Chevalier, 149.

[2] " Pourquoi ne prendrait-on pas la Barbade ? "

[3] Makingthe force up to twenty sail of the line, seven frigates, and two smaller craft.

whose captain was ordered to take them first to Guadeloupe, and
then to a rendezvous at the Azores, where he would again pick up
the fleet. The British men-of-war which had been with the
convoy effected their escape. They were the *Barbados*, 28,
Captain Joseph Nourse, and the schooner *Netley*, 14, Lieutenant
Richard Harward. Immediately after the *Sirène* and her charges
had parted company, Villeneuve, possibly from his prisoners, learnt
that Nelson was in the West Indies in search of him. He seems,
moreover, to have received an exaggerated report of Nelson's force.
The news had an instant effect upon the French vice-admiral.
Hastily putting the troops which he had drawn from Guadeloupe
and Martinique on board the *Hortense*, *Didon*, *Hermione*, and
Thémis, and directing the senior officer to disembark the forces
at Guadeloupe, and then to rejoin him off the Azores, Villeneuve,
instead of waiting any longer in the West Indies, made sail
for home.

The *Hortense* and her consorts had landed their troops and
were returning to the fleet, when, on June 26th, they fell in with
the *Sirène* and her convoy, which had made hardly any progress
since the 9th. The senior officer, reflecting that it must still take
the merchantmen many days to get so far to windward as Guadeloupe, determined to escort the prizes to Puerto Rico ; but, on the
following day, he and they sighted to windward, and chased, the
British sloops *Kingfisher*, 18, Commander Richard William Cribb,
and *Osprey*, 18, Commander Timothy Clinch. The sloops, while
making off, hoisted signals and fired guns, as if to call the attention
of a fleet ahead of them ; and so effective was the ruse that Captain
La Marre La Meillerie, of the *Hortense*, not only bore up, but also
burnt the whole of the prizes lest they should fall into the hands of
the imaginary force below his horizon. On June 30th, he, with
his frigate squadron, rejoined Villeneuve off Corvo, one of the
Azores ; on the same day the *Didon* took and burnt a small
British 14-gun privateer ; and on July 3rd the fleet captured the
privateer *Mars*, of Liverpool, and her prize, the Spanish galleon
Matilda, with treasure worth about £600,000. Beyond a gale of
wind, experienced off Cape Finisterre on July 9th, Villeneuve's
command met with little further adventure, and kept steadily on
its course for Ferrol, until July 22nd, when, as will be seen later, it
encountered Sir Robert Calder.

Nelson had left Antigua on June 13th, having, on the previous

day, sent home the *Curieux* with such news as he had.[1] Villeneuve,
alarmed as it would seem by the news which he had obtained from
the captured Antigua convoy, had started for Europe two or three
days earlier. Nelson had no means of knowing whither the allies
were bound, but his instinct, his reason, and his discretion, led him
also to steer eastward ; and on July 17th he sighted Cape St. Vincent
and then headed for Gibraltar in order to obtain provisions. On the
18th, he fell in with his old friend Vice-Admiral Cuthbert Collingwood, who had his flag in the *Dreadnought*, 98, and had two other
sail of the line in company. Collingwood knew nothing. On the
19th, the fleet anchored in Gibraltar Bay ; and on July 20th,
1805, the indefatigable Nelson went ashore for the first time since
June 16th, 1803. For two years less ten days, indeed, he had not
been over the *Victory's* side. On the 22nd he weighed again, and
at 8 P.M. anchored in Mazari bay to water. On the 24th, he
proceeded for Ceuta, remaining all night in the Gut, with thick
fog and shifting winds. On the 25th, he learnt from the
Termagant, 18, Commander Robert Pettet, which joined from
England, that the *Curieux*,[2] while on her way home from the
West Indies with the Commander-in-Chief's dispatches, had fallen
in with the allied fleets on June 19th, in lat. 33° 12′ N. and long.
58° W., steering first N. by W., and later N.N.W.[3] This was the
first definite piece of intelligence which Nelson had received as to
the proceedings of the enemy. Quitting the Strait, he bore away
to the westward. On August 3rd, being in lat. 39° N. and long.
16° W., he obtained from an American merchantman a log-book and
some other articles which had been found on board an abandoned
and partially burnt vessel ;[4] and from these he deduced to his own
satisfaction that the enemy had taken a more northerly course
across the Atlantic than he. Nelson, therefore, worked up against
a northerly wind, until, on the 8th, the weather, which had been
thick, cleared, and the breeze became favourable. On the 12th, he
was met by the *Niobe*, a frigate detached from the Channel fleet ;
but she was able to tell him nothing. Not until the 15th, when
Nelson himself joined Cornwallis off Ushant, was the Vice-Admiral
informed of all that had happened in the previous weeks. That

---

[1] 'Nels. Disps.,' vi. 457, 473.

[2] The importance of the news brought by her, and the manner in which it was
utilised, will presently appear.

[3] 'Nav. Chronicle,' xiv. 64.

[4] Probably the *Mars*, privateer. Indeed, it is almost certain that it was she.

same evening, in the *Victory*, accompanied by the *Superb*, he steered for Portsmouth, the rest of his command, except the *Belleisle*, which went to Plymouth, continuing with the Channel fleet. On August 18th, the *Victory* anchored at Spithead, and Nelson presently hauled down his flag and went ashore to seek a little of the rest of which, for months, he had been so much in need.

The chase of the allies to the West Indies and back having now, so far at least as Nelson was concerned in it, been followed from its outset to its conclusion, it is time to examine into the measures which were adopted in European waters with a view to obstructing the execution of Napoleon's plans.

On July 6th, news reached the Channel fleet that Villeneuve and Gravina had arrived at Martinique. On the same day, Cornwallis, whose health was by that time restored, appeared off Ushant in the *Ville de Paris*, and, relieving Lord Gardner, resumed the command, the Channel fleet then numbering only eighteen sail of the line.

In the morning of July 7th, the brig *Curieux*, 18, Commander George Edmund Byron Bettesworth, with dispatches from Nelson in the West Indies to the effect that the allies were probably on their return to Europe,[1] anchored at Plymouth; and Bettesworth went up to the Admiralty, where he arrived at 11 P.M. on the 8th. The First Lord had gone to bed; no one cared to disturb him; and consequently he did not see the dispatches until the morning of the 9th. Furious at the waste of time, Lord Barham, without even waiting to dress, wrote an order to Cornwallis to detach Rear-Admiral Charles Stirling (1), with his five sail of the line, from before Rochefort to join Vice-Admiral Sir Robert Calder,[2] who was to be directed to station himself westward of Cape Finisterre, while Cornwallis himself, with the Channel fleet, was to cruise between Cape Finisterre and Ushant.[3] This order reached Cornwallis on his

---

[1] She also, of course, reported the fact, already noted, of her having sighted the enemy.

[2] Off Ferrol.

[3] Barham's strategy in directing Cornwallis to raise the blockade of Rochefort by detaching Stirling to join Calder, and in directing Calder to cruise so far to the westward of Cape Finisterre, has been much criticised. James considers that its policy "does not seem very clear," since it involved the raising of the blockade both of Rochefort and of Ferrol. But the strategy was undoubtedly sound. Whether the enemy would or would not slip out from the liberated ports during the absence of the blockaders was at least problematical. Even if they did slip out, they might still be

station on the 11th, and was, of course, at once acted upon.   Calder, it may be remembered, had himself been detached from the Channel fleet early in 1805, to assume command of the blockade of Ferrol, in lieu of Rear-Admiral the Hon. A. I. F. Cochrane, who, with about half his force, had gone to the West Indies in pursuit of Rear-Admiral Missiessy and the French Rochefort squadron. Calder, in the *Prince of Wales*, 98, had reached his station on March 1st, and had found on it six sail of the line under Captain the Hon. Arthur Kaye Legge, who, in the *Repulse*, 74, had been senior officer since Cochrane's departure.   Although there was always a superior force in port, Calder seems to have rarely, if ever, had more than ten sail of the line with him, until, on July 15th, in pursuance of the orders above alluded to, he was joined by Stirling with five more.

On July 20th, Vice-Admiral Ganteaume, who was still at Brest, received directions to put to sea, and to endeavour to join, first Missiessy and the French Rochefort squadron off the Lizard, and next, Villeneuve and the allied fleets from Toulon and Cadiz.   Ere the directions could be carried out, the receipt at Brest of news of an action having been fought by Villeneuve caused further references to Paris, and further delay.   Ganteaume, therefore, may be left for a time, and attention be devoted to Calder and Villeneuve.

Calder cruised from 90 to 120 miles westward of Cape Finisterre on the lookout for the allies, who, as he then believed, numbered only seventeen sail of the line.[1]   On July 19th, he received a copy of Nelson's dispatch of June 15th, informing the British commanding officer off Lisbon that the allies had passed Antigua on June 8th, and were probably on their way to Europe ; and, at about 11 A.M. on July 22nd, upon the partial clearing up of a fog, he sighted the enemy in lat. 43° 54′ N. and long. 11° 38′ [2] W., steering E.S.E. (*i.e.*, for Ferrol) in three divisions, with a light breeze from

---

beaten in detail.   On the other hand, unless he could be met and checked, Villeneuve would reach his destination, whatever it might be, and restore the whole of his large force to the service of Napoleon.   Barham rightly perceived that the proper strategy was to hurl Calder at once against the strongest of the converging detachments of the foe, while still keeping Cornwallis in the Bay as a screen between Villeneuve and Ganteaume.   His prompt decision did him great honour.   Had Calder possessed Nelson's qualities, the action of July 22nd would, probably, have ended the campaign, and spared Britain the glorious sacrifice of Nelson's life.

[1] 'Nav. Chronicle,' xiv. 64.   This was the report of the *Curieux.*

[2] This was the observation at noon, when Ferrol bore E.S.E. distant 49 leagues, and Cape Finisterre, S.E. distant 39 leagues.   *Prince of Wales's* log.

W.N.W. The British were then on the starboard tack, approaching
the allies from the N.N.E. It was soon seen that the allied fleets
were composed of no fewer than twenty sail of the line, besides
seven frigates, two brigs, and the recaptured galleon, *Matilda*. At
12 A.M., Calder signalled to prepare for battle, and, soon afterwards,
to form the order of sailing in two columns. At about 1 P.M. he
ordered to form line, and, at 1.15 P.M., and again an hour later,
signalled for close order. At 3 P.M., the *Defiance*, 74, which, being
nine miles to windward, had first discovered the enemy, and which
had afterwards stood on to within less than two miles of him,
rejoined, and took her station in the line, which was then in the
following order.[1] The French order, and the losses on the British
side in the action, are also given here for convenience of reference.

BRITISH.						FRANCO-SPANISH.		
SHIPS.	GUNS.	COMMANDERS.	Loss.			SHIPS.	GUNS.	COMMANDERS.
			K.	W.				
Hero	74	{ Capt. Hon. Alan Hyde } Gardner.	1	4		*Argonauta* .	90	{ Adm. Don F. Gravina. } Rear-Adm. Don Ant. Escaño. } Capt. Don. Rafael Hore.
Ajax	74	Capt. William Brown (1).	2	16		*Terrible* . .	74	Capt. Don F. Mondragon.
Triumph . .	74	„ Henry Inman.	5	6		*América* . .	64	„ Don Juan Darrac.
Barfleur . .	98	„ George Martin (2).	3	7		*España* . . .	64	„ Don Bern. Munos.
Agamemnon .	64	„ John Harvey (2).		3		*San Rafael* .	80	Commod. Don F. Montez.
Windsor Castle	98	„ Charles Boyles.	10	35		*Firme* . . .	74	Capt. Don R. Villavicencio.
Defiance . .	74	{ „ Philip Charles C. H. } Durham.	1	7		*Pluton* . . .	74	{ Commod. J. M. Cosmao-Ker- } julien.
Prince of Wales	98	{ Vice-Adm. Sir Robert Calder } (B). } Capt. William Cuming.	3	20		*Mont Blanc* .	74	Capt. G. J. N. La Villegris.
						Atlas . . .	74	„ P. N. Rolland.
						Berwick . .	74	„ J. G. Filhol-Camas.
Repulse . . .	74	{ „ Hon. Arthur Kaye } Legge.		4		*Neptune* . .	80	Commod. E. T. Maistral.
Raisonnable .	64	Capt. Josias Rowley.	1	1		*Bucentaure* .	80	{ V. Adm. Villeneuve. } Capt. J. J. Magendie.
Dragon . . .	74	„ Edward Griffith.		4		*Formidable* .	80	{ R. Adm. Dumanoir Le Pelley. } Capt. J. M. Letellier.
Glory . . .	98	{ Rear-Adm. Charles Stirling } (1) (B). } Capt. Samuel Warren (2).	1	1		*Intrépide* . .	74	„ L. Depéronne.
						Scipion . . .	74	„ C. Bellanger.
Warrior . . .	74	„ Samuel Hood Linzee				*Swiftsure* . .	74	{ Capt. C. E. l'Hôpitalier- } Villemadrin.
Thunderer . .	74	„ William Lechmere.	7	11		*Indomptable* .	80	Capt. J. J. Hubert.
Malta . . .	80	„ Edward Buller.	5	40		*Aigle* . . .	74	Capt. P. P. Gourrège.
						Achille . . .	74	Capt. G. Deniéport.
						Algéciras . .	74	Capt. Le Tourneur.
Egyptienne . .	40	{ Capt. Hon. Charles Elphin- } stone Fleeming.	2	3		*Cornélie* . .	40	Capt. La Marre La Meillerie.
						Hortense . .	40	
						Rhin . . .	40	
Sirius . . .	36	„ William Prowse (1).				*Sirène* . . .	36	
Nile, lugger. .		Lieut. John Fennell.				*Thémis* . . .	40	
Frisk, cutter .		„ James Nicolson.				*Didon* . . .	40	
						Santa Mag- *dalena.*		
						Furet . . .	18	
						Naïade . . .	16	

The British line was on the starboard tack, most of the ships
having their topgallant sails set. The allies, after having hove to

---

[1] The *Dragon*, however, was some way to leeward, struggling up under a press of
sail to get into station.

for a time, filled at 3.30 P.M., and stood under topsails upon the
port tack, rather off the wind, in a close and well-formed line, with
a frigate ahead of them, the *Sirène*, with the rich galleon *Matilda* in
tow, astern, and with the remaining frigates to windward of the
centre and rear. Calder's fleet, which could barely see the enemy
through the mist, was nearly abeam, and distant about seven miles.
Its frigates, the *Egyptienne* and *Sirius*, had been ordered at about

ADMIRAL SIR ROBERT CALDER, BART.

(From the engraving by H. R. Cook.)

1 P.M. to keep sight of the allies; and the *Sirius* had been afterwards able to make, and signal the result of, a very close inspection
of Villeneuve's line.

Calder's signals, after 3 P.M., were: at 3.20, engage the enemy;
at 3.22, tack together; at 3.26, annul tack together; at 3.27, starboard division make all possible sail and steer S.S.W.; at 3.30, the
same, with the *Hero's* pennants; at 3.31, form line of battle in open
order; at 3.53, alter course one point to starboard; at 4.21, tack in

succession ; at 4.30, engage the enemy's centre ; at 4.45, preserve close order ; and at 5.9 P.M., engage the enemy as closely as possible. "The signal to tack in succession," hoisted by the *Prince of Wales* at 4.21 P.M., "appears," says James—

"to have been made by each commander-in-chief about the same time ; but, in the foggy state of the weather, neither fleet saw the commencement of the other's man-œuvre. The British tacked to prevent their opponents escaping them on the opposite tack ; but the Franco-Spaniards, who had hauled close to the wind on getting within about three miles of the British fleet, wore in consequence of the *Sirène*, which had the galleon in tow, making signals, by guns fired in quick succession, that the rear was in danger of being cut off. This was occasioned by the bold approach of the *Sirius*, which, as soon as she had got sufficiently to windward to fetch into the wake of the combined line, had tacked, with the intention of attempting to carry by boarding the great object of the enemy's solicitude. While making the necessary preparation to effect his object, Captain Prowse discovered, through the haze on his lee bow, the enemy's van ship, the *Argonauta*, approaching with the wind nearly abeam. The *Sirius* herself being now in jeopardy, Captain Prowse abandoned his design upon the galleon, and bore up to pass to leeward of the Franco-Spanish line. With a for-bearance highly honourable to Admiral Gravina, the *Argonauta* passed the British frigate without firing ; and so did the *Terrible* and *América*. By the time, however, that the *Sirius* had got abreast of the *España*, which was at about 5.15 P.M., the *Hero*, the British van ship, then with royals set, hove in stays. Instantly the Spanish ships, all of whom had royals and courses set, hoisted their colours and commenced the action, the *Argonauta* firing her larboard guns at the *Hero*, and the *España*, hers at the *Sirius*, which ship, in consequence, had two men killed and three wounded."

Gardner, in the *Hero*, had tacked without signal because he saw what, owing to the mist, the Vice-Admiral could not see, namely, that the enemy had come round on the starboard tack. At 5.20, Gardner opened fire with his starboard battery. At 5.45 P.M., the *Ajax* tacked astern of the *Hero*, but, instead of following Gardner, put her helm up and bore away to speak the *Prince of Wales*, and to inform Calder of the change of position of the two vans ; and, when she had done that, she wore, and took a place in the line astern of the *Glory*. Captain William Brown (1) flung away that day a great chance of distinguishing himself. The Captains astern of him made no similar mistake. By 5.50 P.M., when a signal to tack in succession was hoisted, the *Triumph, Barfleur, Agamemnon, Windsor Castle*, and *Defiance* had already tacked in succession without orders. The flagship followed ; and presently the engage-ment began to become general. By 6 P.M., all the ships, except the *Dragon*, which was still working up from leeward, had come round on the starboard tack ; and most of them had found opponents ; but, as smoke was added to mist and the obscurity deepened, every vessel had to fight her own battle ; and more than one, in the confusion, found herself with several of the enemy about her. Among the ships which, in consequence, suffered most severely were the *Windsor Castle, Malta,* and *Ajax.* On the other hand, the *San Rafael, Firme,* and *España,* which had dropped to leeward, were very badly mauled by an overwhelming British fire. The *Pluton* gallantly bore out of line for a time, in a hopeless effort to cover and save the *Firme;* but the Spaniard's fate had, ere that, been practically decided. The *Pluton* subse-

VICE-ADMIRAL THE HON. ALAN HYDE, 2ND LORD GARDNER.
(*From H. R. Cook's engraving, after the portrait by H. Edridge.*)

quently made an equally brave attempt to relieve the *España;* and in that case, assisted by the *Mont Blanc* and *Atlas,* she was successful. The *Atlas* would, however, have paid dearly for her devotion, had she not, in turn, been relieved by some of her consorts. Just after 8 P.M., the *Firme,* then almost mastless, struck, and, a very little later, the *San Rafael* did likewise. Both vessels, soon after hauling down their flags, lost all their remaining spars. At 8.25 P.M., the British fleet being scattered, the fog and

I 2

smoke being still thick, and night drawing on, Calder signalled to discontinue the action. The enemy was then to windward, still within long gunshot; and, as several ships did not see the private night signal, desultory firing went on until 9.30 P.M. In the meantime the *Dragon* had taken in tow the *Windsor Castle*, which had lost her fore top-mast, and she fell into line astern of the *Triumph*. At about 9.45 P.M., the fleet brought to on the starboard tack, heading S.W. by W., and lay to, repairing damages. Its losses, which, all things considered, were not very heavy, are set forth on the table on p. 112. As regards material, the *Windsor Castle* lost her fore top-mast; the *Agamemnon*, her mizen top-mast and fore topsail-yard; and the *Ajax*, her main-yard and driver-boom. The *Prince of Wales*, *Malta*, and *Defiance* also lost yards, but in few cases were the damages very serious. The allies had 476 killed and wounded in the two prizes, and, in their other vessels, according to their own admission, 171; total 647, as against only 198 on the British side.[1]

By the morning of July 23rd, the centres of the two fleets were about seventeen miles apart. The ships, the British on the port, and the allies on the starboard tack, were lying to, or making very little progress: there was still some haze; and the breeze, a moderate one, was still from N.W. by W.

" The British advanced squadron," says James, " consisting of the *Barfleur*, *Hero*, *Triumph*, and *Agamemnon*, lay about five miles to windward of the main body; and, at the distance of about six miles to windward of the former, lay M. Villeneuve's advanced squadron, consisting also of four sail of the line, besides a few frigates. To windward of these again, at the distance of other five or six miles, lay the crippled *Windsor Castle*, with the *Dragon* approaching to take her in tow; and still further to leeward, at about an equal distance, lay the *Malta*, *Thunderer*, two frigates, and prizes, all of whom were out of sight of the admiral."

At 6.30 A.M., the *Prince of Wales* and the ships near her filled their main top-sails; at 8 A.M., the van ships, by signal, bore up close to the Vice-Admiral. The two bodies then ran to leeward to join the prizes and their escort; and at 9 A.M., having concentrated his command, Calder hauled up on the port tack and steered about N.E., keeping between his crippled ships [2] and the enemy. Choosing

---

[1] Calder to Cornwallis, July 23rd, 1805; Mins. of C.M., Dec. 23rd–26th, 1805; Nav. Chron. xvii., 89; xxviii., 441; and logs of most of the British ships engaged. *See also* Nav. Chron. xiv., 168–171; and Chevalier, 165. Until next morning Villeneuve did not know that he had lost any ships.

[2] The *Windsor Castle*, *Firme*, and *San Rafael*, the first towed by the *Dragon*, the second by the *Sirius*, and the third by the *Egyptienne*.

to imagine, when he saw the weathermost British ships bear up to join the prizes, that Calder was taking to flight, Villeneuve, forgetful for a moment of the Emperor's instructions, and giving rein to his natural impulses, sent some of his frigates to inform his captains that he intended to bring on a conclusive action; and towards noon, with a wind which had more north in it than before, but which was very light, the allies, in order of battle, bore down upon the British, who were then about twelve miles to the E.S.E. Not until 3.10 P.M. was the movement noticed; for very little progress was made. The British then hoisted their colours and hauled closer to the wind to await the attack; but at about 4 P.M. the French and Spaniards hauled to the wind on the same tack as Calder. The reason put forward for this decision not, after all, to renew the engagement was that, with so feeble a wind, the British could not be approached within gunshot before nightfall.[1] The true reason probably was that Villeneuve recollected that he had been ordered, if he elected to effect a junction with the Brest fleet, to endeavour to do it without fighting; and that he considered that the spirit of the order bound him. Calder thereupon resumed his course to the N.E., but the wind shifted to N., then to N.E., and, occasionally, to N.W., and, falling almost altogether, brought the allies nearly astern of the British, who might, perhaps, had they so desired, have obliged the enemy to fight again on the morning of the 24th. Yet Calder made no attempt of the kind. He kept under easy sail to the S.E. by E., accompanied on the same course by the allies, until about 8 A.M. The Franco-Spaniards then began to edge away to the S.E. by S.; and, by 6 P.M., the fleets were wholly out of sight of one another. Villeneuve, as will be seen, went to Vigo, and eventually proceeded to Ferrol.

Calder had won a victory, for, with an inferior force, he had taken two ships from the enemy; but his success had not been decisive. The French declared that he had fled before the allies; the Admiralty suppressed part of the Vice-Admiral's official letter in which he called attention to considerations which might prevent him from following up his advantage; and the public prints insinuated with some freedom that he had not done all that he might have done. Calder therefore demanded a court-martial. The court sat in the *Prince of Wales*, at Portsmouth, from December 23rd to 26th, and, after hearing the evidence, severely

---

[1] 'Vict. et Conq.,' xvi. 143; Chevalier, 168.

reprimanded the Vice-Admiral for not having done his utmost to renew the engagement on July 23rd and 24th, but, at the same time, acquitted him of cowardice or disaffection. A perusal of the minutes shows that, after the action of the 22nd, Calder, who should have thought first and foremost about annihilating Villeneuve and Gravina, allowed himself to be influenced by two considerations, neither of which ought, at such a time, to have had any weight with him. One was his anxiety to preserve his prizes. When it is recalled that, of those trophies, the oldest had been launched fifty-one, and the newest thirty-four years before, it will occur to most critics that, rather than permit himself to be hampered by such craft, the Vice-Admiral should have burnt or scuttled them. The other consideration was the apprehension lest the combined squadrons from Ferrol and the squadron from Rochefort might come out, and, finding him much damaged after a general action, and far from a friendly port, might make an easy prey of him. "They might," he said in his defence, "have gone to Ireland. Had I been defeated, it is impossible to say what the consequences might have been." In short, he seems to have cherished much the same views as Herbert had held about the saving virtues of a fleet " in being." It had surely been his duty, rather, to thrust aside his morbid imaginings of what might befall, and to recollect only that the fleet in front of him was the fleet which he had been sent to stop, and that it formed by far the strongest part of any combination which could be formed against him. Had he taken that course, and renewed, or done his utmost to renew on the 23rd or 24th, the partial action of the 22nd, his name would hold a place very different from the one which it actually occupies in the naval annals of his country. Yet Calder had not acted lightly or without much thought; he had not acted, in fact, without some kind of justification; for he had been specially warned to be on his guard against a junction between Villeneuve and the Ferrol ships; and, in a degree, his judgment was vindicated, for it is now known that, on the 23rd, Rear-Admiral Allemand, from Rochefort, was actually very near the scene of the encounter of the 22nd. In spite of all this, Sir Robert Calder appears to have made a very grave strategical mistake.

After having seen his prizes well on their way to Plymouth, the Vice-Admiral returned to the rendezvous off Cape Finisterre, in hopes of falling in with Nelson; but, seeing nothing of him, proceeded off Ferrol, and, on July 29th, sent in the *Dragon* to reconnoitre.   Concluding, from Captain Griffith's report, that Villeneuve must have gone to the southward, Calder resumed the blockade of the port, though he presently had but thirteen sail of the line [1] wherewith to maintain it.   On August 1st, he was driven off by a south-wester; and on the 2nd, in pursuance of orders from Cornwallis,[2] he detached Rear-Admiral Charles Stirling (1), with four sail of the line, to watch Rochefort.   That night he regained his station; but on the 9th, discovering, when the *Dragon* again reconnoitred the harbour, that Villeneuve lay in the entrance to Corunna, and that, there or in Ferrol, twenty-nine French and Spanish sail of the line were ready to put to sea, the Vice-Admiral raised the blockade, and, on the 14th, joined the main body of the Channel fleet off Ushant.   On the 15th, as has been already shown, Nelson, returning from his long chase, also joined.   When he departed for home, Cornwallis was left with thirty-four sail of the line.   On August 17th, upon receipt of intelligence that twenty-seven or twenty-eight Franco-Spanish sail of the line had been seen off Ferrol, the Commander-in-Chief detached Sir Robert Calder thither with eighteen.   Three days later, the *Captain*, 74, from Plymouth, reached Cornwallis, who then had with him seventeen sail of the line.   Napoleon stigmatised this separation of the Channel fleet as an " *insigne bétise.*" [3]   It certainly was a strategical blunder, such as one would not have expected an officer of Cornwallis's great ability to make.   The detachment of Calder was almost equivalent to an invitation to Villeneuve and his vastly superior force to assume the interior position, and, falling upon one half of the British fleet at a time, to beat the whole in detail. Moreover, it offered Villeneuve an opportunity, if he could evade Calder, of appearing before Brest, and of placing Cornwallis's seventeen ships between twenty-seven or twenty-eight ships of the Franco-Spanish fleet, on the one side, and the twenty-one ships of Ganteaume on the other.   Had he done that, Cornwallis must have fled or have been crushed; and, in either event, the allies would have succeeded in concentrating about fifty line-of-battle ships off the entrance to the Channel.

Happily, Villeneuve missed his chance.   Ganteaume, as will

---

[1] The *Windsor Castle* and *Malta* having been sent home to refit.

[2] Cornwallis heard on July 29th particulars of the action of the 22nd.

[3] Nap. to Decrès, Aug. 29th, in 'Précis des Ev.,' xii. 258.

presently be seen, made ready to co-operate with him, should he show himself off the port ; but Villeneuve never went near it. After losing sight of Calder on the evening of July 24th, he steered as nearly for Ferrol as the N.E. wind which was then blowing would permit. But as he could not readily make that port, as he had many sick and wounded with him, and as the spars of some of his ships were in a precarious condition, he at last bore up for Vigo bay, where he anchored on the evening of July 26th.

In Napoleon's orders of May 8th, Villeneuve was directed, if for any reason he should not be in a position, upon his return from America, to proceed at once to Brest or to enter the Channel,[1] to send away from Ferrol upon a cruise the division of Rear-Admiral Gourdon, accompanied by three or four of the best sailers of Vice-Admiral Grandallana's division, and, joining the rest of the Ferrol ships, and also the Rochefort squadron, himself to gò to Cadiz and enable the squadron from Cartagena to enter that port. He was next to occupy the Strait, and, having seized Gibraltar and the stores there, to steer with all his force for the Channel, and co-operate directly in the scheme for the invasion of England.[2] In pursuance of these instructions, Villeneuve despatched from Vigo a courier to Gourdon and Grandallana ; and, having landed his sick and wounded, watered his ships, done some refitting that could not be postponed, and learnt, on the return of his messenger, that no enemy's vessels had been visible on the 28th off Ferrol and Corunna, he sailed on July 30th with thirteen French and two Spanish ships of the line,[3] seven frigates and two brigs ; and on August 1st, only a few hours after Calder had been temporarily driven from his station there, entered the port.

Learning, soon after his arrival at Ferrol, that Rear-Admiral Allemand, with the Rochefort squadron, was at sea, looking for him, Villeneuve, on August 5th, despatched the *Didon* to search for his friends ; and, on the evening of the 9th, weighed, with twenty-nine sail of the line,[4] besides frigates and smaller craft, and made

---

[1] It was largely because this alternative was left to Villeneuve that Napoleon's combinations so completely broke down.

[2] 'Précis des Ev.,' xi. 254.

[3] He left behind him the *América, España*, and *Atlas*, ostensibly because they were slow, really, perhaps, because they had been the severest sufferers on July 22nd.

[4] *Pluton, Mont-Blanc, Berwick, Neptune, Bucentaure, Formidable, Intrépide, Scipion, Swiftsure, Indomptable, Aigle, Achille, Algéciras, Argonaute, Duguay-Trouin, Fougueux, Héros, Redoutable, Principe de Asturias, Argonauta, Neptuno, Terrible,*

sail. The wind being slight, he was obliged to anchor off the coast on the 10th; but on the 11th, he weighed again, and put to sea with a good easterly breeze. There is no doubt that he then intended, should he fall in with Allemand and his five ships of the line, to make direct for Brest or the Channel. On the 13th, the *Iris*, 32, Captain Edward Brace, sighted him abreast of Cape Ortegal, steering about W.N.W., with the wind still E. On the evening of the 14th, the *Dragon*, 74, Captain Edward Griffith, accompanied by the *Phœnix*, 36, Captain Thomas Baker (1), which had captured the *Didon* and was towing her,[1] saw the allies steering about N.W. with a N.E. wind. But, influenced either by his failure to find Allemand, who, having cruised in vain, anchored in Vigo bay on August 16th, or by the false intelligence, carefully disseminated for him by the *Dragon*, that twenty-five British ships of the line were in his neighbourhood, Villeneuve, apparently during the following night, altered his course to the southward. Keeping out of sight of the coast, he arrived, on August 18th, off Cape St. Vincent, where he took and burnt three merchantmen, but failed to capture the *Halcyon*, 16, which had them under her convoy. At 10 A.M. on the 20th,. his advanced ships chased away to the southward Collingwood's little squadron,[2] which was watching Cadiz; and, late that evening, he and his command entered the port. A few hours afterwards, Collingwood, who had been reinforced at midnight by the *Mars*, 74, Captain George Duff, from Tangier, pertinaciously resumed his station, although he had but four ships, while in the harbour lay, in addition to the twenty-nine which had accompanied Villeneuve from Ferrol, six Spanish ships[3] under Rear-Admiral Alava, making in all thirty-five ready for sea.

Villeneuve, availing himself of the alternative vouchsafed to him by Napoleon's orders of May 8th, went, then, to Cadiz, instead of to Brest or the Channel.

But the Vice-Admiral does not seem to have taken adequate measures to apprise his master of his movements; and, until some

---

Monarca, Montañez, San Agustin, San Francisco de Asis, San Ildefonso, San Juan Nepomuceno, and *San Fulgencio.*

[1] For an account of the action between the *Phœnix* and the *Didon, see* next chapter.

[2] *Dreadnought*, 98, Vice-Adm. Cuthbert Collingwood, Capt. Edward Rotheram; *Colossus*, 74, Capt. James Nicoll Morris, and *Achille*, 74, Capt. Richard King (2).

[3] A seventh Spanish ship, the *Glorioso*, 74, had escaped on May 31st, and joined the squadron at Cartagena.

day after August 22nd, Napoleon hourly expected to learn that
the allied fleets had arrived off Brest. When he knew the truth
he was furious; and, as will be seen, he attempted, not only to
supersede Villeneuve, but also to make a radical change in the
plan of campaign. It was then, however, too late. Villeneuve,
eager to re-establish his reputation, had already sailed again, ere
the fresh orders reached him, and had witnessed the ruin of the
allied cause at Trafalgar.

In the meantime, neither Napoleon nor Ganteaume knew where
Villeneuve was; and, on the assumption that he was on his way
northward, final preparations were made for the anticipated grand
junction of the fleets off Brest. On August 20th, a little before
the time at which, it was conjectured, Villeneuve would appear,
Ganteaume received directions to quit the road and to move to
Bertheaume Bay. He began to do so that evening; and, by
10.30 A.M. on the 21st, the whole of the following powerful fleet
was anchored between Bertheaume and Camaret :—

SHIPS.	GUNS.	SHIPS.	GUNS.	SHIPS.	GUNS.
Impérial [1] . . .	120	*Conquérant* . .	74	*Wattignies* . .	74
Républicain [2] . .	110	*Diomède* . . .	74	*Comète* . . .	36
Invincible . . .	110	*Eole*	74	*Félicité* . . .	36
Foudroyant . .	80	*Impétueux* . .	74	*Indienne* . . .	40
Alexandre . . .	80	*Jean Bart* . . .	74	*Valeureuse* . .	36
Alliance . . .	74	*Jupiter* . . .	74	*Volontaire* . .	40
Aquilon . . .	74	*Patriote* . . .	74	*Diligente* . . .	18
Batave	74	*Tourville* . . .	74	*Espiègle* . . .	16
Brave . . .	74	*Ulysse* . . .	74	*Vulcain* . . .	14
Cassard . . .	74	*Vétéran* . . .	74		

Frigates.

[1] Ex *Vengeur,* flag of V.-Adm. Ganteaume.   [2] Ex *Révolutionnaire.*

Cornwallis, who still maintained a blockade,[1] which deserves
to rank as one of the most wonderful operations of the kind
in history, was, at the time, off Ushant, with seventeen sail of the
line; but the movements of the French were early observed by
his look-outs, under Captain John Tremayne Rodd, in the *Indefatigable,* 44; and on the morning of the 21st, first the *Felix,* schooner,
and afterwards the *Aigle,* 36, Captain George Wolfe, were dispatched to the Admiral with the intelligence. Cornwallis hauled

---

[1] The history of this blockade, from 1803 to 1805, is fully set forth in " Disps. and
Letters Relating to the Blockade of Brest " (Nav. Rec. Soc. 1899), of which, unfortunately, only Vol. I. is available at the time of writing.

to the wind on the larboard tack with a moderate breeze at N.
by E., and, soon after 3.30 P.M., discovered the enemy. He himself,
in the *Ville de Paris*, stood in to reconnoitre, and, at 5.30 P.M., wore
to rejoin his command, being fired at, as he did so, by the shore
batteries. His decision was to attack the French at their anchorage
early on the following morning. At 4.30 A.M. on August 22nd,
therefore, his fleet weighed, and, with a N. by E. wind and some
haze, stood in on the larboard tack in close order of battle, the
Ville de Paris leading, and being next followed by the *Cæsar*, 80,
Captain Sir Richard John Strachan, and the *Montagu*, 74, Captain
Robert Waller Otway (1). At 6.30 A.M., having the Porquelle rock
close ahead, the ships tacked in succession. At 8 A.M., by which
hour the haze had decreased, the French were seen to be getting
under way; and at 9.30 A.M., after the British had again tacked
in succession and stood further in, the *Alexandre*, 80, which was
leading out the enemy in line of battle, and which flew the flag
of Rear-Admiral Willaumez, fired a distant broadside at the *Indefatigable*. For a short time it looked as if an action might result;
but, though Cornwallis made sail towards the enemy, the French
presently tacked for the harbour's mouth. At 10.45 A.M., the *Cæsar*
and *Montagu* hauled out of line to attack the enemy's rear, and
so drew the fire both of it and of the batteries. It then appearing
that the works on shore were far too powerful to be engaged, and
that the French fleet had no intention of accepting combat outside
the range of their shore batteries, the British, at 11.30 A.M., wore
and stood out. In this skirmish the loss on both sides was
insignificant. The *Cæsar* had three men killed and six wounded;
in the *Ville de Paris*, the Commander-in-Chief and a Midshipman
were struck by spent fragments of a shell; and all three of the
leading British ships were somewhat cut about aloft. On the
French side, about twenty people were killed and wounded. It
may be added that the Brest fleet made no further serious attempt
to put to sea until long after Trafalgar had been fought, although
for a week after August 22nd it made daily movements which
indicated that Ganteaume was still expecting the appearance of
Villeneuve in the offing.

On August 22nd, Collingwood, off Cadiz, was reinforced by four
sail of the line under Rear-Admiral Sir Richard Hussey Bickerton,
who, being in bad health, presently proceeded to England in the
Décade, frigate. On August 30th, Collingwood was further re-

inforced by Calder and his eighteen sail of the line which had been detached by Cornwallis on August 17th to cruise off Ferrol, and which, upon discovering that the allies had sailed thence, had followed them. With these ships, or at least with such of them as were not from time to time detached to Gibraltar for water and provisions, Collingwood remained before Cadiz until September 28th, when Lord Nelson arrived to take the command-in-chief.

The long and involved story of the great naval campaign of 1805 has now been followed up to the very eve of the battle of Trafalgar. Before proceeding to describe that memorable action, it may be well to say something, firstly, as to the manner in which Napoleon regarded, and tried to deal with, the situation which had been created by Villeneuve's unexpected appearance at Cadiz instead of off Ushant; and, secondly, as to the circumstances which induced Nelson, in spite of his physical weakness and his need for rest, to take the sea again so quickly, and to relinquish the comforts and attractions of Merton ere he had well begun to enjoy them.

Napoleon was angry with Villeneuve, because the vice-admiral had not done exactly what he had been expected to do in the West Indies; because he had not engaged Calder on July 23rd; because he had gone into Ferrol instead of cruising outside to await the junction with him of the squadron from Rochefort; because he had seen the captured *Didon* and had made no serious attempt to re-take her; because, without sufficient reason, he had gone to Cadiz instead of to Brest; and because, by not sending information of his altered plans to M. Allemand, he had risked the safety of that officer's squadron.[1] The Emperor was also angry because, after having put into Cadiz, Villeneuve appeared to be content to allow Collingwood's very inferior force to prevent the squadron at Cartagena from joining him. He was probably disappointed, too, that the Spaniards had not shown themselves to be better sea-fighters in 1805 than in 1797. But Napoleon was, of course, most angry because all his elaborate scaffolding of plans for the invasion of England had collapsed owing, as it seemed, solely to Villeneuve's failure to co-operate in the right way and at the right time. The failure was irretrievable; for the French fleet had suffered severely in the course of its long cruise; the Spaniards were rapidly becoming disgusted and lukewarm; the season was already advanced; and it was no longer possible to take the British by surprise. The project

---

[1] 'Précis des Ev.,' xii. 84. Nap. to Decrès, Sept. 4th. Chevalier, 172–195.

of invasion, therefore, was abandoned ;[1] and the Emperor decided
no more to seek to employ his fleet at Cadiz in strategic combination
with the squadrons of Rochefort and of Brest, but, instead, to send
it into the Mediterranean, there to do all possible harm to the weak
British force in that sea, and finally to provide him once more at
Toulon with a force which should be strong enough to afford
material assistance to the carrying out of his general European
policy. He had acquired, however, so bad an opinion of Villeneuve's
capacity and courage that he determined to follow the order for the
change of plans with an order for the vice-admiral's supersession.
Villeneuve was to be told about the Mediterranean scheme, and,
it would appear, was to be allowed to make some preparations for it ;
but Vice-Admiral Rosily was to proceed as soon as possible to Cadiz,
with directions to Villeneuve to return to France, there to explain
his conduct, and with instructions to take the place of the discredited
officer.[2] Villeneuve was no naval genius ; but he was a brave man ;
and he did not deserve such treatment, seeing that his hands had
all along been closely tied by the nature of his orders. He soon
knew, or shrewdly suspected, the disgrace that was in store for
him ; and it was with the hope of fending it off, by winning a
success ere he could be supplanted, that he quitted Cadiz on
October 19th.

As for Nelson, he had reached home dissatisfied. He had chased
the allies, but he had not fought them. His work was unfinished.
When, therefore, his friend, Captain the Hon. Henry Blackwood,
of the *Euryalus*, who had been sent home by Collingwood to report
the entrance of Villeneuve and Gravina into Cadiz, called at Merton
on his way up to the Admiralty, the Vice-Admiral, having heard the
news, eagerly accompanied him to Whitehall. Nelson's offer of
service was, as a matter of course, accepted. Very few days were
spent in preparation. On September 15th, the great seaman once
more hoisted his flag in the *Victory*, and, with the *Euryalus* in
company, sailed from Spithead. On the 18th, when off Plymouth,
he was joined by the 74's, *Thunderer* and *Ajax*. On the 26th, the
Euryalus was sent ahead with an intimation to Collingwood that

---

[1] *See also* Nap. to Talleyrand, Aug. 23rd. Napoleon then knew only that Villeneuve had left Ferrol ; but he had apparently arrived at the conclusion already that,
in consequence, partly of what he considered to be Villeneuve's pusillanimity, and
partly of the ever graver aspect of the European situation, he must surrender his great
project.

[2] Nap. to Decrès, Sept. 15th.

Nelson was about to assume command, and with an order that, upon his doing so, no salute should be fired, nor anything done which might hint to the enemy of the arrival of a reinforcement. Two days later, on the evening of the 28th, the *Victory* and her consorts joined the blockading fleet off Cadiz.

In order, if possible, to tempt the allies to put to sea, the Commander-in-Chief withdrew the main body of the fleet, which under Collingwood had cruised only about fifteen miles from the town, to a distance of about fifty miles to the westward of it.[1] Close inshore he stationed the only frigates then with him, the *Euryalus* and the *Hydra* ; and, between them and the main body, he stationed four or five line-of-battle ships within signalling distance of one another, so that, in clear weather, information from the frigates could, in a few minutes, be transmitted to the flagship. But it was not only to tempt the enemy to sea that Nelson kept so far to the westward. The new position diminished the risk that the fleet, in case of a westerly gale springing up, might be forced into the Mediterranean, and might thus give the allies a chance of escaping unchallenged with the first change of wind. Nelson's force at that time consisted of twenty-seven sail of the line, besides the two frigates. When, on October 1st, the *Euryalus* reconnoitred the port, it was seen that in the outer harbour, apparently ready for sea, were eighteen French and sixteen Spanish sail of the line, in addition to four frigates and two brigs.

A force of twenty-seven ships has never been considered theoretically adequate for the effective blockade of a force of thirty-four ; but Nelson could not for long keep even twenty-seven ships before Cadiz. Some of his vessels were very short of water ; and on October 2nd, Rear-Admiral Thomas Louis, with the *Canopus*, *Queen*, *Spencer*, *Tigre*, and *Zealous*, had to be detached to Gibraltar for necessary supplies. On his way eastward, Louis received intelligence that the allies, who had previously set their troops ashore, had re-embarked them on September 30th, with the intention of putting to sea with the first easterly wind. Louis, therefore, took upon himself to return to the Commander-in-Chief on the 3rd ; but the need of water and provisions was so pressing that Nelson directed the Rear-Admiral to proceed as before in execution of his orders, and consoled himself with the reflection that, after all, the news was perhaps merely part of a stratagem to induce the fleet

[1] *See* chart on p. 133 *infra*.

to approach so near to Cadiz that it might be counted. In the meantime the Commander-in-Chief, with his inadequate force, had to keep watch not only against the enemy in Cadiz, but also against the possibility that the Cartagena and Rochefort squadrons, or either of them, might attempt to slip into the port, or that the Brest fleet, having evaded or driven away Cornwallis, might take the blockaders in the rear.

On October 4th, it being calm, some gunboats pulled out from Cadiz and exchanged distant shots with the *Euryalus* and *Hydra*. On the 7th, the *Defiance*, 74, joined from England, and on the 8th, the *Leviathan*, 74, from Gibraltar; and Nelson's effective fleet then amounted to twenty-five sail of the line. It was on the 10th that Nelson sent to his Flag-Officers and Captains the famous memorandum in which he foreshadowed the plan of attack which he actually carried out at Trafalgar. This memorandum is based upon the initial assumption that, before the battle, the enemy's strength would be increased to at least forty-six sail of the line, and his own to forty; and some parts of it, therefore, are of purely academical interest; but the paper is noteworthy because it insists on the advantages to be derived from the cutting of the enemy's line in two places by two parallel lines of British ships.

After declaring his intention of keeping the fleet in such a position of sailing that the order of sailing should be the order of battle, Nelson went on to say :—

"If the enemy's fleet should be seen to windward in line of battle, and that the two lines . . . could fetch them, they will probably be so extended that their van could not succour their rear. I should therefore probably make the second in command's signal to lead through about the twelfth ship from their rear, or wherever he could fetch, if not able to get so far advanced. My line would cut through about their centre. . . . The whole impression of the British fleet must be to overpower [from] two or three ships ahead of their commander-in-chief—supposed to be in the centre—to the rear of their fleet. I will suppose 20 sail of the enemy's line to be untouched. It must be some time before they could perform a manœuvre to bring their force compact to attack any part of the British fleet engaged, or to succour their own ships; which, indeed, would be impossible without mixing with the ships engaged. . . . British to be one-fourth superior to the enemy cut off. Something must be left to chance. Nothing is sure in a sea-fight, beyond all others. Shot will carry away the masts and yards of friends as well as of foes; but I look with confidence to a victory before the van of the enemy could succour their rear; and then that the British fleet would, most of them, be ready to receive their 20 sail of the line, or to pursue them should they endeavour to make off. . . . The second in command will, in all possible things, direct the movements of his line, by keeping them as compact as the nature of the circumstances will admit. Captains are to look to their particular line as their rallying point; but, in case signals cannot be seen or clearly understood, no captain can do very wrong if he places his ship alongside that of an enemy."

Should the enemy wait in line of battle—as he actually did at Trafalgar—to receive an attack from windward—

"the divisions of the British fleet will be brought nearly within gunshot of the enemy's centre. The signal will most probably then be made for the . . . lines to bear up together; to set all their sails, even their steering sails, in order to get as quickly as possible to the enemy's line, and to cut through, beginning at the twelfth ship from the enemy's rear. Some ships may not get through their exact place, but they will always be at hand to assist their friends. If any are thrown round the rear of the enemy, they will effectually complete the business of 12 sail of the enemy. Should the enemy wear together, or bear up and sail large, still the 12 ships composing, in the first position, the enemy's rear are to be the object of attack of the lee line, unless otherwise directed by the Commander-in-Chief, which is scarcely to be expected, as the entire management of the lee line, after the intentions of the Commander-in-Chief are signified, is intended to be left to the judgment of the admiral commanding that line. The remainder of the enemy's fleet . . . are to be left to the management of the Commander-in-Chief, who will endeavour to take care that the movements of the second in command are as little interrupted as possible."[1]

Nelson's small frigate force was gradually strengthened by the arrival of the *Naiad, Phœbe, Sirius, Juno,* and *Niger,* as well as of some smaller cruisers; and some of these vessels were promptly detached to harass the coasting trade, and especially to prevent the landing by nominal neutrals at such ports as Conil, Algeciras, and Ayamonte, of supplies for the fleet in Cadiz. Between October 9th and 13th also, the *Royal Sovereign,* 100, *Belleisle,* 74, *Africa,* 64, and *Agamemnon,* 64, joined the fleet, bringing up its effective strength to twenty-nine sail of the line, in addition to the five which had parted company under Louis. But on the 14th Nelson, in pursuance of orders, detached to England the *Prince of Wales,* 98, with Sir Robert Calder, who went home to take his trial; and on the 17th he was obliged to send the *Donegal,* 74, to Gibraltar to get a new ground tier of casks; so that the eve of the battle found him with but twenty-seven sail of the line under his immediate orders.

Villeneuve's new instructions—those of September 17th, directing him to enter the Mediterranean—had reached him at Cadiz on September 28th, and he had at once begun to make preparations accordingly. The troops were re-embarked; the complements of the short-handed ships were filled up, partly by the division among them of the crew of the Spanish *Terrible,* which had suffered so much on July 22nd as to be unfit again to put to sea; and on October 9th and 10th the combined fleets moved to the entrance of the harbour, so as to be ready to sail at the earliest opportunity.

[1] The entire memorandum is in James, iv. 23–25 (Ed. 1837).

Villeneuve's orders did not tell him to take the Spaniards out with him ; but the Spanish government seems to have considered that the chance of relieving the Cartagena squadron, and of enabling it to put to sea, was not to be neglected ; and Gravina had instructions to accompany Villeneuve. All the ships in Cadiz, therefore, except the *Terrible* above alluded to, and the *San Fulgencio*, 64, which for some reason was detained, were ready, on and after October 10th, to leave the port at a moment's warning. But from the 10th to the 17th there were hard and almost continuous gales from the westward ; and not until midnight on the 17th was there a change for the better. The wind then shifted to east ; and on the 18th, Villeneuve, who had heard of the arrival of Rosily at Madrid, and who feared above all things to be superseded ere he should have time once more to try his fortune, informed Gravina that he would sail on the following day. At 7 A.M., therefore, on October 19th, there being then a light breeze from N. by E., the allies were ordered by signal to get under way.

Their movements were from the first noted and reported by the British inshore squadron ; and Nelson, who at the time lay about fifty miles W.S.W. of Cadiz, at once made sail in chase to the S.E., with a light and unsteady breeze from the S.S.W. That day only twelve sail were able to get out of harbour ; and, in the afternoon, those twelve stood to the northward on the port tack with a breeze that then blew lightly from W.N.W., the *Euryalus* and *Sirius* taking a parallel course two or three miles to windward. At 8 P.M., the breeze shifted to S.W., and the enemy steered N.W. by W., still accompanied by the British frigates. In the evening the British fleet, with the exception of the look-out ships, held slowly on its course for the Strait's mouth. On the following morning early, the rest of the combined fleet weighed and put to sea with a light breeze which blew from S.E. in and near the harbour, but which was found to blow from S.S.W. outside. The ships, therefore, had no sooner begun to make an offing than they were baffled in their progress ; and, to add to their difficulties, the weather became somewhat thick. Nelson, having at daybreak made the entrance to the Strait without seeing anything of the enemy, wore and made sail to the N.W., with a fresh S.S.W. breeze. In consequence of the haze, first the *Agamemnon* (one of the ships forming the line of signalling communication), and

later the *Sirius*, narrowly escaped falling among the enemy in the
course of the morning. By noon the British were about twenty-
eight miles S.W. of Cadiz, standing W.N.W. on the port tack.
Soon after 2 P.M., the weather cleared, the wind shifting at about
the same time to W.N.W. The British were thus taken aback;
and at 4 P.M they wore, and again came to on the port tack,
heading north. Villeneuve, in pursuance of a previously expressed
intention, had in the meantime ordered his fleet to form into five
columns of squadrons, three of which, constituting the van, the
centre, and the rear, and forming together the line of battle proper,
each comprised four French and three Spanish ships. These were
under the orders of Vice-Admiral Alava, M. Villeneuve, the commander-in-chief, and Rear-Admiral Dumanoir Le Pelley, respectively. The remaining two columns, each of six ships, constituted
a "squadron of observation," or a reserve; this being under
Admiral Gravina, with Rear-Admiral Magon de Médine as second
in command [1] (see note, p. 131).

Vice-Admiral Villeneuve, it is worth noting, comprehended
perfectly the kind of tactics which Nelson was likely to employ
against him. "The enemy," he explained to his captains, "will
not content himself with forming a line of battle parallel with ours,
and with engaging us with his guns—a business wherein not
necessarily the most skilful, but rather the most lucky is commonly
successful. He will seek to surround our rear and to pierce our
line; and he will endeavour to concentrate upon, and overpower
with groups of his own vessels, such of our ships as he may manage
to cut off." But the allied commander-in-chief neither purposed
to attack in accordance with the same sound principle, nor pro-
pounded any effective method of meeting and confounding Nelson's
anticipated movements. If the allies should find themselves to
windward, their line was to bear down together, and each ship was
to closely engage her natural opponent in the British line, ultimately
boarding her if possible. If the allies should be to leeward, they
were to await attack in close order of battle. But if the British
should essay to cut the French line and overwhelm its rear by
doubling or concentrating upon it, Villeneuve would apparently
wash his hands of further responsibility. "In that case," he said, "a
captain will do better to look to his own courage and thirst for glory
than to the signals of the commander-in-chief, who, himself in the
thick of the fight and shrouded in smoke, may perhaps be unable to

FATE OF SHIPS. T. Taken. R. Retaken. W. Wrecked. B. Burnt. D. Destroyed. S. Sunk. Bl. Blown-up.

British Fleet

	Ships	Guns	Commanders. († Killed or mortally wounded)	Killed	Wounded
Weather Column	Victory	100	Vice-Adm. Lord Nelson, K.B. (W).†	57	102
	Téméraire	98	Capt. Thomas Masterman Hardy.†	47	76
	Neptune	98	Capt. Eliab Harvey.	10	34
	Leviathan	74	Capt. Thomas Francis Fremantle.	4	22
	Britannia	100	Rear-Adm. William Earl of Northesk (W). Capt. Charles Bullen.	10	42
	Conqueror	74	Capt. Israel Pellew.	3	9
	Africa	64	Capt. Henry Digby.	18	44
	Agamemnon	64	Capt. Sir Edward Berry.	2	8
	Ajax	74	Lieut. John Pilfold (actg.).[1]	2	9
	Orion	74	Capt. Edward Codrington.	1	23
	Minotaur	74	Capt. Charles John Moore Mansfield.	3	22
	Spartiate	74	Capt. Sir Francis Laforey, Bt.	3	20
Lee Column	Royal Sovereign	100	Vice-Adm. Cuthbert Collingwood (B).	47	94
	Belleisle	74	Capt. Edward Rotheram.	33	93
	Mars	74	Capt. William Hargood (1).	29	69
	Tonnant	80	Capt. George Duff.†	26	50
	Bellerophon	74	Capt. Charles Tyler (1).†	27	123
	Colossus	74	Capt. John Cooke (1).†	40	160
	Achille	74	Capt. James Nicoll Morris.	13	59
	Dreadnought	98	Capt. Richard King (2).	7	26
	Polyphemus	64	Capt. John Conn.	2	4
	Revenge	74	Capt. Robert Redmill.	28	51
	Swiftsure	74	Capt. Robert Moorsom.	9	8
	Defiance	74	Capt. William Gordon Rutherfurd.	17	53
	Thunderer	74	Capt. Philip Charles Durham.	4	12
	Defence	74	Lieut. John Stockham (actg.).[2]	7	29
	Prince	98	Capt. Richard Grindall.	0	0
	Euryalus	36	Capt. Hon. Henry Blackwood.		
	Naiad	38	Capt. Thomas Dundas.		
	Phœbe	36	Capt. Hon. Thomas Bladen Capell.		
	Sirius	36	Capt. William Prowse (1).		
	Pickle, schooner	10	Lieut. John Richards La Penotière.		
	Entreprenante	8	Lieut. Robert Benjamin Young.		

Combined Fleet (* Spanish)

	Ships	Guns	Commanders. († Killed or mortally wounded)	Killed	Wounded	Fate of Ships
Rear	Neptuno*	80	Capt. Don H. Cayetano Valdés.		Slight	T., R.
	Scipion.	74	Capt. Charles Bellanger.			(1)
	Rayo.*	100	Capt. Don Enrique Macdonel.			T. 24th, W.
	Formidable	80	Rear-Adm. P. R. M. E. Dumanoir Le Pelley.†		65	(1)
	Duguay Trouin	74	Capt. C. M. Letellier.	Trivial		(1)
	San Francisco de Asis*	74	Capt. Don Luis de Flores.	Slight		
	Mont Blanc	74	Capt. Claude Touffet.	None		(1)
	San Agustin*	74	Capt. J. G. N. La Villegris.	160		T., B.
	Héros*	74	Capt. Don F. X. Cagigal.	Slight		
Centre	Santisima Trinidad*	140	Rear-Adm. Don B. H. de Cisneros. Commod. Don F. X. de Uriarte.	Heavy	209	T., D.
	Bucentaure	80	Vice-Adm. P. C. J. B. S. Villeneuve. Commod. E. T. Maistral.	Heavy		T., R., W.
	Neptune	84	Capt. Don Jose Quevedo.			
	Redoutable	74	Capt. J. J. E. Lucas.	300	222	T., S.
	San Leandro*	64	Capt. Don M. Gaston.	Slight		T., B.
	Intrepide	74	Capt. L. A. C. Infernet.	306		(2)
	San Justo*	74	Capt. J. J. Hubert.			
	Indomptable	80	Capt. Don M. Gaston.			
	Santa Ana*	112	Vice-Adm. Don I. M. de Alava. Capt. Don Jose Gardoqui.	97	141	T., R.
Van	Fougueux	74	Capt. L. A. Baudoin.†	400		T., W.
	Monarca*	74	Capt. Don T. Argumosa.	300		T., W.
	Pluton	74	Commod. J. M. Cosmao-Kerjulien.	216		
	Algésiras	74	Rear-Adm. C. Magon de Médine.† Capt. Le Tourneur.†	400		T., R.
	Bahama*	74	Commod. Don. D. A. Galiano.†	270		T.
	Aigle	74	Capt. P. P. Gourrège.†	250		T., W.
	Swiftsure	74	Capt. C. E. l'Hôpitalier-Villemadrin.	160		T.
	Argonaute	74	Capt. J. Epron.	Slight		
	Montañez*	74	Capt. Don J. Alcedo.	400		
	Argonauta*	80	Capt. Don A. Parejo.	250		T., S.
	San Juan N-pomuceno*	74	Capt. J. G. Filhol-Camas.†	300		T., W.
	Berwick	74	Capt. Don. Cosme Churruca.†			T.
	San Ildefonso*	74	Commod. Don Jose de Varga.			T.
	Achille	74	Capt. G. Deniéport.†	Nearly all		T., Bl.
	Principe de Asturias*	112	Adm. Don Federico Gravina.† Rear-Adm. Don A. Escaño.	41	107	
Squadron of Observation	Rhin	40	Capt. Chesneau.			
	Hortense	40	Capt. La Marre La Mellerie.			
	Cornelie	40	Capt. de Martinenq.			
	Themis	40	Capt. Jugan.			
	Hermione	40	Capt. Mahé.			
	Furet	18	Lieut. Dumay.			
	Argus	16	Lieut. Taillard.			

1 For Capt. William Brown (1). } Absent as witnesses at the court-martial on
2 For Capt. William Lechmere. } Sir R. Calder.

NOTE.—Chevalier, 191, puts the Intrépide between the Scipion and the Rayo, and the San Agustin between the Mont Blanc and the San Francisco d'Asis, if not originally stationed in Dumanoir's division, rapidly joined it. He also transposes the stations of the Argonaute and the Argonauta. There is no question that the Intrépide, if not originally there. I incline to think that she was not originally there.

(1) Taken by Sir R. J. Strachan, Bt., Nov. 3, 1805.

(2) Wrecked off Rota, Cadiz, Oct. 24-25, 1805.

K 2

make signals."[1] It is astonishing to reflect that, after all the hard
lessons which it had received, and in view of what it had learnt to
expect would happen, the French navy was still, in 1805, unable to
shake itself loose from the cramping traditions of the line of battle.

Soon after it had formed in five columns, the allied fleet, upon
receiving news from its advanced frigates that eighteen British
sail were in sight, cleared for action. It continued on the port
tack until about 5 P.M., and then, tacking, stood for the mouth of
the Strait. The news was at once conveyed to Nelson, who
telegraphed that he relied upon Captain Blackwood to keep sight
of the enemy during the night. Soon afterwards, the *Euryalus,
Naiad, Phœbe*, and *Sirius*, which had approached the allies, were
driven off; and Gravina, with his division of the squadron of
observation, was directed to follow them for a time, but to rejoin
the main body before night. At 7.30 P.M., the *Aigle*, belonging
to this detached force, signalled that eighteen British ships were
visible in line of battle to the southward; whereupon the allies
presently wore and stood to the north-west. At 8.40 P.M., Nelson
also wore and stood to the S.W.; and at 4 A.M. on October 21st,
he wore once more, and steered under easy sail to the N. by E.

Just before dawn on the day of the battle, Villeneuve discovered
that the British were to windward and not, as he had expected,
to leeward of him. He also discovered that Nelson had with him
a larger force than had been supposed.[2] The commander-in-chief
of the allies, therefore, instead of restricting his own line to twenty-
one ships, allowed the ships of the three squadrons composing it
to form, without regard to priority of rank, in close line of battle
on the starboard tack upon the squadron of observation, which,
at Gravina's orders, had placed itself ahead, and to steer S.W.[3]
The ships appear, in consequence, to have ranged themselves
in the order given in the table on the previous page,[4] the
Principe de Asturias then occupying the head position in the
van, and the *Neptuno* bringing up the rear. When these directions
had been carried out, and day broke, the hostile fleets were
about eleven miles apart, the allied centre bearing about E. by S.

[1] 'Vict. et Conq.,' xvi. 109.

[2] Villeneuve had expected to encounter only twenty-one sail of the line.

[3] For criticism of Gravina's behaviour, see the preface to this volume.

[4] This arrangement substantially agrees, save as regards the station of the *Intrépide*,
with the one given in 'Préc. des Ev.,' xiii. 187, and quoted by James; but there is no
doubt that, owing to various causes, it altered somewhat ere the opening of the battle.

from the British centre; Cape Trafalgar bearing E. by S. from the *Victory*, distant about twenty-one miles, and the breeze blowing

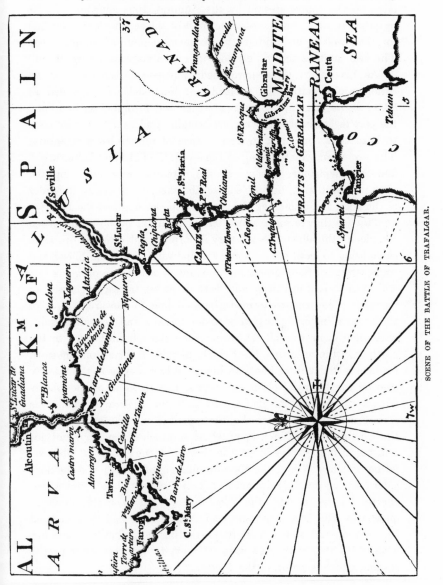

SCENE OF THE BATTLE OF TRAFALGAR.

lightly from W.N.W., accompanied by a heavy swell from the westward.

At 6.40 A.M., Nelson signalled to form the order of sailing

in two columns, and to prepare for battle; and at 6.50 A.M., he ordered both columns to bear up (*i.e.*, in succession), and sail large on the course steered by the Admiral, thus showing that he purposed to carry out the essential part of the scheme which he had foreshadowed to his Captains in his memorandum of October 10th.[1] The two columns accordingly bore up to the eastward under all sail.[1]

As his enemy thus approached, Villeneuve, realising that an action could neither be avoided nor long delayed, signalled at 8.30 A.M. for his ships to wear together and form a close line upon the port tack, his object being, by bringing Cadiz on to his lee bow, to keep that port open to him in case of retreat being necessary. The evolution which, owing to the swell, the light and failing wind, and the ineptitude of some of the captains, was not completed until nearly 10 A.M., had, of course, the effect of reversing the order of the fleet, and of making the *Neptuno* the leading and the *Principe de Asturias* the rearmost ship. Even when the evolution had been completed, the allied line was very ill-formed and crowded up, some ships being to leeward and some to windward, and some ahead and some astern, of their proper stations, much of the column being two and even three ships deep, and part of its centre sagging away to leeward. The frigates formed a second line to leeward. Most of the Franco-Spanish ships were under topsails and topgallant-sails, with their main top-sails shivering; and the column headed to the north. In the meantime the British, in spite of their studding-sails, made only about three knots an hour. While they were thus slowly nearing the enemy, Nelson was approached by some of the officers who were on board his flagship to allow the *Téméraire*, which was then close astern, to pass the *Victory*, it being felt by them that the Commander-in-Chief, upon whom so much depended, ought not unnecessarily to expose himself in the van of the attack. "Oh, yes; let her go ahead," said the Vice-Admiral significantly: and the next astern was accordingly desired to take her station ahead; but when, shortly before 10 A.M., the *Téméraire* ranged upon the *Victory's* quarter in order to assume the lead, Nelson, who had in vain tried to crack on sail with a view to preventing her, bluntly hailed her with, "I'll thank you, Captain Harvey, to keep in your proper station, which is astern of the *Victory*."[2]

---

[1] The intended order of the British ships, with other particulars, will be found in the table on p. 131.

[2] Chamier's note to James, iv. 35, (1837).

Since about 6 o'clock, the Commander-in-Chief had had his frigate Captains with him on board the flagship. He kept Blackwood and Prowse until the very last minute, and did not finally dismiss them until the enemy's shot were already passing over the *Victory.* Captain Blackwood, who, with Captain Hardy, had in the early morning witnessed the paper in which Nelson recommended Lady Hamilton and his little daughter Horatia to the care of his country, has left some valuable memoirs of these last hours.

" He seemed very much to regret, and with reason, that the enemy tacked to the northward, and formed their line on the larboard instead of the starboard tack, which latter line of bearing would have kept the Strait's mouth open.[1] Instead of which, by forming to the northward, they brought the shoals of Trafalgar and St. Pedro under our lee ; and also, with the existing wind, kept open the port of Cadiz, which was of infinite consequence to them. This movement was in a great degree the cause of Nelson's making the signal to prepare to anchor, the necessity of which was impressed on his mind to the last moment of his life. . . . He frequently asked me what I should consider as a victory?—the certainty of which he never for an instant seemed to doubt, although, from the situation of the land, he questioned the possibility of the subsequent preservation of the prizes. My answer was that, ' considering the handsome way in which battle was offered by the enemy, their apparent determination for a fair trial of strength, and the proximity of the land, I thought, if fourteen ships were captured, it would be a glorious result'; to which he always replied : ' I shall not, Blackwood, be satisfied with anything short of twenty.' . . . About 10 o'clock his Lordship's anxiety to close with the enemy became very apparent. He frequently remarked to me that they put a good face upon it; but always quickly added, ' I'll give them such a dressing as they never had before.' . . . Admiral Villeneuve assured me that, on seeing the novel mode of attack intended to be made on the combined fleets, and which at that moment, he confessed, he could not in any way prevent, he called the officers of his ship around him, and, pointing out the manner in which the first and second in command of the British fleet were each leading his column, exclaimed : ' Nothing but victory can attend such gallant conduct.' . . . As we were standing on the front of the poop, I took his hand, and said, ' I trust, my Lord, that on my return to the *Victory,* which will be as soon as possible, I shall find your Lordship well, and in possession of twenty prizes': on which he made this reply : ' God bless you, Blackwood; I shall never speak to you again.' "

The considerations mentioned by Blackwood induced Nelson, between 10 and 11 A.M., to steer a little more to the northward than before, and to telegraph to Collingwood, who led the lee column : " I intend to pass through the van of the enemy's line, to prevent him from getting into Cadiz." At 11.30, A.M.[2] the command was ordered to prepare to anchor at the close of the day; and at 11.40 A.M., after Nelson had remarked to Blackwood, " I'll now amuse the fleet with a signal," and after he had had some conversation with Lieutenant John Pasco as to the precise wording to be

---

[1] *I.e.,* to themselves. Nelson desired them to try to enter the Mediterranean.

[2] At the same hour Villeneuve signalled to Gravina to keep his luff so as to be able to reinforce the allied centre. *See* preface to this volume. Gravina seems to have paid no attention.

adopted, there went up the immortal reminder, " England expects that every man will do his duty "[1]—a signal which, as soon as it was understood, was received with a general shout of enthusiasm throughout the fleet.

It was just noon when the first shot of the great battle was fired by the *Fougueux,* which, in response to a signal, opened upon the *Royal Sovereign.* The sun shone brilliantly; the sea, save for the long Atlantic swell, was smooth; and the wind was so light as barely to fill the huge clouds of white canvas that were spread by the advancing columns. Collingwood, well within gunshot of the allied line, was then heading straight for the *Santa Ana,*[2] Alava's flagship, to which the *Fougueux* occupied the position of next astern; and the *Royal Sovereign* bore about S.E. by S. from the leading ship of the British weather column, distant about two miles, and nearly W. from the *Belleisle,* her own next astern, distant three-quarters of a mile. Nelson, in the *Victory,* was heading at the same time for Ville-neuve's flagship, the *Bucentaure,*[3] but was still far out of gunshot of the enemy's line.[4]

As the enemy opened, the three British Admirals hoisted their flags; and the ships of both British columns hoisted the white ensign; for, although Collingwood was then a Vice-Admiral of the Blue, the Commander-in-Chief had determined that, in order to avoid any possible confusion, the whole fleet should that day wear the same colour. Each British ship had been ordered to carry, in addition, a Union Jack at her fore topgallant-stay, and another at her main topmast-stay; and the *Victory* flew at her main-truck the signal, " Engage the enemy more closely."[5] At about the same time the allies hoisted their ensigns, the Spaniards also displaying a large wooden cross at the end of their spanker-booms. Villeneuve himself seems to have flown no flag;[6] but the other allied flag-officers shook out their flags when the ships hoisted their ensigns.

---

[1] James gives this version; which is to be found in the logs of several of the ships present, the combinations used being, 253, 269, 863, 261, 471, 598, 220, 370, and the alphabetical, 4, 21, 19, and 24 (duty).

[2] The eighteenth ship from the intended, and, probably, the sixteenth from the actual van, and consequently either the sixteenth or the eighteenth from the rear.

[3] The eleventh ship from the actual van.

[4] This situation was due to two causes, viz., Nelson's intention that the lee column should get first into action; and the fact that the *Santa Ana,* and the ships near her, were somewhat further to windward than the ships near the *Santisima Trinidad* and *Bucentaure.*

[5] No. 16, viz. a flag quartered red and white, over a Dutch ensign reversed.

[6] The log of the *Spartiate* nevertheless throws some doubt upon this.

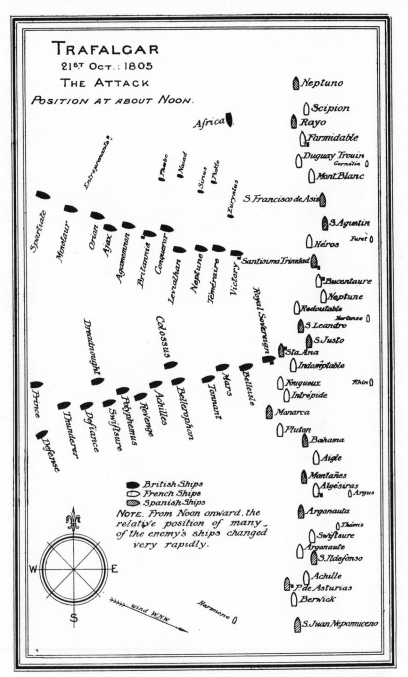

TRAFALGAR

21ST OCT.: 1805

THE ATTACK

POSITION AT ABOUT NOON.

Neptuno
Scipion
Rayo
Farmidable
Duguay Trouin
Cornélie
Mont Blanc
S. Francisco de Asis
S. Agustin
Furet
Héros
Santisima Trinidad
Bucentaure
Neptune
Redoutable
Hortense
S. Leandro
S. Justo
Sta. Ana
Indomptable
Fougueux
Intrépide
Rhin
Monarca
Pluton
Bahama
Aigle
Montañes
Algésiras
Argus
Argonauta
Thémis
Swiftsure
Argonaute
S. Ildefonso
Achille
P. de Asturias
Berwick
S. Juan Nepomuceno

Africa

Entreprenante
Phœbe
Naïad
Sirius
Pickle
Euryalus

Spartiate
Minotaur
Orion
Ajax
Agamemnon
Britannia
Conqueror
Leviathan
Neptune
Téméraire
Victory
Royal Sovereign

Dreadnought
Colossus
Mars
Belleisle
Prince
Thunderer
Defiance
Swiftsure
Polyphemus
Revenge
Achilles
Bellerophon
Tonnant
Defense

British Ships
French Ships
Spanish Ships

NOTE. From Noon onward, the relative position of many of the enemy's ships changed very rapidly.

W   E
S

wind WNW

Hermione

Founded on evidence in British, French, and Spanish Dispatches, James's ' History,' ' Victoires et Conquêtes,' 'Précis des Evènements,' Chevalier, etc.; and on plans in *Naval Chronicle*, Dec., 1805, James's 'History,' Collingwood's 'Collingwood,' Mahan's ' Nelson,' etc., etc.

NOTE.—The distances between the British ships are not accurately indicated, space not permitting. The positions of the *Intrépide, San Juan Nepomuceno, Principe de Asturias*, and one or two other ships, at noon, are open to some doubt. The *Intrépide*, if not more forward in the line at noon than as shown above, rapidly joined the van division.

[To face page 136

At 12.10 P.M., the *Royal Sovereign* slowly passed through the enemy's line between the *Santa Ana* and the *Fougueux*, firing her port guns double-shotted into the stern of the former at very close range, and, it was afterwards acknowledged, killing and wounding by that one broadside alone nearly four hundred people. With her starboard broadside she simultaneously raked the *Fougueux*, and then ranged close along the starboard broadside, and subsequently on the lee bow, of the *Santa Ana*, with which she began a furious contest muzzle to muzzle. In the meantime the *Fougueux*, bearing up, raked Collingwood's flagship from astern, while the *San Leandro*,

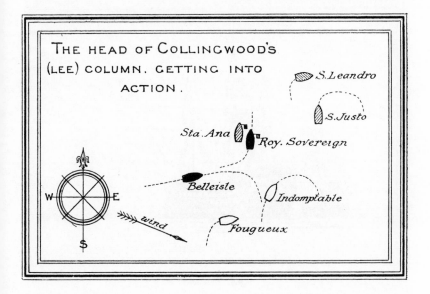

wearing, raked her from forward, and the *Indomptable* and *San Justo*, the one on her starboard quarter and the other on her starboard bow, plied her at a distance of less than three hundred yards with a hail of shot. But the enemy soon discovered that, situated as they were, they were doing almost as much harm to one another as to the *Royal Sovereign*; and Collingwood and Alava were presently left to fight it out alone, the *Fougueux*, *Indomptable*, *San Justo*, and *San Leandro*, finding other occupation.

When the *Royal Sovereign*, alone and unsupported, had been in close action for fully a quarter of an hour, her next astern, the *Belleisle*, drew near, and, hauling up on the port tack, fired her port

broadside into the *Santa Ana's* lee quarter. She had already been
fired at for twenty minutes by the allied rear, and had suffered
heavily, but had replied only with a few shot directed at the
Monarca. Having passed the *Santa Ana,* she bore away a little
towards the stern of the *Indomptable;* but that ship wore in time to
avoid being raked, and, after having exchanged a few broadsides
with Captain Hargood, bore up to the S.E. Already the allied line,
especially the rear of it, was becoming jumbled and confused, some

H.M.S. " VICTORY."

(From a drawing of her at her moorings in Portsmouth Harbour, in 1828, by E. W. Cooke, R.A.)

of the ships astern of the *Fougueux* pressing forward to support the
centre, and others remaining with their sails shivering or aback.
The whole rear, moreover, was soon clouded by the smoke which
rolled slowly to leeward from the guns of the British lee column as,
ship by ship, it drew near enough to reply with effect to the fire of
the enemy.

The *Victory* was first fired at about the time when the *Belleisle* was beginning to engage the *Indomptable.* Nelson had ordered
her to be steered for the bow of the *Santisima Trinidad;* but he
occupied himself, as he approached, in endeavouring to discover some

sign indicating the ship in which Villeneuve was present; for he
desired personally to engage the commander-in-chief, whom he
believed to be in one of the vessels close astern of the four-decker.
The first shot fired at the *Victory*, at 12.20 P.M., seemed to be an
answer to Nelson's unspoken challenge, for it came from the *Bucentaure*. It fell short, the range being then too great; but in a few
minutes it was followed by a second, and then, in quick succession,
by others, one of which, passing through the *Victory's* main top-
gallant-sail, showed that the British flagship could at length be
reached. Two minutes later a very heavy fire was opened upon the
flagship by a considerable part of the allied van. There was no
longer more than the merest stirring of wind, and the progress of
the *Victory*, now heading for the interval between the *Santisima
Trinidad* and the *Bucentaure*, was slower than ever. During her
long approach she suffered terribly; nor, although, it is true, one of
her guns went off by accident, did she or could she make any return.
As she neared the enemy, those ships immediately ahead of her
closed upon one another in order to bar her progress; the result
being that, owing, on the one hand, to the concentration from astern
upon the *Bucentaure*, and, on the other, to the bearing up of the
San Justo, *Indomptable*, and *San Leandro*, to the assistance of the
Santa Ana, which had lost her headway, a considerable gap opened
somewhat ahead of the centre of the allied line. Certainly the
Redoutable, and possibly also the *Intrépide*,[1] though apparently
originally astern of the *San Leandro*, passed her and joined the
foremost group, which thus included about thirteen or fourteen sail.
The *San Leandro*, bearing up, joined the *San Justo* and *Indomptable*
at the head of the rearmost group, which thus included about twenty
sail; and between the two groups there was presently a distance of
at least three-quarters of a mile.

When the *Victory* was about two and a half cables from the
Bucentaure, a shot cut her mizen topmast in two, and another
knocked her wheel to pieces, so that thereafter she had to be steered
from the gun-room. Every sail of the flagship, too, was in shreds,
and all her foremast studding-sail-booms had been shot away. Upon
the *Bucentaure's* lee quarter was the French *Neptune*; and ranging
up between the *Bucentaure* and *Neptune*, as if altogether to close the
interval, was the *Redoutable*. Hardy represented to Nelson that

---

[1] So James believes; but some of the French evidence seems to show that the
Intrépide was still a little astern. Thereafter, if this be so, she rapidly passed to the van.

the *Victory* could not pass through the line without running on
board one or another of those ships. " I cannot help it," replied
the Vice-Admiral. " It does not signify which we run on board of.
Go on board which you please. Take your choice." Hardy headed,
therefore, as if to run on board the *Redoutable*, and at 12.59 P.M.,[1]
as the *Victory* began to pass under the stern of the *Bucentaure*, she
fired in succession every one of her port guns, all double and many
treble shotted, into the cabin windows of Villeneuve's flagship, the
range being so close that, as the *Victory* rolled, her port main-
yard arm in passing struck the vangs of the *Bucentaure's* gaff, and

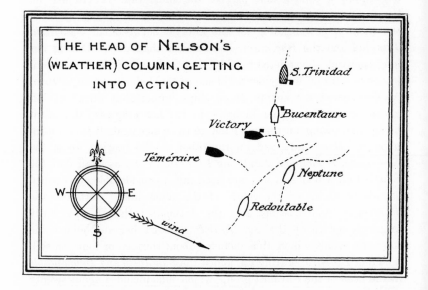

the *Bucentaure's* ensign, if there had been wind enough to blow it
out, must have caught in the *Victory's* rigging. The salvo wrecked
the stern of the French flagship, and, as subsequently appeared,
killed and wounded nearly four hundred of her men, and dismounted
twenty of her guns. But the *Victory* was almost at the same
moment raked from ahead, and terribly mauled, by the French
Neptune, which then, fearing to be run on board of, set her jib, kept
away a little, and ranged ahead. Hardy, however, was still bent
upon running on board of the *Redoutable*, which, while he was

---

[1] *Spartiate's* log, and the balance of probability. The *Victory's* log, which was not
written up till the 22nd, says 12.4 P.M., a time obviously much too early.

passing the *Bucentaure*, had been on his starboard bow. He fired his starboard broadside into her as soon as it would bear, and, putting his helm hard a-port, made directly for her. Ere, however, he could run into her, she also ported her helm a little as if partially to avoid the blow, and, at the same time, in order to avoid being boarded through them, shut her larboard lower-deck ports, from which she had previously been firing both at the *Victory* and at the *Téméraire.* A moment later, the *Victory* fouled her, and, probably with helm a-starboard, dropped alongside her at about 1.10 P.M., the *Victory's* starboard fore topmast studding-sail boom-iron hooking into the leech of the *Redoutable's* foretopsail, and so holding together the two ships, which fell off slowly a few points from the wind. The *Victory* continued for a time to fire some of her port guns at the *Bucentaure*, but that ship gradually moved away to the northward. She also fired distantly at the *Santisima Trinidad.* The *Redoutable*, however, gallantly commanded and admirably fought, demanded and received most of her attention. The French ship used her main-deck guns, and, both from her decks and from her tops, musketry fire, in which Captain Lucas had trained his people to great proficiency. She also fired from her fore and main tops brass cohorns loaded with langridge. The *Victory* employed her starboard 68-pr. carronade with good effect to clear the enemy's gangways, and, of course, utilised her lower batteries ; but her upper-deck guns were soon almost put out of action by the deadly small-arm fire from the *Redoutable.*

In the meantime the ships of the British lee column, as they came up, cut through the grouped mass of the enemy ahead and astern of the *Santa Ana*, and found opponents where they could ; and the ships of the British weather column, pursuing similar tactics, cut through ahead and astern of the *Bucentaure.* By 1.30 P.M., the battle was at its height ; by 3 P.M., the firing had begun to grow less ; by 5 P.M., the day was over. Of the ships in what has been described as the foremost group, six had been taken ; of the ships in what has been described as the rearmost group, twelve had been taken or destroyed. In other words, the allies had lost nine French and nine Spanish sail of the line out of thirty-three originally engaged. Fifteen ships had for the time escaped, four (all French), under Rear-Admiral Dumanoir Le Pelley, to the southward, and eleven (five French and six Spanish) into Cadiz. Such were the general results : but, in view of the vast importance of the occasion, the performances of each of the ships present must be, at least briefly, described ; and, seeing that the *Victory*, and the hero whose flag flew in her, inevitably fill the foreground of any picture that aspires to represent Trafalgar, it may be well to take in order the ships of the weather column before dealing with those of the lee column, although, as has been seen, the latter was the first to get into action.

The *Victory* had been closely engaged with the *Redoutable* for about a quarter of an hour, when, at 1.25 P.M., Lord Nelson, who had been walking backwards and forwards with Captain Hardy between the wheel stanchion and the coaming of the cabin ladder-way, suddenly faced about—not at his usual turning-point, but about one pace short of it. Hardy, who was on the Commander-in-Chief's left, made another step, and, as he turned at the usual point, saw that the Vice-Admiral had sunk to his knees, and was partially supporting himself with his left hand resting on the deck. As Hardy stooped over him, the Vice-Admiral, whose arm gave way, fell on his left side. "I trust," said the Flag-Captain, "that your Lordship is not severely wounded." "They have done for me at last, Hardy," replied Nelson, who realised from the first that his hurt was mortal; and, in answer to a further observation from Hardy, he added : "My backbone is shot through." In point of fact, a musket-ball,[1] discharged, very probably without having been knowingly aimed at the British Commander-in-Chief, from the mizen-top of the *Redoutable*,[2] distant about fifteen yards, had struck Nelson on the fore part of his left epaulette, and, having entered the shoulder, had obliquely passed to the thorax, fracturing the second and third ribs, penetrating the left lung, dividing a large branch of the pulmonary artery, passing through the spine, and finally lodging in the muscles of the back, about two inches below the inferior angle of the right scapula.[3]

---

[1] I had an opportunity, in 1891, of carefully examining the ball with the aid of a microscope. It appeared to bear no trace of having been fired from a rifled piece ; although both Clarke and M'Arthur, and Southey assert that Nelson was shot by a rifleman. There is, indeed, evidence that there were neither riflemen nor rifles in the French fleet. Dupin, ' Voyage,' iv. 10; Clarke and M'Arthur, ii. 445; Southey, ii. 264.

[2] Report of Dr. W. Beatty.

[3] The man who shot the Commander-in-Chief seems to have been ultimately shot by Mr. (later retired Commander) John Pollard, signal Midshipman of the *Victory*. "The attention of Mr. Pollard was arrested by a number of soldiers whom he perceived crouching in the tops of the *Redoutable*, and directing a destructive fire on the poop and quarter-deck of the *Victory*. He immediately seized a musket, and, being supplied

The fall of the Vice-Admiral attracted the attention of Sergeant Secker, R.M., and two seamen, who, by Hardy's order, carried their chief below to the cockpit. Nelson, though in great pain, was perfectly collected; and, taking a handkerchief from his pocket, he deliberately covered his face with it, in the hope of concealing from the people between decks the fact that he had been wounded. He was laid upon a purser's bed; and, when he had been stripped, it was quickly seen by the surgeon that the wound must have a fatal result. Partly covered with a sheet, calling continually for something to allay his burning thirst, and ceaselessly fanned with paper by those in attendance on him, the great seaman, for some time after he had been brought to the cockpit, lay, as might be expected, half stunned by the shock to his system. It would appear, indeed, from Beatty's narrative, that Nelson's mind, save at intervals, remained very confused until he had lain there for about an hour. During that period, the concussion of the firing above and around him tried him intensely; for the *Victory* was in the thick of the action.

Within a few minutes of the Vice-Admiral's fall, nearly everyone remaining upon the flagship's upper-deck was either killed or wounded by the *Redoutable's* musketry fire and by the hand-grenades which her men used very freely. This fact encouraged the French to attempt to board; and a crowd of people quickly gathered in the chains and along the gangway of the 74. They were induced to retire, as much by the discovery that the tumble-home of the two ships rendered boarding exceedingly difficult in any circumstances, as by the rush upon deck of a large body of the *Victory's* officers and men, who plied their small arms with energy, but who lost heavily. Captain Lucas afterwards ordered the main yard of his ship to be lowered in such a manner as to make a bridge for his men to the *Victory's* upper-deck; but ere he was able to utilise this device, the *Téméraire,* as will be seen later, ran foul of the *Redoutable's* starboard, or disengaged side, and effectually distracted the Frenchman's attention. This happened at about 1.40 P.M. Not long afterwards

by the signal-quartermaster, King, with ball-cartridges from two barrels kept on the after-part of the poop for the use of the Marines (who at the time were elsewhere engaged), continued firing at the soldiers every time they rose breast high in the tops, until not one was to be seen. . . . Thus . . . originated the belief that it was he who had shot the man who killed Lord Nelson." O'Byrne, 'Nav. Biog. Dict.,' p. 913. Mr. Pollard used also to relate that, after the action, Capt. Hardy in the *Victory's* wardroom publicly congratulated him upon having avenged the death of the Vice-Admiral.

the *Redoutable* ceased to resist, and Captain Hardy, by means of a boat, sent on board of her Midshipmen David Ogilvie and Francis Edward Collingwood, with the *Victory's* Sergeant-Major of Marines, and a few hands, to assist in extinguishing a fire which was giving trouble to the French crew. The two vessels remained alongside one another until 2.15 P.M., when the British flagship succeeded in freeing herself from her late opponent, and in booming herself off. The *Victory* thereupon got her head to the northward. Beyond firing a few guns at passing enemies, she seems to have done little more fighting; nor, indeed, was she fit for much. She had lost her mizen topmast; all her rigging was badly cut; her fore and main masts and bowsprit, together with their yards, and with the fore and main tops, were greatly knocked about; all her spare spars were too damaged to be of use; her hull was severely mauled; she had several shot-holes between wind and water; her starboard bower and spare anchors were disabled; and, as may be seen in the table, her company had suffered heavily.[1]

As soon as Captain Hardy had taken the most pressing measures to provide for the safety of his ship, he returned for a few minutes to the dying Commander-in-Chief, who had frequently asked to see him. It was at about 2.35 P.M. that the Flag-Captain revisited the cockpit and affectionately took and pressed Nelson's outstretched hand. "Well, Hardy, how goes the battle? How goes the day with us?" demanded the Vice-Admiral, whose mind had by that time regained much of its clearness. "Very well, my Lord," answered Hardy: "we have twelve or fourteen of the enemy's ships in our possession; but five of their van have tacked, and show an intention of bearing down upon the *Victory*. I have therefore called two or three of our fresh ships round us, and have no doubt of giving them a drubbing." "I hope," said Nelson, "that none of our ships have struck." "No, my Lord," returned Hardy; "there is no fear of that." Nelson's next words were: "I am a dead man, Hardy: I am going fast: it will be all over with me soon." A little later the Flag-Captain again went on deck. In a few minutes the *Victory* opened her port battery upon Dumanoir Le Pelley's division, which was then passing at a distance to windward. She also fired some of her foremost starboard guns at the French *Swiftsure*, which was threatening to rake the *Colossus*.

When M. Dumanoir was out of gun-shot to the south-west, and

---

[1] For a list of the British officers killed and wounded at Trafalgar, see p. 157, *infra*.

the *Orion*, ranging athwart the stern of the French *Swiftsure*, had placed herself between that vessel and the British flagship, the *Victory* fired no more; and Hardy, at about 3.30 P.M., found leisure to return to the cockpit. As before, he and his chief exchanged a pressure of the hands, and, while doing so, Hardy congratulated Nelson upon the brilliancy of the result. "The victory is complete," he said; "but as we cannot see every ship distinctly I cannot say exactly how many are taken. I am certain, however, that fourteen or fifteen have struck." "That is well," said Nelson; "but I bargained for twenty." Then, with energy, he added: "Anchor, Hardy; anchor!" "I suppose, my Lord," ventured Hardy, "that Admiral Collingwood will now take upon himself the direction of affairs." "Not while I live, I hope, Hardy," declared the Commander-in-Chief, vainly trying at the same moment to raise himself, as if to give additional force to his words: "no: do you anchor, Hardy!" "Shall we make the signal, sir?" asked the Flag-Captain. "Yes," answered Nelson; "for if I live I'll anchor": his meaning being, apparently, that if he should live until the proper moment for anchoring the fleet, *i.e.*, until resistance should have entirely ceased, he himself would give the order. Hardy had duties which prevented him from remaining below for long. In three or four minutes, having, at Nelson's desire, kissed him, he parted from him for the last time and returned to the deck. The Vice-Admiral's thoughts seemed thenceforward to turn almost exclusively to his private affairs; but more than once he murmured, "Thank God, I have done my duty!" At about 3.55 P.M. he lost the power of speech. At about 4.40 P.M.,[1] having for some time previously ceased to suffer, he, quietly and without a struggle, ceased to breathe.

Nelson and Collingwood had been close friends ever since they had been Lieutenants. To spare Collingwood's feelings as much as possible, Hardy, as soon as he knew that the Commander-in-Chief was dead, sent Lieutenant Alexander Hills, in the *Victory's* only remaining boat, to the *Royal Sovereign* with news that Nelson had been dangerously wounded. At about the same time Captain Blackwood came alongside the *Victory* in his own boat, and, boarding her, saw Hardy and learnt the truth. The two Captains then went together to Collingwood to break the full news, and to carry to

---

[1] *Victory's* time, 4.30 P.M. Log. For the whole story of Nelson's last moments, *see* 'Authentic Narrative of the Death of Lord Nelson,' by Wm. Beatty, M.D., 1807.

him the expression of Nelson's dying desire that, as soon as practicable, the fleet and prizes should be anchored in order to preserve them from the dangers of a lee shore and of a probable gale. Collingwood was overwhelmed with grief; but, when he heard what had been Nelson's wish, he exclaimed: "Anchor the fleet! Why, it is the last thing I should have thought of." And, in spite of the request of his old friend, he did not anchor it. At that time, just as the great battle had ended, Cape Trafalgar bore from the *Royal Sovereign* S.E. by E., distant eight miles.

Although the *Victory* was one of the fastest line-of-battle ships of her day, and although, moreover, she went into action with studding-sails set, the *Téméraire*, her next astern, being very light, had no difficulty in keeping close to the flagship, and, when the latter began to suffer aloft from the enemy's fire, had some difficulty in avoiding passing her. To keep station, in fact, she had to cut away her own studding-sails, and, later, to yaw repeatedly. After receiving a heavy fire as she drew near to the hostile line, and exchanging shot with the French *Neptune* and the *Redoutable*, she presently found herself, reduced by the *Neptune's* raking broadsides to a nearly unmanageable condition, with the *Redoutable* on her port beam, and the *Neptune* on her starboard bow. So she remained until about 1.40 P.M., when the drifting *Redoutable*, still fast to the *Victory*, fell on board the *Téméraire*, the Frenchman's bowsprit passing over the gangway of Harvey's ship on the port side, a little before the main rigging. There the *Téméraires* lashed it, and at once began to pour in as hot a raking fire as they could make. The British vessel had not been long in her new position when the *Fougueux*, which had been attacked by the *Belleisle* and *Mars*, of Collingwood's column, and which had hauled off from them, steered for the starboard side of the *Téméraire*, apparently with the object of passing to windward and raking her, or of boarding her. The *Téméraire*, badly damaged aloft, and with her gaff and colours shot away, may have looked like an easy prey; but she was well prepared for a fresh enemy. She had not yet discharged her starboard broadside, and, waiting until the Frenchman was less than a hundred yards from her, she poured the whole of it into the *Fougueux* with crushing effect, the result being that, no longer under control, the *Fougueux*, at about 2 P.M., ran foul of the *Téméraire*, whose men instantly lashed the French two-decker by her fore-rigging to the British ship's spare anchor. Lieutenant Thomas Fortescue Kennedy then boarded at the head of

a few men, and, within ten minutes, took complete possession of the
prize. Soon afterwards the *Victory* boomed herself off from the
Redoutable's port side, and the *Téméraire*, with the *Redoutable* and
Fougueux still fast to her, swung with her head to the southward.
At almost the same time the *Redoutable* lost her main and mizen
masts, the main falling on the after-part of the *Téméraire*, and
smashing everything there, but forming a bridge between the two
vessels. By means of this bridge, Lieutenant John Wallace (2),
at about 2.20 P.M., took formal possession of the *Redoutable*, which
had long since ceased to make resistance. The subsequent action
of the *Téméraire* seems to have been confined to the firing of some
of her foremost port guns at the French *Neptune*, which quickly
bore away out of range.

The *Leviathan's* original station had been astern of the *Conqueror*. Nelson had given some kind of consent that Captain
Bayntun might precede the *Victory* into action " if he could " ; and
Blackwood, after quitting the *Victory*, had called on board the
Téméraire, and conveyed the permission to the *Leviathan*. Bayntun
crowded sail to reach the head of the column, but was only abreast
of the *Conqueror* when the first shots from the enemy began to reach
the *Victory* ; and, unable to pass ahead, he at length fell into line
astern of the British *Neptune* and a little in advance of the
Conqueror.

Having shortened sail for a time to facilitate the efforts of the
Leviathan, and being further impeded by the increasing lack of
wind, the British *Neptune* was not in close action until about
1.45 P.M. At that hour she hauled up for the nearest ship, and,
passing immediately under the stern of the *Bucentaure*, delivered
her port broadside into it with terrible effect. The *Leviathan* and
Conqueror, following her, did the same, the three discharges
working fearful damage. Fremantle then continued under the
stern and along the starboard side of the *Santisima Trinidad*, and
luffed up to leeward of the huge four-decker, which had already
suffered badly, and which he fought until the Spaniard became
wholly unmanageable. The *Neptune* was afterwards somewhat
severely handled by several ships of the combined van, which
raked her after they bore up. The *Leviathan*, when she had
followed the *Neptune* past the *Bucentaure*, stood towards the
French *Neptune*, which was at that moment annoying the
Téméraire, but which quickly wore round and went away before

L 2

the wind. Bayntun thereupon hauled up on the port tack, and,. perceiving that the ships of the allied van were by that time tacking or wearing, as if to double upon the leading vessels of Nelson's column, he stood confidently to the north-east in their direction. His first opponent was the *San Agustin*, which endeavoured to rake him, but which was easily out-manœuvred,. and which, after receiving a single treble-shotted broadside directed into her starboard quarter, lost her mizen mast, and appeared to have had almost enough of it. Bayntun, who could not back his sails owing to the damaged state of his rigging, put his helm a-starboard and ran on board the Spaniard ; and, a few minutes. later, Lieutenant John Baldwin, with a party of seamen and Marines, boarded and carried her without opposition. For some reason which is not quite clear, the prize was at once lashed to the *Leviathan's* port side. No sooner had the operations been effected than the *Intrépide* crowded up, wore, raked the *Leviathan* from ahead, and then ranged along her starboard side. She did not, however, long remain there, the *Leviathan* being soon assisted by the approach of the *Africa*, and *Orion*, and other ships.

The *Conqueror*, after rounding the *Bucentaure's* stern, hauled up on that vessel's starboard quarter and beam, and very speedily induced the French flagship to haul down her colours. Captain James Atcherley, of the *Conqueror's* Marines, commanded the boat which was sent to take possession, and carried back Villeneuve and his two captains to surrender their swords to Captain Israel Pellew ; but, missing his own vessel, he boarded the *Mars*, instead of the *Conqueror*, her sister ship; and in the *Mars* the French officers remained. The *Conqueror* had, in the meantime, employed her starboard guns, at long range, against the *Santisima Trinidad*, and had subsequently proceeded in chase of Dumanoir's escaping division.

The *Africa* had lost sight of the fleet in the course of the night before the battle, and, when the firing began, was broad on the *Victory's* port beam, and nearly also broad on the port beam of the leading ship of the allied van. Nelson signalled to her to make all possible sail; but Digby seems to have misunderstood the order, which was intended to keep him out of danger, as meaning that he was to lose no time in closing the enemy. He therefore made the best of his way along the Franco-Spanish van, exchanging broadsides with it, and at length bore down ahead of the *Santisima*

Trinidad. Judging from her appearance that that vessel had surrendered, Digby sent Lieutenant John Smith (5) to take possession of her. Smith reached her quarter-deck ere he learnt that the Spaniard had not surrendered; and as he was not in a position to coerce her, he withdrew, no one, strange to say, endeavouring to stop him.[1] The *Africa* then, at about 3.20 P.M., very gallantly brought to action the *Intrépide,* and, for about forty minutes, fought her steadily, until the arrival of the *Orion* upon the Frenchman's starboard quarter relieved the 64, which had been nearly silenced by that time. The *Orion* subsequently wore round the *Intrépide's* stern, and brought to on her lee (port) bow, so covering the *Africa* entirely. After throwing in a heavy fire for about a quarter of an hour from that position, she obliged the French 74 to haul down her colours.[2]

Long ere that time, or, to speak accurately, at about 1.50 P.M., Villeneuve had signalled[3] to those of his ships which were not engaged to take up positions which should bring them into action as soon as possible. This signal applied, of course, to the disengaged van ships; and, in pursuance of it, a few of those which were in a condition to do so began to put about. But the wind was very light; several vessels had to employ their boats to tow their heads round; and no general alacrity was shown. At length ten ships got round on the starboard tack; but while five of them, under Dumanoir Le Pelley—four French and one Spanish[4]—hauled their wind, the other five kept away, as if to join Gravina, who was to leeward in the rear, and who was making off. It was while these confused manœuvres were in progress that the *Orion,* *Ajax,* *Agamemnon,* and *Britannia,* of the British weather column, got among the ships which had kept away, and also exchanged shots with some of those which had hauled their wind. The *Orion,* as has been already said, engaged and reduced the *Intrépide.* The *Ajax* and *Agamemnon* seem to have been more especially in action with Dumanoir's division. The *Britannia* appears to have encountered, at one time the *San Francisco de Asis,* and at another the *Rayo.* But all these British ships were then too far to leeward to offer any effectual resistance to the passage of the French rear-

---

[1] The *Santisima Trinidad* was not taken possession of until about 5.30 P.M., when she was boarded from the *Prince,* and taken in tow.

[2] At 5 P.M.   [3] *See* preface to this volume.

[4] *Formidable,* 80, *Duguay Trouin,* 74, *Mont Blanc,* 74, *Scipion,* 74, and ultimately also the *Neptuno,* 80.

admiral. Only the two last vessels of Nelson's column were in a
position to seriously challenge Dumanoir. At about 3.10 P.M.,
the *Minotaur* and *Spartiate*, having hauled close on the starboard
tack, lay to with their main top-sails to the mast, and exchanged
broadsides with the escaping squadron. As the *Neptuno* was
considerably astern, and to leeward, of her consorts, they succeeded
in cutting her off; and, after they had engaged her closely for
upwards of an hour, they obliged her to strike, at about 5.10 P.M.

It has been seen how the *Royal Sovereign*, the leader of the
lee column, was relieved by the *Belleisle*, after having for a quarter
of an hour been engaged single-handed with several ships of the
enemy. Collingwood's flagship, which ultimately placed herself on
the *Santa Ana's* starboard bow, continued in close and steady
conflict with that ship until about 2.15 P.M., when, having lost
all her masts, and being unable to make further resistance, Alava's
flagship struck to the *Royal Sovereign*. The latter was by that
time scarcely less unmanageable than her late opponent, and was
not in a condition to take much further share in the action.

The *Belleisle*, her next astern, after having obliged the *Indomptable* to bear up,[1] became somewhat distantly engaged on the
starboard side with the *San Juan Nepomuceno*,[2] which, with other
vessels, had pressed up from the rear. At about 1 P.M., the
Fougueux intervened, and, with her port bow, ran on board the
Belleisle, nearly amidships on the starboard side. The two ships
briskly engaged one another for about twenty minutes, when, the
Mars also beginning to fire into her, the Frenchman dropped
astern and hauled to the northward. The *Belleisle* was then a
wreck. Ten minutes later the French *Achille* placed herself upon
the crippled ship's port quarter; and she, with the *Aigle*, far on the
Belleisle's starboard beam, and with the *San Leandro* and *San
Justo*, passing to rearward to join Gravina, and standing across
the British vessel's bows, continued the work of destruction.
Hargood was soon completely dismasted; and, owing to the mass
of spars and rigging that encumbered his port side, he was unable
to make any effectual reply to his nearest and most pertinacious
opponent. At about 2.30 P.M., moreover, the French *Neptune,*
placing herself athwart the *Belleisle's* starboard bow, had begun

---

[1] *See* p. 138.

[2] The name is doubtful, the *San Juan Nepomuceno* having been at the very rear of
the allied line; but the vessel was a Spanish 74.

to rake the devoted vessel; but at 3.15 P.M., the *Polyphemus* interposed on the starboard bow; at 3.20, the *Defiance* diverted the attention of the *Aigle*; and at 3.25, the British *Swiftsure,* passing under the *Belleisle's* stern, fired some terrible broadsides into the French *Achille,* the two British ships warmly cheering one another. The *Belleisle* was thus succoured in time. Though unable to take further active part in the fighting, she subsequently

CAPTAIN GEORGE DUFF, R.N., OF THE " MARS."

(*From the engraving by Ridley and Holl, after the portrait by Geroff.*)

sent her last remaining boat, under Mr. William Hudson, the Master, and Lieutenant John Owen, R.M., to take possession of the *Argonauta,* which had hauled down her colours, and lay not far off.

The *Mars* followed the *Belleisle* into action, and, while endeavouring to find an opening at which to pass through the hostile line, was engaged from astern by the *Pluton.* To avoid running into the *Santa Ana,* she was obliged to turn head to wind,

and so she exposed her stern to the fire of the *Monarca* and
Algésiras, which punished her severely, until the coming up of
the *Tonnant* took off their attention. Quite unmanageable, the
Mars paid off, and was further mauled by the *Fougueux*, and
again by the *Pluton*, one of whose shot carried off the head of
Captain Duff. When help arrived, the *Fougueux* made off to the
northward, and the *Pluton* stood S.E. in order to join Gravina.

The *Tonnant* made for the port bow of the *Algésiras*, but, that
ship backing, Captain Tyler ultimately cut the enemy's line astern
of the *Monarca*, which he raked. He then hauled up, and engaged
the Spaniard yard-arm to yard-arm. But the *Monarca* quickly
dropped astern, and at 1.7 P.M.,[1] struck her colours, though she
subsequently rehoisted them. At that time the *Algésiras* filled,
as if to cross the *Tonnant's* stern, but Captain Tyler, putting his
helm hard a-port, succeeded in running on board his opponent,
and in getting fast entangled on her port bow. The two ships
engaged one another furiously ; and the Frenchman did not strike
until she had made a very determined attempt to board. She
was taken possession of by Lieutenant Charles Bennett at about
2.15 P.M. ; and at 2.30 P.M., the *San Juan Nepomuceno*, which, for
some time previously, had suffered from the fire of the *Tonnant's*
foremost port guns, also surrendered. The boat sent to board her
was swamped, and Lieutenant Benjamin Clement was saved from
drowning only by the devotion of a negro seaman named
Macnamara. The *San Juan Nepomuceno*, which appears to have
rehoisted her colours when she found that she was not boarded,
was ultimately engaged and taken possession of by the *Dreadnought*. The only other service of the *Tonnant* seems to have
been the firing of a few rounds at Dumanoir's squadron when
it passed her to windward.

The *Bellerophon* was unable to cut the enemy's line until about
a quarter of an hour after the *Tonnant* had broken it. By that
time the *Monarca* had rehoisted her colours. Captain Cooke
passed under that ship's stern, and, at about 12.50 P.M., while
luffing up in order to lay her alongside, fouled the *Aigle*, which
was to leeward. The *Bellerophon* was thus closely engaged on
both sides, to port with the *Monarca* and to starboard with the
Aigle; and in a very short time she was also assailed by a Spanish
ship, which fired into her port quarter, by the French *Swiftsure*,

[1] Log of *Spartiate*.

which, from a somewhat greater distance, annoyed her starboard quarter, and by the *Bahama*, which was then so placed as to be able to rake her with a few forward guns from a point nearly astern. The result of all this was that soon after 1 P.M. the *Bellerophon* lost her main and mizen top-masts, the wreckage of which was quickly fired by the flashes from her own guns. About ten minutes later Captain Cooke fell. The situation was soon afterwards relieved somewhat by the appearance of the *Colossus*, which

CAPTAIN JOHN COOKE (1), R.N., OF THE " BELLEROPHON."
(From the engraving by James Fittler, A.R.A.)

engaged the French *Swiftsure* and the *Bahama*, and by the dropping astern of the Spanish vessel (supposed to be the *Montañez*) ; but the *Bellerophon* was still sorely pressed, until, at 1.40 P.M., the *Aigle*, after having made more than one fruitless attempt to board, broke away and dropped astern also, being raked as she went, first by the *Bellerophon* and afterwards by the *Revenge*. The *Bellerophon* was then entirely out of control ; but she still had sufficient fight in her to be able to oblige the *Monarca* to haul down her flag for the second time. Both the *Monarca* and the

Bahama, which had been reduced to submission by the *Colossus*, were taken possession of by parties from the dismantled British 74.

The *Colossus*, as she neared the enemy, made as if to pass astern of the French *Swiftsure*. The Frenchman, to avoid being raked, bore up ; and the *Colossus* ran past her starboard side, and presently found herself locked broadside to broadside with the *Argonaute*, which lay to leeward. Captain Morris's starboard battery had nearly silenced the Frenchman's port one within ten minutes, and the *Argonaute* seemed to be almost ready to strike, when the ships drifted apart. As the Frenchman paid off, however, she was well raked by her antagonist, which, during the whole period, had been steadily engaged also not only with the French *Swiftsure*, which lay on her port quarter, but also with the *Bahama*, which lay nearly on her port beam. Just before 3 P.M., the French *Swiftsure*, which had by that time forged so far ahead as to shut out the fire of the *Bahama*, and as to receive the full broadside of the *Colossus*, dropped astern, practically beaten, and once more exposed the *Bahama*. The *Colossus* quickly obliged the latter to surrender. In the meanwhile the French *Swiftsure* made a last effort, endeavouring to bear up under the *Colossus's* stern ; but Morris wore very smartly, escaped most of the fire that had been intended to rake him, and delivered his starboard broadside. Almost simultaneously the *Orion* poured another broadside into the Frenchman, whereupon the *Swiftsure* signified that she submitted. Both she and the *Bahama* were taken possession of by the *Colossus*, which had the distinction of having suffered more heavily in killed and wounded combined than any other British ship in the fleet.

The British *Achille*[1] followed the *Colossus* closely into action, and, passing astern of the *Montañez*, luffed up and engaged that ship from leeward. When, in about twelve minutes, the *Montañez* sheered off, the *Achille* headed for the *Belleisle*, which lay dismasted to leeward, seeming to be sorely pressed ; but on her way she fell in with the *Argonauta*. Captain King brought to on the Spaniard's port beam, and fought her at close quarters for an hour. The *Argonauta* then endeavoured to make sail, but, not being able to escape, shut her lower-deck ports, ceased firing, and, as was supposed, surrendered. Ere the British *Achille* could attempt to take possession of her, the French *Achille* passed her namesake and

---

[1] Also called *Achilles*, which was, indeed, her proper name, she being not a French prize, but a British-built ship, launched at Cleverley's yard, Gravesend, in 1798.

distracted her attention by firing into her; and the *Berwick*, which had already been distantly engaged with the *Defence*, interposed herself between the British *Achille* and her beaten opponent, the latter subsequently dropping to leeward. A hot action then began between the British *Achille* and the *Berwick ;* and, after more than an hour's fighting, the French ship hauled down her flag and was taken possession of.

At about 2 P.M., the *Dreadnought* got into action with the *San Juan Nepomuceno* ; and, although that ship was to some extent supported by the *Principe de Asturias*, another Spanish vessel, and the *Indomptable*,[1] she was run on board of and taken in little more than a quarter of an hour. It is but fair, therefore, to recall that she had previously been very severely handled by the *Tonnant*, *Bellerophon*, and others of the British lee column. The *Dreadnought* did not wait to take possession, but at once devoted her whole efforts to the subjection of the *Principe de Asturias*. That ship, however, ultimately made sail and got away.

The *Polyphemus* seems to have first encountered the French *Neptune*, and next the French *Achille*. She quitted the latter only when she saw a Union Jack being waved from the French ship's starboard cathead. The *Revenge*, in attempting to pass through the enemy's line and to place herself in an advantageous position athwart the hawse of the *Aigle*, fouled the latter's jib-boom, and, while the ships were interlocked, delivered a couple of broadsides into the Frenchman's bows. Then, standing on, she was in the act of hauling up on the port tack, when a tremendous fire was poured into her lee quarter by the *Principe de Asturias*. Three two-deckers[2] also hemmed her in, and greatly punished her until they were driven off by the approach of other British vessels. She consequently suffered severe damage.

The British *Swiftsure*, having, as already narrated, passed round the stern of the *Belleisle*,[3] began a warm action with the French *Achille*, and set her on fire. The *Defiance*, as she got into the confusion of the allied line, exchanged some shot with the *Principe de Asturias*, and, at about 3 P.M., ran alongside the *Aigle*, to which ship she lashed herself. The enemy was boarded, and appeared

---

[1] The name is perhaps doubtful.

[2] James says, " probably the *Neptune, Indomptable,* and *San Justo,* nearly fresh ships from the centre," iv. 75.

[3] *See* p. 151.

to be subdued ; but, after the boarding-party had hoisted British
colours over her, her people rallied and drove back their foes.
Captain Durham thereupon cut loose the lashings, and, sheering
off ten yards or so, opened so heavy a fire that, in about twenty
minutes, the *Aigle*, which in the meanwhile had gallantly defended
herself, asked for quarter, and was taken possession of. The
Defiance subsequently took possession of the *San Juan Nepomuceno*,
which had struck, as has been seen, to the *Dreadnought*.

The *Thunderer*, after first bearing up to afford relief to the
Revenge, wore across the bows of the *Principe de Asturias*, raked
that vessel, and brought to on the starboard tack. The French
Neptune presently attempted to succour the Spanish three-decker,

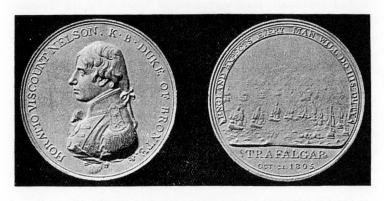

COMMEMORATIVE MEDAL OF THE VICTORY OFF TRAFALGAR.

(From an original lent by H.S.H. Prince Louis of Battenberg, R.N., G.C.B.)

but soon bore up in order to escape. The *Defence* engaged first the
Berwick, and, when that ship, which later encountered the British
Achille, hauled off, the *San Ildefonso*. The Spaniard struck after an
hour's action. The *Prince* directed her fire upon the *Principe de
Asturias* and the French *Achille ;* but, like some other ships of
the rear of the column, she got into action too late to have much
influence upon the fortunes of the day. Indeed, it was 4.30 P.M.
when the French *Achille* received the first broadside from the
British 98. At that time the Frenchman's fore top was in flames.
The *Prince's* broadside brought it down upon deck, and caused the
conflagration to extend to the unfortunate ship's hull. Other broadsides were discharged ere it was perceived that the French *Achille*
was doomed. Captain Grindall then ceased firing, wore, hove to,

and sent his boats to save as many as possible of the French crew. The British *Swiftsure* and the *Pickle* and *Entreprenante* made similar efforts ; but approach was dangerous, owing to the discharge of the burning vessel's guns as they became heated ; and at about 5.45 P.M., when the gallant French *Achille* blew up, most of her crew were, it is to be feared, still in her.   She had been well fought, but whether, as French historians would have it believed, she blew up with her colours still flying, must be doubted ; for it is certain that, earlier in the action, the *Polyphemus*, supposing her to have surrendered, spared her.

Before going further, it may be well to give a list of those officers who were killed and wounded in the British fleet in the course of this ever-glorious engagement.   The names of the commanding officers, and the total numbers of killed and wounded in each ship, have already been set forth in the table on page 131.   It would be pleasant, if space permitted, to chronicle the names of all the British officers whose exertions contributed to so memorable and pregnant a victory ; but it is only feasible to add the names, so far as can be ascertained, of the first Lieutenants to those of the officers who, on October 21st, 1805, perished, or shed their blood in the great struggle which gave to their country a truer mistress-ship of the seas than she had ever previously won, and which, from some points of view, must be regarded as the most decisive battle in the history of the world.

SHIPS AND FIRST LIEUTENANTS.	OFFICERS KILLED.	OFFICERS WOUNDED.
Victory. John Quilliam.[1]	Vice-Adm. V i s c o u n t Nelson, K.B. Lieut. William Ram. Capt. Charles William Adair, R.M. Mids. Robert Smith (1). Mids. Alexander Palmer. Adm.'s Secretary John Scott. Capt.'s Clerk Thomas Whipple.	Lieut. John Pasco. Lieut. George Miller Bligh. Lieut. Lewis Buckle Reeves, R.M. Lieut. James G. Peake, R.M. Mids. William Rivers. Mids. George Augustus Westphal. Mids. Richard Bulkeley. Agent Victualler's Clerk George Geoghehan.
Téméraire. Thomas Fortescue Kennedy.[2]	Capt. Simeon Busigny, R.M. Lieut. John Kingston, R.M. Mids. William Pitts. Carpenter Lewis Oades.	Lieut. James Mould. Lieut. Samuel J. Payne. Master's Mate Francis Swaine Price. Mids. John Eastman. Boatswain John Brooks.

[1] Posted, 24-12-1805.   [2] Commander, 24-12-1805.

Ships and First Lieutenants.	Officers Killed.	Officers Wounded.
Neptune. George Acklom.[2]		Capt.'s Clerk Richard Hurrell.
Leviathan. Eyles Mounsher.[2]		Mids. J. W. Watson.
Britannia. Arthur Atchison.[2]	Lieut. Francis Roskruge.	Master Stephen Trounce. Mids. William Grint.
Conqueror. Robert Lloyd(3), killed. James Couch, 2nd.[3]	Lieut. Robert Lloyd. Lieut. William M. St. George.	Lieut. Thomas Wearing, R.M. Lieut. Philip Mendel, Imp. Russ. Navy.
Africa. John Smith (5).[2]		Lieut. Matthew Hay (actg.). Capt. James Tynmore, R.M. Master's Mate Henry West. Master's Mate Abraham Turner. Mids. Frederick White. Mids. Philip James Elmhurst. Mids. John P. Bailey.
Agamemnon. Hugh Cook.[4]		
Ajax. Jeremiah Brown.		
Orion. John Croft.[2]		Mids. Charles Tause. Mids. Charles P. Cable.
Minotaur. James Stuart (1).[2]		Mids. John Samuel Smith, Boatswain James Robinson.
Spartiate. John M'Kerlie.[2]		Mids. Henry Bellairs. Mids. Edward Knapman. Boatswain John Clarke.
Royal Sovereign. John Ellis (2).[5]	Lieut. Brice Gilliland. Master William Chalmers. Second Lieut. Robert Green, R.M. Mids. John Aikenhead. Mids. Thomas Braund.	Lieut. John Clavell (1). Lieut. James Bashford. Second Lieut. James Le Vesconte, R.M. Master's Mate William Watson (2). Mids. Gilbert Kennicott. Mids. Granville Thompson. Mids. John Farrant. Mids. John Campbell (3a). Boatswain Isaac Wilkinson.

[2] Commander, 24–12–1805.   [3] Commander, 6–9–1817.
[4] Commander, 24–12–1805, but remained as Lieutenant till posted, 31–7–1806.   [5] Commander, 22–1–1806.

Ships and First Lieutenants.	Officers Killed.	Officers Wounded.
Belleisle. 　Thomas Fife.[2]	Lieut. Ebenezer Geall. Lieut. John Woodin. Mids. George Nind.	Lieut. William Ferrie. Lieut. John Owen, R.M. Master's Mate William Henry Pearson. Master's Mate William Cutfield. Mids. Samuel Jago. Boatswain Andrew Gibson. First-Class Vol. J. T. Hodge.
Mars. 　William Hennah, succeeded to command.[1] 　Benjamin Patey.	Captain George Duff. Master's Mate Alexander Duff. Mids. Edward Corbyn. Mids. Henry Morgan.	Lieut. Edward William Garrett. Lieut. James Black. Master Thomas Cook. Capt. Thomas Norman, R.M. Mids. John Young (2). Mids. George Guerin. Mids. William John Cook. Mids. John Jenkins. Mids. Alfred Luckraft.
Tonnant. 　John Bedford.[2]	Mids. William Brown (3a).	Captain Charles Tyler (1). Master's Mate Henry Ready. Boatswain Richard Little. Capt.'s Clerk William Allen.
Bellerophon. 　William Pryce Cumby, succeeded to command.[1] 　Edward Funning Thomas.[3]	Captain John Cooke (1). Master Edward Overton. Mids. John Simmons.	Capt. James Wemyss, R.M. Master's Mate Edward Hartley. Mids. William Nunn Jewell. Mids. James Stone (2). Mids. Thomas Bant. Mids. George Pearson (1). Boatswain Thomas Robinson.
Colossus. 　Thomas Richard Toker.[2]	Master Thomas Scriven.	Captain James Nicoll Morris. Lieut. George Bulley. Lieut. William Forster (2) (actg.). Lieut. John Benson, R.M. Master's Mate Henry Milbanke. Mids. William Allan Herringham. Mids. Frederick Thistlewayte. Mids. Thomas G. Reece. Mids. Henry Snellgrove. Mids. Rawdon Maclean. Mids. George Wharrie. Mids. Timothy Renou. Mids. George Denton. [son. Boatswain William Adam-

---

[1] Posted, 1–1–1806.　　　[2] Commander, 24–12–1805.　　　[3] Retired Commander, 15–12–1830.

Ships and First Lieutenants.	Officers Killed.	Officers Wounded.
Achille. William Westcott Daniel.[1]	Mids. Francis John Mugg.	Lieut. Parkins Prynn. Lieut. Josias Bray. Capt. Palmes Westropp, R.M. Lieut. William Leddon, R.M. Master's Mate George Pegge. Mids. William H. Staines. Mids. William J. Snow. First-Class Vol. William Smith Warren.
Dreadnought.		Lieut. James L. Lloyd. Mids. Andrew M'Culloch. Mids. James Sabben.
Polyphemus. George Moubray.[1]		
Revenge. Lewis Hole.[1]	Mids. Thomas Grier. Mids. Edward F. Brooks.	Captain Robert Moorsom. Lieut. John Berry. Master Luke Brokenshaw. Capt. Peter Lely, R.M.
Swiftsure. James Lilburn.[1]		Mids. Alexander Bell Handcock.
Defiance. William Hellard.[1]	Lieut. Thomas Simens. Mids. James Williamson. Boatswain William Forster.	Captain Philip Charles Durham. Master's Mate James Spratt. Master's Mate Robert Browne. Mids. John Hodge. Mids. Edmund Andrew Chapman.
Thunderer. John Clark (2).[2]		Master's Mate John Coxetter Snell. Mids. Alexander Galloway.
Defence. James Green.[1]		
Prince. William Godfrey.[1]		

1 Commander, 24–12–1805.   2 Retired Commander, 23–10–1837.

Many of the British ships suffered severe material damage. The *Belleisle* lost all three masts and bowsprit; the *Royal Sovereign* lost main and mizen; the *Tonnant* lost all three topmasts; and the *Victory, Téméraire, Leviathan, Conqueror, Africa, Orion, Minotaur, Mars, Bellerophon, Colossus, Dreadnought,* and *Swiftsure* had a

larger or smaller number of important spars shot away or irretriev-
ably injured. It has been seen that thirty-three allied ships of the
line went into action. When the battle ceased, seventeen of these
had been taken, and one had caught fire and blown up.[1] Of the
remainder, four ships,[2] under Dumanoir, having hauled to the
southward, had got away for the time, though they never again
entered a French port ; and eleven, under Gravina, had run to the
north-east. Some of the latter were very little the worse, having
scarcely been in action ; but others, more or less dismasted, were
in tow of the frigates. All Gravina's division anchored, nevertheless,
in the course of the night about a mile and a half from Rota, the
state of the wind [3] preventing them from entering Cadiz.

When, at 6 P.M., Vice-Admiral Collingwood, who had succeeded
to the command-in-chief, shifted his flag from the much-damaged
Royal Sovereign to the *Euryalus*, which subsequently took the
Royal Sovereign in tow and stood off shore, the situation was as
follows. Of the seventeen prizes, eight were entirely and nine were
partially dismasted ; and of the twenty-seven British ships of the
line, half were, comparatively speaking, unseaworthy for the
moment. The fleet was in about thirteen fathoms of water ; the
wind blew with moderate but increasing strength from W.S.W.,
or dead on shore ; there was a nasty swell which greatly distressed
the crippled vessels ; and, only six or seven miles to leeward, lay
the shoals of Trafalgar. Collingwood had ignored Nelson's dying
wish that the fleet should be anchored. At 9 P.M., however, he
ordered his ships to prepare to anchor ; but, the wind veering
towards midnight to S.S.W., and freshening, he signalled to them
to wear with their heads to the westward. With the exception of
four vessels [4] which had previously anchored off Cape Trafalgar, the
whole command obeyed this order and drifted seaward. It has been
urged that many of the vessels which did not anchor were in no
condition to do so, their anchors having been lost or their cables
having been cut to pieces ; but it is certain that some could have held
the ground, and it is more than probable that, had they anchored,
their fate would have been better than that which actually overtook
them ; seeing that all those vessels which did anchor fared well.

---

[1] *See* table on p. 131.

[2] *Formidable, Duguay Trouin, Mont Blanc*, and *Scipion*. All of these were
taken on Nov. 3rd by Sir R. J. Strachan.

[3] In shore it blew from S.S.E. ; in the offing, from W.S.W.

[4] *Defence, San Ildefonso, Bahama*, and French *Swiftsure*.

VOL. V.   M

On the 22nd, the *Neptune*, instead of the *Euryalus*, took the *Royal Sovereign* in tow, and Collingwood issued a general order expressing his thanks to the fleet, and another, directing a day to be set apart for the thanksgiving to God for the victory. The wind, blowing fresh from the south, was squally; but most of the prizes were then under way under sail or were being steadily towed to the westward, to make the appointed rendezvous near the *Royal Sovereign*. At about 5 P.M., however, the *Redoutable*, then in tow of the British *Swiftsure*, signalled that she was in distress. As many as possible of her people were taken off; but, at 10.30 P.M., when she was half under water, the *Swiftsure* had to cut her loose and abandon her for the night. At about 12 P.M., the wind, then blowing with the force of a gale, shifted to N.W. Early on the following morning, more of the *Redoutable's* people were picked up; but many, together with eighteen British seamen, unhappily perished when the ship sank. In consequence of the same gale, the *Fougueux* drove ashore near Torre Bermeja, and became a total wreck, with the loss of all on board save about twenty-five persons; and the *Algésiras*[1] was retaken by her crew, who had been humanely allowed on deck when the ship appeared to be in danger, and was carried into Cadiz. The *Bucentaure*,[2] moreover, was wrecked on the Puercos, after she had been recaptured by her ship's company.

The N.W. wind which blew on the morning of the 23rd, induced Commodore de Cosmao-Kerjulien, the senior French officer[3] in Cadiz, to put to sea with the object of picking up some of the unmanageable prizes. He weighed with his own ship, the *Pluton*, 74, and with the *Indomptable*, 80, *Neptune*, 84, *Rayo*, 100, and *San Francisco de Asis*, 74, and with the five frigates and two brigs which had been present at the battle. Soon after he had made an offing, the wind veered to W.S.W. and blew harder than ever. At noon he found himself near the British ships, ten of which, casting off the vessels in tow, formed line and prepared to protect their prizes. With an unfavourable wind, M. Cosmao did

---

[1] Lieut. Charles Bennett, in command.

[2] Lieut. Richard Spear, in command.

[3] Adm. Gravina, being mortally wounded, could not take command. Julien Marie, Baron de Cosmao-Kerjulien, was born in 1761. In 1805, in command of the *Pluton*, he captured the Diamond Rock, and rendered the services here narrated. He was, in consequence, promoted to be a rear-admiral and made a grandee of Spain. He quitted the navy at the restoration in 1815, and died in 1825.

not venture to attack so formidable a force; but his frigates managed to cut off and retake the *Neptuno* and the *Santa Ana.* On the following day, however, the *Indomptable,* having grounded off Rota, went to pieces; the *San Francisco de Asis* went ashore in Cadiz Bay; and the *Rayo,* anchored off San Lucar to escape going ashore, rolled away her masts, and surrendered to the *Donegal,* Captain Pulteney Malcolm, which had returned [1] a few hours earlier from Gibraltar.[2] The *Rayo,* however, went ashore and was wrecked on the 26th. The rough weather of the night of the 24th also caused the loss of another prize, the *Monarca;* the *Santisima Trinidad* had been scuttled by Collingwood's order on the 24th; the *Aigle* was wrecked off Puerto Santa Maria on the night of the 25th; and between the 28th and the 30th the *Intrépide* and *San Agustin* were burnt as useless, the *Argonauta* was scuttled, it being deemed almost impossible to save her, and the *Berwick* struck and went to pieces off San Lucar.[3] Thus, of the numerous prizes only four remained, namely, the *San Ildefonso,* the French *Swiftsure,* and the *Bahama,* which had anchored after the battle, and the *San Juan Nepomuceno.*

On October 30th, the Commander-in-Chief was . rejoined off Cadiz by Rear-Admiral Thomas Louis, in the *Canopus,* 80, Captain Francis William Austen (1), with the *Queen,* 98, Captain Francis Pender, *Spencer,* 74, Captain the Hon. Robert Stopford, and *Tigre,* 74, Captain Benjamin Hallowell, which had been detached [4] by Nelson on the 2nd. On the following day Collingwood transferred his flag to the *Queen.* In the meantime, the *Victory,* towed by the *Neptune,* had proceeded to Gibraltar, where she arrived on October 28th, and where she partially refitted. On November 3rd she sailed for England, and on December 4th she anchored at St. Helen's, still bearing the Vice-Admiral's flag, but flying it at half-mast. The body of the dead seaman, preserved in spirits, was on board the ship with which his fame had been imperishably associated; but, as preparations for its fitting reception on shore

---

[1] The *Donegal* joined on the 24th. The *Melpomene* had joined on the 22nd, and the *Eurydice* and *Scout* on the 23rd.

[2] *See* p. 128.

[3] An excellent account, based upon documentary evidence, of the experiences of some of the prizes after the battle, may be found in a work, ostensibly a novel, by Don Perez Galdós, a summary of which, by the Author, was printed in the *Cornhill Magazine* of Oct., 1896. *See also* Chevalier, 218, *et seq.*

[4] *See* p. 126.

could not at once be completed, the *Victory* remained off the Isle of
Wight until the 10th.   On the 22nd, being then at the mouth
of the Thames, she was boarded by the *Chatham*, the official yacht
of Captain the Hon. George Grey, then Commissioner at Sheerness.
To this little craft was solemnly transferred the corpse, enclosed
in the coffin which had been made, by order of Captain Benjamin
Hallowell, out of part of the mainmast of the *Orient*, after the
battle of the Nile, and which had been presented to Nelson on
May 23rd, 1799.   A second coffin, of lead, covered the whole.   As
the body was lowered into the yacht, the Vice-Admiral's flag was
struck in the *Victory*, and hoisted at half-mast in the *Chatham*,
which presently passed up the river to Greenwich, where she

COMMEMORATIVE MEDAL OF THE DEATH OF NELSON.

(From an original lent by H.S.H. Captain Prince Louis of Battenberg, R.N., G.C.B.

anchored on the afternoon of December 24th.   At 7 P.M. that
evening the coffin was conveyed to Greenwich Hospital, where it
afterwards lay in state.   On January 8th, with great and impressive
ceremony, it was taken in a state barge, rowed by sixteen seamen
of the *Victory*, to Whitehall stairs, where it was landed, and whence
it was carried to the Captains' Room at the Admiralty.   It remained
there during the following night; and, on January 9th, amid
universal demonstrations of mourning, and with every testimony
of gratitude and love that could be paid by the nation to its hero's
memory, it was borne to St. Paul's Cathedral.[1]

[1] For a full account of the whole ceremony, *see* Campbell's ‘Lives’ (Ed. 1817), viii.
126, 144; *Gentleman's Mag.*, Jan. 1806; *Naval Chronicle*, xv. 45; Clarke and
M‘Arthur, ii. 460, etc.

In his dispatch[1] announcing the victory Collingwood wrote
thus feelingly of the blow which he and his country had suffered
in the death of Nelson :—

"I have not only," he said, "to lament, in common with the British Navy and
the British nation, in the fall of the Commander-in-Chief, the loss of a hero whose
name will be immortal, and his memory ever dear to his country; but my heart
is rent with the most poignant grief for the death of a friend, to whom, by many
years' intimacy and a perfect knowledge of the virtues of his mind, which inspired
ideas superior to the common race of men, I was bound by the strongest ties of
affection; a grief to which even the glorious occasion in which he fell does not bring
the consolation which perhaps it ought."

The country, it is true, had suffered a terrible and, indeed, an
irreparable loss.   Nelson, in his profession, stood head and shoulders
above any of his contemporaries, in spite of the fact that among
those contemporaries were many seamen such as Britain had rarely
had at her disposal in earlier times.   But the loss, though so severe,
was not untimely.   Nelson did not die until he had completed his
work.   The victory at Trafalgar assured not only the eventual
collapse of the Napoleonic system, but also the immediate maritime
supremacy of Great Britain; and, had Nelson survived Trafalgar,
there would have been but little scope for his marvellous energy,
his religious devotion to duty, and his wonderful military genius.
Eminently enviable and eminently appropriate, therefore, was the
fall of such a man at the instant when, having surpassed all his
predecessors, he had placed his country in so strong a position that
he ceased to be necessary to her.   The surgeons who, after his
death, examined his body, decided that, although he had worn
himself to a shadow in the service of the flag, he still preserved
a constitution which might have carried him to a green old age.
We know that men, born no later than he, lived to see the
outbreak of the Crimean War.   Yet surely a venerable Nelson
would be a memory far more sad than a Nelson, smitten in
his prime, but with his life's work well done, breathing his last
breath in the moment of his unexampled triumph.   Nor should it
be forgotten that the hero was compact of weakness as well as of
strength.   In action he was brilliant; in inactivity he was almost

---

[1] Collingwood's dispatches, and especially those of Oct. 22nd, Oct. 24th, Oct. 28th,
and Nov. 4th, 1805, dealing with Trafalgar, have often been admired as models of
what such documents should be; yet it should be noted that they are full of
inaccuracies, many of which are exposed by Mr. James.   To specify them here is,
however, impossible, owing to lack of space.

sordid.   Neither his education[1] nor his tastes fitted him to shine in
civil life.   His true greatness was all inspired by the scent of the
sea, by the needs of his country, and by the presence of the enemy.
If he had lived for many years after Trafalgar, we may be sure
that his memory would be less pleasant than it is, and that his
glory would be no greater.

The Vice-Admiral had no issue by his wife, Frances Herbert,[2]

HORATIA.

(*From a miniature in the possession of her daughter-in-law, Mrs. Nelson Ward.*)

whom he had married at Nevis in 1787.   His honours, therefore,
devolved upon his eldest surviving brother, the Rev. William Nelson,
who, quite undeservedly, was, in addition, made an Earl, granted
a pension of £6000 a year, and presented with £108,000 for the

---

[1] "The hero of the Nile, who fell at Trafalgar, was a man of great mind, but self-
taught: Lord Collingwood, the old companion in arms of the immortal Nelson, was
equally great in judgment and abilities, but had also the advantage of an excellent
education."   Duke of Clarence to Lady Collingwood, 1810, in 'Corr. and Mem. of
Collingwood.'

[2] Widow of Dr. Nisbet.

purchase of an estate.[1] To each of Nelson's surviving sisters, Susannah, wife of Mr. Thomas Bolton,[2] and Catherine, wife of Mr. George Matcham,[3] a sum of £10,000 was voted; and to Lady Nelson[4] an annuity of £2000 was assigned. Nelson had commended to the care of his country Lady Hamilton and his natural daughter, Horatia. It was deemed impolitic on the part of the government to take any public notice of this commendation; and

ADMIRAL THE RT. HON. WILLIAM, EARL OF NORTHESK, K.B.
(*From the engraving by Ridley and Holl,* 1806.)

Lady Hamilton, who, had she been less improvident, might have lived very comfortably on the income which her husband and Nelson had assured for her, fell into poverty ere her death in 1815. Horatia[5] is believed to have received some very slight and indirect recognition of her father's great services from the government of

---

[1] Earl Nelson died in 1835, and was succeeded by Thomas, son of Mrs. Bolton.
[2] Mrs. Bolton died in 1813.
[3] Mrs. Matcham died in 1842.
[4] Lady Nelson died in 1831.
[5] Horatia, born Jan. 30th, 1801; died at Pinner, Middlesex, 1881.

a later day. She married a clergyman ; her sons entered the public services ; and in her numerous descendants runs the only blood which now represents the hero of the Nile, Copenhagen, and Trafalgar.

The surviving sharers in the victory received the unanimous thanks of both Houses of Parliament. Collingwood was made a peer of the United Kingdom, with the title of Baron Collingwood of Caldburne and Hethpoole, and was granted a pension of £2000 a year. Lord Northesk was made a K.B. ; and Captain Hardy, of the *Victory*, was created a Baronet. All the Flag-Officers and Captains who had been present received gold medals. The first Lieutenant of the *Victory*, the Lieutenants acting as Captains of the *Ajax* and *Thunderer*, and the first Lieutenants of the *Mars* and *Bellerophon*, whose Captains had fallen in the action, were made Post-Captains ; and the signal, second, third, and fourth Lieutenants of the *Victory*,[1] the first and second Lieutenants of the *Royal Sovereign*,[2] and the first Lieutenants of all the other ships [3] engaged, were made Commanders. In addition, four Midshipmen of the *Victory*, three of the *Royal Sovereign*, two of the *Britannia*, and one of each other ship and frigate present were promoted to be Lieutenants. Lieutenant La Penotière, of the *Pickle,* who carried home Collingwood's dispatches, was made a Commander immediately after his arrival in England. The patriotism of private societies and individuals conferred numerous other rewards upon those who had been engaged. A medal also was struck and presented, by permission, to seamen and Marines as well as to officers, by Mr. M. Boulton, of the Soho Ironworks ; though no government medal for Trafalgar was awarded to any officers of less than post-rank, or to any seamen or Royal Marines, until 1849, in pursuance of a *Gazette* notice of June 1st, 1847.

Lord Collingwood, who was continued in the chief command of the Mediterranean fleet, remained to watch the enemy's fleet in Cadiz ; but that fleet did not venture to sea. On October 25th, Vice-Admiral François Etienne Rosily arrived from Paris by way of Madrid to supersede Vice-Admiral Villeneuve, who, however, had been taken prisoner in the battle. Villeneuve was released on

---

[1] John Pasco, Edward Williams (2), Andrew King, and John Yule, (all Dec. 24, 1805).

[2] John Ellis (2), Jan. 22, 1806, and William Stephens, (latter not till Jan. 4, 1803).

[3] *See* pp. 157–160. Possibly the exceptions, if there were any—and there seem to have been some—were accidental. It is most difficult to ascertain all the facts.

parole, and landed at Morlaix on April 22nd, 1806. A few days later he was staying at an hotel in Rennes, awaiting Napoleon's directions concerning his future movements. One morning he was found dead in his room, stabbed, so it was said, in five places; and it was alleged that he had perished by his own hand. It was, however, very widely believed among his friends that he had been assassinated; and it is noteworthy that Napoleon, when at St. Helena years afterwards, saw fit, not only to describe in detail how Villeneuve had killed himself, but also to assert that the unfortunate seaman had deliberately disobeyed him.

"Villeneuve," said Napoleon, "when prisoner in England, was so much affected by his defeat that he studied anatomy with a view to taking his own life. To that end, he purchased several anatomical engravings of the heart, and compared them with his own body in order to make certain of the exact position of that organ. Upon his arrival in France, I ordered him to remain at Rennes, and not to come to Paris. Villeneuve, fearing to be convicted by a council of war of having disobeyed my orders, and of having lost the fleet in consequence (for I had directed him not to put to sea, and not to engage the English), determined to put an end to himself. He took his engravings of the heart, again compared them with his breast, made a deep prick with a long pin in the centre of the picture, and then, applying the same pin as nearly as possible to the corresponding place in his own body, drove it in up to the head, pierced his heart, and so died. When they opened his room they found him dead, the pin being in his breast, and the mark on the picture corresponding with the wound on his body. He should not have acted in that way. He was a gallant man, although he had no talent." [1]

This tale is scarcely of a nature to disarm suspicion. The truth, however, can now never be known. Villeneuve, in spite of Napoleon's professed opinion of his gallantry, was, it is certain, buried without honours.

The story of Trafalgar must be completed with an account of the fate which befel Rear-Admiral Dumanoir Le Pelley, and the four ships with which he escaped to the southward, after the battle of October 21st. He would have made for Toulon had he not known that Rear-Admiral Thomas Louis, with several sail of the line, was in the neighbourhood of Gibraltar. He ultimately decided, therefore, to endeavour to reach one of the French Atlantic ports.

It should be explained that the French Rochefort squadron,[2] under Rear-Admiral Allemand, which had quitted its port in the previous July, was still at sea, playing havoc with British commerce, and that several British squadrons, and scores of British cruisers, were looking for it. At the end of October, the *Phœnix*, 36, Captain

[1] 'Méms. du Dr. O'Mear   [2] *See* pp. 118, 120.

Thomas Baker (1), while making, with sealed orders, for a given rendezvous westward of Scilly, learnt from some neutrals that a squadron, supposed to be Allemand's, had been sighted in the Bay of Biscay. Baker took upon himself the responsibility of prematurely opening his orders, and, finding that they were of no great importance, went in search of the enemy. On November 2nd, being in the latitude of Cape Finisterre, he sighted and chased four large ships; and, when he in turn was chased, he steered south, to carry his intelligence to Captain Sir Richard John Strachan, who was cruising off Ferrol,[1] and into whose hands he hoped to lead the foe. In the afternoon Baker sighted four other large ships to the southward; and a little later the vessels which had been chasing him hauled their wind. The *Phœnix* hauled up to keep in sight the latter, which presently wore and stood to the eastward; whereupon the frigate stood again S.S.E. and strove to attract the attention of the other ships, which she believed to be British.

Baker had discovered Dumanoir's squadron, which, at about the same time, had also been sighted and chased by the *Boadicea*, 38, Captain John Maitland (2), and the *Dryad*, 36, Captain Adam Drummond. At 8.45 P.M. on November 2nd, the *Phœnix* saw these vessels; and at 9.30 P.M., these vessels saw the four ships which the *Phœnix* had previously observed to the southward, and which, with three others not far from them, proved to be Strachan's command. The *Boadicea* and *Dryad*, not succeeding in getting any answer to their signals, became suspicious, and, at about 10.30 P.M., tacked to the N.E. and were soon out of sight; but the *Phœnix*, at 11 P.M., though first fired at, hailed the *Cæsar* and informed Strachan that four ships of the enemy were not far away on his lee bow. The British squadron being much scattered, Strachan directed Baker to make sail and hasten forward the stragglers, and himself bore away in chase with a W.N.W. wind. He soon discovered the enemy crowding sail in the E.N.E., and bearing away. At 1.30 A.M. on November 3rd, the moon set, and, the weather being thick and dirty, the French were lost sight of. Strachan, therefore, shortened sail to wait for the ships astern of him; and, at 9 A.M.,[2] he again saw the French in the N.N.E. He had then with him three ships of the line besides his own, together

---

[1] Having been detached from the Channel fleet on October 29th, to look for the Rochefort squadron.

[2] At 7.30 A.M., Cape Ortegal bore S.E. ½ E., distant 36 miles.

with the *Santa Margarita*, 36; and he instantly chased with all possible sail set, the wind having then veered to W.S.W. The forces in presence of one another were:—

BRITISH.				FRENCH.		
Ships.	Guns.	Commanders.	Ships.	Guns.	Commanders.	
Cæsar	80	Capt. Sir Richard John Strachan, Bt.	*Duguay Trouin* .	74	Capt. Claude Touffet.	
Hero	74	Capt. Hon. Alan Hyde Gardner.	*Formidable* . .	80 [3]	Rear-Adm. P. R. M. E. Dumanoir Le Pelley. Capt. J. M. Letellier.	
Courageux . .	74	Capt. Richard Lee.	*Mont Blanc* . .	74	Capt. J. G. N. Le Villegris.	
Namur . . .	74	Capt. Lawrence William Halsted.	*Scipion* . . .	74	Capt. Charles Bellanger.[4]	
Bellona[1] . . .	74	Capt. Charles Dudley Pater.				
Santa Margarita	36	Capt. Wilson Rathborne.				
Æolus . . .	32	Capt. Lord William Fitzroy.				
Phœnix[2] . . .	36	Capt. Thomas Baker (1).				
Révolutionnaire[2]	38	Capt. Hon. Henry Hotham.				

[1] Parted company before the action.   [2] Not of Strachan's squadron. Present accidentally.
[3] The *Formidable* had had three guns dismounted at Trafalgar, and had thrown overboard twelve of her quarter-deck 12-prs. during the chase ; so that she had but 65 guns mounted. Chevalier says only 60.
[4] Chevalier calls him sometimes Bellanger and sometimes Berrenger.

At noon, when the wind blew strong from S.S.W., the French were about fourteen miles distant; at about 3 P.M., the *Santa Margarita*, and, later, the *Phœnix*, well ahead of their consorts, began to draw up with the enemy's rear. In the afternoon, on the other hand, the *Bellona* unfortunately parted company, owing to her inferior sailing. By dawn on November 4th, when there was a moderate breeze from S.E., the leading British ship of the line was but about six miles astern of the rearmost Frenchman, the *Scipion*, which, earlier in the morning, had exchanged shot with the *Santa Margarita*, and subsequently with the *Phœnix* also, and which was thenceforward continually harassed by the frigates. Soon afterwards, the *Cæsar*, *Hero*, and *Courageux* formed in line ahead, and aided by a shift of wind to S.S.E., began to approach so rapidly that, at 11.45 A.M., realising that he could not avoid an action, Dumanoir Le Pelley ordered his ships to take in their small sails, and to haul up together on the starboard tack with their heads to N.E. by E. After having obeyed this signal the French ships formed line ahead in the order given in the above table, the *Scipion* bearing S. by W. from the *Cæsar*, distant a little more than a mile. Both the *Namur* and the *Révolutionnaire*, though they had much improved their positions, were still considerably astern of their consorts, the one bearing S.W., distant fourteen miles, and the other bearing W.S.W., distant seven miles, from the *Cæsar*.

Strachan informed Gardner and Lee that he purposed to attack the centre and rear of the French ; and, at about noon, the three

British ships edged away for the three rearmost of the French ones, the *Cæsar* seeking the *Formidable*, the *Hero* the *Mont Blanc*, and the *Courageux* the *Scipion*. At 12.15 P.M., the *Cæsar*, and shortly afterwards the other ships, opened fire on the port hand, and, the French replying, a warm action began. At about 12.55 P.M., five minutes after Strachan had hoisted his signal for close action, the *Duguay Trouin* luffed up as if to cross the *Cæsar's* bows and rake her from ahead ; but the latter, luffing up also, avoided the danger ; and, the *Duguay Trouin* having gone in stays, both the two leading British ships were able to handle her very severely at close range. The *Formidable*, *Mont Blanc*, and *Scipion* tacked in support of the

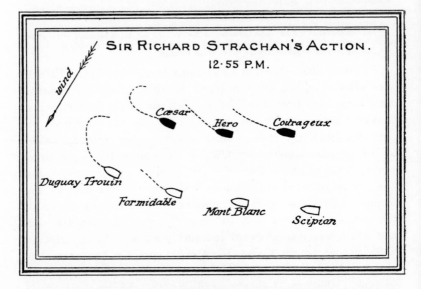

Duguay Trouin, but, in the course of the manœuvre, the French flagship, being somewhat crippled aloft, lost her place in the line and became second instead of third. The French, however, got round on the port tack ; and at 1.20 P.M. the British wore or tacked in chase. The *Cæsar* made but bad progress ; and, seeing that the *Namur* was then on the weather bow of the French, Strachan, at 1.40 P.M., signalled to her to attack the enemy's van, and, to the *Hero*, to lead on the port tack. So impatient was Sir Richard that he presently enforced the order to the *Namur*, with two shotted guns. A little before 2 P.M., the action was recommenced by the *Hero*, which fired her starboard battery into the *Scipion* with such good effect as to bring down the latter's main top-mast and to cause her to fall to leeward, where she was quickly engaged by the *Courageux*, from windward, and by the *Phœnix* and *Révolutionnaire*, then newly come up, from leeward. The *Hero* by that time, having placed herself on the *Formidable's* weather beam, gradually fore-reached her, until she gained a place on the French flagship's port bow. At 2.45 P.M., the *Namur*, arriving astern of the *Hero*, also engaged the *Formidable*, whereupon the *Hero* made sail to close with the *Mont Blanc*. At 3.5 P.M., when the *Cæsar*, having refitted, was about to open fire on her, the *Formidable* struck, and was taken possession of by the *Namur*; at 3.10 P.M., the *Scipion* also struck,

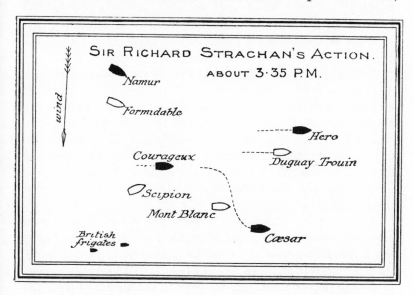

just as the *Duguay Trouin* and *Mont Blanc* were then bearing up to form a fresh line ahead of her. She was taken possession of by the frigates. It was then obvious to the French that the day was hopelessly lost; and the *Duguay Trouin* and *Mont Blanc* endeavoured to escape. But they were quickly overhauled by the *Hero* and *Cæsar*; and, after a hot cannonade which lasted for twenty minutes, both of them struck, at about 3.35 P.M.

The losses on the British side were: *Cæsar*, 4 killed, 25 wounded; *Hero*, 10 killed, 51 wounded; *Courageux*, 1 killed, 13 wounded; *Namur*, 4 killed, 8 wounded; *Santa Margarita*, 1 killed, 1 wounded; *Révolutionnaire*, 2 killed, 6 wounded; *Phœnix*, 2 killed,

4 wounded ; *Æolus*, 3 wounded : total 24 killed, 111 wounded. The officers killed were Second Lieutenant Robert Morrison, R.M. (*Hero*), and Boatswain Thomas Edwards (*Santa Margarita*). The officers wounded were: Lieutenants John Skekel (*Hero*), Robert Clephane (*Courageux*), and Thomas Osborne (*Namur*) ; Captain William Clements, R.M. (*Namur*) ; Second Lieutenant Cornelius James Stevenson, R.M. (*Hero*) ; Midshipmen John Gibbs Bird (*Courageux*), and Frederick Beasley (*Namur*) ; Master's Mate Thomas Daws (*Courageux*) ; Purser Thomas Titterton (*Hero*), and Gunner John Austin (*Courageux*). The *Hero* and the *Cæsar* had suffered most severely aloft. The French ships lost seven hundred and fifty killed and wounded, including among the killed M. Touffet, captain of the *Duguay Trouin*, and among the wounded M. Dumanoir Le Pelley, and M. Bellanger, captain of the *Scipion* ; and all of them had been terribly mauled.[1]

Such was this creditable pendant to the great battle of Trafalgar. A court of inquiry, which, however, was not held until 1809, censured Dumanoir Le Pelley's tactics. In consequence, the rear-admiral demanded a court-martial, and by it he was honourably acquitted. It may still, however, be asked : why did he not, on the day before the action, or even early on the 4th, tack with his four sail of the line, and fall upon the three British sail of the line, which, with the three frigates, were the only vessels then threatening him ?

The four prizes were carried to Plymouth, and all of them were eventually added to the Royal Navy, the *Formidable* as the *Brave*, the *Duguay Trouin* as the *Implacable*, and the other two under their original names. The *Implacable* still (1900) survives as part of the training establishment for boys at Devonport. She is the last of the numerous prizes of the Napoleonic war, and, except the *Victory*, the sole survivor of Trafalgar. For his conduct Strachan, who became a Rear-Admiral on November 9th, was made a K.B. on January 29th, 1806 ; and both he and his officers and men received the thanks of Parliament. Each of the Captains engaged was also presented with a gold medal ; and the first Lieutenants of the ships of the line were [2] promoted.

---

[1] Strachan to Marsden, Nov. 4th, 1805 : ditto, Nov. 8th. Chevalier, 233.

[2] John Thompson (3), of the *Namur*, Robert Clephane, of the *Courageux*, Alexander Cunningham (2), of the *Hero*, and Benjamin Crispin, of the *Cæsar*, were made Commanders on Dec. 24th, 1805.

Napoleon's plans for the invasion of the United Kingdom were doomed when the allied fleets put into Ferrol; and they were finally and hopelessly shattered by the results of Trafalgar and of Strachan's action. When news of Villeneuve's presence at Ferrol reached him, about the second week in August, the Emperor, apprehensive that the allies would be blockaded in that port, prepared to utilise for the marvellous central European campaign of Austerlitz the army which he had assembled against Great Britain. By August 23rd, Napoleon had learnt [1] that the allies had put to sea again; and, hoping that they were heading for Brest and the Channel, he once more, for a brief space, turned to the scheme of invasion, and warned Marmont,[2] in Holland, to be ready to play his part in it, but to be ready also, in case of miscarriage of the fleet, to march inland. A few days later came the intelligence that, instead of making for Brest, Villeneuve had gone to Cadiz. The news obliged the Emperor to recognise that, for that year at least, he must abandon his project of crossing the Channel. Then followed Trafalgar; and the project which, until Trafalgar, had seemed feasible, though perhaps distant, faded into the impossible.

Yet, during more than half the year 1805, Great Britain still saw the invasion flotilla, and the French army, watching from across the Channel for an opportunity to overwhelm her. Unable to follow quickly the movements of the opposing fleets, she knew not from day to day what was in store for her; and until August, when Napoleon first began to withdraw some of his troops to the eastward, the menace seemed to grow hourly more grave. In those anxious months, when the immediate fate of the country was bound up more intimately than at any other period of its history with the fate of its fleets, the real work of defence was done, as has been shown, in the Mediterranean, off Brest, in the West Indies, along the Atlantic coasts of Spain and Portugal, and, finally, at Trafalgar; but, as in previous years, the Navy did something also in the Channel against the huge armaments which lay waiting along the shores of France.

The spring of the year witnessed a systematic effort of concentration on the part of what may be called the right wing of the expeditionary army and flotilla. The corps of Davout moved from

---

[1] Letter to Talleyrand.
[2] Berthier to Marmont, 'Précis des Evénements,' xii. 122.

the neighbourhood of Ostend into the department of Pas de Calais ;
and, at about the same time, part of the Franco-Batavian flotilla,
which was attached to it, and which, in the previous year, had been
driven into Ostend by Sir William Sidney Smith, moved as far to
the westward as Dunquerque, whence it sought an opportunity for
stealing piecemeal along the coast to its new rendezvous at Ambleteuse, a few miles north of Boulogne.

At 9 P.M. on April 23rd, the night being dark and a fresh N.E.
wind blowing, a division of thirty-three gun-vessels and nineteen
transports, which had previously reached Dunquerque road from
Ostend, weighed in further pursuance of this plan of concentration.
It safely passed Gravelines and Calais without being observed by
the British cruisers ; but, just before dawn on the 24th, it was
thrown into some confusion by a shift of wind, first to S.E. and
later to S.S.E., and by the change of tide ; and the greater number
of the craft made for an anchorage between Capes Blanc-Nez and
Gris-Nez, although eight armed schuyts were too far to leeward to
be able to follow.   At break of day the enemy was discovered by a
British squadron, the bulk of which was at anchor off Boulogne.
This consisted of the *Leda*, 38, Captain Robert Honyman, the
sloops *Harpy*, Commander Edmund Heywood, and *Railleur*, Com-
mander Valentine Collard, the bomb *Fury*, Commander John
Yelland, and the gun-brigs *Bruiser*, *Archer*, *Locust*, *Tickler*, *Firm*,
Monkey, *Gallant*, and *Watchful*, the two last being on guard off
Ambleteuse.   The squadron chased to the N.E. ; and at 8 A.M.
the *Gallant*, Lieutenant Thomas Shirley (2), and the *Watchful*,
Lieutenant James Marshall, closed with the schuyts, which were
aided by some of the gun-brigs and by the shore batteries.   The
Gallant, struck between wind and water, had to haul off to stop her
leaks ; but the *Watchful* took one schuyt, and the *Railleur*, with
the *Locust*, Lieutenant John Lake, and the *Starling*, Lieutenant
Charles Napier (1a), presently coming up, took six more, after a
spirited engagement.   On the following morning the *Archer*,
Lieutenant William Price, captured another schuyt which had
drifted off the land.   The only loss on the British side was one
seaman wounded.[1]   The rest of the enemy's flotilla reached Ambleteuse, assisted by armed launches sent out from Boulogne by Rear-

---

[1] *Gazette*, 1805, 554. The schuyts had on board 18 guns, 1 howitzer, and
168 men. Capt. Honyman's letter omits to mention the *Starling*, which seems to have
been present in addition to the eight gun-vessels named by him. James, iii. 306.

Admiral Lacrosse, who, on the death of Bruix, had assumed command of the naval force on the coast.

A somewhat similar effort of concentration began a little later on the left wing; and on June 10th, in pursuance of it, a French division, consisting of the sloops *Foudre*, 10, and *Audacieuse*, 10, fifteen gun-vessels,[1] and fourteen transports, under Captain J. F. E. Hamelin, sailed from Le Hâvre for Fécamp. They were chased by the *Chiffonne*, 36, Captain Charles Adam, *Falcon*, 14, Commander George Sanders, *Clinker*, gun-brig, Lieutenant Nisbet Glen, and *Frances*, hired armed cutter, and brought to action; but, when the French vessels gradually edged in under the protection of the shore batteries, the British began to get the worst of the firing, though some of the hostile craft were by that time aground. The enemy ultimately got under the forts of Fécamp. In this skirmish the *Chiffonne* had two killed and three wounded; the *Falcon* four wounded, and the *Clinker* one killed and one wounded.

On July 15th, the gun-brigs *Plumper*, Lieutenant James Henry Garrety, and *Teazer*, Lieutenant George Lewis Ker, being becalmed, and likely to be carried into danger by the tide, anchored at some little distance from one another near the Chausey Isles, off Granville. They were observed from that town, and during the following night seven gun-vessels, each mounting three long 24-prs. and an 8-in. howitzer, and full of men, were sent out to attack them. The approach was made by means of sweeps; and, at 2.30 A.M. on the 16th, the vessels opened fire on the *Plumper*. She was so situated as to be able to make no adequate resistance, and at length, when Garrety had lost his arm, she surrendered, after having made as gallant a fight as her position allowed. At 8.45 A.M., the French, reinforced by the *Plumper*, attacked the *Teazer*, which set all sail and tried to escape, but was soon surrounded and captured. The brigs seem to have lost somewhat severely, but no exact account of the numbers killed and wounded is to be found.

Nearly all that part of the Ostend division of the invasion flotilla which had not previously passed further to the westward was assembled by the end of May at Dunquerque under Vice-Admiral Ver Huell, who anxiously awaited an opportunity to carry it on to Ambleteuse. The division was, however, prevented, chiefly by

---

[1] Four of three long 24-prs. and one 8-in. howitzer; three of one 24-pr. and one field gun; and eight of two 4- or 6-prs.

adverse winds, from putting to sea until July 17th, when most of it, with a N.E. breeze, went out at 6 P.M., and began to make its way down the coast. Certain small craft remained behind, with instructions to follow if it should be seen that Ver Huell was interfered with by the British. Ver Huell had with him the four French prames, *Ville d'Aix*, *Ville d'Anvers*, *Ville de Genève*, and *Ville de Mayence*, and thirty-two[1] Batavian schooner-rigged gun-vessels of large size ; and he formed his vessels into two lines, so disposed that the openings in the outermost column were covered by the ships of the innermost one. At about 6.30 P.M., the movements of the enemy were observed by a British squadron which lay off Gravelines, and which consisted of the *Ariadne*, 20, Captain the Hon. Edward King, three or four sloops and bombs, and less than half-a-dozen gun-brigs. As soon as King perceived how the enemy was heading, he cut his cables, made sail to meet Ver Huell, and, at about 9.15 P.M., opened fire upon him, eventually driving ashore or disabling eleven of the gun-vessels, and damaging the *Ville de Genève*, in spite of the very heavy fire kept up both by the flotilla and by the batteries.[2] Between 11 P.M. and midnight, the rest of the division succeeded in anchoring off Calais. The noise of the firing brought from the Downs the *Trusty*, 50, Captain George Argles, *Vestal*, 28, Captain Stephen Thomas Digby, and three sloops. The *Vestal*, outsailing her consorts, and joining King at 4 A.M. on the 18th, subsequently recommenced action with the flotilla. But the Dutch were too well protected by the forts ; and, after a two hours' cannonade, the British drew off, and bore away to participate in another engagement which was by that time in progress to the westward, and towards which the *Trusty* and her consorts were already making their way.

Rear-Admiral Lacrosse, at Boulogne, knowing of Ver Huell's movements, had organised a diversion in favour of his colleague, and had ordered several divisions of gun-vessels to get under way as if to attack the British squadron off the port. This squadron, which included the *Immortalité*, 36, Captain Edward William Campbell Rich Owen, the *Hebe*, 32, Captain Macajah Malbon, and the *Arab*, 20, Captain Keith Maxwell, weighed to meet the enemy's craft, one hundred and thirteen in number, and ultimately drove

---

[1] Ver Huell's report; but his 'Life' declares that there were 47 gun-vessels with him. 'Leven,' i. 296.

[2] In this affair the British loss was 4 (1 mortally) wounded.

them, at about 4.30 A.M., under the batteries north-west of Vimereux.

Ver Huell was desirous of continuing his passage; and, as all the coast between Calais and Ambleteuse had been provided with numerous and very powerful batteries, he weighed from Calais road at 3 P.M. on July 18th, taking with him in his schooner, the *Bantam*, Marshal Davout, and accompanied by three out of his four prames, and twenty-one out of his thirty-two gun-vessels, and made for Cape Blanc-Nez, off which lay the *Trusty, Vestal, Ariadne*, and about a dozen smaller craft. At 4 P.M., the French batteries on the heights opened in order to drive off the British vessels; and they worked to such good effect that Ver Huell was able to proceed, without serious annoyance, until he was off the village of Wissant. There, the shore batteries being able to afford less protection, the attack was renewed, the *Arab*, 20, Captain Keith Maxwell, *Calypso*, 18, Commander Matthew Forster, *Flèche*, 18, Commander Thomas White (1), and some of the gun-brigs, succeeding, by 7 P.M., in driving six of the gun-vessels ashore, but being obliged to desist when off Cape Gris-Nez. The *Arab* had seven men wounded, and was considerably damaged; Commander Forster received a wound in the shoulder; and the *Flèche* had five men hurt. The *Immortalité* and *Hebe*, drawing too much water to get within effective range of the smaller Batavian vessels, confined their attention chiefly to the prames; and, though they were ultimately joined by the *Renommée*, 36, Captain Sir Thomas Livingstone, Bart., they managed only to drive ashore two schooner gun-vessels.[1] Soon after 7 P.M., the rest of the flotilla anchored in safety under the forts of Ambleteuse and Andresselles. The *Immortalité* lost four killed and twelve wounded; and the *Hebe* three (one mortally) wounded; and both vessels suffered rather severely in rigging and hull.[2] They were obliged to retire to repair damages; and, while they were away, the whole of the Franco-Batavian flotilla from Dunquerque seems to have found its way towards Boulogne, in the neighbourhood of which place, a few days later, no fewer than 1104 craft were assembled.

The division under Captain Hamelin which, as has been seen,

[1] Among these was the *Crocodil*, on board of which was the Jonkheer Q. Ver Huell, who subsequently wrote the history of the expedition in the life of his uncle, the admiral.

[2] In addition to the English authorities, *see* Ver Huell to Van Royen, July 22nd, 1805, and Davout to Napoleon, in *Moniteur* of 3 Thermidor, as well as 'Leven van Ver Huell,' i. 295–318.

had reached Fécamp from Le Hâvre in June, put to sea again early on the morning of July 23rd in order to continue its progress up the coast to the north-east. According to French accounts, it then consisted of twenty-six; but, according to British accounts, of thirty-four sail. Its movements were at once observed by the *Champion*, 22, Captain Robert Howe Bromley, *Clinker*, gun-brig, Lieutenant Nisbet Glen, *Cracker*, gun-brig, Lieutenant William Henry Douglas (2), and *Frances*, hired armed cutter; and by 10.30 A.M., many of the smaller of the French craft had been forced ashore under the batteries of Seuneville, while all the rest of the flotilla had been driven to take refuge under those of St. Valery-en-Caux. This excellent piece of service was executed with the loss of only two killed and three wounded; but the *Champion* and her consorts were so mauled that they had to proceed to the Downs to refit; and, during their absence, Captain Hamelin made his way to Boulogne without further adventure.

Mr. James [1] gives the following account of the invasion flotilla, which, in July, 1805, was composed of 1339 armed, and 954 unarmed vessels, intended to carry 163,645 men and 9059 horses, and which was made up of six grand divisions :—

"The first, under the designation of the left wing, commanded by Rear-Admiral Jean François Courand, and stationed at the port of Etaples, was destined to carry the troops from the camp of Montreuil, commanded by Marshal Ney; the second and third, called the left and right wings of the centre of the flotilla, under the respective commands of Rear-Admiral Daniel Savary and Capitaine de vaisseau Julien Le Ray, occupied the port of Boulogne, and were destined to carry the troops from the two camps to the right and left of the town, commanded by Marshal Soult; the fourth, named the right wing of the flotilla, commanded by Capitaine de vaisseau François Henri Eugène Daugier, occupied the port of Vimereux, and was to carry the corps of Marshal Lannes. . . . The Gallo-Batavian flotilla, assembled at the port of Ambleteuse, under the command of Vice-Admiral Ver Huell, formed the fifth grand division of the expedition, and was to carry the troops commanded by Marshal Davout. The sixth, or reserve division, lying in the port of Calais, under the command of Capitaine de frégate Charles l'Evêque, was destined to transport the division of Italian infantry, and several divisions of dragoons, mounted and dismounted. The first four grand divisions only had a regular organisation; each was separated into two portions, called *escadrilles*; and each of the latter was to embark a division of the army, composed of four regiments of the line, and one of light infantry, with its cavalry, artillery, and baggage."

Twice, on August 3rd, Napoleon, by way of experiment, caused the entire army to embark. On the second occasion the whole operation was accomplished in ninety minutes. The organisation,

---

[1] James (ed. 1837), iii. 315 and 369. *See also* 'Précis des Evènements,' xii. 304.

therefore, both of the troops and of the flotilla, must have been singularly perfect. Organisation alone, however, could not ensure the success of the Emperor's plans. According to his own admission, when he was in his most sanguine mood, it was necessary also that he should be master of the sea for six hours [1] in order to be able to transport his huge and miscellaneous force across the Channel. But six hours', or even six weeks' mastery of the Channel would, in reality, have not availed him, unless he had not only swept away all the British fleets, but also annihilated or shut up all vagrant British cruisers ; unless, too, he had assembled a vast covering fleet before Boulogne, had been favoured with a continuance of the best of weather, and had met with comparatively little resistance on landing. He could not reasonably expect to command all these advantages, every one of which, nevertheless, was absolutely requisite for the attainment of his objects. The truth is, that never throughout his extraordinary adventures did Napoleon succeed in grasping even the most elementary of the laws which govern maritime operations. [2] Whenever any one of his gigantic combinations was made to depend directly upon the co-operation of fleets, or upon the success of a naval movement, it failed. And it was, probably, because Napoleon ignored the fact that, in nearly all the campaigns upon which he embarked, sea-power was directly or indirectly a determining factor, that his meteoric career terminated as it did. In view of the immense difficulties of all kinds in the way of his successful invasion of England, it has more than once been seriously questioned whether he really cherished the hazardous project, and whether his preparations at Boulogne ought not rather to be regarded as an elaborate mystification intended to mislead the world into believing that he purposed to strike at Great Britain, when, indeed, he was preparing to deal a blow at Austria. But this theory is, after all, untenable. It is absolutely clear, from the testimony of many of the naval and military chiefs who were engaged in the preparations, that Napoleon did intend to cross the Strait of Dover, and that, if his plans had not been rendered palpably hopeless by Cornwallis, Calder, Villeneuve, and Nelson, he would have actually made the attempt.

---

[1] Letter of June 9th, in 'Précis des Evènements,' xi. 270. He later increased his estimate of time to six days, then to fifteen days, and ultimately, according to O'Meara (i. 349), to two months.

[2] *See* Jurien de La Gravière, in ' Rev. des Deux Mondes,' Oct. 1887.

It has already been noted [1] that a French squadron under Rear-Admiral Missiessy, who had succeeded Villeneuve in command at Rochefort, had been ordered by Napoleon in 1804 to proceed to the West Indies, there to carry out certain operations, and ultimately to join, and return to Europe with, Villeneuve. It has also been seen that the intended combination failed, and that Villeneuve and Missiessy did not meet. The Rear-Admiral, as has been said, escaped from Rochefort on January 11th, 1805, during a temporary absence of the British blockading squadron under Rear-Admiral Sir Thomas Graves (3), and, after some delay, crossed the Atlantic. His force consisted of the *Majestueux*, 120, *Jemmapes*, 74, *Magnanime*, 74, *Lion*, 74, *Suffren*, 74, *Gloire*, 40, *Armide*, 40, *Infatigable*, 40, *Actéon*, 16, and *Lynx*, 16 ; [2] and on board the squadron were 3500 troops under General Joseph Lagrange. On February 20th, in the St. Lucia Channel, he chased a British convoy and captured the transport *Prince of Asturias* ; and, later in the day, he anchored before Fort Royal, or Fort de France, Martinique. After throwing ashore supplies, and consulting with the captain-general, Vice-Admiral Villaret-Joyeuse, Missiessy decided to make an immediate attack upon the British island of Dominica, before which he accordingly appeared, under British colours, early on the morning of February 22nd. As the French boats full of troops pushed off from the ships, French instead of British colours were hoisted. Three landings were effected under fire from the squadron ; and ultimately, after a gallant resistance had been offered by some of his subordinates, Brigadier-General George Prevost, the commander-in-chief, was obliged to retreat across the island from Roseau, Fort Young, and Fort Melville, to Fort Prince Rupert. He there, on February 25th, received a summons from General Lagrange ; but, as he did not surrender, the French, for some unexplained reason, decided to withdraw. On the 27th, therefore, after levying a contribution of £5500, destroying some guns and stores, and embarking some trophies and prisoners, they weighed and set sail for Guadeloupe, whither had already been removed twenty-two small merchantmen which had been captured in Roseau road. At Basseterre, Missiessy disembarked certain troops and stores, filled up with water, and sold his prizes ; and on the night of March 2nd he put to sea again. At dawn on the 5th, he appeared

---

[1] *See* p. 77, *antea*.

[2] Joined, apparently in the West Indies, by an armed schooner.

in the absence of Admiral the Hon. William Cornwallis, who had
been driven from his station by foul weather, got away unobserved.
On the 14th, this division separated into two squadrons, one[1] of
which, under Vice-Admiral C. U. Leissègues, was directed to
disembark 1000 troops for the reinforcement of General Ferrand
at San Domingo, and then, before returning to Rochefort or
Lorient, to cruise for two months off Jamaica, or, if the British
were too strong in that quarter, to proceed off the banks
of Newfoundland. The other[2] squadron, under Rear-Admiral
J. B. P. Willaumez, was to make either for the Cape of Good
Hope or for St. Helena, as the rear-admiral might determine, and
thence to go by way of Martinique or Guadeloupe to Cayenne.
It was next to cruise for some months off Barbados, and eventually
to return to Europe by way of St. Helena.

Not until December 24th, 1805, did the Admiralty receive news
of the division having left Brest, and it was even then informed
that only seven sail of the line, instead of eleven, had escaped. Two
British squadrons were at once ordered to prepare to proceed in
search of the enemy. Neither, however, succeeded in quitting the

SHIPS.	GUNS.	COMMANDERS.
[1] *Impérial* *	130	Vice-Adm. Corentin Urbain Leissègues.
		Capt. Julien Gabriel Bigot.
Alexandre †	80	„ Pierre Elie Garreau.
Jupiter	74	„ Gaspard Laignel.
Brave	74	Commod. Louis Marie Coudé.
Diomède	74	Capt. Jean Baptiste Henry.
Comète	40	
Félicité	40	
Diligente	..	Com. Raymond Cocault.

* Ex-*Vengeur*.   † Ex-*Indivisible*.

SHIPS.	GUNS.	COMMANDERS.
[2] *Foudroyant*	80	Rear-Adm. Jean Baptiste Philibert Willaumez.
		Capt. Antoine Henri.
Vétéran	74	„ Jérôme Bonaparte.
Cassard	74	„ Gilbert Aimable Faure.
Impétueux	74	„ Alain Joseph Le Veyer Belair.
Patriote	74	„ Joseph Hyacinthe Isidore Khrom.
Eole	74	„ Louis Gilles Prévost de Lacroix.
Valeureuse	40	
Volontaire	40	„ Bretel.
Two brigs.		

See Chevalier, 246.

coasts of England until late in January, 1806. One[1] of these squadrons, under Vice-Admiral Sir John Borlase Warren, Bart., was to go to Madeira, and, if it there appeared probable that the French had made for the West Indies, to proceed to Barbados and Jamaica, reinforce Rear-Admiral the Hon. Alexander Forester Inglis Cochrane, and Vice-Admiral James Richard Dacres (1), and, unless it should receive definite intelligence as to the enemy's route, return in part to Spithead. The other[2] squadron, under Rear-Admiral Sir Richard John Strachan, Bart., was to look for the French in the neighbourhood of St. Helena, and, in case of not finding them there, to join a force which, as will be noticed later, had been sent out under Commodore Sir Home Riggs Popham to attempt the reduction of the Cape of Good Hope.

On the afternoon of December 15th, 1805, when Leissègues and Willaumez were still almost within sight of one another, both were discovered to leeward by a convoy of twenty-three sail, which was on its voyage from Cork to the West Indies, and which was then in lat. 46° 8′ N. and long. 12° 14′ W., under the protection of the *Arethusa*, 38, Captain Charles Brisbane, *Boadicea*, 38, Captain John Maitland, (2), and *Wasp*, 18, Commander Buckland Stirling Bluett. Leissègues was then steering westward with a N.N.E. wind. Willaumez, heading to the southward, was, as appeared

Ships.	Guns.	Commanders.
[1] *Foudroyant*	80	Vice-Adm. Sir John Borlase Warren, Bart. Capt. John Chambers White.
London	98	„ Sir Harry Burrard Neale, Bart.
Ramillies	74	„ Francis Pickmore.
Hero	74	„ Hon. Alan Hyde Gardner.
Namur	74	„ Lawrence William Halsted.
Repulse	74	„ Hon. Arthur Kaye Legge.
Courageux	74	„ James Bissett.

Ships.	Guns.	Commanders.
[2] *Cæsar*	80	Rear-Adm. Sir Richard John Strachan, Bart. Capt. Charles Richardson.
St. George	98	„ Thomas Bertie (2).
Centaur	74	„ Sir Samuel Hood (2).
Terrible	74	„ Lord Henry Paulet.
Triumph	74	„ Henry Inman.
Bellona	74	„ John Erskine Douglas.

Looking to the work intended to be done by the above squadrons, the absence of frigates and small craft is astonishing.

subsequently, in chase of a convoy [1] from Gibraltar. On the 16th, when only the squadron of Leissègues could be seen by Brisbane, seventeen sail of the British convoy were ordered to the S.W., while the rest, with the men-of-war, tacked and stood to the N.W. Leissègues did the same, and chased until evening, when he tacked and again stood to the S.W. In the meantime Brisbane had detached the *Wasp* to warn the officers off Rochefort, Ferrol, Cadiz, and Gibraltar of the movements of the enemy, and had sent the *Boadicea* with similar news to Cornwallis, off Ushant. At midnight he made sail, with the six vessels of his convoy, to the westward. Leissègues eventually abandóned the chase; and on December 23rd, between Madeira and the Canaries, the *Arethusa* fell in with a British squadron under Vice-Admiral Sir John Thomas Duckworth, K.G. This squadron [2] was mainly composed of ships which, under Rear-Admiral Thomas Louis, had been detached by Collingwood, after Trafalgar, to blockade Cadiz, and which, since November 15th, had been under the orders of Duckworth, who had joined in the *Superb* from Plymouth. The squadron had raised the blockade and proceeded in the direction of Madeira [3] in consequence of information, received on November 26th from the *Lark*, 18, Commander Frederick Langford, that on the 20th a French squadron, conjectured to be the Rochefort one under Allemand, had dispersed a British Gorée-bound convoy off the Salvages. Duckworth was returning to his station off Cadiz when he was fallen in with by the *Arethusa*; and, as he

---

[1] In charge of the *Polyphemus*, 64, and *Sirius*, 36. Willaumez took one or two of the transports and sent in the *Volontaire* with them to Tenerife.

SHIPS.	GUNS.	COMMANDERS.
[2] *Superb*	74	Vice-Adm. Sir John Thomas Duckworth, K.G. Capt. Richard Goodwin Keats.
Canopus `	80	Rear-Adm. Thomas Louis. Capt. Francis William Austen (1).
Spencer	74	,, Hon. Robert Stopford.
Donegal	74	,, Pulteney Malcolm.
Powerful *	74	,, Robert Plampin.
Agamemnon	64	,, Sir Edward Berry.
Acasta	40	,, Richard Dalling Dunn.
Amethyst *	36	,, John William Spranger.

* Before the action off San Domingo the *Powerful* and *Amethyst* were detached, and the *Northumberland*, 74, *Atlas*, 74, *Magicienne*, 36, *Kingfisher*, 16, and *Epervier*, 14, joined. For the names of their commanders, *see* the text *infra*.

[3] For thus leaving Cadiz entirely unblockaded Duckworth was afterwards severely blamed by Collingwood.

was working to the northward, in which direction Leissègues had
been last seen, he held on his course. On December 25th, being in
lat. 30° 52′ N., and long. 20° 16′ W., the British sighted nine strange
sail standing to the southward, and tacked after them in chase, with
every rag of canvas set. On the morning of the 26th, it was
perceived that the enemy's force included six instead of only five
sail of the line ; and the supposition that it was the Rochefort
squadron began, therefore, to be discredited. Until 1 P.M. the
chase was continued, with increasing advantage to the British;
and not more than about seven miles seems to have then intervened between the foremost of the British and the rearmost of the
French ships. But Duckworth's command was drawn out over
a distance of nearly fifty miles ; and, professedly influenced by this
consideration, and by the fear lest the *Superb*, the leading ship,
might be overwhelmed before she could be assisted, the Vice-
Admiral annulled the chase in lat. 28° 25′ N. and long. 19° 10′ W.
It was surely an unfortunate decision. The French were neither
of superior force, nor so concentrated as to be in a position to
crush the British ships had they come up, as they might have
come, in reasonably quick succession ; and it is all but certain that,
if Duckworth had persisted in the pursuit, he might have forced
his opponent, who was none other than Willaumez,[1] either to
abandon his rearmost vessel, or to shorten sail, cover his rear,
and accept a general action.

Duckworth collected his squadron, sent the *Amethyst* to England
with news of the strength and supposed destination of the French,
and then, his stock of water having run low, bore away for the
Leeward Islands. On January 2nd, 1806, he detached the *Powerful*,
74, to fill up with provisions and water at the Cape de Verde Islands
and then to proceed to the East Indies as a reinforcement for Rear-
Admiral Sir Edward Pellew ; and on January 12th, he anchored in
Carlisle Bay, Barbados, and sent forward the *Acasta* to St. Kitts
to make arrangements for the watering of the squadron at that
island. Weighing from Carlisle Bay on the 14th, he reached Basse-
Terre road, St. Kitts, on the evening of the 19th, and on the 21st
was joined by the *Northumberland*, 74, Rear-Admiral the Hon.
Alexander F. I. Cochrane, Captain John Morrison (1) (actg.),[2] and

---

[1] The force of Willaumez was as set forth in the note on p. 184, save that the
Volontaire, having been detached with prizes, was absent.

[2] Confirmed, Feb. 5th, 1806.

the *Atlas*, 74, Captain Samuel Pym. As Cochrane brought no news
of any important movement on the part of the enemy, and as both
he and Duckworth were entirely ignorant of the course which had
been taken by Leissègues, Sir John, without special haste, watered
and refitted preparatory to returning to his station. But on February
1st, the *Kingfisher*, 16, Commander Nathaniel Day Cochrane, brought
intelligence that three French sail of the line had been seen making for

ADMIRAL SIR JOHN THOMAS DUCKWORTH, BART, K.B.

(*From a drawing by W. Evans, after the portrait by Sir Wm. Beechey, R.A.*)

the town of San Domingo, and at once Duckworth weighed and
made sail to look for them. Off St. Thomas, on the 3rd, the squadron
was joined by the *Epervier*, 14, Lieutenant James Higginson. On
the morning of the 5th, off the east end of the island of San Domingo,
it was further joined by the *Magicienne*, 36, Captain Adam Mackenzie, who confirmed the previous news, and who had with him a
Danish schooner which had sailed from San Domingo road after
the French had arrived there. On the following morning at dawn,

the British drew in sight of the roadstead ; and presently the *Acasta*
and *Magicienne*, which had been ordered ahead, signalled the
presence at anchor, first of two frigates, and, subsequently, of
nine sail.

Eight of these vessels composed the force with Vice-Admiral
Leissègues,[1] who, after chasing the *Arethusa* and her convoy on
December 16th, had attempted to pass N.W. of the Azores, and had
fallen in with bad weather, which had not only forced him to bear
up and pass to leeward of the islands, but had also done him much
damage, and had obliged the *Alexandre* and *Brave* to part company.
On January 20th, Leissègues had anchored in San Domingo road ;
and he had subsequently disembarked troops and stores for the relief
of General Ferrand and had been rejoined by the *Alexandre* and
Brave. When discovered, on February 6th, he was practically ready
to proceed in execution of his orders.

At 7.30 A.M., the French, conscious that they were about to be
attacked, slipped their cables and made sail in a westerly direction
with a light N.N.W. breeze. As they approached Punta Palenque,
they formed in line of battle, the *Alexandre* leading, and being
followed in succession by the *Impérial, Diomède, Jupiter*, and *Brave*.
The *Félicité, Comète*, and *Diligente* formed a parallel line closer inshore. The British, formed in two lines, steered to cross the course
of the leading French vessels,[2] Duckworth signalling that the main
object of his attack would be the French admiral and his two seconds,
i.e., the three headmost ships of the enemy. The starboard or
weather line consisted of the *Superb, Northumberland, Spencer*, and
Agamemnon ; and the port or lee one, of the *Canopus, Donegal*, and
Atlas. At 8 A.M. the *Canopus* was nearly abeam of the *Spencer*,
and the ships of each British line were in fairly good order. The
Acasta, Magicienne, Kingfisher and *Epervier*, had taken stations to
windward of the line-of-battle ships.

" Soon after 8 A.M.," says James, " the inequality of sailing among the British ships
began plainly to show itself. By 10 A.M. the *Agamemnon* had dropped considerably
astern, and the *Canopus*, the leading ship of the lee line, was now no further advanced
than the former. The three leading ships of the weather line were in close order, and
gaining fast upon the French squadron ; the ships of which, at about 9.45 A.M.,[3] hoisted
their colours, and, owing to the wind having shifted to N.E. by E., were now steering

---

[1] The other was a merchantman.

[2] This was because Duckworth believed that the French were seeking to join a
friendly force to leeward. Disp. of Feb. 7th.

[3] When Duckworth signalled his ships to take stations for mutual support, and to
engage the enemy as they got up.

with it about a point upon the starboard quarter. At 10.10 A.M. the *Superb*, having shortened sail, opened a fire from her starboard guns upon the *Alexandre*; as, in three minutes afterwards, did the *Northumberland* upon the three-decker, the *Impérial*. In another five minutes, the *Spencer*, who was close upon the *Northumberland's* starboard quarter, joined in the cannonade, taking the *Diomède* as her more immediate opponent, but firing occasionally at the three-decker ahead of her; and all the engaged ships kept running nearly before the wind, at the rate of about eight knots an hour."

After having exchanged three broadsides, the *Alexandre* hauled up on the port tack, passed astern of the *Superb* and *Northumber-*

ADMIRAL SIR PULTENEY MALCOLM, G.C.B.

(*Engraved by Wm. Ward, after the portrait by S. Lane, painted when Sir Pulteney was a Vice-Admiral, 1821–37.*)

land, and tried to cross the bows of the *Spencer*. This ship, however, crossed the *Alexandre's* bows, raked her, and then, wearing, brought the Frenchman to action on the port tack; and the *Alexandre* eventually [1] fell among the British lee division, which dismasted her. The *Spencer's* change of sides was at first unperceived by the *Superb* and *Northumberland*, which were en-

---

[1] At about 10.35 A.M.

veloped in smoke, and which, for a few moments, fired into her. Soon, however, the truth was realised; and, while the *Spencer* and *Alexandre* remained closely engaged with their heads to the southward, the rest of both squadrons continued to the westward, the *Northumberland* pushing up on the *Superb's* starboard quarter, and very gallantly intervening between the British and French flagships. When, at about 11 A.M., the *Spencer* had set the *Alexandre* on fire and reduced her to impotence, she filled and bore up to assist her consorts. The lee division, after passing across and firing into the bows of the *Alexandre*, separated, the *Canopus* standing on towards the *Impérial*, and the *Donegal* and *Atlas* attaching themselves to the *Brave* and *Jupiter*; so that the action was by that time general, save that the *Agamemnon* still remained unable to get up. The *Donegal*, having first poured her starboard battery into the *Brave*, wore under that ship's stern and engaged her with the port battery, the result being that the *Brave* was the next ship of the enemy, after the *Alexandre*, to strike her colours. The *Donegal* then stood on, ranged ahead of the *Jupiter*,[1] and obliged that ship to run her on board, the Frenchman's bowsprit coming over the *Donegal's* port quarter, where it was secured by means of a hawser. This determined action on the part of Captain Malcolm soon induced the *Jupiter* to surrender; and the *Donegal* at once sent a crew on board, and took her prize in tow.

The *Atlas*, having left the *Jupiter* to the *Donegal*, had pushed on and begun to seriously annoy the *Impérial*, when, unfortunately, her tiller became jammed. At almost the same instant she received an unexpected fire from the *Diomède*, and, in the confusion, she fouled the *Canopus* and carried away her own bowsprit. But, quickly heaving aback his after-sails, Captain Pym cleared his consort, and, dropping alongside the *Diomède*, engaged her warmly with his starboard battery, until the *Spencer* came up.

It was then about 11.30 A.M., and—

" the French admiral, much shattered and completely beaten, hauled direct for the land, and, not being a mile off, at twenty minutes before noon ran on shore, his foremast then only standing, which fell directly on her striking; at which time the *Superb*, being only in 17 fathoms water, was forced to haul off to avoid the same evil; but, not long after, the *Diomède* . . . pushed inshore near his admiral, when all his masts went." [2]

---

[1] The *Jupiter* had by that time been quitted by the *Atlas*, which, in pursuance of Duckworth's orders, had stood on after the *Canopus* to assist the attack upon the enemy's van.

[2] Duckworth's Disp. of Feb. 7th.

off St. Kitts ; and, in the course of the day, he landed a column of
troops, which obliged the inhabitants of the capital of the island to
pay an indemnity of £18000. The British garrison, and part of
the local militia, had withdrawn to an impregnable position at
Brimstone Hill. The French, instead of following them, seized
all the merchantmen [1] in Basseterre road, and then proceeded to
Nevis, where they levied a contribution of £4000, disarmed the
batteries, and destroyed such merchant vessels [2] as they could
find. Montserrat was visited on the 9th, and similarly treated.
Upon returning to Fort Royal, Martinique, on March 14th,
Missiessy found the brig, *Palinure*, with dispatches, announcing
the return to Toulon of Villeneuve after his first sortie, and
directing the squadron to return at once to Europe. Most of
the troops still remaining on board were therefore disembarked,
and Missiessy made for France. Calling on his way off the town
of San Domingo, on March 27th, he found General Ferrand, with
the last remnants of the French garrison, sorely pressed by the
negro insurgents under Dessalines. The last battalion of troops,
together with a supply of money and stores, was landed for the
relief of Ferrand ; and, again putting to sea, Missiessy succeeded
in evading the several British squadrons which were looking for
him, and, on May 20th, anchored in safety in Aix road. In
spite of what Missiessy had done, Napoleon was very displeased
with him, and wrote to Decrès : " I choked with indignation
when I read that he had not taken the Diamond Rock. I would
have preferred to lose a ship of the line if only I could have thereby
gained that appanage of Martinique. If he has not departed, you
will make him aware of my dissatisfaction." Napoleon was also
incensed with Missiessy for not having held Dominica, attacked
Barbados, and remained longer before San Domingo. The Rear-
Admiral in consequence fell into disgrace, and was not again
employed until 1809.

The French Brest fleet had no active share in the campaign
of Trafalgar, and not until long after the decisive battle had
been fought did any considerable part of it put to sea. On
December 13th, 1805, however, a division of it, consisting of
eleven ships of the line, four frigates, a corvette, and two brigs
or dispatch-vessels, quitted its anchorage outside the Goulet, and,

---

[1] There were six. Four were burnt and two were carried off.
[2] There were five.

The *Superb* seems to have shown an excessive degree of pre-caution in hauling off, as she did, to the southward when she had still a full hundred feet of water under her ; but her withdrawal was immaterial, for the *Canopus* continued to fire on the *Impérial* until that ship, fast aground, ceased to reply.   The *Diomède* went on firing, however, up to the time when the *Canopus, Atlas,* and *Spencer,* quitted her to rejoin the Vice-Admiral.   During the action the *Comète, Félicité,* and *Diligente,* having got well to leeward, had hauled to the southward ; and, as the British frigates were not ordered to pursue them, they all, unfortunately, escaped.   The two ships which had run ashore lay nearly midway between Punta Nisao and Punta Catalana ; and their bottoms were quickly stove in on the rocks.   The French removed the chief part of the crews, and some of the stores to the shore, and would have destroyed the vessels, had not the British frigates returned to the spot on the 8th, and so interfered with the operation.   The *Acasta* and *Magicienne* took off from the *Diomède* Captain Henry, his surviving officers, and about a hundred of his men, and then burnt both ships.

The losses of the British ships [1] in this action were : *Superb,* 6 killed, 56 wounded ; *Northumberland,* 21 killed, 79 wounded ; *Cano-pus,* 8 killed, 22 wounded ; *Spencer,* 18 killed, 50 wounded ; *Donegal,* 12 killed, 33 wounded ; *Atlas,* 8 killed, 11 wounded ; and *Agamemnon,* 1 killed, 13 wounded : total 74 killed, and 264 wounded.   Among officers killed were Midshipmen David Ridgway (*Northumberland*), and Charles H. Kynaston (*Donegal*), and Boatswain Martin Oates (*Spencer*) ; and among the officers wounded were Captain the Hon. Robert Stopford (*Spencer*), and Lieutenants Charles Patriarch (*Superb*), George Francis Seymour (*Northumberland*), and James Harris (*Spencer*).   The ships were nearly all much knocked about ; but only the *Northumberland* lost any mast by the enemy's fire.   The French loss was much more severe.   It amounted, apparently, in the *Alexandre,* to 300 ; in the *Brave,* to 260 ; in the *Jupiter,* to 200 ; in the *Diomède,* to 250 ; and in the *Impérial,* to nearly 500 killed and wounded.   Of the prizes, the *Alexandre* and the *Brave* were badly cut up ; but the *Jupiter* was little damaged.   The *Brave* foundered on her way to England ; the *Alexandre* was too much shattered to be worth repairing for service ; and the *Jupiter,* re-named *Maida,* was added, as a sea-going ship, to the Navy.

[1] According to the official report ; but the *Superb,* according to her log, had 6 killed and only 30 wounded.

Sir John Duckworth received no new public honour in respect of the services rendered by him at San Domingo, although he, and all who served under him, were voted the thanks of Parliament. Had he, after the fiasco of December 26th, 1805, not brought Leissègues to action, he would in all probability have had to explain to a court-martial his strange conduct when in presence of Willaumez. Rear-Admiral the Hon. A. F. I. Cochrane was, however, made a K.B.,[1] and Rear-Admiral Louis, a Baronet.[2] Commander Nathaniel Day Cochrane, who had been sent home with the dispatches, was posted, and the first Lieutenants of all the ships in line appear to have been made Commanders.[3] James says that some other promotions were made; but I have succeeded in tracing only a few officers who received their first commissions in consequence of their share in the action, and cannot discover that more than five Lieutenants were advanced upon the occasion.

After having been abandoned by Duckworth on December 26th, Rear-Admiral Willaumez in due course reached the neighbourhood of the Cape of Good Hope, and there learnt, from a prize merchantman, that the colony had fallen into the hands of the British. He remained until April in the South Atlantic, and then put into San Salvador, whence he sailed for Cayenne. There he separated his squadron into three divisions, which for a time cruised more or less independently off the coast of Brazil, and, ultimately, after having been chased by British ships, reassembled on June 24th in the Bay of Fort Royal, Martinique. Martinique was watched by Rear-Admiral the Hon. Sir A. F. I. Cochrane; but bad weather prevented the watch from being continuous, and thus enabled the ships of Willaumez not only to get in, but also to put to sea again. The French, indeed, quitted Martinique unobserved on July 1st, and, making for Montserrat, seized three merchantmen lying at anchor there. Another part of the squadron captured three ships and a brig off Nevis, and on the 3rd, in vain, attacked a portion of a convoy anchored under the protection of the guns on Brimstone Hill, St. Kitts. On July 4th, the command, again united, stood for Tortola, where was assembled a large British convoy ready to proceed to England; but at dawn on the

[1] On March 29th, 1806.

[2] On Ap. 7th, 1806.

[3] On April 2nd were promoted Lieutenants George Ravenshaw (*Spencer*), Charles Gill (*Superb*), William Sanders (*Donegal*), Joseph Pearce (*Canopus*), and Richard Harward (*Northumberland*).

6th, when a little to the S.E. of the west end of St. Thomas, it sighted Cochrane's squadron, which was on its way to protect the threatened merchantmen, and which consisted of the *Northumberland*, 74 (flag), Captain Joseph Spear (actg.), *Elephant*, 74, Captain George Dundas, *Canada*, 74, Captain John Harvey (2), *Agamemnon*, 64, Captain Jonas Rose, the frigates *Ethalion*, *Seine*, *Galatea*, and *Circe*, and several small craft. Upon this, Willaumez, as if to avoid an action, bore up and ran through the channel between St. Thomas and Passage. For some hours he was followed by Cochrane, who, however, mindful of the convoy, altered course in the afternoon for Drake's Bay, Tortola, and, anchoring there on the 8th, found no fewer than two hundred and eighty sail of West Indiamen which looked to him for protection.

Although Willaumez never admitted that he had fled before Cochrane, he did admit that, after sighting him, he deemed it wise to shorten his stay among the Antilles. When, therefore, he had filled up with water and provisions at Martinique, he made for the Bahama Bank, with the object of there intercepting the homeward-bound Jamaica convoy. Arrived upon his cruising ground, he unscrupulously seized and detained every neutral vessel that came near him, his aim being to keep secret his presence in these latitudes ; and it is quite likely that he might have been conspicuously successful, had not his plans been turned upside down by the insubordinate action of one of his captains.

Jérôme Bonaparte,[1] commanding the *Vétéran*, 74, was the youngest brother of the Emperor. Born in 1784, he was made an *enseigne de vaisseau* on January 25th, 1802, a *lieutenant de vaisseau* on January 14th, 1803, a *capitaine de frégate* on November 1st, 1804, and, in 1805, after he had first attempted to confer the rank upon himself, a *capitaine de vaisseau*. This young officer, always frivolous and headstrong, speedily discovered that a cruise off the Bahama Bank was not to his liking ; and, on the night of July 31st, he saw fit to part company without permission,[2] and to head for Europe. On August 10th, he fell in with a British homeward-bound Quebec convoy under orders of Captain

---

[1] After his naval experiences, he became King of Westphalia in 1807, but was expelled in 1813. He fought at Waterloo, lived for many years subsequently as the Comte de Montfort, returned to France in 1847, was created a Marshal of the Empire in 1850, and died in 1860. 'Méms. et Corr. du Roi et de la Reine Cathérine,' 5 vols., 1861–64.

[2] Brenton (ii. 143, ed. 1837) erroneously says that Prince Jérôme was "detached."

Robert Howe Bromley, of the *Champion*, 22, and was so fortunate as to take and burn six of the merchantmen. On August 26th, when nearing Belle Isle, he was chased by the *Gibraltar*, 80, Captain Willoughby Thomas Lake, *Penelope*, 36, Captain William Robert Broughton, and *Tribune*, 36, Captain Thomas Baker (1) : but the able officers who had been sent to sea with him succeeded in carrying him safely to an unfrequented anchorage in the Baie de La Forêt in Brittany ; and thither no ship of the line ventured to follow him.[1]

When, early on the morning of August 1st, Willaumez perceived that his unruly pupil had vanished, he naturally became very uneasy, and, while cruising in all directions in search of him, missed the Jamaica fleet, of one hundred and nine sail. He returned at length to his station, and again waited for the expected convoy, until he learnt from a neutral that it was beyond his reach. The delay might easily have cost him an encounter with Vice-Admiral Sir John Borlase Warren,[2] who had reached Barbados on July 12th, but who, upon leaving it again, kept, as afterwards appeared, too far to the eastward. Willaumez next prepared for a cruise off the coasts of British North America; but in the night of August 18th his ships were severely damaged and widely scattered by a hurricane which overtook them in lat. 22° N., long. 63° W. The rear-admiral himself carried the *Foudroyant*, by means of jury masts and a jury rudder, to Havana, but, in order to enter that port, had to fight a very brisk action on September 15th with the *Anson*, 44,[3] Captain Charles Lydiard. The Frenchman proved too heavy an opponent, and the *Anson* eventually had to haul off.[4]

The squadron of Rear-Admiral Sir Richard John Strachan was as unsuccessful as that of Warren in finding any traces of either of

---

[1] In spite of this escapade, Prince Jérôme was presently made a rear-admiral; but, in the year following, he finally abandoned the sea for the army.

[2] For Warren's original squadron *see* note on p. 185. Sir John, after going to Madeira, had returned to Spithead, and sailed again on June 4th with all his former ships except the *London* and *Repulse* (for which, however, were substituted the *Fame*, 74, Captain Richard Henry Alexander Bennett, and one frigate, the *Amazon*).

[3] The *Anson* lost 2 killed and 8 wounded.

[4] There has been much gasconading about this action. Brenton (ii. 143, ed. 1837) says that the *Anson* drove the *Foudroyant* for protection under the guns of Moro Castle; which is untrue. Guérin says that the *Foudroyant* drove the *Anson* for protection under the guns of Moro Castle; which is absurd, seeing that Moro Castle, as a Spanish fortress, was hostile to all British ships. Guérin, vi. 452. The facts, together with part of Lydiard's letter to Dacres on the occasion, are to be found in the 'Nav. Chron.' xix., 447, 448. *See also* Chevalier, 258.

the squadrons which had escaped from Brest, and it returned in
time to Plymouth. But, when it became known in England that
Willaumez, after leaving San Salvador, had gone to the north-west,
Strachan was once more ordered in search of him. Sir Richard's
force on the new cruise consisted of :—

SHIPS.	GUNS.	COMMANDERS.
Cæsar	80	{ Rear-Adm. Sir Richard John Strachan, Bart. { Capt. Charles Richardson.
Terrible	74	„ Lord Henry Paulet.
Triumph	74	„ Sir Thomas Masterman Hardy, Bart.
Bellona	74	„ John Erskine Douglas.
Belleisle	74	„ William Hargood (1).
Audacious	74	„ Thomas Le Marchant Gosselin.
Montagu	74	„ Robert Waller Otway (1).
Melampus	36	„ Stephen Poyntz.
Décade	36	„ John James Stuart.

It left Plymouth on May 19th, and, after cruising off Madeira and
the Canaries, reached Carlisle Bay, Barbados, on August 8th, and
sailed thence again on August 13th. On the night of August 18th,
Strachan and Willaumez were within about sixty miles of one
another. The British squadron fared better than the French one
in the gale which then burst upon both; but it also was dispersed;
and when, on September 14th, the *Bellona, Belleisle,* and *Melampus,*
on the appointed rendezvous off Cape Henry, were searching for
their consorts, they sighted to leeward, and gave chase to, a French
74, which proved to be one of Willaumez's ships, the *Impétueux,*
making for the Chesapeake under jury masts. Being crippled and
pursued by such superior forces, she ran herself ashore, and, upon
being fired at by the *Melampus,* struck. She was, of course, in
neutral waters, and any attack upon her was a breach of international law; yet she was taken possession of, as she lay, by the
boats of the British vessels. Soon afterwards, however, when two
suspicious sail appeared in the offing, Captain Hargood, as senior
officer, ordered the *Bellona* and *Belleisle* to get under way, and
directed Captain Poyntz to burn the prize.[1]

The other ships of Willaumez fared somewhat better. The
Patriote and *Eole* subsequently reached the Chesapeake in safety,
but were blockaded there by some British men-of-war detached from
Halifax. The *Patriote,* after long delay, found her way back to
France; but the *Eole* appears to have never again left the river.

[1] Hargood to Marsden, Sept. 15th, 1806. Chevalier, 258.

The *Valeureuse* made the Delaware, and is said to have been broken up at Philadelphia. The *Foudroyant*, when she had refitted at Havana, returned to Brest in February, 1807. As for the *Cassard*, she headed for Rochefort as soon as the gale had moderated, and made her port without further adventure. In the meanwhile a third British squadron, in addition to the squadrons of Warren and Strachan, had been sent to sea under Rear-Admiral Sir Thomas Louis, Bart., in the *Canopus*, 80, to bar the return of Willaumez. When the news of the French disasters reached him on his station to the west of Belle Isle, Louis proceeded off Cadiz.

The escape of Willaumez and Leissègues, with the best ships of the Brest fleet in December, 1805, left but a comparatively small and ill-found force in the great French port, and materially reduced the responsibilities of the British blockading fleet, which remained under the orders of Admiral the Hon. William Cornwallis until February 22nd, 1806, when that officer struck his flag and was succeeded by Admiral Lord St. Vincent. The blockade, or observation, was continued with great effectiveness; and although, on October 5th, 1806, the *Régulus*, 74,[1] succeeded in entering the harbour, no ship of the line, during the whole year, succeeded in quitting it.

Vice-Admiral Lord Collingwood continued to maintain the blockade of Cadiz; but, in February, learning that four frigates of the fleet which had been defeated at Trafalgar, were awaiting an opportunity to put to sea, he withdrew his larger ships to a distance of about thirty miles from the port, which he left to be more closely watched by the *Hydra*, 38, Captain George Mundy, and the *Moselle*, 18, Commander John Surman Carden, his hope being that he would thus tempt the enemy to venture forth.

On February 23rd, a strong easterly wind sprang up, and, by the 26th, it had driven the blockading force as far to the westward as Cape Santa Maria. Taking advantage of this, Captain La Marre La Meillerie, in the evening of the day last named, put to sea with the frigates *Hortense*, *Hermione*, *Rhin*, and *Thémis*, and the brig *Furet*.[2] The escaping squadron was sighted at 9.15 P.M. by the *Hydra* and *Moselle*, which at first steered a parallel course in order

---

[1] After a long and successful cruise under Captain L'Hermite on the west coast of Africa, the coast of Brazil, and in the West Indies. *See* next chapter.

[2] Of eighteen 8-prs. Collingwood says she had ports for 20 guns, and carried eighteen 9-prs.

to observe the enemy. Finding, however, that the French continued steadily to the westward, Captain Mundy, at 11 P.M.,
detached the *Moselle* to look for the Commander-in-Chief, and
continued the chase alone. At about 4.30 A.M. on the 27th, he
overhauled the *Furet*, which was some distance astern of her consorts, and which, after receiving a broadside, struck.[1] La Meillerie
made no attempt to prevent the *Hydra* from carrying off her prize.
His further adventures will be told in the next chapter.

But for this episode, the station under Collingwood's orders
witnessed no important movement of the allied navies during the
year. In Cadiz, ready for sea, lay five French and six or seven
Spanish ships of the line; at Cartagena lay eight Spaniards; at
Toulon were three Frenchmen, besides frigates; but Trafalgar had
taught them lessons which they were loath to risk any repetition of.
The Mediterranean, nevertheless, was the scene of some naval
activity. By the treaty of Pressburg, signed on December 26th,
1805, Austria had renounced her claims upon the Venetian states
and had assented to their annexation to the Italian kingdom,
retaining only Trieste as a Mediterranean port. Prussia had also,
at about the same time, made temporary peace with Napoleon, who
was thus left free to devote his attention to the punishment of
Ferdinand of Naples for having, in defiance of the treaty of neutrality of October 8th, 1805, allowed British and Russian troops,
under Generals Sir James Craig and Lasey, to be landed in the
bay of Naples, and for having begun military preparations on a
considerable scale. The Emperor promptly decreed the deposition
of Ferdinand and his dynasty; whereupon, doubtful of their ability
to maintain themselves where they were, the Russian troops
embarked for Corfu, and the British troops, about ten thousand
strong,[2] transferred themselves from Naples to Messina in Sicily.
As soon as a French army began to advance, Ferdinand also
abandoned Naples, and, embarking in the *Excellent*, 74, Captain
Frank Sotheron, proceeded to Palermo. By the end of March the
troops of the Emperor were in possession of the whole Neapolitan
kingdom except Gaeta and the inland fortress of Civitella del
Tronto.

To assist Ferdinand, and to impede the progress of the French,

---

[1] Mundy to Collingwood, transmitted to Marsden on Feb. 28th, 1806.

[2] Owing to the illness of Sir James Craig, they passed under the command of Sir
John Stuart.

Rear-Admiral Sir William Sidney Smith was detached by Lord Collingwood. He reached Messina on April 21st in the *Pompée*, 74, and assumed command of the squadron[1] there assembled. Smith at once proceeded off Gaeta, into which place, in spite of all that the French could do, he threw supplies of ammunition, and four lower-deck guns from the *Excellent*. He then went to Naples, in order to make a diversion there, leaving before Gaeta the *Juno*, 32, Captain Henry Richardson, the Neapolitan frigate *Minerva*, and a dozen Neapolitan gunboats. On May 12th, and again on May 15th, the British force at Gaeta was able very materially to assist the commander of the place, the Prince of Hessen-Philippsthal, in the work of defence, Captain Richardson, Lieutenant Thomas Wells (2), and Lieutenant Robert M. Mant, R.M., leading the boats on the second occasion, when the Navy lost four killed and five wounded.[2]

Having arrived in the bay of Naples[3] with the *Pompée*, 74, *Excellent*, 74, *Athénien*, 64, and *Intrepid*, 64, and having been reinforced by the *Eagle*, 74, Sir Sidney set to work to reduce the island of Capri. On May 11th, the *Eagle*, Captain Charles Rowley, with two Neapolitan gunboats, opened a heavy fire at short range upon the defences at the spot which had been selected as a landing place ; and, when the French had been driven out, a storming party of seamen and Royal Marines was disembarked, and mounted the heights with such impetuosity that the garrison quickly agreed to capitulate. In the whole of this affair the British loss was only two killed and ten, including Lieutenant James Crawley, wounded. The storming party was led by Lieutenants John Arthur Morell (*Eagle*) and Edward Reding (*Pompée*), and by Captains Richard Bunce and John Stannus,[4] and Lieutenant George P. Carroll, R.M.[5]

Sir Sidney, having garrisoned Capri, made his way back to Palermo, and, instigated by Ferdinand, induced General Sir John Stuart to invade Calabria. Sir John, and four thousand eight hundred infantry, were set ashore without opposition on July 1st, in the gulf of St. Eufemia, and, on the 4th, attacked about seven

---

[1] *Pompée*, 74, *Excellent*, 74, *Athénien*, 64, *Intrepid*, 64, two or three frigates (including one Neapolitan) and a few small craft.

[2] Richardson to Smith, May 14th and 16th, 1806.

[3] Joseph Bonaparte had been proclaimed King of the Two Sicilies on March 30th.

[4] This officer with his own hand killed Captain Chervet, the French commandant.

[5] Smith to Collingwood, May 24th, 1806.

thousand French troops near the village of Maida.   The enemy, besides his great numerical superiority, had cavalry as well as infantry, but British bayonets completely defeated him.   On the victorious side the loss was only forty-five killed and two hundred and eighty-two wounded.   The French lost in killed, wounded, and prisoners nearly four thousand men.   This action freed Sicily from immediate danger of invasion, and transferred to the victors all the

REAR-ADM. SIR HOME RIGGS POPHAM, K.C.B., F.R.S.

(*From Cardon's engraving, after the painting by M. Brown, of Popham as a Post-Captain.*)

stores and arms which had been prepared for the attempt; but, by the end of July the British expeditionary corps was again withdrawn from the mainland, a garrison being retained, however, at Scilla, and a small detachment of the 78th Regiment being sent round to Catanzaro, under Lieut.-Colonel M'Leod, to encourage the patriots there.   This detachment, supported by the *Amphion*, 32, Captain William Hoste, and by a few Neapolitan gunboats, distinguished itself on July 30th by the reduction· of the fortress of

Cotrone and the capture there of about six hundred French troops and large quantities of stores. These successes caused the enemy to evacuate Calabria, which was thus saved for the moment by the influence of sea-power; but when, on July 12th, Gaeta was obliged to surrender, the French had force and leisure to again occupy the southern province; and, assisted by the new prestige which the capture of Gaeta had given them, they entirely reconquered all of it except Scilla before the close of the year 1806. Their position, however, was always thenceforward extremely precarious in southern Italy, seeing that the sea was persistently denied them.

The only important colonial expeditions of the year 1806 were those which are associated with the name of Sir Home Riggs Popham, who in the autumn of 1805 had been entrusted with a small squadron secretly destined for the reduction of the Dutch settlements at the Cape of Good Hope. The squadron was thus composed:—

Ships.	Guns.	Commanders.
Diadem	64	Commod. Sir Home Riggs Popham. Capt. Hugh Downman (on Jan. 11th, 1806, Lieut. William King (2) (actg. Capt.).
Raisonnable	64	Capt. Josias Rowley.
Belliqueux	64	„ George Byng (2).
Diomède	50	Com. Joseph Edmonds (actg. Capt.).
Leda	38	Capt. Robert Honyman.
Narcissus	32	„ Ross Donnelly.
Espoir	18	Lieut. William King (2) (actg. Com.).
Encounter	14	„ James Hugh Talbot.

Together with a number of transports and Indiamen having on board about 5000 troops under Major-General Sir David Baird, and joined, on January 6th, 1806, by the brig *Protector*, Lieut. Sir George Mouat Keith, Bart.

It assembled from different points at Madeira, proceeded thence to San Salvador on the African coast, sailed again on November 26th, 1805, and on the evening of January 4th, 1806, anchored to the westward of Robben Island, Table Bay. After Blauwberg Bay had been reconnoitred overnight, and a demonstration had been made off Green Island by the *Leda*, and the transports containing the 24th Regiment, the troops were embarked in boats very early on the morning of the 5th, and were assembled alongside the *Espoir*; but, owing to the high surf which was running, it was deemed expedient to send them back to their ships. Sir Home and Sir David, in the *Espoir*, examined the coast for an available landing place, but found nothing more suitable than a spot in Saldanha Bay, to which, accordingly, part of the transports, with some troops [1] under Brigadier-General Beresford, proceeded under the care of the *Diomède* and *Espoir*. When, soon after this detachment had weighed, the westerly wind began to drop, it was seen that the surf greatly diminished. It was therefore determined to land the rest of the army in Blauwberg Bay; and, in the course of the after-noon of the 6th, most of the force was set ashore. In this operation [2] thirty-five men of the 93rd Regiment were unfortunately lost owing to the upsetting of a boat; and, as the surf increased again, the completion of the landing was postponed till the morning of the 7th.

In the course of the 7th, the *Leda*, *Encounter*, and *Protector*, with some of the transports, proceeded to the head of Blauwberg Bay, and drove the enemy from some of his positions in that neighbourhood. On the 8th, the army, formed in two brigades, moved towards Cape Town, dislodged an advanced body of the Dutch from the summit of Blauwberg, and, after a brisk action, in which the bayonet played an important part, obliged the main force of the enemy, under Lieut.-General J. W. Janssens, to retire with a loss of about seven hundred killed and wounded. The British loss was only fifteen killed, one hundred and eighty-nine wounded, and eight missing. On the 9th, the British reached Salt River, and were about to encamp there to await the arrival of their battering train, when a flag of truce arrived with an offer of capitulation. Fort Knocke was at once surrendered and occupied; on the 10th the articles of capitulation were signed, on the one hand by Lieut.-Colonel van Prophalow, and on the other by General Baird and Commodore Popham; and on the 12th, Cape Town and its depen-dencies, in the batteries of which were mounted 113 brass and 343 iron guns, were taken possession of. General Janssens, who, after his defeat on the 8th, had established himself at Hottentot Holland's Kloof, in the direction of Zwellendam, surrendered a little later; and thus the conquest of the colony was completed. In the opera-tions a battalion of seamen and Royal Marines, under Captain George Byng (2), of the *Belliqueux*, made itself most useful; and, among the naval officers doing duty with it were Captain George

---

[1] The 38th Regiment, the cavalry, and part of the artillery.

[2] Which was facilitated by the running ashore of a small transport to serve as a breakwater.

Nicholas Hardinge,[1] and Lieutenants George[2] Pigot (2), Thomas[2] Graham, and William James[2] Mingaye. Captain Downman, in addition, landed with some Royal Marines on the 8th. Popham also wrote with approval of the conduct of Captain William Butterfield, agent with the transports, and of John Cameron, of the *Duchess of Gordon*, Henry Christopher, of the *Sir William Pulteney*, and James Moring, of the *Comet*, masters in the H.E.I. Co.'s service. Before

ADMIRAL HUGH DOWNMAN.

(From H. R. Cook's engraving after a miniature painted about 1806, when Downman was a Post-Captain.)

surrendering the place, the Dutch burnt the *Bato*, 68, lying in Simon's Bay.[3]

On March 4th, while the squadron still lay in Table Bay, the

---

[1] Then on his way to join his ship the *Salsette*. He was killed in 1808, while in command of the *San Fiorenzo* in the action with the *Piémontaise*.

[2] The Christian names of these officers are not mentioned in Byng's report, which also cites Lieuts. Sutherland (? Robert), Carew, and Pearce, whom I cannot certainly identify.

[3] Popham to Marsden, Jan. 13th, in *Gazette Extraordinary* of Feb. 27th, 1806.

French frigate *Volontaire*, 40, which had been detached from the squadron of Rear-Admiral Willaumez, entered the roadstead, deceived by the Dutch flag flying from the forts and shipping, and, passing within hail of the *Diadem*, very sensibly obeyed a summons to strike when that ship changed her colours. In the prize were two hundred and seventeen men of the Queen's and 54th Regiments who had been captured with two transports in the Bay of Biscay.[1] She was added to the navy, and entrusted to the command of Commander the Hon. Josceline Percy, who had been previously appointed to the *Espoir*, but had been unable to join her before her departure, with Captain Downman and the Commodore's dispatches, for England.

Towards the middle of April, Popham received intelligence that the inhabitants of Buenos Aires and Montevideo, which were then under Spanish rule, were so discontented that they would offer no resistance to a British expedition. After consultation, therefore, with Sir David Baird, he determined, upon his own responsibility, to make an attempt upon those important places; and, in pursuance of the decision, he sailed on April 14th with the *Diadem*, *Raisonnable*, *Diomède*, *Leda*, *Narcissus*, *Encounter*,[2] and five transports, having on board the 71st Regiment, some artillery, and a few dragoons, the military force being under Brigadier-General W. C. Beresford. At St. Helena, Beresford persuaded the governor to allow him to embark further troops and artillery sufficient to bring up his little army to a strength of about twelve hundred officers and men,[3] and on May 2nd[4] the squadron continued its voyage. On May 27th, in order to obtain local information, Sir Home proceeded ahead of the squadron in the *Narcissus*; and, on June 8th, he anchored in her off Flores. On the 13th, he was joined by the rest of his command.

It was agreed that Buenos Aires should be first attacked; and, on June 16th, after a naval brigade of one hundred seamen and three hundred and forty Royal Marines, under Acting Captain William

---

[1] Popham to Marsden, Mar. 4th, 1806.

[2] The *Belliqueux* escorted the H.E.I. Co.'s ships back to Madras.

[3] Beresford to Rt. Hon. Wm. Windham, Ap. 30th, 1806. Popham to Marsden, of same date.

[4] In a dispatch of April 30th, he informed the Admiralty of the mission upon which he had quitted the Cape; and as soon as the dispatch reached England, orders of recall were sent after him; but these did not reach him until after he had accomplished his purpose.

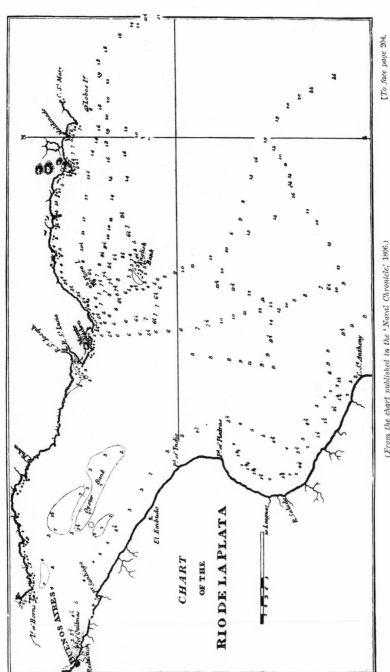

CHART
OF THE
RIO DE LA PLATA

(From the chart published in the 'Naval Chronicle,' 1806.)

King (2), had been put on board the *Narcissus* and *Encounter*, those
two vessels, with the transports and troops, moved up the Rio de la
Plata, while the *Diadem* blockaded Montevideo, and the *Raisonnable* and *Diomède* cruised in the mouth of the river. Having to
contend with adverse currents, shoals, and fogs, the *Narcissus* and
consorts were not able, until the afternoon of June 25th, to anchor
off Point Quilmes, twelve miles below the city; but, in the course of
that evening and the following night, the whole landing force of
1630 men was put ashore without accident or opposition. On the
morning of the 26th, Beresford attacked and easily dispersed a body
of about two thousand Spaniards,[1] and then followed up the retreating foe, hoping to be in time to prevent him from destroying
the bridge over the Rio Chuelo, three miles from Buenos Aires.
The Spaniards succeeded in cutting the bridge, but on the 27th the
British crossed the river in boats and on improvised rafts, under the
conduct of Captain William King (2), and, having summoned the
city, entered it without encountering any resistance. On July 2nd,
the capitulation was formally signed. In pursuance of an agreement
come to on June 28th, a large sum was handed over by the city,
and this, with other captured specie amounting to 1,086,208 dollars,
was embarked in the *Narcissus* for conveyance to England. Lieutenant James Groves, of the *Diadem*, subsequently took possession
of the neighbouring port of Ensenada, and some small vessels which
lay there. The naval brigade was then re-embarked, and Buenos
Aires left in charge of the troops.[2]

The capitulation of the place had been signed by Don Josef de
La Quintana, its governor, the viceroy of the province; and most of
his troops having previously retreated inland to Cordoba. But even
in the city there remained a strong party hostile to the invaders, and
this party was joined on August 4th by Colonel Liniers,[3] whom
Popham describes as "a French officer in the Spanish service, and
on his parole." Liniers managed to reach Conchas, above Buenos
Aires, almost unobserved, with about one thousand men from
Colonia and elsewhere. As early as July 31st, Popham had been
apprised of an intended insurrection, and he had made such dis-

---

[1] Popham says "near 4000 Spanish cavalry." Disp. of July 6th.

[2] Popham to Marsden, July 6th; Beresford to Windham, July 2nd; Terms of
Capitulation; Beresford to Castlereagh, July 11th, and July 16th, 1806.

[3] Marshall (i. 872) calls him de Linières, and says that he was an ex-captain in
the French navy who had fled from France at the Revolution; but he signed himself
"Santiago Liniers."

positions as he could to check it. Beresford, moreover, had defeated and dispersed about one thousand five hundred Spaniards under the patriot leader Pueridon. But continuous bad weather interfered with the carrying out of other measures of repression; and on August 10th, the insurgents summoned the place. It soon became evident that the situation was serious within as well as without the city. Popham desired to embark the wounded, and to move towards Ensenada; but the state of the weather frustrated most of his plans; and after the troops had been obliged to stand on the defensive during most of the night of the 11th, they were attacked on the 12th by overwhelming numbers. After having lost forty-eight killed, one hundred and seven wounded, and ten missing, Beresford, with his whole force, had to surrender, though, happily, terms of a very favourable nature were obtained.[1]

The Commodore and squadron remained in the river blockading the port until, early in October, he received reinforcements from the Cape of Good Hope. He then made an attempt upon Montevideo, but was obliged to abandon it as his vessels could not get near enough to the defences to make any impression upon them. On October 29th, his frigates entered the harbour of Maldonado, and, disembarking a naval brigade, and troops under Brigadier-General T. J. Backhouse, seized the town without much difficulty. On the 30th, he summoned, and received the surrender of the island of Gorrete, which covers the harbour; and thus he gained positions which gave him a comparatively safe anchorage for his ships and also a camping-ground for his men. Such was the situation in the Rio de la Plata at the end of the year.[2]

Ere that time orders had been sent from England for Popham's recall, and Rear-Admiral Charles Stirling (1) had been dispatched to supersede him. The further history of the expedition will be given later; but it should be mentioned here that, upon his recall to England, Popham was tried by court-martial for having quitted his station at the Cape of Good Hope without orders. The court sat on board the *Gladiator* at Portsmouth from March 6th to March 11th, 1807, and the sentence was as follows:—

" The court has agreed that the charges have been proved against the said Captain Sir Home Popham; that the withdrawing, without orders so to do, the whole of any

---

[1] Popham to Marsden, Aug. 25th, 1806.
[2] Backhouse to Windham, Oct. 13th, and Oct. 31st; Popham to Marsden, Oct. 9th, and Oct. 30th.

naval force from the place where it is directed to be employed, and the employing it in distant operations against the enemy, more especially if the success of such operations should be likely to prevent its speedy return, may be attended with the most serious inconvenience to the public service, as the success of any plan formed by his Majesty's ministers for operations against the enemy, in which such naval force might be included, may, by such removal, be entirely prevented.   And the court has further agreed that the conduct of the said Captain Sir Home Popham, in the withdrawing the whole of the naval force under his command from the Cape of Good Hope, and the proceeding with it to Rio de la Plata, is highly censurable; but, in consideration of circumstances, doth adjudge him to be only severely reprimanded; and he is hereby severely reprimanded accordingly." [1]

Napoleon's abandonment of the projected invasion of Great Britain, and his reconciliation with Austria, gave him both leisure and forces for the active prosecution of the campaigns which ended at the peace of Tilsit,[2] where Russia and Prussia were added to the number of his allies.   The northern Powers were aided in their struggle by the presence of British vessels in the Baltic; but the earlier military operations of 1807 were not of a nature which permitted them to be very decisively, or even very directly, influenced by sea-power, the waters bordering upon the scene of hostilities being, for the most part, shallow, the navigation being intricate, and it being impossible to employ large vessels to any advantage under the ruling conditions.   At Danzig, however, while the place was besieged by the French under Marshal Lefebvre, some good work was done by a little British detachment which arrived off the harbour of the beleaguered city on April 12th, 1807, and which consisted of the sloops :—

SLOOPS.	GUNS.	COMMANDERS.
Sally	16	Commander Edward Chetham.[1]
Falcon [2]	16	,, George Sanders.
Charles (hired brig)	..	,, Robert Clephane.

[1] Afterwards Sir Edward Chetham Strode.
[2] Found by Chetham lying in Danzig bay.

The first object of Chetham, who throughout acted upon his own initiative and responsibility, was to prevent the besiegers from receiving succour by sea; and with that object he detached the *Charles* to cruise.   On the 16th, he anchored the *Sally* in Neufahrwasser, so mooring her as to flank the isthmus by which alone the French

[1] For the benefit of those who cannot consult the Mins. of the C. M., it may be said that a good summary of the proceedings is to be found in the 'Nav. Chron.', xvii., pp. 209–242.

[2] July 7th and 9th, 1807.

could advance upon the works; and on the 17th, finding that the French, by taking up a position on the Nehrung, had intercepted communication between Danzig and Neufahrwasser, he lightened his sloop[1] by sending her heavier stores on board the *Falcon*, and entered the mouth of the Vistula. From that position he engaged for two hours and a half a French force of two thousand men and three guns, supported by a small battery; but, though he killed and wounded upwards of four hundred of the enemy, he was unable to clear the Nehrung, and, soon after 9 P.M., had to return to Neufahrwasser. In this gallant effort the *Sally* had about half her crew, including Lieutenant James Edwards Eastman, wounded, her sails and rigging much cut, and more than one thousand musket-balls lodged in her hull.[2] Chetham subsequently co-operated with an attempt by the Prussians to fight their way from Weichselmünde into Danzig, and, aided by the *Valorous*, prame, Commander Reuben Caillaud Mangin, took off the garrison of Fort Weichselmünde just before the occupation of the post by the victorious French. While the siege of Danzig still lasted a magnificent but unsuccessful attempt was made by the *Dauntless*, 18, Commander Christopher Strachey, to run up the river and deliver six hundred barrels of powder to the garrison; but, owing to the difficulties of navigation, she grounded under the enemy's batteries, and, after a plucky defence, was obliged to strike. A few days later Danzig fell, and on May 27th its garrison marched out with the honours of war.[3] Soon afterwards the battle of Friedland opened the way to an armistice, and eventually to the peace of Tilsit.

"That the French emperor," says Mr. James, "had not, in the meantime, wholly neglected his marine, a glance at his naval means at the conclusion of that treaty will show. In the ports of Brest, Lorient, Rochefort, Ferrol, Vigo, Cadiz, Cartagena, and Toulon, were upwards of 45 French and Spanish sail of the line ready for sea, or nearly so, exclusive of 3 French sail of the line in the West Indies and America. Bonaparte flattered himself that he should soon have also at his disposal 9 Portuguese sail of the line in the Tagus, and 5 Russian in the Mediterranean. These 62 sail, even while lying in port, would occupy the attention of an equal number of British ships; and every division that escaped to sea would, in all probability, be pursued by at least two squadrons of equal force. Moreover, it was requisite to have an adequate British force in the colonies, east and west, to be ready to act, in case an enemy's fleet should suddenly make its appearance. Hence, a great portion of the British navy was fully employed in the southern, eastern, and western seas. We have . . . . to show what force

---

[1] This is denied by Marshall, Supp., Pt. I., 230 n.

[2] *Gazette*, 1807, 749. Chetham to Marsden, Ap. 20th.

[3] Marshall, Supp., Pt. I., 228, 233.

might be opposed to the remainder in the northern sea. In the port of Flushing and at
Antwerp . . . were 3 Dutch and 8 new French sail of the line, ready for sea, or fitting
with the utmost expedition. . . . In the Texel were also 3 Dutch sail of the line,
making a total of 14. But these ships were not all. The French emperor . . . flattered
himself with obtaining, either by fair means or by foul, the 11 sail of the line belonging
to Sweden, and the 16 belonging to Denmark. There is also good ground for believing
that one of the secret articles of the treaty of Tilsit placed at the conqueror's temporary
disposal the 19 or 20 fine new ships which the Emperor of Russia had ready for sea or
nearly so, in the ports of Reval and Kronstadt."

With a possibility before her of having to deal with sixty-two
sail of the line elsewhere, and, at the same time, with about sixty
sail of the line in the North and Baltic Seas; and with the knowledge that Napoleon, having brought to his feet Austria, Russia, and
Prussia, would probably revert to his projects of invasion, if only to
find employment for his vast armies, Great Britain realised that
immense danger might result to her if all the Emperor's plans for
banding against her the northern nations should be suffered to take
shape. She, therefore, exerted herself to support Sweden, until it
became clear that Sweden, like the greater Powers, was unable to
make head against the Napoleonic alliance. And, when it appeared
that Denmark, too weak to make objection, was to be coerced into
closing the Sound to British commerce, and into lending her navy to
further the ambitions of Napoleon,[1] the British Government determined that a very bold policy must be adopted, unless the interests
of the country were to be seriously imperilled. On July 19th, in
short, it was decided to ask Denmark to hand over her fleet to Great
Britain upon promise to restore the whole of it at the conclusion of
the war; and, in case of refusal, to seize it by force.

No time was lost in putting this decision into practice; and
as early as July 26th, Admiral James Gambier (2), sailed from
Yarmouth road, with seventeen of the following twenty-five ships
of the line, and with twenty-one—subsequently increased to forty—
frigates, sloops, bombs, and gun-brigs [2] (see next page).

On August 1st, when the main body of the fleet was off Göteborg, Commodore Keats was detached with the *Ganges, Vanguard,
Orion, Nassau, Sibylle,* 38, Captain Clotworthy Upton, *Franchise,* 36,
Captain Charles Dashwood, *Nymphe,* 36, Captain Conway Shipley,
and ten gun-brigs, to occupy the passage of the Great Belt, and so
to prevent assistance being sent over to Seeland from Fünen, Jut-

---

[1] *See* 'Mems. of Fouché,' i. 311; where the suspicion is corroborated.

[2] Besides 377 transports, conveying about 27,000 troops, more than half of whom
were German mercenaries.

Ships.	Guns.	Commanders.
Prince of Wales [1] . . .	98	Admiral James Gambier (2), (B). Capt. Sir Home Riggs Popham, 1st. „ Adam Mackenzie, 2nd.
Pompée [1]	74	Vice-Adm. Hon. Henry Edwyn Stanhope (B). Capt. Richard Dacres.
Minotaur [2]	74	Rear-Adm. William Essington. Capt. Charles John Moore Mansfield.
Centaur [1]	74	Commod. Sir Samuel Hood (2). Capt. William Henry Webley.
Ganges [1]	74	Commod. Richard Goodwin Keats. Capt. Peter Halkett.
Superb [3]	74	„ Donald M'Leod.
Spencer [1]	74	„ Hon. Robert Stopford.
Vanguard [1]	74	„ Alexander Fraser (1).
Valiant [2]	74	„ James Young (2).
Mars [4]	74	„ William Lukin.
Defence [4]	74	„ Charles Ekins.
Maida [1]	74	„ Samuel Hood Linzee.
Brunswick [1]	74	„ Thomas Graves (4).
Resolution [1]	74	„ George Burlton.
Hercule [1]	74	„ Hon. John Colville.
Orion [1]	74	„ Sir Archibald Collingwood Dickson.
Alfred [1]	74	„ John Bligh (2).
Goliath [1]	74	„ Peter Puget.
Captain [1]	74	„ Isaac Wolley.
Ruby [1]	64	„ John Draper (2).
Dictator [1]	64	„ Donald Campbell (1).
Nassau [1]	64	„ Robert Campbell (1).
Inflexible [2]	64	„ Joshua Rowley Watson.
Leyden [2]	64	„ William Cumberland.
Agamemnon [5]	64	„ Jonas Rose.

[1] Sailed with Gambier on July 26th.　　[3] Joined on August 5th, off Helsingör.
[2] Joined on August 7th, off Helsingör.　　[4] Joined on August 8th and 9th.
[5] Joined in the second week of August.

land, and Holsteen. This detached force was eventually joined by the *Superb*, to which Keats transferred his broad pennant.

On the afternoon of August 3rd, having previously ascertained that no opposition would be offered to the passage of the British fleet into the Sound, Gambier exchanged salutes with Kronborg Castle, and anchored in the road of Helsingör, where lay the Danish 32-gun frigate *Frederikscoarn*. During the following week, convoys of transports, both from England, and from the island of Rügen, where a large number of German mercenaries had been embarked, joined the fleet, the military commander-in-chief, Lieutenant-General Lord Cathcart,[1] arriving in the *Africaine*, 32, Captain Richard Raggett, on August 12th.

In the meantime, Mr. Jackson, the British envoy to Denmark,

[1] He had left England on July 5th, had reached Tromper Wiek, Rügen, on July 16th, and had thence proceeded to Stralsund, before joining Gambier.

had conferred with the Crown Prince at Kiel, and had put forward
the British demands. These had been politely rejected; orders had
been sent to Copenhagen to prepare to defend itself; and on
August 11th, the Crown Prince himself had reached the city, which,
on the 12th, was quitted by the King, who proceeded to Kolding, in
Jutland, leaving the defence of the place in the hands of the governor,
General Peyman. This officer appears to have had at his disposal a
regular military force of not more than 5500 men, besides about
4000 seamen, and about 3600 armed citizens. The main body of
the Danish army was at the time in Holsteen. The permanent
defences of the city were not materially different from those which
had existed at the time of Nelson's attack upon them in 1801.[1] The
Trekroner batteries mounted sixty-eight guns, besides mortars; a
pile battery, off the citadel, and apparently new, mounted thirty-six
guns and nine mortars; the citadel itself mounted twenty guns and
three or four mortars; and the arsenal batteries mounted fifty guns
and twelve mortars. All the guns were long Danish 36 and 24-prs.,
and the mortars were of large calibre. The mobile defences consisted of the mastless 64-gunship *Mars*, the 22-gun prame *St.
Thomas*, the 20-gun prames *Elven*, *Eyderen* and *Gluckstad*, and about
thirty gunboats, each carrying two guns. All these craft lay around
the Trekroner, and off the harbour. Inside the port there were
several sail of the line, frigates and sloops, besides three two-deckers
on the stocks.[2]

On the night of August 12th, the *Frederikscoarn*, 32, perceiving
what was likely to happen, slipped her cable, and left Helsingör
road, making for Norway. On the following day Admiral Gambier
sent after her the *Defence*, 74, Captain Charles Ekins, and *Comus*, 22,
Captain Edmund Heywood, with orders to detain the fugitive. As
the wind was light, Ekins subsequently directed Heywood to proceed
ahead and execute the service singlehanded. Early on the 14th, the
Comus descried the chase, and, in the course of the day, steadily
overhauled her, until, at about midnight, she ran alongside the
enemy. Heywood requested the Danish captain to bring to, and
suffer his ship to be detained; but a refusal was, of course, returned;
and there ensued a close action, the *Comus* first taking up a raking
position, and then being fallen on board of by her disabled opponent.
After about forty-five minutes' cannonade, the Dane was boarded by

---

[1] *See* plan, vol. iv., p. 430.
[2] See list *infra*. Two other sail of the line were in Norwegian ports.

a party under Lieutenants George Edward Watts [1] and Hood Knight, and carried without further resistance. The British lost only one man wounded. The *Frederikscoarn*, besides suffering very severely in hull and rigging, had twelve killed and twenty wounded. The capture was a most creditable one; for, although the *Comus* actually carried, in addition to her twenty-two long 9-prs. on the maindeck, two more long 9-prs. and eight 24-pr. carronades on her quarter-

JAMES GAMBIER (2), LORD GAMBIER, G.C.B., ADMIRAL OF THE FLEET.
(*From a drawing by W. Evans, engraved by G. Bartolozzi, after a portrait by Sir Wm. Beechey, R.A,. painted when his Lordship was an Admiral of the Blue.*)

deck and forecastle, the *Frederikscoarn* also exceeded her rated force, carrying at least thirty-six guns; and she had, moreover, 12-prs. on her main-deck.[2] The complement of the Danish ship was 226; that of the British one, only 145.[3]

Delayed by the state of the weather, the fleet did not move

---

[1] Promoted for this service to be Commander, September 17th, 1807.

[2] Heywood to Ekins, August 15th. Another account gives her thirty-two 12- and 6-prs., and six 12-pr. carronades, or thirty-eight guns in all. O'Byrne, 1259, 1260.

[3] *Gazette*, 1807, 1157.

until August 15th, when it worked up to Wedbeck Bay, about half
way between Helsingör and Copenhagen.   There the greater part
of it anchored, while a squadron under Rear-Admiral William
Essington proceeded and anchored closer to the city.   On the
16th, some of the troops were landed at Wedbeck without opposition,
and the rest of the fleet approached Copenhagen.   On the same day
the Commanders-in-Chief addressed a proclamation to the inhabitants;
and the King, from Gluckstad, and General Peyman, from Copenhagen, issued an edict for the detention of all British vessels and
property.   On the 17th, the Danish gunboats, off the harbour,
seized and burnt a British merchantman, fired at the pickets of the
British army, and were fired at by some of the British bombs and
gun-brigs; whereupon they withdrew into the harbour.   Later in
the day, Gambier, with sixteen sail of the line and several frigates,
anchored about four miles north-east of the Trekroner, near the spot
where Parker had anchored in 1801, and ordered his cruisers to
detain all Danish ships.

From the 18th to the 21st, when Gambier declared a blockade of
Seeland, there were several affairs of no great importance between the
British and Danish small craft; and, in the interval, more troops were
disembarked, chiefly in Kjöge Bay, and a battery was erected to the
north of the city.   On the 22nd, while the army was constructing
mortar batteries in advance of this work, three Danish prames, each
of 20 guns, and all the gun-vessels, made preparations to interrupt the
business; and, in order to repel them, a British flotilla, under Captain
Peter Puget, of the *Goliath,* took up a position inside the Trekroner,
over the shoals.   This flotilla consisted of the following :—

SHIPS.	GUNS.	COMMANDERS.
Hebe, hired	18	Commander Edward Ellicott.
Cruiser	18	„ Pringle Stoddart.
Mutine	18	„ Hew Steuart.
Thunder, bomb. . .	8	„ George Cocks.
Vesuvius, bomb . .	10	„ Richard Arthur.
Ætna, bomb . . .	8	„ William Godfrey.
Zebra, bomb . . .	12	„ William Bowles.

With the gun-brigs *Indignant,* 12, Lieut. George Broad; *Kite,* 18, Com. Joseph James;
Pincher, 14, Lieut. James Aberdour; *Urgent,* 14, Lieut. Peter Rigby; *Tigress,* 12,
Lieut. R—— Long; *Safeguard,* 14, Lieut. Robert Balfour; *Fearless,* 14, Lieut. John
Williams (2); and *Desperate,* 14, Lieut. —— Price; three small armed transports, and
ten ships' launches fitted as mortar boats.

At 10 A.M. on the 23rd, these vessels were furiously attacked
by the Trekroner, the prames, the gunboats, and all the Danish

vessels within range.　They returned the fire briskly until 2 P.M., when, being overpowered, they retired, having lost Lieutenant John Woodford (*Cruiser*), and three seamen killed, and Lieutenant John Williams (*Fearless*), seven seamen and five Royal Marines wounded, and having received a considerable amount of damage.　The British shore batteries, however, presently drove off the Danish gun-vessels, with a loss of nine killed and twelve wounded.

On the 25th, some of the gun-vessels, entering the channel between Amager and Seeland, attacked the right of the British army; and on the 26th, others of them made a further attempt to destroy the works to the northward, but had to withdraw after one of their number had been blown up and several more had been badly mauled.　On the 27th, new British batteries were ready, and, opening fire, inflicted some loss on the gunboats; but on the 28th, 29th, and 30th both sides remained quiet.　On the 31st, the Danish vessels near the harbour's mouth began a fresh attack upon the works to the northward, and upon the flotilla which supported them; and on that day the armed transport, *Charles*, was blown up by a shell from the Trekroner, losing her Master, James Moyase, and seven seamen, besides two men belonging to the *Valiant*, and having twenty-one people wounded.

Stralsund had by that time fallen into the hands of the French; and, on September 1st, in order to prevent reinforcements from being sent thence to the Danes, a blockade of the port was proclaimed, and Commodore Keats was ordered to make the dispositions necessary for enforcing it.　On the same day, the preparations for a general bombardment of Copenhagen being nearly completed, General Peyman was summoned to surrender the Danish fleet, and was assured that it and other captured Danish property should be restored immediately upon the conclusion of a general peace.　He declined, but asked for time to communicate the summons to the King.　The British Commander-in-Chief refused to grant this; and at 7.30 P.M. on September 2nd, all the besieging batteries opened upon the town, which was set on fire within a few minutes.　The bombs co-operated, and the fire was returned until about 8 A.M. on the 3rd, when the bombardment ceased.　It was resumed, however, in the evening, and continued, but not hotly, throughout the following night.　On the evening of the 4th, the Danes still remaining obdurate, the batteries opened once more with great fury; and presently enormous conflagrations were raging in the city, the firemen, many of whom had fallen, proving quite unable to cope with them. So matters went on until the evening of September 5th, when, the flames threatening the entire destruction of the place, General Peyman, under a flag of truce, begged for a twenty-four hours' armistice, in which to discuss terms. The request was refused; but the firing was ordered to cease; and in a short time the Governor agreed to accept the surrender of the fleet as a basis for negotiation. By the evening of the 6th, the articles were drawn up; and, on the morning of the 7th, they were signed and ratified, the Danes giving up to the British possession of the citadel, and of the ships and stores. Upon the removal of the latter, or within six weeks, the citadel was to be restored, and Seeland evacuated. In the interim, hostilities were to cease, and prisoners and property taken by either side were to be restored.

The British naval losses during the operations have been noted already. The army lost 42 killed, 145 wounded, and 24 missing.[1] The Danes lost at least 250 combatants killed and wounded, besides a large number of prisoners; and, unhappily, a considerable number of innocent non-combatants also perished, General Peyman having omitted to send the women and children out of the city previous to the bombardment, although he had an opportunity for doing so.

The Danish vessels surrendered under the terms of the capitulation were the following:—

	Guns.		Guns.		Guns.
Christian VII.	84	Nayaden	36	Aalborg	2, & 6 carrs.
Neptunos	80	Nymphen[2]	36	Odense	,,
Waldemaar	80	Triton[2]	28	Langesund	,,
Prindsesse Sophie Frederike	74	Frederiksteen	28	Stavœrn	,,
Justitia	74	Lille Belt	20	Stege	,,
Arveprinds Frederik	74	St. Thomas[1]	22	Christiansund	,,
Kronprinds Frederik	74	Fylla	20	Flensborg	,,
Fyen	74	Elven	16	Wiborg	,,
Odin	74	Eyderen	16	Kallundborg	2, & 4 carrs.
Trekroner	74	Gluckstad	16	Helsingöer	,,
Skjold.	74	Sarpen	16	Nestved	,,
Kronprindsesse Marie	74	Glommen	16	Roeskilde	,,
Danmark.	74	Nidelven	16	Saltholmen	,,
Norge	74	Delphinen[2]	16	Frederiksund	,,
Prindsesse Caroline	74	Flyvendefiske	14	Rödby	,,
Dithmarschen[1]	64	Allart[2]	16	Stubbekjöbing	,,
Seierherre	64	Mercurius	16	Nysted	,,
Mars (mastless)[1]	64	Coureer	16	Svendborg	,,
Perlen	38	Brevdrageren[1]	16	Faaborg	,,
Havfrue	36	Ornen, sch.[1]	12	Holbek	,,
Freja	36	Arendal	2, & 6 carrs.	Middelfart	,,
Iris	36	Nykjöbing	,,	Assens	,,
Rota	38	Nakskov	,,	Kjerteminde[2]	,,
Venus.	36				

[1] Destroyed as useless, as also were the *Neptunos* and 23 of the 2-gun gunboats, while on the way to England.
[2] Not included in Gambier's dispatch. Were discovered later.

(For assistance in compiling the above I am indebted to Dr. Johan Fogh, of the University of Copenhagen.)

[1] These were all lost during petty sorties and skirmishes. No one on the British side suffered during the bombardment.

The Crown Prince had sent to General Peyman an order to burn the fleet, in case he should be obliged to surrender the city; but the bearer of the order, being captured by a British patrol, destroyed his dispatches. Besides the vessels surrendered, three 74's, which were on the stocks, were taken to pieces or otherwise rendered useless; and the *Mars, Dithmarschen, Triton,* and *St. Thomas,* being rotten,[1] were destroyed. The others were removed from the harbour to the road, whence, when the army had been re-embarked, they sailed on October 21st for England with the fleet. Owing to some mismanagement, the *Neptunos,* 80, grounded near the island of Hveen, and eventually had to be destroyed; and in the Kattegat, owing to the rough weather there encountered, all the captured gunboats except three had to be similarly got rid of; but, at the end of the month, the expedition, without further casualties, reached Yarmouth and the Downs. Admiral Gambier announced, with some magniloquence, that his success had "added the navy of Denmark to that of the United Kingdom"; but, of the numerous line-of-battle ships brought to England, four only were found worth refitting for seaservice; so that the real accession of strength was but trifling. These four were the *Christian VII.,* of 2131 tons, the *Danmark,* of 1836 tons, the *Norge,* of 1960 tons, and the *Prindsesse Caroline,* of 1637 tons. The *Christian VII.,* a vessel of very fine type, served as model for the *Cambridge,* which was laid down at Deptford, and launched in 1815.[2]

The attack upon Copenhagen was undoubtedly a wise and indeed a necessary measure. In times of general war, weak powers, which cannot preserve their neutrality, and which may be used as tools by one of the great parties to the strife, are sources of danger to the other party; and it is only prudent of that other party to seize the earliest possible occasion for depriving them of weapons, which, though comparatively harmless in the hands of small and unambitious states, may be formidable under the management of large and aggressive ones. The strict legality of the seizure of the fleet is more open to question. In the conduct of the operation

---

[1] According to Gambier's list, the *Mars* had been built in 1784, the *Dithmarschen* in 1780, the *Triton* in 1790, and the *St. Thomas* in 1779.

[2] Gambier to Castlereagh, Aug. 16th; Procl. of Gambier and Cathcart, Aug. 16th; Cathcart to Castlereagh, Aug. 22nd; Gambier's Journal; Gambier and Cathcart to Peyman, Sept. 1st; Reply of Peyman, Sept. 1st; Gambier and Cathcart to Peyman, Sept. 2nd; Gambier to Pole, Sept. 7th, and Oct. 20th; Corresp. in Chatterton's 'Gambier;' etc., etc.

there was room for the display of promptitude, decision, tact, and good conduct; and these qualities were displayed to the full both by the Navy and by the army. But there was little scope for the acquisition of glory. The Danes were taken at a disadvantage, and were numerically inferior as well by land as by sea; and, looking to the overwhelming nature of the British forces employed, any meed of success short of what was actually achieved would have been disgraceful. Nevertheless it was deemed proper to vote the thanks of Parliament to both branches of the service, to give a peerage to Admiral Gambier, to promote Lord Cathcart from the Scots' peerage to a Viscounty in that of the United Kingdom,[1] and to make Baronets of Vice-Admiral the Hon. Henry Edwyn Stanhope,[2] Lieut.-General Harry Burrard,[3] and Major-General Thomas Blomefield.[4] Captain George Ralph Collier, of the *Surveillant*, who carried home the dispatches, was knighted. But neither then, nor in 1847, were any medals granted in respect of the affair, which presently produced a formal declaration of war by Denmark.[5] Great Britain replied, on November 4th, by ordering reprisals against that country. During the winter, however, hostilities in the north were practically suspended; and a small naval force, cruising in the Belt, sufficed to protect British interests at the mouth of the Baltic.

While Copenhagen was being beleaguered, Denmark was quietly deprived of one of her outlying possessions, the island of Helgoland. On August 30th, the island was summoned by the *Quebec*, 32, Captain Charles John, Viscount Falkland. The governor refused to surrender, and the *Quebec* was about to compel him, when, on the afternoon of September 4th, the *Majestic*, 74, Vice-Admiral Thomas Macnamara Russell, Captain George Hart, appeared upon the scene. This brought a flag of truce from the shore; and, on the following day, articles of capitulation were signed without further dispute.[6] The island remained in British hands until 1890, when it was amicably transferred to Germany, as representing Schleswig-Holstein, in return for concessions in other quarters.

Just as the ambitions of France were responsible for British hostilities against Denmark, so were they, in the same year, responsible for British hostilities against the Sublime Porte. By

---

[1] Nov. 3rd, 1807.
[2] Nov. 13th, 1807.
[3] Nov. 12th, 1807.
[4] Nov. 14th, 1807.
[5] Influenced by the near presence of very large French forces, and by the prospect of Russian support.
[6] Russell to Admlty., Sept. 6th, 1807.

the autumn of 1806, French counsels had become all powerful
at Constantinople, and had disposed Turkey to run counter to all
the projects of Great Britain, and of Russia, her then ally; and,
on September 16th, 1806, the French ambassador demanded, with
threats, that the Sultan should close the Dardanelles to Russian
vessels, which, under treaty, had for some time enjoyed the right
of passing them. To this demand the Porte acquiesced, though,
on October 15th, intimidated by the preparations of the Russian
ambassador to leave Turkey, it reversed the decree.

The attitude of the Sultan induced Lord Collingwood, who
still watched Cadiz, to detach a small division to reconnoitre the
Dardanelles, in case it should become necessary for a British
squadron to force them and to make its way to Constantinople.
Collingwood sent away Rear-Admiral Sir Thomas Louis on
November 2nd, 1806, in his flagship, the *Canopus*, 80, Captain
Thomas George Shortland, with the *Thunderer*, 74, Captain John
Talbot, *Standard*, 64, Captain Thomas Harvey, *Active*, 38, Captain
Richard Hussey Moubray, and *Nautilus*, 18, Commander Edward
Palmer. Louis reached Malta on November 8th, sailed again on
the 15th, and anchored off Tenedos on the 21st to wait for pilots
and a southerly wind. In the early morning of the 27th he weighed
for the Strait, and, having entered it, left the rest of his command
at anchor in Azire Bay, a little below the castle of Abydos, and
proceeded in the *Canopus* alone. By 5 P.M. on November 28th, he
had anchored off Seraglio Point, where he found the *Endymion*, 40,
Captain the Hon. Thomas Bladen Capell, which had brought out
the British ambassador, Mr. Arbuthnot, and was awaiting the result
of his negotiations.[1]

On November 23rd, a large Russian army had entered Moldavia.
News of this invasion caused the Porte to decline to make any
further concessions to the Russian ambassador, who, on December
25th, took refuge on board the *Canopus*. On December 28th, Louis,
leaving the *Endymion* at the disposal of Mr. Arbuthnot, weighed
to return to Azire Bay, where he re-anchored on January 2nd, 1807.
On January 4th, the Russian ambassador removed to the *Active*, for
conveyance to Malta; and on January 31st, the *Endymion* joined
the squadron, having quitted Constantinople on the 29th, with the
ambassador and the entire British commercial colony on board.

---

[1] Collingwood's 'Collingwood,' 263 *et seq.*

Capell had hurriedly carried them off upon an assurance that the Porte had intended to seize both them and his ship in order to secure hostages. Louis at once made the best of his way out of the Strait, and, on February 1st, was again at anchor off Tenedos.

As early as November 22nd, 1806, the British Government, in anticipation of the probable course of events, had sent directions to Lord Collingwood, ordering him to detach a larger squadron to the Dardanelles, and indicating Vice-Admiral Sir John Thomas Duckworth for the command of it; but Collingwood, off Cadiz, did not receive these instructions until January 12th, 1807. On the 15th, nevertheless, Duckworth, in the *Royal George*, 100, Captain Richard Dalling Dunn, quitted the Commander-in-Chief.

Collingwood's directions [1] to his subordinate were not as clear and precise as they might have been. Duckworth, after assembling certain ships, was to proceed with all speed to Constantinople, and to so place himself as to be able to bombard the city in case of the refusal of the Porte to deliver up the Turkish fleet and stores sufficient for its equipment. But he was to consult with Mr. Arbuthnot, the British ambassador, on the measures proper to be pursued; and he was not to demand the Turkish fleet until the ambassador should be of opinion that hostilities ought to commence. Again, he was recommended, after having made the demand, not to allow the Turks to gain time by prolonged negotiations, none of which should be permitted to " continue for more than half an hour "; and, upon receiving " an absolute refusal," he was either to cannonade the town or to attack the fleet, wheresoever it might be found, bearing always in mind that to secure the fleet, or, if not, to destroy it, was the first object to be kept in view. Collingwood explained that he was sending on the service a larger force than had been originally intended, as he was doubtful whether the Russians would be able to co-operate; but he added that he had asked Vice-Admiral Seniavine, who was then in the Archipelago, to detach four of his ships to serve under Duckworth in the expedition.

Duckworth reached Gibraltar on January 17th, picked up the *Windsor Castle* and *Repulse*, sailed again on the 18th, and anchored on the 30th at Valetta, whence he dispatched the *Active* to Sir Thomas Louis to apprise him of the projected plan of operations. At Malta, Duckworth was joined by the *Ajax*, and *Pompée*, from the

---

[1] Collingwood to Duckworth, Jan. 13th, 1807.

coast of Sicily; on February 4th, he sailed for the Levant, and on the 10th he arrived off Tenedos, where his entire command consisted of the following men-of-war :—

SHIPS.	GUNS.	COMMANDERS.
Royal George	100	Vice-Adm. Sir John Thomas Duckworth, K.B. Capt. Richard Dalling Dunn.
Canopus	80	Rear-Adm. Sir Thomas Louis. Capt. Thomas George Shortland.
Pompée	74	Rear-Adm. Sir William Sidney Smith. Capt. Richard Dacres.
Windsor Castle . . .	98	„ Charles Boyles.
Repulse	74	„ Hon. Arthur Kaye Legge.
Ajax	74	„ Hon. Henry Blackwood.
Thunderer	74	„ John Talbot.
Standard	64	„ Thomas Harvey (1).
Endymion	40	„ Hon. Thomas Bladen Capell.
Active	38	„ Richard Hussey Moubray.
Lucifer, bomb	8	Com. Robert Elliot.
Meteor, bomb	8	„ James Collins.

The fortifications of the Dardanelles had by that time been discovered to be somewhat less formidable than had been previously supposed. About a mile within the Strait, where the channel is two miles wide, were the outer castles of Europe and Asia, Sedil Bahr and Koum Kaleh[1]; nine or ten miles further, where the channel's width contracts to three-quarters of a mile, were the inner castles of Europe and Asia, Kilid Bahr and Chanak Kaleh.[2] Yet further, at another constriction, were other forts, which had to be passed ere the Sea of Marmora could be reached; but the batteries were everywhere either in bad condition or but partially armed. As for the Turkish fleet, most of it was reported to be moored at Constantinople and to be not yet fit for sea; but a division of it, consisting of one 64-gun ship, four frigates, four corvettes, two brigs, and three gunboats, lay in the Dardanelles, under Point Pesquies.

Duckworth weighed at 11 A.M. on February 11th, but, the wind not being fair, had to anchor at 1 P.M. off Cape Janissary. While he lay there, he wrote, on the 14th, to Collingwood a letter in which occurs the following obscurely ominous passage :—

"I think it a duty I owe to his Majesty and my own honour, to observe to your Lordship that, our minister having left Constantinople sixteen days since, and the Turks [having] employed French engineers to erect batteries to flank every turn in our passage through the Dardanelles, I conceive the service pointed out in my instructions as completely altered; and, viewed in whatever light it may be, [it] has become the most arduous and doubtful that ever has been undertaken; for, as I am instructed by

---

[1] Sand Castle.　　[2] Castle of Sultanieh.

your Lordship to communicate and consult with his Majesty's ambassador, and to be guided in my proceedings by such communication, it is on that principle that the resolution has been adopted ; for the honour and character of the nation appear pledged ; and in our hands they never can be tarnished. Of the hazard which attends such an enterprise I am fully aware. We are to enter a sea environed with enemies, without a possible resource but in ourselves ; and, when we are to return, there cannot remain a doubt but that the passage will be rendered as formidable as the efforts of the Turkish empire, directed and assisted by their allies, the French, can make it. I entreat your Lordship, however, to believe that, as I am aware of the difficulties we have to encounter, so I am resolved that nothing on my part [shall] be left undone that can ensure the means of surmounting them."

Duckworth had been nominated for the command because the service would assuredly call for " much ability and firmness."[1] This dispatch indicates neither ability nor firmness on the part of the writer ; and it must have greatly disturbed Collingwood. It was obviously designed to prepare the mind of the Commander-in-Chief for the news of a failure ; and it betrayed a lack of self-confidence which was almost predestined to be fatal. If Duckworth really felt that the enterprise was beyond his strength, he should, even at that late hour, have declined, either absolutely, or failing the receipt of reinforcements, to attempt it. His letter shows, moreover, that he fully realised that the fortifications were from day to day becoming more formidable, and that, granting that he might pass up without much loss, he would certainly be unable to return without greatly increased risk. Such a consideration as this would have spurred a strong man to more than usual promptitude in all his operations ; but it seems to have affected Duckworth in precisely the opposite way ; and, from the time when the dispatch, from which the above is an excerpt, was written, the Vice-Admiral, as if paralysed by his responsibilities, vacillated, procrastinated, and neglected his opportunities so conspicuously as to prove that the Admiralty had lamentably misunderstood his character.

While the squadron lay wind-bound off Cape Janissary, a terrible disaster overtook the *Ajax*. At 9 P.M. on February 14th, a fire broke out in her cockpit. The flames rapidly spread ; a dense smoke quickly rendered it almost impossible either to fight them or to hoist out the boats ; and at length, when only 381[2] out of her complement of 633 souls had saved themselves or been picked up, she drifted ashore on the island of Tenedos, and, at 5 A.M. on the 15th, blew up. Captain Blackwood and his surviving officers and

---

[1] Parl. papers ordered Mar. 23rd, 1808.

[2] Marshall says 384 (i. 649). Among the sufferers were Lieutenants Mitchell and Sibthorpe, and Captain Boyd, R.M.

men were honourably acquitted of blame ; and, although rumour
attributed the origin of the fire to carelessness, the truth was
never established, and it is quite probable that the catastrophe was
due to spontaneous combustion.[1]   During the subsequent operations,
Blackwood served as a volunteer in the *Royal George*.

The wind having shifted to S.S.W., the Vice-Admiral weighed
at 7 A.M. on the 19th, with his fleet formed in the following line of
battle : *Canopus, Repulse, Royal George, Windsor Castle, Standard*
(towing the *Meteor*), *Pompée, Thunderer* (towing the *Lucifer*), *Endymion*, and *Active*.   He had previously directed Sir William Sidney
Smith, with the *Pompée, Thunderer, Standard*, and *Active*, to
specially devote himself to the Turkish squadron under Point
Pesquies, in case that force should show a hostile demeanour.
At about 8 A.M., as the *Canopus* drew abreast of the outer castles
or forts, she was fired on by both of them.   They also fired on the
ships astern of her as they arrived in succession within range of
their guns ; but the bomb-vessels alone made any reply, and even
they threw only a few shells.   Mr. Arbuthnot, the British ambassador, who was on board the *Royal George*, dissuaded the Vice-
Admiral from ordering any more general return ; but Duckworth
seems to have been ill-advised in holding his hand, for, as he had
written to Collingwood, the works were being steadily improved and
they had to be repassed ; and, had they been vigorously replied to at
once, their ability to obstruct the return passage would have been
proportionably lessened.   The inner pair of castles, which were
passed at 9.30 A.M., also fired ; but their fire was returned by all the
ships, and there is reason to believe that the reply caused a considerable amount of damage.   On neither side, however, were the losses
in these preliminary encounters very serious.   The ships suffered
little harm aloft, and they had but six killed and fifty-one wounded—
all in the *Canopus, Repulse, Royal George*, and *Windsor Castle*.
The *Meteor*, unfortunately, burst her 13-inch mortar.

Above the inner castles, and below Point Pesquies, or Nagara
Burun (Abydos), on the Asiatic side, lay the Turkish squadron already
mentioned.   It consisted of a 64-gun ship bearing a rear-admiral's
flag, one 40-gun frigate, two 36-gun frigates, one 32-gun frigate, one
22-gun corvette, one 18-gun corvette, two 10-gun corvettes, two
brigs, and three gunboats, anchored under the protection of an

---

[1] Court of Inquiry, Feb. 16th, 1807, in *Canopus*, ordered by Duckworth ; C. M., in
Royal Sovereign, ordered by Collingwood.

unfinished 31-gun redoubt on the Point.   As the British approached, one of the brigs cut her cables, and made sail unpursued
for Constantinople.   The other Turkish ships gallantly opened fire

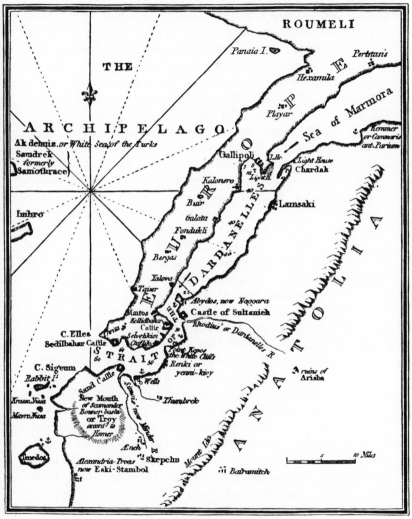

STRAIT OF THE DARDANELLES.
(After a chart published by Joyce Gold in 1811.)

on the British van.   The main body of the squadron stood on,
delivering its reply as it went, and anchored about three miles
higher up.   Sir William Sidney Smith, with his division, "closed into

the midst,"[1] and, anchoring within musket-shot of the enemy's vessels
and redoubt at about 10 A.M., opened so heavy a cannonade that in
half an hour all the Turkish craft, except a corvette and a gunboat,
which struck and were taken possession of, ran ashore. One of the
frigates, endeavouring to make off, was driven ashore by the *Active*,
and then boarded by her boats under Lieutenants George Wickens
Willes and Walter Croker. When her people had been removed,
she was set on fire. The three other frigates were boarded and
burnt by boats of the *Thunderer* and *Standard* under Lieutenants
John Carter, John Waller (2), and Thomas Colby; and the line-of-
battle ship was destroyed by the *Repulse*, aided by the boats of the
Pompée. In the meantime the redoubt on Point Pesquies, having
continued its fire after the Turkish ships had run ashore, had been
shelled until the enemy evacuated it, and had been entered by seamen and Royal Marines under Lieutenant Lestock Francis Boileau,
and Lieutenants Edward Nicolls and William Finmore, R.M.,
who partially destroyed it, and spiked the guns. The destruction
was subsequently completed, under the direction of Captain
Moubray, by Lieutenants William Fairbrother Carroll and Septi-
mus Arabin, of the *Pompée*, and Lieutenant William Lawrie, R.M.
Among other officers who were employed in the operations on
shore were Lieutenants Mark Oates and David Holt, R.M., Master's
Mate David Sinclair, and Midshipmen George Parkyns, Thomas
Smith (7), Norfolk King, and Edmund Lyons. The *Active* was
instructed to remain in the Dardanelles, pending the receipt of
further orders. The whole British loss in this affair was only four
killed and twenty-six wounded.[2]

At 5 P.M., Sir Sidney's division, except the *Active*, weighed and
passed up to rejoin the main body, which also weighed, and, pursuing
its course with a fair wind, but with little sail, anchored off Prince's
Isles, about eight miles from Constantinople, at 8 P.M. on February
20th. This anchorage might have been reached many hours earlier,
had the Vice-Admiral taken all possible advantage of the breeze,
which at first was brisk, but which afterwards became light. At
dawn on the following morning, when there was a moderate S.E.
wind, Duckworth, instead of pressing on and putting the city within
range of his guns, began a series of consultations with Mr. Arbuthnot, and presently sent the *Endymion*, with dispatches and a flag of

[1] Duckworth's Disp. of Feb. 21st.
[2] *Gazette*, 1807, 595.

truce, to approach as closely as possible to Constantinople.   At
11.30 A.M., Captain Capell, unable to get nearer, anchored four miles
from the place,[1] and endeavoured to send on shore the ambassador's
somewhat weakly worded declaration, to which a reply, not in half
an hour, but by sunset on the following day, was required.   It was
accompanied, however, by Duckworth's demand for the surrender of
the fleet and of stores for its equipment, and for a reply within half
an hour of the translation of his note.   The Vice-Admiral did not
expressly say what he would do in case of refusal, but he darkly
hinted that, " having it in his power to destroy the capital and all
the Turkish vessels, the plan of operation which his duty prescribed
to him was, in consequence, very clearly marked out."[2]   The Turks
declined to allow the flag of truce to land.   Later in the day,
Mr. Arbuthnot addressed to the Porte a letter saying that " the
answer to the Admiral's note must be delivered in half an hour " ; [2]
and at midnight, Duckworth followed this up with a declaration
that, " As it has been discovered by our glasses that the time
granted the Sublime Porte to take its decision is employed in
warping the ships of war into places more susceptible of defence,
and in constructing batteries along the coast, it is the duty of the
Vice-Admiral to lose no time." [2]   This feeble language was being
held twelve hours after the expiration of the time-limit originally
specified ; and, if the letter was ever received by the Porte, it is not
astonishing that it encouraged the Turks in their obduracy.

Early on the 22nd the *Royal George* made the signal to prepare
to weigh ; but, though the S.E. wind freshened in the course of the
morning, and lasted until after 4 P.M., the signal to weigh did not
follow, and by 5 P.M. there was almost a calm.   Thus, the threats
which had been so freely made use of were again not carried out.
That day Mr. Arbuthnot fell ill, and the Vice-Admiral, on the 23rd,
continued the one-sided and ridiculous correspondence with the
shore.

" I must tell you frankly," he wrote, " I will not consent to lose any more time.   I
owe it to my Sovereign and to my own honour not to suffer myself to be duped ; and
those who are capable of thinking so meanly of others justly become themselves the
object of suspicion.   You are putting your ships of war in motion ; you take every
method of increasing the means of defence ; but if the Sublime Porte really wishes to

---

[1] Duckworth to Collingwood, Feb. 21st, 1807.
[2] Translations in the *Times* and other London papers from the dispatches published
in the *Moniteur*, and forwarded to it, it is believed, by General Sébastiani.

save its capital from the dreadful calamities which are ready to burst upon it, the thought of which is shocking to our feelings of humanity, you will be sent here very early to-morrow morning with full powers to conclude with me the work of peace, which Mr. Arbuthnot would by this time have set out to conclude on shore, if he had not been prevented by a very serious indisposition. I now declare to you, for the last time, that no consideration whatever shall induce me to remain at a distance from your capital a single moment beyond the period I have now assigned; and you are sufficiently acquainted with the English character not to be ignorant that, in a case of unavoidable necessity, we are less disposed to threaten than to execute. But understand me well. Our object is peace and amity: this depends on you."

The Turks would have been little short of foolish at that period if they had paid serious attention to the man who, after demanding the Turkish fleet in half an hour, and declaring again and again that he would lose no time, asked, two days later, for peace and amity, and begged for a reply " early to-morrow morning." It was, perhaps, because they had learnt to despise Sir John that they took delight in prolonging the situation. They agreed to treat; but they were still far from having seen the last of his vacillation and indecision. On February 24th, he announced that he intended to conduct the negotiations in person, and that he would either meet a Turkish plenipotentiary on board the *Endymion* or *Royal George*, or would himself land for the purpose on one of the Prince's Isles. The Turks suggested Kadikiöi, on the Asiatic coast, as a suitable meeting-place. To this Duckworth advanced two objections. Firstly, an admiral or commander-in-chief could not quit his command. Secondly, the place was too far distant. While these objections remained unovercome, the jolly-boat of the *Endymion*, having on board Midshipman Harwell and four boys who were going to the isle of Prota [1] to buy provisions, was seized by Turks and carried up to Constantinople. The return of the lads was demanded, and flatly refused; [2] and still the Vice-Admiral did nothing.

It is not astonishing that the Turks by that time thought of assuming the offensive. On the morning of the 27th, it was seen that they were erecting a battery on Prota island, within range of the nearest ships of the British squadron. Pending a disembarkation of Royal Marines, the *Repulse* and *Lucifer* scoured the shore of the island with grape; whereupon a number of Turks made off

---

[1] One of the Prince's Isles.

[2] The prisoners were found on board the Turkish flagship which was taken by Vice-Adm. Seniavine at the battle off Lemnos on July 1st, 1807, and were afterwards handed over by him to Capt. Edward Oliver Osborn, of the *Kent*, 74.

in boats, one of which was captured. Later in the day it was found
that there were still Turkish forces in the island, and the Marines
of the *Canopus*, under Captain R. Kent, R.M., were landed to capture
them.[1] The detachment, pursuing the enemy to a loopholed
monastery, was badly handled, and had to signal for help ; whereupon further Marines from the *Royal George, Windsor Castle*, and
Standard were sent ashore, " with particular directions to bring off
the *Canopus's* people, but to avoid being drawn into danger." [2]
While the Marines were warmly engaged with the foe, Duckworth
sent ashore an officer with orders for both detachments to return to
the ships, the result being that the incompleted action, which, if
persisted in, would probably have ended in the capture of General
Sébastiani, French ambassador to the Porte, who was on the island,
involved the useless sacrifice of seven people[3] killed and nineteen
wounded. Had Sir John only made up his mind either that the
Turks must be ousted, or that they might be suffered to remain in
Prota and erect batteries to annoy the British squadron, this
disaster would not have occurred. Nor was the escape of the
enemy prevented. The launches of the squadron rowed guard
round the island during the night; but, by the morning, the Turks
had all disappeared.

On the 27th, a westerly wind sprang up, and blew during the
whole of the 28th. This would have enabled the Vice-Admiral
to bombard the city, or destroy the Turkish fleet, had he pleased
to do either. But, apparently influenced by the consideration that,
if he allowed his ships to be partially disabled he would never
succeed in getting back to the Mediterranean, he remained idle,
while the Turks went on steadily completing the equipment of their
men-of-war and the arming of their batteries, both near the city
and in the Dardanelles.[4] On March 1st, the wind blew from the
north-east. It gave Sir John, therefore, an opportunity for quitting
" the territories of a people so ignorant and foolhardy, that no
rhetoric could persuade, no threats intimidate them." [5] The Vice-

----

[1] Sir John Duckworth allowed Sir. Thomas Louis to send the party upon the
contradictory understanding " that no risk whatever must be run." If no risk was to
be run and the people were not to be hazarded, it was surely useless to suffer anyone
to be landed.

[2] Duckworth to Collingwood, Feb. 28th.

[3] Among the killed were Capt. R. Kent and Lieut. George Lawrence Belli, R.N.

[4] Duckworth to Collingwood, Feb. 28th, 1807.

[5] James, iv. 308 (Ed. 1837).

Admiral signalled to weigh ; and by 8.25 A.M., all the ships were
under sail in line of battle. It was, of course, most improbable, in
the circumstances, that the Turks, who had then but five sail of the
line and four frigates ready for sea, would accept his challenge to
come out and fight him ; yet, for the sake of appearances, he stood
on and off during the day within sight of the city. At night,
relinquishing the pretentious farce, he bore up for the Dardanelles,
and, at 5 P.M. on March 2nd, anchored about six miles above Point
Pesquies, in order to be able to pass the narrows in daylight. He
was there joined by the *Active*.

At 7.30 A.M. on the 3rd, the squadron weighed again, and, at
8.15 A.M., bore up under topsails with a fresh north-east wind. The
order of the ships, on going down, was *Canopus, Repulse, Royal
George, Windsor Castle, Standard, Pompée, Thunderer* (towing
Lucifer), *Active*, and *Endymion* (towing *Meteor*). As the squadron
neared the higher pair of castles, Duckworth weakly and unnecessarily fired a salute of thirteen guns. It cannot be determined whether the Turks believed that the guns were shotted, or
whether they were determined to bestow a parting kick upon their
foe, no matter how politely servile he might be ; but certain it is
that the salute produced a general discharge of heavy shot both
from the castles and from the repaired and re-armed battery on
Point Pesquies. From that point the squadron, as it passed,
received the fire of every gun that would bear upon it. It replied
warmly, but probably inflicted much less damage than it suffered.
By about 11.35 P.M., it was out of range of the last of the
batteries, and before noon it was once more at anchor off Cape
Janissary.[1]

The loss of officers and men in each ship during the passage
down was as follows : *Canopus*, 0 killed, 3 wounded ; *Repulse*,
10 killed, 10 wounded ; *Royal George*, 3 killed, 27 wounded ;
Windsor Castle, 3 killed, 13 wounded ; *Standard*, 8 killed, 47
wounded ; *Pompée*, 0 killed, 0 wounded ; *Thunderer*, 2 killed,
14 wounded ; *Lucifer*, 0 killed, 0 wounded ; *Active*, 0 killed, 8
wounded ; *Meteor*, 0 killed, 8 wounded. The material damage
done to the ships was, upon the whole, less serious than might
have been expected from the enormous size of the shot employed
by the Turks. The *Canopus* and *Repulse* had their wheels carried

---

[1] Duckworth to Collingwood, Mar. 6th, 1807.

away; the *Windsor Castle's* main mast was nearly cut in two; an
explosion was caused on board the *Standard*; and the *Meteor*,
having parted her hawser, and being left behind by the *Endymion*,
narrowly escaped total destruction.[1] All the ships, except the
Pompée, were more or less knocked about, and several, when they
came out of action, had huge shot sticking in them. One, which
struck the *Windsor Castle*, weighed 800 lbs.; another, which entered
the *Standard*, weighed 770 lbs. and measured 2 feet 2 inches in
diameter; a third, which came to rest in the *Active*, was 6 feet
6 inches in circumference, and weighed 800 lbs. The only officers
killed while the squadron was within the Dardanelles seem to have
been Lieutenant George Lawrence Belli (*Royal George*) and Captain
R. Kent, R.M. Among those wounded were Lieutenants John
Forbes (3) and Nisbet Josiah Willoughby (*Royal George*), John
Waller (2) and Thomas Colby (*Thunderer*), Daniel Harrington
(*Standard*), and John Langdon (*Endymion*).

Never, perhaps, did a British naval officer of high rank succeed
in making himself, his squadron, and his country so ridiculous as
Sir John Thomas Duckworth. He allowed his flag to be fired at,
and made no adequate return; he wasted valuable time; after
threatening instant action in case of refusal of his demands, he
waited for days and did nothing; he sacrificed his men uselessly at
Prota; he permitted himself to be trifled with and laughed at by
the Porte; he tacitly abandoned all his demands when the Turks
refused to take him seriously; he made pretence of a demonstration
which imposed upon nobody; he went out of his way to do honour
to the flag which had insulted his own; and, finally, he departed
ignominiously, pursued by the enemy's shot. Yet, strange to say,
this officer's conduct was never reviewed by any tribunal. The
House of Commons,[2] when asked to order the production of the
log of the *Royal George*, refused on the ground that any inquiry
which might arise out of such production should be made, not by
the House, but by a court-martial. Subsequently, when asked to
censure the Grenville ministry, which had planned the expedition, it
declined, chiefly on the strength of Windham's [3] submission, that

---

[1] In going down, the *Meteor* burst her 10-in. mortar. She was a converted
merchantman, and, as her magazine was above water, there was great danger of its
being exploded by the sparks struck from her ironwork by the Turkish stone shot.

[2] May 16th, 1808.

[3] Windham had been Secretary for War in the Grenville ministry.

"the failure of the expedition could not be attributed to any misconduct on the part of the late government"; although Canning [1]
declared "that the expedition might have done more than it did."
Duckworth, however, did not demand an inquiry; and the British
public, awed by tales of shot six feet in circumference, and blinded
by an exaggerated estimate of what had been accomplished off Point
Pesquies, had not the heart to formally question the conduct of the
Vice-Admiral. But although Sir John was to blame, the Grenville
government was to blame too. It ought to have known better than
to mistake Duckworth for an officer of exceptional "ability and
firmness"; and it ought never to have given its chosen admiral an
excuse for supposing that he was to be directed from hour to hour
by Mr. Arbuthnot. It should have clearly told Duckworth what
he was to do; and it should have called him to account [2] had he
failed to do it.

After his return to the anchorage off Cape Janissary, Duckworth
was joined by eight Russian sail of the line under Vice-Admiral
Seniavine, who, according to Brenton, "requested Sir John to
return with him and renew the attack or the negotiations; but this
was declined, and it was observed, perhaps with too much national
vanity, that where a British squadron had failed no other was likely
to succeed." [3]

While Duckworth's squadron was still up the Dardanelles, preparations were in progress for supporting the demonstration before
Constantinople by means of action elsewhere; and on March 6th,
1807, an expedition consisting of thirty-three transports, having on
board about five thousand troops under Major-General Fraser, left
Messina for Alexandria, under convoy of the *Tigre*, 74, Captain
Benjamin Hallowell, *Apollo*, 38, Captain Edward Fellowes, and
Wizard, 16, Commander Edmund Palmer. Part of the force reached
its destination on March 15th, and the remainder on the 19th. In
the meantime, on the 16th, the place had been summoned; on the
17th, the governor had replied that he would defend it to the utmost;
on the evening of the 17th, about six hundred and fifty troops, five
guns, and a few seamen under Lieutenant James Boxer had been
landed near Lake Mareotis; and on the 18th, an additional three

---

[1] Canning was Foreign Secretary in the Duke of Portland's ministry.

[2] The Grenville ministry did not fall until April, 1807—more than a month after
Duckworth had repassed the Dardanelles. The *Nav. Chron.* at one time announced
that Duckworth was about to apply for a C. M.

[3] Brenton, ii. 194 (Ed. 1837).

hundred men had been put ashore, and the enemy's advanced works had been carried, with a loss of only seven killed and ten wounded. On the 20th, Aboukir castle was secured; and the rest of the army was disembarked, chiefly in Aboukir Bay. The effect of these operations was to induce the governor to reconsider his position; and on the 21st, the city of Alexandria was surrendered and taken possession of. In the harbour were found a 40-gun and a 34-gun Turkish frigate, and a 16-gun sloop.[1]

On March 22nd, Sir John Duckworth, with part of the squadron from Cape Janissary, appeared upon the scene. His arrival encouraged Major-General Fraser to attack Rosetta; but in an attempt upon that town the troops were defeated and driven back to Alexandria with a loss of about four hundred killed[2] and wounded. This was but the beginning of their misfortunes; and by the middle of September they had been so reduced by hardships and reverses that they were glad to conclude a convention, in pursuance of which they were allowed to evacuate the country. In the interim Duckworth had returned to England in the *Royal George*, leaving the naval command on the coast of Egypt to Rear-Admiral Sir Thomas Louis, who, however, died on board the *Canopus* on May 17th. In every respect, therefore, British action against Turkey in 1807 was disappointing.

The Russians did better. Seniavine,[3] with a fleet of ten sail of the line and two frigates, took Lemnos and Tenedos, blockaded the Dardanelles, chased back thither a Turkish fleet which, during his temporary absence, had issued thence in May, and, on July 1st, defeated the same fleet off Lemnos, subsequently retaking Tenedos, which had been recaptured. But, on August 24th, as a result of the Treaty of Tilsit, he concluded an armistice with the Porte, and, after detaching a few ships to take possession of Corfu, set out for the Baltic with the remainder of his force, anxious, if possible, to get home ere the outbreak of hostilities between Russia and Great Britain, and so to avoid the necessity for taking a personal part in a conflict with a service in which he counted many friends. How he fared on his voyage will be seen later.

---

[1] Hallowell to Duckworth, Mar. 24th, 1807.

[2] Among the killed was Fraser himself.

[3] Dmitri Nicolaevich Seniavine; born 1765; served in the British Navy; was present at the battle of Varna, 1791; held command at Corfu, 1806; after the rupture with Great Britain consequent upon the Treaty of Tilsit, he temporarily retired from the service, rather than act against England; died 1831.

As early as the autumn of 1806, Napoleon had begun to threaten Portugal, with a view to forcing that country to take sides against her old ally Great Britain; and Lord St. Vincent had, in consequence, been sent with a squadron to Lisbon to lend assistance to the Prince Regent Dom João, son of the insane Queen Maria II. Temporarily preoccupied by his difficulties with Prussia and Russia, Napoleon neglected, until 1807, to carry out his threats. He then, however, demanded that Portugal should close her ports to British commerce, detain British subjects, sequestrate British property, and assist France with a squadron. Dom João held out as long as he could; but, upon the approach of General Junot with a large army, he agreed, on October 20th, to obey Napoleon's behests. Sir William Sidney Smith had returned from the Mediterranean in the summer; and when, early in November, news of the coercion of Portugal reached England, a squadron,[1] which had been already assembled at Portsmouth and Plymouth, was dispatched, under his command, to the Tagus.

Dom João, on November 8th, allowed himself to be further intimidated into ordering the seizure of a few British subjects and a little British property at Lisbon; whereupon the British minister, Lord Strangford, demanded his passports, and, after lodging a final protest, joined the squadron of Sir Sidney Smith on the 17th. That squadron at once began a rigid blockade of the Tagus. On November 27th, Lord Strangford, in the *Confiance*, 20, Commander James Lucas Yeo,[2] returned to Lisbon under a flag of truce, and informed the Portuguese government that the blockade would be raised if the Portuguese navy were surrendered to Great Britain, or if the Regent and royal family chose to utilise it for transferring

[1] SHIPS.	GUNS.	COMMANDERS.
Hibernia	120	Rear-Adm. Sir William Sidney Smith (B). Capt. Charles Marsh Schomberg.
London	98	„ Thomas Western.
Foudroyant	80	„ Norborne Thompson.
Elizabeth	74	„ Hon. Henry Curzon.
Conqueror	74	„ Israel Pellew.
Marlborough	74	„ Graham Moore.
Monarch	74	„ Richard Lee.
Plantagenet	74	„ William Bradley (1).
Bedford	74	„ James Walker (2).

[2] Com. Yeo was afterwards sent home with dispatches, and was posted on Dec. 19th. He distinguished himself, as will be seen, on many occasions, and died, still a Captain, on Aug. 21st, 1818, having been previously knighted.

themselves to Brazil, pending the termination of the troubles with France. Dom João needed but little convincing that Great Britain was really his best friend, and that Napoleon aimed at the deposition of the house of Braganza; and he readily agreed to proceed with his family to America, leaving his European dominions to be governed by a regency until he should be able to return to them. The greater part of the Portuguese fleet happened to be ready for sea; and on November 29th, after only a few hours of preparation, the Regent, with Queen Maria II., the whole of the royal family, and a very large number of adherents, embarked in it,[1] and left the Tagus, accompanied by a fleet of about twenty armed merchantmen. The fleet, being met outside by the British squadron, was given, and returned, a salute of twenty-one guns.[2] On the following day the troops of General Junot entered Lisbon.

Sir Sidney escorted the Portuguese ships [3] as far as lat. 37° 47' N. and long. 14° 17' W., and then, on December 6th,[4] detached Captain Graham Moore, with the *Marlborough, London, Monarch,* and *Bedford* to see them to Bahia [5] and Rio de Janeiro, while he himself, with the rest of the squadron, returned to look for the Russian sail of the line which, under Vice-Admiral Seniavine, were attempting, as has been seen, to get round from the Mediterranean to the Baltic. They were nine in number, and they had with them one frigate. Deterred by the large force of British ships in and about the Bay of Biscay, they had put into the Tagus; and, when Sir Sidney found them there, he took the responsibility of retaining with him the *Foudroyant, Conqueror,* and *Plantagenet,* which he had been previously ordered to detach to Rear-Admiral John Child Purvis (1), off Cadiz. With these ships, and with the *Hibernia* and *Elizabeth,* he cruised off the Tagus, until he was joined by the *Ganges,* 74, Commodore Peter Halkett, *Defence,* 74, Captain Charles Ekins, *Alfred,* 74, Captain John Bligh (2), *Ruby,* 64, Captain John Draper (2), and *Agamemnon,* 64, Captain Jonas Rose,

---

[1] *Principe Reale,* 84, *Rainha de Portugal,* 74, *Conde Henrique,* 74, *Medusa,* 74, *Principe de Brazil,* 74, *Affonso de Albuquerque,* 64, *Dom João de Castro,* 64, *Martino de Freitas,* 64, *Minerva,* 44, *Golfinho,* 36, *Urania,* 32, a frigate, name unknown, *Voador,* 22, *Libre,* 22, *Vinganza,* 20, and *Curioza,* 12. These constituted the whole of the serviceable Portuguese navy except the *Vasco da Gama,* 74, repairing.

[2] Smith to Pole, Dec. 1st, 1807.

[3] Except one ship of the line, which, being unseaworthy, bore up for England.

[4] Smith's dispatch of Dec. 6th, 1807.

[5] Where the Prince Regent landed on Jan. 19th, 1808.

which had left Portsmouth on December 6th, three days after the news of Russia's hostile declaration of October 31st had been received in England. Thus reinforced, Sir Sidney maintained an effective blockade of Lisbon, and of Seniavine's squadron, until the end of 1807. At the same time a squadron[1] under Sir Samuel Hood (2), with troops under Major-General W. C. Beresford, proceeded to Madeira, effected a landing without any opposition on December 24th, and, on December 26th, took over the island from the Portuguese authorities in accordance with the terms of capitulation.[2]

The appointment of Rear-Admiral Charles Stirling to supersede Sir Home Riggs Popham in the Rio de la Plata has been already noted. Stirling, with a small convoy, reached Maldonado on January 5th, 1807. He was presently followed by Brigadier-General Sir Samuel Auchmuty, who had been sent out to take over command of the troops from Brigadier-General Backhouse. The Rear-Admiral's view was that Maldonado was too exposed and resourceless to serve as a good base at which to prepare for the recovery of Buenos Aires. He therefore evacuated it on January 13th, leaving only a small garrison on Gorrete island, and took measures to make himself master of Montevideo, which, though strongly defended and held, seemed to be the best position on the river for his purpose. On the 16th, accordingly, a landing was effected about eight miles to the eastward of the city; on the 19th, the troops, with about eight hundred seamen and Royal Marines under Captain Ross Donnelly and Commander John Palmer, of the *Pheasant*, moved forward, and the ships and transports anchored off Chico Bay; on the 25th, the batteries were opened; on February 2nd, a breach was made; and before daybreak on February 3rd, the city was gallantly stormed and carried. During the whole of the operations the army lost 192 killed, 421 wounded, and 8 missing.[3]

The water in front of Montevideo is so shallow, and such high winds and heavy swells prevailed, that the ships of the squadron could do but little towards the reduction of the place beyond landing

---

[1] *Centaur*, 74, Rear-Adm. Sir Samuel Hood (2), Capt. William Henry Webley; *York*, 74, Capt. Robert Barton; *Captain*, 74, Capt. Isaac Wolley; *Intrepid*, 64, Capt. Richard Worsley; and frigates *Africaine*, *Alceste*, *Shannon*, and *Success*.

[2] Hood to Pole, Dec. 29th, 1807.

[3] *Gazette*, 1807, 473.

men and guns, and cutting off communication with Colonia and Buenos Aires. The ships employed were :—

SHIPS.	GUNS.	COMMANDERS.
Diadem	64	Rear-Adm. Charles Stirling (1) (W.) Capt. Samuel Warren (2).
Raisonnable	64	„ Josias Rowley.
Ardent	64	„ Ross Donnelly.
Lancaster	64	„ William Fothergill.
Leda	38	„ Robert Honyman.
Unicorn	32	„ Lucius Ferdinand Hardyman.
Medusa	32	„ Hon. Duncombe Pleydell Bouverie.

Besides sloops, brigs, transports, etc.

The Navy lost on shore six killed, twenty-eight wounded, and four missing, among the wounded being Sub-Lieutenant George Stewart (2), and Midshipmen the Hon. Charles Leonard Irby, Henry Smith (1a), and John Morrison (2). The siege had almost exhausted the stock of powder in the squadron, and the fall of the city did not provide the victors with any large fresh supply. Nor were the Spanish vessels[1] taken at Montevideo of much value. The expedition remained, in consequence, comparatively inactive until May, when Sir Samuel Auchmuty was superseded in the military command by Brigadier-General Crauford, who brought with him about five thousand troops from Europe, and who was himself superseded on June 15th by Lieutenant-General J. Whitelocke. At the same time, Rear-Admiral George Murray (3), in the *Polyphemus*, 64, Captain Peter Heywood, arrived from England to assume the chief naval command, Stirling remaining as second. The shoal water before Buenos Aires prevented the squadron from having more than a very small share in the disastrous and indeed disgraceful operations which were undertaken against that city. The army was landed on June 28th; the place was attacked on July 5th; the troops gained a Pyrrhic and terribly costly success;[2] and on the 6th, Whitelocke weakly agreed to the proposal of Liniers that all prisoners should be delivered up, conditional upon the attack being discontinued and the Rio de la Plata being evacuated by the British forces within two months.[3] For this miserable surrender,

---

[1] A 28-gun corvette (burnt), two or three unserviceable sloops, and 21 gunboats, besides a number of merchantmen.

[2] Losing 2500 men.

[3] Whitelocke to Windham, July 10th; Murray to Marsden, June 30th, July 8th, July 10th, 1807.

and for his general mismanagement and ill-conduct, Whitelocke
was subsequently tried, cashiered, and declared "totally unfit and
unworthy to serve his Majesty in any military capacity whatever."
Happily no blame fell upon the Navy.

By far the most brilliant exploit of the year 1807 was witnessed
in the West Indies.   Vice-Admiral James Richard Dacres (1), who
commanded on the Jamaica station, desired to ascertain the state of

REAR-ADM. SIR CHARLES BRISBANE, KT., K.C.B.

*(From H. R. Cook's lithograph, after the painting by J. Northcote, R.A., of Brisbane
as a Post-Captain.)*

affairs in the Dutch island of Curaçoa, and to make practical test of
whether it had been truly reported to him that the inhabitants were
anxious for a British alliance.   On November 29th, 1806, therefore,
he dispatched from Port Royal the *Arethusa*, 38, Captain Charles
Brisbane, *Latona*, 38, Captain James Athol Wood, and *Anson*, 44,
Captain Charles Lydiard,[1] with directions to Brisbane to also take

---

[1] The *Morne Fortunée*, 10, Lieut. John James Rorie, also took some part in the
operations to be described.   O'Byrne, 1003.   Admiralty Order of Jan. 25th, 1849.
But Brisbane's dispatch mentions neither the brig nor the officer.

under his orders, upon falling in with her, the *Fishguard*, 38,
Captain William Bolton (1). The squadron, delayed by adverse
winds and currents, did not reach the island òf Aruba until
December 22nd. There it anchored ; and, on the 23rd, it was joined
by the *Fishguard*. Realising that Curaçoa was strongly fortified,
that his force was but a modest one, and that parley or procrastina-
tion would be all to his disadvantage, Brisbane, an officer of distinguished bravery, resolved to give the Dutch as little time as possible
for preparation, and, sailing straight into the harbour, to negotiate
only when the muzzles of his guns should be pointed directly upon
the town and forts. He therefore weighed on the 24th, with the
intention of striking the blow on New Year's Day, 1807. He had
already clearly made known his plans to his Captains. At 1 A.M. on
January 1st, he sighted the high land at the east end of the island,
having decided to utilise the regular south-east trade wind for
running for the harbour of St. Anne, which lies on the south-east
side. The ships then hove to, hoisted out their boats, and took
them in tow. The task which Brisbane had set himself was an
heroic one.

"The entrance to the harbour, according to Mr. Mantor's chart," says James, " is
only 50 fathoms wide, and is defended by regular fortifications, the principal of which,
Fort Amsterdam, standing on the right of the entrance, mounts 60 pieces of cannon,
in two tiers. Athwart the harbour, which nowhere exceeds a quarter of a mile in
width, were the Dutch 36-gun frigate *Kenau Hasselaar*, Captain Cornelis G. Evertsz,
and 22-gun ship corvette *Suriname*, Captain Jan van Nes, exclusive of two large
armed schooners. There was a chain of forts on Misselburg heights; and that almost
impregnable fortress, Fort Republiek, situated upon a high hill at the bottom of the
harbour, and almost within grape-shot distance, enfiladed the whole." [1]

At 5 A.M., after he had made every preparation for an immediate
storming of the town, Brisbane, with an easterly wind, bore up for
the mouth of the harbour, the *Arethusa* leading, and being followed
in order by the *Latona*, *Anson*, and *Fishguard*. At daylight, under
a flag of truce, the *Arethusa* entered the port; but the Dutch, ignoring the flag, opened fire on her. At that moment a shift of wind to
the north checked the frigate's progress; but within a few minutes
another shift enabled all the squadron, except the *Fishguard*, which
grounded on the west side, to take up its assigned position and

[1] James (Ed. 1837), iv. 352. I have corrected the spelling of proper names, etc.,
and should add that, so far as I can discover from the Dutch official reports, there were
not two armed schooners, but only one, the *Vliegende Visch*, and she was not manned.
Brisbane, however, mentions two armed schooners. Disp. to Dacres, of Jan. 1st ; C. M.
on Changuion ; Ver Huell to Louis, July 31st ; Rep. of de Quartel.

anchor in the harbour.   The *Arethusa's* jib-boom was then
over the town wall, and Brisbane, going to her capstan, wrote
upon it the following summons to the governor, M. Pierre Jean
Changuion :—

"The British squadron are here to protect, and not to conquer you ; to preserve to
you your lives, liberty, and property.   If a shot is fired at any one of my squadron
after this summons, I shall immediately storm your batteries.   You have five minutes
to accede to this determination."

But the governor, taking no notice of the summons, did his utmost
to destroy the British frigates ; and, having hauled down the flag of
truce, the British, at 6.15 A.M., began action.   When his ships had
fired about three broadsides apiece, Brisbane, at the head of some of
his men, boarded and carried the *Kenau Hasselaar ;* and the *Latona*,
warping alongside, took possession.   Almost simultaneously, Lydiard,
with some of the *Anson's*, boarded and took the *Suriname*.   Both
Brisbane and Lydiard then pulled ashore, as did Wood and Bolton,
landed, and, at 7.30 A.M., stormed Fort Amsterdam, carrying it with
a rush in ten minutes, and subsequently carrying also one or two
minor works, the citadel, and the town.   They next returned to
their ships, opened fire on Fort Republiek, and in half an hour
silenced it.   By 10 A.M. it had fallen, and by noon the whole island
had submitted.   Brisbane, with his own hands, struck the Dutch
colours, first in the *Kenau Hasselaar*, and then on Fort Amsterdam.
This extraordinary exploit cost the Navy a loss of only three killed
and fourteen wounded.   The Dutch, on the other hand, lost very
nearly two hundred men, among the killed being Captain Evertsz,
and among the dangerously wounded Captain van Nes.[1]   They
fought most bravely afloat ; and, if the forts offered less resistance
than the ships, it was chiefly because they were surprised.

For their services Captains Brisbane and Wood were knighted ;
Brisbane was granted an honourable augmentation of his armorial
bearings, together with supporters ; each of the four frigate
Captains concerned was awarded a gold medal ; and several promotions were made among the subordinate officers engaged.[2]

[1] *Gazette Extraordinary*, Feb. 22nd, 1807; Dacres to Marsden, Jan. 11th;
Brisbane to Dacres, Jan. 1st, 1807 (with enclosures); De Jonge, v. 633.

[2] Lieut. John Parish, first of the *Arethusa*, had already been promoted on
Nov. 28th, though he did not receive his commission until after the action; but
Lieut. Henry Higman, also of the *Arethusa*, and Lieuts. William Mather (*Fishguard*),
Thomas Ball Sulivan (*Anson*), and Samuel Jeffery (*Latona*), were made Commanders
on Feb. 23rd, 1807.

Just as the hostility of Holland cost her Curaçoa, so did the hostility of Denmark cost her the island of St. Thomas, which was peaceably surrendered on December 21st to a joint expedition from Barbados under Rear-Admiral the Hon. Alexander Forester Inglis Cochrane[1] and General Bowyer. The neighbouring island of St. Croix also surrendered on the 25th. At neither place was any ship of war found, but at each were a number of merchantmen.

In the East Indies, where Rear-Admiral Sir Edward Pellew commanded, the most important operation of the year 1807 was the expedition to Griessee. On the occasion of his descent upon Batavia in the previous year,[2] Sir Edward had expected to find there the two Dutch 68-gun ships *Revolutie* and *Pluto*, but had been disappointed. Hearing that they had taken refuge in the fortified roadstead of Griessee, on the Sourabaya River, at the eastern end of Java, he, in June, sent from Madras the *Caroline*, 36, Captain Peter Rainier (2), and the *Psyche*, 36, actg. Commander Fleetwood Broughton Reynolds Pellew (actg. Captain),[3] to reconnoitre. These officers ascertained from a prize taken on August 30th that the ships in question were at Griessee, but were beyond repair. Later on the same day the *Caroline* went in chase of a strange sail, and the *Psyche*, having stood to the westward, anchored at midnight off the port of Samarang. At dawn on the following morning, Pellew sent in his boats under Lieutenant Lambert Kersteman and acting Lieutenant Charles Sullivan; and these, in spite of a heavy fire, brought out an armed schooner and a large merchant brig. In the course of the same day, after having destroyed her prizes, the *Psyche* chased and drove ashore three vessels, which soon struck, and proved to be the *Scipio*, 24, Commander Carrega, who was mortally wounded, and the armed merchantmen *Resolutie* and *Ceres*. All three were, by great exertions, got afloat that night, and were eventually carried to Madras.[4]

Upon the return of his frigates, Sir Edward Pellew, with a small

---

[1] With his flag in the *Belleisle*, 74.

[2] *See* next chapter, p. 392.

[3] Capt. Pellew was then really only a Lieutenant, for he was not confirmed as Commander until Oct. 12th, 1807, nor as Captain till Oct. 14th, 1808. Even at the latter date he was not quite nineteen. But Sir Edward was his father.

[4] *Gazette*, 1808, 537. Pellew to Pellew, Sept. 3rd. Verhaal v. d. Min. van Marine, of Apr. 27th, 1808. Rapp. aan K. Lodewijk, of July 30th, 1808.

squadron,[1] having on board troops under Lieut.-Colonel Lockhart, proceeded to Panka Point, at the eastern end of Java, and, on December 5th, sent thence under a flag of truce a summons for the surrender of the vessels at Griessee. The boat bearing the flag was detained, and an officer was sent to Sir Edward with an unconditional refusal of the demand. On the 6th, therefore, the *Culloden* and *Powerful*, having been lightened, continued their course to Griessee with the rest of the force, passing and silencing a 12-gun battery at Sambilangan, on the island of Madura, but receiving little damage, and suffering no loss. When the squadron reached Griessee, the authorities of Sourabaya disclaimed the action of the Dutch senior officer, Captain Cowell,[2] returned the boat and those who had been detained with her, and consented to deliver up the ships in dispute. Cowell had, however, already scuttled everything in the roadstead; and the British had only the satisfaction of setting fire to what remained above water of the *Revolutie*, 68, the *Pluto*, 68, the *Kortenaar*, sheer hulk (late 68-gun ship), the armed colonial vessel *Rusthof*, and a large transport. Sir Edward also destroyed the guns and stores at Griessee, and procured the demolition of the battery at Sambilangan. From that time forward there was for a long period no Dutch naval force in the East Indies.[3]

Speaking of the year 1808, James says :—[4]

"A new era was commencing in the navy of France. Such had been Napoleon's exertions since the disastrous affair of Trafalgar, that the spring of this year saw him possessed of upwards of 80 sail of the line, including 20 recently ordered to be laid

[1] Ships.	Guns.	Commanders.
Culloden . .	74	Rear-Adm. Sir Edward Pellew. Com. George Bell (actg. Capt.) [Capt. 31–7–1809].
Powerful . .	74	Lieut. Fleetwood Broughton Reynolds Pellew (actg. Capt.) [Com. 12–10–1807 ; Capt. 14–10–1808].
Caroline . .	36	Com. Henry Hart (actg. Capt.) Capt. [1–8–1811].
Fox	32	Capt. Hon. Archibald Cochrane.
Victor . . .	18	Lieut. Thomas Groube (actg. Com.) [Com. 31–7–1809].
Samarang . .	18	„ Richard Buck (actg. Com.) [Com. 28–12–1807].
Seaflower . .	14	„ William Fitzwilliam Owen.
Jaseur . . .	12	„ Thomas Laugharne (2).*
Worcester, transport.		

* Lost with the *Jaseur*, Aug. 1809.

[2] De Jonge (v. 630) says that this officer was an American by birth, who had been in the Dutch navy for several years.

[3] Pellew's disp. of Dec. 15th to Madras Govt. Disps. of Govs.-Genl. Wiese and Daendels of Dec. 31st, 1807, and Jan. 22nd, 1808, in Dutch Col. Archives.

[4] James (Ed. 1837), v. 2.

down at Antwerp, Brest, Lorient, Toulon, and other ports. In Brest a squadron of eight sail of the line and four frigates was, in the course of the summer, got ready for sea, and only remained in port because unable to elude the vigilance of the Channel fleet under Admiral Lord Gambier, who, since March, had succeeded to the command of it. Early in the year . . . a French squadron of six sail of the line sailed from the road of Isle d'Aix, and large and powerful frigates were occasionally slipping out of other ports along the French Channel and Atlantic frontier. Of the minor ports of France, Cherbourg was fast rising into importance : the basin there constructing and nearly finished, would, in a year or two, it was expected, be capable of holding a fleet of line-of-battle ships. It had long been a celebrated port for frigates, and several very fine and powerful ones had sailed from, and were constructing within it."

Five French sail of the line and a frigate remained, at the beginning of the year, in Cadiz. Five sail of the line were in Toulon road, and three or four more were on the stocks. At Genoa a 74, and at Venice one or two ships of the same class, were building; and Spezzia was fast becoming a first-rate naval port.

The escape, above alluded to, of the Rochefort squadron, under Rear-Admiral Allemand, from the road of Isle d'Aix, occurred in January in the following circumstances. The British force assigned to the watching of the port consisted, towards the end of the year 1807, of seven sail of the line, besides frigates, under Rear-Admiral Sir Richard John Strachan, in the *Cæsar ;* and the squadron generally anchored in Basque road. In November, shortness of provisions induced Sir Richard to put to sea in order to look for some victuallers which had been ordered to meet him at a rendezvous to the south-west of Roche Bonne. North-east gales drove him beyond his rendezvous ; delay took place in the sailing of the victuallers from England ; and it was the middle of January ere his squadron had taken on board the supplies intended for it. On January 4th, 1808, the *Patriote,* 74, Captain J. H. I. Khrom, from Chesapeake Bay, dropped anchor in Aix road ; and, on January 17th, Rear-Admiral Allemand, perceiving only a frigate and a brig in the offing, put to sea with a moderate N.E. by N. breeze, with the *Majestueux,* 120, *Ajax,* 74, *Lion,* 74, *Jemmapes,* 74, *Magnanime,* 74, *Suffren,* 74, a frigate, and a brig. The British frigate in the offing was the *Phœnix,* 36, Captain Zachary Mudge ; the brig was the *Raleigh,* 18, Commander Joseph Ore Masefield. These vessels, after observing the French for a short time, were chased, and made all sail to the W. by N. Upon losing sight of the enemy, Mudge sent the *Raleigh* to England with the intelligence, and himself proceeded in search of Strachan. While looking for him on the 19th, the *Phœnix* fell in with the *Attack,* 14, brig, Lieutenant Thomas

Swain (2), and communicated the news, directing Swain to seek for
Sir Richard. On the 20th, the *Phœnix* looked into the road of
Isle d'Yeu, and there saw a partially-rigged ship of the line and
three brigs. She then made for England, and anchored in Cawsand
Bay on January 24th. The *Attack* did not find Strachan until January 23rd. The squadron was then fifty miles S.W. of Chassiron
lighthouse, working back against a strong N.E. wind. Sir Richard
headed for Cape Finisterre; but soon afterwards he had to contend
for several days with a violent gale from the westward. On the
29th he detached the *Donegal*, which was leaky,[1] to England; and
on February 2nd, having cleared the Bay of Biscay, he crowded
sail for the Strait of Gibraltar, whither he rightly concluded that
Allemand was bound. On February 4th, he spoke Commodore
Sir Richard King (2), who, with the *Achille*, 74, *Audacious*, 74,
and *Theseus*, 74, was watching Ferrol. On the 9th, he spoke
the division off Cadiz under Rear-Admiral John Child Purvis (1);
on the 10th, he passed Gibraltar; and on the 21st, anchoring
off Palermo, he joined Vice-Admiral Edward Thornbrough. The
squadrons thus united were composed of the following ships of
the line:—

SHIPS.	GUNS.	COMMANDERS.
Royal Sovereign . . .	100	Vice-Adm. Edward Thornbrough (B). Capt. Henry Garrett.
Formidable	98	„ Francis Fayerman.
Cæsar[1]	80	Rear-Adm. Sir Richard John Strachan, Bart., K.B. (B). Capt. Charles Richardson.
Eagle	74	„ Charles Rowley.
Kent	74	„ Thomas Rogers.
Thunderer	74	„ John Talbot.
Spartiate[1] . . .	74	„ Sir Francis Laforey, Bart.
Colossus[1]	74	„ James Nicoll Morris.
Cumberland[1] . . .	74	„ Hon. Philip Wodehouse.
Renown[1]	74	„ Samuel Jackson.
Superb[1]	74	Lieut. Thomas Alexander (2), actg. Capt. [Com. 11–4–1809.]

[1] Joined with Sir R. J. Strachan.

In the meantime Allemand had suffered as much as Strachan
from the bad weather, and had been obliged to send back the
Jemmapes, in a crippled condition, to Rochefort. With his other
ships he passed Gibraltar unseen on January 26th, and, on

[1] And out of which he had taken the main yard to supply his flagship.

February 6th, joined Vice-Admiral Ganteaume in Toulon road.
On his way, he had destroyed several merchantmen ; and, off Toulon,
he had driven from her post of observation the *Apollo*, 38, Captain
Edward Fellowes. Ganteaume, thus reinforced, left Toulon on
February 7th with ten sail of the line, three frigates, two sloops,
and seven armed transports, and made the best of his way to
Corfu, where he arrived on the 23rd, and landed troops, stores,
and provisions. From the 25th until March 15th, when he
returned to Corfu, he cruised, chiefly among the islands.

Ganteaume had been sighted on February 23rd by the *Porcupine*, 22, Captain the Hon. Henry Duncan (3), then on her way
to join the *Standard*, 64, Captain Thomas Harvey (1), which had
been stationed to watch the Ionian Islands. As soon as the
Porcupine had ascertained that the strange fleet was French, she
headed for Syracuse, where Lord Collingwood, the Commander-
in-Chief, then lay [1] : but, on the 24th, she was fallen in with by
the *Active*, 38, Captain Richard Hussey Moubray ; and, as
Moubray happened to know that the *Standard* had gone to
Syracuse, he took the *Porcupine* under his orders, and with her
stood back to observe the French. From February 24th to
March 13th, these two vessels, or one or other of them, were
always in company with Ganteaume. On March 16th, the French
vice-admiral again put to sea, and cruised along the coasts of
Africa, Sicily, and Sardinia, re-anchoring off Toulon on April 10th.
During part of the time he was watched by the *Spartan*, 38,
Captain Jahleel Brenton (2), which, since February 23rd, had, with
the *Lavinia*, 40, Captain John Hancock (1), been detached by
Vice-Admiral Thornbrough to gain intelligence of the Rochefort
squadron. Thornbrough had, immediately afterwards, weighed from
Palermo with all the ships in the above list, and had gone in search
of the Commander-in-Chief. Brenton, with news of Ganteaume's
departure from Toulon, had joined Collingwood, off Marittimo, on
March 3rd ; and the Commander-in-Chief, detaching the *Lavinia*
for further intelligence, had stood with the fleet towards the Bay
of Naples, whence he had sent the *Spartan* to Palermo. At
Palermo, where he had found Rear-Admiral George Martin (2) with
three sail of the line, Brenton had received orders to cruise between
Cape Bon and Sardinia ; and, on that station, he had sighted the
French on April 1st, standing under a press of sail to the westward.

---

[1] With the *Ocean*, *Canopus*, *Malta*, *Repulse*, and *Montagu*.

He had kept sight of them until night, when he had dispatched his launch, under Lieutenant Thomas Coffin,[1] with the intelligence, to Trapani; and he had subsequently hung on to the French with great doggedness and excellent seamanship for several days. Upon his return to Toulon, Ganteaume found there the frigates *Pénélope* and *Thémis*, which, having escaped from Bordeaux on January 21st, had cruised for a time in the Atlantic, passed Gibraltar on March 17th, called at Ajaccio on March 23rd, and anchored at Toulon on March 28th, having taken or destroyed British vessels alleged to be worth nearly a quarter of a million sterling.

Collingwood has often been blamed for having thus allowed Ganteaume to roam the Mediterranean unchallenged from February 7th to April 10th. His failure to find the French and bring them to action seems to have been chiefly due to a succession of accidents. He was at Syracuse until February 24th, when, without any knowledge that the enemy was at sea, he sailed for Palermo with the *Ocean*, 98 (flag), Captain Richard Thomas (2), *Canopus*, 80, Rear-Admiral George Martin (2), Captain Charles Inglis (2), *Malta*, 74, Captain William Shield, and *Montagu*, 74, Captain Robert Waller Otway (1), leaving behind him the *Repulse*, 74, Captain the Hon. Arthur Kaye Legge. Scarcely had the Commander-in-Chief departed, ere the *Standard*, which, as has been seen, had news of Ganteaume's appearance at Corfu, reached Syracuse; and no sooner had she entered the port than a change of wind occurred to keep her there for several days. An express was sent to Cape Passaro to communicate with Collingwood; but the Vice-Admiral had, unfortunately, already passed to the westward. On March 2nd, near Marittimo, he was joined by Thornbrough and Strachan; and on the 3rd, with fifteen sail of the line, he headed for Palermo, still without intelligence that the French were out; and not until March 6th, when off Cape St. Vito, was he fallen in with by the *Apollo*, 38, Captain Edward Fellowes, which brought news of Ganteaume having left Toulon a month before. Collingwood thereupon stood across to the Bay of Naples, where he received the further news which had been collected by the *Standard*. From Naples he sailed round the west end of Sicily, and, on March 21st, was again off Syracuse. On the 22nd, he made for the mouth of the Adriatic; on the 23rd, he detached Rear-Admiral Martin with

---

[1] Who proceeded from Trapani to Rear-Admiral Martin at Palermo, sending on the launch to Malta.

three sail of the line to Palermo; and until the 28th he maintained a
position which would probably have enabled him to bar Ganteaume's
return, had the French been still to the eastward. But on the
28th, he learnt that Ganteaume had quitted the Adriatic about a
week before. He then turned to the westward, and cruised between
Sardinia and Sicily until April 28th, when he was informed by the
Proserpine, 32, Captain Charles Otter, that the enemy had long
since re-anchored at Toulon. The fleet, in consequence, proceeded
thither, and on May 3rd sighted Cape Sicié; but Ganteaume then
had no further thought of cruising. Thus a chance of bringing
the enemy to action was lost. It must, however, be admitted that
Collingwood does not appear to have taken all the precautions
which he might have taken for ensuring that news should promptly
reach him of the motions of the French.[1] He did not suffer from
that terrible lack of frigates which so often hampered and distressed
Nelson; and there can be little doubt that, had he utilised his
scouts as Nelson would have utilised them, Ganteaume would have
hardly carried his fleet back to Toulon.

Leaving Vice-Admiral Thornbrough, with a division, to watch
Toulon, Collingwood, with the rest of the fleet, sailed for the south
coast of Spain to lend assistance to the Spanish patriots. Thornbrough's task proved to be one of wearisomeness rather than of
difficulty; for, during the rest of the year, Ganteaume made no
serious effort to put to sea.

In the south of Italy, the success of the French arms had
already led to the abandonment of Reggio by its British and
Neapolitan garrison, which retired to Scilla; and on January 30th,
1808, Commander Philip Cosby Handfield, of the *Delight*, 16, while
endeavouring to recapture some Sicilian gun-vessels at Reggio,
was killed. His brig-sloop, which had previously grounded under
the batteries, was set on fire to prevent her from being of use to
the enemy. Among the prisoners who fell into French hands on
the occasion was Captain Thomas Seccombe, who, though he commanded the *Glatton*, happened to be in the *Delight* at the time.
He was mortally wounded. On February 17th it became advisable
also to evacuate Scilla; and the garrison, under Lieut.-Colonel
Robertson, was on that day safely withdrawn by Captain Robert
Waller Otway (1), of the *Montagu*, 74, and Commander George

---

[1] Nor does his correspondence, during most of the time, indicate that he was
thinking as much of Ganteaume as of events in the Levant. 'Collingwood,' 342–362.

Barne Trollope, of the *Electra*, 18.[1]   Scilla was the last post held
by the British in Lower Calabria.

On the Spanish coast Lord Collingwood found plenty to do.
The Spaniards, in the course of the first half of the year 1808,
had discovered that subserviency to Napoleon was intolerable ; and
on June 4th, a junta at Seville, acting in the name of the captive
king, Ferdinand VII., declared war against France.   This event
placed in peril the French squadron[2] which still lay in Cadiz,
and which was at once removed by its commander, Vice-Admiral
Rosily, from the port to the channel leading to Caraccas,[3] where
it was out of range of the town batteries.   Rear-Admiral John
Child Purvis (1), who was off the harbour with about ten sail of
the line, offered to co-operate with the Spaniards in reducing the
French to submission ; but the patriots preferred to act alone, and
on the afternoon of June 9th, a division of their gun and mortar
boats, aided by specially erected batteries, began hostilities with the
French squadron.   On the afternoon of the following day, Rosily
proposed terms, which were considered inadmissible and were
consequently refused ; but on the 14th, finding that additional
guns were ready to open upon him, he surrendered, and his ships
were taken possession of by the Spaniards.   This event was quickly
followed by the departure for England of Spanish commissioners
who were empowered to ask for the aid of the British Government,
the result being that, on July 4th, hostilities between Great Britain
and Spain were ordered to cease.   Thenceforward, as will be seen,
immense assistance was rendered by British cruisers to the patriot
cause.   Portugal took similar steps, negotiating in the first instance
with Admiral Sir Charles Cotton, who blockaded the Tagus, and
watched the Russian[4] squadron which lay there.   The upshot of
these communications was that in August a small British army,
under Lieut.-General Sir Arthur Wellesley, was landed on the
coast ; that, on August 21st, the battle of Vimeira was fought ; and
that on August 30th, the Convention of Cintra was signed.   By a

---

[1] *Gazette,* 1808, 503.   The *Electra* was wrecked on March 25th following off Port
Augusta.

[2] *Neptune,* 80 ; *Algésiras,* 74 ; *Argonaute,* 74 ; *Pluton,* 74 ; *Héros,* 74 ; *Cornélie,*
frigate ; and a corvette.

[3] See plan, Vol. ii., 378.

[4] Russia had issued a hostile declaration on October 31st, 1807 ; and on
December 18th, 1807, reprisals had been ordered in London against Russian ships
and goods.

separate convention[1] concluded on September 3rd, between Sir Charles Cotton and Vice-Admiral Seniavine, the Russian ships at Lisbon—nine sail of the line and a frigate[2]—were transferred to Great Britain, to be held until six months after the signature of peace between Great Britain and Russia; and the Russian officers and seamen were conveyed by Great Britain to Russia.

Of the Northern Powers, Denmark and Russia were now ranged with France, and Sweden was allied with Great Britain. If for no other reason than to protect Sweden, it was necessary to send a strong expedition to the Baltic in 1808; for, although Denmark had but few men-of-war left to her, Russia's fleet was, numerically at least, much more formidable than that of king Gustavus IV.; and Byam Martin has recorded that the state of the Swedish fleet was bad. Before the end of May, therefore, the undermentioned fleet,[3] accompanied by more than two hundred transports, having on board about fourteen thousand troops, under General Sir John Moore, assembled in the Baltic. Owing to misunderstanding between the king and Moore, the army was not employed, and it presently returned to England.

[1] Cotton to Pole, Sept. 3rd and 4th, 1809: Ho. of Com. return ordered on Feb. 9th, 1809.

[2] The ships were *Tverdoi*, 74; *Skoroi*, 60; *S. Helena*, 74; *Salafael*. 74; *Ratvizan*, 66; *Silnoi*, 74; *Mochnoi*, 74; *S. Rafael*, 80; *Jaroslav*, 74; and *Koldun*, 26. The *S. Rafael* and *Jaroslav*, being unseaworthy, were left in the Tagus.

[3] SHIPS.	GUNS.	COMMANDERS.
Victory	100 '	Vice-Adm. Sir James Saumarez, Bart.. K.P. (B), Capt. George Hope (1) (1st). ,, Philip Dumaresq (2nd).
Centaur.	74	Rear-Adm. Sir Samuel Hood (2), K.B. (W). Capt. William Henry Webley.
Superb	74	Rear-Adm. Richard Goodwin Keats (B).[1] Capt. Samuel Jackson.
Implacable	74	,, Thomas Byam Martin.
Edgar	74	,, James Macnamara (2).
Brunswick	74	,, Thomas Graves (4).
Mars	74	,, William Lukin.
Orion	74	,, Sir Archibald Collingwood Dickson, Bart.
Goliath	74	,, Peter Puget.
Vanguard	74	,, Thomas Baker (1).
Africa	64	,, John Barrett.
Dictator	64	,, Donald Campbell (1).

With 5 frigates, and numerous sloops, bombs, brigs, and fire-vessels.

[1] Had his flag for a time in the *Mars*.

The Navy, however, rendered excellent service.[1] Early in August a Russian fleet of nine sail of the line, three 50-gun ships, eight frigates and large corvettes, two brigs and two cutters, left Kronstadt, and, on the 19th of the month, anchored in the Bay of Hangö, a port of Swedish Finland then in Russian occupation. At that time Saumarez, with a few ships, lay off Langeland, one of the Danish islands ; another part of the fleet was off Copenhagen ; and yet another part was off Nyborg in the island of Fünen ; while a Swedish squadron of seven sail of the line and four frigates was at anchor in Öresund. This squadron was joined on August 20th by Rear-Admiral Sir Samuel Hood (2), with the *Centaur* and *Implacable*. Later on the same day, the Russian fleet from Hangö appeared and anchored outside, and in the evening of the 22nd it weighed and stood off and on. On the 22nd, four more Swedish sail of the line joined Hood and the Swedish rear-admiral, bringing up the force in Öresund to eleven sail of the line besides small craft ; but the allied fleet was very sickly, and a third of the Swedish seamen were down with scurvy, so that the ships were inefficient. Nevertheless, early on the 25th, the allies weighed, and, with a fresh N.E. breeze, made sail in pursuit of the enemy, which, at 9 A.M., was seen to the S.E. off Hangö Head. The Russians made all sail to get away, and were followed ; but the uncoppered Swedish ships, with their weak and inexperienced crews, made but slow progress in a windward chase, and soon the *Centaur* and *Implacable* drew ahead of their friends. By 4 A.M. on the 26th, the *Implacable* was two miles to windward of the *Centaur*, and only four or five miles behind the Russians ; and the *Centaur* was about ten miles to windward of the nearest Swede. The Russians were scattered, and evidently making all possible efforts to get away. At 4.30 A.M., the *Implacable*, then on the port tack, observed a Russian two-decker well to leeward of her consorts; and at 5.30 A.M., the Russian, which was the *Sewolod*, 74, Captain Roodneff, being on the starboard tack, passed the bow of the *Implacable*, which at once tacked after her. At 6.30 A.M. the *Sewolod* tacked, and at 6.45 A.M., when the ships again crossed one another, the Russian opened fire, the *Implacable*, of course, replying promptly. The British ship tacked again, and when, at 7.20 A.M., she had overtaken the *Sewolod*, she closed her within pistol-shot to leeward, and brought her to action with such

---

[1] A full account of the operations of the fleet is to be found in 'Letters and Papers of Adm. of the Fleet, Sir T. Byam Martin,' Vol. ii. (Nav. Rec. Soc. xii.), 1898.

determination that in less than half an hour the Russian struck.[1] Before, however, the *Implacable* could take possession, she was recalled by Hood, who having observed the Russians bear up, desired to save Captain Martin from being cut off and overwhelmed. Martin rejoined Hood at about 8 A.M., and with him ran towards the Swedes. In this action the *Implacable*[2] had six killed and twenty-six wounded,[3] among the latter being Master's Mate Thomas Pickernell and Captain's Clerk Nicholas Drew. The loss of the Russians amounted to forty-eight killed and eighty wounded.

The Russian admiral, having ordered a frigate to take in tow the almost entirely disabled *Sewolod*, hauled his wind. Soon afterwards, when the *Implacable* had made good such slight damages as she had suffered, she and the *Centaur* again made sail in chase, soon obliging the frigate to cast off the *Sewolod* and the Russian fleet to bear up in support of the cripple. But presently, rather than bring on a general engagement, the enemy took advantage of a change of wind to the N.E. and stood for the port of Roggersvik or Port Baltic, in which he anchored at about noon. He left the *Sewolod* aground on a shoal outside the harbour ; but she soon floated and rode at her anchors ; and, in the afternoon, numerous boats were sent out to tow her into the road. At 8 P.M., while the operation was in progress, the *Centaur*, thanks to the excellent seamanship of her officers and men, managed to run on board the Russian 74. For a few moments the Russian's starboard bow scraped along the *Centaur's* starboard side and was fired into by every gun that would bear upon it. Then the Russian's bowsprit, or what remained of it, was lashed under a withering fire to the *Centaur's* mizen rigging by Captain Webley, Lieutenant Paul Lawless,[4] and Mr. Edward Strode, Master. Hood had hoped to be able to tow off the Russian ship ; but she had dropped an anchor in six fathoms, and could not be moved. For about half an hour each vessel fought hard, and made ineffectual attempts to board the other. At 8.40 P.M., however, ten minutes after the *Implacable* had arrived and had anchored in a favourable position for assisting her consort, the *Sewolod* again hauled down her colours. In this action the *Centaur* had three killed and twenty-

---

[1] *I.e.*, she struck her pennant ; for her colours had been shot away early in the action. She had previously ceased firing.

[2] Whose first Lieutenant, Augustus Baldwin, was highly spoken of by Captain Martin, and was promoted on September 19th following.

[3] Martin, in his ' Remarks,' says six killed and twenty-four wounded.

[4] Promoted to be Commander, September 19th, 1808. He was severely wounded.

seven wounded;[1] and the Russian ship, which had been reinforced
with one hundred men since her action with the *Implacable*, had
one hundred and eighty killed, wounded, or missing.   Both the
Centaur and her prize grounded soon after the latter had surrendered; and this encouraged the Russian admiral to send out
a couple of ships to attempt their capture; but the *Implacable* was
soon successful in getting her consort afloat again, whereupon the
Russians returned to port.   In the course of the following night the
Sewolod was burnt by the victors.   The port of Roggersvik was
blockaded until early in October by the Anglo-Swedish fleet, which
was joined on August 30th by Sir James Saumarez, with the *Victory*,
Mars, *Goliath*, and *Africa*, and some smaller craft.   Plans were
prepared for burning the Russian ships at their anchorage by means
of fire-vessels; but upon the harbour being reconnoitred by the
Salsette, 36, Captain Walter Bathurst, and the Swedish frigate
Camilla, 44, it was found to be so excellently defended by means of
a boom, that the project had to be abandoned.   When, in consequence of the advancing season, the blockading force was withdrawn, the Russians made sail, and, in due course, found their way
back to Kronstadt.

In the meanwhile, measures were taken by Rear-Admiral Richard
Goodwin Keats for withdrawing from the shores of the Baltic the
Spanish troops which, during the subserviency of Spain to France,
had been sent thither to further the ambitions of Napoleon.   Keats,
who commanded among the Danish islands, had with him, besides
his flagship the *Superb*, 74, the *Brunswick*, 74, the *Edgar*, 74, and
several small vessels.   In pursuance of arrangements come to
between him and the Spanish general, the Marques de La Romana,
the latter, on August 9th, seized the town and fortress of Nyborg,
in Fünen.   The Danes on shore submitted to the force of circumstances; but the captains of two Danish vessels in the port, the
Fama, 18, and the *Salorman*, 12, decided to resist any attempt of the
British squadron to take off the Spaniards, and moored their little
craft across the harbour.   It became necessary, therefore, to attack
them.   A flotilla of boats was assembled for the purpose under
Captain James Macnamara (2), of the *Edgar*, who gallantly went in
and captured both brig and cutter, with a loss on the British side of
only one killed (Lieutenant Robert Harvey, of the *Superb*) and two
wounded.   The Danes lost in the encounter seven killed and thirteen

---

[1] Martin, in his ‘Remarks,’ says two killed and several wounded.

wounded. The Spaniards were then embarked in such smacks and doggers as could be laid hands upon, and they and most of the other Spanish troops in Denmark, to the number of about ten thousand, were presently collected in the island of Langeland,[1] whence they were carried to England, and eventually to their own country. For the ability and tact which he displayed while engaged in these services, Rear-Admiral Keats was made a K.B.

In more distant seas little of importance was done during the year 1808. In the West Indies, French privateers still gave trouble, using Guadeloupe as their base, and, when they could not at once make it, sheltering themselves under the batteries of Marie Galante and Désirade until opportunity presented itself for running across to the larger island. In February, Captain William Selby, who, in the *Cerberus*, 32, with the *Circe*, 32, Captain Hugh Pigot (3), and the *Camilla*, 20, Captain John Bowen (1), was cruising off Pointe-à-Pitre especially to repress the privateers, conceived that, if he could surprise Grand Bourg, the chief town of Marie Galante, he would greatly facilitate his labours. He therefore, on the morning of March 2nd, suddenly disembarked two hundred seamen and Royal Marines under Captain Pigot, who, marching upon the town, was met by a flag of truce. The unconditional surrender of the island followed.[2]

The news of the ease with which this little conquest had been effected decided Rear-Admiral Sir Alexander Forester Inglis Cochrane to entrust Captain Selby with the conduct of an attack on Désirade; and on March 30th the *Cerberus*, accompanied by two sloops, two brigs, and a schooner,[3] appeared off the island. The boats of the squadron, under Commander William Henry Shirreff, of the *Lily*, approached under a smart fire, which, however, was soon silenced by the guns of the *Cerberus* and her consorts, and by 4.30 P.M. the island had surrendered.[4] It was not deemed worth while to hold it. Its batteries—not very formidable ones—were, therefore, destroyed; the place was evacuated; and the *Lily*, with the brig *Express* and the schooner *Mozambique*, was left to cruise under Commander Shirreff for its protection, and to prevent it from being re-garrisoned from Guadeloupe.

---

[1] Keats to Pole, Aug. 13th (with enclosures).
[2] Selby to Cochrane, Mar. 3rd; Pigot to Selby, Mar. 2nd, 1808.
[3] *Lily*, 18; *Pelican*, 16; *Express*, 6; *Swinger*, 14; and *Mozambique*, 14.
[4] *Gazette*, 1808, 661. Selby to Cochrane, Mar. 30th, 1808.

An attack made upon the French part of the island of St. Martin had, unfortunately, a less successful termination. On the night of July 3rd, Commander Edward Lowther Crofton, of the *Wanderer*, 18, who had with him the *Subtle*, 4, Lieutenant George Augustus Spearing, and the *Ballahou*, 4, Lieutenant George Mills, saw fit to land one hundred and thirty-five men, under Lieutenant Spearing, upon the island. The party at first met with trifling loss, and took and spiked six guns in a lower battery, but, ascending to the assault of a fort on higher ground, was met by overwhelming forces and obliged to surrender, after having lost seven killed, including Lieutenant Spearing, and about thirty wounded.

The French Brest squadron, observed by Admiral Lord Gambier, remained in its roadsteads until after the middle of February, 1809. At that time Gambier had been driven from his station off Ushant by long-continued westerly gales. Rear-Admiral Willaumez had received orders to take an opportunity to put to sea and drive from its station the British blockading squadron off Lorient, in order that Commodore Troude, with three sail of the line and five frigates, might issue thence and join him. But Willaumez had been instructed that if, when he was off Lorient, Troude should be prevented by the tide from going out, the Brest squadron should at once proceed to Basque road, and drive thence any British force which might be lying there. He was then to anchor in Aix road, take under his orders not only the Lorient, but also the Rochefort squadron of three sail of the line, together with the *Calcutta*, armed *en flûte*, and several frigates, and proceed with dispatch to Martinique, which was supposed to be about to be attacked by the British. At dawn, therefore, on February 21st, 1809, Willaumez put to sea with his flagship, the *Océan*, 120, the two 80's, *Foudroyant* and *Varsovie*, the five 74's, *Jean Bart, Tourville, Aquilon, Tonnerre*, and *Regulus*, the two 40-gun frigates *Elbe* and *Indienne*, the brig *Nisus*, and the schooner *Magpie* (late British).

At about 9 A.M., the rearmost of the French ships doubled the Vaudrée rock ; and, with a fresh N.N.E. breeze, the squadron stood in line of battle for Pointe du Raz. As soon as the headmost vessels had cleared the Passage du Raz, they were discovered by the *Revenge*, 74, Captain the Hon. Charles Paget, which at once headed for the Glénan Isles to give information to Captain John Poo Beresford, who, in the *Theseus*, 74, with the *Triumph*, 74, Captain Sir Thomas Masterman Hardy, and the *Valiant*, 74, Captain

Alexander Robert Kerr, was blockading the three sail of the line and five frigates at Lorient.   Soon after 3 P.M., the *Revenge*, well ahead of the French, but in sight of them, exchanged numbers with the *Theseus* off Isle Groix.   Not, however, until about 4.30 P.M. were the squadrons of Willaumez and Beresford within view of one another.   The British were then steering nearly E.S.E. with a fresh N.N.E. breeze, and the French were almost close hauled on the port tack.   Four French sail of the line, presently followed by the remaining vessels, bore up in chase; upon which the British tacked and steered W.N.W.   They thus soon left open the port of Lorient; and the French, having thus far succeeded in their object, hauled their wind.   By 6 P.M., when Beresford tacked and shortened sail, and when Willaumez arrived off Isle Groix, the two squadrons were out of sight of one another.   Shortly afterwards it fell calm. On the following morning, there being a N.W. breeze, Willaumez sent the *Magpie* into Lorient to communicate with Troude, and himself steered for Antioche passage.[1]   By 9 A.M., the British were again in sight, and so they continued until late in the afternoon, when the French, passing inside of Belle Isle, continued towards Isle d'Yeu [2] with the wind then again at N.E.   At 10.30 P.M., when the enemy was abreast of Pointe des Baleines, the western end of Rhé, he was seen by the *Amethyst*, 36, Captain Michael Seymour (1), the look-out frigate of the Rochefort blockading squadron, which consisted of the *Cæsar*, 80, Rear-Admiral the Hon. Robert Stopford, Captain Charles Richardson, *Defiance*, 74, Captain the Hon. Henry Hotham, and *Donegal*, 74, Captain Peter Heywood (actg.),[3] and which was at anchor off the Tour de Chassiron.   The *Amethyst*, by means of rockets, warned Stopford, who got under way and stood to the N.W. towards the frigate.   At midnight, the squadron of Willaumez was seen to the eastward, approaching the Antioche passage.   Stopford chased until, at dawn on the 24th, he saw the French entering Basque road.   Then, confident that the strangers had escaped from Brest, he detached the *Naiad*, 38, Captain Thomas Dundas, to carry the news to Lord Gambier.

The *Naiad* had not run far to the N.W., ere she signalled three

---

[1] 'Pertius d'Antioche:' one of the channels leading into Rochefort, between Rhé and Oleron.

[2] Often written Isle Dieu.

[3] In the absence of Captain Pulteney Malcolm, who was attending a court-martial. Captain Heywood was the officer who had been condemned to death in 1792 for complicity in the mutiny of the *Bounty*, and subsequently pardoned.

suspicious sail approaching from the northward. Stopford, in consequence, left the *Amethyst*, and the *Emerald*, 36, to observe Willaumez, and, wearing, made sail in the direction of the newcomers. These were the French 40-gun frigates *Italienne*, *Calypso*, and *Cybèle*, which, soon after Willaumez had passed Isle Groix, had left Lorient, under Commodore Pierre Roch Jurien, with an E.N.E. wind, Troude himself, with his heavier ships, not being then able, owing to the state of the tide, to put to sea. They had already seen Beresford in the offing, and, when discovered by the *Naiad*, were being chased by the *Amelia*, 38, Captain the Hon. Frederick Paul Irby, and the *Doterel*, 18, Commander Anthony Abdy. As soon, therefore, as he perceived Stopford in the south-east, or nearly to windward [1] of him, Jurien, realising that he was cut off, headed for Sables d'Olonne with the *Amelia* and *Doterel* at his heels. By 10 A.M., the *Cæsar*, *Defiance*, and *Donegal* were also in close pursuit; and very shortly afterwards the French anchored in line of battle, with springs on their cables, immediately under the Sables d'Olonne batteries. Half an hour later, the British stood in, the *Defiance* leading, and being followed in order by the *Cæsar*, *Donegal*, and *Amelia*; and at 11 A.M. fire was opened upon the enemy, who replied from the frigates as well as from the powerful forts on shore. At 11.50 A.M., the *Italienne* and *Cybèle*, in flames, cut their cables and ran on to the beach, and later the *Calypso* drove thither stern foremost. As the tide then began to fall, Stopford ordered his ships to stand out; and the French frigates, having taken the ground nearly at the top of high water, became total wrecks. In this action the *Cæsar*, though she, like her consorts, suffered somewhat aloft, had no one hurt. The *Donegal* had one killed and six wounded; and the *Defiance*, which was the most hotly engaged, had two killed and twenty-five wounded. The French lost twenty-four killed and fifty-one wounded, in addition to the losses which they may have sustained on shore. [2]

Having accomplished this service, Stopford returned to his anchorage off the Tour de Chassiron, on the northern point of Oleron, and was there joined on February 25th by Commodore Beresford with the *Theseus*, *Revenge*, *Triumph*, and *Valiant*. [3] On the 26th Willaumez weighed and stood for Aix road; but while he

---

[1] The wind was then about S.E. by E.

[2] *Gazette*, 1809, 289. Stopford to Pole, Feb. 27th, 1809.

[3] Stopford had also five frigates. Stopford to Pole, Feb. 27th, 1809.

was on his way thither, the *Jean Bart*, 74, grounded on the Palles shoal, off Isle Madame, and, in spite of the efforts that were made to get her off, became a wreck.[1]　The remaining Brest ships joined the Rochefort squadron [2] under Commodore Gilbert Aimable Faure, and anchored with it between the south end of Isle d'Aix and the tail of the Boyart shoal.　The *Hero*, 74, Captain James Newman Newman, presently joined Stopford, who continued to blockade Willaumez until March 7th, when Admiral Lord Gambier, who had learnt on February 23rd of the escape of the French,[3] arrived. When, a little later, the Commander-in-Chief had detached the *Defiance* and *Triumph*, there remained in the Antioche passage eleven British ships of the line, the names of which are given below,[4] together with those of the smaller craft which were already there or which joined later.　On March 17th, Gambier anchored his fleet in Basque road, posting his frigates about a mile nearer than his main force, now towards Aix, and now towards La Rochelle,

---

[1] Seymour to Stopford, Feb. 27th.

[2] *Cassard*, 74; *Jemmapes*, 74; *Patriote*, 74; *Calcutta*, flûte, 30; *Pallas*, 40; *Hortense*, 40.

[3] Upon learning of their escape, Gambier had detached Duckworth, with eight sail, in pursuit of them, and had himself gone to Cawsand Bay, whence he had sailed on March 3rd, with five ships of the line.

[4]

SHIPS.	GUNS.	COMMANDERS.	SHIPS.	GUNS.	COMMANDERS.
Caledonia . .	120	Admiral Lord Gambier (B). Capt. Sir Harry Burrard Neale, Bart., 1st. ,, William Bedford.	Beagle . . .	18	Com. Francis Newcombe (posted 11–4–1809).
			Doterel . .	18	,, Anthony Abdy.
			Foxhound . .	18	,, Pitt Burnaby Greene.
Cæsar . . .	80	Rear-Adm. Hon. Robert Stopford (B). Capt. Charles Richardson.	Lyra . . .	10	,, William Bevians.
			Redpole. . .	10	,, John Joyce (posted 11–4–1809).
Gibraltar . .	80	,, Henry Lidgbird Ball.	Thunder, bomb[1]	8	,, James Caulfield (1) (posted 11–4–1809).
Hero . . .	74	,, James Newman Newman.			
Donegal . .	74	,, Pulteney Malcolm.	Ætna, bomb .	8	,, William Godfrey (posted 11–4–1809).
Resolution . .	74	,, George Burlton.			
Theseus. . .	74	,, John Poo Beresford.	Insolent . .	14	Lieut. John Row Morris.
Valiant . .	74	,, John Bligh (2).	Encounter . .	14	,, James Hugh Talbot.
Illustrious. .	74	,, William Robert Broughton.	Conflict . .	12	,, Joseph B— Batt.
			Contest . .	14	,, John Gregory (1).
Bellona. . .	74	,, Stair Douglas (2).	Fervent . .	12	,, John Edward Hare.
Revenge . .	74	,, Alexander Robert Kerr.	Growler . .	14	,, Richard Crossman.
			Martial . .	14	,, Joseph Marrett.
Indefatigable .	44	,, John Tremayne Rodd	Whiting, sch. .	4	,, Henry Wildey.
Imperieuse. .	38	,, Lord Cochrane.	Nimrod, hired}		
Amelia[1] . .	38	,, Hon. Frederick Paul Irby.	cutter . .}	..	Master's Mate Edward Tapley.
Aigle . .	36	,, George Wolfe. [(2).	King George,}		
Emerald . .	36	,, Frederick Lewis Maitland	hired cutter .}	..	,, ,, Thomas Mercer.[2]
Unicorn . .	32	,, Lucius Ferdinand Hardyman.	And the *Cleveland*, transport, 20 fireships, 3 explosion vessels, storeships, etc.		
Pallas . . .	32	,, George Francis Seymour.			
Mediator (flûte)	32	Com. James Wooldridge (posted 11–4–1809).			

---

[1] Not present at the attack on the vessels in Basque road on April 12th. The *Thunder*, however, was employed against the *Regulus* at the mouth of the Charente on April 20th and 24th.

[2] James (v. 105) says Thomas Mekeek. The Admiralty Order of 1849 says Mercer.

according to the direction of the wind. Lest his command should
be attacked by fireships, he kept every vessel ready for instant action
and for slipping her cables, leaving buoys upon them. Boats were
also held prepared with grapnels, and all other desirable precautions
were taken; though it does not appear that the French ever
meditated any movements of the nature which Gambier had in his
mind. His precautions, in fact, seem to have been chiefly suggested
by his own half-formed intentions; for as early as March 11th, in
a letter to a Lord Mulgrave,[1] he hinted that fireships might be
advantageously employed against the enemy, though, he added, "it
is a horrible mode of warfare, and the attempt very hazardous, if
not desperate." The Admiralty, however, had, even earlier, decided
that fireships should be utilised; for on March 7th it had ordered
that a number of vessels of that class should be prepared; and on
March 19th, the very day on which Gambier's letter of the 11th
reached London, the Secretary was directed to inform the Admiral
that twelve transports were fitting as fireships, that Mr. Congreve[2]
was to proceed, with rockets and men to work them, to Basque road,
and that five bombs were getting ready to join the fleet.

"All these preparations," wrote the Secretary, "are making with a view to enable
your Lordship to make an attack on the French fleet at their anchorage off Isle d'Aix,
if practicable; and I am further commanded to signify their Lordships' directions to
you to take into your consideration the possibility of making an attack upon the
enemy, either conjointly, with your line-of-battle ships, frigates, and small craft,
fireships, bombs, and rockets, or separately, by any of the above-named means."[3]

On March 19th, also, there arrived at Plymouth, from the
Mediterranean, the *Impérieuse*, 38, Captain Lord Cochrane. Cochrane was instantly ordered by telegraph to attend at the Admiralty.
He reached London on the 21st, and was privately interrogated by
Lord Mulgrave as to the possible destruction of the French fleet in
Aix road. Cochrane expressed a decided opinion that an attempt
by means of fireships would be successful. Would he then, he was
asked, undertake to make it ? He objected that his appointment to
such a service would excite jealousy in the minds of officers already

[1] Chatterton, 'Gambier,' ii., 96. M. of C. M. by Gurney, p. 115.
[2] Afterwards Sir William Congreve, Bart. This distinguished engineer was born
in 1772 at Woolwich, and died in 1828 at Toulouse. In 1806 he had invented the
incendiary rocket which bears his name.
[3] Gurney's Mins. of C. M., p. 116. The letter was received by Gambier on
Mar. 26th.

on the spot; [1] but, subsequently reflecting that, as he had advocated the measure and declared it to be easily practicable, his motives in refusing to carry it out might be misconstrued, he consented to assume command of the adventure. On March 25th, therefore, the Admiralty wrote to inform Lord Gambier that Lord Cochrane had been selected to conduct the operation under the Admiral's direction; [2] and the letter to that effect was delivered to Cochrane, who hurried back to Plymouth, sailed in the *Impérieuse* as soon as possible, and joined Lord Gambier on April 3rd. [3]

On March 26th, the Admiral had received [4] the Board's orders of the 19th. In reply, Lord Gambier wrote on the same day two letters to the Secretary of the Admiralty. In these he admitted that "their ships certainly lie exposed to an attack upon them with fire-vessels with a hope of success;" but he also gave reasons why his heavier ships could not, in his opinion, be advantageously utilised

---

[1] The appointment did, in fact, excite jealousy, Cochrane being then a Post-Captain of less than eight years' standing. It led, moreover, to a very regrettable naval scandal. When news arrived in Basque road that the French were to be attacked by means of fireships, the Commander-in-Chief, through the other flag-officers then in company, asked for volunteers. Among these flag-officers there happened to be then present Rear-Admiral Eliab Harvey, whose flag flew in the *Tonnant*, 80. Harvey thereupon went on board the *Caledonia*, and offered to direct the contemplated operations. Gambier explained that the Admiralty had nominated Cochrane for the service. In reply, Harvey violently and disrespectfully declared "that if he were passed by, and Lord Cochrane, or any other junior officer, appointed in preference, he should immediately desire to strike his flag and resign his commission." Gambier entered into further explanations, and remonstrated with the Rear-Admiral; but Harvey "continued his vehement and insulting language," criticised Gambier's conduct while in command, declared that he could impeach the Commander-in-Chief for bad management, "and concluded by saying, with the same insulting tone and manner, that he would go in the *Tonnant*, or any old rotten 74, to board the enemy's three-decked ship in Aix road, and bring her out." Harvey also spoke disparagingly and disrespectfully of Gambier to various officers in the fleet. In consequence of all this, Harvey was tried by court-martial on board the *Gladiator*, at Portsmouth, on May 22nd, 1809. Harvey apologised both to Gambier and to the court; pleaded that he had spoken under the influence of great irritation; and submitted that he had sinned by excess of zeal for the Service; but the court held the charges to have been proved, and sentenced the Rear-Admiral to be dismissed the service. Harvey was, however, quickly reinstated. His rash conduct appears to have been to a large extent instigated by some vague dislike to Gambier's private character, for, speaking of the Commander-in-Chief to Lord Cochrane in the cabin of the Captain of the Fleet, he said : "I am no canting Methodist, no hypocrite, nor a psalm-singer. I do not cheat old women out of their estates by hypocrisy and canting." Min. of C. M.

[2] Gurney's Mins. of C. M., p. 22.

[3] Much of what follows is based upon Dundonald's (Cochrane's) 'Autobiog. of a Seaman,' i., 338–428, and ii., 1–126, on Lady Chatterton's 'Memorials of Adm. Lord Gambier,' ii., 95–327, and on the Mins. of C. M. on Gambier.

[4] By the gun-brig *Encounter*.

against the enemy, and he appeared doubtful as to the practicability
of employing bombs with effect.   Indeed, he even went so far as to
hint that an attack by means of fireships might be without result,
seeing that the French had the Charente open to them, and that
" the tide and wind that are favourable to this kind of annoyance to
the enemy serve equally to carry them up the river."   They were
not sanguine, strong, confident letters.   They were the dispatches
of a Duckworth or a Persano rather than those of a Nelson or a
Saumarez.   Nevertheless, the second of them terminated with a
formal declaration " that, if their Lordships are of opinion that an
attack on the enemy's ships by those of the fleet under my
command is practicable, I am ready to obey any orders they may
be pleased to honour me with, however great the risk may be of the
loss of men and ships." [1]

Pending the arrival of the fireships, bombs, and rockets, Lord
Gambier did little beyond ordering the *Amelia*, 38, Captain the
Hon. Frederick Paul Irby, to dislodge some French who were
endeavouring to erect defensive works on the south end of the
Boyart shoal.   Captain Irby executed this service on April 1st, and
then, sending in his boats, destroyed whatever the enemy had
already constructed. [2]

On April 3rd, when Gambier was apprised of the Admiralty's
selection of Cochrane by the letter brought by that officer, the
fireships, [3] some of the transports [4] intended to be fitted as fireships, a large expected consignment of carcasses for 18-prs., and
various promised combustibles had not reached the fleet.   The
Commander-in-Chief, however, ordered eight of the transports then
with him, and, at Cochrane's suggestion, the *Mediator*, flûte, to be
prepared as fireships with such materials as the fleet could supply.
Three explosion vessels were also equipped.   On April 6th, the
Ætna, having Mr. Congreve on board, anchored with the fleet;
and on the 10th, the expected fireships, twelve in number, joined
under convoy of the *Beagle* and *Redpole*, and in company with the
transport *Cleveland*.   The force to be employed was then practically
complete.

After the French Brest squadron had entered the road of Aix,

---

[1] 'Autobiog. of a Seaman,' i., 350.

[2] The *Amelia* was soon afterwards detached to the north coast of Spain.

[3] Twelve lay in the Downs awaiting a fair wind.

[4] Six had been ordered to sail from Plymouth.

Captain Jacques Bergeret, dissatisfied with the behaviour of Willaumez when in presence of Commodore Beresford on February 21–23, had written to the Minister of Marine a letter which occasioned not only the recall of Willaumez, but also the super-session, or transfer to new commands, of Bergeret and some other captains. In place of Willaumez, Vice-Admiral Allemand hoisted his flag in the *Océan*, on April 17th.

Allemand's orders were precise; and he must not be held responsible for what followed. The real responsibility for the disaster to the French squadron rests upon Napoleon, who gave the orders under which Allemand acted, and who cherished not only a general and invincible conviction of the security of a naval fórce well moored under batteries, but also a particular conviction of the safety of a fleet lying in Aix road. As early as June, 1805, he had written [1] :—

"You may quiet your apprehensions that the enemy will attempt something against Isle d'Aix. . . . Nothing can be more insane than the idea of attacking a French squadron at Isle d'Aix. I am annoyed to see you with such notions. . . . What on earth do you imagine is to be feared by a squadron of five ships of the line, with plenty of powder and supplies, well protected, and ready to fight, lying at Aix?"

As was almost invariably the case when he expressed any opinion on naval subjects, Napoleon was wrong. On the other hand, it must be said in favour of MM. Willaumez and Allemand that they did what they could under the conditions by which they were bound. The French fleet was moored, with the ships' heads to the north-ward, in three lines, on a nearly north and south bearing, in the passage between the south end of Isle d'Aix and the western tail of the Palles shoal, which runs out north-westward from Isle Madame. The inner, or easterly line, lying in about six fathoms, consisted, counting from the north end, of the *Elbe*, 40, *Tourville*, 74, *Aquilon*, 74, *Jemmapes*, 74, *Patriote*, 74, and *Tonnerre*, 74, moored, at intervals of about ninety fathoms, each with one cable to the north-west and another to the south-east. The middle line, parallel with the former and about 250 yards to the westward of it, consisted, still counting from the northward, of the *Calcutta*, flûte, 50, *Cassard*, 74, *Regulus*, 74, *Océan*, 120, *Varsovie*, 80, and *Foudroyant*, 80. These ships were moored in the same manner and with the same intervals between them as those of the inner line; but they were so stationed as to close the openings left by the inner

---

[1] Napoleon to Decrès, from the Château de Monteronne.

line, and thus to form a double *ligne endentée*. The *Calcutta* bore
due south, distant 640 yards, from a battery on the south point of
Aix. The third, or western line, lay nearly parallel with the others,
about 740 yards outside the middle one, and consisted, again counting
from the north, of the *Pallas*, 40, *Hortense*, 40, and *Indienne*, 40.
About 100 yards to the eastward of this third line was a very strong
and firmly anchored boom of floated cables,[1] half a mile in length.
This boom seems to have been laid down without the knowledge of
the British, and not to have been discovered by them until the
moment of the attack. Protecting the boom and anchorage were
several batteries, mounting, in all, at least thirty guns, chiefly long
36-prs., besides some heavy mortars. Most of the guns were on
Isle d'Aix, where there were about two thousand troops, all of them,
however, conscripts.

Having noted the arrival of the fireships in Basque road on
April 10th, Vice-Admiral Allemand issued very careful directions
for the conduct of the numerous boats and armed launches of his
fleet, which he ordered, some to row guard at night, and others to lie
near the boom, so as to be ready to board and tow away any vessels
that might threaten the safety of his command. He also strengthened
the garrison of Aix, caused his larger ships to strike their topmasts
and send down their top-gallant masts, and directed his advanced
frigates to be always prepared for getting under way at a moment's
notice.

Early in the afternoon of April 11th, the *Impérieuse* moved in
towards the enemy, and came to in nine fathoms, close to the
north-east edge of the Boyart shoal, and about a mile and three-
quarters from the nearest French frigate. The *Aigle, Unicorn,* and
Pallas, anchored outside of her, in readiness to receive the crews of
the fireships upon their return, and to render general assistance.
The *Whiting, King George,* and *Nimrod*, fitted for throwing rockets,
took station close to the tail of the Boyart. The *Ætna*, bomb,
covered by the *Indefatigable* and *Foxhound*, placed herself north-
west of Isle d'Aix, as near as possible in that direction to the fort on
its southern extremity.[2] The *Emerald, Beagle, Doterel, Conflict,*
and *Growler*, were stationed off the east end of Aix to make a

---

[1] These cables were, some of them, 31½ inches in diameter, or nearly a third thicker
than a British first-rate's bower cable.

[2] Joyce Gold's plan of the action, published in the *Naval Chronicle*, shows the
Ætna only in her later position, three-quarters of a mile to the S.E. of the tail of the
Boyart.

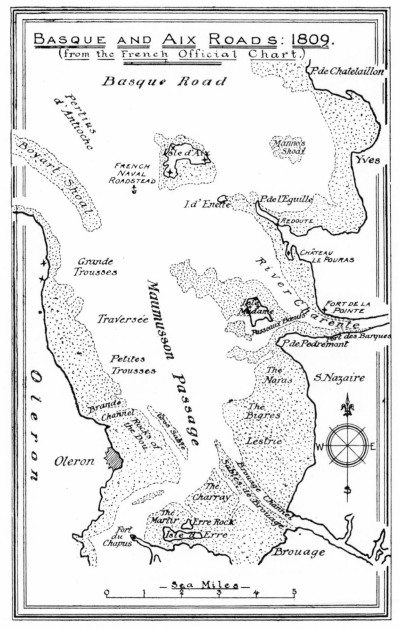

BASQUE AND AIX ROADS: 1809.
(from the French Official Chart.)

P. de Chatelaillon

Basque Road

Pertius d'Antioche

Boyart Shoal

Isle d'Aix

Manne's Shoal

Yves

FRENCH
NAVAL
ROADSTEAD

I. d'Enette

P. de l'Eguille

REDOUTE

CHÂTEAU
LE FOURAS

Grande
Trousses

River Charente

Traversée

Maumusson Passage

Isle
Madame

Passeaux Bœufs

FORT DE LA
POINTE

Fort des Barques

P. de Pedremont

Petites
Trousses

The
Naras

S. Nazaire

Oleron

Brande
Channel

Rocks of
the Dou

Bon Sable

The
Bigres

Lestrie

W   E

Oleron

The
Charray

Brouage Channel

Sables de Brouage

S

The
Martir

Erre Rock

Fort
du
Chapus

Isle d'Erre

Brouage

— Sea Miles —

0   1   2   3   4   5

Note.—The Palles shoal is the shoal running N.W. from Isle Madame.

[To face page 260.

diversion; and the *Redpole* and *Lyra*, with lights hoisted, were anchored, one off the shoal running out to the north-west of Aix, and the other off the tail of the Boyart, so as to serve as guides during the attack. The British ships of the line, which had lain in Basque road, about six miles north-west from the enemy's fleet, unmoored with a view to co-operating if necessary; but, being in a strong tide-way, with a brisk north-west wind, they had to be moored again to prevent them from falling on board one another when the weather tide made. The fireships lay ready at anchor about a mile nearer to the enemy than the ships of the line.

It had been intended to chain together the fireships in divisions of four; but, owing to the strength of the wind, this idea was at the last moment abandoned, and the vessels were left to act independently. At 8.30 P.M., by which time it was very dark, all of them, including the *Mediator*, cut their cables and made sail, with a two-knot tide in their favour, in the direction of the enemy. Two of the three explosion vessels [1] also proceeded, one of them having on board Captain Lord Cochrane and Lieutenant William Bissell, a volunteer. [2] Both craft are believed to have been fired when within less than three-quarters of a mile from the enemy's line. The effect produced by them will be shown later. But several of the fireships were fired and abandoned when more than two miles from the nearest French ship; and they, in consequence, were simply thrown away. Five or six, however, including the *Mediator*, were most admirably handled. Cochrane's own explosion vessel, it should be mentioned, contained about one thousand five hundred barrels of powder, started into puncheons placed end upwards and jammed fast together with hawsers, wedges, and wet sand. Upon them were placed about three hundred and fifty fused shells, and many thousands of hand-grenades.

The *Mediator*, under the united impulses of wind and tide, broke the boom, and opened a passage for such other fireships as drove so far. Commander Wooldridge, in his anxiety to carry out his dangerous service satisfactorily, remained on board until the very last moment, and, with Lieutenants Nicholas Brent Clements [3] and

---

[1] The third was fouled by a prematurely abandoned fireship, and, when she was fired, her fuse failed to act.

[2] He had just returned in the *Brunswick*, 74, from the Baltic. For his services in Aix road he was made Commander April 11th, 1809.

[3] Promoted April 11th, 1809.

James Pearl,[1] and a seaman, was actually blown out of the exploding ship, and so badly burnt that he never wholly recovered from his injuries. His gunner, Mr. James Segges, was killed. Of the people serving in the remaining fireships, Lieutenant William Flintoft (actg.) and a seaman died of fatigue, two other seamen were killed, and Master's Mates Richard Francis Jewers[2] (*Theseus*) and John Conyers[3] (*Gibraltar*) were badly scorched. Among the officers who, besides Commander Wooldridge, commanded fireships or explosion vessels, were Commanders Francis Newcombe and John Joyce, and Lieutenants John Cookesley[3] (*Gibraltar*), Thomas Alexander[3] (2) (*Resolution*), John Cook Carpenter,[3] Robert Hockings[3] (*Caledonia*), Henry Jones[3] (*Cæsar*), Henry Montresor[3] (*Revenge*), Thomas Goldwyer Muston[3] (*Caledonia*), Christopher Nixon,[3] Thomas Percival,[3] William Robert Smith[3] (*Theseus*), and William West.[3] Several of them experienced great difficulty and no small danger in regaining the advanced frigates.

According to the French accounts, the fireships and explosion vessels did little actual damage. One of them blew up at the boom, within about 120 yards of the *Indienne*, but did her no injury. Ten minutes afterwards, another one blew up, also at the boom, and also close to the *Indienne*. This, likewise, did little harm, beyond covering the frigate with a shower of sparks and small fragments. A few minutes later the boom was broken by the *Mediator ;* and she and her advancing consorts were at once fired at by the entire French fleet, the enemy seeming to take little pains to avoid hitting his own advanced frigates, which, possibly for that reason, soon cut their cables. The *Hortense* made sail, and, passing to windward of some of the fireships, threw several broadsides into them, ere, with her consorts, she sought refuge behind the lines of heavier ships. The *Regulus* and *Océan* were presently grappled by fireships; and, although both vessels almost miraculously escaped from immediate destruction, the British onslaught threw the French into such confusion that they not only cut their cables,[4] but also began to foul one another. The *Regulus*, for example, ran on board the *Tourville ;* and the *Océan*, having grounded, was collided with by

---

[1] He was not promoted until September 29th, 1827. At his death in 1839 he was still only a Commander, but he had previously been knighted.

[2] Promoted to be Lieutenant, July 5th, 1809.

[3] Promoted April 11th, 1809.

[4] The *Foudroyant* alone kept her station.

the *Tonnerre* and *Patriote*. By midnight, in short, all the French
ships in Aix road, except the *Foudroyant* and *Cassard*, were aground,
several of them being, in addition, considerably damaged. James,
summarising from French accounts, thus describes the position of
the stranded ships :—

" The *Océan* lay in the mud at the distance of a full half-mile to the E.S.E. of the
anchorage in Aix road. Having on board, in common with the other ships, a quantity
of provisions for the supply of the colony to which she had been destined, the *Océan*
was very deep, drawing not less, perhaps, than 28 or 29 feet. Hence she grounded
while still in a part of Aix road, and not on the Palles shoal. . . . At about 500 yards
to the S.W. of the *Océan*, upon a rocky bed named Charenton, lay the *Varsovie* and
Aquilon, and close to them, but upon somewhat better ground, the *Regulus* and
Jemmapes. The *Tonnerre*, with her head to the S.E., lay on a hard bottom about
200 yards to the eastward of the rock of Pontra, and bore N.W. of Isle Madame,
situated on the S.W. side of the entrance to the Charente, and N.E. of the isle of Enette,
which forms the northern extremity of the opposite side of the same river. . . . She
had already bilged. . . . At some distance to the S.W. of the *Tonnerre*, nearly on
the extremity of the Palles in that direction, and close to the wreck of the *Jean Bart*,
lay the *Calcutta*, with her head to the S.E. . . . The *Patriote* and *Tourville* lay on
the mud off Isle Madame, and at no great distance from the channel of the Charente.
With respect to the four frigates, the *Indienne* lay about three-quarters of a mile to
the eastward of the *Océan*, upon the mud off Pointe de l'Eguille, near Enette isle. The
Elbe and *Hortense* lay upon the Fontenelles, and the *Pallas* upon the mud off the little
fort of Barques, just at the entrance of the Charente." [1]

Although, therefore, Cochrane's night assault had destroyed no
vessel of the enemy, it had reduced nearly the whole of his ships to
a state of comparative helplessness and impotence, and had left them
at the mercy of a new and different species of attack, if promptly
made. When, on the morning of April 12th, the state of affairs had
been noted on board the *Impérieuse*, her Captain made the following
telegraphic signals to the *Caledonia*, which was then twelve miles
from the grounded ships :—

At 5.48 A.M. " Half the fleet can destroy the enemy. Seven on shore."
At 6.40 A.M. " Eleven on shore."
At 7.40 A.M. " Only two afloat."
At 9.30 A.M. " Enemy preparing to heave off."

Upon getting the last of these signals, Lord Gambier telegraphed
to his fleet to " prepare with sheet and spare anchors out of stern
ports, and springs ready " ; [2] and a few minutes later he signalled to
weigh, though he postponed weighing until about 10.45 A.M., in the
meantime summoning all the Captains on board the flagship. At

[1] James (ed. 1837), v. 110, 111.
[2] But not " to prepare for battle." It was because he wished to omit this direction
from the signal (No. 14) that he used the telegraph.

11.30 A.M., the fleet re-anchored in about twelve fathoms, three miles from Aix flagstaff, and still six miles from the grounded French. The Admiral deemed it unwise to run any unnecessary risk, seeing that, in his view, the object sought had already been practically attained.[1]   But he directed the *Ætna*, covered by the *Insolent*, *Conflict*, and *Growler*,[2] to take up a position from which to throw shells over the stranded vessels ; and he ordered Captain John Bligh (2), in the *Valiant*, with the *Bellona*, *Revenge*, and the frigates and sloops, to anchor as close as possible to the Boyart, so as to support the brigs and the bomb.   Bligh and his division consequently brought up a mile nearer to the enemy than the remainder of the ships of the line.   These dispositions induced the *Foudroyant* and *Cassard* to cut and make sail for the Charente ; but, in endeavouring to enter the river, both vessels grounded nearly opposite the Château Le Fouras.   Before high water, the *Océan*, *Patriote*, *Regulus*, and *Jemmapes*, having floated, also moved towards the mouth of the river, and piled up on the mud there.

Perceiving that the enemy was thus gradually placing himself out of reach of attack, Lord Cochrane, at 1 P.M., adopted the bold course of getting under way in the *Impérieuse*, and dropping down, without orders, towards the French.   He made for the vessels which were still aground upon the Palles shoal, and, with the deliberate purpose of forcing his chief's hand, hoisted in succession the following signals :—

> At 1.30 P.M. No. 405. "The enemy's ships are getting under sail."
> At 1.40 P.M. No. 378. "The enemy is superior to the chasing ship."
> At 1.45 P.M. No. 364. "The ship is in distress, and requires to be assisted immediately."

By 2 P.M. the *Impérieuse* had so anchored, with a spring, as to bring her starboard broadside to bear upon the *Calcutta's* starboard quarter, and to be able to fire with her starboard forecastle and bow-guns at the *Varsovie* and *Aquilon*.   Cochrane soon observed that the 24 and 18-pr. carronades of the *Insolent*, *Conflict*, and *Growler*, and even the heavier carronades of the *Beagle*, were producing no visible effect.   He therefore desired to order the brigs to approach closer.   On the other hand, he was quite satisfied with the position of the *Ætna* ; and, as the signal which would have served part of his purpose would have made no distinction between

---

[1] Broughton's evidence at the C. M.

[2] The *Beagle* subsequently anchored somewhat closer in.

the brigs and the bomb, he adopted the rather brusque, but perfectly effective expedient of firing his main-deck guns at or near the former, which, understanding the hint, dropped into better stations. Not until after 2 P.M. did Lord Gambier adopt any measures for supporting the *Impérieuse*. He then sent the *Indefatigable*, followed by the remaining frigates and small craft, to Cochrane's assistance; and at 2.30 P.M. he also ordered the *Valiant* and *Revenge* to proceed towards her. But, as the wind was light and the tide was ebbing, these vessels made but slow progress, and not until about 3.20 P.M. were the *Indefatigable* and her consorts cheered by the *Impérieuse* as they neared her. Just at that time, Cochrane sent a boat[1] to take possession of the *Calcutta*, which had ceased firing and was being abandoned by her people. One by one the *Aigle, Emerald, Unicorn, Valiant, Revenge* and *Pallas*, joined Cochrane and Rodd, and anchored in a semi-circle, with springs, around the grounded French ships, upon which they opened a heavy fire,[2] while the *Beagle* most gallantly ran still closer in and placed herself under the stern of the *Aquilon*. At 5.30 P.M., the *Varsovie* and *Aquilon* struck. At nearly the same moment, the *Theseus*, from the fleet, joined the attacking squadron. At 6 P.M., the *Tonnerre* was fired and abandoned by her crew, and at 7.30 P.M. she blew up. At 8.30 P.M., the *Calcutta*, which had probably been fired by the British boarding party without orders, also exploded.

There remained in more or less assailable positions the *Océan, Cassard, Regulus, Jemmapes, Tourville,* and *Indienne;* but the British had, unfortunately, expended all their regular fireships; and but a single bomb, the *Ætna*, was then present. Three transports were hurriedly converted into fireships, and at 5.30 P.M., Stopford, in the *Cæsar*, weighed with them and some launches fitted as rocket-boats, and stood towards Aix road under a heavy fire from the Aix and Oleron batteries. At 7.40 P.M., the *Cæsar* grounded[3] on or near the tail of the Boyart, and was delayed until 10.30 P.M.,

[1] This boat had to be withdrawn after she had reached the *Calcutta*, owing to the danger to her people from British shot.

[2] In this phase of the operations the *Revenge* had 3 killed and 15 (including Lieutenant James Garland) wounded; and the *Impérieuse* had 3 killed and 11 wounded. The other vessels suffered no loss; but the *Indefatigable* and *Beagle* were more or less damaged. The French, especially in the *Varsovie*, were much more severely handled.

[3] The *Valiant* also was aground for a time, as were the *Indefatigable* and *Impérieuse*, on the edge of the Palles shoal, but none of them were any the worse.

when she floated. Ere that hour, the *Revenge*, with all the frigates and brigs except the *Impérieuse*, had anchored in the Maumusson passage between the Boyart and Palles shoals. The fireships were delayed as well, until, at 2 A.M. on the 13th, the wind, after some chopping about, settled in the south-west. This enabled the *Cæsar* to leave Aix road again and to anchor in Little Basque road ; but it also prevented, for the moment, the employment of the fire-ships,[1] which had been entrusted to Captain John Bligh (2). That officer, therefore, contented himself with setting fire to the *Varsovie* and *Aquilon*. The burning vessels were mistaken by some of the uncaptured French craft for British fireships, and were accordingly fired at ; and the *Tourville's* people were so alarmed at what seemed to be a fresh attack, that they incontinently abandoned their ship after ineffectually setting her on fire. They subsequently returned to her when they found that she had been neither burnt nor taken possession of.

At 5 A.M., by signal from Stopford, Bligh, with the *Valiant*, *Theseus*, *Revenge*, *Indefatigable*, *Unicorn*, *Aigle* and *Emerald*, got under way in order to proceed to Little Basque road. The *Im-périeuse* was at that time on her way to anchor in the Maumusson passage ; and, passing within hail of the *Indefatigable*, Cochrane proposed to Captain Rodd to go with him and attack the *Océan*. Rodd, however, declined, on the grounds that his ship had a shot through her main topmast, and drew too much water for the service, and that, being in the immediate presence of two senior Captains,[2] he could not act without orders. Cochrane dropped anchor in the Maumusson passage at 6 A.M., and, half-an-hour later, was hailed by the *Pallas*, then under sail to follow Bligh to Basque road. Captain Seymour asked whether or not he should remain, and Cochrane desired him to do so, unless he had received contrary orders. For a fresh attack Cochrane thus retained with the *Impérieuse* the *Pallas* as well as the *Beagle*, the gunbrigs, the *Ætna*, and the small craft.

The fresh attack was ordered at 8 A.M., which was as early as the tide suited. Cochrane sent the brigs and the bomb to reduce the nearest of the French ships which were aground in the mouth of the Charente, but was unable to follow them with the frigates, there not

---

[1] One of the fireships, while working out to avoid the expected explosion of the *Aquilon* and *Varsovie*, ran ashore off Aix.

[2] Bligh and Beresford.

being sufficient depth of water. At 11 A.M., the *Beagle, Ætna, Conflict, Contest, Encounter, Fervent, Growler, Whiting, Nimrod* and
King George, anchored, and opened fire on the *Océan, Regulus*, and
Indienne.[1] The *Beagle*, which gallantly posted herself on the
Océan's stern and quarter in barely more water than sufficed to float
her, fought hotly for five hours, and suffered much more severely
than any of her consorts, although none of the British vessels is
noted as having lost any men.[2] At 4 P.M., owing to the falling
water, the flotilla had to weigh, and work back to its anchorage,
leaving the *Océan* and *Regulus* busily engaged in preparing to push
further up the river at the next rise of tide.

During the engagement, the *Doterel, Foxhound, Redpole*, and
two rocket-boats from Basque road, joined Cochrane in the Maumusson passage. They brought to him two letters from Lord
Gambier. One, a public one, ordered Cochrane to make an attempt
upon the *Océan* with the bomb and the rocket-vessels, but expressed
doubt as to the attempt being successful. It also ordered Cochrane
to proceed to Basque road so soon as the tide should turn. The
other, a private one, beginning " My dear Lord," deprecated any
action that would, by attempting impossibilities, jeopardise the
brilliant effect of what Cochrane had already accomplished, and
urged Cochrane to join the flag as soon as possible. Cochrane
replied : " I have just received your Lordship's letter. We can
destroy the enemy's ships on shore ; of which I hope you will
approve." In his evidence at the subsequent court-martial, Cochrane declared that, at " about four or five o'clock in the afternoon,"
or at about the time when he received the letters, it was reported to
him that the *Caledonia* had made the *Impérieuse's* signal of recall,
and that he replied telegraphically that the enemy could be destroyed ; but it is more than doubtful whether the signal of recall
was made.

Early on the 14th, the *Tourville* and the *Océan* got afloat, and
pushed further up the river ; but both of them ultimately grounded
again near Le Fouras. The *Patriote, Hortense, Elbe* and *Pallas,* were
more successful, and entered the Charente so far as to be beyond
danger of further attack. That day, Lord Cochrane, in compliance

---

[1] The *Cassard, Tourville* and *Jemmapes* were too distant to have more than a very
slight part in the engagement.

[2] The *Ætna* split her 13-in. mortar. The heavy mortars of those days hardly
ever survived the strain of a few hours' use in action.

with a signal from Lord Gambier, handed over the command of the
Aix flotilla to Captain George Wolfe, of the *Aigle*, and proceeded
with the *Impérieuse* to Basque road, whence, on the 15th, he sailed
for England, carrying home Captain Sir Harry Burrard Neale, with
the Admiral's dispatches. At about 3.30 P.M. on the 14th, the *Ætna*
and brigs again attacked the ships that were still aground outside
the mouth of the river; but they appear to have done little damage,
and they did not prevent the *Jemmapes*, during the firing, from
getting off and entering the Charente. On the following days,
moreover, the *Océan*, *Cassard*, *Foudroyant* and *Tourville*, thanks to
the prolonged exertions of their people, were moved to positions of
safety, and the *Indienne* was burnt by her crew; so that only the
Regulus, on the mud off Le Fouras, remained assailable. On the 19th,
the *Thunder*, bomb, arrived, and on the 20th, covered by the gun-
brigs, she went to the attack of the French 74; but she quickly split
her 13-in. mortar,[1] and had to desist. Other vain attempts were
made to destroy the *Regulus*, which, however, succeeded, on the
29th, in getting afloat and rejoining her consorts before Rochefort.
There being nothing more to be done, Lord Gambier, on the same
day, sailed for England.

There can be no question that the affair of Aix road was mismanaged both by the Admiralty at home and by the Admiral on the
spot. Until the arrival of the *Thunder*, Gambier had only a single
bomb-vessel with him. He ought to have been supplied with half-
a-dozen. The British gun-brigs of that day almost invariably carried
18-pr. carronades instead of long guns. Gambier had five brigs[2] of
the 12-18-pr. carronade class; but the Admiralty should have known
that, for attacking a squadron posted and defended as that of
M. Allemand was, light carronades were of little use. Small craft
carrying either long guns or 68-pr. (8 in.) carronades should have
been sent. As for Gambier, he surely did not employ to the best
advantage such force as he had. He despatched the *Cæsar* and
Revenge to Aix road, while he kept in inactivity in Basque road the
Bellona and *Resolution*, which drew less water than either. He did
not send the *Doterel* and *Foxhound*, with their 32-pr. carronades, to
Cochrane until the 13th. He might, had he known how, have

---

[1] Service mortars, in consequence of the experience gained at Aix road, were
afterwards made heavier.

[2] *Encounter*, *Conflict*, *Contest*, *Fervent* and *Growler*. Some of these however,
carried, in addition, a couple of long guns.

carried all his 74's, and possibly even his 80's, into Aix road, and, silencing the batteries, have destroyed the French at their anchors.

Cochrane, who was firmly of opinion that Gambier had not done all that lay in his power against the enemy, intimated to the First Lord that, from his seat in Parliament,[1] he would oppose the passage of any vote of thanks to the Admiral. Apprised of this, Gambier demanded a court-martial; and, on July 26th, he was duly tried at Portsmouth. The proceedings lasted until August 4th. The charge was—

"That Admiral the Right Honourable Lord Gambier, on the 12th of April, the enemy's ships being then on shore, and the signal having been made that they could be destroyed, did, for a considerable time, neglect or delay taking effectual measures for destroying them."

And the sentence was that the court considered that the charge had not been proved, but—

"that his Lordship's conduct on that occasion, as well as his general conduct and proceedings as Commander-in-Chief of the Channel Fleet in Basque road, between the 17th day of March and the 29th day of April, 1809, was marked by zeal, judgment, ability, and an anxious attention to the welfare of his Majesty's service, and did adjudge him to be most honourably acquitted."

Gambier was, accordingly, most honourably acquitted. He was fortunate. James points out with truth that several members of the court, notably Admiral Sir Roger Curtis, the president, and Admiral William Young (1), showed strong partiality in favour of the accused; and that Captain Frederick Lewis Maitland (2), of the *Emerald*, who was known to hold strong opinions concerning the Admiral's conduct, was one of the only two Aix Captains who were not called as witnesses. Napoleon's opinion, as expressed to O'Meara, was that Cochrane might and would have carried the French ships out, had the British Admiral supported him as he ought to have done; and that the French admiral was a fool, but that the British one was every bit as bad.[2]

Lord Gambier eventually received the thanks of both Houses, though in neither were the members unanimous.[3] Votes of thanks to the other officers, and to the seamen and Royal Marines concerned, passed unopposed, though the thanks were given as well to

---

[1] He was one of the members for Westminster, and had retained his seat, as did many another naval officer of the time, while serving at sea on full pay.

[2] 'Nap. in Exile,' ii. 292.

[3] In the Lords there were dissentients, but a division was not taken. In the Commons the resolution was carried by 161 to 39.

those who lay in Basque road and did nothing, as to those who went through the boom in the fireships. Gambier received no other recognition. Cochrane, however, had been promptly[1] created a K.B. He is the only officer, except Jervis, who, as a Post-Captain, ever attained to that high distinction.[2] Numerous other subordinate officers who had specially distinguished themselves received a step in rank.

The affair of Aix road led to courts-martial in France as well as in England. Captain Clément de La Roncière, of the *Tonnerre*, was acquitted on a charge of misconduct; but Captain Charles Nicolas Lacaille, of the *Tourville*, was cashiered, deprived of his cross of the Legion of Honour, and imprisoned for two years. Captain Guillaume Marcellin Proteau, of the *Indienne*, was condemned to three months' confinement; and Captain Jean Baptiste Lafon, of the *Calcutta*, was sentenced to be shot, and was duly executed on September 9th.[3] It may be that these officers were to blame; but it should be recollected that when a squadron of sea-going ships does as M. Allemand's command did, and, as it were, entrenches itself to await attack behind a boom in a practically open roadstead, it invites disaster. If, moreover, M. Willaumez had been less cautious than he was, and had fought Commodore Beresford in February, Cochrane might have been deprived of the opportunity which he used so well in April. A great naval commander never loses an occasion to attack when the conditions are favourable to him; and, if he be driven to bay, he takes care to assume the offensive.

The story of the defence of Anholt will have to be told in the next chapter among the events of the year 1811. It is, therefore, well to say here that in May, 1809, Vice-Admiral Sir James Saumarez, Commander-in-Chief in the Baltic, detached the *Standard*, 64, Captain Aiskew Paffard Hollis, with a frigate, three sloops and a brig, to reduce that Danish island with a view to utilising the lighthouse which stood upon it, and which, prior to the war, had been of great assistance to vessels navigating the Kattegat. On May 18th, the island was seized by a party of seamen and Royal Marines under Captain William Selby, of the *Owen Glendower*, 36, and Captain Edward Nicolls, R.M., after a brief resistance, in which one Marine was killed and two were wounded.

---

[1] April 26th, 1809.

[2] Though Nelson was awarded the K.B. while he was still *serving* as a Commodore, but while he was actually of flag-rank.

[3] Chevalier, 241.

The naval preparations of France in the West Schelde have already been spoken of more than once. Antwerp was found to be insufficient as a port and arsenal for the fleet which was in time collected there; and Napoleon, in consequence, induced his brother, Louis, King of Holland, to make over to him the Dutch port of Flushing, on the Isle of Walcheren. By the summer of 1809, there were ready for sea, near the mouth of the river, ten 74-gun ships[1] under Rear-Admiral Missiessy; and on the stocks at Antwerp and Flushing there were six 80's[2] and four 74's,[3] besides smaller craft. Missiessy waited only for the British blockading force to give him an opportunity to quit the river and sail to the southward.

The Admiralty had more than once experienced the advantages resulting from a strong offensive naval policy; and in May, 1809, it was determined, if possible, to seize the mouth of the Schelde, and to take or destroy the French fleet there ere it could leave its ports. The project, which should have been kept secret, was well advertised by the public press; and, as large British military forces were already serving in Spain and Portugal, it was not easy to quickly collect the troops necessary for an expedition of the kind intended. While, therefore, preparations were completing, the French had warning and time to perfect their scheme of defence. Not, indeed, until the early morning of July 28th, did the main body of the expeditionary force leave the Downs. When at its full strength, this huge armament, the greatest which ever left England, consisted of no fewer than 37 sail of the line,[4] two 50-gun ships, three 44-gun ships, 23 frigates, one 20-gun post ship, 31 sloops, 5 bombs, 23 brigs, about 120 hired cutters, gunboats and tenders, and nearly 400 transports, having on board 39,219 troops, including about 3000 cavalry. The fleet was commanded by Rear-Admiral Sir Richard John Strachan,[5] and the army by Lieutenant-General the Earl of Chatham, brother of William Pitt. The former, as has been seen, was an excellent officer; the latter was destitute alike of energy and of military capacity. Strachan was instructed to take or destroy all the enemy's

---

[1] *Charlemagne, César, Albanais, Anversois, Commerce de Lyon, Dalmate, Dantzig, Duguesclin, Pultusk* (ex-*Audacieux*), and *Ville de Berlin* (ex-*Thésée*).

[2] *Auguste, Tilsit, Conquérant, Friedland, Illustre,* and *Pacification.*

[3] *Trajan, Gaulois, Superbe* and another.

[4] Many of these had their lower-deck guns removed, and the main holds fitted to receive horses.

[5] Having as his immediate subordinates Rear-Admirals William Albany Otway, Sir Richard Goodwin Keats, and Alan Hyde, Lord Gardner.

ships in the Schelde and at Antwerp ; to demolish the yards and
arsenals at Antwerp, Flushing, and Ter Neuze, and, if possible, to
render the Schelde no longer navigable for big ships.   To facilitate
the operations, Cadzand, on the south side of the West Schelde,
and the islands of Walcheren and Zuid Beveland, on the north,
were to be occupied by the army.

The Commander-in-Chief, in the *Venerable*, 74, Captain Sir
Home Riggs Popham, anchored in West-Kapelle road in the evening
of July 28th, and there found the *Fishguard*, 38, Captain Sir William
Bolton (2).   That officer had already stationed small craft as marks
upon some of the neighbouring shoals.   In the course of the night,
the Roompot channel, between Noordland and Walcheren, was
sounded, and marks were placed to show its entrance.   On the 29th,
a large flotilla of transports, having on board Sir John Hope's
division, anchored between Noord Beveland and Schouwen, opposite
Zierikzee ; and a few hours later, the transports with Sir Eyre
Coote's division, 17,000 strong, also arrived, in charge of Rear-
Admiral William Albany Otway.   Coote's troops were destined
exclusively for operations against Walcheren, and should have been
at once landed ; but bad weather prevented any disembarkation
being attempted until 4.30 P.M. on the 30th, when, under cover of
the hired cutter *Idas*, 10, Lieutenant James Duncan, and under
direction of Captains Lord Amelius Beauclerk, of the *Royal Oak*, 74,
and George Cockburn, of the *Belleisle*, 74, Coote's division, after
very slight opposition, established itself on the northern extremity of
Walcheren.[1]   In the evening, some bombs and gunboats entered the
Veere Gat, or creek, and, on the 31st, opened fire on the fortified
town of Veere, one of the chief places in the island ; but, towards
nightfall, after three gunboats had been sunk by Dutch shot, the
flotilla had to withdraw, without, however, having lost a man.
Middelburg, the capital of the island, had, in the meantime, peace-
fully surrendered, and Veere had been invested.   In addition, a
naval brigade, landed on the 30th, under Captain Charles Richardson,
of the *Cæsar*, 80, and Commander George William Blamey, of the
Harpy, 18, had greatly annoyed the place with guns and Congreve
rockets.   During the night, therefore, the Dutch commandant offered
to capitulate, and on August 1st Veere surrendered.   Thereupon the
army advanced.   Fort Rammekens fell on August 3rd, and, immediately afterwards, Flushing was besieged.   Sir John Hope's

[1] *See* maps, Vol. II. 312 ; and facing p. 274 *infra*.

division, under the conduct of Sir Richard Goodwin Keats, had been already landed without opposition on Zuid Beveland, and had occupied some posts there, including Fort Bath,[1] at the eastern end of the island.

On July 29th, as soon as he had been apprised of the approach of the British fleet, Rear-Admiral Missiessy, who had been lying at anchor off the Calot Sand, had weighed and proceeded up the

ADMIRAL SIR RICHARD GOODWIN KEATS, K.B.
(From an engraving by Ridley and Blood, after the painting by H. Matthews.)

Schelde. By the evening of the 30th, six of his ten ships of the line were above a boom which had been thrown across the river at Lillo. The other four remained below Fort Bath until a few hours before the British occupied it, and so obtained control, to some extent, both of the East and of the West Schelde.

It has been seen that one division of the British army landed

[1] *Or* Bathz.

on Walcheren, and another on Zuid Beveland. A third should, according to the original plans, have been almost simultaneously disembarked at Cadzand, where General Rousseau commanded a small force. Owing, however, to some mistake, the transports which ought to have put their troops ashore at Cadzand moved round to the Veere Gat. This error enabled Rousseau, on August 1st and 2nd, to send over about 1600 men in schuyts to reinforce the threatened garrison of Flushing. But on the 3rd, his efforts to send more were frustrated by the extremely gallant action of the *Raven*, 16, Commander John Martin Hanchett.[1] That brig-sloop, by direction of Captain Edward William Campbell Rich Owen, of the *Clyde*, 38, stood in to cover some boats which, under Lieutenant Charles Burrough Strong, had been ordered to sound and buoy the channel between Flushing and Breskens. She quickly became exposed to a heavy fire from the batteries of both places ; but, instead of withdrawing, she returned it, and, assisted by some gunboats, also drove back to the Cadzand side a flotilla of enemy's boats which had been in the act of crossing. As she returned down the river, she passed through a perfect hail of shell, grape, and red-hot shot from the batteries on both shores, and lost her main and fore topmasts, besides receiving other serious damage, having two of her guns dismounted, and drifting on to the Elboog sand, whence she could not be moved until the following morning. In this creditable affair, Commander Hanchett and eight of his men were wounded. Their plucky action produced, however, no permanent result, for, on August 4th, communication between Cadzand and Flushing was re-opened, and between that day and the evening of the 6th, General Rousseau succeeded in sending across about 1500 more men, a reinforcement which brought up the strength of the Flushing garrison to about seven thousand.

Possession of Fort Rammekens opened to the British the Sloe channel, which is one of the connections between the East and the West Schelde, and facilitated the passage into the latter of the flotilla which had been operating against Veere. Part of this was destined to watch the river opposite Flushing, and to prevent further intercourse with Cadzand and Ter Neuze ; and part to proceed up

---

[1] A Commander of September 22nd, 1807. He was posted on October 18th, 1809, and died in 1819. It is believed that he was a natural son of the Prince of Wales, afterwards George IV.

CHART
TO ILLUSTRATE THE
OPERATIONS
DURING THE
WALCHEREN EXPEDITION,
1809.

Scale of Nautic Miles

(From the Chart published by Fisher, Son, and Jackson, 1833.)

the West Schelde, and to co-operate in a naval advance in the direction of Lillo; but, owing to bad weather and the difficulties of the navigation, Flushing was not effectively blockaded until the 6th; and not until the 9th was a division, under Sir Home Riggs Popham, able to push up the West Schelde in order to sound and buoy the Baerlandt channel in preparation for the passage of the larger ships.

On the afternoon of August 11th, with a light westerly breeze, the following frigate squadron, under Lord William Stuart, weighed from below Flushing, and, in line of battle ahead, in the order given, forced the channel between the batteries of Flushing and Cadzand.

SHIPS.	GUNS.	COMMANDERS.
Lavinia	40	Capt. Lord William Stuart.
Heroine	32	„ Hood Hanway Christian.
Amethyst	36	„ Sir Michael Seymour (1), Bt.
Rota	38	„ Philip Somerville (1).
Nymphen	36	„ Keith Maxwell.
Aigle	36	„ George Wolfe.
Euryalus	36	„ Hon. George Heneage Lawrence Dundas.
Statira	38	„ Charles Worsley Boys.
Dryad	36	„ Edward Galwey.
Perlen	38	„ Norborne Thompson.

In consequence of the little wind, and the opposing tide and current, the frigates were exposed to the fire of the enemy for about two hours; yet their loss was small, amounting only to two killed and nine wounded; and, except the *Aigle*, they reached the upper part of the river without having suffered any material damage. The *Aigle* had her stern frame shattered by a shell. In the meantime, an attack upon Fort Bath by Missiessy's small craft had been repulsed; and Sir Richard Goodwin Keats, who was in command below Lillo, had obliged the French to move the rest of their line-of-battle ships above the boom which spanned the river at that spot.

It had been arranged that when the siege batteries of the army should open upon Flushing, a squadron of ships of the line should move up the river and second their efforts. The bombardment was begun at 1.30 P.M. on August 13th; and it was promptly taken part in by two divisions of bomb and gun-vessels respectively commanded by Captain George Cockburn, of the *Belleisle*, 74, who went on board the *Plover*, 18, Commander Philip Browne (2), and Captain

Edward William Campbell Rich Owen, of the *Clyde*, 38. On that day the lightness of the wind prevented the line-of-battle ships from moving to the attack; but at 10 A.M. on the 14th, the following ships, in the order named, weighed from off Dijkshoek, and stood in:—

SHIPS.	GUNS.	COMMANDERS.
San Domingo	74	{ Rear-Adm. Sir Richard John Strachan, Bt. (W). { Capt. Charles Gill.
Blake	74	{ Rear-Adm. Alan Hyde, Lord Gardner (B). { Capt. Edward Codrington.
Repulse	74	„　Hon. Arthur Kaye Legge.
Victorious	74	„　Graham Eden Hamond.
Danmark[1]	74	„　James Bissett.
Audacious	74	„　Donald Campbell (1).
Venerable	74	„　Andrew King (*pro tem.*).

[1] Generally spelt *Dannemark* in the British navy lists. Her Danish name (she had been taken in 1807) was as given above.

Soon after approaching near enough to open fire, the *San Domingo*, and then the *Blake*, which attempted to pass inside of her, grounded on the Dog-sand; whereupon the other ships were signalled to haul off and anchor. The two flagships, in about three hours, got off and anchored with the rest, having lost only two killed and eighteen wounded. The remaining ships of the line had no one hurt. It does not appear what effect was produced by the fire of the squadron; but at 4 P.M. the garrison of Flushing ceased to reply; and at 2 P.M. on the 15th, the French commandant, General Mounet, offered to surrender. Terms were soon agreed to; and, on the following afternoon, ratifications were exchanged.

Apart from the loss sustained by the line-of-battle ships and by Lord William Stuart's squadron, the Navy had 7 killed (including Lieutenant George Rennie) and 22 wounded on board the bombs and gun-vessels; and 7 wounded in the brigade which served on shore with great distinction under Captain Charles Richardson. Among the officers employed with this brigade were Lieutenants John Wyborn,[1] Richard St. Lo Nicholson, Eaton Stannard Travers, Stephen Hilton, John Allen Meadway, and John Netherton O'Brien Hall. The army, in the various operations on the island of Walcheren up to the surrender of Flushing, had 103 killed and 443 wounded. On the day of the surrender, the *Impérieuse*, 38, Captain Thomas Garth, exposed herself to the fire of the fort at

[1] Commander, December 18th, 1809.

Ter Neuze, and, in return, fired some shrapnel shells[1] from her carronades. One of these blew up the magazine of the battery, and caused the death of 75 men. What loss the French sustained in Walcheren is unknown, but it was probably severe. On August 17th, the islands of Schouwen and Duijveland, northward of the East Schelde, surrendered peaceably to Sir Richard Goodwin Keats and Lieutenant-General the Earl of Rosslyn.

From that time forward the campaign collapsed. The Earl of Chatham, who moved his headquarters on the 21st from Middelburg to Veere, transferred them thence on the 23rd to Goes, in Zuid Beveland. He left 10,000 men in Walcheren to hold in check the ever-increasing force of the enemy at Cadzand; and he therefore had but about 29,000 nominally available for the remaining objects of the expedition, namely, the reduction of the strong forts of Lillo and Liefkenshoek, and of the great fortress of Antwerp. At those places, and in Bergen-op-Zoom, there were discovered to be at least 35,000 French; while, from the 19th onward, the British effective strength was daily reduced by malarious sickness.[2] Chatham, moreover, was intimidated by the reports which reached him of the defences of Antwerp, which he had believed to be easily assailable, and of the impossibility of destroying the docks and arsenal there while the citadel remained unreduced. He learnt, too, that there was nothing to prevent the French ships of the line from moving, with everything on board, to Ruppelmonde, five miles beyond Antwerp, or, without their guns and stores, to Dendermonde, fifteen miles higher; and, losing heart, he held a council of war on the 26th. This council declared in favour of abandoning the enterprise ·rather than of running any risk of failure. Zuid Beveland was accordingly evacuated at once, and Walcheren in December, after the basin, arsenal, and sea-defences had been blown up. Two small vessels on the stocks there were also destroyed; but a 74, that was in frame, was taken to pieces, and the timbers, being subsequently put together at Woolwich Yard, formed the skeleton of the *Chatham*, 74.[3] The only other material

---

[1] So called from their inventor, Lieut.-Gen. Henry Shrapnel, an artillery officer who died in 1842. They were shells filled with bullets and a bursting charge, exploded by means of a time-fuse. They were invented in 1792, and adopted for the services in 1803.

[2] Known among the troops as "polder" fever. About 14,000 officers and men suffered from it from first to last, and about a fourth of that number died.

[3] Of 1860 tons, launched in 1812.

spoil of the expedition was a new frigate, the *Fidèle*, which was added to the Navy as the *Laurel*, 38. The whole affair was mismanaged, ill-planned, and ill-timed; but its failure was in no-wise due to any remissness either on the part of the Navy in general or on the part of the naval Commander-in-Chief in particular.[1] Nor can it be said that blame rested upon anyone so heavily as upon the Government and the Earl of Chatham.

In the Mediterranean, Vice-Admiral Lord Collingwood still continued to watch Vice-Admiral Ganteaume at Toulon; but, for various reasons, he was unable to watch him so closely and persistently as always to prevent vessels from quitting or entering the port; and Rear-Admiral François André Baudin, with five sail of the line, two frigates, one corvette, and sixteen small craft, got out in April, carried troops and stores to the relief of Barcelona, and returned safely to Toulon in May, closely followed, however, by the British fleet. This experience, and the knowledge that a further effort was to be made to throw supplies into Barcelona, induced Collingwood, in October, to abandon his station off Cape Sicié, and, leaving as look-outs off the port the *Pomone*, 38, Captain Robert Barrie, and *Alceste*, 38, Captain Murray Maxwell, to cruise between Cape San Sebastian and Barcelona. There were at that time in Toulon, ready for sea, fifteen French and six Russian sail of the line, whereas Collingwood had with him fifteen sail of the line only.

On October 21st,, Rear-Admiral Baudin, in the *Robuste*, 80, Captain François Legras, with the *Borée*, 74, Captain Gaspard Laignel, *Lion*, 74, Captain Eustache Marie Joseph Bonami, the 40-gun frigates *Pomone* and *Pauline*, and a number of armed transports and storeships, left Toulon for Barcelona with an easterly wind. Captain Robert Barrie discovered the enemy an hour or two later, and, making sail to the W.S.W., fell in, at 9 P.M. on the following day, with Collingwood, off the Catalonian coast, having previously spoken the *Alceste*. Barrie was unable to report exactly how many French ships were out; and the Commander-in-Chief, feeling sure that the force, whatever might be its strength, was bound westward, prepared for action, and stationed his frigates as scouts to windward. At 8 A.M. on the 23rd, the *Volontaire*, 38, Captain Charles Bullen, signalled a fleet to the eastward; and at 10 A.M., Captain Barrie signalled that the strangers had hauled to

---

[1] For many interesting particulars of the naval operations in the Schelde, see Bourchier's 'Codrington,' i. 129–167.

the wind. Thereupon Rear-Admiral George Martin (2), with eight of the best sailers in the British fleet, was ordered to chase to the E.N.E. At 3 P.M., Baudin, with his three ships of the line and two frigates, separated from his convoy, which steered in confusion to the N.N.W., while he made for the E.S.E., with a north-easterly wind. That afternoon and evening, Captain Barrie, in the *Pomone*, 38, picked up and destroyed two brigs, two bombards, and a ketch belonging to the convoy; but the rest got away. The five French men-of-war, chased by Martin, soon disappeared in the other direction.

Martin, at 8 P.M., when the wind was nearly east, tacked to the northward, since he judged that the enemy would make for his own shores. A little later, two of the chasing ships parted company by accident, leaving the following to continue the pursuit:—

SHIPS.	GUNS.	COMMANDERS.
Canopus	80	Rear-Adm. George Martin (2), (R). Capt. Charles Inglis (2).
Renown	74	„ Philip Charles Henderson Calderwood Durham.
Tigre	74	„ Benjamin Hallowell.
Sultan	74	„ Edward Griffith.
Leviathan	74	„ John Harvey (2).
Cumberland	74	„ Hon. Philip Wodehouse.

The French were not seen until early in the morning of the 24th, when four of them were sighted in the N.N.E. The *Pomone*, it afterwards appeared, had left her consorts and proceeded independently for Marseilles. Martin crowded sail as much as possible, but could not come up with the enemy, and, at nightfall, owing to the proximity of the lee-shore and the shallowness of the water, was obliged to haul off. Early on the 25th, however, the French were again seen to the northward, running under the coast with a fresh S.E. breeze. Martin once more crowded sail, and prepared to anchor with springs. At 11.45 A.M. the *Robuste* and *Lion* put up their helms and ran ashore near Frontignan, about six miles N.E. of Cette, in the little harbour of which the *Borée* and *Pauline*, though closely pressed, succeeded in finding precarious shelter.[1] Martin hauled his wind and stood off, and, on the 26th, having regained eight of the grounded ships, had the satisfaction of finding that their people had set them on fire. That night both the *Robuste* and the

---

[1] They subsequently got back to Toulon.

Lion blew up. Having executed this service, the Rear-Admiral rejoined Collingwood, who presently resumed his old station off Cape Sicié.[1]

The remains of the convoy which Rear-Admiral Baudin had had in his charge put into Rosas Bay, and anchored under the guns of Rosas Castle, Fort Trinidad, Fort Bouton, and other batteries. This flotilla consisted of seven merchantmen, under the care of the *Lamproie*, 16, armed storeship, the armed bombards *Victoire*, 14, and *Grondeur*, 8, and the armed xebec *Normande*, 10. Learning of its whereabouts, Collingwood detached Captain Benjamin Hallowell to endeavour to take or destroy it. Hallowell had under his orders the vessels named below :—

SHIPS.	GUNS.	COMMANDERS.
Tigre	74	Capt. Benjamin Hallowell.
Cumberland	74	,, Hon. Philip Wodehouse.
Volontaire	38	,, Charles Bullen.
Apollo	38	,, Bridges Watkinson Taylor.
Topaze	38	,, Henry Hope.
Philomel	18	Com. George Crawley.
Scout	18	,, William Raitt.[1]
Tuscan	16	,, John Wilson (3).

[1] This officer had been posted on September 16th, but had not learnt of his promotion.

The larger ships of the squadron anchored at about five miles from Rosas on the night of October 31st, the brigs remaining under way. The boats of all the vessels were at once manned and armed, and, without delay, they pushed off under command of Lieutenant John Tailour,[2] first of the *Tigre*. The French had made full preparations to resist attack, and were not taken by surprise. The *Lamproie* was, nevertheless, quickly boarded and carried; the *Victoire*, *Grondeur*, *Normande*, and a felucca full of musketeers, soon shared the same fate in spite of the gallant resistance which they made, and of a heavy fire from the forts, and from troops posted on the beach ; and by daylight on November 1st, every vessel in the harbour had been either burnt at her moorings, or carried out. The British loss was somewhat heavy, for fifteen (including Lieutenant Dalhousie Tait, of the *Volontaire*, and Master's Mate James Caldwell, of the *Tigre*) were killed, and fifty wounded. Among the latter were Lieutenants John Tailour (*Tigre*), John Forster (*Apollo*),

[1] Collingwood's 'Collingwood,' 550–553 ; Collingwood to Pole, Oct. 30th, enclosing Martin's disp. of Oct. 27th, 1809.
[2] Promoted November 1st, 1809 ; posted October 26th, 1813.

Richard Stuart (*Cumberland*), James Begbie (*Apollo*), and the Hon.
James Ashley Maude (*Ville de Paris*), Master's Mate John Webster
(*Cumberland*), and Midshipmen Dey Richard Syer (*Tigre*), William
Hollinshed Brady (*Cumberland*), and John Armstead (*Ville de Paris*).
The French loss must have been even heavier.[1] The complete
defeat of this attempt on the part of Rear-Admiral Baudin to
succour Barcelona illustrates the great importance of command of
the sea in cases where military operations are in progress on or near
the seaboard; but the ease with which Baudin was detected and
checkmated on this occasion causes one to feel astonishment that
his previous cruise in April and May began and ended without any
British interference whatsoever. Nor, on the other hand, is it
possible to avoid wondering why Admiral Ganteaume, who had
with him superior forces, who realised the necessity for relieving
Barcelona, and who must have known that Collingwood was not the
man to decline an action, did not put to sea with his fifteen French
and six Russian sail of the line, and endeavour not only to force a
way to the Catalonian coasts, but also to cripple for ever the enemy
who sought to bar his passage thither. Napoleon, however, always
loved to husband his ships; and Trafalgar had made French
admirals somewhat chary of risking decisive encounters when they
had in their favour a numerical advantage of not more than twenty-
five per cent. or thereabouts.

At the eastern end of the Mediterranean the year 1809 witnessed
other misfortunes to the cause of France. In October, Zante,
Cephalonia, and some outlying islands surrendered without opposition to British forces commanded by Captain John William
Spranger, of the *Warrior*, 74, and Brigadier-General John Oswald.[2]
Cerigo similarly fell to Captain Jahleel Brenton (2), of the *Spartan*, 38,
and Major Charles William Clarke, of the 35th regiment;[3] and
Ithaca, to Commander George Crawley, of the *Philomel*, 18, and
Captain R. Church.[4] The consequence of these operations was the
liberation of the Archipelago from French rule, and the re-establish-
ment of the Republic of the Seven Islands.

In extra-European waters France experienced worse disasters,

---

[1] *Gazette*, 1809, 1907. Collingwood to Pole, Nov. 1st, enclosing Hallowell's disp.
of same date. Marshall, Supp. Pt. iii. 157.

[2] Spranger to Martin, Oct. 3rd, and Oct. 16th, 1809.

[3] Brenton to Spranger, Oct. 13th.

[4] Crawley to Spranger, Oct. 10th.

losing Sénégal, Martinique, and Cayenne, as well as several minor possessions. Early in the summer of 1809, the depredations of numerous small privateers, which used Sénégal as their head-quarters, drew attention to the importance of that settlement; and, in consequence, Captain Edward Henry Columbine, of the *Solebay*, 32, who was senior officer at Gorée, arranged with Major Charles William Maxwell, commanding the garrison, to attempt to reduce the French colony. The expeditionary force assembled for the purpose consisted of the *Solebay*, *Derwent*, 18, Commander Frederick Parker, *Tigris*, brig, Lieutenant Robert Bones, *Agincourt*, transport, *George*, colonial schooner, six other armed schooners and sloops, and several unarmed vessels which were added to give an appearance of force. On board were 166 officers and men under Major Maxwell. The flotilla left Gorée on July 4th, and anchored off the bar of Sénégal on the 7th. On the following day 160 soldiers, 120 seamen, and 50 Royal Marines were, with much difficulty, got over the bar. This operation, unfortunately, involved the grounding of the *George*, the total loss of a schooner and a sloop, and the drowning of Commander Parker, of the *Derwent*. It was then discovered that a French force of about 400 men lay at Babaqué, twelve miles above the bar, and five miles below St. Louis. The British troops and Marines were accordingly landed on the left bank, and established in a position where it was purposed that they should await the refloating of the *George* and the disembarkation of supplies. On the 9th, the enemy advanced to the attack, but retired before Maxwell, who was supported by the boats of the squadron, and again took post at Babaqué, an island battery which covered a flotilla of seven armed vessels, mounting thirty-one guns, and which also commanded a boom spanning the whole river. On the 11th, the *George* being again afloat, the *Solebay* and *Derwent* [1] proceeded to a spot whence they cannonaded Babaqué across the intervening land with good effect. In the following night, however, the *Solebay* took the ground, and she ultimately became a total wreck, though happily no lives were lost, and many of her stores were saved. On the 12th, the forces which had been landed were re-embarked, and the expedition proceeded up the river until within gunshot of Babaqué. An attack was postponed owing to the receipt of information that the enemy desired to capitulate; and on the 13th it was found that the boom was broken,

---

[1] Then commanded by Commander Joseph Swabey Tetley, who was confirmed in that rank on August 31st, 1809.

and that the battery and vessels were abandoned. Later in the day Sénégal was formally surrendered.[1]

In the summer of 1808 it had become known to the British ministry that Martinique was in want both of provisions and of troops; and preparations had been subsequently begun at Barbados for taking advantage of the distress of the most important of the French West-Indian possessions, which was at the time governed by Vice-Admiral Villaret-Joyeuse, the officer who had been defeated by Lord Howe in 1794. These preparations were completed by the end of January, 1809, when the naval force set forth below,[2] together with a fleet of transports, having on board about 10,000 troops under Lieutenant-General Beckwith, assembled at Carlisle Bay. The expedition sailed on January 28th, and arrived on the 30th off Martinique, which was garrisoned by about 2400 effective regulars, and 2500 militia, and which mounted in its various batteries about 290 guns. In the harbour of Fort Royal lay the *Amphitrite*, 40, which had left Cherbourg on November 12th, 1808; at St. Pierre lay the *Diligente*, 18; and at Marin lay the *Carnation*, 18, which had been taken by the *Palinure* from the British on October 3rd, 1808.

Early on January 30th, about 3000 men, commanded by Major-General Frederick Maitland, were landed without opposition at Pointe Sainte Luce, under the superintendence of Captain Fahie;

[1] Columbine to Pole, July 20th; Maxwell to Castlereagh, July 18th, 1809.

²

SHIPS.	GUNS.	COMMANDERS.	SHIPS.	GUNS.	COMMANDERS.
Neptune [1]	98	Rear-Adm. Hon. Alexander F. I. Cochrane, K.B. (R.) Capt. Charles Dilkes.	*Frolic* [1]	18	Com. Thomas Whinyates.
			Recruit [1]	18	,, Charles Napier (2).
			Wolverine [1]	18	,, John Simpson.
Pompée [1]	74	Commod. George Cockburn.	*Express* [1]	6	Lieut. William Malone (1).
York [1]	74	Capt. Robert Barton.	*Haughty* [1]	14	,, John Mitchell (2).
Belleisle [1]	74	,, William Charles Fahie.	*Swinger* [1]	14	
Captain [1]	74	,, James Athol Wood.	*Pelorus*		
Intrepid [1]	64	,, Christopher John Williams Nesham.	*Fawn*	18	Com. Hon. George Alfred Crofton.
Ulysses [1]	44	,, Edward Woollcombe.	*Gloire*	36	Capt. James Carthew.
Acasta [1]	40	,, Philip Beaver.	*Hazard*	18	Com. Hugh Cameron.
Penelope [1]	36	,, John Dick.	*Mozambique,* sch.	14	Lieut. James Atkins.
Ethalion [1]	38	,, Thomas John Cochrane.			
Æolus [1]	32	,, Lord William Fitzroy.	*Port d'Espagne*	16	Com. Alexander Kennedy (1).
Circe [1]	32	,, Hugh Pigot (3).	*Surinam*	18	,, John Lake. [(actg.)
Cleopatra	38	,, Samuel John Brooke Pechell.	*Supérieure.*	16	,, William Ferrie.
			Ringdove	18	,, George Andrews (2).
Eurydice [1]	24	,, James Bradshaw.	*Bellette*	18	,, George Sanders.
Cherub [1]	18	Com. Thomas Tudor Tucker.	*Snap*	...	,, James Pattison Stewart.
Gorée [1]	18	,, Joseph Spear.	*Demerara*	16	,, William Dowers.
Star [1]	18	,, Francis Augustus Collier.	*Pultusk*	20	,, George Pringle.
Stork [1]	18	,, George Le Geyt.	*Liberty*	14	Lieut. John Codd.
Amaranthe [1]	18	,, Edward Pelham Brenton	*Subtle*	10	,, — Brown.
Eclair [1]	12	[(2).	*Bacchus*	10	,, Charles Deyman Jermy.
Forester [1]	18	,, John Richards.	*Cuttle,* sch.	..	,, Thomas Bury (2).

[1] These vessels only were mentioned in Cochrane's dispatch of February 25th.
[2] Lieut. James Hay acted while Brenton served on shore.

and 600 men, under Major Henderson, were put ashore at Cape Solomon. Upon the appearance of the former in Marin Bay, the French destroyed the *Carnation*. In the meanwhile, nearly 6500 men, commanded by Lieut.-General Sir George Prevost, were landed on the north side of the island, at Baie Robert, under the direction of Captain Beaver. These, also, were unopposed, the militia assembled near the landing-places retiring before them, and going to their homes. On February 1st and 2nd, the advancing British army gained successes against the French regulars, the main body of whom then fell back on Fort Desaix. Major Henderson possessed himself of a fort or battery on Pointe Salomon; and on February 4th, Pigeon Island [1] surrendered after it had been heavily bombarded for twelve hours. The fall of this post was largely due to the exertions of a body of seamen employed ashore under Captain Cockburn; and the capture of its little garrison of 136 men was owing to retreat having been cut off by the *Æolus*, *Cleopatra*, and *Recruit*, which had pushed up to the head of Fort Royal Bay, and which, by their appearance there, induced the French to burn the *Amphitrite* and other vessels in harbour. When Sir Alexander Cochrane, with the squadron, afterwards stood into the bay, the enemy on that side of the island concentrated themselves in Fort Desaix, the investment of which was then begun. Cas des Navires was occupied on February 8th; St. Pierre and the *Diligente* surrendered on the 9th; and Fort Royal itself was taken possession of on the 10th. On the 19th the bombardment of Fort Desaix was opened, and until noon on the 23rd it continued without cessation. After a fruitless parley it was recommenced, and continued until 9 A.M. on the 24th, when white flags were hoisted. In the course of that day, the place, and the whole colony, formally surrendered by capitulation. In the acquisition of Pigeon Island the Navy lost two seamen killed; in the siege of Fort Desaix it lost six killed and nineteen wounded. The seamen who served on shore were, as usual, of the greatest use in getting heavy guns and mortars into position on commanding heights, and in helping to man the batteries.[2] For mismanagement of the defence, Vice-Admiral Villaret-Joyeuse and some other officers were broken by a court which tried them in Paris in December, 1809.

---

[1] Or Ilot aux Ramiers.

[2] Cochrane to Pole, Feb. 4th, Feb. 18th, Feb. 25th 1809: Cochrane's mem., Feb. 26th, etc. Beaver to Cochrane, Jan. 31st, 1809. Brenton, ii. 259.

The capture of Cayenne was a more brilliant if not a more important exploit. On December 8th, 1808, the *Confiance*, 20,[1] Captain James Lucas Yeo, two Portuguese brigs, the *Voador* and *Infante*, some small craft, and about five hundred and fifty Portuguese troops under Lieut.-Colonel Manoel Marques, with the concurrence of Rear-Admiral Sir William Sidney Smith, had seized Oyapok, in French Guiana, and, on the 15th, had reduced Appruague. These successes encouraged Lucas and Marques to make a descent upon Cayenne, which is the capital of the colony, and which lies upon an island between the rivers Cayenne and Mahuy.

The troops, with a body of British and Portuguese seamen and Marines, having been embarked in small vessels, entered the mouth of the Mahuy, eastward of the island, early in the morning of January 6th, 1809. In the evening of the same day, Yeo, with about two hundred and fifty of the men in ten canoes, proceeded to attack some forts commanding the entrance to the river, having directed Commander Salgado, of the *Voador*, to follow after dark with the rest of the troops, and, upon being apprised of the fall of the forts, to land the men as promptly as possible. Yeo's venture was difficult and dangerous, for some of his canoes could not keep up with the others, and those which landed their people were all wrecked in the surf. Nevertheless, one detachment of the party, under Major Joaquim Manoel Pinto carried an 8-gun battery called Dégras de Cannes ;[2] and another, under Yeo himself, rushed Fort Diamant, where three guns were mounted. The loss on the side of the attack was not heavy, that of the British being only six wounded. Among the officers engaged in this affair were, in addition to Yeo, Lieutenants William Howe Mulcaster[3] and Samuel Blyth,[4] Lieutenant John Read, R.M. (killed), Midshipmen George Forder and David Irwin, Mr. Thomas Savory, Purser, and Carpenter William Taylor. Commander Salgado, as agreed upon, landed with the remainder of the troops ; but as General Victor Hugues was known to be advancing from the town of Cayenne, only twelve miles distant, with one thousand men, Yeo left Lieutenant Mulcaster, with a few men from the *Confiance*, to dismantle Fort Diamant, and concentrated the bulk of his command at Dégras de Cannes. Upon

[1] 18-pr. carronades only.   [2] Called " Grand Cane " in the disp.
[3] Made Commander May 13th, 1809.
[4] Made Commander Sept. 5th, 1811 ; killed in the *Boxer*, Sept. 5th, 1813.

reaching that position he discovered, higher up the Mahuy, two other forts, one, named Trio, on the right bank, commanding a creek leading up to the town of Cayenne, and the other [1] on the left bank. The two Portuguese cutters *Lion* and *Vinganza* had already anchored between the forts, and were cannonading them with their 4-prs.; but, perceiving that such weakly armed craft could effect nothing alone, and that, in fact, their people were suffering severely, Yeo quickly decided that both batteries must be stormed. Accordingly Mr. Thomas Savory and some Portuguese were directed against the battery on the left bank, and Yeo, with Lieutenant Samuel Blyth, led the attack upon Trio. Both parties had to land under the muzzles of the French guns, and each was exposed to a heavy fire of grape and musketry; but the assailants quickly carried their point and drove out the defenders.

No sooner had the forts been taken than General Victor Hugues, from Cayenne, attacked Colonel Marques at Dégras de Cannes, while a detachment of the French forces appeared before Fort Diamant, where Lieutenant Mulcaster was still engaged. Yeo instantly pushed off from Trio to assist Marques; and the allies, after a three hours' hot action, obliged Hugues to return to Cayenne. At Fort Diamant the resolute attitude of the small body of seamen decided the two hundred and fifty of the enemy not to risk an attack, but to follow their general. On the following day Yeo sent a summons to a strong French fort which defended Hugues's private house and plantation, not far from the left bank of the Mahuy, and which was held by one hundred picked men; but a boat, carrying a flag of truce, was twice fired upon at short range and had to retreat; whereupon Yeo effected a landing near the house. Again a flag of truce, intended to cover Lieutenant Mulcaster, was fired at; and presently the French, most of whom were well ambushed in a wood, opened upon the allies with musketry and a field-piece. The British and Portuguese could not bring up their own gun; but they charged with pike and bayonet, and soon made themselves master of the French field-piece, and drove the enemy in confusion from the position. The allies then advanced towards Cayenne; and on the 10th the town was summoned. An armistice was agreed to; and on January 14th the place was taken possession of, the enemy's troops, to the number of 400 regulars, 600 white militia, and 200 blacks, giving up their arms. Thus, with a loss to the British of

---

[1] Each fort mounted two 8-prs.

only 1 killed and 23 wounded (2 mortally), and to the Portuguese
of only 1 killed and 8 wounded, was acquired the whole territory
of what is now French Guiana, from the Maroni to the Oyapok.[1]

"It is but just," says Yeo, in his letter of January 15th to Sir W. S. Smith, "that
I should take notice of the exertions of Mr. J. Arscott,[2] acting Master, who has passed
for Lieutenant, whom I left in charge of the ship, and who proved himself worthy of
the confidence reposed in him. The *Topaze*,[3] French frigate, appeared in the offing on
the 13th, with a reinforcement for the garrison. Though with only twenty-five
Englishmen and twenty negroes, and no other officers than two young gentlemen,
Messrs. George Yeo[4] and Edward Bryant,[5] he contrived, by his skilful manœuvres, to
drive her off the coast."

The capture of Cayenne is one of the most striking examples of
the accomplishment of great ends with what were apparently
altogether inadequate materials; and seldom has naval officer better
deserved than Captain Yeo the exceptional honours which his
bravery and ability won for him,[6] and for all who served with him.[7]

As regards important actions at sea, the year 1810 was less
eventful than any year that had preceded it since the renewal of the
war in 1803. Great Britain had so far established her maritime
supremacy that France was unable, during the whole of the period,
to send a fleet of any kind out of sight of port; yet Bonaparte, still
apparently believing that he might retrieve his position, made
unceasing efforts to increase and improve his navy. At Antwerp he
launched two 80-gun ships, the *Friedland* and *Tilsit*, and laid down
two vessels intended to carry 110 guns each; and, both in the
Schelde and at Toulon, his squadrons were kept in good order and
were continually exercised. At Brest and in the Channel ports there
was little activity. Brest had in its road but three sail of the line
and three or four frigates; and at Lorient and Rochefort there was
scarcely a sail of any consequence. The force in the Schelde was
watched by Rear-Admiral Sir Richard John Strachan; that in the
various harbours and estuaries of the Channel, by Admiral Lord
Gambier; and that in the Mediterranean, by Vice-Admiral Lord

---

[1] Yeo to Sidney Smith, Jan. 15th, 1809, capitulation enclosed.

[2] James Arscott, promoted to be Lieutenant, Apr. 14th, 1810: died Sept. 27th, 1816,
James gives all the credit of this affair to young Yeo.

[3] A 40-gun frigate, which was taken by the *Cleopatra*, 32, and others, off
Guadeloupe on Jan. 22nd. *See* next chapter.

[4] Brother of the Captain, a Midshipman.

[5] Midshipman.

[6] James Lucas Yeo; born Oct. 7th, 1782; Commander June 21st, 1805; Captain,
Dec. 19th, 1807; died a K.C.B. Aug. 21st, 1818.

[7] For an account of these honours, *see* Marshall, Supp. iii. 222, 223.

Collingwood until his regretted death on March 7th, and afterwards by Admiral Sir Charles Cotton. When, towards the end of the year, Sweden, which had recently witnessed the adoption of Marshal Bernadotte as heir to the throne, took an active part with France against the British Crown, a squadron under Vice-Admiral Sir James Saumarez sufficed to prevent either the Swedes or the Russians from attempting to give trouble in the Baltic.[1]

Immediately after Lord Collingwood's death, and while Rear-Admiral George Martin (2) held temporary command, a successful expedition was undertaken against the island of Santa Maura, one of the Ionian group, which, with Corfu, still remained in French hands. The force employed for the purpose consisted of the *Magnificent*, 74, Captain George Eyre, *Belle Poule*, 38, Captain James Brisbane, *Imogene*, 16, Commander William Stephens, three gunboats, and five transports, subsequently joined by the *Leonidas*, 38, Captain Anselm John Griffiths, which, pending the assemblage of the squadron, cruised to prevent supplies from reaching the island from Corfu, and by the *Montagu*, 74, Captain Richard Hussey Moubray, which was detained by an accident to her rudder.[2]

The main part of the squadron left Zante early in the morning of March 21st, and arrived off Santa Maura in the evening. It had on board a body of troops under Brigadier-General Oswald. Early on the 22nd, a landing was effected under cover of the *Imogene* and gunboats, and a strong position was secured ashore, though not until Captains Eyre and Stephens had been wounded. On April 8th the batteries were opened against the fortress, which capitulated on the 16th, after the British had sustained a loss of 24 killed, 127 wounded, and 17 missing.[3]

At Toulon, in the meanwhile, Vice-Admiral Ganteaume had been succeeded as commander-in-chief by Vice-Admiral Allemand. There lay thirteen sail of the line, made up of one 130, two 120's, one 80, and nine 74's, including the *Borée*, which had returned from Cette after her sortie of the previous year. There were also about nine frigates, and several armed storeships ; and under construction were the *Wagram*, 130, launched on June 30th, the *Sceptre*, 80, and the *Trident*, 74. The British fleet cruising outside consisted generally of not more than thirteen sail of the line, with an unduly small

---

[1] See ' Letters of Sir T. Byam Martin' (Nav. Rec. Soc.), ii.

[2] The *Kingfisher*, 18, Com. Ewell Tritton, also joined on Apr. 5th from Malta.

[3] Eyre to Martin, Apr. 18th.

proportion of frigates. In the middle of July, after Sir Charles
Cotton had arrived to assume command, a succession of strong gales
drove the main body of the observing fleet as far to the eastward as
Villefranche; and the only vessels remaining off the port were the
Warspite, 74, Captain the Hon. Henry Blackwood, *Ajax*, 74,
Captain Robert Waller Otway (1), *Conqueror*, 74, Captain Edward
Fellowes, *Euryalus*, 36, Captain the Hon. George Heneage
Lawrence Dundas, and *Shearwater*, 10, Commander Edward
Reynolds Sibly. This division, during the absence of the
Commander-in-Chief, chased into the little port of Bandol, a few
miles to the westward of Toulon, a convoy of French coasters,
bound east. On the 17th eight ships of the line and four frigates
stood out of port, either to exercise, or to make a demonstration
which should enable the coasters to reach the road in safety; and
one of the 74's exchanged some innocuous broadsides with the
Euryalus. On the day following, two French sail of the line and a
frigate were seen at anchor under Cape Cepet, and eleven sail of the
line and seven frigates, in the outer road. It was evident that the
enemy was still determined to attempt the release of the convoy at
Bandol; and Blackwood kept on the alert until 7 A.M. on the 20th,
when six sail of the line and four frigates put to sea from Toulon,
while at almost the same moment, the craft at Bandol got under
way with a useful land wind. Blackwood, with his small force,
could not hope to prevent the intended junction; but he recalled his
inshore craft, the *Euryalus* and *Shearwater*, with the object of
offering as good a front as possible to the enemy in case he should
be attacked. Unfortunately, says Blackwood, " owing to the
situation of the *Euryalus* and *Shearwater*, who were obliged to cross
their headmost ships, and the wind rather failing them, whilst the
enemy preserved it so entirely as to render the capture of the
Shearwater certain, if not the *Euryalus*, it became a matter
imperatively necessary that I should risk an action, though at the
door of the enemy, and with a force so superior." At 9.15 A.M. the
Shearwater began to receive the fire of the leading French ships,
the *Ajax*, 74, and the *Amélie*, 40. By judicious manœuvring,
however, Blackwood saved his imperilled vessels, neither of which
suffered any damage; but the Bandol convoy entered Toulon in
safety. The gallant Blackwood's letter [1] on the subject to Sir
Charles Cotton contained some rather unworthy boasting; and upon

[1] Blackwood to Cotton, July 20th.

it, and certain correspondence sent to the newspapers by an officer of the British *Ajax*, the French were able to found a tolerably fair complaint that their attitude had been misrepresented. In point of fact, they effected their object, and were not "driven back to port."

An exploit of a somewhat analogous nature was performed a few weeks later single-handed by the *Repulse*, 74, Captain John Halliday.[1] On August 31st, the *Philomel*, 18, Commander Gardiner Henry Guion, while endeavouring to prevent the passage of two storeships from Bandol to Toulon, was threatened with capture by a division of the French fleet which stood out as before to cover the approach. Halliday, with the greatest bravery and coolness, interposed between the British sloop and three French 40-gun frigates which, closely supported by several ships of the line, were attempting to cut off the *Philomel;* and, after a quarter of an hour's firing, he forced them to retire.

On distant stations the Navy had better opportunities for actively distinguishing itself. In the West Indies, Vice-Admiral the Hon. Alexander Forester Inglis Cochrane, who probably knew that sickness raged on the island and that the colonial militia was disaffected, appeared before Guadeloupe on January 27th, with troops under Lieut.-General Sir George Beckwith. On the following day landings were effected without opposition, one under the direction of Commodore William Charles Fahie, of the *Abercrombie*, 74, and the other under that of Commodore Samuel James Ballard, of the *Sceptre*, 74. After some fighting, in which the Navy was not engaged, terms of capitulation were proposed, and the island surrendered on February 6th. Between that date and February 22nd the Dutch islands of St. Martin, St. Eustatius, and Saba were peaceably taken possession of by the same forces.[2]

The chief services of the fleet were, however, performed in the East Indies, where Rear-Admiral William O'Brien Drury commanded, and on the Cape Station. Early in the year, Drury decided to attempt the capture of the important Dutch settlement of Amboyna, in the Moluccas; and on February 9th, in compliance with his directions, the *Dover*, 38, Captain Edward Tucker,

---

[1] Marshall, i. 747; and Supp. ii. 445: James, v. 220.

[2] Cochrane's dispatches of Feb. 8th and Feb. 27th. Fahie to Cochrane, Feb. 17th and Feb. 22nd. Lieut. Thomas Wells (3), of *Morne Fortunée*, to Fahie, Feb. 22nd.

Cornwallis, 44, Captain William Augustus Montagu, and *Samarang*, 18, Commander Richard Spencer, anchored before the place, which was strongly defended by Victoria Castle, mounting, with its outlying batteries, 215 guns, Wagoo battery, mounting 9 guns, a detached battery, built on piles in the sea and also mounting 9 guns, and two highly placed works, Wannetoo, with 9, and Batto-Gautong, with 5 guns.   On the 16th, after the defences had been reconnoitred, the ships weighed, as if intending to relinquish their project and to proceed to sea.   Tucker had previously put a landing force into boats, which he kept carefully concealed behind his vessels ; and he so managed his squadron that, while it appeared to be working out, it was in reality drifting towards the landing place which had been already selected.   When the situation was favourable the boats were slipped by signal, and a force of four hundred and one men, drawn from the Madras European regiment, and from the seamen and Royal Marines of the squadron, was successfully thrown ashore. Wannetoo battery was soon carried, and, after some arduous marching by the troops, the enemy was induced to abandon Batto-Gautong.   The fall of these works enabled the ships, which had been exposed in the interval to a heavy fire, to anchor in Portuguese Bay in positions where they could be no longer annoyed.   That night Commander Spencer landed with a party and a couple of field-pieces ; and, on the following day, the British fire obliged the foe first to abandon Wagoo and the pile battery, and finally to surrender Victoria Castle and the entire island.   The only loss on the part of the Navy during the operations was two killed and four or five wounded.   The loss on the part of the troops was almost equally insignificant.   Three Dutch vessels of war had been sunk in the inner harbour before the surrender.   One of these, the *Mandarin*, 12, was subsequently weighed by the captors.   The fall of Amboyna was speedily followed by the bloodless acquisition of the neighbouring Dutch Islands of Harouka, Nasso-Laut, Bouru, Manipa, and Saparoua, and by the acceptance by the Sultan of Gorontale, in Celebes, of British instead of Dutch suzerainty.   Captain Tucker proceeded later to Menado, another important post in Celebes, and received its surrender on June 24th.   With Menado fell several dependent ports of considerable commercial value.   On August 31st Captain Tucker also reduced Ternate, after some sharp fighting, in which Lieutenant Charles Jefferis behaved with great gallantry. During the cruise, the boats of the *Cornwallis*, under Lieutenant the Hon. Henry John Peachey,[1] pluckily cut out of a bay in the island of Amblaw the Dutch man-of-war brig *Margaretta*.[2]

Upon receipt of news of the capture of Amboyna, Rear-Admiral Drury despatched from Madras a force carrying troops and supplies for the place. This force consisted of the *Caroline*, 36, Captain Christopher Cole, *Piedmontaise*, 38, Captain Charles Foote, *Barracouta*, 18, Lieutenant Richard Kenah (acting Commander), and *Mandarin*, 12, Lieutenant Archibald Buchanan, with one hundred officers and men of the Madras European regiment. Cole had permission from the Commander-in-Chief to attack certain of the enemy's settlements on his route, and he made up his mind to attempt the reduction of the Spice Islands. The expedition sailed on May 10th, and, having called at Penang for a few additional artillerymen, two field-pieces, and some scaling ladders, left that island on June 10th, to make the passage into the Java Sea against the south-east monsoon. On the 15th, in the Strait of Singapore, the *Samarang* was met with; and from her commander, Cole learnt that in the island of Banda there were more than seven hundred regular troops.

The course taken by the expedition was a very difficult one; and, the winds being often baffling, the Banda Islands were not sighted until the evening of August 8th, when shots were unexpectedly fired at the ships from the island of Rosensgen. At first Cole abandoned all idea of trying to surprise the foe; but, the night becoming very dark and squally, and it being supposed that, in the circumstances, the Dutch would be lulled to a feeling of security, it was determined, after all, to attack Great Banda at once. Accordingly, at about 11 P.M., the boats, having on board less than four hundred people all told, pushed off from the *Caroline* under the command of Captain Cole in person. Owing to the badness of the weather and the pitchy darkness, the boats could not be kept together; and it was not until dawn that a certain number of them, carrying about 180 men, could be assembled off the appointed landing place. The Dutch troops[3] had been warned by the guns from Rosensgen, and had collected to repel the British; but, anticipating that the point threatened would be the one at which

---

[1] Afterwards Lord Selsey.

[2] Drury to Croker, Apr. 22nd; Tucker to Drury, Feb. 20th; Capt. M. H. Court (Mad. regt.) to Tucker, Feb. 27th; Tucker to Drury, Mar. 1st, June 16th, June 25th; Montagu to Tucker, Mar. 3rd; Tucker to Drury, Aug. 31st.

[3] Seven hundred regulars, and eight hundred militia.

Rear-Admiral Peter Rainier's forces had landed in 1796, they had collected in the wrong spot. In the confusion of the storm the British boats grounded on a reef within one hundred yards of the Voorzichtigheid battery, where the men were at their guns with matches lighted; but the gloom and rain prevented the invaders from being detected; and, a little later, the battery was so success-fully attacked from the rear by a party under Lieutenant Kenah and Lieutenant Thomas Carew (1) that it was captured without the firing of a shot. Kenah was then recalled to join the main body, which pushed on to storm the principal work, half a mile away. This bore the name of Casteel Belgica, and mounted no fewer than fifty-two heavy guns. By that time bugles were sounding to alarm the island; but the wind rendered them almost inaudible, and the assailants arrived within one hundred yards of the castle ditch ere they were discovered. In the face of hot opposition they stormed the fortress; and full daylight saw the British flag instead of the Dutch waving above it. Below, and covered by, Casteel Belgica, lay Casteel Nassau, the town, and the sea defences. The governor, however, had to be twice summoned ere he agreed to surrender. That day 1500 Dutch troops laid down their arms, after reduc-tion by but about 180 British, most of whom were seamen and Royal Marines.[1] For his magnificent exploit Cole received the thanks of the Commander-in-Chief, of the Governor-General of India, and of the Admiralty, besides many gratifying testimonials from his subordinates. He was also awarded a gold medal, and on May 29th, 1812, he received the honour of knighthood. In 1815 he was made a K.C.B.[2] It should be added that among the naval officers who most distinguished themselves at the capture of Banda were Lieutenants Richard Kenah,[3] Thomas Carew (1),[4] Samuel Allen,[5] George Pratt,[6] Robert Walker,[7] and Edmund Lyons.[8]

The force on the Cape station, where Vice-Admiral Albemarle Bertie commanded, had received so many accessions of strength by the autumn of the year 1810, that it was determined to attempt the reduction of the island of Mauritius, then known as Isle de

[1] Cole to Drury, Aug. 10th, 1810. Marshall, ii. 505.
[2] Sir Christopher Cole died, still a Captain, in 1836.
[3] Confirmed Commander, July 1st, 1811; killed in the *Ætna*, Oct 3rd, 1814.
[4] Commander, June 6th, 1814.   [5] Never promoted.
[6] Commander, June 15th, 1814.   [7] Commander, Dec. 8th, 1813.
[8] Commander, Mar. 21st, 1812; died V.-Adm. Lord Lyons, Nov. 23rd, 1858.

France. At Port Louis, the chief port of the colony, lay the frigates *Bellone, Minerve, Manche, Astrée,* and *Iphigénie,*[1] the corvette *Victor,* the brig *Entreprenante,* and another brig, besides several French merchantmen. After October 19th these were blockaded by the English frigates *Boadicea,* 38, Commodore Josias Rowley, *Nisus,* 38, Captain Philip Beaver, and *Néréide,*[2] 38, Commander George Henderson (actg. Captain).

The entire expeditionary force was ordered to assemble off Rodriguez ; but, a division from Cape Town not having arrived by November 21st, it was decided to start without it. On the following morning, therefore, the fleet set sail ; yet, owing to adverse winds, it did not sight its destination until the evening of the 28th. A military force of about 10,000 men, under Major-General the Hon. John Abercromby, was embarked on board the ships, which numbered about seventy sail, and which ultimately included, besides transports, the vessels named in the note.[3]

On November 29th the whole fleet anchored in Grande Baie, about twelve miles to the north-east of Port Louis ; and, the approaches having been most carefully sounded beforehand, the army, some Royal Marines, and a large body of seamen under Captain William Augustus Montagu, who had relinquished command of the *Cornwallis* to take charge of the naval brigade ashore, were landed without opposition or casualty. The force advanced on the three following days, driving back the enemy, and suffering a loss of only 28 killed, 94 wounded, and 45 missing ; and on December 2nd, realising that he could make no effective stand, the French general Decaen proposed terms. On the 3rd, in consequence, the island was formally surrendered. About 1300 regular

---

[1] Late British *Iphigenia,* which had been captured on Aug. 28th, 1810.

[2] Late French *Vénus,* which had been captured on Sept. 18th, 1810.

[3]

Ships.	Guns.	Commanders.	Ships.	Guns.	Commanders.
		V.-Ad. Albemarle Bertie.	*Psyche*	32	Capt. John Edgcumbe.
Africaine . . .	38	Capt. Charles Gordon (1) (actg.).	*Ceylon*	32	Com. James Tomkinson (actg. Capt.).
Illustrious . . .	74	,, William Robert Broughton.	*Hesper*	18	,, David Paterson. Lieut. Henry Lynne (actg. Com.).
Cornwallis . . .	44	,, James Caulfeild (1).	*Eclipse*	18	
Boadicea . . .	38	,, Josias Rowley.	*Hecate*	18	Lieut. George Lucas Rennie (actg. Com.).
Nisus . . .	38	,, Philip Beaver.			
Clorinde. . . .	38	,, Thomas Briggs.	*Actæon*	16	Com. Ralph Visct. Neville.
Menelaus . . .	38	,, Peter Parker (2).			
Néréide . . .	38	Com. George Henderson (actg. Capt.).	*Staunch*	14	
Phœbe . . .	36	Capt. James Hillyar.	*Emma,* armed ship		Lieut. Benjamin Street (actg. Com.).
Doris . . .	36	,, William Jones Lye.	*Egremont,* hired .		,, Robert Forder.
Cornelia. . . .	32	,, Henry Folkes Edgell.	*Farquhar,* hired . *Mouche,* hired . .		

troops laid down their arms, among them being nearly 500 Irish
renegades. Decaen had also under his orders fully 10,000 militia ;
but they were insubordinate and disaffected, and he could not count
upon them. In the batteries were 209 heavy guns, all in excellent
condition ; and in the harbour were the men-of-war already mentioned, the late British Indiamen *Charlton*,[1] *Ceylon*,[2] and *United
Kingdom*,[1] and twenty-four French merchantmen.[3] The old *Néréide*
which, after so gallant a defence under Nisbet Josiah Willoughby,
had been taken on the previous 23rd of August,[4] was also recovered,
but she was in so battered a condition that she could not be
restored to the Navy.

The year 1811 witnessed even fewer active operations of great
fleets than 1810, though the minor actions fought during the period
were both numerous and important. In the North Sea Admiral
William Young (1) watched the ports of Holland, wherein lay a
considerable force. In the mouth of the Schelde was Vice-Admiral
Missiessy, with fifteen sail of the line, a frigate, and nine brigs ; at
Antwerp were three ships of the line repairing, and several on the
stocks ; other ships of the line were building at Flushing and
Ter Neuze ; and in the Texel seven sail of the line were ready for
sea. But no squadron ventured out to challenge Young. Nor was
the Channel fleet, which, in the second half of the year, passed to
the command of Admiral Sir Charles Cotton, able to induce the
enemy to issue from Brest, Cherbourg, Lorient, or Rochefort, in all
of which the building slips were kept fully occupied.

When Cotton quitted the Mediterranean for the Channel the
command of the former station was given to Vice-Admiral Sir
Edward Pellew, whose duty it became to watch Toulon, where the
command had by that time devolved upon Vice-Admiral Maurice
Julien Emeriau. In the latter half of the year several slight
collisions occurred between the blockaded and the blockading forces.

On July 19th two French frigates, the *Amélie*, 40, and *Adrienne*,
40, returning from Genoa with naval conscripts, were endeavouring
to enter Toulon. Emeriau, apprised of their presence off the coast,
weighed with the intention of proceeding into the offing to cover

---

[1] Taken Nov. 18th, 1809, in lat. 6° 30′ N., long. 90° 30′ E., by two French
frigates and a corvette.

[2] Taken 1810.

[3] Bertie to Croker, Oct. 13th, Dec. 6th ; Montagu to Bertie, Dec. 4th ; Abercromby's
General Orders of Dec. 1st and 5th ; Rowley to Croker, Feb. 19th, 1811.

[4] *See* next Chapter.

them; and just as Pellew, then off Cape Sicié with sixteen sail of
the line and three frigates, signalled to his two inshore battleships,
the *Conqueror*, 74, Captain Edward Fellowes, and *Sultan*, 74,
Captain John West, to chase the frigates, the French vice-admiral
left the road with thirteen sail of the line and the *Incorruptible*, 40.
By 11.30 A.M. the *Conqueror* was near enough to the *Amélie* and
Adrienne to open fire upon them; but, very soon afterwards, both
she and the *Sultan* were exchanging distant broadsides with the
four most advanced of the French battleships, and were obliged,
in consequence, to shorten sail and tack off to the fleet, the French
frigates joining their friends and returning with them to Toulon.
No one seems to have been hurt on either side.

In the early days of August, Pellew having anchored off Hyères,
and having left only a ship of the line and two or three frigates off
Cape Sicié, M. Emeriau several times sailed out and "chased the
enemy from off the port," always, however, returning ere Pellew
had an opportunity of bringing him to action. On August 13th
the French were tempted out by the fact that the *Téméraire*, 98,
Rear-Admiral Francis Pickmore, Captain Joseph Spear, while getting
under way, drifted under a battery at Pointe des Mèdes, and was for
some time in a disagreeable position; but, as usual, M. Emeriau
attempted nothing. His most ambitious cruise during the year
was one which he began on November 20th, when the only British
force off Toulon, and that at some distance, consisted of the
Volontaire, 38, Captain the Hon. Granville George Waldegrave,
and the *Perlen*, 38, Commander Joseph Swabey Tetley (actg.
Captain). The French remained cruising about Capes Sicié and
Cepet, with fourteen sail of the line and several frigates, until, on
the morning of the 23rd, their advanced division, of three sail of
the line and two frigates, fell in with the *Volontaire* and *Perlen*,
and chased them. The *Perlen* drove off the first frigate that drew
near her, but was then engaged at gradually decreasing range by
the other frigate and a 74. The *Volontaire*, in the meanwhile,
exchanged only distant shots with the enemy. At 1 P.M. the *Perlen*,
finding that her pursuers were gaining upon her, cut away four of
her anchors. At 2.30 P.M. she had the *Trident*, 74, on her lee,
and the *Amélie*, 40, on her weather quarter, both keeping up a
heavy fire, which was steadily returned. Later, the *Trident* yawed
in order to discharge a broadside; but this occasioned her to drop
so far astern that she soon abandoned her designs upon the *Perlen*,

and, with her consort, stood instead for the *Volontaire*. The French
ships, however, were by that time too much damaged aloft to chase
successfully, and presently they bore away for Toulon. The *Perlen*,
though somewhat cut up, had no one hurt. The *Volontaire* was
not struck. Emeriau continued his manœuvres outside Toulon
until the 26th, when he re-anchored in the road. On that day
Pellew and the British fleet were off the south-east end of Minorca.
M. Emeriau's last sortie for the year was made on December 9th.
Informed that twelve British sail of the line were in the offing, he
put to sea with sixteen sail of the line and two frigates; but he
returned in a few hours without giving Pellew a chance of trying
conclusions with him.

It is exceedingly difficult to understand the French naval policy
of that time. Napoleon is said to have cherished a gigantic project
for moving a great fleet, having on board a large number of troops,
to the East Indies, and for striking a blow at the British power
there. He may have had some such design. Certainly, one would
imagine, he must have had extensive naval designs of some sort,
seeing that he continued to spend immense sums upon his navy,
that he carefully increased its efficiency, and that little good could
accrue to him from the mere stay in port, or the inadventurous
cruise in the offing, of fleets, no matter how excellent. Yet, though,
in 1811, he had in commission at least fifty-six sail of the line, not
one of those vessels ever went out of sight of her harbour. Better
would it have been, nevertheless, to keep his fleets in port altogether
than to kill the *moral* of the men by suffering a French vice-admiral,
with sixteen sail of the line, to be driven back to his anchorage by
a British vice-admiral with only twelve.

While Napoleon, if report may be credited, was meditating great
exploits in eastern waters, Britain continued her vigorous action
there. Vice-Admiral William O'Brien Drury died while still in
chief command on March 6th, 1811; yet, while lying on his death-
bed, he completed his preparations, and issued his final orders, for
the conquest of Java. He entrusted the preliminary direction of
the affair to Captain Christopher Cole, of the *Caroline*, 36. On
April 18th the first division of the expeditionary force, under Cole
himself and Colonel Robert Gillespie, sailed from Madras, and on
May 18th it anchored at Penang. The second division, under
Captain Fleetwood Broughton Reynolds Pellew, of the *Phaeton*, 38,
and Major-General Wetherall, left Madras on April 24th, and

reached Penang on May 21st. On May 24th the two divisions sailed for Malacca, where they were joined by troops from Bengal, and by Commodore William Robert Broughton, in the *Illustrious*, 74, and Lieutenant-General Sir Samuel Auchmuty, the naval and military Commanders-in-Chief. The entire military force thus assembled consisted of 11,960 officers and men, of whom 5344 were Europeans ; but, of the whole number, 1200 were sick, and had to be left behind. Leaving Malacca on June 11th, the fleet proceeded by way of Singapore, the High Islands, and Port Sambar, in Borneo, to its final rendezvous off the Island of Boompjes, which lies near the mouth of the Indramayo, on the coast of Java. There the Commanders-in-Chief awaited intelligence which they expected to be brought them by craft which had been detached in order to gain it.

While the expedition [1] was still on its way, several preliminary operations were carried out by the vessels already on the station. On May 23rd the *Sir Francis Drake*, 32, Captain George Harris, discovered fourteen Dutch gunboats under the shore near Rembang, Java. Five were forced to anchor and strike. The remaining nine were cut out by the frigate's boats under Lieutenants James Bradley and Edward Brown Addis (actg.).[2] A little later an extraordinary exploit was performed by Lieutenant Edmund Lyons, then of the *Minden*, 74, Captain Edward Wallis Hoare. Lyons knew that the harbour of Marrack was regarded by the French as

[1] The ships and commanding officers engaged in the reduction of Java were :—

SHIPS.	GUNS.	COMMANDERS.	SHIPS.	GUNS.	COMMANDERS.
Scipion	74	R.-Ad. Hon. Robert Stopford. Capt. James Johnstone (2). Commod. Wm. Robert Broughton.	*Caroline* [1] . . .	36	Capt. Christopher Cole.
			Modeste	36	„ Hon. George Elliot (3).
			Phœbe	36	„ James Hillyar.
			Bucephalus . . .	36	„ Charles Pelly.
Illustrious . . .	74	Com. Robt. Worgan Geo. Feeting (actg. Capt.).	*Doris*	36	„ Wm. Jones Lye.
			Cornelia	32	„ Hy. Folkes Edgell.
			Psyche	32	„ John Edgcumbe.
			Sir Francis Drake.	32	„ George Harris.
Minden	74	Capt. Edward Wallis Hoare.	*Procris*	18	Com. Robert Maunsell.
Lion	64	„ Henry Heathcote.	*Barracouta* . .	18	„ Wm. Fitzwm. Owen.[2]
Akbar	44	Lieut. Henry Drury (actg. Capt.).	*Hesper*	18	„ Barrington Reynolds.
Nisus	38	Capt. Philip Beaver.	*Harpy*	18	„ Henderson Bain.
Présidente . . .	38	„ Samuel Warren (2).	*Hecate*	18	„ Hon. Hy. Jno. Peachey.
Hussar	38	„ Jas. Coutts Crawford.			Lieut. Benedictus Marwood Kelly (actg. Com.).
Phaeton	38	„ Fleetwood Broughton Reynolds Pellew.	*Dasher*	18	
Leda	36	„ George Sayer (1).	*Samarang* . . .	18	„ Joseph Drury (actg. Com.).

and the H. E. Co.'s cruisers, *Malabar, Aurora, Mornington, Nautilus, Vestal, Ariel, Thetis*, and *Psyche*, together with transports and captured craft.

[1] Detached home, Aug. 29th.　　　　　[2] Captain, May 2nd, 1811.

[2] Harris to Broughton, May 23rd.

the only unassailable harbour in Java, and that the French convoys expected for the succour of the island would be almost certain to run for it. He knew also that a projected attack on Marrack by the boats of the *Minden,* and of the *Leda,* 36, Captain George Sayer (1), had shortly before been deliberately abandoned because of the arrival of military reinforcements at the threatened spot. Nevertheless, being detached in the *Minden's* launch, with her cutter, on July 25th to land some prisoners at Batavia, and then, returning down the coast, to gain what useful information he might, he determined on his own responsibility to make a midnight dash at Marrack, although he had with him only thirty-five people all told, and the post was well fortified and strongly held. He made the attack on the night of July 29th, and, although he failed to surprise the defenders, he carried the fort in the most dashing manner. Very early on the following morning, however, the fire from a detached Dutch battery, and from two gunboats in the harbour, decided Lyons that he could not hold the place. By strategy he induced the troops in the neighbourhood to attempt an assault in which they lost heavily, and then, taking advantage of their temporary discouragement, he sank one of the gunboats, destroyed the fort, left the British flag flying above it, and withdrew, having had but four of his gallant companions slightly wounded. Midshipmen William Langton and Charles Henry Franks shared the honours of the day. But for the fact that the whole affair was undertaken without orders, Lyons would undoubtedly have won his immediate promotion.[1] On the night of July 30th another creditable service was performed. The *Procris,* 18, Commander Robert Maunsell, anchored near the mouth of the Indramayo, and there discovered six gunboats, each mounting a couple of guns and having about sixty men on board. Under their charge were about fifty proas. On the 31st, after endeavouring in vain to get within effective gunshot of the enemy, Maunsell sent in his boats under Lieutenant George Majoribanks. These boarded and carried five of the gunboats, and would have taken the sixth had she not blown up. The success, which was effected with the loss of but eleven wounded on the British side, was shared in by some officers and men of the 14th and 89th regiments.[2]

[1] Lyons to Hoare, July 31st. Lyons was not promoted to be Commander till Mar. 21st, 1812.

[2] Maunsell to Sayer, July 31st.

The Java expedition left Boompjes island on August 2nd, and on the afternoon of the 4th were off the village of Chillingching, about twelve miles to the eastward of Batavia, where it had been decided to disembark. Before dark about 8000 men had been put ashore without opposition. That night there was a slight affair of outposts, but the governor-general, Janssens, and his army of about 10,000 effective troops, held the strongly-entrenched camp of Meester Cornelis, nine miles from Batavia, and did not move out from it. In consequence of these dispositions, Batavia, which was unprotected, surrendered on August 8th, upon being threatened by the Navy and army, and was occupied by the troops, its roadstead being also utilised as an anchorage for the men-of-war and trans-ports. On the day following Rear-Admiral the Hon. Robert Stopford arrived and superseded Commodore Broughton, who, since the death of Vice-Admiral Drury, had commanded the station.

On August 20th, after the Dutch had been defeated in a smart skirmish on the 10th, the formal siege of Meester Cornelis, in which no fewer than 280 guns were mounted, was begun. A brigade of 500 seamen, under Captain George Sayer (1), and Commanders Robert Worgan George Festing, Robert Maunsell, Barrington Reynolds, and Edward Stopford (1) (volunteer),[1] served in the batteries ; and a detachment of Royal Marines, under Captain Richard Bunce, R.M., was also employed ashore. On August 22nd the Dutch made a sortie, which was at first successful, but which ended in their repulse. On the 24th there was a furious cannonade on both sides ; and, at midnight on the 25th, the formidable works were stormed and carried, after a very determined and bloody struggle. Janssens escaped ; but about 5000 troops were taken prisoners, and more than 1000 more fell in the action and pursuit. The total British loss from August 4th to 27th inclusive was only 156 killed, 788 wounded, and 16 missing. The Navy's share of these casualties was 15 killed, 55 wounded, and three missing. Among the wounded were Com-mander Edward Stopford, Lieutenant Francis Noble, and Lieu-tenants (R.M.) Henry Elliot and John Stepney Haswell.[2]

In the meantime the French frigates *Nymphe*, 40, and *Méduse*, 40, which, under Commodore François Raoul, had escaped from Nantes in the previous spring, lay in Sourabaya harbour, where

---

[1] Edward Stopford was in the *Scipion*, waiting for his own ship, the *Otter*.
[2] Stopford to Croker, Aug. 28th. Dispatch of Auchmuty. Stopford to Croker, Aug. 30th.

they were watched, from the middle of August onwards, by the
Akbar, 44, Lieutenant Henry Drury (actg. captain) *Phaeton*, 38,
Captain Fleetwood Broughton Reynolds Pellew, *Bucephalus*, 36,
Captain Charles Pelly, and *Sir Francis Drake*, 32, Captain George
Harris. On September 3rd, the two French frigates weighed, and
began to warp towards the north-west into the outer road. The
Bucephalus, observing them, closed, and early on the 4th was joined
by the *Barracouta*, 18, Captain William Fitzwilliam Owen, in
company with which she chased as soon as the frigates were clear
of the harbour. The *Barracouta* soon began to fall astern, and,
during the whole of the 5th, 6th, 7th and 8th, was barely in sight
of her consort. She then dropped entirely out of view, but the
Bucephalus alone continued the pursuit, until, early on the 12th,
off Great Pulo Laut, the frigates, having, as they doubtless conceived, their enemy at a disadvantage, turned upon her. In danger
of being embayed, she made off, and, for about an hour and a half
after 1 P.M., was engaged by the Frenchmen. A little later Pelly
endeavoured to decoy his pursuers among some shoals which lay
ahead of him; but they, discovering the risk, tacked away, and
finally disappeared. The *Bucephalus* had no one hurt. Commodore
Raoul's conduct in the affair is difficult to explain. When near the
Java coast, on the 4th and 5th, he may have been justified in
fleeing from a single British frigate, owing to the proximity of
Stopford's fleet; but, when off Borneo on the 12th, he had no
reason to fear any interference. Nevertheless, he abandoned what
would have been an almost certain prize had he been Pelly's equal
as a navigator. Pelly's [1] behaviour, on the other hand, was
admirable throughout. He chased so long as there was a hope that
he might separate his foes and find an opportunity of engaging one
of them; and he out-manœuvred them as soon as circumstances
put him in a perilous position. The fugitives reached Brest in
safety on December 22nd.

Although the *Sir Francis Drake* and the *Phaeton* missed the
frigates, they were not idle while they kept watch off the east end
of Java. In the small hours of August 31st, having previously sent
the *Dasher*, 18, Lieutenant Benedictus Marwood Kelly (actg.
Com.), to make a diversion on the seaward side, the Captains
of these two frigates landed and rushed the fort of Sumenap, in
the island of Madura. They then summoned the governor of the

---

[1] Capt. Pelly unfortunately died a few weeks later.

town of Sumenap to surrender. He replied by requiring them to instantly evacuate the fort. Although the Franco-Dutch disposed of upwards of 2000 men, and the British of only about 190, Captain George Harris, the senior officer, never hesitated. He from one direction, and Pellew from another, advanced, and, after discharging a few volleys, charged; whereupon the enemy fled, abandoning his colours and guns. In these operations, in which some Royal Marines from the *Hussar* participated, the British loss was only 3 killed and 28 wounded. The effect of the success was that Madura and the neighbouring islands were presently completely reduced.

On September 4th, the *Nisus*, *Présidente*, and *Phœbe*, which had been detached thither by Stopford, received the surrender of the seaport of Cheribon. On the 12th, Taggal also submitted. In the meantime the army on shore pressed General Janssens so vigorously that on September 16th, having been driven into the fort of Salatiga, near Samarang, he offered to capitulate. On the 18th, in consequence, Java and all its dependencies were formally handed over to Great Britain.[1]

The events of the war which broke out between Great Britain and the United States in 1812 will be found hereafter narrated in a separate chapter. Although, for about three years, America and France were both hostile to the United Kingdom, there was no co-operation of any sort between them. Indeed, America, at the time, was scarcely less exasperated with France than she was with her mother-nation.

From the beginning of the year 1812, until the conclusion of the war three years later, the fleets of France were practically impotent. Only on very few occasions did any of them venture out of port. When they did so, their commanders concentrated their energies upon evading the numerous British squadrons which were on the look out for them; and this they did with so much cleverness that no fleet action deserving of the name was fought during the whole of the period. On the other hand, France had long since been deprived of nearly all her over-sea possessions; so that Great Britain had no opportunities of injuring her enemy by embarking on colonial adventures such as had been successfully carried out during the

---

[1] Stopford to Croker, Sept. 29th; Harris to Stopford, Sept. 1st; Beaver to Stopford, Sept. 7th and 11th; Hillyar to Stopford, Sept. 12th; Harris to Stopford, Sept. 13th (two dispatches).

earlier phases of the war. The steadily employed influence of sea power had at length confined the might of Napoleon to the land ; and, during the last years of the long campaign, by remorselessly preventing him from using the highways of the ocean, either to move troops or to obtain supplies, the same power slowly yet surely brought the great Corsican to his knees. On March 19th, 1812, Russia declared war against France. On July 12th following, Russia and Sweden signed at Örebro a treaty with Great Britain ; and thus the Emperor lost the last of his friends.

Yet France, as if still hoping for a chance of breaking loose from her thralls and springing again upon her foes, continued to add to her navy. In the Schelde about twenty, and in the Texel about nine sail of the line occupied the careful attention of the British blockaders during many months of 1812 ; and in the autumn new ships were ordered to be laid down at Amsterdam and elsewhere. Continual efforts were made to assemble once more a large fleet at Brest ; and there was ceaseless activity in the yards of Toulon, Genoa, Naples, Spezzia, and Venice.

The most noteworthy incident of the year occurred off the Atlantic seaboard. Throughout January and February Vice-Admiral Allemand lay in Lorient with five ships of the line, waiting to elude the vigilance of Captain Sir John Gore (2), who blockaded him with four. On March 9th and 10th, while reconnoitring the port, Sir John discovered that Allemand, with four of his ships, had escaped. He had, in fact, left port in the night of the 8th, with the *Eylau*, 80, and *Guillemard, Marengo*, and *Vétéran*,[1] 74's, besides two corvettes, with a view to reaching Brest. Soon after midday on the 9th, Allemand was sighted by the *Diana*, 38, Captain William Ferris, which was joined on the 10th by the *Pompée*, 74, Captain Sir James Athol Wood. In the meantime the *Tremendous*, 74, Captain Robert Campbell (1), and *Poictiers*, 74, Captain John Poo Beresford, which had been cruising off Ushant, had also sighted the French and chased them ; and later the pursuing force was joined by the *Bulwark*, 74, Captain Thomas Browne, and *Colossus*, 74, Captain Thomas Alexander (1), both of Gore's squadron ; but ere then Allemand had been lost sight of in a fog. He remained at sea for three weeks, and picked up a few small prizes. In the course of his cruise, which was prolonged owing to the fact that two or three

---

[1] This ship had managed to get to Lorient from Concarneau, where she had long been blockaded.

British divisions were looking for him, he fell in with, and exchanged shots with the *Nayaden*, 32, Captain Farmery Predam Epworth, which, however, managed to escape from him; and on March 29th, he anchored safely in Brest road. The pursuit seems to have been mismanaged, and led to the holding of a court of inquiry : but the matter proceeded no further.

The French Brest fleet was thus reinforced by four ships of the line. Some vessels which were in Aix road, and two more which lay in Cherbourg, though equally anxious to reach the great Atlantic port, were so well watched that they did not venture to put to sea.

Toulon was jealously and closely observed by Sir Edward Pellew. Within lay a superior fleet under Vice-Admiral Comte Emeriau. Part of it made a brief demonstration outside the harbour on January 14th, and a bigger force issued forth once or twice during the month of May; but the British fleet was never allowed to get within gunshot of it. Only once, indeed, was there any actual collision off the port. On May 28th, the French *Pauline*, 40, and *Ecureuil*, 16, from the Adriatic, were discovered by one of the inshore British frigates, the *Menelaus*, 38, Captain Sir Peter Parker (2), Bart. They were endeavouring to enter Toulon, under the protection of their fleet, which had weighed to cover them. Parker, though unsupported, did his best to cut them off, and did not desist until he had had his fore topmast shot nearly through, and had suffered considerable damage to his sails and rigging. By the end of the year the number of ships of the line ready for sea in Toulon was eighteen, five of which were three-deckers.

In 1813 there was an equal absence of startling incident. The forces in the Schelde and at Brest remained inactive, nor were they materially increased by the arrival of ships from elsewhere. The *Regulus*, 74, however, succeeded in moving, undetected, from Roche-fort to the Gironde; and the improvements made at Cherbourg, which was formally opened on August 27th as a naval port, permitted ship-building on a large scale to be begun there.

The fleet in Toulon continued to be added to ; and in the early autumn of the year it included twenty-one sail of the line and ten 40-gun frigates ready for sea, besides three more ships of the line on the stocks. Parts of it frequently weighed and manœuvred for a few hours at a time ; but the fleet as a whole was badly manned, owing to the enormous demands of the army, which more than once borrowed seamen from the navy and never returned them. On

November 5th, during one of the usual sorties for exercise, there was a partial action. The main body of Pellew's fleet had been blown from its station, and was but just in sight to the southward ; but an inshore squadron, consisting of the four 74's, *Scipion*, Captain Henry Heathcote (senior officer), *Mulgrave*, Captain Thomas James Maling, *Pembroke*, Captain James Brisbane, and *Armada*, Captain Charles Grant, was close off Cape Sicié. M. Emeriau went out with twelve, or, as Pellew says, fourteen sail of the line, six frigates and a schooner. He left port with a wind from E.N.E., but, as soon as his leading squadron was just outside, the wind shifted to N.W. Thereupon the French made every effort to get back to port, while Heathcote exerted himself to cut off some of their leewardmost ships, in spite of the fact that Rear-Admiral Baron Cosmao-Kerjulien, who commanded the enemy's van in the *Wagram*, 130, had five sail of the line and four heavy frigates, and that the main British force was coming up only slowly. At 12.34 P.M., when Heathcote had been joined by the *Pompée*, 74, Captain Sir James Athol Wood, a running engagement began. At 1 P.M. the *Caledonia*, 120, Vice-Admiral Sir Edward Pellew (Captain of the Fleet Rear-Admiral Israel Pellew), Captain Jeremiah Coghlan, *Boyne*, 98, Captain George Burlton, and *San Josef*, 112, Rear-Admiral Sir Richard King (2), Captain William Stewart, stood inshore across the bows of Heathcote's division, and took up the fighting ; but the French quickly got out of gunshot and escaped. In this affair the losses on the British side were one killed and fourteen, including Lieutenant of Marines William Clarke, and Midshipman William Cuppage, wounded.[1] The enemy had seventeen wounded. Soon afterwards Pellew proceeded to Minorca, leaving but a small squadron off Toulon ; but although the force there was augmented in December by the launch of the *Colosse*, 74, M. Emeriau made no further effort to put to sea.

By the end of the year the outlook was black indeed for the fortunes of the Emperor. Great Britain, Spain, Portugal, Russia, Prussia, Austria, Denmark, and Sweden were allied against him ; and the Prince of Orange had been proclaimed King of the United Netherlands. On January 11th, 1814, Murat, King of Naples, formally deserted Napoleon, and made his peace with the Allies. The Emperor, nevertheless, still appeared to have hopes that his navy would save him from final disaster, and still he continued his

---

[1] Pellew to Croker, Nov. 6th, 1813.

efforts to concentrate it. In pursuance of this project three sail of the line, including the *Romulus*, Captain Rolland, and three frigates, including the *Adrienne*, quitted Toulon on February 12th, 1814, to meet and escort into port a new French 74 which was expected from Genoa. Sir Edward Pellew had by that time returned from Minorca, and at daybreak on the 13th he sighted the enemy, under Rear-Admiral Baron Cosmao-Kerjulien, steering south. The French soon tacked in order to return, and, with a strong E. wind, headed for Porquerolles, subsequently passing through Hyères Bay. Pellew's fifteen sail of the line endeavoured to cut them off; and the *Boyne*, 98, Captain George Burlton, and *Caledonia*, 120 (flag), pressed the rear ship, the *Romulus*, so closely and so hotly that, only by a magnificent display of seamanship on the part of her commander, was she enabled to get back to her anchorage. The *Adrienne* also had a narrow escape. She lost eleven, and the *Romulus* no fewer than seventy, killed and badly wounded. The ship from Genoa, in spite of the failure of her escort, seems to have safely got into Toulon on the following day. In this skirmish, in which the French shore batteries took part, the *Boyne* suffered severely aloft and had two guns disabled, besides losing two, including Midshipman George Terry, killed, and forty wounded. The flagship had but one person injured.[1]

In the meantime, on January 5th, Cattaro, in the Adriatic, had surrendered, after a ten days' cannonade, to the *Bacchante*, 38, Captain William Hoste, and *Saracen*, 18, Commander John Harper. The ships lost only one seaman killed and Lieutenant of Marines William Haig wounded. On January 28th, Ragusa surrendered to the same vessels, assisted by detachments of British and Austrian troops;[2] and on February 13th the island of Paxo was taken without resistance by the *Apollo*, 38, Captain Bridges Watkinson Taylor, and troops under Lieutenant Colonel Church. All these operations were carried out under the direction of Rear-Admiral Thomas Francis Fremantle, who, ere the beginning of March, with the co-operation of Austrian troops, had reduced every remaining French possession in the Adriatic.[3] In March and April Spezzia and Genoa fell to a squadron under Captain Sir Josias Rowley, who had with him British troops and two Sicilian vessels. At Genoa there was

---

[1] Pellew's dispatch of Feb. 13th, enclosing Burlton's return.

[2] Hoste to Fremantle, Jan. 3rd and 29th.

[3] Fremantle to Pellew, Feb. 16th.

found a 74, the *Brillant*, ready for launching. She was ultimately launched, and added to the Navy as the *Genoa*. There were also found another 74 in frame, and four corvettes, the *Coureur*, 18, *Renard*, 16, *Endymion*, 16, and *Sphinx*, 18.[1]

The British advance from Spain, which resulted, on March 31st, in the entry of the Allies into Paris, and the signature, on April 24th, of the preliminary treaty between Great Britain and France, was materially assisted by the co-operation of a naval squadron under Rear-Admiral Charles Vinicombe Penrose. The passage of the Adour, on February 23rd, was greatly facilitated by the exertions and excellent dispositions of Captain John Coode of the *Porcupine*, 24, Commander Dowell O'Reilly (commanding the force in the river), of the *Lyra*, 10, and Lieutenants George Cheyne, commanding the *Woodlark*, John Cheshire, commanding a gunboat, and John Debenham, transport officer. The losses on the occasion included Commander George Elliott, of the *Martial*, 14, Mr. Henry Bloye, Master's Mate of the *Lyra*, and eleven British seamen, besides numerous soldiers and others drowned, and Surgeon Charles Norman, of the *Martial*, killed.[2] Simultaneously with Marshal Beresford's approach to Bordeaux, Penrose, with his flag in the *Egmont*, 74, entered the Gironde. Lieutenant Robert Graham Dunlop, with the boats of the *Porcupine*, captured or destroyed a number of French craft, which, protected by troops from Blaye, had run ashore near Tallemont. This service, which was performed on April 2nd, cost the Navy fourteen seamen and Royal Marines wounded, and two missing. Four days later, after preparations had been made by the *Egmont* and the *Centaur*, 74, Captain John Chambers White, to attack the *Regulus*, 74, three corvettes, and other vessels which lay under batteries in the river, the French burnt the whole flotilla. At or about the same time, the various works commanding the river were entered and destroyed by a force under Captain George Harris, of the *Belle Poule*, 38.[3]

In April Louis XVIII. embarked at Dover in the *Royal Sovereign* yacht, and, escorted by the *Jason*, 32, on board of which was Admiral of the Fleet the Duke of Clarence, and by the French frigate *Polonais*, landed at Calais on the 24th. On the 28th of the same month, Napoleon embarked at Fréjus in the *Undaunted*, 38,

---

[1] Rowley's dispatches of Mar. 31st and Apr. 18th.
[2] Penrose to Keith, Feb. 25th, and O'Reilly's return of casualties.
[3] Penrose to Keith, Apr. 6th and 9th. Coode to Penrose, Apr. 2nd.

Captain Thomas Ussher; and on May 4th he was landed at Porto
Ferrajo in Elba, the sovereignty of which little island had been
assigned to him by the Powers. The definitive treaty with France
was signed at Paris on May 30th.

But definitive peace was not yet. On February 26th, 1815, after
the British fleet in commission had been nearly everywhere reduced,
Napoleon suddenly left Elba in an armed brig, and, accompanied by
about a thousand men in pinks and feluccas, landed in Golf Juan,
near Cannes, on March 1st. On March 21st he entered Paris.
Pellew, who since May 14th, 1814, had been deservedly raised to
the peerage with the title of Lord Exmouth, was at once reappointed
Commander-in-Chief in the Mediterranean, with his brother, Sir
Israel Pellew, as Captain of the Fleet. Lord Keith was given

COMMEMORATIVE MEDAL OF THE SURRENDER OF NAPOLEON.
(*From an original lent by Capt. H.S.H. Prince Louis of Battenberg, G.C.B.*)

command in the Channel, and measures were promptly taken to
strengthen the Navy on all stations. But ere many of these
measures could be completely carried out, the decisive battle of
Waterloo, on June 18th, put an end for ever to Napoleon's active
career. On July 15th, finding that he had no chance of escaping,
as he had hoped, to the United States, the ex-Emperor surrendered
himself to Captain Frederick Lewis Maitland (2), of the *Bellerophon*, 74, in Basque road, and was conveyed, first to Torquay, and
then to Plymouth, where he arrived on July 26th. On August 7th,
he was transferred to the *Northumberland*, 74, Rear-Admiral Sir
George Cockburn, Captain Charles Bayne Hodgson Ross; on the
following day the ship sailed; and on October 16th Napoleon was
disembarked at his final place of detention, the island of St. Helena.
A general peace was again signed at Paris on November 20th.

During the brief revival of hostilities consequent upon the return of Napoleon to France, the Navy had few opportunities of effecting much. Off Ischia, on April 30th, the *Rivoli*, 74, Captain Edward Stirling Dickson, after a quarter of an hour's action, captured the *Melpomène*, 40, Captain Joseph Collet, which was on her way to Naples to carry Madame Mère [1] to France. The frigate lost 6 killed and 28 wounded, while the line-of-battle ship had but three or four people hurt, including one mortally. Again, on June 17th, the *Pilot*, 18, Commander John Toup Nicolas, being off Cape Corso, chased the Bonapartist *Légère*, 22, Commander Nicolas Touffet, and ultimately engaged her at short range. After less than two hours' action the *Légère* was obviously beaten; but, as the *Pilot* had had most of her running gear and some spars shot away, she was unable to manœuvre in order to oblige her opponent to strike; and the Frenchman eventually got away, having lost no fewer than 22 killed and 79 wounded, out of a complement which James estimates at 170 men. The *Pilot* had one killed, one mortally wounded, and 14, including Lieutenant William Keigwin Nicolas and Purser Thomas Rowe, less severely hurt. [2]

In more distant waters, almost the only naval events of the revived war took place in the West Indies. To assist in the preservation of Martinique to Louis XVIII., Rear-Admiral Sir Philip Charles Durham and Lieut.-General Sir James Leith landed a body of British troops in the island; and, in August, the same officers, assisted by French Royalists from Martinique, conducted an expeditionary force to Guadeloupe, where the celebrated Comte de Linois, a staunch Bonapartist who had been retained as governor, had proclaimed Napoleon. On August 10th, after a slight action, Linois capitulated. [3]

The Peace of Paris was extremely favourable to France. Under its provisions she received back every foreign possession which she had held on January 1st, 1792, except only Tobago, St. Lucia, the Isle of France (Mauritius), Rodriguez, and the Seychelles. France, however, was condemned to pay an indemnity of 700,000,000 francs, or about £28,000,000 sterling; and the terms granted her were upon

---

[1] Napoleon's mother, *née* Maria Letitia Ramolino, born 1750, died 1836. She had been given the title of Madame Mère in 1804.

[2] O'Byrne, 815. Nicolas was posted on Aug. 26th, 1815.

[3] Durham to Croker, Aug. 15th; Brit. procl. of Aug. 3rd; Capit. of Aug. 10th.

the whole considerably less advantageous than those which she had obtained in 1814.

The net gain to Great Britain was, nevertheless, enormous. The conclusion of the war found her firmly established not only as the supreme naval power in the world, but also as the leading commercial one. France, which for centuries had been her continual enemy, was exhausted and no longer dangerous. The social peril born of the excesses of the Revolution had at length been strangled. The European menace resulting from the unscrupulous ascendency of Napoleon had been annihilated ; and, although immense sacrifices had been made, they left the victor, like a trained athlete, really stronger than ever. What the sacrifices were may be gathered, to some extent, from the fact that the war, between 1793 and 1815, necessitated the raising, in addition to the ordinary income of the United Kingdom, of loans to the total amount of upwards of £600,000,000. On the other hand, peace for a long course of years was practically assured by the nature and issue of the gigantic and prolonged struggle ; and peace, as subsequent events have shown, was what Great Britain most needed. Until the crisis of the struggle with Napoleon, the position of her Empire was everywhere precarious ; after 1815 she was freed from all her most besetting anxieties, and was enabled to begin in earnest the work, till then too much neglected, of social, industrial, financial, and political reform. Since 1815, civilisation, not only in Great Britain, but also throughout Europe, and, indeed, all over the world, has made greater comparative advances than it had made during the previous five centuries. This is largely because the close of the conflict marked the end of an age when war had been a normal condition, and the beginning of a period when peace became the rule rather than the exception. But for the dogged work of the British Navy, the result must have been very different. For years that Navy stood almost alone between Europe and obliteration. Had there been no British Navy, Napoleon might well have reduced the greater part of the Old World to subjection, and have inscribed the name of France right across the map from Kerry to Celebes.

CHAPTER XL.

MINOR OPERATIONS OF THE ROYAL NAVY, 1803–15.

Recommencement of the War in 1803—Capture of the *Affronteur*—Detention of British residents in France—Capture of the *Franchise* and *Impatiente*—Of the *Colombe* and *Pélagie*—Of the *Endymion*—Cutting-out of the *Venteux*— Taking of the *Mignonne* and escape of the *Poursuivante*—Capture of the *Créole* —Loss of the *Minerve*—Cutting-out of the *Providence*—Capture of the *Alcion* and *Lodi*—Chase and capture of the *Duquesne*—Escape of the *Duguay Trouin* and *Guerrière*—Temerity of the *Vénus*—Escape of Jérôme Bonaparte—Taking of the *Atalante*—Defence of the *Juno*—Taking and retaking of the *Lord Nelson* —Destruction of the *Mutine*—Gallantry of Lieutenant Rowed—Defence of the *Princess Augusta*—The *Atalante* in Quiberon Bay—The *Racoon* off Guantanamo —Boarding of the *Resource*—Destruction of the *Sept Frères*—Cutting-out of the *Albion*—Gallantry of Midshipman A'Court—Cutting-out of the *Harmonie*— Capture of the *Vautour*—Burning of the *Bayonnaise*—The *Goliath* and French convoys—Wreck of the *Shannon*—Of the *Grappler*—1804, Occupation of the Diamond Rock—The *Scourge* in the Vlie—Cutting-out of the *Curieux*—The *Eclair* and *Grand Décidé*—Nathaniel Dance and Linois—The *Drake* at Trinité— The *Curieuse* repels the boats of the *Blenheim*—Capture of the *Mosambique*—The *Drake* at Deshaies—Destruction of the *Renommée*—The *Osprey* and the *Egyptienne* —Loss of the *Wolverine*—Capture of the *Egyptienne*—Cutting-out of the *Athalante* —Loss of the *Swift*—The *Wilhelmina* and *Psyché*—Capture of *No. 360*—Repulse of the *Hippomenes*—Boat attack in Hyères Bay—Destruction of the *Charente* and *Joie*—Loss of the *Lily*—Cutting-out of the *Hirondelle*—Futile attack on the *Général Ernouf*—Capture of the *Blonde*—Defence of the *Centurion*—The *Fortunée* mistaken for a privateer—Action with the Spanish treasure ships— Chase of the *Contre-Amiral Magon*—Capture of the *Bonaparte*—Wreck of the *Apollo*—1805, Escape of the *Gipsy*—The *Arrow* and *Acheron* with the *Hortense* and *Incorruptible*—Capture of the *Dame Ernouf*—The *San Fiorenzo* takes the *Psyché*—Loss of the *Cleopatra*—Retaking of the *Cleopatra* and taking of the *Ville de Milan*—Blowing up of the *Général Ernouf*—Cutting-out of the *Antilope* —The *Bacchante* at Mariel—The *Gracieuse* off San Domingo—The *Papillon* off Jamaica—Capture of the *Tape-à-Bord*—The *Seine* off Puerto Rico—The *Seahorse* off San Pedro—Successful cruise of the *Pallas*—Boat attack in Camarinas Bay— Yeo at Muros—Capture of the *Maria* and *Matilda*—Pigot in River St. Mary— Defence of the *Blanche*—Taking of the *Faune* and *Torche*—Attempt upon the *Sémillante*—Troubridge and Linois—Case of Lord William Fitzroy—The *Phœnix* and *Didon*—Cutting-out of the *Caridad Perfecta*—Loss of the *Calcutta*—Taking of the *Cyane* and *Naïade*—The *Serpent* at Truxillo—Capture of the *Libre*—1806, Capture of the *Napoléon*—Cutting-out of the *Raposa*—The *Pitt* and the *Sémil- lante*—Cutting-out of the *Alcide*—Capture of the *Belle-Poule* and *Marengo*— Ussher on the Spanish coast—Repulse of the *Reindeer*—Capture of the *Phaëton* and *Voltigeur*—Taking of the *Néarque*—Of the *Dame Ernouf*—Capture of the *Vigilante, Giganta, etc.*—Cutting-out of the *Tapageuse*—Cochrane in the Gironde —The *Pallas* and *Kingfisher* in Aix Road—The *Sirius* off Civita Vecchia—Clever

off the Wielings—Simmonds off Boulogne—Capture of the *Nayaden, Laaland, Samsö,* and *Kiel*—Capture of the *Eole*—And of the *Ville de Caen*—Recapture of the *Urania*—Repulse at Santander—Capture of Danish cutters—Cutting-out affair at Port San Stefano—Michael Dwyer at Benidorm—Defence of the *Attack*—O'Brien in the Canale di Leme—Capture of the *St. Esprit* and *Fidèle*—Loss of the *Laura*—Boats of the *Eagle* at the mouth of the Po—Capture of a convoy off Tremiti—Boats of the *Minstrel* at Peniscola—Loss of the *Spy* and *Linnet*—Affair at St. Cataldo—1813, Boats of the *Bacchante* off Cape d'Otranto—Capture of *No.* 8—Capture of Lagosta and Curzola—Boats of the *Kingfisher* off Merlera—Loss of the *Daring*—The *Amelia* and the *Aréthuse*—Capture of the *Alcinous*—Hall at Pietra Nera—Capture of Ponza—The *Brevdrageren* in the Elbe—The *Undaunted* near Marseilles—Cutting-out affair at Morgiou—Boats of the *Havannah* off the coast of the Abruzzi—The *Apollo* and *Cerberus* off Corfu—Capture of the *Invincible*—The *Weazel* and gunboats in Bassoglina Bay—The *Apollo* at St. Cataldo—Boats of the *Elizabeth* and *Eagle* off Goro—Cutting-out affair at Morgiou—Capture of Carlopago—Action in Cavalaire Road—The *Apollo* and *Cerberus* near Brindisi—Capture of a convoy off Apulia—Collier on the north coast of Spain—Supposed pirates at Chiliodromia—Landing in the Canale di Maltempo—Storming of Farasina—Capture of Umago—Hood off Giulianova—Seizure of Giuppana—Capture of Dignano—Storming of Fiume—Capture of Rovigno—Capture of Rogoznica—Taking of the *Auguste* and *Tonnante*—Attack on Cassis—Blowing up of the *Alphea*—Capture of the *Guerrier*—Capture of a convoy at Anzio—Capture of the *Neptune*—Hoste at Cattaro—Capitulation of Triest—Destruction of the *Flibustier*—The *Furieuse* at Sta. Marinella—Capture of the *Weser* and *Trave*—Capture of the *Lion*—Boats of the *Revenge* at Palamos—Attack on La Nouvelle—Capture of the *Charlemagne*—Farquhar in the Elbe—Taking of the *Cérès*—The *Eurotas* and the *Clorinde*—Capture of the *Alcmène*—And of the *Iphigénie*—The *Creole* and *Astræa* with the *Etoile* and *Sultane*—The *Hebrus* and the *Etoile*—Capture of the *Sultane*—Capture of the *Terpsichore*—Fatal mistake of the *Primrose* with the *Duke of Marlborough*—End of the War.

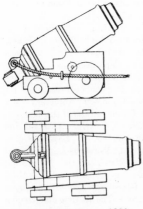

BOAT CARRONADE, *ca.* 1820.
(*From Ch. Dupin.*)

ON May 16th, 1803, Cornwallis, then Commander-in-Chief on the Channel station, acting in obedience to instructions, issued an order to detain and send into port all French and Dutch vessels. Four days previously the British Ambassador had left Paris, delayed much longer than he wished, after his demand for his passports, by " the infamous chicanery and difficulties which have occurred." As the French Government affected to regard Cornwallis's order as a violation of the law of nations, this point is important.

On the 18th occurred the first action of the war. The French hired lugger *Affronteur*, 14 (long 8's), Lieutenant M. A. Duthoya, was cruising off Ushant to observe

Cornwallis's fleet, which had put to sea from Torbay on the 17th,
when a vessel, which she is said to have mistaken for a British
West Indiaman, came in sight.   The French craft approached to
board, but, soon discovering her mistake, set all sail to escape.
The stranger was the British frigate *Doris*, 36, Captain Richard
Harrison Pearson, and she at once fired a shot wide of the *Affronteur*
to bring her to.   Gaining fast upon the lugger, the frigate fired
a second shot, and a running fight began which could, from the
disproportion of the combatants, have but one issue.   The *Doris*
drew alongside of the *Affronteur*, engaged her closely and compelled
her to strike, after a singularly gallant resistance.   The French loss
out of a very small crew was heavy.   Lieutenant Duthoya and 8,
or, according to Chevalier, 11, men were killed and 14 others were
wounded, 1 mortally.   The *Doris* had only 1 man wounded and
some slight injuries to her rigging.   Next day the French brig
Jeanne,[1] on her way from Brest to Quimper, was chased by two
British frigates.   She took refuge under a battery, the guns of
which her crew manned, but the British boats promptly cut her out
and carried her off.   A *chasse marée*, laden with salt, was also
seized near Brest.[2]

These incidents, and the embargo laid upon French and Dutch
shipping by the British Government, led Napoleon to the extreme
and unprecedented measure of detaining in France all the British
residents upon whom he could lay his hands.   Amongst them were
included certain members of the British Embassy in Paris.   The
measure was justified by Napoleon as an act of reprisal, but the
recall of Lord Whitworth, Ambassador in Paris, six days before the
capture of the *Affronteur*, had been by common usage equivalent to
an intimation that a state of war existed.   The issue of a formal
declaration of war all through the eighteenth century had been
commonly preceded by acts of hostility, and France in this respect
was just as great a sinner as England.[3]   Napoleon himself afterwards confessed that his conduct in this matter had savoured of
the pirate.   His action only exasperated British opinion, and did
him no good.

On May 28th, the British 74's, *Minotaur*, Captain Charles John

---

[1] Apparently not belonging to the French navy.

[2] 'Blockade of Brest' (Nav. Rec. Soc.), i. 11, 14; Browning: 'England and Napoleon in 1803,' 240; Chevalier, iii. 82; James (ed. 1837), iii. 186.

[3] Hall: 'International Law,' 378–9.   Snow: 'International Law,' 84.

Moore Mansfield, *Albion*, and *Thunderer*, of the Channel fleet, chased and captured the French frigate *Franchise*, 40, Captain Jurien.[1]   The *Franchise* was on her way home from the disastrous San Domingo expedition, and was in no condition to offer any resistance to this overwhelming force.   Of her guns, ten were in her hold ; and her crew numbered only 187.   She was conducted to England by her captors, and was subsequently purchased for the Navy, where she retained her old name, but was rated as a 36.   On the 29th, the *Naiad*, 38, Captain James Wallis (1), captured the French corvette *Impatiente*, 10, Lieutenant Arnous, in the Bay of Biscay, on her way home to Rochefort from Sénégal.   The *Impatiente*, according to Captain Wallis's despatch, was considered one of the fastest sailers in the French fleet.[2]   During the chase, the French crew cut away her anchors and threw several of her guns overboard.

On June 18th, the French corvette *Colombe*, 16, Lieutenant Caro, returning to France from Martinique, fell in off Ushant with the British ships *Dragon*, 74, Captain John Aylmer, and *Endymion*, 44, Captain the Hon. Charles Paget.   The *Colombe* had left all her guns in San Domingo, and was compelled to strike without offering any resistance.[3]   On the 25th, the *Doris* captured and scuttled the Nantes privateer *Pélagie*, which was on a cruise, but had made no prizes.

On the same day (June 25th), the *Endymion* fell in with the French corvette *Bacchante*, 18, Lieutenant F. L. Kerimel, then on her way home from San Domingo.[4]   The *Bacchante* gave a good deal of trouble.   She was chased for eight hours, and exchanged fire with the British frigate before she struck.   The *Endymion's* bow guns killed 1 French lieutenant and 7 men, besides wounding 9 others.   The *Bacchante's* fire did the British ship no harm.   The prize was a large and fine vessel, quite new and a fast sailer, with a crew of 200 men.   She had been sent out to San Domingo with despatches.   She was purchased for the Navy, and was rated as a 20-gun ship, seeing that she was superior in tonnage to the general run of vessels of that class in the British service.

---

[1] James, iii. 186 ; Troude, iii. 285 ; 'Blockade of B.,' 23.

[2] Troude gives her 6 guns and calls her a brig (iii. 285) ; Captain Wallis ('Blockade of B.,' i. 26) gives her 10 guns.   James does not notice this or the following capture.

[3] Troude, iii. 286 ; 'Blockade of B.,' i. 40.

[4] 'Blockade of B.,' i. 51–2 ; Troude, iii. 286.

Two days later, the boats of the *Loire*, 38, Captain Frederick
Lewis Maitland (2), were despatched to cut out the French brig
Venteux, 10, Lieutenant Montfort, which was lying under the shelter
of a battery on the Ile de Batz.[1] The boats, three in number, were
commanded by Lieutenants Francis Temple and James Bowen (2).
One of the three failed to arrive. The other two dashed at the brig,
which was found fully prepared ; but, nevertheless, they boarded her,
and carried her after a brief struggle. The French loss was 1 officer
and 2 seamen killed, and Lieutenant Montfort, 4 officers, and 8 men
wounded. The British loss was only 6 wounded. It appears from
a letter of the Prefect of Brest that the battery did not fire a shot,
Its guns were mounted on rotten carriages, and the troops in charge
—there were only 7 artillerymen and 70 infantry—did not know how
to handle their weapons. For two hours after her capture, the brig
remained within range.

On June 28th, the *Cumberland*, 74, Captain Henry William
Bayntun, *Goliath*, 74, Captain Charles Brisbane, and *Hercule*, 74,
Lieutenant John B—— Hills (actg.-Captain), discovered inshore,
near Cape Nicolas Mole, two French vessels. These were the
Poursuivante, 44, Captain J. B. P. Willaumez, and *Mignonne*, 16,
Lieutenant Bargeau, both on their way from Aux Cayes to Cape
Nicolas, with crews weakened by the climate. The *Mignonne* had
but ten guns on board, having landed six of her long 12-prs.
She was chased by the *Goliath*, which speedily overtook her, fired
a few shot at her, and obliged her to strike. She had on board
only 80 men and boys, and was taken somewhat by surprise, as this
was the first act of hostility on the part of the British against the
French forces off San Domingo. The *Mignonne* was a fast sailer,
and was purchased for the Navy.

Whilst the *Goliath* was securing the *Mignonne*, the *Hercule* had
been directed to turn her attention to the *Poursuivante*, the *Cumberland*, according to Troude, being in charge of a convoy, and having
apparently remained by it to protect it. The *Hercule* was not skilfully handled. The wind was very light, and the frigate had the
better of her in sailing qualities. The British ship added to her
mistakes by opening fire too soon. At length the two closed very
near the land ; and a short action followed, in which the frigate
managed to rake the ship of the line, but suffered severely herself.
Her masts and rigging were much damaged, and she lost 6 killed

---

[1] 'Blockade of B.,' i. 57 ; James, iii. 187 ; *Nav. Chron.* x. 157.

and 15 wounded. The *Hercule* was damaged in her rigging and had some men wounded. The action ended by her withdrawal— probably because of the proximity of shallow water. The *Poursuivante* escaped into St. Nicolas Mole. She must be esteemed very fortunate in escaping from an adversary of twice her weight of metal, possessing also all the advantage of stouter scantling. It is clear that she was skilfully handled. From Mole St. Nicolas she proceeded, as soon as she had repaired her injuries and the British cruisers had disappeared, to make her way home to Rochefort.[1]

On June 30th, the *Cumberland*, 74, Captain Henry William Bayntun, and *Vanguard*, 74, Captain James Walker (2), whilst cruising off St. Nicolas Mole, discovered a ship approaching the port. This was the French frigate *Créole*, 40, Captain J. M. P. Lebastard, with 530 French troops on board, but a crew greatly weakened by disease, as was almost invariably the case with French vessels in San Domingo waters, owing to the prevalence of yellow fever in the French expeditionary force. The British ships of the line gave chase, overhauled her, and compelled her to strike after firing a few shots. She was purchased for the Navy, but foundered on her way to England.[2]

On the night of July 2nd, the British frigate *Minerve*, 38, Captain Jahleel Brenton (2), one of the Guernsey squadron under the command of Rear-Admiral Sir James Saumarez, being stationed off Cherbourg to blockade that port, was so unfortunate, through the fault of a pilot, as to run aground upon one of the huge cones, filled with stones, which marked the first beginnings of the breakwater. She struck upon the westernmost cone, about a mile, or a little less, from Fort Liberté. As soon as she had struck, the fog lifted and showed her position to the enemy. Fort Liberté opened fire upon her, and the two gun-brigs, *Chiffon* and *Terrible*, got under way. Captain Brenton lowered and manned his boats, and despatched them to cut out a craft which lay under the batteries, and which was large enough to carry out his bower anchor. At the same time, the frigate's launch, with a carronade, was sent to engage the French gun-boats. The first of the British boats away was one commanded by Lieutenant the Hon. William Walpole, who, under a heavy fire, dashed at, and carried without assistance, a French lugger laden with stone. The lugger was taken alongside the *Minerve*. Up to that

---

[1] James, iii. 187; Troude, iii. 286; *Nav. Chron.* x. 334.
[2] James, iii. 188; Troude, 288; *Nav. Chron.* x. 333.

time, the *Chiffon* and *Terrible* had caused little trouble, as their commanders had expected the frigate to assail them. They at length, however, discovered her real situation, and at once took up positions on her bows, whence they could rake her. The lugger had to be veered clear of the frigate, and emptied of the stone which was on board; and this was slow and awkward work under a heavy fire. The moon had come out, so that the French were able to see their target clearly. The British crew, busy trying to save the ship, could make little or no reply, and then only from the guns on the forecastle, those on the main-deck having been run aft to lighten her. The lugger was repeatedly struck, and the carpenters were kept busy plugging the shot holes. At last, when, at about midnight, the bower anchor was ready on board the lugger, and when the latter had begun to warp, by means of a hawser attached to a kedge anchor, to the position where the anchor was to be dropped, the hawser was shot away. The boats, however, came to the lugger's help, and took her in tow; and the anchor was finally let go in its proper place. But the trials of the *Minerve* did not end there. The wind completely dropped towards the morning, leaving the frigate helpless. Despairing of saving her, Captain Brenton ordered the wounded to be placed in the lugger, and fires to be prepared, whilst he destroyed his papers and private signals. No sooner had this been done than the wind rose, rendering it possible to get the ship away. The wounded were returned to the cock-pit: under a heavy fire which killed or wounded several men at the capstan, the crew hove in upon the bower anchor; and at length, at about 5 A.M. on the 3rd, their persevering efforts were rewarded by the floating of the *Minerve*. But just as all were congratulating themselves upon their escape, the wind fell once more; and the inset of the tide carried the frigate into the harbour and laid her upon a cone. There she remained under a heavy fire till six, when, seeing that the position was hopeless, Brenton struck his flag. The *Minerve's* loss was 11 killed and 16 wounded. All her masts were much injured.

Brenton, perhaps indignant at the fact that the *Chiffon* and *Terrible* claimed the whole credit of the success, wrote to the officer commanding the French troops at Cherbourg, that he had handed his sword to the captain of the *Chiffon*, but that the fire of Fort Liberté had been the determining cause of his surrender. This started a pretty quarrel between the French navy and army.

According to the navy, there were only three guns in Fort Liberté; and those soon ceased firing and waited for daylight, finding the range too great—it is variously given at from 1338 to 2338 metres, whilst the point-blank range of the French 36-pr. was only 779 metres. According to the army, the *Minerve* was "excessively annoyed by the well-served artillery of the fort." British accounts give Fort Liberté 70 guns and 15 mortars, so that the discrepancy in the stories is greater than usual. After this lapse of time, it cannot easily be determined who told the truth; but, at least, no discredit rests upon Captain Brenton and his crew, who did all that bravery and skill could do amid the most untoward circumstances. Brenton was kept a prisoner for thirty months; many of his men were confined for eleven years. Napoleon characteristically announced in Brussels that a "superb frigate of the enemy's has just surrendered to two of our gun-boats," suppressing all mention of the fact that the "superb frigate" was helplessly aground. The *Minerve*, upon being got off by the French, was nevertheless renamed *Canonnière*, in honour of her supposed captors. The force of the French gun-boats is uncertain. Each probably mounted three 24-prs. and two 36-pr. carronades.[1]

On the night of July 4th, the boats of the *Naiad*, 38, Captain James Wallis (1), watching the Passage du Raz, were despatched to cut out the French schooner *Providence*, 2, which was lying amongst the rocks of Ile de Seins. Led by Lieutenants William Dean, and John Louis, R.N., and Robert Irwin, R.M., and three Midshipmen, they brought her off, notwithstanding the impetuous currents, the shoals, and the fact that their quarry had been made fast to the shore. She proved to be a very valuable prize, as she was laden with twenty-eight French 36-, 24-, and 18-prs., and with a quantity of ship timber. The maritime prefect of Brest complained that her crew neither defended her nor set her on fire. The British suffered no loss.[2]

On July 7th, the French brig *Alcion*, 16, Lieutenant Lacuée, was chased by the British frigate *Narcissus*, 36, Captain Ross Donnelly, off the west of Sardinia. The *Alcion* in vain attempted to shake her pursuer off, was overtaken, and at 2 A.M. on the 8th, after returning a few shots, struck her flag. She was apparently on her way back to Toulon from Alexandria, ignorant that war had

---

[1] Brenton (ed. 1837), i. 596; Troude, 288; James, iii. 189; C. M., Feb. 7, 1807.
[2] 'Blockade of B.,' i. 67; James, iii. 191.

broken out. As she was a fine vessel of her class, prodigiously fast, she was purchased for the Navy as the *Halcyon*.[1]

On July 11th, the *Racoon* (two 6-prs., and sixteen 18-pr. carronades), Commander Austin Bissell, whilst cruising between the islands of Gonave and San Domingo, discovered the French corvette *Lodi*, 10 (6-prs.), Lieutenant P. I. Taupier, at anchor off Léogane, with springs on her cables. The *Racoon* closed to three hundred yards, anchored with springs, and opened fire. After half-an-hour of this, the *Lodi* cut her cable, and attempted to make off, but the *Racoon* followed her closely, and speedily compelled her to strike. The *Lodi* lost 1 killed and 14 wounded; the *Racoon* only 1 wounded.[2]

Amongst the French ships blockaded in the harbour of Cap François, San Domingo, were the *Duguay Trouin*, 74, Captain P. L'Hermite, *Duquesne*, 74, flying the broad pennant of Commodore P. M. J. Querengal, and *Guerrière*, 40, Captain L. A. Baudoin, forming part of the command of Rear-Admiral Latouche-Tréville. Peremptory orders had arrived from France directing that all the ships should be sent home; and accordingly, during a violent squall on the afternoon of July 24th, the above-mentioned vessels put to sea, the British squadron, commanded by Commodore John Loring, having been driven to some distance from the harbour by the weather. When, however, the French ships cleared the harbour, they were seen and chased by several of Loring's vessels, including the 74's, *Bellerophon*, with the Commodore's broad pennant, *Elephant*, Captain George Dundas, *Theseus*, Captain John Bligh (2), and *Vanguard*, Captain James Walker (2), with the frigates, *Æolus*, 32, Captain Andrew Fitzherbert Evans, and *Tartar*, 32, Captain John Perkins.[3] As darkness came on, the French ships separated, the *Duguay Trouin* standing to the east, and the *Duquesne* to the west, the latter intending to regain the harbour. The *Elephant* followed the *Duguay Trouin*, the *Bellerophon, Æolus*, and *Tartar*, the *Duquesne*. The latter group of ships was joined at midnight by the *Theseus* and *Vanguard*. The *Duquesne* was prevented by the lightness of the wind—the weather having abated—from making the harbour, and was compelled to follow the coast, annoyed the while by the distant fire of the *Tartar*. A Haytian battery also opened on

[1] Troude, 291; Nicolas, 'Nelson Despatches,' v. 155; *Nav. Chron.*, x. 423.

[2] James, iii. 193; Troude, 291.

[3] *See* Vol. IV. 471 n.

the Frenchman as he passed, and received his fire in return. At 2.45 P.M. on the 25th, the *Vanguard* and *Tartar* were close enough to attack with effect. The *Duquesne*, luffing to avoid being raked by the *Vanguard*, found herself surrounded by British ships. The *Bellerophon* and *Æolus* were within gunshot of her; the *Cumberland*, 74, Captain Henry William Bayntun, was also coming up; and the *Tartar*, on her starboard quarter, and the *Vanguard*, just astern, maintained a heavy fire on her. Her own crew was physically and numerically weak, by reason of disease. According to Troude, she had not a man for her 18-pr. battery, or for her quarter-deck and forecastle guns. The only weapons manned were twelve of her 36-prs. on the lower deck. Unable to offer any effective resistance to such odds, she struck her flag, when some fifteen miles to the east of Cape Maysi. A certificate given to her captain by Latouche-Tréville, when she was ordered out, shows that her whole crew numbered only 275, of whom 60 or more were either in sick-bay or just recovering. In this total were none of the most important ratings, such as carpenters and sail-makers. Her decks were crowded with wounded or sick passengers. Altogether, she was in no condition to resist an enemy. She was added to the British Navy under her own name. In the British squadron, the *Vanguard* had 1 killed and 1 wounded.[1]

While the *Duquesne* was thus being run to earth, the *Duguay Trouin* had stood to the east; and at daylight of the 25th she found the *Elephant* close upon her. The Frenchman opened with his stern-chasers, and the British ship drew up on the starboard quarter and maintained a long range fire, until the *Guerrière* came into view, when the *Elephant* retired. In failing to push his attack home, Dundas made a great mistake. All the French ships at San Domingo were sickly, and wanted proper crews. Moreover, the *Duguay Trouin* had some time previously grounded at Jérémie, and had thrown twenty of her guns overboard before she could get off. These had never been replaced. A well-found British 74 should have been fully a match, under such conditions, for both the *Duguay Trouin* and the *Guerrière*. The *Elephant* might have had the assistance of the British sloop *Snake*, 18, which was within sight. Captain L'Hermite was, naturally enough, only too pleased to get away under such circumstances, and made no attempt to

[1] James, iii. 192; Troude, 291; 'B. of Brest,' i. 139, 143, 158; Logs of *Elephant* and *Tartar*.

pursue the *Elephant*. By the afternoon, the French ships had the sea to themselves.[1]

They steered direct for Europe, and sighted no other ship till August 29th, when, 140 leagues W.N.W. of Cape Ortegal, they fell in with the *Boadicea*, 38, Captain John Maitland (2), cruising in the Bay. The *Boadicea*, though alone, and much smaller and weaker than either of the French ships, boldly gave chase. The weather was thick, and night came on, but she persisted in her pursuit till 3 P.M. of the 30th, when she made out the *Duguay Trouin* to be a large ship of the line, and the *Guerrière* a large frigate. The French vessels then altered course and chased their daring enemy, exchanging fire with her. After two hours, however, the British frigate succeeded in shaking off their pursuit. The *Boadicea* sustained some slight injury in her sails and rigging, but she hulled the *Duguay Trouin* several times, and seems to have damaged that ship's fore topsail, since, after the action, the French were seen unbending it. The *Boadicea* then proceeded to Ferrol to warn Sir Robert Calder's squadron of the proximity of the French ships.[2]

On September 2nd, at 4 A.M., Calder, in the *Prince of Wales*, 98, whilst running in for Cape Ortegal, sighted the *Duguay Trouin* and the *Guerrière*. They immediately headed for Corunna; and Sir Edward Pellew's squadron, which was watching Ferrol, got under full sail and endeavoured to cut them off. The wind, however, was so strong in favour of the French that they escaped, after a hot chase by the *Culloden*, 74, Captain Barrington Dacres, and the *Tonnant*, 80, Captain Sir Edward Pellew. The *Culloden* alone got close enough to open fire. At about 11.50 A.M. she attacked the *Duguay Trouin*, and, a little later, the *Guerrière*. The *Tonnant's* main topgallant tie carried away and her jib split, which kept her behind the *Culloden*. The *Duguay Trouin* was the first to reach Corunna. The *Culloden* maintained her pursuit of the *Guerrière*, firing steadily the while, till, at 12.10 P.M., Calder made the signal to discontinue action, the British ships being at that time close to the neutral Spanish waters. The *Tonnant*, indeed, appears to have actually entered Spanish waters, as a Spanish fort fired at her. The *Culloden's* casualties were four men wounded. The *Duguay Trouin* seems to have come out of this second encounter with the British without loss or injury;

---

[1] James, iii. 192.
[2] 'Blockade of Brest,' 158; James, iii. 192; Marshall, i. 843.

but the *Guerrière*, according to information received by a British officer visiting Corunna, had 5 or 6 men killed, about 17 wounded, and her masts and yards crippled. Troude adds that her fore mast and mizen mast were so damaged as to be rendered unserviceable, and that amongst the wounded was Captain Baudoin.[1]

On July 26th, the *Thunderer*, 74, Captain William Bedford, whilst blockading Lorient, was approached by a vessel which asked if she was English, and, upon receiving an affirmative reply, let go a broadside. This only cut a few of the *Thunderer's* ropes; and the 74 at once gave chase to the stranger. Overtaking her, and firing a broadside, she compelled her to strike. The strange ship was the *Vénus*, 16, a Bordeaux privateer, manned by 150 men. She was a new and very fast ship.[2]

On July 27th, the *Egyptienne*, 40, Captain the Hon. Charles Elphinstone Fleeming, captured the French brig *Epervier*, 16, on her way from Guadeloupe to Lorient. This capture excited unusual interest, as Jérome Bonaparte was supposed to be on board her. He had commanded her; and, when she was taken, a careful search was made for him, it being thought that he might be concealed amongst her crew. It afterwards turned out that he had sailed for Europe in the American ship *President*, and had thus eluded his would-be captors. The *Epervier* had despatches on board, and, being a fine vessel of her class, was purchased into the Navy, and rated as a 14-gun brig.[3]

On the 27th, the *Plantagenet*, 74, Captain Graham Eden Hamond, a ship without a poop, and for that reason, as her force could not easily be perceived by the enemy, detached to cruise in the Bay, fell in with the British sloop *Rosario*, 10, Commander William Mounsey, in chase of an enemy. The *Rosario*, during the afternoon, got very close to the chase, but was then disabled by her fore mast being shot away. The *Plantagenet* took up the pursuit, and, by 8 P.M., came up with the chase and compelled her to strike. The enemy proved to be the *Atalante*, 22, a Bordeaux privateer, and remarkably fast. She had taken nothing on her cruise, and when captured had only fourteen guns on board, the others having been thrown overboard during the pursuit.[4]

---

[1] Troude, 292; James, iii. 193; 'Blockade of B.,' i. 139.

[2] 'Blockade of B.,' i. 118.

[3] 'Blockade of B.,' i. 102, 110, 149.

[4] 'Blockade of B.,' i. 105, 108; *Nav. Chron.*, x. 254; the *Atalante* took the *Plantagenet* for an East Indiaman.

On August 14th, the French frigate *Poursuivante*, 44, Captain J. B. P. Willaumez, on her way home to France from Mole St. Nicolas, came up with the British Liverpool merchantman *Juno*, 18, Lutwidge Affleck, master, 200 miles from Wilmington. Affleck had a crew weak in numbers, and an armament which was ludicrously inferior to that of the French frigate. But, worthy of the fighting names he bore, and, as he says, "knowing that I had a set of the bravest fellows that ever swam salt water," he "was deter-mined to defend the ship to the last extremity." Accordingly, he fought his enemy for two hours, when with 2 men killed, his mate wounded, and hull, sails, and rigging, much shattered, he struck. Captain Willaumez returned him his sword, and received him with all the courtesy due to a gallant opponent.[1] The *Juno* was so damaged that the *Poursuivante* took her into Charleston, intending to repair her there. This was forbidden by the American authorities, and the prize had to be burnt. Affleck was presented with 120 guineas for his valiant resistance.

On August 14th, the British East Indiaman *Lord Nelson*, 26 (twenty long 18's, and six long 12-prs.), Robert Spottiswoode, master, with a crew of 102, was attacked to the west of Brest by the French privateer *Bellone*, 34, with a crew of 260 men. The French vessel had much the lighter battery—twenty-four of her guns were only long 8-prs.—but, closing after a sharp action, she boarded, and brought her superiority of men into play. The *Lord Nelson* was carried, after the *Bellone* had been once repulsed, with a loss to the British of 5 killed and 31 wounded. A prize crew of 41 men, was placed on board the capture, and, in company with her, the *Bellone* proceeded towards Corunna. On the way, a British frigate gave chase, but was drawn off by the *Bellone*. When the *Lord Nelson* had thus been left to herself, the gallant little Plymouth privateer *Thomas and John*, of only fourteen 6-prs., made an attempt to retake her. For one hour this craft fought, but was then forced to clear off. Next a hired cutter dogged the *Lord Nelson* for a day, but did not molest her. On the 25th the *Seagull*, 18, Commander Henry Burke, sighted her, and, after five hours' chase, closed her at about 7 P.M. The two fought the whole night, but at 6 A.M. on the 26th, the *Seagull*, with her masts and rigging much cut up, and two shots between wind and water, was compelled to haul off for repairs. The *Lord*

---

[1] Williams, ' History of Liverpool Privateers,' 384.

Nelson, however, did not escape. Burke had refitted, and was just bearing down to renew the attack, when Sir Edward Pellew's squadron of four sail of the line hove in sight. The *Lord Nelson* then struck her colours to the *Seagull*. The British loss was 2 killed and 8 wounded. Pellew writes that "the effects of Captain Burke's vigorous assaults are so evident on the *Lord Nelson*, and the comparative size and force of the ship he engaged are so manifest, as to strike the beholder with the highest admiration." [1]

On August 17th, the *Racoon*, 16, Commander Austin Bissell, cruising off Santiago de Cuba, sighted a brig and a schooner whose movements were suspicious. In the afternoon, she succeeded in closing the brig and engaging her, whereupon her adversary ran ashore and struck her colours. The *Racoon* wore and stood out to avoid grounding, and the French colours were rehoisted. Thereupon, the British vessel stood on and off, firing at her, till she brought down the Frenchman's main mast. The *Racoon* was so weakly, and the enemy, by all appearances, so strongly manned, that Bissell thought it inexpedient to send in his boats and burn her. The French vessel, however, became a perfect wreck. She was believed to be the *Mutine*, a brig of 18 guns, but all particulars of her must be doubtful. [2]

On the morning of September 9th the *Sheerness*, cutter, 8, Lieutenant Henry Rowed, cruising with the inshore squadron off the Brest Goulet, observed two French *chasse-marées* on the southern side of Douarnenez Bay. She at once gave chase, and, after an hour's pursuit, the leewardmost of the French vessels ran ashore to the east of Pointe du Raz. The Mate and seven seamen were despatched with the largest of the cutter's boats to bring her off; and they succeeded in this, as the crew of the *chasse-marée* fled ashore on the boat's approach, and only kept up a weak musketry fire, which did no one any harm. The cutter waited till the success of her boat was assured and then pushed on after the other *chasse-marée*. At 10 A.M. the weather fell calm. The *chasse-marée* was still about four miles from the *Sheerness*, and was, with the use of her sweeps, drawing steadily inshore. Rowed, under these circumstances, arrived at the amazingly daring determination of pursuing her with his skiff, which would only hold five men. Mr. John Marks, the Boatswain, and three men at once volunteered

---

[1] 'Blockade of B.,' i. 137; *Nav. Chron.*, x. 259, 260; James, iii. 196.
[2] James, iii. 194; *Nav. Chron.*, xi. 239.

to accompany him. The skiff pushed off, and, after a couple of hours' hard rowing, the British seamen saw their quarry run ashore under a battery near Audierne, while a number of French soldiers hurried towards her along the beach. Nevertheless, the boat dashed up alongside and boarded. The French crew, after cutting the halyards, had bolted ashore, though supported by the musketry fire of nearly thirty French soldiers. This fire was maintained all the time that the British five were getting the *chasse-marée* off, but no one was hit. After taking the prize in tow and proceeding some little distance, Rowed perceived that a boat with ten French soldiers on board, armed with muskets, was chasing him. He immediately moved with his four men on board the *chasse-marée*, and showed such a bold front that the French boat dropped back, though she had been almost alongside. She fired a few ineffectual shots and then gave up the game. The battery, which was probably in much the same plight as those of the Ile de Batz, fired only two shots. Marks showed remarkable daring in this brilliant little affair. It is not particularly creditable to Cornwallis and the men at the head of the British Navy that Lieutenant Rowed was in no way officially rewarded for this singular piece of gallantry. He was, however, presented with £50 to buy a sword, and Marks with a silver call and chain, by the Committee of the then recently established Patriotic Fund.[1]

On September 20th the *Princess Augusta*, 8 (4-prs.), Lieutenant Isaac William Scott, one of the smallest cutters in His Majesty's service, with a crew of only twenty-six men, whilst off the Texel, was closed by two schooners. The larger of the two approached under British colours, but suddenly hauled them down and substituted the Dutch flag. At the same time she hailed the *Princess Augusta*, and, on receiving the British reply, discharged a broadside which killed the Gunner (William Lavender) and Boatswain (William Cornelius) and mortally wounded Lieutenant Scott. That officer, however, urged the Master, Mr. Joseph Thomas, to fight the ship to the last and to tell his Commander-in-Chief that he had done his duty. The *Princess Augusta*, though grievously overmatched, was brilliantly defended. She beat off several attempts of her two enemies to board, and finally repulsed them and escaped, with much

---

[1] 'Blockade of B.,' i. 147; James, iii. 197. Mr. Rowed was not made a Commander until June 15th, 1814; and he died, still in that rank, Jan. 6th, 1831. Marshall, iv. Part I., 218.

injury to her hull and rigging. In addition to the killed or mortally injured she had two men wounded. The Dutch schooners were the *Union*—according to British accounts, which probably exaggerated her force, of 12 guns and 70 men—and *Wraak* of 8 guns and 50 men. The *Wraak* had one man killed and several wounded.[1]

On October 9th, the *Atalante*, 16, Commander Joseph Ore Masefield, was directed by Captain Thomas Elphinstone of the *Diamond*, 38, cruising in Quiberon Bay, to give chase to two ketches and a brig close inshore. The *Atalante* accordingly stood after them and drove them into the Penerf Estuary, off which she waited till nightfall to cut them out. Two boats were then despatched, one under Lieutenant John Hawkins and the other under the Master, Richard Burstal. Hawkins boarded the innermost vessel, but found her aground and was very warmly received. A force of troops, with two field pieces, kept up a hot fire upon him from the beach, and he had to withdraw. He went to the assistance of the other boat, which had boarded the brig, in spite of the resistance of ten or twelve soldiers, of whom six were killed and two pitched overboard. The British party then cut the cable, but could not get the vessel off, she being aground. Nothing was, therefore, possible but retreat. The vessel was not set on fire, as there seemed to be wounded on board. Burstal, who showed exceptional gallantry, had 1 man killed and 2 men wounded.[2]

On October 13th, the indefatigable *Racoon*, 36, cruising off Guantanamo in Cuba, and still under Commander Austin Bissell, saw several vessels proceeding along the coast. On the 14th, she observed that they were becalmed, and stood towards them with a land wind behind her. She first closed a brig, which proved to be the *Petite Fille*; exchanged fire with her, and compelled her to strike. She next pushed on to a schooner and cutter, which had been firing at her. These vessels were crowded with troops, and attempted, but unsuccessfully, to board. The *Racoon* maintained a running fight with them, giving the cutter especial attention. At last, reduced to a complete wreck, the latter struck. She proved to be the *Amélie*, 4, with seventy troops on board. The schooner, which was the *Jeune Adèle*, 6, alone remained; and she was speedily disposed of and obliged to surrender. But in the meantime the French on board the *Petite Fille* had overpowered the

---

[1] James, iii. 199; *Nav. Chron.*, x. 420. De Jonge apparently overlooks the affair.
[2] 'Blockade of B.,' i. 167; James, iii. 199.

prize-crew and run the vessel ashore. The *Racoon's* arrival soon
put matters right, and the prize-crew was rescued. The British
loss was 1 wounded. The French loss is said to have been 40 on
board the schooner and cutter alone.[1]

On October 26th, the *Osprey*, 18, Commander George Younghusband, cruising off Trinidad, chased a suspicious sail. The
weather fell calm, and the stranger, using sweeps, drew away. On
this, three of the *Osprey's* boats were despatched under Lieutenant
Robert Henderson to secure the vessel. Henderson outstripped the
other boats, and, with only seventeen seamen, boarded and carried
the enemy, which proved to be the French privateer *Resource*,
four 4-prs. and forty-three men. The *Resource* had 2 killed and
12 wounded. Of the British, Henderson and four seamen were
wounded.[2]

On October 27th, the *Merlin*, 16, Commander Edward Pelham
Brenton, and *Milbrook*, 14, Lieutenant Mauritius Adolphus Newton
de Starck, observed the French lugger privateer *Sept Frères*
endeavouring to get into Calais. The *Milbrook* cut off her retreat;
and she ran ashore near Gravelines to escape the *Merlin's* boats.
The *Milbrook* then stood inshore, picked up the boats, and, in spite
of a heavy fire from the beach, destroyed the *Sept Frères*.[3]

On November 3rd, the *Blanche*, 36, Captain Zachary Mudge,
discovered the French cutter *Albion*[4] (two 4-prs., six swivels, forty-
three officers and men) lying under the guns of Monte Christi in the
island of San Domingo, with a cargo of cattle for Cape François.
Four of the *Blanche's* boats were thereupon despatched to capture
her, with sixty-three officers and men under Lieutenant William
Brathwaite. The attempt was badly ordered and managed. The
boats attempted to row in, in broad daylight, under the muzzles of
four 24-prs. and three field pieces mounted in the Monte Christi
battery; and the wind was blowing inshore, so that, even if the
cutter had been carried, she could not have been got out of the bay.
It was soon evident that nothing could be done without inordinate
and unnecessary waste of life. Brathwaite therefore retired.

A night attack was next determined on, and Lieutenant Edward
Nicolls, R.M., volunteered to lead it. On the 4th he set out with
only the cutter containing thirteen men. Such a force was quite

[1] James, iii. 195.
[2] James, iii. 200; *Nav. Chron.*, xi. 153; Marshall, Supp., Pt. I., 114.
[3] *Nav. Chron.*, x. 497; James, iii. 200.
[4] Apparently not a national vessel.

inadequate for the work; which fact seems to have struck Captain
Mudge very speedily, for he sent the barge with twenty-two men
under Lieutenant the Hon. Warwick Lake to follow, reinforce, and
supersede Nicolls. When the two boats were near the French
cutter, Lake insisted on rowing off in another direction, asserting
that the cutter was to be found there ; and Nicolls, left to himself,
rowed towards the *Albion*. The French were ready for him and
received him with two volleys, as his men with three hearty cheers
dashed in. Three men were wounded before he was able to board.
Then, followed by the other ten, he leapt into the cutter. The
French commander fired at him at the same moment, and the bullet
passed right round his stomach and lodged in his arm. The
Frenchman was at once shot ; and the *Albion* was carried. Her
loss was five wounded besides the commander killed. The battery
ashore opened fire, but Nicolls resorted to a most judicious
stratagem to stop its attack. He directed his men to discharge
their muskets vigorously as if the conflict on board were still
proceeding, anticipating that in that case the battery would hold
its fire. The cutter was just clearing the shore when Lake in his
boat arrived, stopped the firing, and, as the reward of his stupidity,
had two of his men killed. The cutter then ran out of gunshot.[1]

Captain Mudge added to the other mistakes which he made on
this occasion that of failing to draw attention to the splendid
courage of Nicolls. He did not mention the fact that that officer
had been wounded, and he gave Lake even more credit than the
other. James suggests that " Mudge had a favourite, whom he was
determined to serve, no matter at whose expense." In 1806, Lake
was made Commander, and in 1808 he was posted. He deserved no
such favours. He was a thoroughly worthless officer, and, in 1810,
was dismissed the service for having marooned a seaman on the
desert island of Sombrero.[2]

On the morning of the 4th, the *Blanche's* launch under Master's
Mate John Smith (10A)[3], had attacked and carried a privateer
schooner of one gun and thirty men. A day or two later a boat
of the same ship under Midshipman Edward Henry A'Court[4] with

---

[1] James, iii. 201.

[2] C. M., Feb. 5th and 6th, 1810; James, iv. 348.

[3] I ticket this officer as " John Smith (10A)," but I cannot certainly identify him,
or discover when, if ever, he was promoted.

[4] This officer in later life assumed the name of Repington. He died, a vice-
admiral on the retired list, in 1855.

eight men had boarded and captured a French schooner with over thirty French soldiers on board. A'Court had only five or six muskets among his men, as he had been sent to get sand, and when on such errands, to prevent rash enterprises, the seamen were not allowed to carry arms. The soldiers appear to have been seasick, which may explain a most astonishing affair.[1]

Whilst the *Blenheim*, 74, Captain Thomas Graves (4), was at anchor off Fort de France, Martinique, blockading the place, the news arrived that a peculiarly destructive French privateer, the *Harmonie*, was lying at the small port of Marin, near at hand. On November 16th, Graves proceeded to Marin, reconnoitred the place, and determined to cut out the *Harmonie*. Lieutenants Thomas Cole (1) and Thomas Furber, with sixty seamen, were to attack the privateer, whilst simultaneously Lieutenants George Beatty and Walter S. Boyd, with sixty Marines, assaulted a work on the east side of the harbour, known as Fort Dunquerque, which had to be carried to prevent the enemy from annoying the retreat of the boats engaged. As the expedition was pushing off, the *Drake*, 14, Commander William Ferris, and hired cutter *Swift* arrived. Ferris volunteered his services, and was directed to take charge of the seamen, adding fourteen from his sloop. The *Drake* towed the seamen's boats; the *Swift*, the Marines'. The seamen had to be given some start, as the privateer lay high up the harbour, whereas the battery was at the mouth. They passed the battery undiscovered, and, so admirable were the arrangements, attacked the *Harmonie* at the very moment when the Marines assaulted the work. The latter was surprised. Fifteen prisoners were taken, and nine guns spiked and dismounted; and the magazine was exploded, without the loss of a man. The seamen speedily made themselves masters of the *Harmonie* with the loss of only one killed and five wounded; but sixteen French on board, out of a crew of sixty-six, were killed or wounded, and some others were drowned. Everyone in this affair showed gallantry and good judgment.[2]

On November 24th, the *Boadicea*, 38, Captain John Maitland (2), captured off Finisterre the French lugger *Vautour*, 12, Lieutenant Bigot. The lugger was on her way home from San Domingo with despatches, and had during the chase thrown ten of her twelve guns overboard. She was a fast and fine vessel.[3]

---

[1] James, iii. 204; O'Byrne, 2.   [2] James, iii. 205; *Nav. Chron.*, xi. 157.
[3] *Nav. Chron.*, xi. 64.

On November 28th, the *Ardent*, 64, Captain Robert Winthrop, forming part of Pellew's squadron off Ferrol, chased the French *flûte, Bayonnaise*, 32 (six mounted), Captain Leblond-Plassan, on her way back from Havana to Ferrol. Despairing of escape, the French officer ran his ship ashore near Cape Finisterre, landed his crew, and set the *Bayonnaise* on fire. At midnight she blew up.[1]

On December 9th, the *Goliath*, 74, Captain Charles Brisbane, cruising off Sables d'Olonne, discovered a French convoy stealing along the coast. With nightfall she despatched two cutters under Lieutenant Bartholomew Kent (1), of the Marines. The convoy had the protection of formidable batteries at Sables d'Olonne; yet so bravely did the British attack under a heavy fire, that they drove several French vessels ashore, and recaptured a British brig of six guns which had been taken some days before by a French privateer. Kent and Lieutenant Joseph Langston, R.M., paid the penalty for their bravery, both being mortally wounded. Besides them, one Marine was mortally wounded. The *Goliath* next cruised in the Pertuis Breton, chasing a convoy and completely dispersing it, whilst at the same time she interrupted communication with Ile de Rhé.[2]

On December 10th, the *Shannon*, 36, Captain Edward Leveson Gower, in company with the *Merlin*, 16, Commander Edward Pelham Brenton, on a very dark and stormy night, was swept by the tide under the island of Tatihou, as she was making her way from Cape de La Hève to Cape La Hougue; and the *Shannon* ran fast aground. The *Merlin* saw the land by the light of a flash of lightning, and wore in time. The *Shannon's* crew was saved, but made prisoners. Some days later the *Merlin* approached the wreck, sent her boats in under a heavy fire, and set fire to the frigate without suffering any loss.[3]

On December 31st, the *Grappler*, 12, Lieutenant Abel Wantner Thomas, was wrecked on the Chausey Reefs. Thomas, attacked by a number of soldiers and sailors in fishing-boats, was severely wounded in the head and captured.[4]

To the south-west of Martinique lies the islet known by the name

---

[1] 'Blockade of B.,' i. 218; Troude, iii. 299.

[2] 'Blockade of B.,' i. 214–5, 242; *Nav. Chron.*, xi. 361; O'Byrne, 609.

[3] James, iii. 206; Troude, 306; Brenton, i. 603.

[4] Troude, 306; O'Byrne, 1167. Thomas received a pension in 1815. He had been made a Commander in 1814, and, retiring as a captain in 1851, he died in the same year.

of the Diamond Rock. It is roughly of the shape of a haystack, rising precipitously from the sea. The extreme height is 600 feet, the circumference about a mile, and the distance from Martinique three-quarters of a mile. On the south the cliffs fall almost sheer into the sea, and access is impossible. On the east and south-west are caves and overhanging rocks which prevent any landing from being effected in those quarters. Only from the west is access possible, and even there the risks are great. There are breakers to be confronted, and the rocks to be scaled are difficult. Working round high up to the north-west side a number of caves and grottoes are reached, offering excellent shelter. The island is thereabouts wooded and covered with vegetation.

As the rock offered excellent opportunities for annoying ships which, in spite of the British blockade, ran in and out of Fort Royal, it was seized in January, 1804, by a party of men from the *Centaur*, 74, Commodore Samuel Hood (2), Captain Murray Maxwell. At the base of the rock two batteries were constructed, each mounting a gun from the ship. In the Centaur battery was a 24-pr. fronting north-east; in the Queen's battery, another weapon of the same calibre on a centre-pivot carriage, commanding the entrance of the harbour. On a higher level, reached only by the aid of a rope ladder, was another 24-pr. in Hood's battery. Lastly, at the summit were placed two 18-prs. The guns were got up to the top by the ingenious method of carrying from the ship to the summit of the rock a hawser, along which, by means of a traveller, the guns and gun-carriages were hauled. Ammunition was taken up in the same manner, and Lieutenant James Wilkes Maurice,[1] with 120 men, took command of what was commissioned as the sloop-of-war *Diamond Rock*. There was one grave defect in the position. The water on the island was scanty and bad, so that the garrison had to be supplied from the ships. Tanks were constructed, however, to catch such rain as fell.[2]

On January 10th, the boats of the *Scourge*, 16, Commander William Wooldridge (1), cut out a captured British merchantman laden with naval stores, which lay under the Dutch batteries in the Vlie. She was carried off without the smallest loss, though she

[1] Born, 1775; Com., May 7th, 1804; Capt., Jan. 18th, 1809; retired r.-adm., Oct. 1st, 1846; died, 1857.

[2] James, iii. 242; *Nav. Chron.*, xii. 205. The taking of the Rock by the French has been described in the previous chapter, p. 106.

mounted eight guns. The *Scourge*, navigated by Wooldridge himself, against the advice of his pilot, worked her way into the intricate
and difficult Vlie, and supported her boats in the enterprise.[1]

Early in February, 1804, Commodore Hood determined that an
attempt should be made to cut out the *Curieux*, a fine French brig
of sixteen 6-prs. and 70 men, under the command of Commander[2]
J. M. E. Cordier, which was lying in the harbour of Fort Royal,
Martinique, under shelter of the guns of Fort Edouard, and was
nearly ready for sea. The French, anticipating such an attempt,
were prepared, as they said, to defy any force which could be sent
against them. Boarding nettings were triced up, guns and swivels
loaded with grape, numerous sentries posted, and the whole watch
kept under arms. On the night of February 3rd, four boats of the
Centaur, 74, with 60 seamen and 12 Marines, under Lieutenant
Robert Carthew Reynolds (2), delivered the attack after a hard pull
of twenty miles. There was a moon, and they were seen and hailed
by the Frenchmen long before they could close, and the *Curieux's*
guns were discharged, though with little effect. The British Marines,
as the boats rowed in, kept up a steady fire. The first boat, the
barge, found a rope ladder hanging over the *Curieux's* stern.
Reynolds climbed up it and cut away the boarding netting, whereupon the British seamen poured on board and began a hand-to-hand
struggle with the French. The officers especially offered a most
determined resistance, but, indifferently supported by their men,
they were speedily flung below, and wounded or killed. The *Curieux's*
cables were then cut and the vessel was got under way, under a
smart fire from the French batteries, which did, however, no
damage. The British loss was 3 officers and 6 seamen wounded,
the gallant Reynolds mortally, and Lieutenant Edmund Byron
Bettesworth and Midshipman John Tracy slightly. Reynolds received no fewer than five wounds. Among the French the havoc
was greater. Cordier was thrown overboard and seriously injured ;
his first lieutenant had three wounds ; and an *enseigne de vaisseau*,
4 midshipmen, the carpenter and gunner, and 30 men, were killed
or wounded. So many were the wounded that Hood sent them in
the *Curieux*, as a cartel-ship, to Fort Royal. On the *Curieux's*
return, Reynolds[3] was given command of her, but, disabled by his

---

[1] *Nav. Chron.*, xi. 159.   [2] 'Capitaine de frégate.'

[3] Robert Carthew Reynolds (2) was a son of the R.-Adm. Robert Carthew Reynolds (1) who perished in the *St. George* in 1811, and a brother of V.-Adm. Sir Barrington Reynolds. He lingered until early in Sept., 1804, when he died.

wounds, was succeeded by Bettesworth, who some months later was
to carry home the news of Villeneuve's return to Europe in the
Trafalgar campaign.   One French account reckoned the British
boarding party at 225, and asserted that the weather was dark and
that the *Curieux* was surprised.   This, however, was contradicted
by the gallant Cordier when he recovered.[1]

On February 5th, the British schooner *Eclair*, 12 (18-pr. carronades), Lieutenant William Carr, to the north of Tortola, chased and

SIR NATHANIEL DANCE, KT., H. E. I. CO.'S SERVICE.
(From Fittler's engraving, after a drawing by Geo. Dance, R.A.)

closed the French privateer *Grand Décidé*, 22 (8-prs.), M. Gory,
master.   The *Grand Décidé* showed no desire to shirk battle, and at
about 4.30 P.M. the two vessels engaged within pistol-shot. After
three-quarters of an hour's hot fighting, the Frenchman had had
enough, and made all sail. He was at once pursued by the *Eclair*, but
the British vessel was unable to overhaul him. As the *Grand Décidé*
carried about 220 men to the British schooner's 60, and as she was

[1] James, iii. 243; *Nav. Chron.*, xii. 65, 380; O'Byrne, 967.

far better armed, her retreat was decidedly discreditable, even for a privateer, though it should be remembered that craft which preyed upon trade had nothing to gain, except hard knocks, by assailing men of-war. The British loss was 1 killed and 4 wounded. A great part of the *Eclair's* standing and running rigging was shot away, and the masts and yards were much damaged.[1]

During January and early February, the French Rear-Admiral Comte C. A. L. D. de Linois's squadron, consisting of the *Marengo*, 74, flagship, Captain J. M. Vrignault, *Belle Poule*, 40, Captain A. A. M. Bruilhac, *Sémillante*, 36, Captain L. B. Motard, *Berceau*, 22, Commander E. Halgan, and the Dutch brig *Avonturier*, 16, borrowed at Batavia by Linois, cruised at the eastern entrance of the Straits of Malacca, waiting for the rich British convoy of East Indiamen which usually left Canton at the beginning of the year. On February 14th this convoy came in sight, and the French observed that sixteen vessels[2] were ranged in line of battle. The leading ship was the *Earl Camden*, Nathaniel Dance,[3] senior officer of the squadron. All were regular East Indiamen of large size—in tonnage, each equal or superior to a 64-gun ship of the line. With them were twelve country ships, two merchantmen, and the Company's armed brig *Ganges*. At that date, it should be remembered, merchantmen were generally armed. The regular East Indiamen, in fact, each carried from thirty to thirty-six guns, chiefly "medium" 18-prs.,

---

[1] James, iii. 246; *Nav. Chron.*, xii. 66.

[2]

H. E. I. Co.'s Ships.	Master.
Earl Camden	Nathaniel Dance.
Warley	Henry Wilson.
Alfred	James Farquharson.
Royal George . . .	John Fam. Timins.
Coutts	Robert Torin.
Wexford	William Stanley Clarke.
Ganges	William Moffat.
Exeter	Henry Meriton.
Earl of Abergavenny .	John Wordsworth.
Henry Addington . .	John Kirkpatrick.
Bombay Castle . . .	Archibald Hamilton.
Cumberland . . .	William Ward Farrer.
Hope	James Pendergrass.
Dorsetshire . . .	Robert Hunter Brown.
Warren Hastings . .	Thomas Larkins.
Ocean	John Christopher Lochner (actg.).

The country ships were *Lord Castlereagh, Carron, David Scott, Minerva, Ardeseer, Charlotte, Friendship, Shaw, Kissataw, Tahaungeer, Gilwall,* and *Neptune*.

[3] Nathaniel Dance, born in London 1748; entered E. I. Co.'s service, 1759; obtained his first command, 1787; Kt., 1805.

midway between the gun and the carronade, and ordinary 18-pr. carronades, or long 12's and 6's. This did not make them a match for men-of-war of even their own number of guns, since their crews and scantlings were weak, and their decks naturally much encumbered. These particular ships had, however, been newly painted, which, with their two decks, gave them the appearance of men-of-war.

As soon as the French ships were sighted, Dance directed the *Alfred*, *Royal George*, and *Hope*, with the *Ganges*, brig, in which Lieutenant Robert Merrick Fowler, R.N., was a volunteer, to reconnoitre and ascertain who they were. Dance was speedily informed of the truth, and made all his dispositions—not for retreat, but for battle. His sixteen East Indiamen formed in line; the other vessels were stationed under their lee. Linois, instead of at once pushing home a reconnaissance and ascertaining the character of the sixteen vessels in line, was filled with vague alarm at the fact that the convoy numbered thirty-one sail instead of twenty-four, as he had expected, and fancied that he could distinguish three ships of the line amongst the East Indiamen. He kept away, collecting his ships; and he informed his captains that he did not care to risk a night action, but would attack next day. It would appear that his real object in delaying was to ascertain whether the British vessels would employ the hours of darkness in attempts to get away from him. He argued that if they were all merchantmen, such would certainly be their course. Dance, however, acted with singular judgment and daring. Noting, doubtless, the shyness of the enemy, he lay-to all night, and three of his ships showed their lights, as if challenging battle. With morning, these three and the brig hoisted blue ensigns, and the others red; which more and more confirmed Linois in his belief that he had to deal with at least four warships. He might, one would think, have reasoned that three British two-deckers, of at least 64 guns apiece, would not hesitate to attack one French 74, and four frigates or smaller vessels, even though placed in charge of a most valuable convoy. He was to windward; and, when it was seen by Dance that he did not bear down, the British convoy, in excellent order, headed south, continuing on its course, under easy sail. The movement seems to have given Linois fresh confidence, and he at last approached the rear of the convoy.

Dance thereupon gave the order to tack in succession and engage the enemy. The movement was well executed, the *Royal George* leading, followed by the *Ganges* and *Earl Camden.* All the British vessels crowded sail and attempted to get into action. Linois then feared that the British, with superior force, were manœuvring to place him between two lines. His ships were formed in very close order, and moved towards the *Royal George* and her sisters, opening upon them a fire, which was not returned till the British closed. Before the vessels astern of the *Earl Camden* could get near enough to support their leaders, the French hauled their wind and retired ignominiously to the east under all the sail they could spread. Dance signalled a general chase, and from 2 P.M. to 4 P.M. the East Indiamen pursued their enemy, till at last, fearing to be carried too far from the mouth of the Straits of Malacca, he tacked.   On

MEDAL COMMEMORATING THE SETTLEMENT OF BOMBAY, AND DANCE'S
ACTION WITH M. DE LINOIS.

(*From an original lent by H.S.H. Capt. Prince Louis of Battenberg, R.N., G.C.B.*)

February 28th, the convoy picked up the British 74's, *Albion* and *Sceptre,* which saw it safe to St. Helena.

The British loss was insignificant. The *Royal George* was the most hotly engaged, and lost 1 killed and 1 wounded. She had many shot in her hull, and was fought splendidly. The courage and skill of Dance were honoured, as they deserved, upon his arrival in England. He was knighted, and received a sword of honour, and the usual services of plate and sums of money which were presented to merchant officers who had saved their ships. A sum of £50,000 was distributed among the officers and crews by the East India Company.

"Admiral Linois," says the French historian Chevalier, "would have certainly made himself master, if not of the whole convoy, at

least of the greater part, had he determined to attack." His timidity
and want of enterprise threw away a great opportunity. Napoleon
was justly indignant with his admiral. "All the enterprises at sea,"
he wrote to Decrès, the Minister of Marine, who had defended
Linois, "which have been undertaken since I became the head of
the Government have missed fire because my admirals see double,
and have discovered, I know not how or where, that war can be
made without running risks . . . Tell Linois that he has shown
want of courage of mind, that kind of courage which I consider
the highest quality in a leader." The Emperor's judgment was
severe, but not, on the whole, unfair.[1]

It is extraordinary that such a valuable convoy as Dance's—it
was estimated to be worth £8,000,000—should have been hazarded
without any proper escort.

On the night of February 19th, the boats of the *Drake*, 14,
Lieutenant William King (1) (actg.), attempted to cut out three
vessels from the harbour of Trinité, in Martinique. Led by Lieutenant William Cumpston, the seamen carried the craft, but, having
no wind, could not bring them off. On the night of the 24th,
Lieutenant King landed with a party of thirty men, and stormed a
battery which commanded the anchorage, spiking five guns. The
loss was one man mortally, and Lieutenant Cumpston and one other
man slightly wounded.[2]

The boats of the *Blenheim*, 74, Captain William Ferris, on the
night of March 4th, attempted to cut out the French schooner
Curieuse from St. Pierre harbour, Martinique. The cutting-out
party was fifty strong, under Lieutenant Thomas Furber. The
schooner was found to be fully prepared. Boarding-nets, well triced
up, prevented the British from getting into her; and she was secured
with chains to the shore, and supported by a heavy fire from guns
and troops on the beach. The British party cut the cables, but was
then compelled to retreat with 3 killed, 19 wounded (including
Furber), and 3 missing—or nearly half its strength *hors de combat*.[3]

On March 5th, the *Eclair*, 12, Lieutenant William Carr, chased
the French privateer-schooner *Rose* into Deshaies, Guadeloupe. In
the evening, the cutter was sent in, under the orders of Mr. John

---

[1] *Nav. Chron.*, xii. 137, 345 ; James, iii. 247 ; Troude, iii. 311 ; Chevalier, iii. 295 ;
Hardy, 'Register of E. I. Co.'s Ships' (1811), App., 119.

[2] *Nav. Chron.*, xii. 68 ; James, iii. 252.

[3] *Nav. Chron.*, xii. 68 ; James, iii. 252 ; O'Byrne, 383.

Salmon, the Master, with the Surgeon and ten men, to bring her out. The privateer opened fire as soon as the boat entered the harbour, but was boarded and carried off, though she is said to have had 49 men in her, though batteries on shore fired vigorously at the British, and though there was no wind, so that she had to be towed and rowed off to the *Eclair*. The British suffered no loss; the French had 15 killed or wounded.[1]

On March 13th, Lieutenant Thomas Forrest, with thirty volunteers from the *Emerald*, 36, Captain James O'Bryen,[2] proceeded in the *Fort Diamond*, armed sloop, to capture the French privateer *Mosambique*, 10, which had taken shelter under a battery at Seron, near St. Pierre, Martinique. At the same time, the boats of the *Emerald* and those of the *Pandour*, 44, were despatched in another direction to divert attention. The *Fort Diamond* laid herself alongside the privateer, in so doing breaking a chain by which the latter was secured to the shore. The French crew, after discharging one broadside, precipitately bolted and swam ashore. The British loss in this affair was but two wounded.[3]

The *Drake*, 14, which was still commanded by Lieutenant William King (1), sent two boats, on the morning of March 14th, to capture a large French 18-gun privateer which had taken shelter under the guns of Deshaies, Guadeloupe. The French crew abandoned the ship on the boats' approach, only one man being discovered on board. A little later, however, the prize blew up, killing six officers and men, and injuring several others. Whether the explosion was accidental or designed is not clearly stated in the official letter. At the same time, the *Drake* recaptured a valuable British prize which had been taken by the French.[4]

On March 17th, the *Penguin*, 16, Commander George Morris, drove the French privateer *Renommée*, 12, ashore upon the Sénégal bar. A week later, surf having in the meantime prevented any operations, the *Penguin* opened fire upon the privateer and two schooners which had come to her help, but could not get near enough to produce any effect. She then sent in a boat which, under Lieutenant Charles Williams, destroyed the *Renommée* without any loss to the British.[5]

[1] *Nav. Chron.*, xii. 70; James, iii. 247.
[2] Afterwards Marquis of Thomond.
[3] James, iii. 253; *Nav. Chron.*, xii. 69.
[4] *Nav. Chron.*, xii. 72; James, iii. 253.
[5] *Nav. Chron.*, xii. 131; James, iii. 254; O'Byrne, 788.

On March 23rd, the *Osprey*, 18, Commander George Younghusband, cruising near Barbados, chased four ships, one of which
had the appearance of a frigate. This was the Bordeaux privateer
Egyptienne, 36, a vessel which, under the name of *Railleuse*, had
formerly figured as a frigate in the French Navy. The *Osprey*
closed and engaged her, despite the disparity of force, the privateer
carrying twenty-six 12-prs., ten 6-prs., and 248 men, to the
Osprey's sixteen 32-pr. carronades, two 6-prs., and 120 men. A
close action of eighty minutes followed, in which the French had so
much the worst of it that they ceased firing and set all sail, while
the three ships which had been with the *Egyptienne* scattered, and
steered different courses. The *Osprey* sailed so badly that she was
quite unable to overtake her enemy, which, however, as will be seen,
was taken a few days later. The British loss was 1 killed and 16
wounded; the French loss 8 killed and 19 wounded.[1]

On March 24th, the sloop *Wolverine*, 13, Commander Henry
Gordon, on her way to Newfoundland in charge of a convoy, sighted
two strangers. As they showed an intention to attack the rear of
the convoy, the *Wolverine* stood to intercept them, signalling the
convoy to escape as best it could. At 4 in the afternoon, the larger
of the two enemies, the *Blonde*, 30, a French privateer, was within
range. To explain what followed, it should be stated that the
Wolverine carried her ports very low, and that her battery consisted
of two 18-pr. long guns and six 24-pr. carronades on the main
deck, all of which could be fought on the same side. In addition to
these, she carried four 12-pr. carronades on the quarter-deck and
one on the forecastle. On this occasion, one of her two 18-prs.—
the best guns she carried—jammed, and could not be moved to the
engaged broadside. Her ports being so extremely near the waterline, she was compelled to engage to leeward, in order to be able to
fight her heavy guns. Her enemy was higher out of the water, and
carried long 8-prs. on the main deck. These, except at very close
quarters, were far more accurate and deadly than carronades. The
two ships fought at a distance of fifty yards for fifty minutes before
the *Wolverine* lowered her colours. Her sails and rigging were cut
to pieces, her hull riddled between wind and water, and, of her small
crew, 5 were killed and 10 wounded. Testimony to the fact that
the British ship held out to the last possible moment is afforded by
the fact that the *Wolverine* sank soon after the prisoners had been

[1] *Nav. Chron.*, xii. 71 ; James, iii. 254.

removed. Of the convoy, six ships escaped, and only two were taken.[1] The comparative force of the two vessels was as follows :—

—	Tons.	Guns.	Broadside.	Men.	Killed.	Wounded.
Blonde	580?	30 [2]	Lbs. 135	240?	1	5
Wolverine . . .	286	13	198	76	5	10

On March 27th, the French privateer *Egyptienne*, 36, which had been so severely handled by the *Osprey*, was captured by the *Hippomenes*, 14, Commander Conway Shipley. She was chased for fifty-four hours, and then engaged in a running fight for three hours and twenty minutes, but ceased all resistance and struck as soon as the *Hippomenes* got alongside her. Shipley very generously attributed this result to the sharp punishment she had received from the *Osprey*. Only one man was wounded in the British ship.[3] The *Egyptienne* became the British prison ship *Antigua*.

On the night of March 31st, the boats of the *Scorpion*, 18, Commander George Nicholas Hardinge, and *Beaver*, 14, Commander Charles Pelly, cut out the Dutch brig *Athalante*, 16, Commander G. S. Carp, from the Vlie. She could not be attacked by the *Scorpion*, owing to the shoals and difficulties of navigation. The cutting-out party was led by Hardinge himself, and mustered sixty officers and men. It arrived alongside the *Athalante* at 11.30 P.M., and found her ready, with boarding-nets triced up. But her men do not seem to have offered any very obstinate resistance, since, in the words of a private letter of Hardinge's, " the noise, the alarm, etc., so intimidated her crew that many of them ran below in a panic, leaving to us the painful duty of combating those whom we respected the most." Hardinge fought the Dutch captain hand to hand, but was disarmed by him, and was rescued by one of his own people. The Dutch captain was urged to accept quarter, refused, and was killed—most reluctantly—by the British seamen, who admired his valour. The hatches were secured, and the *Athalante* passed into British hands. The British loss was Lieu-tenant Buckland Stirling Bluett (who was at once promoted), two

---

[1] James, iii. 255; O'Byrne, 408. Gordon was posted, Apr. 8th, 1805 ; and, upon his return to England in Nov. 1811, was honourably acquitted by C. M.

[2] All her guns were long 9-prs. [French 8-prs.] ; the *Wolverine's*, mostly short-range carronades.

[3] *Nav. Chron.*, xii. 72 ; James, iii. 255.

other officers and two seamen wounded; the Dutch loss, out of a total crew of 76, Commander Carp and 3 seamen killed, and the first lieutenant and 11 others wounded. A gale sprang up after the capture of the ship, and detained the *Athalante* for two days in the Vlie, and not till the third was she able to effect her exit.[1] Hardinge was posted on April 4th.

On April 3rd, off Palermo, the British hired cutter *Swift*, 8, Lieutenant William Thomas Martin Leake, was chased, overhauled and taken, by the French privateer *Espérance*, 10, but only after a fierce struggle. Leake was killed in the act of throwing overboard the despatches from the Admiralty, which he was carrying out to Nelson. Nelson was right in asking " how the Government can think of sending papers of consequence in such a vessel." The *Swift* carried only twenty-three men, and was, in Nelson's judgment, " not equal to cope with any row-boat privateer." [2]

On April 9th, the 32-gun frigate *Wilhelmina*, Commander Henry Lambert (2), armed *en flûte*, and as such carrying only light guns —eighteen 9-prs., two 6-prs., and one 12-pr. carronade—and manned with a very weak complement, whilst escorting a country ship towards Trincomale, fell in, to the east of Ceylon, with the powerful French privateer, formerly a frigate in the French Navy, *Psyché*, 32, Trogoff master. During the night of the 9–10th, the *Psyché* closed the British vessel fast, and Lambert, directing his charge to beat a retreat, lay-to to await his enemy. The *Wilhelmina*, being jury-rigged, had the look of a merchantman; which may explain the readiness of the privateer to attack. At daylight on the 11th, the two ships were within pistol-shot, the *Wilhelmina* to windward of the *Psyché*. They exchanged their first broadsides, passing on opposite tacks, and the *Psyché* hailed Lambert, bidding him surrender. The *Psyché* tacked, and the *Wilhelmina* wore, and, as the two ships' heads pointed the same way, a running fight began. The French fired alternate guns at the British vessel's rigging and hull. The damage which they thus inflicted upon their enemy brought the *Wilhelmina*, disabled, upon the starboard tack with her sails aback, and enabled the Frenchman to pass under her stern and deliver a raking fire. Lambert, however, succeeded in getting his ship again before the wind, and engaged the *Psyché* with his port broadside. The *Psyché* closed to board; but, finding the

---

[1] *Nav. Chron.*, xi. 410; xii. 49; De Jonge, v. 589; James, iii. 261.
[2] *Nav. Chron.*, xi. 413; Nicolas, 'Nelson,' v. 505, 508; James, iii. 262.

Wilhelmina ready to give boarders a warm reception, sheered off a little, and continued the action yard-arm to yard-arm. Then she crossed the *Wilhelmina's* bows, raking the British ship; and, tacking to close again, was herself raked in turn. The two vessels were now once more steering the same course. They closed for the last time, yard-arm to yard-arm, and fought till, at 7 A.M., two hours and ten minutes after the beginning of the combat, the *Psyché* had had enough. She crowded all sail, and, being faster and less damaged in her sails, masts, and rigging than the *Wilhelmina*, succeeded in effecting her escape. The latter was in no plight to pursue. She had lost her main topmast; her bowsprit and main and mizen masts were badly wounded; her boats were shot to bits; and her hull was pierced in several places.

The *Wilhelmina's* previous Captain had attached the greatest importance to gunnery, and the effects of his care were seen in this action. Though the *Wilhelmina* was so much cut up, she succeeded with her weak battery in reducing the *Psyché* almost to a sinking condition. At the close of the action the privateer had 44 men *hors de combat*, and some feet of water in her hold, whereas the *Wilhelmina* suffered a loss of only 10. The *Psyché* was in many respects as good a ship as, or better than, most frigates in the French Navy. She had an excellent, indeed, a famous, skipper and a well-trained crew, whilst her preponderance in force, whether of guns or men, was immense. In the circumstances, Lambert deserves especial praise for his splendid resistance to such odds, and though his opponent was " only a privateer," his Admiral evidently thought so, since he took the first opportunity of promoting [1] him to post rank. Lambert will be met with again in the pages of this history. Till the day when he fell in the service of his country his career was one of exceptional distinction.[2]

The force of the two ships was as follows :—

	Tons.	Guns.	Broadside.	Men.	Killed.	Wounded.	Total.
Wilhelmina .	827	21	Lbs. 99	134	4	6	10
Psyché . .	848	36	240	250	11	33	44

On the night of April 29th, the boats of the *Doris*, 36, Captain Patrick Campbell (1), one of Cornwallis' squadron off Brest, were

[1] Confd. Ap. 10th, 1805.	[2] James, iii. 263; *Nav. Chron.*, xii. 491.

sent in, under Lieutenant —— Anderson, to attack a flotilla of
French gunboats under Captain C. Le Bozec, which was observed
anchored at the entrance to Audierne Harbour.   The British party
brought off gunboat *No. 360*, under Enseigne Dubois, notwithstanding the vigorous efforts of the French to protect her.   The
British loss was one man killed.[1]

On June 21st, the *Hippomenes*, 14, Captain Kenneth M'Kenzie,[2]
was sighted to the east of Antigua by the French privateer
Bonaparte, 18, Paimpéni master.   The Frenchman boldly bore
down, believing the British vessel, from her build, which was
peculiar, and from the careful disguise which M'Kenzie had adopted,
to be a merchantman.   At 1.50 P.M. the two closed and began a
close action.   In this the *Bonaparte* had the worst of matters, and
she dropped on board the *Hippomenes*, her bowsprit touching the
latter's main mast.   M'Kenzie at once had the bowsprit lashed to
the mast, and dashed on board the *Bonaparte*, calling upon his crew
to follow him.   However, only his officers and about eight men
obeyed.   The Frenchmen were rapidly driven from their quarters
to the poop, where they gathered, and, perceiving the weakness of
the British boarding-party, regained heart.   Half the boarding-party
was cut to pieces, M'Kenzie was badly wounded, and the others
were forced back from the *Bonaparte's* forecastle to the *Hippomenes's* deck.   At that critical moment the lashing which had held
the privateer parted, and M'Kenzie, wounded in fourteen places, had
only just time to leap back on board his ship.   The British loss was
heavy.   Two officers and two men were taken prisoners; five men
were killed, and eight, including the Captain and the Master,
wounded.   In the crew of the *Hippomenes*, according to the *Naval
Chronicle*, were many foreigners; which may explain, if it cannot
condone, the cowardice displayed by the men.   The *Bonaparte* had
5 killed and 15 wounded, besides suffering much damage in her
hull and rigging.[3]

On July 11th, ten boats of the *Narcissus*, 32, Captain Ross
Donnelly, *Seahorse*, 38, Captain the Hon. Courtenay Boyle, and
Maidstone, 32, Captain the Hon. George Elliot (3), forming part
of Lord Nelson's squadron blockading Toulon, attacked a dozen

---

[1] 'Blockade of B.,' i. 309 ; *Nav. Chron.*, xii. 79.
[2] M'Kenzie, a Commander of 1802, had been posted on June 6th, 1804; but was
not aware of the fact.   He died in 1824.
[3] *Nav. Chron.*, xii. 422, 492 ; James, iii. 268 ; Marshall, ii. 899.

small French craft at Lavandou in Hyères Bay, just before midnight. The enemy was found fully prepared, and received the British boats, which were under the orders of Lieutenants John Thompson (3a.), John Richard Lumley, Ogle Moore, and Hyde Parker (3), with a tremendous fire. The British force, however, was led and handled in a manner which won warm praise from Nelson, and destroyed most of the French small craft, but only with terrible loss. One vessel was brought away. The killed numbered 4, including Midshipman Thomas Owen Roche, and the wounded 23, including Lumley. "Wounds," said Nelson in a general order on this affair, "are marks of honour; they must be expected." [1]

On July 12th, the *Aigle*, 36, Captain George Wolfe, off the mouth of the Gironde, sighted the French vessels *Charente*, 20, and *Joie*, 8, on their way from the Gironde to Bayonne. The British vessel at once gave chase; and the two French ships precipitately ran ashore on the coast to the south of the Gironde. Owing to the heavy surf, the *Aigle* was not able to get them afloat, or to remove any part of their valuable cargo of ordnance. They were therefore destroyed by the British boats. [2]

On July 15th, the *Lily*, 16, Commander William Compton, off the coast of South Carolina encountered the French privateer *Dame Ambert*, 16, C. Lamarque master. The British vessel, armed mainly with carronades, and inferior in sailing qualities to her enemy, was attacked at long range by the latter's long guns, which knocked her sails and rigging to pieces with almost absolute impunity. The *Dame Ambert* [3] then had her completely at her mercy; took up a raking position; and secured the *Lily's* bowsprit to her taffrail. The Frenchmen made eight attempts to board, all of which were beaten off, notwithstanding their great advantage of position. The ninth was successful and the *Lily* passed into their hands. Her Commander, first Lieutenant, and great part of her crew were killed or wounded. The French loss was 16. The force of the two ships was as follows :—

----	Tons.	Guns.	Broadside.	Men.	Killed.	Wounded.
Dame Ambert . .		16	Lbs. 48	75 ?	5	11
Lily	200	16	88	80	Most of the crew.[4]	

[1] *Nav. Chron.*, xii. 316; Nicolas, 'Nelson,' vi. 108; James, iii. 270.
[2] James, iii. 270.   [3] *Ex* British packet *Marlborough*.   [4] Including Compton.

This action clearly illustrates the tactical danger of a short range armament when the enemy cannot be closed. The *Dame Ambert* carried nothing but long 6-prs.; the *Lily's*[1] carronades, fourteen in number, were 12-prs. of old and weak pattern. She had only two 4-pr. long guns.[2]

On July 31st, the *Tartar*, 32, Captain Keith Maxwell, chased the small French privateer *Hirondelle*, 10, into the difficult channel between the islands of Saona and San Domingo. The channel being impassable, the *Hirondelle* anchored in it under a reef. As the *Tartar* could not get at her, three boats were despatched under Lieutenants Henry Muller and Nicholas Lockyer to destroy her or bring her off. The boats rowed gallantly in under a heavy fire in broad daylight with the wind against them, and carried the privateer. In this dashing affair the British loss was only 2 wounded. The French had 15 killed or wounded, besides 3 missing, supposed to have been drowned while attempting to swim ashore. The *Hirondelle* was an exceedingly fast sailer. She had often been chased but had always escaped.[3]

On the night of August 12th the boats of the *Galatea*, 32, Captain Henry Heathcote, were despatched to cut out the privateer *Général Ernouf* (late British *Lily*) from Anse à Mire, Guadeloupe. The boats, however, failed to find the privateer, and returned without accomplishing anything beyond placing the French thoroughly on their guard. The latter reinforced the *Général Ernouf's* crew with 31 men, and moored a vessel athwart the privateer's hawse so as to rake the cutting-out party, should the attempt be repeated. Further, the French batteries were enjoined to allow the enemy to approach and not to open fire till he was in retreat.

On the 15th the *Galatea* reconnoitred the privateer, drawing a heavy fire from the batteries, which, however, did her no damage. At 10 P.M. she despatched four boats with 90 officers and men, under Lieutenant Charles Hayman, for the desperate enterprise. The French were apprised by a guard-boat of the British approach; but no shot was fired, and, with growing confidence in the belief that the enemy would be surprised, the cutting-out party pushed in. The barge with Hayman took the lead, and was just alongside, when she

---

[1] She was renamed by her captors *Général Ernouf*, and became, as will be seen, a well-known privateer.

[2] James, iii. 271.

[3] James, iii. 272; *Nav. Chron.*, xii. 318.

was received with a murderous fire. Hayman was mortally injured, and, of 27 officers and men in his party, only 3 were not severely wounded. The other boats were not one whit more fortunate. They were so roughly handled that, after a magnificent display of pluck and determination, they were forced to turn back, abandoning the barge. On the retreat the batteries opened fire and inflicted fresh loss. In this terrible affair, out of 90 British officers and men engaged, no fewer than 65 seem to have been killed or wounded—a loss which speaks volumes for the bravery and resolution of the attack. The French acknowledged only 4 killed, but had also some wounded.

There can be no disputing the fact that the attack under such circumstances was injudicious. Yet the reader will recall instances, already narrated, in which vessels, perfectly prepared and on their guard, were cut out without heavy loss. The recapture of the *Hermione,* and the cutting out of the *Curieux* are striking examples. Yet it is a good rule that for such enterprises surprise is essential, and that nothing whatsoever shall be done, before they are attempted, to put the enemy on his guard. The French, in their reports of this action, as was often their habit, looked at their own forces through the wrong end of their glasses, and so converted what was really a most heroic passage into a dishonourable defeat for the British. No force which loses more than two-thirds its strength can be held to have fought badly. Fortune and judgment, not valour, were wanting on the defeated side.[1]

On August 17th, the *Blonde,* 30, French privateer, which in March had sunk the *Wolverine,* was taken in the North Atlantic by the *Loire,* 38, Captain Frederick Lewis Maitland (2), after a long running fight in which the *Loire* had 6 and the *Blonde* 7 wounded, 2 mortally. The prize was disguised as an Indiaman, and had been a serious annoyance to British trade.[2]

On September 15th, the *Centurion,* 50, Lieutenant James Robert Phillips (actg. Captain),[3] whilst at anchor in Vizagapatam Roads, waiting for two ships, the *Princess Charlotte* and the *Barnaby,* to load, observed three strange sail approaching from the south-west. These were the *Marengo,* 74, *Atalante,* 40, Captain C. C. A. Gaudin-Beauchêne, and *Sémillante,* 36, Captain Motard,

---

[1] James, iii. 273 ; Marshall, ii. 123.

[2] *Nav. Chron.,* xii. 236, 336 ; James, 282.

[3] The ship's Captain, James Lind, was on shore during the early part of the action.

of Linois's squadron. After having committed many depredations on British commerce, Linois had received information that at Vizagapatam were two merchantmen in charge of the British frigate *Wilhelmina*, and he had determined to capture all three vessels.

The nature of the approaching vessels, with the fact that they were enemies, was speedily ascertained by the *Centurion*; and at about 9.45 A.M. she opened fire on the leading frigate, at the same time directing the merchantmen to retire to a neighbouring port. The *Barnaby* cut her cable, drove on shore, and was totally lost; the *Princess Charlotte*, being covered by the *Centurion*, did not move. At 10 A.M., the *Centurion* cut her cable and sheeted home her topsails, thus bringing her broadside to bear upon the *Atalante*, which was then close at hand on the port quarter, and which seemed inclined to board. The *Marengo* and *Sémillante* also closed on the starboard quarter and hotly engaged the British ship. To them the *Princess Charlotte* struck precipitately in a most craven manner, without firing a shot. Both the *Marengo's* and the *Centurion's* colours were early shot away, but replaced. The British fire was directed mainly upon the *Marengo*, which kept at a distance of under half a mile. At about 10.45 A.M., the French trio retired, the *Marengo* having, according to French accounts, touched the bottom. The *Centurion* retreated inshore, in shallow water, but out of reach of the three guns of a battery which had hitherto supported her; and at about that time was rejoined by her Captain, James Lind. Her sails and rigging were very much cut up.

The French ships again approached at about 11.30, and the *Marengo*, perhaps afraid of the shoals, opened fire when about a mile away. Only the *Centurion's* lower deck guns (eleven 24-prs. on the broadside) could be used effectively at that range; but almost all the *Marengo's* shot fell round the *Centurion*. The *Atalante*, nearer in on the *Centurion's* quarter, maintained a galling fire, whilst the *Sémillante* busied herself in carrying off the *Princess Charlotte*, instead of in subduing the British warship. At last, at about 1.15 P.M., after two hours of cannonading, the French ships made sail and tamely stood away to sea, though one of the *Marengo's* last shot cut the *Centurion's* cable and brought her a good distance off-shore, and into deeper water, before the sheet anchor could be let go. The *Centurion* made a fine defence against heavy odds. In battery she was only equal to the two French frigates; and, of course, she was hopelessly outclassed by the French 74. Her masts and rigging were badly damaged, and she had several shot between wind and water, yet of her crew only 9 were wounded, 1 mortally. The force of the four ships engaged was as follows :—

—	Guns.	Broadside.	Men.	Killed.	Wounded.
Centurion . . .	54	Lbs. 698*	345 n.	1	8
Marengo . . .	78	990	690 n.	2	1 ?
Atalante . . .	44	410	330 n.	2	6
Sémillante . . .	40	280	300 n.	0	0

n., nominal complement : probably all four ships had crews under the strength given.

* Of this 416 lbs. was from short range carronades, against 72 lbs. in the *Marengo* and 36 lbs. in each of the French frigates.

Linois's half-hearted and timid action on this occasion cannot but provoke censure. If the *Marengo* could not get at the poor little 50-gun ship, the frigates could have done so, and were, combined, much more than a match for her. There is little room for surprise that, after such a miserable display, Napoleon told Linois, " France cared for honour, not for a few pieces of wood," when the Admiral strove to excuse his weakness.[1]

Late in September, off the coast of Hayti, the British armed trader *Leander*, 12, Lewis, master, in company with the brig *Dolly*, met and mistook for a privateer the British frigate *Fortunée*, 44, Captain Henry Vansittart. The error had fatal consequences, since the *Leander* poured a broadside into the frigate, which, owing to a recent gale, had all her guns in the hold, and killed a man before she discovered her mistake. The *Leander's* master showed courage and want of judgment in equal parts, by thus daring to attack a powerful ship, and by the precipitate manner of attack. He was punished by the impressment of twenty-six of his men and a fine of 1500 dollars.[2]

On October 3rd, the British frigates *Indefatigable*, 44, Captain Graham Moore, *Lively*, 38, Captain Graham Eden Hamond, *Medusa*, 32, Captain John Gore (2), and *Amphion*, 32, Captain Samuel Sutton, assembled off Cadiz, whither they had been ordered to intercept four

[1] James, iii. 276; Troude, iii. 315; *Nav. Chron.*, xiii. 218; Chevalier, iii. 301 ; O'Byrne, 900.
[2] *Nav. Chron.*, xiii. 160.

Spanish frigates laden with treasure, which were due to arrive from
Montevideo. Of the British frigates, the first two were from Cornwallis's fleet, and the last two from Nelson's. The latter Admiral,
with his usual judgment, had despatched also the line of battleship
Donegal, 74, wishing to make the British force so strong that resistance to it would be hopeless. Unhappily she failed to arrive in
time, and there was much unnecessary waste of life. Spain was
nominally at peace with Great Britain, though she was at that very
moment paying to France a large subsidy, which was, of course, used
against England. The treasure expected in the Spanish frigates was
therefore destined to be employed by an enemy. But no notice of
our intention was given to the Spanish Government [1]; and a British
officer, Captain Sir Robert Barlow, Kt., was actually on his way
in the *Triumph*, 74, to Cadiz, to pick up and convoy home the
British traders who had gathered there. These circumstances led
what followed to be severely denounced both at home and abroad.

On the 5th, the Spanish vessels came into sight. They were
four in number, the *Fama*, 34, *Medea*, 40, Rear-Admiral Don José
Bustamente, *Mercedes*, 34, and *Clara*, 34, a squadron much weaker
in force than the British quartette, and suffering the great disadvantage of being taken unprepared. They formed line of battle
in the order given above, whereupon the *Medusa*, the leading British
ship, placed herself upon the *Fama*'s weather beam, and the *Indefatigable*, *Amphion*, and *Lively* also paired off with their antagonists
in order, the *Lively* taking her position to leeward, abeam of the last
Spanish ship. Captain Moore, the senior British officer, then hailed
the Spanish admiral to shorten sail, and, as no reply was made, fired
across his ship. The *Medea* shortened sail, and a boat was sent
from the *Indefatigable* urging Bustamente to allow his squadron to
be detained without bloodshed. Honour compelled him to refuse,
whereupon the *Indefatigable* fired a shot across his bows and closed.
The *Mercedes* promptly fired into the *Amphion;* the *Medea* fired into
the *Indefatigable*; and the British senior officer made the signal for
close action. In ten minutes the *Mercedes* blew up; in half an hour
the *Medea* and *Clara* struck their flags. The *Fama* attempted to
escape, and gained on the *Medusa*, but the *Lively* was despatched to
join in the chase, which was overhauled and captured, with the help
of the *Medusa*, early in the afternoon. The boats of the other British
ships, having secured the *Medea*, turned their attention to the un-

[1] There had been an angry diplomatic correspondence.

happy survivors of the *Mercedes*. One officer and 45 men were saved, but with that exception, all on board, including several women and children, perished. The prizes had cargoes of great value, in addition to specie, on board, and their total worth was placed at about £1,000,000. In the *Mercedes*, one-third as much more was lost. The British casualties were only 2 killed and 7 wounded. The Spaniards lost 20 killed and 80 wounded, besides those who perished in the *Mercedes*.[1]

On October 16th, the *Cruiser*, 18, Commander John Hancock (1), blockading Ostend, sighted and chased the French privateer *Contre-Amiral Magon*, 17, a vessel which had committed terrible depredations upon British commerce. The pursuit continued for 97 miles, but at last the privateer was overhauled. She struck after a few shots. So scarce were seamen in France that instead of her complement of 200 men she had gone to sea with 84 men only, among whom were many Danes, Swedes, and Americans.[2]

On November 8th, the merchantmen *Thetis*, *Ceres*, and *Penelope* encountered the French privateer *Bonaparte*, 18, off Barbados. The *Thetis*, John Charnley, master, closed and fought her. The other two held aloof. The *Thetis*, however, proved quite a match for her, knocked her badly about, and left her almost disabled.[3]

Amongst the British ships lost by shipwreck in 1804 was the *Apollo*, 36, Captain John William Taylor Dixon. While in charge of a convoy for the West Indies, she struck on the Portuguese coast during a heavy gale on April 2nd. Her Captain and 60 of her crew perished.[4]

On January 21st, 1805, the *Gipsy*, 10, Lieutenant Michael Fitton, whilst cruising on a rendezvous off Cape San Antonio with despatches, was chased by five privateers. These she succeeded in separating by a feigned flight; and, attacking the leading vessel, which at once in its turn took to flight, drove it ashore after a running engagement.[5]

On February 3rd, at daylight, the sloop *Arrow*, 28, Commander Richard Budd Vincent,[6] and the bomb *Acheron*, Commander Arthur

---

[1] James, iii. 280; Nicolas, 'Nelson,' vi. 241; *Nav. Chron.*, xii. 322, 500; xiii. App. (for diplom. correspondence); Chevalier, 126.

[2] *Nav. Chron.*, xii. 457, 417.

[3] *Nav. Chron.*, xiii. 273.

[4] James, iii. 257; Narr. of Mr. Lewis; C. M., May 22nd, 1804.

[5] James, iv. 117.

[6] Com., Apr. 29th, 1802; Capt., Apr. 8th, 1805.

Farquhar (1),[1] whilst escorting a convoy of merchantmen from Malta to England, sighted two strange sail off the Algerian coast. These were the *Hortense*, 40, Captain L. C. A. La Marre La Meillerie, and *Incorruptible*, 38, Captain S. Billiet, of Admiral Villeneuve's squadron. They had separated from the French fleet to chase away the British look-out frigates, and had not been able to rejoin. They were speedily made out by the British vessels to be enemies, and the

CAPTAIN RICHARD BUDD VINCENT, R.N.
From H. R. Cook's lithographed portrait in the "Naval Chronical," 1807.

convoy was ordered to close. The *Arrow* cast off a vessel which she had in tow and joined the *Acheron*; and the two ships placed themselves between the enemy and the convoy, directing the latter to make all possible sail for the rendezvous appointed in case the ships should have to disperse. Late in the afternoon it fell calm, and not till night had fallen did a breeze spring up from the W.S.W. All day and night the frigates in pursuit were making all the sail they

[1] Com., Apr. 29th, 1802; Capt., Apr. 8th, 1805; R.-Adm., Jan. 10th, 1837.

could, but they were not within range till 4.45 A.M. of the 4th. The Hortense then passed under the lee of the *Arrow* on the opposite tack, hailed her, and, passing the *Acheron*, hailed again and fired a broadside into the bomb, which did great damage, carrying away the main yard slings and the main topgallant yard. The *Acheron* returned the fire, and was supported by the *Arrow*, which bore up and raked the *Hortense*. The *Incorruptible*, from the lightness of the wind, had fallen away from her sister frigate; and when, at about 5.30 A.M., she appeared to be wearing, she was distantly fired into by the *Acheron*. She eventually stood after the *Hortense*. In this brief respite which followed, the *Acheron* attempted to repair the damage to her rigging.

The convoy was at that time about four miles to windward. The French frigates bore down a second time; and at 7.30 A.M. the *Incorruptible*, which was leading, opened on the *Arrow* and exchanged broadsides with her. As the French ships were on the opposite tack to the two British vessels, the *Incorruptible* went on to the *Acheron*, whilst the *Hortense* gave the *Arrow* her attention. Having passed, the two Frenchmen wore to renew the action. The *Arrow* attempted to rake them, but failed in her manœuvre, and was attacked by both the frigates. The *Hortense*, however, soon left her in order to look after the *Acheron*. The *Arrow*, hopelessly outmatched, protracted her resistance till 8.30 A.M., when, with her rigging shot to pieces, her masts wounded, her hold full of water and four guns dismounted, she struck. The *Acheron* had attempted to escape, but with the much faster *Hortense* in pursuit, and retarded by the injuries which she had sustained in her masts and rigging, she also surrendered at about 8.45.

Both British ships had sustained such damage in their heroic defence as to render them worthless to their captors. The *Acheron* was burnt by the French; the *Arrow* sank immediately after her crew had been transferred to the enemy's ships. Nor was the stubborn courage displayed by the British seamen without effect, since, of the convoy, only three vessels were taken. The *Arrow* and the *Acheron*, from the circumstance that both were armed entirely with carronades— excepting the *Acheron's* two mortars, which of course were useless— could do little outside the very closest range, and the French vessels with their long guns had them at their mercy. The *Acheron*, in Nelson's judgment, was not the equal of a strong privateer. The force and losses of the four ships were as follows :—

—	Guns.	Broadside.	Men.	Killed.	Wounded.
		Lbs.			
Hortense . . .	44	410	340 n.		
Incorruptible . .	40	280	300 n.	1	5
Arrow	28	448	132	13	27
Acheron . . .	8	96	67	3	8

The *Arrow's* fire probably did the *Incorruptible* some damage, since the latter took no further part in Villeneuve's operations.[1]

On February 8th, the *Curieux*, 16, Commander George Edmund Byron Bettesworth, chased and overhauled a large brig off Barbados. This was the notorious French privateer *Dame Ernouf*, 16. A sharp action of 40 minutes' duration followed, and then the *Dame Ernouf* attempted to board on the *Curieux's* leeward quarter. The *Curieux* starboarded her helm, caught the privateer's jibboom between her after fore-shroud and fore mast, and held her in that position till the enemy's deck was cleared. Just as the British in their turn were about to board, the vessels parted and the *Dame Ernouf's* fore top-mast came down. She fired a few shot, and then struck. Each craft carried sixteen long French 6-prs. Of the *Curieux's* crew of 67, 1 officer was killed and 4 officers and men were wounded. Of her 120 men, the *Dame Ernouf* lost 30 killed and 40 wounded.[2]

On February 13th, the *San Fiorenzo*, 36, Commander Henry Lambert (2) (actg. Captain), searching for the French frigate *Psyché*, 32, Captain Jacques Bergeret, discovered three sail off Ganjam, on the Malabar coast, and, approaching, made them out to be the *Psyché* and two prizes. The three crowded all sail away, but on the evening of the 14th the rearmost of the prizes was overhauled by the *San Fiorenzo* and secured. At 8 P.M. the *Psyché* was within range and the first shot was fired. At 8.20 P.M. close action began, broadside to broadside, at half a cable's distance, between the *Psyché* and *San Fiorenzo*. The other French prize, the *Pigeon*, had been armed by the French with 4 guns, manned with 34 men, placed under the command of Lieutenant Ollivier, and renamed the *Equivoque;* but she held aloof from the action and gave the *Psyché* little assistance.

[1] James, iv. 118; Troude, iii. 412; *Nav. Chron.*, xiii. 223, xvii. 281; Nicolas, 'Nelson,' vi. 263; Marshall, ii. 912, 929; C. M., Mar. 28th, 1804, and June 17th, 1805.

[2] *Nav. Chron.*, xiii. 403; James, iv. 121.

In the close engagement between the *Psyché* and *San Fiorenzo*,
both ships suffered severely. The French, as was their usual
custom, seem, from the damage which they inflicted upon the
San Fiorenzo's rigging, to have fired high. The British fire, directed
at the enemy's hull, put many of her guns and carronades out of
action. At about 9 P.M. the *Psyché* passed under the *San Fiorenzo's*
stern and raked the British ship, but without causing very serious
injury, owing to the damage which had been sustained by the
French vessel's guns. The *San Fiorenzo* speedily recovered her old
position and brought her broadside to bear. Bergeret saw that his
solitary chance of success lay in boarding. He ran the *Psyché* upon
the *San Fiorenzo*; but his boarders were received with so furious a
fire from the British small-arms' party that their attempt was easily
beaten off. At that moment a fire broke out on the *Psyché's* orlop
deck, and diverted the attention of a large part of her crew from the
battle. The two ships parted, but the British seamen continued
their deadly fire at something outside pistol range. The *Psyché's*
main yard was shot away; and she was left, if French accounts can
be believed, with only two serviceable guns, the others having been
either dismounted or disabled. At about 11.30 P.M. the British ship
hauled off to effect repairs to her masts and rigging. Thirty minutes
later she bore down again, before the *Psyché* had cleared her decks
or made ready for the renewal of the action. The *San Fiorenzo* was
on the point of re-opening fire, when a boat from the *Psyché*, with
an officer on board, came off to her with a message from Captain
Bergeret stating that he was prepared to surrender. French
accounts assert that he stipulated for terms, but the terms were only
such as would always be granted to a brave opponent—the right of
the officers to keep their swords, the seamen to retain their private
effects, and Captain Bergeret to remain one night on board his ship
to see that the wounded received proper attention. The French say
that the *Equivoque* only fired four or five shots. The *Psyché*, it
should be admitted, was skilfully and bravely defended against a ship
of very superior size and force.

—	Tons.	Guns.	Broadside.	Men.	Killed.	Wounded.
San Fiorenzo . . .	1032	42	Lbs. 467	253	12	36
Psyché	848	36	250	240	57	70

The damage which the *San Fiorenzo* had sustained rendered it impossible for her to pursue the *Equivoque*.[1]

Early on February 16th, the *Cleopatra*, 32, Captain Sir Robert Laurie, Bart., to the south-east of Bermuda, sighted the French *Ville de Milan*, 40, Captain J. M. Renaud, on her way from Martinique to France with despatches and orders not to speak any ship on her voyage. The *Cleopatra* gave chase, and, at about 11 A.M., ascertained that the French vessel was of very superior force. As the stranger did not shorten sail, Laurie resorted to the device of hoisting American colours; but the *Ville de Milan* paid no attention. The *Cleopatra* then made all possible sail and continued her pursuit all the 16th. At 10.30 A.M. on the 17th she was within three-quarters of a mile. At about noon, the stranger hoisted French colours and the *Cleopatra* showed the British ensign. The British ship, then within long range, opened with her bow chasers, as the *Ville de Milan* seemed to draw ahead. The French vessel replied from time to time with those of her guns which would bear. The French fire was so well directed, and of such weight, that the *Cleopatra*, to avoid being continuously raked, was forced to steer for a point broad on the *Ville de Milan's* quarter. At last, at about 2.30 P.M., the *Cleopatra* closed to within a cable's length, whereupon the *Ville de Milan* luffed and fired two broadsides. The *Cleopatra* held her fire till only one hundred yards parted her from her enemy, and then began a close action in which she quite held her own. At length she knocked away the *Ville de Milan's* main topsail yard and at once shot ahead, though she herself had sustained very serious injuries to her masts, sails, and rigging. Her running rigging, in Laurie's words, was " cut to pieces so as to render it impossible to either shorten or back a sail, and both main and spring-stays were shot away." In such a plight he determined to attempt to rake the *Ville de Milan* by hauling up and crossing her bows. But, at the critical moment, a shot struck the wheel, jamming the broken spokes against the deck; and simultaneously the rudder-head was choked with splinters, and with a number of pistols which had been placed near it. Thus the *Cleopatra* was left ungovernable, at the mercy of her opponent. The *Ville de Milan* at once drove her bows upon the British ship abaft the main rigging; and her men, covered by a heavy fire of musketry, attempted to board. They were beaten back for the moment, and a hot fire was maintained by the *Cleopatra's*

---

[1] *Nav. Chron.*, xiv. 164; James, iv. 122; Troude, iii. 413; Chevalier, iii. 302.

small-arm men and by the only two guns which she could bring to
bear, without, however, inflicting much of either loss or injury
upon the enemy. The condition of the *Cleopatra* was, in fact,
desperate. The French, from the fact that the *Ville de Milan* was
a so much bigger and higher vessel, were able to fire down upon
their enemy's deck and to clear it of men. At the same time, the
great weight of the French frigate, pressing upon the *Cleopatra's*
hull, threatened to break it in two at each heave of the ship.
There was a heavy sea running, and the *Cleopatra's* sails were
shivering or aback. At the suggestion of his first Lieutenant,
William Balfour, Laurie ordered the fore topmast staysail and the
spritsail to be set; but the order could not be obeyed, as every
seaman who showed himself on deck was struck by the French
bullets. At 5.15 P.M. the French boarded and carried the *Cleopatra*,
then a complete wreck, and with more than one-fourth of her crew
killed or wounded. Immediately after the surrender the bowsprit,
and main and fore masts went by the board, leaving only the
mizen mast standing.

The *Ville de Milan*, according to her captor's account, carried
only long guns—twenty-six 18-prs. and twenty long 8-prs.; the
Cleopatra carried twenty-six 12-prs., two 9-prs., and ten 24-pr.
carronades—a great part of her broadside being thus delivered from
weapons of very limited range and power.

—	Tons.	Guns.	Broadside.	Men.	Killed.	Wounded.
Ville de Milan . . .	1097	46	Lbs. 340	350	10 ?	?
Cleopatra	689	38	282	199	22	36 [1]

[1] Including Lieuts. William Balfour, James Crooke, Charles Mitchell (actg.), and William Bowen (2) (supernumerary), and Lieut. Thomas Appleton, R.M.

The *Ville de Milan* had her captain killed, and her second in
command wounded. Her main and mizen masts went by the board
during the night after the action, and her hull was much cut up by
the British shot. She was so much the stronger ship in every
way that no surprise can be expressed at the result of the fight.
Captain Laurie was probably led to conclude that his enemy was
weakly manned or ill prepared for battle, by her seeming anxiety to
get away when chased. His courage was fully rewarded when,

some days later, the *Ville de Milan* fell an easy victim to a larger British vessel, and the *Cleopatra* was recaptured.[1]

On February 23rd, the two vessels were sighted in squally weather by the *Leander*, 50, Captain John Talbot. The *Cleopatra* was jury rigged and had a French crew of 50 men on board ; the *Ville de Milan* had been also in some measure refitted, with a topmast for mast and a top gallant mast for topmast. The *Leander*, in these circumstances, being herself undamaged in masts and rigging, closed very rapidly upon the two. At 4 P.M. she was within range, whereupon the French frigate and her prize separated. The *Leander* pursued the *Cleopatra*, and, in half an hour, was within musket-shot of her. One gun was fired from the British 50-gun ship's lower deck, and the *Cleopatra* hauled down her colours. Several of the British crew on board her came on deck when she struck, and they were hailed by Talbot and directed to take possession of her and make all sail after the *Leander*, which gave chase to the *Ville de Milan*. In an hour's time the latter was overhauled, and struck at once, without a shot being fired on either side. Unquestionably this was due to the very severe handling which the *Ville de Milan* had sustained from the *Cleopatra's* guns. The French officers were enthusiastic and generous in their praise of Laurie and his crew. Though there was no real dishonour in the surrender of a virtually disabled vessel to a ship of superior force, perfectly fresh, French official accounts pretended that the 40-gun British frigate *Cambrian* had assisted the *Leander* in her capture of the *Ville de Milan* and *Cleopatra*. The *Cambrian's* log proves that she was at Bermuda at the date of the action. The *Ville de Milan* was purchased for the Navy and, under the name *Milan*, rated as a 38. Laurie was her first Captain.[2]

On March 20th, the *Renard*, 18, Commander Jeremiah Coghlan, to the north of Hayti, encountered the notorious French privateer *Général Ernouf*, 20 (ex *Lily*), and, after an action of thirty-five minutes' duration, set her on fire. Very little later the *Général Ernouf* blew up. Only 55 out of her crew of 160 could be saved by the British boats.[3] Three days later, on the coast of Puerto Rico, the boats of the *Stork*, 18, Commander George Le Geyt, cut out the

---

[1] James, iv. 124; *Nav. Chron.*, xiii. 409; Troude, iii. 416.

[2] *Nav. Chron.*, xiii. 407; James. iv. 127; 'Précis des Evèn.,' xi. 259; Log of *Cambrian*; O'Byrne, 635, 1157.

[3] James, iv. 129; *Nav. Chron.*, xiii. 502.

Dutch privateer *Antilope*, 5, and a brig, with the loss of only two wounded.[1] On April 5th, the boats of the *Bacchante*, 22, Captain Charles Dashwood, were sent in to the small harbour of Mariel, in Cuba, to cut out three French privateers which had committed great depredations upon British trade. To secure a safe retreat it was necessary to carry a martello tower at the entrance to the harbour, forty feet high and loopholed for muskets. This was gallantly stormed by Lieutenant James Oliver[2] and only thirteen men, without any loss, though in the tower were thirty-one Spanish soldiers. The British boats then pushed into the harbour, but found to their chagrin that the privateers had gone. They carried off, however, two sugar-laden schooners, and regained the *Bacchante* with the loss of but one man badly wounded.[3]

The constant recurrence of actions with privateers in the West Indies at about that time proves that such craft were both numerous and troublesome, though they seem rarely to have been able to make a good fight against British warships of anything like equal force. On April 8th, the schooner *Gracieuse*, 12, Midshipman John Bernhard Smith, after a smart exchange of fire, drove a French armed schooner ashore on the San Domingo coast. The *Gracieuse* sent in a boat, which removed from the schooner a long 12-pr. and burnt the wreck, and this with the loss of only 3 wounded.[4] On April 15th, the *Papillon*, 14, Commander William Woolsey, while lying in the Jamaican harbour of Savanna La Mar, placed twenty-five men under Lieutenant Peter Stephen Prieur on board a coasting vessel, which was borrowed for the purpose, and sent them out to capture a small Spanish privateer which was cruising off the west of the island. The coasting vessel was fallen in with by the privateer, which promptly lashed herself alongside. The British seamen as promptly boarded; and the enterprise had quite a different ending from that which the privateersmen had anticipated. The British loss was 2 wounded. The Spaniards, out of 25 men, had 7 killed or drowned and 8 wounded.[5] On May 6th, off the island of San Domingo, in a dead calm, the *Unicorn*, 32, Captain Lucius

---

[1] James, iv. 130; *Nav. Chron.*, xiii. 495.

[2] James wrongly ascribes the exploit to Lieutenant William Sandford Oliver.

[3] James, iv. 130. Dashwood captured on April 3rd the *Elizabeth*, 10, and on May 14th the *Felix*, 6, both Spanish letters of marque. O'Byrne, 263; *Nav. Chron.*, xiii. 496.

[4] James, iv. 131.

[5] James, iv. 132.

Ferdinand Hardyman, sighted the French cutter-privateer *Tape-à-bord*, and sent boats to capture her. In this they succeeded without loss.[1] On May 27th, the boats of the *Seine*, 32, Captain David Atkins, captured a small armed schooner off the Puerto Rican coast, and later destroyed an armed felucca.[2]

Turning to a different field: on May 4th, the boats of the *Seahorse*, 38, Captain the Hon. Courtenay Boyle, cruising in the Mediterranean off the south coast of Spain, cut out an ordnance

CAPTAIN SIR JAMES LUCAS YEO, KT., K.C.B., R.N.
From H. R. Cook's engraving, after the portrait by A. Buck.

brig, laden with powder and stores, from the harbour of San Pedro, while the frigate herself engaged three gunboats and two armed schooners. The *Seahorse* had one man killed.[3]

In March, 1805, the *Pallas*, 32, Captain Lord Cochrane, returned from a month's very successful cruise in the latitude of the Azores. She had taken several rich Spanish prizes, amongst them the *Fortuna*, with 432,000 dollars on board. This was the occasion

---

[1] *Nav. Chron.*, xiii. 503.   [2] James, iv. 133.   [3] *Ib.*, iv. 133.

when the *Pallas* entered port with gold candlesticks five feet high at each masthead.   On her way home she had a narrow escape, as she was chased and overhauled by three French line-of-battle ships—possibly belonging to Missiessy's squadron.   She got away by the manœuvre of suddenly clewing up and hauling down every sail, and putting the helm 'hard a-weather, so as to wear the ship.   Her pursuers, unprepared for this, shot past her, and she went off on the opposite tack.   This was a very clever piece of seamanship, worthy of so fine an officer as Lord Cochrane.   The story of it, as told by himself, deserves study.[1]

On June 1st, the boats of the *Loire*, 38, Captain Frederick Lewis Maitland (2), were sent in after dusk, under the orders of Lieutenant James Lucas Yeo, to cut out a small privateer from the bay of Camarinas in north-western Spain.   The boat party, thirty-five strong, did not reach the privateer till daybreak on the 2nd, and then discovered that there were two privateers instead of one, both moored under a battery of ten guns.   Nevertheless, under an ill-directed fire from the battery, both the privateers were boarded and captured with the loss of but three men on the British side.   Only one of the two, however, the *Esperança*, could be carried off, as the weather was perfectly calm.   On his way out, Yeo seized three small Spanish merchantmen laden with wine.

A day later, the *Loire* proceeded to the neighbouring port of Muros to capture a French privateer, which was supposed to be at anchor there.   She towed in her boats, with fifty men in them, under the command of Yeo, at about 9 A.M., and was promptly attacked by a Spanish battery mounting two guns upon the point under Mount Louro.   To seize this, and secure the British retreat, Yeo, with the boats, was sent in.   The Spanish force in the battery was much too weak to offer any effective resistance.   It numbered only eighteen, and took to flight as the British party landed.   The two guns were spiked, and the British, flushed with success, advanced quickly along the land towards a fort mounting twelve guns, which was then hotly engaged with the *Loire*.   This fort was a regularly-constructed masonry work, with a deep ditch, and was strongly garrisoned.   To assail it with a force of less than fifty men was an act savouring of temerity; yet the very audacity of the attack was the cause of its success.   The Spanish garrison had all attention centred upon the *Loire*, and had left the gate to the rear of the fort open.   Through

---

[1] Dundonald, ' Autobiog. of a Seaman ' (ed. 1861), i. 174 *et seq.*

this the British seamen burst, and met the garrison, headed by the
Spanish commander of the fort, at the inner gate. Yeo dashed at
the commander and killed him with a single blow. A fierce hand
to hand struggle between the British and Spaniards followed ; and
the latter, though about one hundred strong, were driven to a corner
of the fort, and compelled to surrender. Their loss was exceedingly
heavy, amounting to 12 killed and 30 wounded, whereas the British
loss was only 6 wounded, including Yeo. The guns in the fort were
spiked, the carriages destroyed, and as much damage as possible
was done to the embrasures before the British party re-embarked.

The *Loire*, whilst Lieutenant Yeo was thus occupied ashore, had
engaged the Spanish fort, anchoring very close to it, with springs on
her cable. The embrasures, however, were too small to allow her
broadsides to inflict any serious damage, and she was herself struck
repeatedly by the Spanish projectiles, losing nine men wounded.
But for the opportune capture of the fort by the landing-party, she
could scarcely have maintained her position. In the harbour were
found two large French privateers without armament, the *Confiance*
and the *Bélier*, and one merchantman in ballast. Maitland offered
that, if the stores and guns of the privateers were given up, he would
not trouble the place further. His offer was accepted ; but the guns
could not be embarked, and were left behind. The gallant Yeo was
made a Commander on June 21st, 1805, and given command of the
captured *Confiance*.[1]

On June 13th, the boats of the *Cambrian*, 40, Captain John Poo
Beresford, to the south-east of Bermuda, boarded and captured the
Spanish privateer *Maria* ; and on July 3rd, the French privateer
Matilda, 10, on the Floridan coast. A crew was placed on board the
latter, under the command of Lieutenant George Pigot (2),[2] and the
vessel was despatched to the River St. Mary, then the boundary
between the Spanish colony of Florida and the United States, to
destroy a Spanish privateer which was thought to be lying in the
river. The *Matilda* proceeded twelve miles up the river, under a
continual fire from Spanish sharpshooters on the banks, found the
privateer moored with two prizes across the river, and then ran
aground. Pigot, however, led his men in their boats to the enemy,
carried all three craft in succession, turned their fire upon the
enemy's sharpshooters, and finally brought them off. The British

---

[1] *Nav. Chron.*, xiii. 498, 501, xxiv. 269 ; James, iv. 134.
[2] Com., Aug. 15th, 1806 ; Capt., Sept. 17th, 1808.

loss was 2 killed and 14 wounded, among the latter being Pigot himself. The Spaniards are said to have had 25 killed and 22 wounded.[1]

On July 19th, the *Blanche*, 36, Captain Zachary Mudge, on her way from Jamaica to Barbados with despatches for Lord Nelson, was so unfortunate as to run up against a small French squadron some distance to the north of Puerto Rico. The French ships were the *Topaze*, 40, Captain F. A. Baudin, *Département des Landes*, 22, Lieutenant R. J. H. Desmontils, *Torche*, 18, Lieutenant N. P. Dehen, and *Faune*, 16, Lieutenant C. Brunet. They had, at various times, arrived in the West Indies with despatches for Villeneuve, had missed him, and were then returning. At first sight, as the day was hazy, and as they carried British colours,[2] Captain Mudge took them for part of the homeward-bound West India fleet, which he knew was to be expected thereabouts. But as they made no reply to his signals, and closed him fast, he took alarm, and endeavoured to make off. The *Blanche* was close-hauled upon the port tack, with the wind from the east. She sailed badly, owing to the damaged condition of the copper on her bottom, and was speedily overtaken by the *Topaze*, which had drawn ahead of her consorts. The *Topaze* came up on the *Blanche's* starboard quarter, fired a broadside, and closed to within pistol-shot, whereupon the British ship returned the fire. The two ships ran large under easy sail. On the *Blanche's* starboard quarter was the *Département des Landes*, and astern were the other two corvettes. Both the *Département des Landes* and the *Torche*, according to the evidence of the *Blanche's* officers, were firing upon the British frigate, though, if French accounts can be believed, they contributed very little to the *Blanche's* defeat, the first only firing eighteen shots, and the second three broadsides. After half an hour's close action, the *Blanche* attempted to cross the *Topaze's* bows and rake her, but was thwarted in that manœuvre by the French captain's sharply luffing, grazing the *Blanche's* mizen shrouds, and passing under her stern, there delivering a raking fire. At 11 A.M., after two and a quarter hours' resistance, the *Blanche* struck, being then in a thoroughly disabled condition, with several of her guns dismounted, her sails and rigging shot to pieces, her masts badly wounded, and her hold full of water.

---

[1] James, iv. 138; *Nav. Chron.*, xiv. 260.

[2] Mudge, however, "from the make of the Union and colour of the bunting," later concluded that they were French. This deserves consideration by flag-makers.

The force of the ships engaged was as follows :—

—	Tons.	Guns.	Broadside.	Men.	Killed.	Wounded.
Topaze	1132	44	Lbs. 500	340	3	9
Dépt. des Landes . .	—	22	96	200	0	0
Torche	—	18	120	196	0	0
Faune	—	16	52	98	0	0
Blanche . . .	951	44	476	215	8	15

The *Topaze* sustained only very trivial injuries, but the *Blanche* sank some hours after the action. She was infected with dry-rot, and, in consequence, her timbers offered little resistance to the enemy's shot.

The fact that the *Blanche* struck without having suffered heavy loss, and that she inflicted little damage upon her enemies, subsequently excited some unfavourable comment; and it was suggested that Mudge had been surprised and attacked before his ship was cleared for action. The force on the side of the French could, however, be fairly described as overwhelming. It is nothing unprecedented to find British ships striking in such circumstances with but small loss. In this case it is clear that the *Blanche* was in a desperate condition when she surrendered. The usual court-martial on the loss of the ship honourably acquitted Captain Mudge, and congratulated him upon his "able and gallant conduct." [1]

On their way back to France, two of the four French ships were taken. The *Faune*, having separated from the other three, was chased by the British *Camilla*, 20, and *Goliath*, 74, and struck on the morning of August 15th, some hundreds of miles to the west of Rochefort. The *Camilla*, Captain Bridges Watkinson Taylor, with the prize, steered for England, while the *Goliath*, Captain Robert Barton, proceeded southwards to look for the other French vessels, and was joined by the *Raisonnable*, 64, Captain Josias Rowley. The two sighted the *Topaze*, *Torche*, and *Département des Landes* in the afternoon, when the French ships scattered. The *Goliath* followed

---

[1] James, iv. 139; 'Vict. et Conq.,' xvi. 150; *Nav. Chron.*, xiv. 166, 186, 341; Troude, iii. 422; C. M. Oct. 14th, 1805. Mudge retired, when a full Admiral, in 1852.

and captured the *Torche*. The *Raisonnable* gave chase to the *Topaze* and on the 16th was able to get near her. The *Topaze*, however, as soon as her enemy was within range, opened so effective and accurate a fire from her stern chasers at the *Raisonnable's* rigging, that the British battleship was unable to close and bring her heavy broadside to bear. Favoured by the wind, the *Topaze* gradually drew away, and finally escaped to Lisbon, having had 3 men wounded by the British fire. The *Département des Landes* also made good her escape.[1]

On August 2nd, the *Phaeton*, 38, Captain John Wood (2), and sloop *Harrier*, 18, Commander Edward Ratsey (actg.),[2] discovered the French *Sémillante*, 36, Captain L. B. Motard, at anchor in the harbour of San Jacinto in the Philippines. The *Sémillante* had been despatched from Mauritius to warn the Spanish governor of the colony of the outbreak of war, and, after performing that mission, had been requested by him to proceed to Mexico and obtain funds, which were urgently required in the Philippines, where the Spanish treasury was empty. The *Sémillante* was on her way to Mexico, but had been compelled to anchor at San Jacinto, owing to the feebleness of the wind, which would not permit her to attempt the passage of the San Bernardino Strait. As soon as the British vessels were made out, the *Sémillante* warped to a position where on one side she had a reef of rocks, and on the other two batteries, mounting in all two 12 and two 9-prs. These guns were manned by seamen from the frigate. The *Harrier* led in and opened fire; the *Phaeton* followed; and, after an hour's cannonade, the British sloop took fire. The flames were speedily got under, but a little later both British vessels retired, as it was impossible to get at the enemy without warping. Each of the British ships had 2 men wounded, and both were much damaged in sails and rigging. The *Sémillante* does not seem to have suffered any loss. During the night she landed several guns and prepared for a fresh attack, but the British ships, having reconnoitred her position next day, withdrew. The *Sémillante*, when they had disappeared, retired to Mauritius and abandoned her voyage to Mexico, judging that the enemy would keep a sharp look-out for her.[3]

---

[1] James, iv. 145.

[2] Com., Feb. 4th, 1806; Capt., Sept. 5th, 1806; R. Ad., Nov. 23rd, 1841. Ratsey became a retired V.-Adm. in 1850, and a retired Adm. in 1857.

[3] James, iv. 152; Troude, iii. 418.

On August 6th, the *Blenheim*, 74, Captain Austin Bissell,
carrying the flag of Rear-Admiral Sir Thomas Troubridge, on her
way to Madras with a convoy of ten East Indiamen, sighted two
of the ships of Admiral Linois's squadron, some hundreds of miles to
the east of Mauritius. These two ships were Linois's flagship, the
Marengo, 74, Captain Vrignault, and the *Belle Poule*, 40, Captain A.
Bruillac, on their way to the Cape from the Gulf of Aden, where
they had been cruising. They opened fire upon the Indiamen, and
then exchanged several broadsides with the *Blenheim*. A heavy sea
was running, and the British ship had the windward position,
which prevented her from using her lower-deck guns. But Linois
had no desire to risk a close action with so powerful an opponent.
His object was commerce-destruction rather than fighting, and he
drew off, preferring to hover about the convoy. This, however,
showed him a bold front; and on the evening of the 7th, his ships
disappeared to the south.[1] The *Marengo* and *Belle Poule* had
between them 10 wounded; the *Blenheim* had a passenger killed,
and one of the Indiamen also lost a man. The convoy safely
reached Madras.

At the end of July, 1805, the *Æolus*, 32, Captain Lord William
Fitzroy, was detached from the Channel fleet to reinforce Vice-
Admiral Calder's squadron, then cruising to the west of Finisterre,
on the look-out for Villeneuve and the Franco-Spanish fleets. Lord
William's instructions were to obtain all possible information of the
enemy's whereabouts, and, in case he should meet with the allied
squadron, to follow it till he could discover its route. On August
5th, he fell in with Allemand's squadron from Rochefort, followed it
at a great distance for nine hours, and then, losing sight of it, made
all sail to inform Calder. On the 7th, he sighted the French *Didon*,
40, Captain P. B. Milius, on her way from Villeneuve with despatches and orders for Allemand. She made no attempt upon him,
and Lord William, after reconnoitring her, went on his way. The
enemy was so greatly his superior in force, that any engagement
would not improbably have resulted in the *Æolus's* loss, the British
broadside being only 372 lb. to the French 563. But there are
many instances to prove that in that war, British Captains had
no hesitation in attacking far more superior adversaries. What
held Lord William back was beyond doubt the fact that he wished.

[1] James, iv. 150; Troude, iii. 424.

as speedily as possible to communicate to Calder the despatches which he carried, and the news of Allemand's movements. James, overlooking this fact, virtually accuses Lord William Fitzroy of cowardice. The charge is a little unjust, for in war, if Captains entrusted with important despatches went out of their way to fight purposeless actions, great strategic combinations could rarely be effected. Fitzroy was a tyrannical officer, as subsequent events showed, but that does not prove him to have been a coward or incapable.[1]

In the end the *Didon* did not escape. She was sighted on August 10th by the *Phœnix*, 36, Captain Thomas Baker (1), at daylight. Baker immediately gave chase, and, strange to say, the French vessel made no attempt to get away, having received very erroneous information from an American craft as to the *Phœnix's* force. The American had represented her as a 20-gun ship, and her appearance, at a distance, gave some support to this story, since she had been disguised to look like a sloop. What happened is a good illustration of the folly of captains who are charged with despatches giving way to their instinct of pugnacity.

At about 8.45 A.M., the *Didon* opened on the *Phœnix*, which ship was steering to close on the French vessel's leeward quarter, so as to frustrate any attempt to escape. The *Didon*, also with the object of preventing the British ship's escape, wore three times as the *Phœnix* approached, on each occasion delivering a broadside at the British vessel's rigging. Her adroit manœuvres compelled the *Phœnix* to abandon her attempt to pass round the enemy, and forced her to bear down and draw up on the windward side. At 9.15 A.M. the two ships were within close range, both standing on the port tack, when they began a broadside action. The *Phœnix*, however, had so much way on her that she speedily shot ahead, upon which the *Didon* passed under her stern, and fired some shots at her, but at too long a range to do much damage. The *Didon* was then to leeward, and used her position with effect, suddenly bearing up, passing a second time under her opponent's stern, and delivering a raking broadside, which, nevertheless, failed to inflict heavy loss,

---

[1] James, iv. 154; Log of *Æolus*. Fitzroy, a Captain of 1804, was dismissed the service for tyranny and oppression by C. M. April 7th, 1811, but reinstated Aug. 22nd following, though never again employed. He died a full Admiral, May 13th, 1857.

as the British crew, as soon as the manœuvre was noted, was
ordered to lie down. Again the French ship attempted to cross the
Phœnix's stern, but was foiled by the British crew smartly backing
her sails. The way on the *Phœnix* was arrested, and the Frenchman, as he attempted to turn, ran his port bow against the *Phœnix's*
starboard quarter. In that position the French endeavoured to
board, but were beaten back, though in greatly superior force.
Meantime, one of the *Didon's* 36-pr. forecastle carronades poured in
a steady fire upon the British ship.

It had become a matter of absolute necessity for the *Phœnix*, if
she was not going to be beaten, to bring one or more of her main-
deck guns to bear. Singularly enough, though action after action
had showed the want of gun-ports which would allow the heavy
guns to play upon an enemy in any position, British frigates, and
the *Phœnix* amongst them, were built without ports on the quarters.
But in the *Phœnix's* case the mistake of the constructor had in some
degree been remedied by the Captain's forethought. A port on each
quarter had been cut. Unfortunately, however, the gunner had
failed to provide the tackle needed for the transfer of the aftermost
maindeck guns to their new position. In consequence, whilst the
crew were with makeshift appliances moving one of the guns, under
Baker's direction, very heavy losses were inflicted by the fire of the
French small-arm parties, directed through the *Phœnix's* stern
windows. When, at length, the 18-pr. could be brought to bear, it
fired with devastating effect. Its first shot is said to have killed or
wounded 25 of the French.

Slowly the *Didon* drew ahead, and one by one the broadside guns
in each ship came into action. Happily the *Phœnix's* people had
been thoroughly trained in gunnery, practising with powder and
shot where most Captains would have been content to go through
the gunnery drill. They fired three shots to the *Didon's* two, and
each shot was more effective. They brought down the enemy's
main topmast, and so badly wounded the fore mast that it fell a
little later. On her part, the *Phœnix* had her main royal-mast, main
topsail yard, and gaff shot away. The two ships parted and made
what repairs they could. The British crew, however, showed such
smartness that the *Phœnix* was ready first; and this ability of hers
to resume action whilst her antagonist was still disabled, virtually
decided the issue of the engagement. There was a brief interchange
of broadsides, and then, at about 12.15 P.M., the *Didon* struck, after

a most gallantly fought encounter. The force of the two ships was
as follows :—

—	Tons.	Guns.	Broadside.	Men.	Killed.	Wounded.
Phœnix	884	42	Lbs. 444	245	12 [1]	28
Didon	1091	46	563	330	27	44

[1] Including Lieut. John Bounton, and Master's Mate George Donalan.

Both ships were commanded by brave and skilful captains, and
manned with exceptionally good crews. So far as can be ascertained,
the contest was decided in the _Phœnix's_ favour by superior gunnery.
She carried, instead of long 18-prs., guns of medium length, midway
between the long gun and the carronade ; and these could be better
handled by a numerically small crew. They would have handicapped
her seriously in a long range action, but seem to have worked in
her favour on the present occasion, as her weapons could be fired
with great rapidity. The spirit of the British crew is shown by
the fact that sick men left their cots to join the powder-passing
division.[1]

Four days after the action, the _Phœnix_ and _Didon_ fell in with
the _Dragon_, and in her company, on August 15th, were sighted and
chased by a division of Villeneuve's fleet, but escaped, though at
one time the enemy was almost within range. Steering southwards, the British vessels passed into thick fog, and heard on all
sides the firing of guns and the ringing of bells. It was Villeneuve's
fleet once more. Yet again the _Phœnix_ and _Didon_ escaped—the
Dragon had before parted company—and made good their way to
Plymouth. Baker[2] received no public reward for this brilliant
success, nor was his first Lieutenant, Mr. Samuel Brown, made
Commander until August 1st, 1811. The _Didon_ was purchased
for the Navy, but, though a superb sailer, was never employed on
active service.

On August 13th, two small boats from the _Mariamne_, Lieutenant
James Smith (3), a prize of the _Swift_, 18, Commander John Wright
(3), boarded a Spanish revenue cruiser, the _Caridad Perfecta_, 12,

[1] James, iv. 163 ; _Nav. Chron._, xiv. 258 ; Troude, iii. 425.
[2] Thomas Baker, Com., Nov. 24th, 1795 ; Capt., June 13th, 1797 ; C.B., June 4th,
1815 ; Col. of R. M., Aug. 12th, 1819 ; R.-Adm., July 19th, 1821 ; K.C.B., Jan. 8th,
1831 ; V.-Adm., Jan. 10th, 1837 ; died, Jan. 26th, 1845.

and carried her off from under the guns of the port of Truxillo. The *Swift* covered this operation, and returned the fire of the batteries.[1]

On September 25th, the British ship *Calcutta*, 54, Captain Daniel Woodriff, convoying, from St. Helena to England, six merchantmen, one of which, the *Brothers*, was a very slow sailer, fell in with the French squadron from Rochefort, under Rear-Admiral Allemand, some leagues to the W.N.W. of Ushant. This squadron consisted of five ships of the line, three 40-gun frigates, and three brigs, and had already captured, on July 17th, the *Ranger*, 16, Commander Charles Coote. The wind was light, and, on the 25th, the French were not able to close the *Calcutta* and her convoy; but, early on the 26th, they drew very near her, the *Calcutta* keeping between the merchantmen and the enemy, with the *Brothers* some distance astern. As soon as the nature of the approaching ships was made out, the *Calcutta* signalled to the convoy to make all sail ahead, and herself turned to engage the French *Armide*, 40, which was fast closing. After a short interchange of fire, the French frigate's rigging was so badly cut up as to disable her. But, in the meantime, the French battleships had closed the *Calcutta*, and she found herself compelled to engage the *Magnanime*, 74, Captain P. F. Violette. Such an engagement could have but one end. The French fired mainly at the *Calcutta's* rigging, and completely disabled her, whereupon she was obliged to strike, with 6 killed and 6 wounded. She saved the convoy, with the exception of the slow-sailing *Brothers*, which the French secured.[2]

On October 5th, the *Princess Charlotte*, 38, Captain George Tobin, by disguising herself as a merchantman, attracted the attention of the French *Naïade*, 16, Lieutenant J. P. M. Hamon, and *Cyane*,[3] 26, Lieutenant C. L. Menard, cruising off Tobago. The *Cyane* was very close before she discovered what the disguise covered; and she was brought to action and captured. Her loss was 3 killed and 8 wounded. The British ship had 1 killed and 6 wounded. The *Naïade*, further off, made all sail, and got away for the time, but only to be taken on the 13th by the *Jason*, 32, Captain William Champain.[4]

---

[1] James, iv. 172.
[2] James, iv. 147; Troude, iii. 336; *Nav. Chron.*, xix. 170.
[3] *Ex* British; taken May 12th, 1805.
[4] James, iv. 173; *Nav. Chron.*. xiv. 508; Troude, iii. 430.

On November 29th, the boats of the *Serpent*, 16, Commander John Waller (1), cut out a small Spanish revenue cruiser and a privateer from the harbour of Truxillo without any loss.[1]

On December 24th, the French *Libre*, 38, Captain H. Descorches, was chased off Rochefort (to which port she was returning owing to having sprung a leak, though she was under orders for San Domingo), by the British frigates *Egyptienne*, 44, Lieutenant Philip Cosby Handfield (actg. Capt.), and *Loire*, 38, Captain Frederick Lewis Maitland (2). The *Loire* was the first to close and bring the enemy to action, but she was quickly followed by the *Egyptienne*. Against such overwhelming force—for the *Egyptienne* alone was far more than a match for the *Libre*—the chances of the French were quite hopeless. In thirty minutes, all the *Libre's* masts were very badly injured, and twenty of her crew put *hors de combat*, Captain Descorches being twice wounded. She struck, and during the following night her masts went by the board. The *Loire* had no losses, and very slight damage to report. The *Egyptienne* was much cut up in her rigging, and had 1 killed and 9 wounded. The *Libre* was too old and worn out to be purchased for the Navy.[2]

On January 2nd, 1806, the *Malabar*, 54, Captain Robert Hall (1), and *Wolf*, 18, Commander George Charles Mackenzie, chased two French privateers into the Cuban harbour of Aserraderos. The *Wolf*, with the boats of the *Malabar*, worked her way into the port and brought off one of the two, the *Napoléon*, 4, the other sinking from her numerous shot wounds.[3]

On January 6th, the *Franchise*, 36, Captain Charles Dashwood, proceeded to Campeche, though that harbour lay outside the limits of her station, Dashwood having heard that there were several Spanish vessels in the Mexican port. The shallowness of the water prevented her from approaching within fifteen miles of the shore. In consequence, three boats were sent in, in the evening, with 64 officers and men, under Lieutenants John Fleming[4] (2) and Peter John Douglas,[5] to bring off the enemy's ships. They were not able to reach Campeche till after the moon had risen and had revealed their movements to the Spaniards. Several Spanish ships

---

[1] James, iv. 174.

[2] James, iv. 173; *Nav. Chron.*, xv. 73; Troude, iii. 433.

[3] James, iv. 219.

[4] John Fleming (2): Lieut., 1800; Com., 1814: died in that rank, 1847.

[5] Peter John Douglas: Lieut., 1804; Com., 1807; Capt., 1811; R.-Adm., 1848; V.-Adm., 1856.

of war of small size were waiting for their attack, fully prepared. These opened a heavy fire upon the British boats; but Fleming dashed at the nearest, the *Raposa*, 16, a brig with 90 men on board, and carried her. The British loss was only 7 wounded, and the prize was successfully brought off.[1]

On January 26th, the *Pitt*, 36, Captain Walter Bathurst, blockading the harbour of Port Louis, Mauritius, had a brush with one of the French batteries, and lost a man. Next day, the French warship *Sémillante*, 36, and the *Bellone*, privateer, put to sea to capture the *Pitt*, as the British vessel was known to be very weakly manned. The two ships, however, actually allowed themselves to be chased by the *Pitt*, without, so far as can be discovered, making any serious attempt to bring her to action.

On March 8th, the boats of the *Egyptienne*, 44, Captain the Hon. Charles Paget, cut out a large French privateer, the *Alcide*, from under batteries in the port of Muros, in north-western Spain, without suffering any loss. No particulars are recoverable of the exact number of guns mounted by the *Alcide*; she was "pierced for" thirty-four, but the number of guns actually mounted was very often found to be much below that for which a ship had portholes.[2]

On March 13th, the depredations on commerce of Admiral Linois's two ships—the *Marengo*, 74, and *Belle Poule*, 40—came at last to an end. They were on their way back to France after a very unsuccessful cruise on the trade route to India, between St. Helena and the Canaries, when, very early in the morning of the 13th, they saw several sail to the eastward, and, taking them for merchantmen under convoy, approached them. These were really the *London*, 98, Captain Sir Harry Burrard Neale, *Foudroyant*, 80, Captain John Chambers White (flag of Vice-Admiral Sir John Borlase Warren), and *Amazon*, 38, Captain William Parker (2), forming part of the squadron then on its way to the West Indies to look after Leissègues's and Willaumez's divisions[3] which had escaped from Brest. Five other ships of the British squadron were some miles astern. At 3 A.M., the *London*, which, by reason of her bad sailing, had been placed to windward of the flagship *Foudroyant*, made signals, whilst on the port tack with wind at W.S.W., that an enemy was at hand. The night was so dark that the other ships could perceive nothing; but the *Amazon*, on discovering that the *London* was altering course,

---

[1] James, iv. 220; *Nav. Chron.*, xv. 345.   [2] James, iv. 221; *Nav. Chron.*, xv. 254.
[3] *See* p. 184.

and apparently giving chase, made sail after her. As day broke, the
British ship was seen to be close to a line-of-battle ship and a frigate,
which vessels she at once engaged, opening a heavy fire at about
5.30. The *Belle Poule*, however, was directed by Linois to make off;
and she left the *London* and *Marengo* to fight their battle out. Some
minutes later, the *Marengo*, having received a heavy fire from the
London, herself attempted to get away. She had inflicted so
much damage on the *London's* rigging that that ship speedily
dropped astern ; but she had herself sustained such injuries that the
other British battleships gained on her slowly. At about 11 A.M.,
the *Ramillies*, 74, Captain Francis Pickmore, was near enough to
open fire upon her, whereupon she struck, with the *Repulse*, 74, and
Foudroyant also almost within range. She had 63 killed and 83—
including Linois and Captain Vrignault—wounded, whilst the *London*
had 10 killed and 22 wounded.

The *Amazon*, on seeing the *Belle Poule's* attempt to escape, had
boldly made all sail ahead, passing the *Marengo*, and receiving from
that formidable vessel several broadsides, which, however, she
returned with effect. At about 9 A.M. she was near enough to the
French frigate to begin a running action, but was unable to close to
decisive range, since she had been driven far to leeward in her efforts
to avoid the *Marengo's* fire. At 11 A.M., nevertheless, the *Belle
Poule* followed the *Marengo's* example and struck, with 6 killed and
24 wounded.   The *Amazon's* loss was 3—including Lieutenant
Richard Seymour—killed and 7 wounded, of whom one afterwards
died.[1]

The French ships offered a brave resistance, and might have
done better, had not the overwhelming force against them rendered
resistance hopeless.

On March 21st, the hired armed brig *Colpoys*, 16, Lieutenant
Thomas Ussher, chased three Spanish luggers into the Spanish port
of Aviles. Lieutenant Ussher, in a boat with only six men, rowed
in under a heavy fire from a Spanish battery, and boarded and
captured all three. Two were successfully brought off. A month
later, on April 19th, the same daring officer[2] landed a party of
seamen, and, assisted by a party from the *Attack*, 12, Lieutenant
Thomas Swaine (2), stormed a two-gun battery at Doëlan, on

---

[1] James, iv. 222; *Nav. Chron.*, xv. 433; Troude, iii. 455; 'Life of Sir W. Parker,'
i. 319; Chevalier, 305.

[2] Lieut. Ussher was made Com., Oct. 18th, 1806. He died a R.-Adm., 1848.

the Breton coast, carried off two French *chasse-marées*, and destroyed a signal station—all this, too, without the loss of a single man.[1]

On March 24th, to the south of Puerto Rico, the *Reindeer*, 18, Commander John Fyffe, sighted the *Phaëton*, 16, Lieutenant L. H. Saulces de Freycinet, and *Voltigeur*, 16, Lieutenant J. Saint Cricq, and approached them. They immediately attacked her, and, after some hours of desultory fighting, inflicted so much damage upon the *Reindeer's* sails and rigging that she was unable to keep up with them. They then made off, having, it is supposed, despatches on board for M. Leissègues at San Domingo. The *Reindeer* had no killed or wounded, and only a few shots in her hull. For close action she was the better armed vessel, carrying 32-pr. carronades against her enemies' long 6-prs. Two days later, the *Pique*, 36, Captain Charles Bayne Hodgson Ross, whilst on her way from San Domingo to Curaçao, sighted these same two French brigs, neared them, and at about 1 P.M. opened upon them at long range. An hour later she was able to begin a close action, and speedily damaged the *Phaëton's* rigging so much that the Frenchmen were unable to prevent Ross from placing the *Pique* across their hawse, whereupon the *Phaëton* was boarded and carried, though not without a desperate struggle, in which the French lost nearly half their men. The *Voltigeur*, whilst the *Pique* was thus engaged, had attempted to make her escape, crowding all sail to reach the land ; but she was pursued, promptly overtaken, and compelled to strike. The British loss was 9 killed and 14 wounded. The French in the two vessels are said to have lost nearly 100 people. James charges the crew of the *Phaëton* with treachery, because they resorted to a ruse when the British boarded. This consisted in the Frenchmen lying concealed behind the boom of the mainsail, and suddenly rushing out and opening fire upon the British boarding-party, who, seeing the deck apparently deserted, were off their guard. A less prejudiced critic will admit that this was a perfectly fair stratagem, and that no discredit attaches to the French for making use of it.

Both ships were added to the British Navy, the *Phaëton* first as *Mignonne* and afterwards as *Musette*, the *Voltigeur* as *Pelican*.[2]

On March 28th, the French vessels *Revanche*, 40, *Guerrière*, 40,

---

[1] James, iv. 224; O'Byrne, 1144, 1222.
[2] James, iv. 225; *Nav. Chron.*, xvi. 78; Troude, iii. 466.

Sirène, 36, and *Néarque*, 16, put to sea from Lorient to harass the British whale-fisheries. They were quickly seen and chased by the *Niobe*, 38, Captain John Wentworth Loring, which overtook, and, dropping two boats under Lieutenant Barrington Reynolds, captured, the *Néarque*, the other French ships making no attempt to come to the help of their comrade.[1]

On March 29th, off Barbados, the *Agamemnon*, 64, and *Heureux*, 16, captured the notorious French privateer *Dame Ernouf*, 17, which had apparently been recaptured by the French some time after her capture by the *Curieux* in February, 1805.[2]

On April 3rd, the *Renommée*, 36, Captain Sir Thomas Livingstone, and *Nautilus*, 18, Commander Edward Palmer (1), were chased away from off Cartagena by two Spanish ships of the line and a frigate, covering the Spanish brig *Vigilante*, 18, and a small convoy. The *Nautilus* was sent off to Collingwood with the news that the Spanish vessels of the line were at sea, and the *Renommée*, having shaken off her pursuers, steered for Cape de Gata, where she expected to discover the brig and the convoy. The brig was found anchored under a battery on Punta del Corralete, and was attacked, and captured with a loss to the British of only two wounded. Exactly one month later the boats of the *Renommée* and *Nautilus* cut out the Spanish schooner *Giganta*, 5, from the harbour of Vieja, near Cartagena, with the loss of only 7 wounded, though the Spaniards were fully prepared, had boarding-nettings triced up, were moored close under the guns of a battery, and were assisted by troops on the beach. On October 21st, the *Renommée's* boat performed another feat of much the same nature, carrying off two small coasters from Puerto Colon, in Majorca, and destroying a tartan. On October 22nd, they captured yet another coaster, and carried her off from the same port. In these last operations, the only British loss was 2 wounded.[3]

On the night of April 5th, the boats of the *Pallas*, 32, Captain Lord Cochrane, were despatched, with about 160 men under the orders of Lieutenant John Haswell, to cut out the French corvette *Tapageuse*, 14, which was lying in the Gironde. The *Tapageuse* was twenty miles up the river and close to two powerful batteries; but, the weather being thick, the British boats surprised their enemy and

[1] *Nav. Chron.*, xv. 430 ; O'Byrne, 633, 968.
[2] *Nav. Chron.*, xv. 432.
[3] *Nav. Chron.*, xv. 436, xvi. 82; James, iv. 227.

carried her without the loss of a man killed, and with only three
wounded. At daybreak her captors hoisted her sails to take her
out, whereupon another French vessel attacked her, but was quickly
driven off. The guns of the French battery de Graves, did not fire
a shot, and the *Tapageuse* made good her retreat.

In the meanwhile, however, the *Pallas*, with a mere handful of
men, had been in the gravest danger. Three French sail had
appeared in the offing steering for the Gironde, and Cochrane had
only 40 men to work and fight his ship. He was not the officer to
abandon the cutting-out party, and in such straits he showed a bold
front, and had recourse to a most ingenious stratagem. The sails
were first furled with rope yarns, and then, on a signal, the yarns
were cut away by a few hands, so that all the sails were instantly
let drop together, as though they had been handled by a numerous
and well-trained crew. The *Pallas* gave chase to the leading enemy,
fired a few shot at her, and drove her ashore. She was the *Garonne*,
20. A second French vessel, the *Malicieuse*, 16, suffered the same
fate. The third, the *Gloire*, 20, is said by Cochrane to have been also
run on shore. After this extraordinary performance, the British
Captain coolly rejoined his prize, the *Tapageuse*.[1] It is satisfactory
to be able to note that Lieutenant Haswell was promoted on
August 15th following; but Cochrane, being unpopular with the
Admiralty, never received the thanks which he deserved. Numerous
instances of this kind of neglect occur in the period 1803–1815,
and, no doubt, contributed, in their way, to lower the efficiency
of the Navy.

Having " nothing better to do," as he remarked in his despatch,
Lord Cochrane determined next to interfere with the French coast
signal-service. Detachments from the *Pallas* seized and demolished
three signal stations on the Pertuis Breton ; and on May 9th, aided
by the *Frisk*, cutter, and *Contest*, brig, a party of seamen under
Lord Cochrane stormed a French battery on the Pointe de l'Aiguillon
and spiked three 36-pr. guns.[2]

On May 14th, the *Pallas* stood in to the Isle of Aix to reconnoitre
Allemand's squadron, and anchored just within range of the French
batteries. The *Kingfisher*, 16, Commander George Francis Seymour,
was in the offing, but had been given strict orders by Vice-Admiral

---

[1] James, iv. 229; 'Autob. of a Seaman,' i. 188; *Nav. Chron.*, xv. 347; Troude,
iii. 459. Cochrane incorrectly says that Haswell was not promoted.

[2] 'Autob.,' i. 196; James, iv. 230.

Thornbrough [1] not to pass Chassiron Lighthouse, as Seymour was thought to be prone to run great risks. As soon as the French admiral realised Cochrane's audacious intentions, he directed the frigate *Minerve*, 40, Captain J. Collet, and *Lynx*, *Sylphe*, and *Palinure*, of 16 guns each, to get under way to attack the Englishman, whilst the *Armide*, 40, and *Infatigable*, 40, were to hold themselves ready to assist at a signal.

Cochrane weighed and waited for his four enemies under topsails. The French came up with every inch of canvas—studding-sails and royals—spread. A broadside, as soon as the French vessels were within range, brought down the main topsail yard of one of the brigs, and put her out of action. The *Minerve* and the second brig then engaged the *Pallas* closely; but the action was not continuous, as each side had frequently to tack to avoid the shoals. At about 1 P.M., or almost two hours after the action had begun, Cochrane succeeded in getting to windward of the *Minerve*, and between her and the French batteries on the Isle of Aix, which had constantly fired at him. He then gave her two or three broadsides in quick succession. Her fire slackened, and, as there were signs that she meditated making off, he ran the *Pallas* on board her. Unfortunately, the *Minerve* had grounded on a shoal just before the *Pallas* struck her, so that the force of the concussion was very great indeed. The guns on board the British ship were driven back into the ports, and the fore topmast, fore-sail, jib-boom, sprit-sail yard, tcp-sail yards, fore-rigging, cat-head, and bower anchor were torn away. With the bower anchor, Cochrane had intended to grapple the *Minerve*; and he was unable to hold the two ships together. In the *Minerve*, the fore-yard came down, and much damage was done to the rigging. Three pistol shots were the only reply she made to a broadside from the *Pallas*; and the French crew fled below, Collet alone gallantly keeping his place on deck. The British were setting to work to clear away the wreckage from the *Pallas's* deck, preparatory to boarding, when it was seen that the *Armide* and *Infatigable* were getting under way and coming to the *Minerve's* help. There was nothing for it but to withdraw. Meantime Seymour, in the *Kingfisher*, observing that the *Pallas* had lost her fore-sail, came up with all possible speed, passed inside Chassiron light—in defiance of orders—and sent a cable to the *Pallas*. The three French frigates,

---

[1] Commanding a small squadron off the Vendéean coast.

presently reinforced by the *Gloire*, 40, positively allowed those two vessels to retire unmolested, though any one of them was a match in guns for the *Pallas* and *Kingfisher* together.[1]

Cochrane's whole career is so wonderful—his judgment was so excellent, his resourcefulness so capable of surmounting any emergency—that one hesitates to accuse him of rashness in thus assailing an enemy of enormously superior force in full sight of a strong French squadron. But a lesser genius would probably have sacrificed his ship by such an act. The force of the two frigates engaged was apparently as follows :—

—	Tons.	Guns.	Broadside.	Men.	Killed.	Wounded.
Pallas	667	38	Lbs. 300	214 n.	1	5
Minerve.	1101	44	530	330	7	14

The two corvettes engaged probably had between them a broadside of about 140 lbs., and 180 or 200 men. Their loss is unknown.

On April 17th, the *Sirius*, 36, Captain William Prowse (1), cruising to the east of Civita Vecchia, sighted a French flotilla, consisting of the *Bergère*, 18, Commander C. J. C. Chaunay-Duclos, *Abeille*, 18, *Légère*, 12, and *Janus*, 12, one bomb-vessel, three gunboats and a cutter, then on their way to attack the Neapolitan frigate, *Minerve*, off Gaeta. As soon as the *Sirius* was observed, the flotilla was moored in close order, in shoal water. The *Sirius* drew within pistol shot and opened fire, apparently sailing right in amongst the small craft; for we are told that she used both broadsides. She was most hotly engaged by the *Bergère* and *Abeille*. After two hours' hard cannonading, most of the French small craft retired to the shoals, where the *Sirius* could not follow them. The *Bergère*, however, offered a determined resistance, and did not strike till she was disabled and had suffered heavy loss. In the *Sirius*, 9 men were killed and 20 wounded. The *Bergère's* exact losses are not known. Great fault was found by the French authorities with the conduct of the commanders of the gunboats; but two were acquitted by court-martial, and only the third was found guilty

---

[1] James, iv. 231; 'Autob.,' i. 197; O'Byrne, 1053; 'Vict. et Conq.,' xvii. 290; Allemand to Min. of War.

and rendered incapable of holding any command for three years.
The sea being smooth and the weather calm, the small vessels
with their sweeps should have been able to effect more against
the *Sirius,* since she was too large to employ like means of
locomotion.[1]

On April 21st, the *Tremendous,* 74, Captain John Osborn, and
Hindostan, 50, Captain Alexander Fraser (1), convoying a number
of East Indiamen home, fell in off the coast of Natal with the
French frigate *Canonnière,* 40, Captain C. J. Bourayne. The
Canonnière had been despatched from France to reinforce M. Linois,
had failed to find him at Mauritius, and was on her way to the
Cape. The wind was E.N.E., and the *Canonnière* was steering
S.S.W., and was to leeward of the British vessels. The *Hindostan*
was at once ordered by Osborn to take charge of the convoy, whilst
the *Tremendous* went in chase of the French frigate. Osborn
succeeded in closing her sufficiently, at about 3.30 P.M., for the
chasers of both vessels to come into action. The *Canonnière,* which
had been going before the wind, then hauled up on the port tack.
The *Tremendous,* on her port quarter, did the same, but, having too
much sail spread and being to windward, heeled so much that her
fire was not effective. The *Canonnière* drew ahead and yawed,
bringing time after time her whole broadside to bear; but this
manœuvre enabled the *Tremendous* to gain upon her. The 74-gun
ship had drawn slightly ahead, and was preparing to cross her adversary's bows and pour in a raking fire, when a skilfully directed
broadside from the *Canonnière* shot away the jib-stay and fore top-
yard ties and slings, and brought the yard down on the cap. The
loss of so important a stay and the damage to the fore-rigging
retarded the *Tremendous.* She dropped back and passed under the
frigate's stern, directing, but at too long a range for any effect, a
raking broadside upon her enemy. The *Canonnière* then rapidly
drew away, and, in spite of an attempt of the leading Indiaman in
the convoy to cut her off, escaped.

In this action the French ship was handled with remarkable
skill. The same cannot be said of the *Tremendous*; and the decline
of British gunnery is clearly shown by the fact that the 74-gun ship's
powerful broadside failed to disable her enemy. The *Canonnière's*
loss was 7 killed and 25 wounded. As she fired high, to injure her

---

[1] James, iv. 233; *Nav. Chron.,* xvi. 80; Troude, iii. 460.

opponent's masts and rigging, she inflicted no loss upon the *Tremendous*. Her main mast, fore-yard, and mizen mast were all badly wounded, and one of her guns was smashed.[1]

Nine days after this encounter, the *Canonnière*, unaware that the Cape had fallen into the hands of the British, put in to Simon's Bay, anchored, and sent a boat ashore. She was fired upon, and immediately cut her cable and put out to sea, abandoning her boat, but herself escaping without injury.

On April 25th, off New York, an unfortunate incident occurred, which did much to embitter relations between Britain and the United States. British cruisers regularly hovered off the port and searched all neutral vessels for French goods or contraband of war. That in itself was likely to lead to ill-feeling, as the British officers always insisted with a high hand upon their rights. On the day in question the *Leander*, 50, Captain Henry Whitby, *Cambrian*, 40, Commander John Nairne (actg. Captain), and *Driver*, 18, were at this work.

Whitby went on board the *Cambrian* to dine; and, in his absence, the *Leander's* first Lieutenant, John Smith Cowan, took charge of the ship. Several small American vessels were standing in for New York; and, to make these heave to, the *Cambrian* occasionally fired shots ahead or astern of them. At length the *Leander* fired twice at an American coaster, the *Richard*. The second shot struck the taffrail and drove a splinter upon the master's brother, John Pierce, killing him on the spot. It was further asserted by some of the witnesses on the American side that this happened when the *Richard* was in American waters. That, too, was practically admitted[2] by the officers of the *Leander*. The British case was that British ships had the right to search for hostile goods, that American vessels regularly refused to bring to unless fired at, and that the killing of the man was a pure accident. Captain Whitby, as he had been out of his ship at the time of the firing, was acquitted by a British court-martial of all blame; but wonder can scarcely be felt that the verdict caused some indignation in the United States. The *Leander, Cam-*

---

[1] James, iv. 234; *Nav. Chron.*, xvi. 173; Troude, iii. 461.

[2] At that date the maritime frontier was regarded by British naval officers as lying at a gunshot from the shore. As guns varied in range, this was a very elastic limit. The Americans had sound sense on their side in placing the limit at three miles, and British international lawyers are now in agreement with their contentions. Snow, 27–29.

brian, and *Driver* were forbidden by the United States Government to enter American ports.[1]

On May 6th, the *Adamant,* 50, Captain John Stiles, fell in with the Spanish frigate-privateer *Nuestra Señora de los Dolores,* 26, in the southern Atlantic and captured her. Her crew, according to Captain Stiles, were " a desperate set of French, Spaniards, Portuguese, and Americans, the principal officers French." [2]

About May 20th, the British cutter *Dominica,* 14, Lieutenant Robert Peter, was carried off by her crew to the French at Guadeloupe. She was retaken, sailing as a privateer under the name of *Napoléon,* on May 24th, by the *Wasp,* 18, Commander Buckland Stirling Bluett.[3]

On May 25th, the *Renard,* 18, Commander Jeremiah Coghlan, sighted the French brig *Diligent,* 16, Lieutenant V. Thevenard, in the Mona Passage and gave chase. All the 25th and 26th the pursuit continued without the British vessel being able to overhaul her enemy. On the 27th, the *Renard* had recourse to her sweeps, and, aided by them and by a light breeze which opportunely sprang up, got within range of the *Diligent* at midday on the 28th. The French crew were exhausted by the long chase, during which they had had to keep on the alert to be ready for any opportunity. They refused to go to quarters when ordered, and, from captain downwards, seem to have supposed that the *Renard,* of 18 guns, was the *Magicienne,* of 32. So extraordinary a mistake is difficult to explain. It looks as though it were only an excuse for cowardice. The *Diligent* struck her flag without firing a shot. Thevenard was acquitted by a court-martial which afterwards tried him for this surrender, but was blamed for his "mistake" and for showing insufficient energy in taking steps to counteract the discouragement of his crew.[4]

On June 21st, the East Indiaman *Warren Hastings,* 36, Thomas Larkins, master, on a voyage home from China, fell in with the French frigate *Piémontaise,* 40, Captain J. Epron, cruising to the south of Réunion. The latter was under British colours, but failed to answer the private signal. At 12.20 P.M., with the wind at N.E. by E., and the *Warren Hastings* steering west, the *Piémontaise*

---

[1] James, iv. 236; *Nav. Chron.,* xviii. 72, 160 (C. M. Apr. 16th and 17th, 1807).
[2] *Nav. Chron.,* xvi. 173.
[3] *Ib.,* xvi. 85.
[4] James, iv. 238; *Nav. Chron.,* xvi. 86; Troude, iii. 465.

came up astern upon the Indiaman's port quarter, selecting the leeward position on account of the rough state of the sea, which heeled the frigate so that only her windward broadside could fire, and beginning action. The *Warren Hastings* returned the fire as her guns bore; and, after fifteen minutes' sharp fighting, the *Piémontaise* drew ahead, tacked, and passed the Indiaman to lee-ward, exchanging shot. The ships were so near to one another that there was danger of the yard-arms interlocking. The *Piémont-aise* passed astern, leaving the *Warren Hastings* in a terrible plight, with fore mast badly wounded, all the port shrouds shot through, and fore and main running-rigging and ensign shot away. Before repairs could be made the *Piémontaise* put about and got up along-side, and, after about twenty minutes' furious firing, again drew ahead and prepared to repeat her previous manœuvres. The short respite was employed by the weak crew of the Indiaman in, as far as was possible, refitting their ship. The fore mast had again been wounded, and the fore topsail had, in consequence, to be kept on the cap. Again the *Piémontaise*, on the opposite tack, closed, and this time inflicted such damage upon the Indiaman's masts and rigging that the latter ship was left a complete wreck aloft, with only the main topsail untouched, and with all braces shot away, so that to tack or manœuvre was an utter impossibility. The *Piémontaise*, as before, turned astern of the *Warren Hastings* and came up for the last time on the port quarter. There she could use her guns with the utmost effect; and the *Warren Hastings's* mizen mast was shot through till it fell forward, preventing the service of the British guns on the upper deck. The gun-room was set on fire; the guns' crews on deck were reduced to two men; the surgeon's instruments were carried away by a shot which penetrated the sick-bay; finally, the tiller-rope slipped on the wheel-barrel. As further resistance was quite out of the question, Larkins struck his flag at 4.50 P.M., having splendidly upheld the honour of the East India Company. The *Warren Hastings* was so utterly out of control—a fact which the mere recital of her injuries in Larkins's official letter clearly establishes—that she ran on board the *Piémontaise* whilst the latter vessel was lowering her boats to take possession of the prize. In a frenzy of rage, a French party under Lieutenant Charles Moreau, who, it is said, was drunk, dashed on board her and stabbed with daggers Larkins, the surgeon, the second officer, a midshipman, and a boatswain's mate. For this horrible outrage, inflicted in cold blood, there can be no excuse; and it will ever stain the annals of the French Navy.[1]

The force of the two ships was as follows :—

—	Tons.	Guns.	Broadside.	Men.	Killed.	Wounded.
Piémontaise . . .	1093	46	Lbs. 533	385	7	5
Warren Hastings . .	1356	36	312	138	7	13

but the grave inferiority of a merchantman pitted against a warship must also be taken into account. The Indiaman's decks were necessarily encumbered, and her crew was too weak to sail and fight the ship at the same time.

The Indiaman mounted twenty-two medium 18-prs.,[2] and ten 18-pr. and four 12-pr. carronades. The *Piémontaise* carried twenty-eight long 18-prs., four 9-prs., two 8-prs., and twelve 36-pr. carronades. Besides these, she had appliances fitted to her fore and main yard-arms for dropping large shells on an enemy's deck.

On June 22nd, two boats of the *Minerva*, 32, Captain George Ralph Collier, having entered Finisterre Bay, carried a fort mounting eight guns—which the British seamen spiked—and cut out five Spanish coasting vessels, without the loss of a man. On July 9th, the barge of the same vessel proceeded north from Oporto to look after certain very troublesome privateers from the Spanish port of La Guardia, which lurked along the coast. On the 11th, the barge came up with and captured, without loss, one of these craft. On September 29th, the ship's cutter cut out two *chasse-marées* off Pontevedra. In both of these affairs Lieutenant William Howe Mulcaster distinguished himself. Finally, on October 2nd, the same barge, whilst the *Minerva* was lying at anchor off Ons Island, entered Arosa Bay and carried off a Spanish gunboat.[3]

On June 25th, the *Port Mahon*, 18, Commander Samuel Chambers, chased the Spanish privateer *San Josef*, 7, into the Cuban harbour of Puerto de Banes. That same night the British boats went in, under a heavy fire from the privateer's guns and

---

[1] James, iv. 239; *Nav. Chron.*, xvi. 479, 484; xx. 193.

[2] Medium 18-pr.; length, 6 ft.; weight, 26·7 cwt.

[3] James, iv. 244; *Nav. Chron.*, xvi. 84, 170, 350.

from the guns of a Spanish battery, and cut her out, without any loss whatsoever.[1]

On July 9th, the *Rattlesnake*, 16, Commander John Bastard, sighted off the coast of Ceylon the very notorious French privateer *Bellone*, 34, and gave chase to her. The wind was south-west, and both ships were going free before it with all sail spread, when the *Powerful*, 74, Captain Robert Plampin, unexpectedly came into sight ahead. The *Bellone*, her escape thus cut off, did not at once strike, but for nearly two hours maintained a running fight with the 74, in which, extraordinary to relate, she inflicted more damage than she suffered. She then surrendered, with 1 killed and 6 wounded to the *Powerful's* 2 killed and 11 wounded. This action serves to again illustrate the lamentable decline in British gunnery. As James notes, it was the second occasion in those seas within one year on which a British ship of the line had failed to do any serious injury to a vessel of far inferior force and scantling.[2]

On the night of July 15th, twelve boats, under Lieutenant Edward Reynolds Sibly, from the ships *Prince of Wales*, 98, *Centaur, Conqueror, Monarch*, and *Revenge*, all of 74, *Polyphemus*, 64, *Indefatigable*, 44, and *Iris*, 32, proceeded into the Gironde to cut out two French corvettes and a convoy lying in that river. The boats approached, boarded the *César*, 16, Lieutenant L. F. H. Fourré, and captured her, though she was perfectly prepared; but only with terrible loss. As many as 9 of the party, including Lieutenant Charles Manners, were killed, 39 wounded, and 20 taken prisoners through the sinking of the *Revenge's* boat. The *César* was carried off by her captors. Sibly, who was wounded, was deservedly promoted [3] for his bravery.[4]

On July 18th, the *Blanche*, 38, Captain Thomas Lavie, sighted, off the Färöes, the French frigate *Guerrière*, 40, Captain P. M. Hubert, which had, in March, with her two sister frigates, so poor-spiritedly abandoned the *Néarque*. The *Blanche* was one of a squadron of three British frigates which had been despatched northwards to put a stop to the three French vessels' depredations on our whale fisheries. The *Guerrière*, according to French accounts, was in a deplorable state, foul in hull, with 80 men

---

[1] James, iv. 245; *Nav. Chron.*, xvi. 506.

[2] James, iv. 245; *Nav. Chron.*, xvii. 259. *Cf.* the case of the *Tremendous* and the *Canonnière*, p. 380.

[3] Aug. 4th, 1806. Sibly was posted, Mar. 8th, 1814, but died still a Captain.

[4] James, iv. 246; *Nav. Chron.*, xvi. 168.

sick of scurvy—to which disease 36 officers and men had already
fallen victims. For that reason the French frigate endeavoured to
escape; but at about 12.45 A.M. on the 19th, the *Blanche* closed her
and poured in two rapid broadsides. The *Guerrière* returned this
fire feebly, aiming at the enemy's rigging. Her masts were quickly
wounded; her mizen topmast fell; and, at 1.30 A.M., she struck.
The *Blanche* suffered scarcely any damage in the brief action.[1]

—	Tons.	Guns.	Broadside.	Men.	Killed.	Wounded.
			Lbs.			
Blanche	1036	46	520	314	0	4
Guerrière	1092	48	516	265	20	30

Captain Lavie, for his success, was knighted; and his first
Lieutenant, Henry Thomas Davies, was made Commander on
July 28th, 1806. The other two French frigates, *Revanche* and
Sirène, succeeded in regaining France, but in a miserable condition.
They captured in all twenty-nine whalers or merchantmen. As for
the *Guerrière*, she was added, under the same name, to the British
Navy.

On July 25th, the *Greyhound*, 32, Captain Charles Elphinstone,[2]
and sloop *Harrier*, 18, Lieutenant Edward Thomas Troubridge
(actg. Com.), sighted, off the south of Celebes, the Dutch *Pallas*, 36,
Captain N. S. Aalbers, and *William*, 16, Commander P. Feteris,
convoying the Dutch armed Indiamen *Victoria*, and *Batavier*.
The Dutchmen lay to all the night of the 25th off the Celebes
coast; and the British vessels did the same, as they had not been
able to ascertain whether one of the Indiamen was not a ship of the
line—which at a distance she resembled. At daylight the British
ships attacked the Dutch, who had meantime drawn up in line of
battle. The *Greyhound* engaged the leading Dutch ship, the
Pallas, whilst the *Harrier* bore up, passed between the *Pallas* and
her next astern, and poured her fire into both Dutch vessels.
Immediately after this the *Greyhound* crossed the *Pallas's* bows,
delivered a raking broadside, and gained a position on the enemy's
starboard bow, which she succeeded in maintaining, while the
Harrier on the Dutchman's quarter kept up a galling fire, to which
the enemy was able to make little return. Thus out-manœuvred,

[1] James, iv. 248; *Nav. Chron.*, xvi. 162; Troude, iii. 436.
[2] Elphinstone was lost (supernumerary) in the *Blenheim*, 1807.

the *Pallas* struck after forty minutes' hard fighting. The *Victoria* and *Batavier* followed her example. The *William*, which had taken no part in the fighting, succeeded in making good her escape. The *Pallas* and *Greyhound* were about equal in force. The Dutch East Indiamen were probably more heavily armed than the *Harrier*, but were not warships, and did not carry fighting crews. The British loss in the action was 1 killed and 8 wounded in the *Greyhound*, and 3 wounded in the *Harrier*. The Dutch had 12 killed and 39 wounded.[1]

On July 27th, the French frigates *Hortense*, 40, *Hermione*, 40, *Thémis*, 36, and *Rhin*, 40, Captain M. J. A. Chesneau, returning from the West Indies to Rochefort, were sighted by the *Mars*, 74, Captain Robert Dudley Oliver, look-out ship of Captain Richard Goodwin Keats's squadron blockading that port. She at once gave chase, and the pursuit continued all night. With daylight the *Rhin* was much astern of the remaining three, and the *Mars* was gaining on her fast. The other French vessels tacked, and formed in line of battle to support their comrade; but, as the *Mars* came resolutely on, they apparently concluded that discretion was better than valour, crowded all sail, and left her. The *Mars* then overhauled the *Rhin*, which struck at the first shot. The *Hortense*, *Thémis*, and *Hermione* escaped to Bordeaux, where their commodore, Captain La Marre La Meillerie, pretended that serious damage, sustained during his cruise, had alone prevented him from going to the *Rhin's* help. Chevalier blames his conduct, which was apparently most cowardly. Four large frigates, acting in combination, ought to have been able to make a good defence even against a vessel of the line such as the *Mars*.[2]

On August 14th, Lieutenant William James Hughes, in the fire-brig *Phosphorus*, 4, displayed a high degree of valour in beating off the privateer *Elise*, 12. He had but 24 men against the French 70 or 80; but he fought the enemy, chiefly at close quarters, for an hour and ten minutes, and pursued him when he made sail. The British loss was 8 wounded, including Hughes, who was deservedly promoted on September 25th.[3]

On August 18th, the barge of the *Galatea*, 32, Captain George Sayer (1), under Lieutenant Andrew M'Culloch, destroyed a Spanish

---

[1] James, iv. 251; *Nav. Chron.*, xvii. 339; De Jonge, v. 622.
[2] James, iv. 253; Troude, iii. 471; *Nav. Chron.*, xvi. 172; Chevalier, 265.
[3] *Gazette*, 1806, 1065; James, iv. 255.

privateer near Puerto Cabello on the Venezuelan coast. On the
21st, another small privateer of the same description was driven on
shore by Lieutenant Henry Walker, and burnt. On October 11th,
several Spanish vessels were cut out of the Venezuelan harbour of
Barcelona by the boats of the same ship under Lieutenant Richard
Gittins. On November 12th, the *Galatea* chased and captured the
French privateer *Réunion* off Guadeloupe.[1]

On August 23rd, the boats of the *Alexandria*, 32, Captain the
Hon. Edward King, and *Gracieuse*, 10, Lieutenant William Smith
(4a), rowed, under Lieutenants Joseph Lewis and Edmund Nagle (2),
into the port of Ensenada on the La Plata coast, under a heavy fire
from three Spanish batteries, a Spanish brig, and a Spanish revenue
cruiser, boarded the brig and cruiser, destroyed them, and retired.
The British loss was very heavy : 6 were killed and 12 wounded—a
great price to pay for so insignificant a success.[2]

On August 23rd, the *Arethusa*, 38, Captain Charles Brisbane, and
Anson, 44, Captain Charles Lydiard, sighted the Spanish *Pomona*,
34, two miles from Moro Castle at the entrance to the harbour of
Havana, for which she was making against a strong current. As
the British ships approached, the *Pomona* anchored close under the
guns of Moro, whilst twelve large Spanish gunboats came out of the
harbour, and advanced in line abreast against the *Arethusa* and
Anson. Disregarding their fire, the *Arethusa* anchored close alongside the *Pomona*, and the *Anson* on the *Arethusa's* port bow, and
began action. So steady and accurate was the British fire that in
thirty-five minutes the *Pomona* struck. Six of the gunboats were
sunk, three blown up, and the other three driven ashore. Thereupon the Moro guns began firing red-hot shot, and speedily set the
Arethusa on fire. The flames, however, were extinguished before
much damage was done. Shortly afterwards an explosion occurred
in Moro, and the Spanish guns ceased firing. The *Pomona* was
safely carried off; but a large quantity of specie which had been
on board her had been landed just before the action began. Her
loss was 21 killed and 32 wounded. The *Anson* suffered no loss, but
the *Arethusa* had 2 killed and 32, including Brisbane, wounded. The
Arethusa fought throughout in shoal water with only a foot between
the bottom and her keel.[3] The prize was added to the Navy as the
Cuba, 38.

---

[1] James, iv. 256.   [2] *Ib.*, iv. 255.
[3] *Ib.*, iv. 257; *Nav. Chron.*, xvi. 504.

On August 29th, the boats of the *Bacchante*, 24, Captain James Richard Dacres (2), rowed, under a heavy fire, into the port of Santa Marta, on the coast of what is now Colombia, and cut out three small Spanish armed vessels.[1] On August 30th, the *Stork*, 18, Commander George Le Geyt, *Supérieure*, 14, Commander Edward Rushworth, *Flying Fish*, 12, Lieutenant James Glassford Gooding, and *Pike*, 4, Lieutenant John Ottley, arrived off the Isle of Pines, off Cuba, whither they had been despatched by the Commander-in-Chief on the station, to clear out the privateers who frequented Batabano and Trinidad. Off Cape Frances, a Spanish coastguard schooner was captured. As the *Stork* drew too much water to enter the Gulf of Matamano, the *Supérieure*, *Flying Fish*, and *Stork* were detached under Rushworth for the service. Twenty-two miles from Batabano, on September 2nd, 64 officers and men of the three vessels landed, and on the 3rd advanced through bush and marshes upon a fort near Batabano; and, though opposed by a considerable force of Spanish soldiers and militia, captured the fort, in which six guns were mounted, and carried off, or destroyed, eleven French and Spanish vessels. This was effected with the loss of only one man wounded.[2]

On September 9th, the *Constance*, 22, Captain Alexander Saunderson Burrowes, *Sharpshooter*, 14, Lieutenant John Goldie, and *Strenuous*, 14, Lieutenant John Nugent, whilst cruising off St. Malo, sighted the French ship *Salamandre*, 26, armed *en flûte*, on her way from St. Malo to Brest with ship-timber. The *Salamandre*, having no chance against the squadron, precipitately ran ashore to the east of Cape Fréhel. There she had the help of a battery ashore, and of a number of troops on the beach. Owing to the strength of her position, the three British vessels were unable to send their boats in to destroy her. They considered that she must beat to pieces on the reefs, and they withdrew. No sooner, however, were they gone than she got afloat again and returned to St. Malo. After her damages had been repaired she started once more on October 12th, and was promptly discovered by the *Constance* and *Strenuous*, then in company with the *Sheldrake*, 16, Commander John Thicknesse, and the hired cutter *Britannia*. She entered the inlet to the west of Cape Fréhel, known as the Bouche d'Erquy, and there went aground, at a point close under a battery of two

---

[1] James, iv. 258; *Nav. Chron.*, xvi. 507.
[2] James, iv. 258; *Gazette*, 1806, 1537.

guns. Field artillery and a few troops at once went down to the
beach to support her. In spite of this the *Constance*, *Sheldrake*,
and *Strenuous* worked in and opened fire, and, after two hours' hot
action, the *Salamandre* struck. The *Constance*, however, unhappily
lost her Captain, Burrowes, in the action, and went fast aground on
the rocks under the battery. She was afterwards got off by the
French and taken to St. Malo. The *Salamandre* was set on fire by
her captors and destroyed. In all, the British loss was 10 killed,
23 wounded, and 38 prisoners, who were taken by the French in an
attempt to float the *Constance*. The French loss is unknown, but
was probably about 40 killed and wounded.[1]

On September 24th, the French frigate *Gloire*, 40, Commodore
E. J. N. Soleil, *Infatigable*, 40, Captain J. M. Girardias, *Minerve*,
40, Captain Joseph Collet, *Armide*, 40, Captain J. J. J. Langlois,
and *Thétis*, 36, Captain Jacques Pinsum, with the corvettes *Lynx*
and *Sylphe*, left Rochefort, having on board troops and stores for
the French West Indies. Late that same night they were sighted
by the *Monarch*, 74, Captain Richard Lee, one of Commodore Sir
Samuel Hood's squadron off Rochefort. The squadron consisted
of the following ships besides the *Monarch* : *Windsor Castle*, 98,
Captain Charles Boyles, *Centaur*, 74, Commodore Sir Samuel Hood
(2), *Achille*, 74, Captain Richard King (2), *Revenge*, 74, Captain Sir
John Gore (2), *Mars*, 74, Captain William Lukin, and *Atalante*, 16,
Commander Joseph Ore Masefield. At first it was thought by the
British Commodore that some of the Frenchmen were ships of the
line ; and he accordingly ordered line of battle to be formed ; but,
when the enemy were seen to be making all sail away to the S.S.W.,
the signal was hoisted for a general chase. The *Monarch*, *Centaur*,
and *Mars* speedily took the lead in the British squadron ; and at
5 A.M. on the 25th the *Monarch* was near enough to the *Armide* to
open fire upon her. The *Armide*, *Gloire*, and *Minerve* kept close
together, going S.W. before the wind, which was N. by E. The
Infatigable hauled her wind and stood to the N.W. ; and the *Thétis*,
with the corvettes, steered due S. The *Mars* pursued the *Infatigable ;* and the *Windsor Castle*, the *Thétis ;* but the British 98 sailed
too badly to be able to overtake the frigate.

At about 10 A.M. the *Monarch* was close enough to the *Gloire*
and *Armide* to open on those ships from her starboard broadside a
very heavy fire, which was returned with great effect. The frigates

[1] James, iv. 260; *Nav. Chron.*, xvi. 263, 348.

had the best of matters, as the swell at times prevented the 74 from using her lower deck guns. Her masts, sails and rigging were much cut up and she suffered a serious loss of men. With 4 killed and 25 wounded, she dropped astern of the *Armide* and *Gloire*, and engaged the *Minerve*, which was also considerably injured. The *Centaur* came up and relieved the *Monarch* at 11 A.M., and, an hour later, the *Armide* struck to the flagship, and the *Minerve* to the *Monarch*. Of the group of three French frigates, the *Gloire* alone remained. At about 3 P.M. she struck to the *Centaur* and *Mars*— the latter ship having got up after overhauling and capturing the *Infatigable* without difficulty or loss. The resistance offered by the French to a force so superior was in every way creditable. It would, however, seem that the gunnery of the *Monarch* could not have been very good, for even without her lower deck guns, her long 18's and her carronades should have sooner crushed the French frigates opposed to her. She had the great advantage of stouter scantling.

The total British loss was 9 killed and 29 wounded, among the latter being Hood, who lost an arm. The French loss is unknown, but Commodore Hood speaks of "much slaughter on board them," and the loss would be increased by their being crowded with troops.[1]

On September 24th, off the Malabar coast, the British East Indiaman *Fame*, 16, James Jameson, master, was captured by the French frigate *Piémontaise*, 36, Captain Epron, after a gallant resistance, which cost the French no fewer than 6 killed and 11 wounded. On board the East Indiaman 1 was killed and 6 were wounded.

On September 27th, the French frigate *Présidente*, 40, Captain G. Labrosse, which had been cruising in African and West Indian waters for a year, fell in with Rear-Admiral Sir Thomas Louis's squadron, cruising in the Bay to intercept Willaumez on his return. The *Présidente* was closed by the *Dispatch*, 18, Captain Edward Hawkins,[2] which, though some distance from the rest of the squadron and so greatly inferior in force to the *Présidente*, opened fire, and, according to French accounts, inflicted on the frigate so much damage that the *Présidente* was overtaken by the *Canopus*; whereupon the French flag was lowered. The *Dispatch* sustained

---

[1] James, iv. 262; *Nav. Chron.*, xvi. 346; Chevalier, 266; Troude, iii. 483.
[2] Posted Sept. 25th, 1806, but not yet aware of it.

severe damage as the result of her bold action, but had no one killed or wounded on board. The *Présidente* was, it would appear from British accounts, practically uninjured ; and she was purchased for the Navy,[1] and known, first as *Présidente*, and, after 1815, as *Piémontaise.*

On October 18th, the *Caroline*, 36, Captain Peter Rainier (2), captured off Batavia the Dutch brig *Zeerob*, 14. Whilst she was taking possession of the prize, the Dutch frigate *Phoenix*, 36, was seen making for Batavia roads, and was at once chased. The *Phoenix* succeeded in making good her escape, but another Dutch frigate, the *Maria Reijgersbergen*, 36, Captain Claas Jager, was found at anchor in the road, with the Dutch vessels *Maria Wilhelmina*, *William*, 14, and *Zeeploeg*, and the colonial vessel *Patriot*, 18. The *Caroline* at once closed with the *Maria Reijgersbergen*, opened a heavy fire on her, and in thirty minutes forced her to strike. Several Dutch gunboats, besides the *Phoenix*, were close at hand but gave no help, whilst the *William*, *Zeeploeg*, and *Patriot* appear to have rendered only the very slightest assistance. The force of the two ships was as follows :—

—	Tons.	Guns.	Broadside.	Men.	Killed.	Wounded.
Caroline	—	42	Lbs. 498	204	3	18
Maria Reijgersbergen .	—	40	256	270	50	

The *Caroline* was very little damaged, but the Dutch frigate's rigging, masts, and hull were much cut up.[2]

On November 27th, Rear-Admiral Sir Edward Pellew, the Commander-in-Chief on the East India station, arrived off Java with the 74's *Culloden*, *Powerful*, and *Russell*, *Belliqueux*, 64, *Sir Francis Drake*, 38, *Terpsichore*, 32, and *Seaflower*, 14. The Dutch had been expecting a French squadron, and mistook Pellew's force for it. In consequence, the Dutch warship *Phoenix*, 36, *Avonturier*, 18, *Zeeploeg*, 14, *William*, 14, *Maria Wilhelmina*, 14, with the *Patriot* and two other colonial ships, were caught unprepared in Batavia roads, and were run aground by their crews. The boats of the British squadron were sent in to complete their destruction,

---

[1] James, iv. 264; *Nav. Chron.*, xvi. 346; Troude, iii. 472.
[2] James, iv. 266; *Nav. Chron.*, xix. 341; De Jonge, v. 623.

which was accomplished with a loss of 1 killed and 4 wounded. Two Dutch 68-gun ships had, unfortunately, proceeded to the east of the island just before Pellew's arrival, and thus escaped.[1]

On October 24th and 25th, the schooner *Pitt*, 12, Lieutenant Michael Fitton, engaged the famous French West India privateer *Superbe*, 14, off the Cuban port of Baracoa, and, on the 26th, drove her ashore, and sent in her boats to take possession and get the prize afloat. In the latter work she was aided by the *Drake*, 16, Commander Robert Nicholas. The *Superbe* was for all practical purposes a pirate. She preyed alike upon British, American, and Spanish ships. There were many vessels of her type making their headquarters in the creeks and inlets of the Cuban coast; and the smaller vessels of the Navy in these waters were kept very busy watching them and stopping their depredations. It is characteristic of the indifferent administration of the Navy during the years which followed Trafalgar, that Lieutenant Fitton was never promoted for the skill and gallantry which he had shown in capturing the *Superbe*. He was actually superseded in his command by a follower of Rear-Admiral Dacres.[2]

On November 11th, the *Sceptre*, 74, Captain Joseph Bingham, and *Cornwallis*, 38, Captain Charles James Johnston, made a dash upon the French frigate *Sémillante*, 36, which with other vessels was lying in the harbour of St. Paul, Réunion, but finding that she was protected by very numerous heavy guns, drew off, after a brisk interchange of fire with the batteries.[3]

On November 20th, the *Success*, 32, Captain John Ayscough, sent her boats, under Lieutenants William Duke and Charles Spence, into Hidden Port, on the south coast of Cuba, to cut out the privateer felucca *Vengeur*. The French, who had landed with their only gun, covered their vessel with a brisk fire, which killed Duke, and obliged Spence, who had 7 men wounded, to desist from further attempts to dislodge the privateersmen, and to content himself with capturing their abandoned craft.[4]

On November 20th, the barge of the *Orpheus*, 32, Captain Thomas Briggs, under Lieutenant George Ballard Vine, most gallantly boarded and carried the schooner *Dolores*, 3, which had

[1] James, iv. 267; Osler, 'Exmouth,' 242; De Jonge, v. 625.
[2] James, iv. 269.
[3] O'Byrne, 587.
[4] James, iv. 270; *Nav. Chron.*, xvii. 163.

been despatched a few hours earlier from Campeche to annoy the frigate's boats.[1]

On the night of December 1st–2nd, off Tobago, the *Dart*, 28, Commander Joseph Spear, and *Wolverine*, 18, Commander Francis Augustus Collier, attacked the Liverpool slaver *Mary*, 24, Hugh Crow, master, mistaking her for a French privateer. The conflict was a close and terrible one, each side displaying the utmost tenacity. After seven hours of give and take, the *Mary* was at last overpowered,

CAPT. AUSTIN BISSELL, R.N.

From a miniature in the possession of his family.
(Kindly lent by Mr. F. Broad Bissell.)

and one of the warships boarded her. The British then discovered, to their consternation, that they had been fighting Englishmen. Six men on board the *Mary* died of their wounds, and many of the wretched negroes were killed or injured. Crow was an excellent and determined leader, and he had a good crew under him. The *Mary* did not strike till he had been stunned by a splinter.[2]

On December 13th, the *Halcyon*, 16, Commander Henry Whit-

---

[1] James, iv. 271; *Nav. Chron.*, xvii. 345.
[2] Williams, ' Liverpool Privateers,' 641.

marsh Pearse, cruising off the eastern coast of Spain, sighted, 20 miles from Cape San Martin, the armed vessels *Neptune, Dios de los Mares*, 14, *Virgen de Soledad*, 14, and *Vivaz*, 12. Some distance away from these three were five settees[1] following them. The *Halcyon* boldly attacked the three larger vessels, drove off with her fire the *Virgen de Soledad* and *Vivaz*, drew alongside the *Neptune*, and captured her—all this, too, without any loss to the British. The settees, when they saw what had happened, beat a prompt retreat.[2]

Among the losses of the time, few were more sad than those of the *Blenheim*, 74, and *Java*, 32, which foundered off Rodriguez, in the Indian Ocean, possibly early in March, 1807. In the former vessel, which dated from the year 1761, and was asserted to be hogged, were the gallant Rear-Admiral Sir Thomas Troubridge, Bart., Captain Austin Bissell, Captain (supr.) Charles Elphinstone, Midshipman George Lord Rosehill, eldest son of the Earl of Northesk, etc. In the latter, which was badly manned and very crank, was Captain George Pigot (1). Not a soul belonging to either ship's company was ever seen again.

On the night of January 2nd, 1807, the boats of the *Cerberus*, 32, Captain William Selby, cut out two French privateers from the harbour of St. Pierre, Martinique, in face of a tremendous fire. The British loss was small. Two men were killed and 10 wounded, including Lieutenant William Coote,[3] who was in command of the party. Two Russian officers, serving as midshipmen in the *Cerberus*, were warmly praised by Selby in his despatch.[4]

On January 7th, the boats of the *Impérieuse*, 38, Captain Lord Cochrane, under Lieutenant David Mapleton, landed a detachment of seamen, stormed Fort Roquette, protecting the French port of Arcachon, spiked four 36-prs., two field guns, and a 13-inch mortar, and burnt the fort. The shipping in the harbour, consisting of several gunboats and some small merchant vessels, was then destroyed. Lord Cochrane did not lose a man; which indicates that his plans were skilfully laid.[5]

Early on January 21st, the *Galatea*, 32, Captain George Sayer (1), cruising off Caracas, sighted the French corvette *Lynx*, 16,

---

[1] *Settee* (Fr. *scitie*), a Mediterranean vessel with long prow, single deck, two or three masts, and lateen sails.

[2] James, iv. 271; *Nav. Chron.*, xvii. 78.

[3] Com., May 6th, 1807.

[4] *Nav. Chron.*, xvii. 335.

[5] James, iv. 319; 'Autobiog. of a Seaman,' i. 213.

Lieutenant J. M. Farjenel, carrying a detachment of troops from Guadeloupe to Venezuela. The *Lynx* was very poorly manned. She had been cruising in the West Indies, and had lost many of her original crew; and to fill the dead men's places, 60 foreigners had been forcibly impressed at Guadeloupe. Aided by her sweeps, as the wind was excessively light, she drew fast away from the *Galatea*, and, in the afternoon, only her topgallant sails showed above the horizon. It was hopeless for the frigate to attempt to overtake her. Sayer decided to send his boats after her; and lowered six, with 75 officers, seamen, and Marines under Lieutenants William Coombe,[1] Henry Walker, and Robert Gibson (? 1 or 2 [2]), with Master's Mates John Green, and Barry Sarsfield. At about 6 P.M. they were only 12 miles off the enemy, who was working his sweeps and moving very slowly. At 8.30 P.M. the leading boat was within musket-range. A stop was made for the men to get weapons ready and prepare for the desperate onset which was to follow. At the same time, the boats formed in two separate lines, one of which was to board on each quarter of the enemy. As they came on, the *Lynx* received them with a heavy fire from her great guns and small arms, to which, from the nature of things, the boat party could reply only with musketry. Two attempts to board were repulsed in quick succession, and the gallant Coombe was wounded. Nevertheless, the British boats remained close under their enemy, who probably, for that very reason, could not bring his great guns to bear on them. The British small arms' fire through the ports was so destructive as to have a most de-moralising effect upon the ill-disciplined French crew; and, in a third desperate effort, the Frenchman's deck was gained, Lieutenant Henry Walker, who led the onset, there falling dead with three wounds in his body. There was a fierce and sanguinary struggle on the deck as the British forced the French back from the poop, and then below from the upper deck. At about 9.15 the *Lynx* was in British hands.

The loss was so heavy in this gallant but temerarious enterprise, as to lead one to question whether the game was worth the candle. Two good officers were killed or severely wounded, 8 men killed, and

---

[1] Lieut. Coombe had lost his left leg in a previous action. In this gallant affair he was wounded in the left thigh. Coombe was made Com. on Apr. 23rd, 1807, and given command of his prize, which was renamed *Heureux*. In her this brave officer was killed in action at Martinique, Nov. 29th, 1808.

[2] *See note*, p. 487.

21 wounded. It should, however, be remembered that such small French craft inflicted great injury on British commerce. They sailed too well to be often caught at sea, and consequently, if they were to be got out of the way, they had to be cut out of fortified harbours, or captured, as was the *Lynx*, by the daring use of boats. The French loss was 14 killed and 20 wounded.[1]

On January 27th, the *Lark*, 18, Commander Robert Nicholas, captured two Spanish revenue cruisers, the *Postillon* and *Carmen*, off Puerto Bello, on the Panama Isthmus. On February 1st, she drove two gunboats and an armed schooner into Puerto Cispata, under shelter of a small battery, silenced the battery, and sent in her boats with the captured revenue cruisers. Unfortunately, these latter were run aground by the pilot, and had to be abandoned and destroyed. The Spanish schooner and one of the gunboats ran ashore, or escaped up the river; and the boats returned, having carried one of the gunboats, but having lost 19 men wounded.[2]

On January 27th, the *Jason*, 32, Captain Thomas John Cochrane, cruising off the Guiana coast in search of two small French warships, fell in with the *Favourite*, 18, Lieutenant G. E. L. Le Marant-Kerdaniel. The *Favourite* was a British sloop which had been taken on January 6th, 1806, by L'Hermite's squadron off the Canaries. She was speedily brought to action, and, against the *Jason's* great superiority of force, could make no effective resistance. The brig *Argus*, 16, which was in her company, escaped whilst the prisoners were being transferred. The British loss was 1 wounded; the French had 1 killed and 1 wounded.[3]

On February 14th, the *Bacchante*, 20, Captain James Richard Dacres (2), captured off the San Domingo coast the French schooner *Dauphin*, 3. A little later, having taken under his orders the *Mediator*, 32, Captain William Furlong Wise (actg.), Dacres determined to attack a notorious nest of privateers in Samana Bay. For that purpose the *Dauphin*, under French colours, led in, followed by the *Mediator*, a ship of merchant build, under neutral colours, and the *Bacchante*, disguised as a prize. Deceived by this ruse, the enemy allowed the three British vessels to get within long range of a fort in the bay before they opened fire. The fort was cannonaded

---

[1] James, iv. 319; *Nav. Chron.*, xvi. 346; Troude, iii. 480.

[2] James, iv. 323; *Nav. Chron.*, xvii. 516. Nicholas, still commanding the *Lark*, was lost in her in 1809.

[3] James, iv. 322; *Nav. Chron.*, xvii. 348; Troude, iii. 481.

for four hours, and then gallantly stormed by landing parties from
the ships under the orders of Captain Wise, and Lieutenants Henry
Loraine Baker, John Norton (2), and James Shaw. In the harbour,
two French schooners were found fitting for sea, as well as a British
and an American vessel, which had been captured. The British
losses were chiefly on board the *Mediator*, which ship suffered
severely from the fire of the French fort. Two were killed and 16
wounded. The French retired into the forest, so that their losses
could not be ascertained.[1]

On March 1st, the boats of the *Glatton*, 50, Captain Thomas
Seccombe, and *Hirondelle*, 16, Lieutenant George Augustus Elliott
Skinner, were sent in under the command of Lieutenant Edward
Watson to cut out a Turkish treasure-ship from the harbour of
Sigri in Mitylene. The vessel was brought off, but with a loss of
5 killed and 9 wounded, among the killed being Watson.[2]

On March 15th, the boats of the *Comus*, 22, Captain Conway
Shipley, cruising off Gran Canaria, cut out several small vessels
from Puerto de Haz. On May 8th, three boats of this same ship
rowed in, in the evening, to capture a large felucca lying in Las
Palmas harbour under the guns of a fort and two batteries. The
cutter, under Lieutenant George Edward Watts,[3] outstripped the
other boats, singly dashed at the felucca under a severe fire, and
boarded her, the Spaniards being almost driven from the deck before
the two laggards arrived. The vessel was carried, and the boats
tried to take her in tow; but she was kept back by a hawser which
had been made fast under water astern, and led into the fort.
Before this hawser could be discovered and cut, she had been hauled
almost to the muzzles of the Spanish guns. She was got away,
however, and carried off to the *Comus*, with a loss to the British of
only 1 killed and 5 wounded.[4]

On April 19th, the *Richmond*, 12, Lieutenant Samuel Scudamore
Heming, sent in her boats and cut out a small Spanish privateer
from the Portuguese harbour of Pederneira. The French and
Spanish privateers on that coast gave constant trouble, and, from
their proximity to the great routes, were able to plunder British
commerce too often with complete impunity.[5]

---

[1] James, iv. 323; *Nav. Chron.*, xvii. 349.
[2] James, iv. 323; *Nav. Chron.*, xvii. 435.
[3] Com., Sept. 17th, 1807, as a reward for this service. He died a retired vice-admiral.
[4] James, iv. 324; *Nav. Chron.*, xvii. 515.   [5] James, iv. 334.

During May and June, the British *Uranie*, 38, Captain Christopher Laroche, watched Cherbourg, in which port lay the *Département de La Manche*, 40, and *Cygne*, 16. These vessels regularly got under way, and stood a short distance out of the harbour, to give their crews exercise. On May 15th, the enemy came some way out, and the *Uranie* cleared for action; but, a thick fog coming on, she lost her adversaries. On June 7th, the *Département de La Manche* was out again, but, on the *Uranie* attempting to close, promptly withdrew. On the 18th, the *Uranie*, then in company with the *Defender*, 12, Lieutenant George Plowman, saw her elusive enemy once more leaving the harbour. A fresh attempt to close was unsuccessful, however, as the *Uranie* only set her foresail, whereas the *Département de La Manche* had topsails and topgallant sails spread. The French ship easily drew away, and regained Cherbourg. Finally, on the 22nd, the *Département de La Manche* and *Cygne* came out at about noon by the eastern passage. The *Uranie*, with the *Defender*, made sail in a leisurely manner towards the enemy, and, at about 3.20, with mainsail, topsails, topgallant sails and royals set, was gaining decidedly, when she fired a distant broadside at the *Département de La Manche* without inflicting any damage, shortened sail, and lay to. The *Département de La Manche* and *Cygne* retired quietly to harbour.

No clearer proof of the contempt entertained in the British fleet for the French Navy can be found than the fact that Laroche was accused by his crew of cowardice for refusing to force a decisive encounter upon so greatly superior an adversary. The *Département de La Manche*, it should be said, fired a broadside of 440 lbs., mainly from long guns; the *Uranie* one of 373 lbs., mainly from carronades, so that the Frenchman had a considerable advantage, whilst the *Uranie* was further very foul and an old ship.[1] Laroche was tried by court-martial, and the charge against him was found to be partly proved. In the evidence, it was sworn that, on June 22nd, there was great confusion on board the British frigate; that Laroche changed colour, and showed signs of fear; that his ship did not carry all possible sail; and that he could not have failed to bring the *Département de La Manche* to action when he abandoned the chase. On his part, Laroche contended that there was a conspiracy against him, that he was in bad health, and that he had simply

---

[1] Capt. Laroche remained on the active list until 1830, when he retired on half pay. For certain facts not here touched upon, *see* O'Byrne, 633.

refused to be decoyed under the guns of the land batteries. It was allowed by all that he had often anchored close inshore, and it is certain that he was very unpopular among his officers. It would seem that he was severely treated, since he was dismissed his ship. We should have expected the French captain to have been tried for declining to give battle with a considerable advantage on his side, but no action was taken by Napoleon or his Minister of Marine.[1]

On May 14th, the *Spartan*, 38, Captain Jahleel Brenton (2), was becalmed off Nice whilst chasing a small vessel which seemed to be unarmed. Her boats were lowered to row to the enemy and board, but were received with a deadly fire of great guns and small arms which killed or wounded 63 out of the 70 of the party. Among the killed or mortally wounded were Lieutenants —— Weir, and Woodford Williams. The survivors retreated as best they could.

Some days later, the *Spartan* fell in with the French ships *Annibal*, 74, *Pomone*, 40, *Incorruptible*, 38, and *Victorieuse*, 14, followed them, and was then chased by them, having a very narrow escape of being captured. She got away only by the judgment of her Captain, who held his fire, whereas the leading French frigate opened too soon, killed the breeze, and, surrounded by a dense cloud of smoke, lost sight of her enemy.[2]

On June 5th, the British *Pomone*, 38, Captain Robert Barrie, sighted three armed French brigs and a convoy, close inshore on the Vendéean coast, making for Sables d'Olonne. He sent in his boats, which, under Lieutenants John Jones (3) and James Wallace Gabriel, captured and drove ashore without loss seventeen small vessels.[3]

On June 6th, a party of men on board a prize schooner, disguised as a neutral, was sent from the *Port d'Espagne*, 14, Lieutenant James Pattison Stewart (actg. Com.), to capture the Spanish privateer *Mercedes*, lying in the Gulf of Paria. The Spanish vessel was taken with a loss of only 2 wounded.[4]

On July 10th, the *Bombay*, 74, Captain William Jones Lye, captured the French *Jaseur*, 12, to the south-east of the Andaman Islands. The *Jaseur*, on a three months' cruise, had made no captures.[5]

---

[1] James, iv. 337; *Nav. Chron.*, xviii. 158; C. M. July 20th–24th, 1807.
[2] Brenton, ii. 197; James, iv. 334.
[3] James, iv. 336; *Nav. Chron.*, xvii. 517.
[4] James, iv. 337; *Nav. Chron.*, xviii. 227.
[5] *Nav. Chron.*, xix. 79.

On August 7th, the *Hydra*, 38, Captain George Mundy, having
on the previous evening driven three armed vessels[1] into the
Catalan port of Bagur, a narrow rocky harbour defended by a tower
and a battery, anchored off the entrance and opened fire on the
Spanish works. The fire was returned; but the reply presently
slackened, and the boats were sent in under Lieutenant Edward
O'Brien Drury, in spite of a·hail of bullets. The seamen landed,
and rushed the battery, which was evacuated by the enemy as the
storming column pressed in. A detachment was left to garrison the
battery, whilst the rest of the landing-party, covered by the fire of
the *Hydra*, hurried forward towards the town, entered it, driving
out the enemy, and secured the French vessels. A galling fire was,
however, maintained by such of the crews as had fled ashore and
taken post on the heights overlooking the harbour. Nevertheless,
the vessels were carried off, and the party at the battery re-embarked.
The British loss in this gallant enterprise was absurdly small. Only
1 man was killed, and but 6 were wounded. Drury, for his brave
and skilful conduct, was deservedly promoted to be Commander.[2]
Lieutenant James Little, and Lieutenants (R.M.) John Hayes and
Edward Pengelly, likewise distinguished themselves.[3]

On August 18th, the Spanish schooner *Cautela*, 12 (only six
mounted), with despatches for South America, was captured in the
Bay by the *Narcissus*, 32, Captain Charles Malcolm. On the
evening of this same day, the boats of the *Confiance*, 18, Commander
James Lucas Yeo, under Lieutenant William Hovenden Walker,
cut out a small Spanish privateer, the *Reitrada*, 3, from La Guardia,
without loss.[4]

During August, in conformity with the stipulations of the treaty
of Tilsit, Corfu was transferred from Russia to France. On August
20th, the first detachment of Neapolitan and French troops landed
there. A second force, under General César Berthier, left Otranto
on the 22nd. On the 23rd, the *Weazel*, 18, Commander John
Clavell (1), cruising off Corfu, was informed by the Russians of the
change, and at once prepared to proceed to Malta with the news.
Whilst on her way she sighted several small craft laden with men
making for Corfu. She gave chase, and drove three ashore,

---

[1] *Principe Eugenio*, 16; *Bella Carolina*, 12; *Carmen del Rosario*, 4.
[2] Com., Oct. 9th, 1807; Capt., Jan. 1st, 1817.
[3] James, iv. 340; *Nav. Chron.*, 344.
[4] James, iv. 341; *Nav. Chron.*, xviii. 226, 343.

capturing four more, on board of which were found 280 French soldiers and the colonel of the 6th Regiment.   Joseph Bonaparte magnified the poor little *Weazel* into " five ships of war."   Napoleon was greatly annoyed at the capture, but, in spite of the British naval superiority, 7400 men were speedily thrown into the Ionian Islands. In   October,   however,   Joseph   wrote   that   Corfu   was   rigorously blockaded ;   and   Napoleon,   to   drive   off   the   British   cruisers,   des-patched two frigates and a corvette from Toulon on the 7th.   On November 29th, nevertheless, the *Glatton*, 50, Captain Thomas Seccombe, captured another 300 French troops on their way to the island, in precisely the same manner as the *Weazel* had done.[1]

On August 25th, the boats of the *Clyde*, 38, cruising off Fécamp, were sent in, under Lieutenant Thomas Strong, in face of a heavy fire,   to   capture   a   French   coasting-vessel   which   was   hugging   the shore.   The vessel was brought off without loss.[2]

Early in August, the French privateer *Jeune Richard*, 7, fell in with the Liverpool brig *Pope* off Barbados, and got a very warm reception.   The *Pope* was only carried after 6 of her people had been killed and 4 wounded.   The *Jeune Richard* must have lost at least as heavily.   In the following two months, this privateer captured five other fine merchantmen, but on October 1st she met her match in the packet *Windsor Castle*, 8, William Rogers, com-mander (actg.).   The *Windsor Castle* cleared for action, and, with 28 men at quarters, received the privateer's attack at about 11.50 A.M. At 1.15 P.M., the enemy grappled the packet on the starboard quarter, but could not board owing to the *Windsor Castle's* high boarding-nettings.   Rogers showed the utmost bravery.   Ten of his crew were killed or wounded almost at once, and he was left with ten to hold the deck ; and these he had to rally again and again.   At last, at about 3 P.M., the enemy fled from his quarters, and Rogers boarded at the head of five men.   The *Jeune Richard* was speedily carried, though she had begun the fight with a crew of 92—more than three times that of the British vessel.   The losses were 3 killed and 10 wounded in the *Windsor Castle*, 21 killed and 33 wounded in the privateer.[3]

On   September   17th,   the   British   schooner   *Barbara*,   10,   Lieu-

---

[1] 'Méms. de Jos. Napoléon,' iii. 429, 436, 442; James, iv. 342; Log of *Weazel* ; *Nav. Chron.*, xix. 155.

[2] James, iv. 341.

[3] James, iv. 343; 'Liverpool Privateers,' 409; *Nav. Chron.*, xix. 184.

tenant Edward d'Arcy, was captured in the West Indies by the
French privateer *Général Ernouf*, 14.

Several successful cutting-out expeditions took place on the
Dalmatian coast during October and November, when the British
small craft displayed great activity.   On the night of October 7th,
the boats of the *Porcupine*, 22, Captain the Hon. Henry Duncan (3),
under Lieutenant George Price, cut out the Venetian gunboat
Safo from a harbour on the coast of the island of Giuppana; on
November 27th, they carried off two small Ragusan craft; and on the
29th, they destroyed several French supply vessels, and captured a
coaster laden with guns and artillery stores.[1]   On October 25th, the
boats of the *Herald*, 18, Commander George John Honey, under
Lieutenant Walter Foreman, cut out the French privateer *César*, 4,
from under the guns of the Otranto batteries.[2]

On the night of November 6th, the boats of the *Renommée*, 36,
Captain Sir Thomas Livingstone, Bart., and *Grasshopper*, 18, Commander Thomas Searle, cut out a French and a Spanish merchantman which were lying under the Torre de Estacion, near Cartagena.
As soon as the vessels had been carried, they were unhappily swept
ashore by the current, just under the tower, in a position where the
Spanish guns could bear upon them.   Two of the British, and several
of the prisoners, were wounded before it was decided to abandon the
prizes.   On December 11th, the same two British ships drove the
Spanish brig of war *San Josef*, 12, ashore, under Cape Negrete, and
compelled her to strike.   In spite of a heavy fire from troops on the
cliffs above, the *San Josef* was floated off by the exertions of the
Grasshopper's men.   Lieutenant Cornelius Willes, of that sloop,
specially distinguishing himself.[3]

On November 24th, off Tarifa, the British hired armed brig
Anne, 10, Lieutenant James Mackenzie (2),[4] in company with the
Vencejo,[5] 7, a small Spanish privateer which she had taken, was
attacked by ten Spanish gunboats.   The wind was so light, as to
favour the tactics of these pulling craft.   Seven assailed the *Vencejo*
and speedily forced her to strike, after she had had 3 killed.
Three rowed towards the *Anne*, but were very warmly received,
though the British crew only numbered 30 all told.   One of the

---

[1] Marshall, Supp. Pt. iii. 2; James, iv. 344; *Nav. Chron.*, xix. 155, xxiii. 391.
[2] James, iv. 345.
[3] James, iv. 346; *Nav. Chron.*, xix. 342, 505.
[4] Com. for this service, Jan. 22nd, 1808.   Drowned in the *Foxhound*, 1809.
[5] Disps. say " *Vansigo*," which is obviously an error.

gunboats was dismasted, and the two others were so mauled that they struck, but could not be taken possession of. Thereupon, five of the boats which had been engaging the *Vencejo*, approached, but, receiving a hot fire from the *Anne*, retreated with their prize. The *Anne* had not a man hurt. Her battery consisted of 12-pr. carronades, against which the gunboats mounted twenty long 24-prs. and as many 8-prs. The latter showed a great want of courage and combination; but all through the war the Spanish Navy had little heart in its work.[1]

On December 3rd, to the east of Barbados, the *Curieux*, 18, Commander John Sherriff, encountered the privateer *Revanche*, 25, Vidal, master. The *Revanche*[2] had been a Liverpool slave ship, and, like all such craft, was heavily armed. The two closed, and engaged at about 2 P.M., and the *Curieux* was soon severely injured in her running rigging. Thereupon the *Revanche* ran on board the British sloop, and, with her small arms' fire and a traversing 18-pr., swept the *Curieux's* deck, killing Sherriff and several men. The French, however, could not board, and, on the other side, Lieutenant Thomas Muir (2), upon whom the command of the *Curieux* had devolved, could not induce enough of his men to follow him on to the enemy's deck. The two vessels parted, and the *Revanche* made off with 2 killed and 13 wounded, leaving the *Curieux* with 8 killed and 14 wounded. Muir was court-martialled, and reprimanded for not having done his utmost to take the enemy. As the *Revanche* was very superior in force to the *Curieux*, and as, at that date, the best French seamen were usually to be found in privateers, the sentence may have been unduly severe.[3]

The growing audacity of the small French privateers in the Channel is a striking feature of these middle years of the war. The seaboard of Normandy and Brittany, and the French shore of the Straits of Dover, sent forth by the dozen luggers and rowing boats, which plundered British merchantmen and compelled them to hug the British coast, often with the consequence that they became embayed and were lost. Numerous small British vessels were told off to watch these troublesome depredators, yet without much success; for although many were taken, there were always more to take their place. Privateers were found, too, as far north as Flam-

---

[1] James, iv. 345; *Nav. Chron.*, xviii. 510.
[2] Ex *British Tar*.
[3] James, iv. 347.

borough Head, where on January 7th and 8th, 1808, the *Ariadne*, 20,
Captain Arthur Farquhar (1), assisted in capturing two, the *Trente
et Quarante* and the *Aglaé* ; and, when Denmark and Norway, after
the attack on Copenhagen in 1807, became hostile, privateers
swarmed in the North Sea, North Atlantic, and Baltic.   The very
insignificance of the craft employed made them more dangerous.
Ships of frigate and corvette build, if lost by the privateer owners,
could not be replaced; but luggers and rowing boats could be
built in a few days or weeks.   The batteries on the French coast
gave these vessels a measure of security when they retreated to
their own waters.   Among the more important British captures
in January were the *Courier*, 18, taken by the *Linnet*, 14, Lieutenant John Treacy,[1] on the 16th, and the *Entreprenant*, 16,
taken by the *Pandora*, 18, Commander Henry Hume Spence, on
the 13th.[2]

On February 7th, 1808, the *Découverte*, 8, Lieutenant Colin Campbell (2), cruising off San Domingo, discovered two enemy's schooners
and a British prize.   One of the schooners escaped ; the other was
driven ashore and bilged.   The prize, being on the reefs, was burnt.
Two days later the *Découverte* brought to action, and captured, the
privateer *Dorade*, 3, with a loss of Campbell and 6 seamen wounded.
Three of the *Découverte's* wretchedly mounted carronades were upset
in the combat and put out of action.[3]

In February, the *Impérieuse*, 38, Captain Lord Cochrane, was
directed to harass the French and Spanish coasts to the best of her
Captain's ability.   Her proceedings are instructive, as they show what
can be done by a single ship's crew when well led.   Her first exploit,
on February 19th, was to dash in amongst four Spanish gunboats which
she caught some miles from Cartagena.   One was taken, another
escaped, and two were sunk.   On the 21st, a French ship laden with
supplies was captured by the boats with the loss of only one officer,[4]
and this close under the batteries of Almeria.   In the next six weeks
the *Impérieuse* captured ten brigs, schooners, and coasting vessels,
and destroyed a new signal tower on the Minorca coast.   On April
13th, she bombarded a barrack at Ciudadela, in the same island, and
all but demolished it.   A little later, being fired upon by a small

---

[1] Sometimes spelt Tracy.   He was made Com. June 11th, 1814, and died in that
rank.

Nav. Chron., xix. 79, 82, 83, 336, etc.

[3] James, v. 19 ; *Nav. Chron.*, xix. 345.   [4] Lieut. Edward Caulfield.

tower on the island of Majorca, she landed a party which carried the tower and destroyed it without loss. At the end of April she filled her casks with water on the Spanish coast, overawing a considerable body of troops by the discharge of a few round-shot. On May 9th, she chased a large Spanish xebec, and captured her under a tower near the mouth of the Ebro, having first silenced the guns mounted in the tower. A fortnight later she caught a flotilla of Spanish gunboats off Cape Palos and destroyed two vessels. In June, Cochrane learnt that the Spaniards had risen against the French and that he was to assist them in every possible way. The French were reported to be plundering and burning the Spanish villages along the coast, and committing horrible atrocities. Cochrane determined to annoy them in retaliation to the utmost. He damaged the important road along the coast of Catalonia, so that it was rendered temporarily impassable for cavalry or artillery ; and seized French batteries and carried off their guns with admirable audacity and impudence. On July 31st, in combination with the Spanish insurgents, he captured the fort of Mongat, an important position on the road between Barcelona and Gerona, receiving the surrender of the French garrison, and blowing up the work.

In August, Cochrane determined to transfer the war to the enemy's coast, and on the 15th, with the *Impérieuse* and a gunboat, anchored off the mouth of the Rhône. On the 17th he destroyed a French semaphore station at that point, another at La Pinède, and yet another at Frontignan ; and he followed this up by capturing two more close to Marseilles, and destroying a French battery, with a loss of only one man. The French signal-books were carried off in every case, and burnt paper was strewn about to make it appear that they had been destroyed. The French, for that reason, did not trouble to change the code ; and the British ships were able to read every message which they despatched. On September 3rd, Cochrane bombarded La Ciotat, the inhabitants of which town had fired upon him. A few days later, in concert with the *Spartan*, 38, Captain Jahleel Brenton (2), he destroyed a signal station in the Gulf of Fos, captured a battery at Port Vendres, threw rockets into Cette, burnt two pontoons near Montpellier, and captured or destroyed a convoy of coasters. In want of water, he ran into the Rhône mouth and filled his casks, diverting his seamen by blowing up a new signal tower at Fos, while thus engaged. For these services Cochrane was deservedly commended by Collingwood. The Admiralty, however, showed its dislike of him by making no recognition of such brilliant work.[1]

In October the *Impérieuse* renewed her exploits upon the Spanish coast, this time harassing the French troops, and capturing French vessels laden with stores for the enemy's army. In November, hearing that the French were at Rosas, Cochrane proceeded thither and found that Captain John West, of the *Excellent*, 74, had garrisoned Fort Trinidad, a work to the east of Rosas, and held it in the face of all attacks till he was relieved by Captain Richard Henry Alexander Bennett, of the *Fame*, 74, who was succeeded by Cochrane. In the face of heavy batteries, and constant attacks by a greatly superior enemy, Cochrane clung to the fort, which was of great importance as commanding the chief road from French territory to Barcelona. The skill and resourcefulness displayed by Cochrane in this defence were above all praise. He did not abandon the fort till its defence was hopeless, and he withdrew all his men. His loss was only 3 killed and 7 wounded; for he was an officer who contrived to secure great results with small bloodshed.[2]

On February 8th, the boats of the *Meleager*, 36, Captain John Broughton, cut out the French privateer *Renard*, from Santiago de Cuba. On the 19th, the same frigate captured the Spanish privateer *Antilope*.[3]

On the night of February 13th, two boats of the *Confiance*, 20, Captain James Lucas Yeo, under Master's Mate Robert Trist,[4] rowed in under the forts at the mouth of the Tagus and captured a French gunboat without loss.[5]

Whilst cruising off Scarborough on March 2nd, the *Sappho*, 18, Commander George Langford,[6] chased and brought to action the Danish brig *Admiral Jawl*, 28, Commander Jorgen Jorgenson. The *Sappho*, in spite of her nominal inferiority, was at close quarters the more powerful vessel, and in half an hour compelled her opponent to strike. The *Sappho* had 2 wounded; the enemy, 2 killed.[7]

On March 8th, the long cruise of the *Piémontaise*, 40, Captain J. Epron, came to an end. Whilst lying in wait on the Ceylon

---

[1] Cochrane was an impetuous, headstrong and irascible person, and had quarrelled bitterly with Lord St. Vincent. This, probably, was the result.

[2] 'Autob. of a Seaman,' i. 240 *et seq.*

[3] *Nav. Chron.*, xix. 346.

[4] Promoted Lieut., Mar. 24th, 1808.

[5] *Nav. Chron.*, xix. 259.

[6] Posted, Mar. 5th, 1808.

[7] *Nav. Chron.*, xix. 253.

coast for three East Indiamen, she was sighted early on March 6th
by the *San Fiorenzo*, 36, Captain George Nicholas Hardinge, and
chased. She took to flight, but late in the same night was closed.
After two or three broadsides, directed at the British ship's rigging,
she made all sail and once more drew away. The *San Fiorenzo*
could not overtake her till daylight on the 7th. At 6.25 A.M., the
Piémontaise opened fire at a range of 800 yards, and the *San*

CAPT. GEORGE NICHOLAS HARDINGE, R.N.

(From H. R. Cook's engraving after the portrait by Lethbridge.)

Fiorenzo promptly replied. The two slowly closed till within 400
yards, the French all the time directing their fire mainly at the *San
Fiorenzo's* rigging. By 8.15, serious damage had been done. The
fore topsail yard was shot through ; the main royal-mast, main topmast stays, spring stay, most of the running rigging, and the sails
were shot to pieces. As the *San Fiorenzo* had made the hull of her
enemy the target, similar injuries had not been inflicted upon the
French ship's motive power, and she was able to draw away. The

San Fiorenzo turned to the work of making good the damage done.
Thus far the loss on board had been only 8 killed and 17 wounded.
The French ship must have suffered far more severely, but was so
strongly manned, if British accounts may be trusted, that she could
scarcely have felt the loss.

All day the *San Fiorenzo* was busied with her repairs.   With the
evening the *Piétmontaise* disappeared to the east under a press of
sail, but was picked up again towards midnight.   From that hour
onwards she was kept in view, about ten or twelve miles ahead.
With daylight, the *San Fiorenzo*, completely refitted, gained slowly
on her opponent, and at about 4 P.M. was within range.   The
Piémontaise, as escape without fighting an action was now seen to
be hopeless, turned and encountered the British frigate, passing her
on the opposite tack at 50 yards' distance, and exchanging several
broadsides.   Unhappily, the gallant Hardinge[1] was struck by a
grape shot and killed.   Lieutenant William Dawson[2] thereupon
took command.   The *Piémontaise* wore astern of the *San Fiorenzo*
and engaged her closely, but proved no match in gunnery for the
British ship.   At 5.50 P.M. she struck, with masts and rigging cut to
pieces, and a great part of her crew killed or wounded.

According to statements of the French officers who survived the
action, the *Piémontaise*, when she struck, had fired away all her
18-pr. and 8-pr. shot.   This is one of the rare occasions on which
ammunition ran short; but it should be remembered that the vessel
had been cruising since early in 1806 in the Indian Ocean, and may
not have been able to replenish her store of projectiles at Réunion or
Mauritius.   Her gun-locks are also stated to have been out of order
at the beginning of the final action, and her match to have been
extremely bad.   She is said in the British accounts to have had a
crew of 366 Frenchmen and 200 Lascars ; but 50 of the French seem
to have been absent in prizes.

—	Tons.	Guns.	Broadside.	Men.	Killed.	Wounded.
San Fiorenzo . . .	1032	42	Lbs. 467	186	13	25
Piémontaise . . .	1093	46	533	316?	49	92

[1] Born, Apr. 11th, 1781; Lieut., Oct. 15th, 1800; Com., May, 1802; Capt.,
Apr. 10th, 1804.

[2] Posted, Mar. 9th, 1809, but died Sept. 29th, 1811.

The *San Fiorenzo's* crew had been weakened by sickness and by prize crews detached. One at least of her Lieutenants was on shore, an invalid. In these circumstances her rapid refit and ultimate victory were most creditable. The *Piémontaise's* masts went by the board in the night following the action.[1]

On March 13th, the *Emerald*, 36, Captain Frederick Lewis Maitland (2), was on her way with despatches from Lord Gardner to the squadron blockading Ferrol, when a large French schooner was observed in Vivero Harbour, under the protection of two forts, one on the west and the other, a mile further in, on the east side of the entrance. Maitland arrived at the conclusion that it would be easy to cut the schooner out. Accordingly, at dusk, he despatched a party under Lieutenant Charles Bertram to storm the west fort, whilst the *Emerald* stood in and engaged the east one. The western fort was carried without much difficulty, and, after a brisk bombardment, a party landed to storm the east one, but missed its way and was compelled to retire. Meantime, a third boat party, under Midshipman Daniel Baird, had rowed to the schooner under a heavy fire, and, being joined by Bertram's[2] boats, drove off her crew, but found her aground. She was set on fire and totally destroyed. The British loss was heavy : 9 were killed and 16 wounded.[3]

On March 14th, the *Childers*, 14, Commander William Henry Dillon, whilst cruising off Midby on the Norwegian coast, sighted a small Danish vessel inshore, and sent in her boats to cut her out. The boats had done this and were on their way to rejoin the *Childers* when the Danish brig of war *Lügum*,[4] 20, Commander Wulff, suddenly came into sight and bore down upon the British ship, but, when the latter fired a shot and stood boldly towards her boats, altered course and kept inshore. The *Childers*, having hoisted in her boats, made all sail after the *Lügum*, overhauled her, and began action at short range. The two vessels were on opposite tacks. At the first broadside the *Lügum* took fire. Night had fallen, and the Danish ship, under the heavy shadow of the coast, could be

---

[1] James, v. 21; *Nav. Chron.*, xx. 145, 383, 430, 483; Log of *San Fiorenzo*; Chevalier, 313; Troude, iii. 499.

[2] For this service Bertram, who was wounded, was made Com., Mar. 28th, 1808. He retired with the rank of R.-Adm. in 1849.

[3] *Nav. Chron.*, xix. 257; James, v. 24.

[4] Called *Lougen* in most of the accounts; in some, *Lugn*; in a few, *Lyn* (i.e., *Lightning*). Lügum is a place in Schleswig. I cannot find any official Danish report.

made out only by the flashes of her guns. The British craft, armed
entirely with feeble 12-pr. carronades, soon found that most of her
shots fell short, whereas the Dane, with long 18-prs., was able to fire
with great effect, repeatedly hulling the *Childers*. Dillon determined
to try to tempt the enemy out to sea, where his hull could be better
seen. At 11 P.M. the *Lügum* was three miles from the land. The
Childers then passed close under her lee, pouring in a broadside of
round shot and grape, which had so much effect, that the Dane
retired inshore. The *Childers* was too much battered to pursue or
renew the battle. She had five feet of water in her hold, and 11,
out of a total crew of 56, killed or wounded. Her Commander[1]
displayed extraordinary bravery in forcing so powerful an enemy
to battle. The *Childers's* broadside was only 84 lbs. in weight,
all from carronades; the *Lügum's* was 168 lbs., all from long guns.
Further, the *Childers* was a very old and rotten vessel, dating
from 1778.[2]

Three months later, on June 19th, this same *Lügum* was sighted
by the *Seagull*, 16, Commander Robert Cathcart, off the Naze of
Norway. The *Seagull* at once attempted to close her, using sweeps
as the wind fell to a calm, whilst the *Lügum* maintained a steady fire
at a range at which the *Seagull's* fourteen 24-pr. carronades were
ineffective. In short, this action, like the last, serves to demonstrate
the tactical weakness of short range large calibre guns against a
speedy and intelligent enemy. When the *Seagull* at last succeeded
in closing her adversary, she found herself trapped. Six Danish
gunboats, each carrying two long 24-prs., appeared from amongst the
islands, and took up a raking position on her quarters. Against
such odds the *Seagull* was helpless; and she struck after two and a
half hours' gallant resistance, with 8 killed (including Lieutenant
Abraham Harcourt White and Master Andrew Martin), and 20
wounded, out of a crew of 94. She sank as soon as the crew and the
wounded had been transferred to the captor. The *Lügum* had 14
killed or wounded.[3] Cathcart was subsequently posted, as from the
day of the action.

After her action with the *Phaeton* and *Harrier* in the Philippine
Islands in August, 1805, the *Sémillante*, 40, Captain Motard, pro-

---

[1] Dillon was posted as from Mar. 12th, 1808, and lived to become a V.-Adm.

[2] *Nav. Chron.*, xix. 282; James, v. 27.

[3] James, v. 30; C. M. Nov. 21st, 1808; Cathcart to Wells, June 20th, and Wells
to Pole, Sept. 17th, 1808.

ceeded to Mauritius, where she was eventually blockaded by the *Pitt*, 36, Captain Walter Bathurst. In company with the privateer *Bellone*, 34, the *Sémillante* sallied out, and, after a cruise, returned again, to issue forth a second time in April, 1806. She made many prizes, and more than once narrowly escaped capture by British cruisers, especially by the *Dédaigneuse*, 36, Captain William Beauchamp Proctor, on November 22nd, 1806. She cruised again in 1807, and, returning to Mauritius to refit, put to sea once more in February, 1808. On March 15th she had just captured, and sent off to Mauritius, a prize, when she sighted the *Terpsichore*, 28, Captain William Augustus Montagu, and stood to meet her, taking her for a merchantman. The *Terpsichore*, it should be said, had been carefully disguised with the express object of enticing the French frigate *Canonnière*, then commerce destroying in the East Indies, to battle. At about 7 P.M. the two ships closed and opened fire, and a fierce engagement began. The *Sémillante*, when almost on board the *Terpsichore*, threw into the British ship a hand-grenade which, unhappily, fell through one of the hatches on to the main-deck, fired some powder charges, and put out of action the crews of no fewer than four guns on the engaged side. The ship at once took fire, and, had the French boarded, they might have carried her with ease in the confusion which resulted. Instead of doing this, Captain Motard sheered off, aiming his guns at the *Terpsichore's* rigging; and, when the fire on board her had been extinguished and she bravely pursued, he was able to evade all attempts to close. The *Terpsichore* had her masts badly wounded, most of her running rigging and stays shot away, and her sails cut to pieces. By mid-night she was far astern. Undaunted by the force of her opponent, however, she continued the pursuit all the 16th, 17th, and 18th, while her crew did their best to repair the damage.

On the 19th, the *Sémillante* was only just in view. On the morning of the 20th the *Terpsichore* at last gained upon the French-man, and came up so fast that the *Sémillante* had to cut away several of her boats, throw overboard some of her guns, start her water and jettison stores and lumber. Thus lightened, and having with her stern chasers inflicted fresh damage, she drew out of sight in the night of the 20th–21st.

The *Terpsichore* was much the weaker ship, as she was unable, from age, to carry carronades, or her proper complement of 6-prs., on the upper deck. The force of the two was as follows :—

—	Tons.	Guns.	Broadside.	Men.	Killed.	Wounded.
Terpsichore	682	28	Lbs. 158 n.	180	20	22
Sémillante	940	40	279 n.	300?	22	

Her determined attack did, however, produce the required effect.
The *Sémillante* was so much damaged in her hull by the *Terpsichore's* broadsides that, on her return to Mauritius, she was judged
incapable of further cruising, and was in consequence loaded with
Motard's plunder and with colonial produce to the value of £300,000,
with which she reached France in February, 1809. She was at once
replaced by the 40-gun frigate *Manche*.[1]

On the afternoon of March 22nd, the British squadron blockading
Lorient sighted the frigates *Italienne*, 40, Captain H. Méquet, and
Sirène, 38, Captain Duperré, on their way back from Martinique,
where they had been landing troops. The vessels composing the
British squadron were the *Impétueux*, 74, *Saturn*, 74, *Aigle*, 36,
Captain George Wolfe, *Narcissus*, 32, and *Cuckoo*, 4. The wind
was north-north-west; the enemy's ships were upon the port tack
and close to the western end of the Ile Groix; and the British
squadron lay between that island and the Glénans. To cut the
French vessels off, the *Aigle* steered straight into the Basse des
Bretons, and was fired upon by the French batteries. She came
near enough to the sternmost of the French frigates to open fire,
whereupon that vessel abandoned the attempt to reach Lorient, bore
up, and anchored under the guns of Groix. The other frigate, the
Sirène, was, by that time, close to the entrance of Port Louis; and
the only possible means of stopping her was by boarding. Captain
Duperré, however, was too adroit for his opponent, and, as the *Aigle*
bore up, he too bore up, and ran aground on the Pointe des Chats.
The ships of the British squadron which had followed the *Aigle*
through the Basse des Bretons could do nothing, as the *Sirène* lay
under powerful batteries; and they had to withdraw. She was got
off by the French some days later, and, with the *Italienne*, reached
Lorient safely. The *Aigle* had 22 killed or wounded in this affair,
amongst the severely injured being Captain Wolfe.[2]

---

[1] James, v. 67; Troude, iii. 501; Chevalier, iii. 309; *Nav. Chron.*, xxi. 24.
[2] James, v. 25; Troude, iii. 502. James wrongly supposes Duperré's frigate to
have been the *Seine*.

On March 22nd, the *Stately*, 64, Captain George Parker, and *Nassau*, 64, Captain Robert Campbell (1), were on their way into the Great Belt, when, some miles south of Grenaa, they sighted the *Prinds Christian Frederik*, a Danish 74, commanded by Captain Jessen. The enemy, as soon as the nationality of the two 64's was made out, evidently prepared to run ashore. Before this intention could be carried out, first the *Nassau* and then the *Stately* closed and engaged. After two hours' action, at 9.30, the Dane struck, and almost immediately afterwards ran aground. As she could not be got off the rocks, she was set on fire on the 23rd, and destroyed by her captors. The *Prinds Christian Frederik* had 55 killed and 88 wounded ; the British ships, 5 killed and 45 wounded or missing.[1]

On March 27th, the boats of the *Ulysses*, 44, *Castor*, 32, *Hippomenes*, 18, and *Morne Fortunée*, 12, attempted to cut out the French brig *Griffon*, 16, from the harbour of Marin, in Martinique, but were driven back, after capturing a battery, and suffering heavily from the fire of the brig.[2]

On April 4th, a small British squadron, consisting of the *Alceste*, 38, *Mercury*, 28, Captain James Alexander Gordon, and *Grasshopper*, 18, Commander Thomas Searle,[3] under Captain Murray Maxwell, of the *Alceste*, discovered a large Spanish convoy to the north of Cadiz, under the convoy of about twenty gunboats. When off Rota, the British vessels attacked, the *Grasshopper* especially distinguishing herself by drawing close to the Spanish batteries at Rota, and silencing them with grape from her guns, at the same time holding in check a division of gunboats which came out from Cadiz. The *Alceste* and *Mercury* opened fire on the convoy, destroyed two gunboats, and drove several others ashore. Then the boats were sent in, under Lieutenants Allan Stewart and Watkin Owen Pell, and brought off seven small craft from under the Spanish guns, though all the barges and pinnaces of the combined Franco-Spanish fleet lying in Cadiz had come up to the help of the convoy.[4] The British lost only 1 mortally and 2 less severely wounded.

On April 22nd, the *Gorée*, 26, Commander Joseph Spear, whilst at anchor in one of the harbours of Marie-Galante, a small island off Martinique, which had been occupied by the British in March,

---

[1] James, v. 31; *Nav. Chron.*, xix. 338.

[2] Troude, iii. 503.

[3] Posted for this service, Apr. 25th, 1808.

[4] *Gazette*, 1808, 570; James, v. 37.

sighted the French vessels *Palinure*, 16, Commander P. F. Jance,
and *Pilade*, 16, Lieutenant J. M. Cocherel, and gave chase to them,
after signalling to the *Supérieure*, 12, Commander Andrew Hodge, at
anchor some miles off, that they were enemies. The *Gorée* succeeded
in closing, but was speedily disabled by her two French antagonists,
who fired high. She inflicted, however, heavy loss upon them,
killing or wounding 10 in the *Pilade*, and 19 in the *Palinure*, at
the cost of only 1 killed of her own crew. Later in the day the
Supérieure came up, with the *Circe*, 32, and *Wolverine*, 18, astern
of her; but the French vessels reached the shelter of the forts on the
Saintes before they could be overpowered.[1]

On April 23rd, upon the Danish coast, the boats of the *Daphne*,
20, Captain Francis Mason, and *Tartarus*, 18, Lieutenant William
Russell (2) (actg. Com.), were sent in, in tow of the *Forward*, 12,
Lieutenant David Sheils, to destroy a convoy which was assembling
at Fladstrand for the purpose of carrying stores and provisions to
Norway. All the laden vessels of the convoy, ten in number, were
carried off from under the guns of a Danish fort, with a loss of only
5 wounded.[2]

Another and less successful cutting out affair took place on the
same day at Lisbon. Captain Conway Shipley, of the *Nymphe*, 36,
with the boats of the *Nymphe* and *Blossom*, 18, Commander George
Pigot (2), attempted to carry the *Garrota*, 20, a Portuguese naval
vessel which had been seized by the French, and which was lying
just above Belem. The boats, when they closed to board, found
that the *Garrota* had the support not only of the guns of Belem
Castle, but also of a formidable floating battery. Moreover, the tide
was ebbing at the rate of seven knots, so that the men were much
exhausted. Shipley was shot dead whilst attempting to gain the
Garrota's deck, and fell into the water. His brother Charles, who
was not a naval officer, ordered the boat's crew to shove off and pick
up the body; and, in attempting to do this, she fouled a cutter and
drove her into one of the launches. Owing to this unwarrantable
interference, the whole attack fell into confusion; and the boats,
unable to row against the tremendous current, retired with 1 killed,
besides Shipley, and 2 wounded.[3]

On the same day the *Grasshopper*, 14, Commander Thomas

[1] James, v. 41; Troude, iii. 504.
[2] James, v. 32; *Nav. Chron.*, xix. 433.
[3] James, v. 38; *Nav. Chron.*, xxxix. 350.

Searle, and *Rapid*, 14, Lieutenant Henry Baugh, captured two Spanish gunboats, drove two others ashore, and made prizes of two richly-laden Spanish merchantmen from South America, off Faro in southern Portugal.[1]

On April 29th and the following days, the *Falcon*, 16, Lieutenant John Price (3) (actg. Com.), destroyed several small craft on the Danish coast, and on May 7th carried off two Danish coasters laden with artillery material, from under the guns of Lundholm.[2]

On May 2nd, the *Unité*, 36, Captain Patrick Campbell (1), captured the Italian corvette *Ronco*, 16, in the Gulf of Venice, after a few broadsides had been exchanged without loss. Two other Italian vessels were observed to the north and chased, but without result. A month later, on June 1st, the *Unité*, after a long pursuit, overtook two Italian brigs, the *Nettuno*, 16, and *Teuliè*,[3] 16, inflicted upon them a loss of 14 killed and 29 wounded, without a single man being hurt in the British crew, and captured them.[4]

On May 7th, the *Redwing*, 18, Commander Thomas Ussher, attacked seven Spanish armed vessels in charge of a convoy, off Cape Trafalgar. She drove ashore and destroyed four of the armed craft, captured one of them, and took or sunk most of the merchantmen. All this was achieved with the loss of 1 killed and 3 wounded.[5] The Spanish gunboats, however, rarely fought or manœuvred with any spirit. It was quite different, as we shall see in the next instance, when our Navy had to deal with Danish craft of the same type.

On May 15th, the *Tartar*, 32, Captain George Edmund Byron Bettesworth, an officer of the most distinguished gallantry, and famous for having brought the first news to Europe of the return of Villeneuve's fleet from the West Indies in 1805, worked her way through the islands to the town of Bergen, and sent in her boats to bring off the shipping in the harbour. This the boats were unable to do, as the entrance was closed by a chain. They had only just returned to the ship, which was lying becalmed in a narrow rocky inlet, when a Danish schooner and five gunboats, each mounting two long 24-prs., appeared and opened fire. Bettesworth fell at almost

---

[1] James, v. 40; *Nav. Chron.*, xix. 432.

[2] *Nav. Chron.*, xix. 508.

[3] Mr. W. H. Wilson suggests that the name should be *Giulia*. I can find no evidence in Randaccio, or elsewhere. I therefore leave the name as it appears in the disps.

[4] James, v. 52; *Nav. Chron.*, xx. 77; Marshall, ii. 293

[5] James, v. 47; *Nav. Chron.*, xix. 505; O'Byrne, 1223.

the first shot, the command then devolving on Lieutenant Herbert
Caiger.   The *Tartar* was end-on to her little enemies; and, manned
by a raw crew, few of whom had ever served on ship-board before,
she appeared to be in a desperate position.   The depth was too great
for her to anchor with springs, and then bring her broadside to bear.
At last, however, she succeeded in warping round, and then, by her

VICE-ADMIRAL SIR EDWARD BRACE, K.C.B.

(By permission, from a family portrait in the possession of F. G. O. Brace, Esq.)

fire, she sank one gunboat and damaged the others.   At that point
a light breeze sprang up, and she was able to make sail in pursuit
of her enemies, and to drive them under the guns of Bergen.   Her
loss was 2 officers (Bettesworth and Midshipman Henry Fitzburgh)
killed, and about 10 men wounded.   Her hull was pierced between
wind and water in several places, and the sails and rigging were
much cut up.   Bettesworth, though only twenty-three years
of age, had been wounded no fewer than twenty-four times in the

course of the war; which is, probably, a record in the British
Navy.[1]

The *Tartar's* real object had been to intercept the Dutch frigate
Gelderland, 36, Captain Bartholomeus Jacobus Pool, which was
believed to be at Bergen.   She had sailed, however, a fortnight
before the *Tartar* put in an appearance, but she did not, for all that,
escape the vigilance of the British cruisers.   On the evening of May
19th she was sighted to the south-west of Ireland by the *Virginie*,
38, Captain Edward Brace, and brought to action late in the
night.   A heavy sea was running, and the night was very dark; but
this did not apparently affect the accuracy of the British fire.   Three
times the Dutchman wore, probably with the object of raking the
Virginie.   Attempting that manœuvre a fourth time, the *Gelderland*
ran on board the British ship, but soon got free again.   At last, after
ninety minutes' hard fighting, with their ship on fire, all masts and
the bowsprit shot away, and one-fourth of the crew killed or wounded,
the Dutch struck.   Pool deserted his quarters during the action,
having received two slight wounds.   For this he was afterwards
cashiered.   The Dutch shooting appears to have been most indifferent, seeing that the loss and damage to the British ship was
insignificant, whereas the gunnery of the British crew must have
been surprisingly good.[2]

—	Tons.	Guns.	Broadside.	Men.	Killed.	Wounded.
Virginie	—	46?	Lbs. 494	277 n.	1	2
Gelderland	—	40?[1]	232	253[2]	25	{ 40 or more

<small>[1] De Jonge says only 36.   [2] De Jonge says only 230, including passengers.</small>

On May 10th, the *Wizard*, 16, Commander Abel Ferris, sighted
and chased, to the south of Toulon, the *Requin*, 16, Commander C. R.
Bérar, and, after a long pursuit, engaged her in close action on the
morning of the 11th.   The *Requin* fired high and inflicted sufficiently
severe injuries to be able to draw away from her adversary.   The
British crew refitted their ship, and, on the morning of the 12th,
were near enough to the *Requin* to open a long range fire.   The
firing killed the breeze, and the *Requin* drew ahead once more;

[1] James, v. 34; *Nav. Chron.*, xix. 420, 440.
[2] James, v. 36; *Nav. Chron.*, xix. 506; De Jonge, v. 647.   For this service Lieut.
John Davies (2) was made Com. on June 3rd, 1808.

but the *Wizard* stuck to her enemy all the 12th and 13th, now
gaining and now losing ground, and exchanging shots whenever
near enough for the guns to carry. On the 14th, however, the
Requin entered the neutral harbour of Goletta in Tunis, and the
pursuit ceased, having continued through 88 hours over 369 miles
of sea. The *Requin* was ultimately taken on July 28th, to the
north of Corsica, on her way back from Tunis to Toulon, by the
Volage, 22, Captain Philip Lewis J—— Rosenhagen, after a long
chase. The *Wizard's* total loss was 1 killed and 5 wounded; the
Requin's is unknown.[1]

On May 11th, the *Bacchante*, 20, Captain Samuel Hood Inglefield, captured, off Cape San Antonio, in Cuba, the French brig
Griffon, 16. The *Griffon*, though much inferior in force, offered
a brave resistance, and did not surrender till she was almost
amongst the breakers.[2]

On May 12th, the *Amphion*, 32, Captain William Hoste, whilst
on her way from Toulon to Majorca, found the French storeship
Baleine, 26, Captain Gaudran, at anchor in Rosas Bay, on the north-
east of Spain. The *Baleine* had parted from the squadron of
Ganteaume, on its voyage from Toulon to the Adriatic, during a
storm. Despite a fire of red-hot shot from the Spanish forts, the
Amphion worked in and cannonaded the *Baleine*. It was believed
that the French crew were abandoning her, and therefore a British
boat was despatched to take possession of her. On its approach,
the boat was so warmly received that she had to retire; and the
Amphion, after she had picked her up, withdrew, as nothing more
could be attempted under the guns of the Spanish batteries.[3]

On May 24th, the hired cutter *Swan*, 10, Lieutenant Mark
Robinson Lucas, when off Bornholm, attacked a Danish cutter,
which blew up in twenty minutes, without a single man being saved.
The *Swan* sustained no loss.[4]

During June, and the later months of the year, the Danish gunboats caused a great deal of trouble to the British cruisers and
convoys in the narrow waters of the Belts and Sound. The Danish
battleships and frigates had been carried off by the expedition of
1807, so that there was no lack of good seamen to man such small

[1] James, v. 48; Troude, iii. 505.
[2] *Nav. Chron.*, xx. 153; James, v. 51; Troude, iii. 506.
[3] James, v. 53; Troude, iii. 506.
[4] *Nav. Chron.*, xix. 509; James, v. 33.

craft. On June 14th, the *Tickler*, gun-brig, Lieutenant John W—
Skinner, was captured by four gunboats, after a desperate resistance,
in which she had 36 men killed or wounded out of 50, and in which
Skinner himself fell. On June 9th, the bomb *Thunder*, Commander
James Caulfeild (1), and gun-brigs *Charger*, Lieutenant John Aitken
Blow, *Piercer*, Lieutenant John Sibrell, and *Turbulent*, Lieutenant
George Wood, in charge of a convoy of 70 vessels, were attacked off
Saltholm by 25 Danish gunboats in a calm. The boats surrounded
the *Turbulent* and captured her, but, on proceeding to assail the
Thunder, were driven off, after they had inflicted some damage.
Several vessels of the convoy were taken. On July 1st, the *Exertion*,
12, ran aground in the Great Belt and was attacked by a Danish
schooner and two gunboats, which shot through her fore mast and
bowsprit, and badly wounded five men. On August 2nd, the *Tigress*,
12, Lieutenant Edward Nathaniel Greensword, was caught in the
Great Belt by sixteen gunboats, and taken, after she had had 10 men
killed or wounded. The run of ill-luck did not cease till October 1st,
when the *Cruiser*, 18, Lieutenant Thomas Wells (2) (actg. Com.),[1]
off Göteborg, was assailed by about twenty cutters and gunboats.
She drove them off and succeeded in capturing one.[2]

At times, even vessels of the line were hard put to it to hold
their own against these wasp-like enemies. On October 20th, the
Africa, 64, Captain John Barrett, while escorting a convoy, was
attacked in a dead calm by twenty-five gun and mortar boats off
the island of Amager, in the Sound. The enemy took up positions
on her bows and quarters, where her guns would not bear, and
poured in a terrible fire. At nightfall only did they withdraw,
leaving the *Africa* in such a state that, had their attack only been
continued, she must have struck. Her loss was 9 killed and 53
wounded. Her masts and yards were badly damaged, her boats were
disabled or destroyed, and her running rigging was cut to pieces.
One or two of the Danish boats were sunk, but their loss is not
likely to have been large.[3] The gunboat of those times, like the
torpedo boat of to-day, offered a very small mark.

During June and July, the boats of the *Porcupine*, 22, Captain
the Hon. Henry Duncan (3), cruising on the Italian coast, executed
several cutting-out operations. On June 23rd they destroyed a

---

[1] Com., Nov. 26th, 1808, for this service.
[2] James, v. 74; *Nav. Chron.*, xx. 76, 451; xxi. 98.
[3] James, v. 76.

French merchantman which had run aground near Civita Vecchia. On July 9th, as the *Porcupine* lay becalmed, they carried off a merchantman from two French gunboats under Monte Circeo, and drove the gunboats to take shelter near a neighbouring battery at Porto d'Anzio. On the night of the 10th the boats rowed in to that harbour, and cut out a polacca with a loss of 8 wounded. On the 21st the *Porcupine* drove ashore and destroyed, near Monte Circeo, another French polacca. Finally, on August 8th, she chased a vessel into a harbour in the little island of Pianosa, whence, during the following night, the boats, under Lieutenant Francis Smith,[1] cut her out with a loss of 3 killed and 7 wounded.[2]

On June 22nd, the *Cossack*, 22, Captain Charles George Digby, and *Comet*, 18, Commander Cuthbert Featherstone Daly, despatched their boats into the Spanish port of Santander, to destroy the forts commanding the harbour, as the French, under General Merle, were approaching the town. With the co-operation of the Spaniards, then thoroughly hostile to France, all the guns in two of the forts were spiked, and further disabled by wedging shot in the chambers, and a magazine of 500 barrels of powder was destroyed. In accomplishing this, two British officers were badly scorched. The French appeared just as the work had been completed.[3]

On June 26th, the boats of the *Standard*, 64, Captain Thomas Harvey (1), under Lieutenant Richard Cull and Captain Edward Nicolls, R.M., captured off Corfu the Neapolitan gunboat *Volpe*; and another boat, under Lieutenant John Alexander (3), took the French despatch-boat *Léger*.[4]

On July 1st, the *Seahorse*, Captain John Stewart, whilst anchored off the island of Syra in the Archipelago, received intelligence that a Turkish force, consisting of the *Badere-i-Zaffér*, 52, Captain Scandril Kichuc Ali, and *Alis Fezzan*, 26, Captain Duragardi Ali, was off the island of Chiliodromia. Captain Stewart at once proceeded towards that place, and, on the afternoon of the 5th, sighted his two enemies, who were standing to the south with the wind at north-east. At 9.30 P.M., the *Seahorse* was near enough to the *Badere-i-Zaffér* to hail her and order her to surrender.

---

[1] Smith, a Lieut. of Jan. 22nd, 1806, was never promoted, owing to an unfortunate miscarriage of despatches.

[2] James, v. 54; *Nav. Chron.*, xx. 382; xxiii. 394.

[3] *Nav. Chron.*, xx. 75.

[4] James, v. 56; *Nav. Chron.*, xxi. 72.

The Turks paid no attention to the demand, whereupon the *Sea-horse* poured a double-shotted broadside into the *Badere-i-Zafför's* lee quarter at a range of only twenty yards, and a close action began.

The *Seahorse* was to windward, as it was important that the Turks, with their enormous number of men, should not be permitted to board. The *Badere-i-Zaffér* was slightly before her port beam, and between her and the *Alis Fezzan*, which latter ship was thus

CAPT. JOHN STEWART, R.N.

(From Page's engraving, after a drawing sometime belonging to Mr. W. Adam.)

unable to engage. The larger frigate, after a few minutes' firing, attempted to run on board the *Seahorse*, but the manœuvre was foiled by the British ship luffing and tacking astern of her. This brought the *Seahorse* upon the *Alis Fezzan*. Three broadsides were poured into the smaller Turkish ship with so much effect that her guns were silenced. The powder under the forecastle exploded, and the vessel was set on fire. After this the *Alis Fezzan* seemed to have had enough, for she retired amidst dense clouds of smoke, which entirely hid her from view. The *Badere-i-Zaffér*, which had fallen to leeward, with almost every one of her sails shot to rags, was again closed by the *Seahorse* at about 10.35, and engaged broadside to broadside. A little later, the Turk attempted a second time to board, collecting 300 or so men on her forecastle. The *Seahorse*, however, shot ahead of her and cleared her, though the Turkish ship's bowsprit fouled, and carried away, the gaff vangs and the mizen mast standing rigging. The *Seahorse's* stern-chasers poured a terrible fire into the would-be boarders.

For two hours more the *Seahorse* plied her enemy with deadly broadsides, hailing at intervals to know if the Turks would strike. The Turkish ship was gradually reduced to a complete wreck, but knowing the temper of his enemy, Stewart did not care to waste life in boarding. At about 1.15 A.M. the British discontinued their fire, and stood by the *Badere-i-Zaffér* until daylight, only discharging an occasional shot or two " to keep the Turks awake." When daylight came, as the Turkish colours were seen to be still flying, the *Seahorse* came up under the Turk's stern, and poured in a raking broadside. The Turkish captain had hitherto shot, or threatened with death, all those who suggested surrender. He was at length seized by his own men, and the colours were lowered. Possession was then taken by the British.[1] The force of the ships was as follows :—

—	Tons.	Guns.	Broadside.	Men.	Killed.	Wounded.
Seahorse.	998	42	Lbs. 462	251	5	10
Badere-i-Zaffér. . .	1300	52	484	543	165	195
Alis Fezzan . . .	730	26	156	230	?	?

The enormous losses of the Turks show plainly the desperate nature of the resistance; and their complete failure to inflict heavy loss upon the *Seahorse* shows that their gunnery was of the most rudimentary kind. The two Turkish ships did not work together, and thus greatly simplified the task of the *Seahorse*. Still, the action does Captain Stewart the greatest credit. The chief injuries which the *Seahorse* sustained were in her mizen mast, which was so wounded that it fell.

---

[1] James, v. 57; *Nav. Chron.*, xxi. 330.

On July 17th, the French *Serpent*, 18, which had carried to La Guaira the news of Joseph Bonaparte's accession to the Spanish throne, was captured by the British frigate *Acasta*, 40, Captain Philip Beaver. The Spanish forts would not give her any protection, nor would they fire on the British vessel.[1]

On August 1st, the boats of the *Kent*, 74, Captain Thomas Rogers, and *Wizard*, 16, Commander William Ferris, were despatched to cut out ten coasters lying close to the Italian town of Noli. The boats, under Lieutenants William Cashman (2), and Alexander Bisset, reached the coasters, but found them firmly secured to the beach, whereupon they rowed in under a heavy fire from French troops and field-pieces, drove back the troops, and released the vessels. At the same time they captured a French gunboat. The total British loss was only 2 killed.[2] Lieutenants James Lindsay and Fairfax Moresby, besides the officers already mentioned, greatly distinguished themselves in this affair.

On August 11th, the *Comet*, 18, Commander Cuthbert Featherstone Daly, sighted in the Bay, and boldly chased, the *Diligente*, 18, *Espiègle*, 16, and *Sylphe*, 16, Lieutenant L. M. Clément. The *Diligente* and *Espiègle* easily outsailed the British vessel; but the *Sylphe* was overtaken, brought to action, and, after twenty minutes' fighting, forced to surrender. The *Comet* had no one hurt. The French lost 6 killed and 5 wounded out of a crew of 98.[3]

The *Espiègle* and *Diligente* made all sail for Martinique; but on August 16th the *Espiègle* was unlucky enough to be overhauled and captured by the *Sibylle*, 38, Captain Clotworthy Upton. The *Diligente* once more escaped by the speed of her sailing. On September 6th, however, when to windward of Antigua, she was discovered by the British sloop *Recruit*, 18, Commander Charles Napier (2). Though the *Recruit's* main mast was sprung, the British vessel made all sail in chase, and, at about 8.30 A.M., brought her opponent to close action. The *Diligente's* second shot broke Napier's right thigh, the bone protruding from the flesh. A little later, the only Lieutenant on board, Mr. Moses de Willetts, was mortally wounded. Napier having left the deck, the action was continued by the Master. Soon after 11 A.M., the mainstay

---

[1] *Nav. Chron.*, xx. 327.

[2] James, v. 87; *Nav. Chron.*, xxi. 74.

[3] James, v. 77; Troude, iii. 509.

was shot away, and the main mast fell, its wreck grievously hampering the British crew. In consequence, the *Diligente* was able to rake the *Recruit* twice; and the action seemed about to terminate disastrously, when a lucky broadside caused an explosion on board the French corvette. After that she sheered off, and made all sail to escape, whilst the *Recruit's* men refitted their ship. The British loss was 6 killed and 23 wounded—half of the latter mortally—out of a total crew of 106; the *Diligente's* loss is unknown.[1] She reached Martinique, where she was afterwards captured.

On August 18th, the wretched little schooner *Rook*, 4, Lieutenant James Lawrence, whilst on her way from Jamaica to England, was captured by two French privateers, but only after a heroic resistance, in which 13 out of the 20 men on board were killed or wounded. Lawrence himself perished.[2]

On September 3rd, the *Kite*, 16, was attacked by Danish gunboats off Nyborg in a calm, and very severely handled. The ship was reduced to a wreck, and 2 were killed and 13 wounded of the crew. She only escaped by a breeze opportunely springing up.

On September 12th, the British ship *Laurel*, 22, Captain John Charles Woollcombe, whilst watching the harbour of Port Louis in Mauritius, sighted the French frigate *Canonnière*, 40, Captain C. J. Bourayne, which, after a long cruise in the Pacific, had arrived at Mauritius in July. The officers of the *Laurel* were in some doubt as to the identity and force of their opponent, some taking her for the *Sémillante*, 36, and others for an East Indiaman. Even when they made out her formidable nature, they did not shun an encounter, though the *Laurel* was enormously inferior in every respect. On the 15th, the French frigate having left port, the two closed, in a very light wind, and fought desperately for ninety minutes. In that time the *Laurel's* rigging was destroyed. Unable to manœuvre, the British Captain was compelled to haul down his flag, though his loss was insignificant. The *Canonnière* sustained such injuries in her hull that, after seven months' cruising in company with the *Laurel*, during which time neither vessel captured a single prize, she proved unfit for further service as an armed ship, and had to be sold. From the trivial loss sustained by the *Laurel*, it is clear either that the French fired very high, or

[1] James, v. 78; 'Life of Napier,' i. 16.   [2] James, v. 46.

that their gunnery was bad.[1]   The force of the two ships was as
follows: —

—	Tons.	Guns.	Broadside.	Men.	Killed.	Wounded.
			Lbs.			
Canonnière	1102	48	570	420	20?	19?
Laurel	526	30	159	144	0	9

The *Canonnière's* crew was larger than usual, as she had embarked
a detachment of soldiers from the garrison at Port Louis.

On September 24th, the packet *Cornwallis*, Anthony, master,
encountered and beat off the French privateer *Duquesne*, 12, to the
east of Barbados.   The privateer is said to have had 14 killed and
30 wounded—a good deal more than the *Cornwallis's* whole crew.
The packet lost 2 killed and 2 wounded.[2]

On September 29th, off Guadeloupe, the *Maria*, 14, Lieutenant
James Bennett, with astounding audacity, chased and brought to
action the *Département des Landes*, 22, Commander J. F. Raoul.
The British vessel had a broadside of just 76 lbs. to the Frenchman's
230 lbs., and a crew of 65 to the French 160.   Such temerity had
its natural result.   The gallant Bennett was killed, and his ship,
in a sinking condition, captured.   The British loss was 6 killed
and 9 wounded.   The French craft was little damaged, and suffered
trivial loss.[3]

It must always be a question whether it is right and wise for an
officer to encounter such odds as Lieutenant Bennett faced.   " Des
chocs irréfléchis ne constituent pas la guerre "—to quote Napoleon.
In this case nothing was effected, a British vessel was lost, and
many valuable lives were thrown away.   The explanation, probably,
is that the corvette was mistaken for a privateer.

On October 3rd, the *Carnation*, 18, Commander Charles Mars
Gregory, fell in with the French brig *Palinure*, 16, Commander
P. F. Jance, to the north-eastward of Martinique, and brought her
to action.   Unfortunately, Gregory was killed, and most of the
officers[4] were killed or wounded, in the earlier stages of the fight,

---

[1] James, v. 70; Troude, iii. 513; *Nav. Chron.*, xxi. 348; Chevalier, 309; C. M.,
Mar. 2nd, 1810.

[2] *Nav. Chron.*, xxi. 16.

[3] James, v. 79; Troude, iii. 515; *Nav. Chron.*, xxi. 76.

[4] Including Lieutenants Samuel Bartlett Deecker and James Fitzmaurice, severely,
and Master Anthony Metherell mortally wounded.

and when the *Palinure* fell on board the *Carnation*, the British
crew deserted their quarters and fled below, with some few exceptions, among whom was the Boatswain, William Triplet.   The
British vessel was, in consequence, captured by an enemy of much
inferior force, after having had 10 killed and 30 wounded out of a
crew of 117.   The survivors of the crew were afterwards tried for
misconduct.   One sergeant of Marines, John Chapman, was hanged,
and 32 seamen and Marines were transported to New South Wales.[1]

On October 8th, the British frigate *Modeste*, 36, Captain the
Hon. George Elliot (3), captured in the Bay of Bengal the French
corvette *Jéna*, 18, Lieutenant N. Morice, after a running fight, in
which the French suffered no loss, and the British had her Master,
William Donovan, killed, and a seaman wounded.[2]

On October 20th, the *Pompée*, 74, Captain George Cockburn,
captured to the eastwards of Barbados the French corvette *Pilade*,
16, Lieutenant J. M. Cocherel, without any resistance on the part
of the French.   On October 31st, the vanquisher of the *Carnation*,
the *Palinure*, was at last captured by the *Circe*, 32, Captain Hugh
Pigot (3), under the Diamond Rock, after a brief action in which
the *Palinure* lost 15, and the *Circe* 2 men.[3]

On the evening of November 10th, the French *Thétis*, 40,
Captain Jacques Pinsum, on her way from Lorient to Martinique
with troops and provisions on board, was sighted by the *Amethyst*,
36, Captain Michael Seymour (1), off Groix, and chased.   At 9 P.M.
the two ships began a running action, engaging with bow or stern
chasers, and the *Amethyst* signalled the presence of an enemy to the
other British ships off the coast.   The *Triumph*, 74, Captain Sir
Thomas Masterman Hardy, at once made sail to the *Amethyst's*
help.   At 9.15 a close action between the *Amethyst* and *Thétis*
began.   The *Thétis*, after going before the wind, suddenly came
round on the starboard tack, intending to cross the bows of the
Amethyst, which ship was also going before the wind, and rake her.
The *Amethyst*, however, frustrated the manœuvre by also turning,
inside the *Thétis's* circle, and engaging the enemy broadside to
broadside.   Both ships described a complete circle, and then resumed their course before the wind.   A second time the *Thétis*
attempted to rake, the *Amethyst* having drawn slightly ahead of

[1] James, v. 42; Troude, iii. 511; C. M. Feb. 1st, 1809, and Feb. 28th, 1809.
[2] James, v. 73; *Nav. Chron.*, xxi. 431.
[3] James, v. 42; *Nav. Chron.*, xxi. 76.

her; but, miscalculating, the French ship ran her jib-boom on board
the *Amethyst*, between the main and mizen rigging. She quickly
cleared the British ship, and resumed the broadside action until
about 10, when the *Amethyst*, then some distance ahead, turned to
port, crossed the *Thétis's* bows, pouring in a raking fire, and again
turned to starboard before the wind. At that point the *Amethyst's*
mizen-mast came down, doing much damage, and encumbering the
quarter-deck. Fortunately, the *Thétis's* mizen mast also fell a few
minutes later, so that both ships were left on even terms.

At 11, the *Thétis's* captain determined to board, and use his
superiority of men. He steered to strike the *Amethyst's* bow, struck
it, rebounded, and fell alongside, whereupon the British, who had
reserved their fire, poured in a terrible broadside. The two ships
became entangled, and, in that state, the British crew poured broadside after broadside into the enemy, setting her on fire, and shatter-
ing her hull and masts. At last, at 12.20 A.M. on the 11th, the
Amethyst's men boarded and carried their determined adversary.
The *Thétis* had three-quarters of her crew killed or wounded; 13
of her guns were dismounted; on the engaged side, the timbers
between her portholes had been, in many places, beaten in, so
that she showed huge gaps. Her two remaining masts fell just
after the close of the action.[1] The force of the combatants was as
follows :—

—	Tons.	Guns.	Broadside.	Crew.	Killed.	Wounded.
Amethyst	1046	42	Lbs. 467	261	19	51
Thétis	1090	44	524	436	135	102

In this case, as in many others, the number of troops on board the
Thétis—106 in all—largely swelled the losses. An hour after the
action was over, the *Triumph* and the *Shannon*, 38, came up, and
assisted in the transfer of prisoners, and in clearing the prize.

On November 11th, the *Franchise*, 36, Captain Charles Dashwood, *Aurora*, 28, *Dædalus*, 32, *Reindeer*, 16, and *Pert*, 14, seized
the harbour of Samana in San Domingo without opposition, just
before the batteries which the French were erecting had been

---

[1] James, v. 81; Troude, iii. 518; *Nav. Chron.*, xx. 417, xxi. 95. For this service
Capt. Seymour received the gold medal, and his first Lieutenant, Goddard Blenner-
hassett, was made Com., Nov. 11th, 1808.

completed. The move was important, as it secured British shipping
from the attacks of the privateers, who had always made that place
a principal base.[1]

On November 14th, the boats of the *Polyphemus*, 64, Captain
William Pryce Cumby, cut out the French war schooner *Colibri*, 3,
from the harbour of San Domingo, with a loss of 1 killed.[2] On
November 28th, the boats of the *Heureux*, 16, Commander William
Coombe, who led them, made an unsuccessful attempt to carry off
seven vessels from the harbour of Mahaut, in Guadeloupe, whilst a
detachment, under Lieutenant Daniel Lawrence, was told off to
attack two French batteries, under the guns of which the vessels
lay. Two armed vessels were carried, and the landing-party stormed
one of the two batteries. The fire of three field-guns on the beach
and of the other battery, however, compelled the British boats to
retreat. Coombe was killed, and Lawrence wounded.[3]

On December 12th, the *Cygne*, 16, and two schooners, on their
way from Cherbourg to Martinique, were discovered at anchor off
the Pearl Rock in the latter island, by the *Morne Fortunée*, 12,
Lieutenant John Brown (2). He summoned by signal the *Circe*, 32,
Commander Francis Augustus Collier (actg. Capt.), *Stork*, 18, Commander George Le Geyt, *Epervier*, 16, Commander Thomas Tudor
Tucker, and schooner *Express*, Commander William Dowers,[4] which
vessels were watching St. Pierre. One of the two schooners was
speedily driven ashore by the *Stork*, under the guns of three
batteries. The remaining schooner and the *Cygne* took shelter close
inshore under the guns of four other batteries. There they were
cannonaded by the *Circe*, *Stork*, and *Express*, and attacked by a
party of 68 men, under Lieutenant Charles Henry Crooke, in three
of the *Circe's* boats. This attack was repulsed with terrible loss.
One boat was sunk, one was taken, and, of the 68 men, 9 were killed,
26 were missing (prisoners or drowned), and 21 were wounded.[5]
On the 13th, the *Amaranthe*, 18, Commander Edward Pelham
Brenton, which had just joined, renewed the fight. The *Cygne*
was then working into St. Pierre, keeping close under the shore.
Brenton, aided by the boats of the *Circe* and *Stork*, worked in under
a heavy fire from the batteries, drove the *Cygne's* crew to their boats

[1] *Nav. Chron.*, xxi. 163.
[2] James, v. 87 ; *Nav. Chron.*, xxi. 162.
[3] James, v. 44 ; *Nav. Chron.*, xxi. 101.
[4] Promoted Com., Nov. 4th, 1808.
[5] James, v. 85.

with grape, and then sent in a boat party, under Lieutenant James Hay, to destroy her. The remaining French schooner, which was ashore, was also destroyed. The *Amaranthe's* loss was 1 killed and 5 wounded. In the other vessels there were 2 killed and 5 wounded.[1]

On December 30th, the *Imperieuse*, 38, Captain Lord Cochrane, sailed into Caldagues Bay, where were several French vessels laden with supplies for the besieged garrison of Barcelona. In spite of the fire of a battery, and of the French *Gauloise*, 7, and *Julie*, 5, Cochrane sank the two vessels ; with a landing-party captured the battery ; and took possession of 11 ships laden with provisions—all this without loss to his crew. A few days later, he captured a battery at Silva, and rolled all the guns into the sea. As a return for his hard and splendid work, Cochrane was positively reproached by the Admiralty for using too much powder, shot and stores ![2]

So troublesome had French privateers in the Channel become, that, at the close of 1808, steps were taken to arrange a system of signals by which warships could be informed of the whereabouts of such craft. The system was rudimentary, the direction of the enemy being indicated by a number of shots fired from alarm guns.

On January 1st, 1809, the sloop *Onyx*, 10, Commander Charles Gill, cruising in the North Sea, encountered the Dutch *Manly*,[3] 16, of superior force, brought her to close action, and, after two and a half hours' fighting in heavy weather, forced her to strike. The *Onyx* lost only 3 men wounded. The *Manly* had 5 killed and 6 wounded.[4] On the following day, off the Dutch coast, the *Aimable*, 32, Captain Lord George Stuart, gave chase to the French corvette *Iris*, 24, Lieutenant J. J. Macquet, and captured her on the 3rd, after twenty-four hours' pursuit. The *Iris* was laden with flour, and was under orders for Martinique. She was purchased for the Navy, and became the *Rainbow*, 28.[5]

On January 5th, the French corvette *Hébé*, 20, laden with flour for San Domingo, was taken by the *Loire*, 38, Captain Alexander

---

[1] James, v. 86; Brenton, ii. 255; *Gazette*, 1809, 146.

[2] 'Autob.,' i. 325, 336. The *Gauloise* and *Julie* were subsequently raised by Cochrane.

[3] *Ex* British; captured in the Ems, Jan., 1806. She was restored to the service.

[4] James, v. 146; De Jonge, v. 656; *Nav. Chron.*, xxi. 78. Gill was posted Jan. 16th, 1809, and his first Lieut., Edward William Garrett, was made a Com. on the same day.

[5] James, v. 147; Troude, iv. 61; *Nav. Chron.*, xxi. 171.

Wilmot Schomberg, in the Bay, after a slight resistance.   The *Hébé*
was caught in the act of taking possession of a prize.   She was
added to the Navy as the *Ganymede*, 34.[1]

On January 16th, the *Melampus*, 36, Captain Edward Hawker,
captured the French brig *Colibri*, 16, to the north of Barbuda.[2]

On December, 1808, the *Topaze*, 40, Captain P. N. Lahalle, with
a cargo of flour for Cayenne, had escaped from Brest, after a brush
with the *Loire*, 38, in which she suffered some damage.   On reaching
Cayenne, she had found the port blockaded, and had steered for
Guadeloupe.   Reaching that island on the night of January 21st–
22nd, 1809, she was sighted by the *Hazard*, 18, Commander Hugh
Cameron, *Jason*, 38, Captain William Maude, and *Cleopatra*, 32,
Captain Samuel John Brooke Pechell, and took refuge under the
guns of a battery on Pointe Noire.   The *Cleopatra* was the first of
the British ships to get near her, and at about 4.30 P.M. on the 22nd
anchored with springs and opened fire.   The *Topaze* had moored with
springs, and she poured in her fire as the *Cleopatra* approached.
Almost at once one of the *Topaze's* springs was shot away, and the
French frigate swung round, exposing herself to be raked.   Though
unable to bring the greater part of her broadside to bear, she held
out till the *Jason* and *Hazard* came up, when she struck, with
12 killed and 14 wounded.   The British loss was 2 killed and
1 wounded.[3]

On February 7th, the *Junon*, 40, Captain J. B. A. Rousseau,
after having been for some weeks blockaded in the harbour of the
Saintes, escaped to sea.   She was sighted next day by the British
vessels *Supérieure*, 14,[4] Commander William Ferrie, and *Asp*, 16,
Commander Robert Preston.   The *Supérieure* gave chase; but
the *Asp* soon dropped behind.   In the afternoon of the 9th the
Supérieure was still bravely pursuing, when the *Latona*, 38, Captain
Hugh Pigot (3), opportunely hove in sight, and joined in the chase.
On the 10th, the two vessels were some distance astern of the
Junon.   At that point, two more British vessels, the *Horatio*, 38,
Captain George Scott (1), and *Driver*, 18, Commander Charles
Claridge, came into sight, steering on the opposite tack.   Their
appearance compelled the *Junon* to turn and go before the wind,

---

[1] James, v. 147; *Nav. Chron.*, xxi. 172; Troude, iv. 61.

[2] *Nav. Chron.*, xxi. 261.

[3] James, v. 148; *Nav. Chron.*, xxi. 318.

[4] But with only 4 guns (18-pr. carr.) on board.

whereupon she was headed off by the *Latona*, and forced to double back and meet the *Horatio*. She passed the *Horatio* on the opposite tack, exchanging a hot fire, and then wore, and hauled up. But the *Horatio* outstripped her in speed of wearing, and was able to rake her. The *Junon* hauled up again on the starboard tack, and was brought to close action by her antagonist, running on the same tack. The *Horatio's* main and mizen topmasts, fore top-gallant mast, and fore topsail tie were shot away, and her Captain was wounded. The *Junon* soon drew away, with less serious injuries to her rigging but greatly shattered in hull. The *Supérieure* pluckily opened fire on her, the *Latona* being too far away to give any help ; and the *Driver* not hastening up to engage. At last the *Latona* got within range and opened fire, and the *Driver* got near enough to attack. The *Junon's* main and mizen masts fell in an attempt to tack, where-upon the French flag was struck, after a most creditable and skilful resistance to greatly superior force. The *Junon* lost 130 out of a crew of 323 ; the British loss was 7 killed and 33 wounded.[1]

On February 8th, the boats of the *Amphion*, 32, Captain William Hoste, and *Redwing*, 18, Commander Edward Augustus Down, cut out an armed brig and a coaster from the Dalmatian harbour of Melada. Three guns mounted ashore were carried off.[2]

On February 15th, the *Belle Poule*, 38, Captain James Brisbane, attacked the French storeship *Var*, 26, moored under the guns of Valona, on the Albanian coast, and cut her out with very little trouble. The guns ashore did not open fire.[3]

During January and February the *Proserpine*, 32, Captain Charles Otter, acted as look-out ship close inshore for the British squadron off Toulon, and showed such boldness that the French determined to trap her. During the night of February 27th, whilst she was becalmed to the south of Toulon, the *Pénélope*, 40, Captain Bernard Dubourdieu, *Pauline*, 40, Captain F. G. Montfort, and *Pomone*, 40, worked out to the west under Cape Sicié, hidden from view by the deep shadow cast by the moon. They then turned before an E.N.E. wind, and bore down upon the *Proserpine*. The British cruiser saw them too late, attempted escape, and was quickly brought to action by the *Pénélope* and *Pauline*, one on each quarter.

---

[1] James, v. 149; Troude, iv. 62; *Gazette*, 1809, 543; Logs of *Horatio* and *Supérieure*.

[2] James, v. 153; *Nav. Chron.*, xxi. 433.

[3] James, v. 153; *Nav. Chron.*, xxi. 432.

Against such a superiority of force she had no chance of success, especially as the *Pomone*, with the *Ajax*, 74, and *Suffren*, 74, was coming up astern.   After 40 minutes' firing, in which she inflicted no loss whatsoever upon the enemy and had her own rigging cut to pieces, she hauled down her flag, with 1 killed and 10 wounded. The French vessels suffered some slight damage to their rigging.[1]

On March 12th, the *Topaze*, 36, Captain Anselm John Griffiths, and *Kingfisher*, 18, Commander Ewell Tritton, chased and attacked the French frigates *Danaé*, 40, and *Flore*, 40, in the Adriatic. In spite of their great inferiority in force, the British vessels escaped loss or serious damage.   It can only be conjectured that the French frigates had received orders not to fight, or were upon some important mission.[2]

At daylight on March 15th, the boats of the *Arethusa*, 38, Captain Robert Mends, were sent, under Lieutenant Hugh Pearson, into the port of Lequeitio, on the northern coast of Spain, where 20 guns, mounted in the batteries, were destroyed and several prisoners captured.   On the 16th and 20th, other damage was done in the river Andero and at Baigno and Paissance.[3]

In the evening of April 1st, the boats of the *Mercury*, 28, Captain the Hon. Henry Duncan (3), under Lieutenant Watkin Owen Pell, rowed into the port of Rovigno under a heavy fire, and boarded and carried the French gunboat *Léda*, with a loss of 5 killed and wounded.   On May 15th, a party from the same ship, under Lieutenant Robert James Gordon, destroyed seven coasters in the Italian harbour of Rodi.[4]

On April 5th, the French frigate *Niémen*, 40, Captain J. H. J. Dupotet, on her way from France to Mauritius with stores and food, was sighted in the Bay by the *Amethyst*, 36, Captain Michael Seymour (1), and *Emerald*, 36, Captain Frederick Lewis Maitland (2), which were engaged in watching the Gironde.   The British ships gave chase ; but, as the evening of the 5th was very dark, they lost sight of one another and of the enemy.   The *Amethyst*, however, made a good guess at the *Niémen's* course and sighted her again at about 9.40 P.M.   Two hours later she was near enough to open with her chasers ; and, at 1.15 A.M., she succeeded in bringing

[1] James, v. 154; Troude, iv. 64; C. M. Oct. 30th, 1814.
[2] James, v. 171.
[3] *Ib.*, v. 156; *Nav. Chron.*, xxi. 430.
[4] James, v. 178; *Nav. Chron.*, xxiii. 395.

her starboard broadside to bear. On this the *Niémen* wore from
the port to the starboard tack with the wind at E.N.E. The
Amethyst imitated the manœuvre, again closed with her adversary,
drew ahead, and passed under the Frenchman's bows, pouring in a
very effective raking fire. She then bore up, and, a second time, was
passing under the *Niémen's* bows, when the French ship fell on
board her and received a heavy fire from the after guns of her

REAR-ADM. SIR MICHAEL SEYMOUR (1), BART., K.C.B.

(*From H. R. Cook's engraving, after the painting by J. Northcote, R.A., of Seymour
as a Post-Captain.*)

starboard battery. Apparently neither side attempted to board, and
the two ships soon drew clear. The action was continued broadside
to broadside. Soon after 3 P.M. the *Niémen* caught fire in her port
hammock-nettings, and, in quick succession, lost her mizen mast and
main topmast. The fire in her hammock-nettings was barely got
under ere another broke out in her main top. The attention of her
crew was thus distracted from the battle, and her guns were all
but silent. The *Amethyst*, observing this, bore up to pass under

her stern and rake her ; but the British ship's main mast suddenly
fell, bringing down with it the mizen mast. At the same moment
the *Niémen's* main mast went by the board. The wreckage
prevented the *Amethyst* from answering her helm ; but the British
frigate *Arethusa*, 38, Captain Robert Mends, which had steered to
the sound of the firing, opportunely came up, and received the
surrender of the enemy whom the *Amethyst* had so skilfully
overcome.

—	Tons.	Guns.	Broadside.	Men.	Killed.	Wounded.
Amethyst	1046	42	Lbs. 467	222	8	37
Niémen	1090?	46	563	339	47	73

An absurd French story[1] represents the British ship as hailing
to say that she had struck after her two masts fell. No un-
prejudiced person can believe that, with the *Arethusa* within
signalling distance and fast coming up, Seymour ever dreamt of
striking to an enemy whom he had punished so severely.[2]

In March, Commodore A. G. Troude, with the three French
74's *Courageux*, *Polonais*, and *d'Hautpoult* (flagship), and the storeships *Furieuse* and *Félicité*, freighted with supplies for Martinique,
anchored in the harbour of the Saintes, having heard of the capture
of Martinique[3] by the British. Their appearance at that point led
the British commanders on the station to determine upon an expedition[4] for the purpose of capturing the Saintes and so driving
the enemy out. On April 14th, a body of about 2500 men was
landed on one of the islands. A height overlooking the harbour was
seized, and from it two 8-inch howitzers were directed upon the
French ships. That night the three line-of-battle ships put to
sea. Their movements, however, were seen, and immediately
signalled, by Commander Hugh Cameron of the *Hazard*, 18, to
the blockading squadron, which consisted of the *Neptune*, 98,
Captain Charles Dilkes, with Rear-Admiral Sir Alexander F. I.
Cochrane's flag, *York*, 74, *Pompée*, 74, Captain William Charles
Fahie, *Polyphemus*, 64, *Recruit*, 18, Commander Charles Napier (2),

---

[1] *Moniteur*, July 13th, 1809.
[2] James, v. 157; Troude, iv. 65; Log of *Arethusa*; *Nav. Chron.*, xxi. 343.
Seymour was created a Bart., May 31st, 1809; and his first Lieut., William Hill, was
made Com., Apr. 6th, 1809.   [3] *See* p. 283.
[4] Under the naval command of Capt. Philip Beaver, of the *Acasta*, 40.

and some small craft. At about 10 P.M. the *Pompée* and *Recruit*
closed with the sternmost Frenchman, the *d'Hautpoult*, and fired
into her, without effect. The *Neptune* also succeeded in getting
near enough to open fire ; but soon the French vessels drew away
from all but the *Recruit*. The *Recruit* during the whole night kept
on the quarter of the *d'Hautpoult*, the outer ship of the line abreast
which was formed by the French, and at daylight began annoying
her and her consorts. More than once by her temerity she compelled the line-of-battle ships to yaw and fire broadsides at her. As
the evening of the 15th came on, the *Pompée* had drawn so close to
the French line that the three 74's scattered. The *d'Hautpoult*
steered W.N.W., and was followed by the *Pompée*, while the
Recruit and *Neptune* chased the other two. All the 16th the
pursuit continued, and in the forenoon the *Pompée* was joined by
the *Latona*, 38, Captain Hugh Pigot (3), and *Castor*, 32, Captain
William Roberts. On the 17th, early, the *Castor* was near enough
to the *d'Hautpoult* to open fire ; and she delayed the French ship
so much that the *Pompée* was able to come up and bring the enemy
to close action. British ships were showing on the horizon in every
direction, all standing towards the scene of action, when at 5.15 A.M.
the *d'Hautpoult* struck, with rigging and sails cut to pieces, masts
wounded, hull riddled, and between 80 and 90 killed or wounded.
The British loss was 10 killed and 35 wounded, mostly on board the
Pompée.[1]

The *d'Hautpoult* was purchased for the Navy and renamed
Abercrombie. For his gallantry Napier was appointed her acting
Captain.[2] As for the other two French ships of the line, they
reached Cherbourg in safety. The *Furieuse* and *Félicité* put to sea
on the night of the 15th, and, in spite of a hot pursuit, reached
Guadeloupe. They escaped from Basse-Terre on the night of
June 14th, but were again hotly pursued ; and, on the 18th, the
Félicité was overtaken and captured by the *Latona*, 38, Captain
Hugh Pigot (3). The *Furieuse* got away for the time, but, on
July 5th, fell in with the British *Bonne Citoyenne*, 20, Commander
William Mounsey, in mid-Atlantic, and was chased. On the 6th,
the British sloop was near enough to begin close action. The
handling of the *Bonne Citoyenne* was clever in the extreme. With

---

[1] James, v. 162; *Nav. Chron.*, xxi. 437, 501; 'Life of Napier,' i. 17; Troude,
iv. 26.
[2] Confirmed in post-rank, May 22nd, 1809.

her superiority of sailing she was able to steer a zig-zag course, using each broadside in turn; and thus she got off 129 broadsides to the *Furieuse's* 70 in a space of 7 hours. Thus, too, her carronades were kept from overheating. Her ammunition being exhausted by this long cannonade, she took up a position athwart the *Furieuse's* hawse, and prepared to board, whereupon the Frenchman struck. Both vessels were much damaged, but the injuries of the *Furieuse* were far severer than those of the *Bonne Citoyenne*.[1]

—	Tons.	Guns.	Broadside.	Men.	Killed.	Wounded.
Bonne Citoyenne . .	511	20	Lbs. 297	127	1	5
Furieuse	1085	20[1]	279[1]	200	35	60 ?

[1] Troude, 14 guns; broadside, 245 lbs.

Good gunnery and skilful manœuvring evidently gave the victory. Both ships were carried safely into Halifax. Mounsey was most deservedly posted, as from the day of his success, for his gallantry. His first Lieutenant, Joseph Symes, could not, however, be promoted until March 13th, 1810, as he did not till then complete the necessary two years' service as Lieutenant.

On April 23rd, the boats of the *Spartan*, 38, Captain Jahleel Brenton (2), *Amphion*, 32, Captain William Hoste, and *Mercury*, 28, Captain the Hon. Henry Duncan (3), supported by those frigates, bombarded the town of Pesaro on the Adriatic coast, and, driving out the French troops, destroyed the castle and carried off every vessel which had not been scuttled by the enemy. All this was achieved without loss. Lieutenants George Wickens Willes, Charles George Rodney Phillott, and William Augustus Baumgardt commanded the various divisions of boats.[2] On May 2nd, the *Spartan* and *Mercury's* people, at Cesenatico, seized the town and captured twelve coasters without loss.

On May 1st, the *Royalist*, 18, Commander John Maxwell, fell in with five French lugger privateers in the Channel, and captured the largest of them, the *Princesse*, 16. The others escaped while the *Royalist* was taking possession of her prize.[3]

The boats of the *Melpomene*, 38, Captain Peter Parker (2), on

[1] James, v. 165; *Nav. Chron.*, xxii. 346; Troude, iv. 69, 71.

[2] James, v. 169; *Nav. Chron.*, xxii. 152.

[3] *Nav. Chron.*, xxi. 433.

May 11th destroyed a Danish 6-gun cutter which had been chased ashore on the Jutland coast. Lieutenant George Rennie and 5 men were severely wounded in the affair. On May 23rd, the *Melpomene*, then commanded by Captain Frederick Warren, when becalmed in the Great Belt, was attacked by 20 Danish gunboats, and suffered very severe damage and loss, 5 men being killed and 29 wounded. The ship was so much shattered as to be incapacitated for further cruising, and had to return to England two or three months later. It would appear that she must have been captured or sunk, had not a light wind opportunely sprung up and enabled her to make sail and bring her broadside to bear.[1]

On May 15th, the *Tartar*, 32, Captain Joseph Baker, chased a Danish 4-gun privateer ashore on the Courland coast, sent in her boats, under Lieutenants Thomas Sykes and Frederick Augustus Hargood Parker, and brought off the vessel without loss.[2] On May 31st the *Cruizer*, 18, Commander Thomas Richard Toker, captured a small Danish cruiser, the *Christianborg*, 6, off Bornholm.

On May 17th, the *Goldfinch*, 10, Commander FitzOwen George Skinner, gave chase to the French corvette *Mouche*, 16, in lat. 44° 6′ N., long. 11° 20′ W. The *Mouche*, though greatly superior in force, attempted to avoid an action. She was overtaken on the 18th, but, firing high, inflicted so much injury upon the *Goldfinch's* masts and sails that she was able to escape. On the 21st, she exchanged some broadsides with the hired armed lugger *Black Joke*, Lieutenant Moses Cannadey, and entered the Spanish port of Santander, where she was captured on June 10th by the British frigates *Amelia*, 38, and *Statira*, 38.[3]

On May 20th, the boats of the *Princess Caroline*, 74, Captain Charles Dudley Pater, boarded and carried off from the Vlie the Dutch schooner *Piet Hein*, 7, without loss of life.[4]

On May 31st, the boats of the *Topaze*, 36, Captain Anselm John Griffiths, under Lieutenant Charles Hammond, were sent into Demata Bay, in the island of Santa Maura, to cut out nine French and Italian craft which had been observed lying there. The vessels were brought off with the loss of 1 man killed and 1 wounded.[5]

[1] James, v. 179; *Nav. Chron.*, xxi. 434.
[2] *Nav. Chron.*, xxi. 507 ; James, v. 179.
[3] James, v. 169; *Nav. Chron.*, xxii. 78.
[4] *Nav. Chron.*, xxi. 500; De Jonge, v. 657.
[5] James, v. 173.

At the close of 1808, four French 40-gun frigates, the *Vénus*, *Manche*, *Bellone*, and *Caroline*, had escaped unobserved from various ports in the French empire, and had sailed for Mauritius, with orders to avoid all British warships, and to harass commerce. The *Caroline*, Lieutenant J. B. H. Feretier, proceeded to the Bay of Bengal, and there, on May 31st, 1809, sighted the Indiamen *Streatham*, 30, John Dale, master, *Europe*, 30, William Gelston, master, and *Lord Keith*, 12, Peter Campbell, master, of whose force and character full particulars had been obtained from an American skipper. The three Indiamen formed line of battle as well as they could, but a great distance separated the two most powerful ships, the *Streatham* and the *Europe*. The *Caroline* attacked the sternmost of the three, the *Europe*, and, after half an hour's sharp fighting, left her in a disabled state. The French frigate then made sail ahead, engaged the *Streatham*, which had not as yet fired a shot, and, in an hour, disabled her and compelled her to strike. The *Lord Keith* remained, but the *Caroline* could not secure her without sacrificing one or other of the two craft that had been already engaged. Accordingly, after firing a few shots at her, the Frenchman returned to the *Europe*, and resumed action. The *Europe* at first answered the fire, but soon attempted to escape. She was speedily overhauled and captured by the *Caroline*, after that ship had placed a party on board the *Streatham*.[1] The British vessels were indifferently manœuvred, and were in consequence beaten in detail. In force, three weakly-manned, heavily-laden, and encumbered Indiamen were, however, no match for one powerful frigate.[2]

On June 13th, the *Pomone*, 38, Captain Robert Barrie, captured in the Mediterranean a new Neapolitan privateer, the *Lucien Charles*, 3.[3]

On June 14th, a landing party from the *Scout*, 18, Commander William Raitt, under Lieutenant Henry Robert Battersby, attacked a battery about ten miles to the east of Cape Croisette, stormed it, spiked the guns, and carried off seven vessels which had been moored under it; all this with the loss of only 1 killed and 5 wounded. On July 14th, following, Lieutenant Battersby headed

---

[1] Both the *Streatham* and the *Europe* were re-taken Sept. 21st, 1809, at Mauritius.

[2] James, v. 193; *Nav. Chron.*, xxiii. 97; xxiv. 76.

[3] James, v. 173; *Nav. Chron.*, xxii. 261.

an attack upon a battery at Carri, carried it without loss, killed 5 Frenchmen, and made 7 prisoners.[1]

On June 19th, the boats of the *Bellerophon*, 74, Captain Samuel Warren (2), were despatched, under Lieutenant Robert Pilch, into an anchorage near Hangö, on the Finland coast, to cut out three vessels. The vessels were boarded and carried off. To secure the retreat it was necessary to storm a battery mounting four guns, a business which was accomplished with trivial loss.[2]

In June it was determined to attack the Neapolitan islands of Ischia and Procida; and, on the 24th, a number of transports, under convoy of the *Canopus*, 80, Captain Charles Inglis (2), carrying the flag of Rear-Admiral George Martin (2), *Spartiate*, 74, *Warrior*, 74, *Cyane*, 22, Captain Thomas Staines, *Espoir*, 18, Commander Robert Mitford, and numerous British and Sicilian gunboats, anchored to the north of the islands. The *Cyane*, *Espoir*, and twelve gunboats were presently detached to the south to blockade on that side. Whilst on their station, on the 25th, they sighted the Neapolitan ships *Cerere*, 40, Commander Giovanni Bausan,[3] *Fama*, 30, Commander Sozi Carafa, and several gunboats, coming out of Pozzuoli Bay. They at once approached the enemy and opened fire. After a few broadsides the enemy fell back. Ischia surrendered on the morning of the 25th, though a fort on the south-east of the island held out for some days longer; Procida, in the evening. On the morning of the 26th the *Cyane*, *Espoir*, and gunboats attacked a flotilla of gunboats, which was coming up from the south, with such effect that eighteen were taken and five sunk. The British loss was small. In the afternoon the guns of a Neapolitan battery on Cape Miseno were spiked. Next day another battery in Pozzuoli Bay was attacked and silenced, and its guns were spiked. That evening the *Cerere*, *Fama*, and twenty gunboats made a fresh attempt to get from Pozzuoli Bay to Naples, but were at once assailed by the *Cyane*. Drawing ahead of the *Espoir* and the British gunboats, and using her sweeps, she closed with the *Cerere*, and fought her till all her powder was exhausted, when she drew off in a disabled condition with 2 killed and 20 (including the gallant Staines and

---

[1] James, v. 171; *Nav. Chron.*, xxii. 253.

[2] James, v. 180; *Nav. Chron.*, xxii. 84.

[3] Giovanni Bausan, a Neapolitan, born, 1757; served in British Navy under Rodney for three years; co-operated with British fleet in 1794–96. Assisted French at siege of Genoa, 1806. Was posted for his services in the *Cerere*, 1809. Commanded expedition against rebels of Palermo, 1820. Died, 1821.

Lieutenants James Hall and John Ferrier (2)) wounded. The *Cerere* is said to have lowered her flag, but, on receiving a reinforcement of men from Naples, to have hoisted it again. Her losses were about 50 killed or wounded. The *Fama* gave no help to her consort.[1]

In June a small British force, under Major-General Carmichael, sailed from Jamaica to co-operate with the Spaniards in the reduction of San Domingo. The *Polyphemus*, 64, Captain William Pryce Cumby, *Aurora*, 46, and eight small craft, meantime blockaded the city on the seaward side, and the *Polyphemus* landed eight of her lower-deck guns for service in the batteries. The blockade was so effective that, on July 2nd, the French governor opened negotiations for a capitulation, which took place on the 6th.[2]

On July 7th, the boats of the *Implacable*, 74, Captain Thomas Byam Martin, *Bellerophon*, 74, Captain Samuel Warren (2), *Melpomene*, 38, Captain Peter Parker (2), and *Prometheus*, 18, Commander Thomas Forrest, were sent into Barö Sound on the Finland coast to attack eight Russian gunboats, and a number of merchantmen, at anchor behind the fringe of islets which encircles the shore. Under a tremendous fire the British boats approached, and, boarding the gunboats, captured six. One other was sunk, and the eighth escaped. Of the merchantmen, twelve were captured. This result was not, however, achieved without terrible loss. Lieutenant Joseph Hawkey, first of the *Implacable*, who was in command, was killed with the cry on his lips, " Hurrah ! push on. England for ever ! " Of the 270 officers and men who took part in the affair, 17 (including Lieutenants Hawkey and James Stirling) were killed, and 37 wounded. Though the Russians lost over 120 men, it may be questioned whether the sacrifice was wholly justifiable. That it was not, was the decided opinion of Sir James Saumarez, the Commander-in-Chief in the Baltic, who wrote that he did not consider " the object in view to have been adequate to the risk and danger attending so hazardous an enterprise, and to the severe loss that must inevitably have ensued from the very strong position the enemy appears to have taken." Elsewhere, however, Saumarez stated that the affair had results of importance, since it stopped the

---

[1] James, v. 173; *Nav. Chron.*, xxii. 257; Randaccio, 'Storia delle Marine,' i. 98 ; *Corr. di Napoli*, June 28th and July 1st, 1809.

[2] *Nav. Chron.*, xxii. 253.

coast traffic, and compelled the Russians to provision their garrisons by land—a work of great difficulty.[1]

An enterprise of similar nature was one carried out, on July 25th, by seventeen boats from the *Princess Caroline*, 74, Captain Charles Dudley Pater (senior officer), *Minotaur*, 74, *Cerberus*, 32, and *Prometheus*, 18, against four Russian gunboats and a brig in the harbour of Frederikshamn. Four of the five vessels were boarded and carried off, after a terrible struggle, in which the British loss was 9 killed (including Lieutenant John James Callenan), and 51 wounded, among the latter being Commander Thomas Forrest,[2] of the *Prometheus*, who led the party.[3]

On July 7th, a squadron of ten small British craft, under Commander William Goate, of the *Mosquito*, 18, proceeded into the Elbe, presumably with the intention of co-operating with the German insurgents under the Duke of Brunswick, who was at Zwickau with a guerilla force. The flotilla anchored off Cuxhaven, and, on the 8th, landed a strong party which captured the town, hoisted the flags of Great Britain and of Hamburg, and destroyed the French batteries. The force then re-embarked. On the 29th, a detachment was landed from the same vessels and from the *Aimable*, 32, Captain Lord George Stuart, for the purpose of cutting off a small body of French troops which had shown itself near Cuxhaven. The landing-party advanced as far as Geestendorf, captured and destroyed a French battery, and returned to the ship with a great quantity of merchandise which had been seized and confiscated by the enemy.[4] In these operations Commanders William Goate, Robert Pettet (*Briseis*), and George Edward Watts (*Ephira*), greatly distinguished themselves.

On July 28th, the boats of the *Excellent*, 74, Captain John West, aided by the *Acorn*, 18, Commander Robert Clephane, and *Bustard*, 16, Commander John Duff Markland, entered the harbour of Duino, near Triest, with the object of cutting out a convoy that had taken shelter there. At the same time a party of Marines landed to hold the cliffs round the harbour. The operations were completely successful, six gunboats and ten coasters being brought off with a loss of but 8 wounded.[5]

---

[1] James, v. 180; 'Letters of Sir T. B. Martin,' i. 126; *Nav. Chron.*, xxii. 136; Ross, 'Saumarez,' ii. 161.

[2] Posted as from July 25th, 1809, for this service.

[3] James, v. 182; *Nav. Chron.*, xxii. 249.   [4] *Nav. Chron.*, xxii. 84, 139.

[5] James, v. 176; *Nav. Chron.*, xxiii. 72.

On August 12th, the *Lynx*, 18, Commander John Willoughby Marshall, and gun-brig *Monkey*, 14, Lieutenant Thomas Fitzgerald, attacked three Danish luggers under Issehöved, and drove them ashore. The British boats were then sent in, under Lieutenant Edward Kelly, and brought them off in safety, notwithstanding arrangements which had been made by the enemy for blowing up one of the luggers.[1]

On August 14th, the *Otter*, 18, Commander Nisbet Josiah Willoughby, discovered three French vessels at anchor under the batteries of Rivière Noire, in Mauritius, and sent in her boats at night, under Lieutenant John Burns, to cut them out. One of the three vessels was boarded and carried; but the alarm was given, and the batteries opened a heavy fire. The prize was found to be so firmly secured to the shore that she could not be brought off, and had to be abandoned. The British boats then retired, with a loss of 1 killed, 1 wounded.[2]

On August 27th, the boats of the *Amphion*, 32, Captain William Hoste, landed a party of seamen and Marines on the Venetian coast. This party, under Lieutenant Charles George Rodney Phillott, stormed a battery defending the entrance to the river Piave at Cortellazzo, and turned its guns upon six Italian gunboats lying in the river. Simultaneously another boat party from the *Amphion*, under Lieutenant William Slaughter, dashed up, boarded the gunboats, and carried them off, at the same time destroying or capturing seven coasting vessels. The loss was only 1 man wounded.[3]

On the night of September 7th, the boats of the *Mercury*, 28, Captain the Hon. Henry Duncan (3), under Lieutenant Watkin Owen Pell, cut out the schooner *Pugliese*, 7, from the harbour of Barletta, in Manfredonia. Though exposed to a heavy fire the party escaped without loss.[4]

On September 10th, the *Diana*, 10, Lieutenant William Kempthorne,[5] discovered the Dutch brig *Zefir*, 14, at anchor off Amurang in the island of Celebes, and, when night fell, sent in her boats to cut out the enemy. The *Zefir*, however, had sailed for Menado, where there was a strong fort, so was missed by the boats. Kempthorne pursued, and at daylight saw her near the fort. The wind from the sea blew so strong, unfortunately for the Dutch, that they

---

[1] James, v. 182; *Nav. Chron.*, xxii. 345.

[2] James v., 195.

[3] *Ib.*, v. 177; *Nav. Chron.*, xxii. 506.

[4] James v., 178.

[5] Com., Apr. 3rd, 1811, for this service.

could not anchor, and the *Diana* was able to draw near. Even
then the *Zefir* might have escaped, had not a land breeze suddenly
laid her sails aback and allowed the British brig to close. A hot
engagement began, in which the damage was all on one side, as
the Dutch failed to hit their target. After seventy minutes' fighting
the *Zefir* hauled down her flag. Five gunboats were coming out to
her assistance, but when they saw what had happened, and had
received a few shot, they retired.[1]

In September, Commodore Josias Rowley, in concert with
Lieut.-Colonel Henry S. Keating, commanding the British garrison
at Rodriguez, a small island which, being eastward of Mauritius,
had been previously occupied as a base for the British blockading
squadrons off Réunion and Mauritius, determined upon a conjoint
expedition for the capture of St. Paul, the only good harbour in the
island of Réunion. The vessels engaged were :

SHIPS.	GUNS.	COMMANDERS.
Raisonnable	64	Commodore Josias Rowley.
Sirius	36	Capt. Samuel Pym.
Boadicea	38	Capt. John Hatley.
Néréide	36	Capt. Robert Corbett.
Otter	18	Commander Nisbet Josiah Willoughby.
Wasp (East India Co.'s Schooner) .	—	— Watkins.

A force of 368 troops was embarked. On September 21st the
Néréide disembarked the troops, and 236 seamen and Marines under
Commander Willoughby, at Pointe des Galets, five miles from
St. Paul. The men advanced rapidly, seized the causeway over
the Etang de St. Paul, captured three batteries with but trifling
resistance, and turned the guns on the shipping in the harbour,
where lay the French 40-gun frigate *Caroline*. Two other batteries
completely dominating the harbour were carried in quick succession,
while the British squadron in the bay stood in close, poured a heavy
fire into the *Caroline*, and finally anchored off the town. The
Caroline,[2] *Grappler*, 16,[3] and the Indiamen *Streatham* and *Europe*,

---

[1] James, v. 183.

[2] Added to the Navy as *Bourbonnaise*.

[3] Pierced for 16, but with only 11 on board. She was probably a British privateer
prize ; as no man-of-war of the name seems to have fallen into the hands of the enemy
between 1803 and 1809.

had cut their cables when the British squadron approached, and had, in consequence, drifted ashore. They were all got off without injury by the seamen of the squadron, and St. Paul, with 125 guns of all kinds, fell into the hands of the British.

The naval loss was 7 killed, 18 wounded, and 1 missing. The place was taken by surprise from the land, in spite of strong defences which fronted towards the sea. As the roads ran along the coast, and troops moving by them could be attacked by the fire of the British ships, it was difficult, if not impossible, for the French to recover the ground which they had lost. The British force was re-embarked, after destroying the fortifications and guns, but, on the 22nd, as French troops could be seen approaching from the hills to the south of the town, a party of Marines and seamen was again landed under Willoughby.[1] It destroyed a government store-house, containing silk to the value of £500,000, and re-embarked. On the 23rd, terms were arranged with the French, by which all public property was to be surrendered, and the British were to be unmolested in removing it. On the 28th, the British withdrew from St. Paul, carrying with them their prizes.[2]

On October 17th, the *Hazard*, 18, Commander Hugh Cameron, and *Pelorus*, 18, Commander Thomas Huskisson, sent in their boats, under Lieutenants James Robertson (2) and Edward Flin, to destroy a privateer which lay secured under the guns of Sainte Marie, Guadeloupe. She was boarded and blown up under a heavy fire, the British losing 6 killed and 9 wounded, many of them by the explosion.[3]

On October 30th, the *Surveillante*, 38, Captain Sir George Ralph Collier, captured the French corvette *Milan*, 18, Commander Touffet, in the Bay, with despatches for Guadeloupe.[4]

On November 2nd, the British sloop *Victor*, 18, Commander Edward Stopford (1), was chased in the Bay of Bengal by the French frigate *Bellone*, 40. The British vessel had her masts and rigging badly damaged, and was compelled to strike, having had 2 wounded.[5]

In November, a conjoint expedition, in which the *Chiffonne*, 36,

---

[1] Succeeded Corbett (who commissioned the *Bourbonnaise*) in command of the *Néréide*, but not confirmed in post rank till Sept. 5th, 1810.

[2] James, v. 196; Troude, iv. 83; *Nav. Chron.*, xxiii. 251 *et seq.*

[3] James, v. 184; *Nav. Chron.*, xxiii. 164.

[4] *Nav. Chron.*, xxii. 437.

[5] James, v. 203; *Nav. Chron.*, xxiv. 81.

Captain John Wainwright (2), and *Caroline*, 36, Captain Charles
Gordon (1), took part, with several cruisers of the East India Com-
pany's service, and a body of troops, cleared out the pirate strong-
holds of Ras-el-Khyma (on the 13th), Lingeh (on the 17th), and
Laft (on the 27th), at the entrance of the Persian Gulf.   The entire
British loss was 4 killed and 35 wounded, 1 mortally.[1]

On December 12th, the *Thetis*, 38, Captain George Miller,
Pultusk, 16, Commander William Elliot (2), *Achates*, 10, Commander Thomas Pinto, *Attentive*, 12, Lieutenant Robert Carr, and
armed schooner *Bacchus*, 16, Lieutenant Charles Deyman Jermy,
discovered the French corvette *Nisus*, 16, at anchor under a battery in
the harbour of Deshaies, Guadeloupe.   The boats, under Lieutenant
Nathaniel Belchier, were sent in that night to cut her out, after
a party of seamen and Marines, under Commander Elliot, had
landed and attacked the battery from the rear.   The battery was
carried, and the corvette was boarded and captured, with a loss of
5 wounded.[2]

On December 13th, to the east of Antigua, the *Junon*, 38,
Captain John Shortland, and *Observateur*, 16, Commander Frederick
Augustus Wetherall, sighted the *Renommée*, 40, and *Clorinde*, 40,
convoying the two *flûtes*, *Loire*, 40, and *Seine*, 40 (then mounting
20 guns apiece only).   The British vessels boldly gave chase and
closed.   The strangers showed the Spanish flag, and made the correct
answer to the private signal.   This led the *Junon* to approach within
a quarter of a mile of her antagonists, whereupon the French hoisted
their national colours, and the *Renommée* fired a broadside.   The
Clorinde ran almost foul of the *Junon's* starboard side; the *Renommée* closed yard-arm to yard-arm on the port side; and the two *flûtes*
opened a raking fire ahead and astern of the British frigate.   Thus
circumstanced, and though her deck was swept by the enemy's
small-arms fire, she fought heroically for half an hour, and did not
haul down her flag till more than a quarter of her crew had been
placed *hors de combat*, and her gallant captain wounded no fewer
than five times.   Of those wounds he died on January 21st following.
Out of 224 officers and men, she lost 20 killed and 40 wounded.
Her enemies had among them 21 killed and 18 wounded.   The
Junon's hull was in such a shattered state that, as soon as the

---

[1] James, v. 204; *Nav. Chron.*, xxiv. 73.   The *Chiffonne* often figures in the list
of the time as the *Chiffone*.

[2] James, v. 185; *Nav. Chron.*, xxiii. 166, 169.

prisoners had been transferred, the frigate was set on fire by the French.

The *Observateur*, seeing that her aid would be fruitless, escaped as soon as her consort was surrounded. She made sail for Guadeloupe, and there warned the *Blonde*, 38, Captain Volant Vashon Ballard, *Thetis*, 38, Captain George Miller, *Hazard*, 18, Commander Hugh Cameron, and *Cygnet*, 18, Commander Edward Dix. All these

CAPTAIN JOHN SHORTLAND, R.N.

(From a lithograph by H. R. Cook, after the painting by R. Field.)

vessels took post in the channel between the Saintes and Guadeloupe, where they were joined on the 16th and 17th by the *Scorpion*, 18, Commander Francis Stanfell, *Ringdove*, 18, Commander William Dowers, and *Castor*, 32, Captain William Roberts, the latter having been chased by the Frenchmen off Désirade. The *Scorpion* and *Ringdove* were detached to reconnoitre Basseterre. It was still early on the 17th when the *Loire* and *Seine* were made out by the squadron, steering down the west of Guadeloupe towards Basseterre.

The British gave chase, and drove them into Anse la Barque, where they anchored. A battery to the south of the Anse fired at the squadron, but its activity induced a somewhat startling result, for Commander Dowers instantly landed with a boat party, stormed it, and destroyed it, without loss. The British then stood off and on off the port, preparing to attack. There they were joined by the *Freija*, 36, Captain John Hayes (1), and *Sceptre*, 74, Captain Samuel James Ballard. In the afternoon of the 18th, the *Blonde* and *Thetis* closed within 400 yards of the French ships, and attacked them, whilst the *Sceptre* and *Freija* cannonaded the batteries, and a large landing party attacked from the shore side. The French *flûtes* were speedily compelled to strike, though they afterwards took fire. At about the same time the most important of the shore batteries was stormed by a party under Commander Cameron. The losses of the *Blonde* and *Thetis* were 9 killed (including Lieutenant George Jenkins) and 22 wounded. Those of the other British vessels are not known. The *Renommée* and *Clorinde* saw the British squadron at a distance, and, in endeavouring to escape, ran aground off Antigua, sustaining severe injury. This led their captains, when, by throwing overboard many of their guns, they had lightened their ships and got them afloat, to return to Brest, where they arrived late in January, 1810. The British vessels, busy with the *flûtes*, do not seem to have paid any attention to them.[1]

On December 14th, the *Melampus*, 36, Captain Edward Hawker, captured the French brig *Béarnais*, 16, off Guadeloupe. On the 19th, a French sister-ship, the *Papillon*, 16, was taken in the same neighbourhood by the *Rosamond*, 18, Commander Benjamin Walker.[2]

On January 10th, 1810, the boats of the British squadron, then under Captain Sir Joseph Sydney Yorke, in Basque Road, cut out several French coasters from under the guns of a battery near La Rochelle. The attack was led by Lieutenant Gardiner Henry Guion. On the 20th, they repeated their exploit, without, on either occasion, any loss of life. Troude notices the growing difficulty of carrying on the coasting trade, as the British blockading squadrons grew bolder and bolder. On February 13th, another boat affair took

---

[1] James, v. 186 ; Troude, iv. 47; *Nav. Chron.*, xxiii. 168, 170, 346; xxiv. 12; *Moniteur*, Feb. 3rd, 1810; C. M., Feb. 19th and 20th, 1810. The *Junon's* first Lieut., Samuel Bartlett Deccker, was made Com., April 17th, 1810, for his defence of her.

[2] James, v. 186.

place, in which three French coasters were destroyed by parties from the same squadron.[1]

On January 11th, the *Cherokee*, 10, Commander Richard Arthur,[2] dashed into the mouth of Dieppe harbour, and boarded and carried off a privateer, the *Aimable Nelly*, 16, from under the guns of the batteries.[3] It may here be noticed that the French privateers during the years 1810 and 1811 became more and more troublesome, and that the bitterest complaints were made by merchants and ship-owners of the inadequate protection afforded by the Navy in the Channel. In the course of 1810, the following notice was posted up at Lloyds : " The committee feel it their duty to make known to the subscribers to this House that, in a communication with the Admiralty this morning, they have been informed that the increase of the number of French privateers fitted out and fitting from the various ports in the Channel and North Sea is beyond precedent." On one occasion a French privateer lay for a fortnight off the eastern coast of England, unmolested, waiting for a prize ; on another occasion the same vessel took no fewer than 30 sail out of a fleet of coasters. It was complained that the excessive cost of condemning these privateers, which were usually beggarly little vessels, was so great as to render naval officers unwilling to touch them. Insufficient small craft were assigned to duty in the Channel, and they were too slow. Nor was a close enough watch kept off the French ports from which the privateers chiefly issued. In spite of this, a great many of the marauders were laid by the heels by the Royal Navy. The *Gazette* records, for instance, the capture of four in the Channel between January 2nd and 13th.[4]

On January 11th, the *Scorpion*, 18, Commander Francis Stanfell,[5] was sent into Basseterre harbour by Captain Volant Vashon Ballard, senior officer of the squadron off Guadeloupe, to bring out the brig *Oreste*, 16. After a running fight with the Frenchman, who was found under way, the *Scorpion* succeeded, aided by the barge of the *Blonde*. The British loss was only 4 wounded.[6] On January 17th, Captain John Hayes (1) of the *Freija*, 36, learnt that three French vessels were at anchor in

---

[1] James, v. 229; Troude, iv. 100; *Nav. Chron.*, xxiii. 428.
[2] Posted, Jan. 11th, 1810, for this service.
[3] James, v. 221; *Gazette*, 1810, 57.
[4] *Nav. Chron.*, xxiv. 491; xxv. 291.
[5] Posted, Mar. 19th, 1810, for this service.
[6] James, v. 221; Troude, iv. 98; *Nav. Chron.*, xxv. 461.

Baie Mahaut, on the north coast of the same island, and at once
made her way in towards them through the reef-strewn waters of
the Grand Cul-de-Sac Marin. On the 21st, he sighted his quarry,
and, as evening came on, despatched four boats, under Lieutenant
David Hope, to cut out the enemy's vessels. The boats, in the face
of a sharp fire, boarded and captured a brig. A few men were left
in charge of the prize ; and the rest of the party pushed on, landed,
stormed, and destroyed two batteries mounting 10 guns. They
then returned to the brig ; destroyed the two other French vessels
in the bay and carried off the brig. All this was accomplished with
the loss of 2 men wounded.[1]

On February 3rd, the *Valiant*, 74, Captain John Bligh (2), was
so fortunate as to fall in with the late French frigate *Canonnière*[2]
(fitted as a merchantman, renamed *Confiance*, and armed with
14 guns only), off Belle Isle. She was captured after a long chase,
with cargo on board to the value of £150,000. As showing the
ubiquity of the British cruisers, it is interesting to record that on her
voyage from Mauritius to the Bay of Biscay she had been chased no
fewer than fourteen times.[3]

On February 9th, just after the capture of Guadeloupe by the
British, the French frigate *Néréide*, 40, arrived off Basseterre.
She was at once chased by the British squadron lying there, but
succeeded in escaping with the loss of a boat which she had sent
into the port. On the 13th, however, she was again chased by the
Rainbow, 22, Captain James Wooldridge, off San Domingo ; and on
the 14th, the *Avon*, 18, Commander Henry Tillieux Fraser, joined
in the chase. In the afternoon the *Néréide* turned on the *Rainbow*,
engaged her in close action, and reduced her sails and rigging to
a wreck. The *Avon* came up and was treated in much the same
manner. Leaving her two antagonists in very damaged condition,
the *Néréide* returned to Brest without further incident. The British
loss was 10 wounded in the *Rainbow*, and 2 killed and 7 wounded in
the *Avon*.[4]

On February 10th, some distance to the south-east of Bermuda,
the *Thistle*, 10, Lieutenant Peter Procter, chased the Dutch colonial
corvette *Havik*, 10, and at about 5 P.M. closed her sufficiently to

---

[1] James, v. 222 ; *Gazette*, 1810, 308 (abstract only).

[2] *Ex* British *Minerve*, 38, taken July 2nd, 1803. She had been originally taken
from the French in 1795.

[3] James, v. 231 ; *Nav. Chron.*, xxiii. 171.

[4] James, v. 226 ; Troude, iv. 98.

bring her to action. After the best part of two hours' fighting, in which three of the *Thistle's* carronades were dismounted, the Dutchman made all sail to escape. The *Thistle* pursued, but could not a second time close her antagonist till 8.30 P.M., when the action was renewed, and, after more than an hour's hard fighting, the enemy was compelled to strike. The British loss was 1 killed and 6 wounded ; the Dutch, 8 wounded.[1]

On February 21st, the *Horatio*, 38, Captain George Scott (1), fell in with the French *flûte*, *Nécessité*, 26, in the Atlantic, and, after a long chase, captured her without loss on either side.[2]

On April 4th, the boats of the *Success*, 32, Captain John Ayscough, and *Espoir*, 18, Commander Robert Mitford, were despatched to destroy three vessels which were seen loading near Castiglione on the Calabrian coast. Though three of the boats, which were all under Lieutenants George Rose Sartorius and Robert Oliver, struck on a ledge of rocks and filled with water, the men from them swam ashore under a heavy fire from two 6-prs., captured and spiked the guns, destroyed two of the three vessels, and, baling out the swamped boats, returned to the ships, having lost but 2 men drowned and 2 wounded.[3]

On April 6th, the cutter *Sylvia*, 10, Lieutenant Augustus Vere Drury, destroyed a Malay proa, and, on the 7th, captured another off the Java coast. On the 11th, she sank a third. These vessels made Krakatoa their headquarters, and caused a great deal of trouble to commerce. On the 26th, she captured the Dutch brig *Echo*, 8, after a short but sharp action in which she had 4 killed and 3 wounded, and the enemy 3 killed and 7 wounded. She also captured two small Dutch transports.[4]

On April 12th, off the isle of Rhé, the ex-British ship *Laurel*, 22, which had been captured on September 15th, 1808, and had since been known as the *Espérance*, was retaken by the *Unicorn*, 32, Captain Alexander Robert Kerr. She was restored to the Navy as the *Laurestinus*.[5]

---

[1] James, v. 225; *Nav. Chron.*, xxiii. 515; De Jonge, v. 632. *Havik* is Dutch for Goshawk; but the name was corrupted in the British service into *Havick* and so to *Havock*, and, as such, it has been handed down to this day. The first *Havik* captured was taken in 1796.

[2] James, v. 231.

[3] *Ib.*, v. 245; *Nav. Chron.*, xxiv. 255.

[4] James, v. 260; *Nav. Chron.*, xxiv. 510.

[5] James, v. 231; *Nav. Chron.*, xxiii. 436.

On April 21st, the cutter *Surly*, 10, Lieutenant Richard Welch, with the gun-brigs *Firm*, 14, and *Sharpshooter*, 14, chased ashore the French privateer *Alcide*, 4, in Granville Bay, sent in their boats under a heavy fire, hove her off, and, losing only 1 killed and 1 wounded, brought her away.[1]

In the course of this year, beginning in April, a most important series of operations began in the Indian Ocean. The ultimate result of these was the capture of the last remaining French bases in those waters—Réunion and Mauritius.[2] The French ships on the station were the *Vénus*, *Bellone*, and *Manche*, all of 40 guns, to which must be added the *Minerve* (ex *Minerva*), also of 40 guns, which had been captured from the Portuguese, and the brig *Entreprenante*. If James can be believed, to complete the crew of the *Minerve* the French had recourse to prisoners taken from the various British ships captured, a large number of whom were Irish Catholics. The British squadron, which comprised the *Leopard*, 50, *Iphigenia*, 36, *Magicienne*, 36, and some small craft, was unable to maintain a strict blockade. Late in April, it was reinforced by the *Néréide*, 36, Commander Nisbet Josiah Willoughby (actg. Capt.). The *Néréide* proceeded to Rivière-Noire on the south coast of Mauritius, off which was to be her cruising ground. There, on April 24th, she discovered the French frigate *Astrée*, 36, also newly arrived, at anchor under the batteries ; and she opened fire on her at long range without much effect. On the 30th, she observed a large merchant-man at anchor under the batteries of Jacolet, and in the evening sent in her boats, Willoughby himself taking command, to capture the ship. In spite of the fire of two French batteries, the boat party landed, stormed the first battery and spiked its guns, and then drove back a detachment of French militia, capturing from them two field pieces. Day broke and revealed to the British the second battery beyond the river Galet, which, it could be seen, was held by a strong body of French militia. The British seamen, however, boldly swam the stream or forded it, carried the second battery and drove the militia before them in ignominious flight. Returning, they found that the garrison of the first battery had rallied. Willoughby immediately threatened its line of retreat, whereupon it ran, leaving him leisure to destroy the signal-station, to carry off the schooner *Estafette*, and to examine the merchantman, which proved to be American and was for that reason not touched. The British loss

---

[1] *Nav. Chron.*, xxiii. 513.   [2] *See also* previous Chapter, p. 293.

was only 1 killed and 7 wounded.   Of the French, three officers were
made prisoners.[1]

Willoughby, a few weeks later, was most severely wounded
by the bursting of a musket whilst exercising his men on Flat
Island, an islet to the north of Mauritius, which was used by
the British squadron as its base.   His jaw was fractured, and his
larynx was laid bare, but happily he recovered.[2]   He will soon be
again met with.

Meanwhile operations were in progress on other stations.

On April 25th, the *Spartan*, 38, Captain Jahleel Brenton (2),
Success, 32, Captain John Ayscough, and *Espoir*, 18, Commander
Robert Mitford, being to the eastward of Monte Circeo, discovered
a ship, three barks, and several feluccas at anchor under the castle
of Terracina.   The boats of the squadron were therefore sent in
under Lieutenants William Augustus Baumgardt and George Rose
Sartorius, supported by the fire of the men-of-war, and, in spite of
much resistance, took, and brought off, the ship and the three barks,
with a loss of only 1 killed and 2 wounded.[3]

On May 1st, the *Spartan* was cruising with the *Success* off
Ischia, when, late in the afternoon, two ships, a brig, and a
cutter were discovered in the Bay of Naples.   These were recognised as the Neapolitan *Cerere*, 40, Captain Ramatuelle, *Fama*, 30,
Captain Giuseppe de Cosa, *Sparviero*, 8, Commander Raffaele de
Cosa, and *Achille*, 8, Commander Vincent.   That evening those
vessels were chased nearly within the mole.   On the morning
of the 2nd, they were seen at anchor.   Having stood towards
them, and satisfied himself that they would not fight the force
then at his disposal, Brenton that evening detached the *Success*
to a rendezvous south-west of Capri.   The Neapolitans, however,
intended to fight, and had already made preparations to that
end, putting 400 Swiss troops into the *Cerere* and *Fama*, and
adding six or seven gunboats, each carrying a long 18-pr., to
the squadron.   Very early on May 3rd, the *Spartan* stood into
the bay with a light S.E. breeze in order to attack; and soon
she found that the enemy was already standing out for the same
purpose.   The *Cerere*, followed in line of battle by the *Fama* and
Spárviero, after manœuvring in vain to get to windward, held on,
and, at 7.58 A.M., being then within pistol shot on the *Spartan's*

[1] James, v. 266; *Gazette*, 1810, 1325.   [2] O'Byrne, 1303.
[3] James, v. 245.

port, or lee, bow, the *Cerere* opened fire. The *Spartan* waited to reply to the best advantage, and then returned a destructive broadside, having treble-shotted the guns on her main deck. As the ships were moving slowly through the water, she was subsequently able to throw broadsides into the *Fama* and *Sparviero* in succession. By that time the *Achille* and gunboats had hauled to the south-east. Standing on to within easy range of them, the frigate hove in stays, and, coming round, gave them the whole of her port broadside, while she discharged her starboard one at the larger craft. These, instead of tacking to meet the *Spartan*, wore, and stood towards the Baia batteries. When, therefore, she was round on the port tack, the *Spartan* kept her helm up and went after the *Cerere*; but, at about 9 A.M., the failing breeze left the British ship with the *Cerere* nearly across her bows, the *Fama* and *Sparviero* on her port bow, and the *Achille* and gunboats sweeping up astern. She was thus exposed to a concentrated fire, which wounded Brenton, and caused the command to devolve upon Lieutenant George Wickens Willes. Soon, however, the light S.E. breeze sprang up again, and enabled the *Spartan* to place herself on the starboard quarter of the *Cerere* and the starboard bow of the *Fama*. Then, although the *Sparviero*, *Achille*, and gunboats still annoyed her on the stern and quarters, the *Spartan* quickly began to assert herself. The *Cerere* hauled to windward of her consort and gained the protection of the Baia batteries; the *Fama*, after having been raked and terribly damaged, was gallantly towed away by the gunboats; and the *Sparviero*, by a broadside from the frigate's port guns, was compelled to strike, after the action had lasted for about two hours. In this well-fought affair, 95 guns and about 1400 men were opposed by 46 guns and 259 men, and beaten. The *Spartan* lost 10 killed, including Master's Mate William Robson, and 22 wounded, including Brenton and Lieutenant Willes. The total loss of the enemy in killed and wounded seems to have been 131.[1] Brenton, who was rendered useless for further service, was made a Baronet on December 24th, 1812. Willes was made a Commander on June 2nd, 1810. Among the others who distinguished themselves on the occasion were Lieutenants William Augustus Baumgardt and Henry Bourne, and Captain George Hoste, R.E., who was a passenger, together with

---

[1] Report of Ramatuelle in *Corr. di Napoli*, May 9th–12th, 1810; *Nav. Chron.*, xxiv. 163; *Spartan's* Log; James, v. 246; Randaccio, i. 103; Brenton, ii. 345.

Master Henry George Slenner, and Purser James Dunn, who took charge of some of the main-deck guns.

While cruising off Lindesnäs, the southern point of Norway, the *Tribune*, 36, Captain George Reynolds, chased two Danish brigs, which hove to in the port of Mandal, at about 2.30 P.M. on May 12th. When the frigate was firing at them, several gunboats and two more brigs appeared from behind the rocks, and, with the vessels first seen, began to work out towards the *Tribune*, which thereupon stood in nearer to the enemy and hove to. The four brigs, which together mounted 74 guns, tacked and formed line of battle, and, at 4.30, the *Tribune* having filled and wore, a smart action began. It continued for two hours and a quarter, at the expiration of which time the Danes ceased firing, and crowded sail to regain the harbour of Mandal. The frigate tacked, and made sail in chase, but failed to get up with the enemy, whose return was covered by several more gunboats. The *Tribune* suffered severely aloft and in her hull, and had 9 killed and 13 wounded. As the Danish guns engaged were all long or medium 18-prs., the frigate was fortunate. The enemy's loss is unknown.[1]

On May 22nd, the *Alceste*, 38, Captain Murray Maxwell, chased several French vessels into a fortified bay near Fréjus. A battery, having great command, stood on each side of the entrance. Maxwell detached two parties, one under Lieutenant Andrew Wilson, and the other under Master Henry Bell, to storm the works that night. Wilson's party was unsuccessful, and had to retire; Bell's, though it carried its battery and spiked the guns, had to abandon its conquest, as the opposite battery had not been reduced. Maxwell then made use of a ruse. On the night of the 25th, he sent his barge and yawl, manned and armed, under Mr. Bell and Midshipman James Adair, to lie in a cove near the mouth of the bay; and, in the *Alceste*, he stood to sea. On the following morning, the French, supposing the blockade to have been raised, sailed out boldly, the result being that, in spite of resistance and the fire from above, four feluccas were captured, two forced ashore, and the rest driven back to harbour. On the British side there was no loss.[2]

During June, the *Amphion*, 32, Captain William Hoste, *Active*, 38, Captain James Alexander Gordon, and *Cerberus*, 32, Captain Henry Whitby, cruised in the gulf of Triest. On the 28th, several

---

[1] James, v. 232; *Nav. Chron.*, xxiii. 515.
[2] James, v. 250; *Nav. Chron.*, xxiv. 253.

vessels, reported to be laden with naval stores for Venice, were
chased into Grado harbour ; and, in the evening, the boats of the
Amphion and *Cerberus,* under Lieutenants William Slaughter,
Donat Henchy O'Brien, and James Dickinson (2), went in, and, by
daylight of the 29th, landed near the town without opposition. As
the party advanced to attack the place, above which lay the vessels
sought for, it was met by troops and peasantry, and obliged to retire
to a line of hillocks ; but, being there charged with the bayonet, it
drove off its assailants, took 40 prisoners, entered the town, and
seized the vessels, 25 in number. In the meantime a division from
the *Active,* under Lieutenant James Mears, had also landed ; and at
about 11 A.M., when a small detachment of French troops from
Maran attacked, the whole of that little force, of 22 men and an
officer, over and above 2 who were killed, was obliged to surrender.
Before night, fourteen of the prizes were safely carried out to the
squadron, the remainder being burnt. The British loss in these
operations was only 4 killed and 8 wounded.[1] In addition to the
officers already mentioned, Lieutenants (R.M.) Thomas Moore and
Jeremiah Brattle (who was wounded) greatly distinguished themselves.

Early on July 3rd, off Mayotte, the outward-bound Indiamen
Ceylon, Henry Meriton (senior officer), *Windham,*[2] John Stewart,
and *Astell,* Robert Hay, discovered on their starboard bow the
French men-of-war *Bellone,* 40, Captain Victor Guy Duperré,[3]
Minerve, 40, Captain Pierre François Henri Etienne Bouvet, and
Victor, 22, Commander Nicolas Morice. As soon as the Indiamen
had satisfied themselves that the strangers were enemies, they
prepared for action, while trying at first to avoid it ; but, the
Frenchmen pressing, Meriton ultimately formed a close line of the
Windham, Ceylon, and *Astell,* in the order named, and awaited the
attack, which began at about 2.15 P.M. A most determined and
gallant fight was made of it, both by the crews of the ships and by
the numerous troops[4] in them ; and it was not until 7.20 that the
Ceylon, having had 7 killed and 21 (including Meriton) wounded,
hauled down her colours. The *Windham* continued the struggle

---

[1] James, v. 251; *Nav. Chron.,* xxiv. 501.

[2] Had been taken by *Vénus,* Nov. 22nd, 1809, and retaken by *Magicienne,*
Dec. 29th, 1809.

[3] Created Baron in 1812; Min. of Mar., 1834–6 and 1840–3; died an Admiral,
1846, aged 71.

[4] About 250, in each ship, all of the 24th Regt.

for 25 minutes longer, and struck only when she had had nine guns dismounted, and had lost 6 killed and 18 wounded. The *Astell*, after losing 8 killed and 37 (including Hay) wounded, put out her lights and escaped in the darkness. The losses on the French side were 22 killed and 38 wounded. Seldom has a braver defence been made by peaceable vessels against an overwhelming force of men-of-war.[1] The prizes were carried to Mauritius.

Early in the summer of 1810, elaborate preparations began to be made for the capture of Réunion, or, as it was then called, Bourbon. Large numbers of British and Indian troops, together with transports, were assembled at Rodriguez; and on June 24th, the *Boadicea*, 38, Captain Josias Rowley, and *Néréide*, 36, Captain Nisbet Josiah Willoughby, from off Mauritius, arrived to escort the expedition. On July 3rd, they sailed again; and on the 6th, made a rendezvous, about 50 miles from Réunion, with a small squadron which, under Captain Samuel Pym, of the *Sirius*, 36, had previously been cruising off Mauritius. This squadron consisted of the *Iphigenia*, 36, Captain Henry Lambert (2), and *Magicienne*, 36, Captain Lucius Curtis, besides the *Sirius*. At the rendezvous the troops, 3650 in number, were divided, and arrangements were perfected; and on the 7th, the ships bore away for the different points of disembarkation. The first brigade, under Lieut.-Colonel Frazier, was to land at Grande Chaloupe, about six miles west of St. Dénis, the capital, and the remaining three brigades, under Lieut.-Colonels Henry S. Keating (senior officer), Campbell, and Drummond, were to be thrown ashore at Rivière des Pluies, about three miles to the eastward. In the afternoon, while the enemy, who had about 600 regulars and 2700 militia in the island, was distracted by a demonstration off Ste. Marie, Frazier, with 950 men and some howitzers, was landed at Grande Chaloupe without opposition; and Lieutenant John Wyatt Watling, of the *Sirius*, occupied a height which protected the force from molestation during the following night. At Rivière des Pluies, on the weather side of the island, conditions were less favourable; and, although Willoughby, still suffering from his musket accident, effected a landing with a few seamen and about 150 troops, the operation was not carried out without the drowning of four people in the surf, and the loss of several boats. Further disembarkation at that point was therefore abandoned for the time. Willoughby,

---

[1] James, v. 262; *Nav. Chron.*, xxv. 158, 234.

and Lieut.-Colonel M'Leod, who was in command of the detachment of troops, occupied, and spent that night in, Fort Ste. Marie.
On the 8th, the *Boadicea* disembarked Keating and some troops at
Grande Chaloupe; and the *Iphigenia* and transports landed some
more; but, in the meantime, Frazier had been so active that Colonel
Ste. Susanne, the military commander, asked for a truce. At 6 P.M.,
the island capitulated, the conquest having cost the victors only
22 killed and drowned, and 79 wounded. It fell to the *Sirius* to take
possession of the shipping in the bay of St. Paul. On the 9th, the
privateer brig *Edward*, of Nantes, made sail and put to sea to
escape; but the frigate's barge, under Lieutenant William Norman,
rowed hard after her for nearly twelve hours, and, catching her,
boarded and carried her most gallantly, having 3 men slightly
wounded. She had dispatches for France on board.[1] Mr. Robert
Townshend Farquhar,[2] who had been sent out for the purpose,
assumed the post of governor of Réunion.

Immediately after the surrender of Réunion, the *Sirius* returned
to her station off Mauritius, where her boats, under Lieutenants
William Norman and John Wyatt Watling, destroyed a schooner
which was aground, covered by two field pieces and 300 men. In
retiring, the British lost 1 killed and 1 wounded.[3]

On July 22nd, three Danish gun-vessels, the *Balder*, 8, *Thor*, 8,
and another, were discovered in a deep bay near Studtland, on the
coast of Norway, by the Master of the *Belvidera*, 36, who had been
sent in by Captain Richard Byron (2) to take soundings. On the
following morning Byron despatched seven boats from his ship, and
from the *Nemesis*, 28, Captain William Ferris, under Lieutenants
Samuel Nisbett, William Henry Bruce (2), Thomas Hodgskins, and
Marmaduke Smith, to capture or destroy the gunboats. Under a
heavy fire, but without loss, the service was accomplished, the
Balder and *Thor* being taken, and the remaining craft being burnt.[4]

At dawn on July 25th, the *Thames*, 32, Captain the Hon.
Granville George Waldegrave, and *Pilot*, 18, Commander John
Toup Nicolas, were standing along the Calabrian coast, when, off
Amantea, there appeared the *Weazel*, 18, Commander Henry
Prescott, signalling the presence of an enemy's convoy, which, as

---

[1] *Nav. Chron.*, xxiv. 427 *et seq.*; James, v. 269; O'Byrne, 821.
[2] Bart., 1821.
[3] James, v. 273.
[4] James, v. 232; *Nav. Chron.*, xxiv. 333.

afterwards shown, consisted of thirty-two transports intended for Murat's army at Scilla, escorted by seven gunboats, four armed vessels, and an armed pinnace, the whole under Commander Giovanni Caracciolo. Upon the approach of the British, the transports ran themselves ashore under the batteries, and the other craft drew up in line to protect their charges. As soon as he could get within grape-shot range, Waldegrave drove the Neapolitans from their ships, and then anchored. Without delay, the boats, under Commander Prescott,[1] and Lieutenants Thomas John James William Davis, Edward Collier (1),[2] Francis Molesworth, Francis Charles Annesley (2), and George Penruddock, pushed off, and, in spite of entrenchments and a heavy fire, brought away all the vessels except two transports, two armed vessels, and one gunboat. The British lost only 1 killed and 6 wounded.[3]

Events in the eastern seas may now be returned to.

Towards the end of July, in addition to the *Sirius*, 36, Captain Samuel Pym, the *Iphigenia*, 36, Captain Henry Lambert (2), *Néréide*, 36, Captain Nisbet Josiah Willoughby, and *Staunch*, 14, Lieutenant Benjamin Street, cruised off Mauritius. In the *Néréide* were 12 Madras artillerymen, 50 grenadiers of the 69th Regt., and 50 of the 33rd Regt., the whole under Captain Todd of the 69th. These had been put on board by Lieut.-Colonel Keating, with a view to co-operating in a projected attack on Ile de la Passe, a small island off Grand Port on the south-east side of Mauritius, which it was intended to use as a base for political agitations as well as for military operations in the colony. Accordingly, on August 10th, having left Lambert, in the *Iphigenia*, off Port Louis, on the west coast, Pym, with the other vessels, proceeded off Grand Port, and, that evening, in terrible weather, tried to effect a landing on Ile de la Passe. The boats, however, lost their way, or fouled one another; and the attempt had to be abandoned. On the following morning Pym picked up his people, and, to lull suspicion, bore away and rejoined Lambert off Port Louis. It was there arranged that the frigates should return to the eastward by different routes, the *Sirius* going round by the longer or northern way, and the *Néréide*, accompanied by the *Staunch*, beating up from the south end of the island, so that the enemy should not readily perceive that any organised

---

[1] Posted for this service, as from July 25th, 1810.

[2] Com. for this service, as from July 25th, 1810.

[3] James, v. 256; *Nav. Chron.*, xxiv. 505; *Moniteur*, Aug. 5th, 1810.

movement was in progress. Lieutenant Henry Ducie Chads, with two boats, was temporarily lent by the *Iphigenia* to the *Sirius*.

The *Sirius* reappeared before Ile de la Passe on August 13th, when, however, the other craft were still far to leeward. Anxious to effect a surprise, Pym decided not to wait for his consorts, and in the evening sent in five boats, containing 71 officers and men under Lieutenants William Norman, John Wyatt Watling, and Henry Ducie Chads, together with Lieutenants (R.M.) James Cottell and William Bate. The attack was most successful, although the enemy opened fire before the boats had landed. Norman[1] fell, shot through the heart as he was endeavouring to enter a battery; but Watling took his place, carried the work in spite of a determined resistance, and then, crossing the islet, joined hands with Chads, who had been similarly successful on the south-east side. Thereupon the French garrison, of about 80 regulars, surrendered, having inflicted a loss of 7 killed and 18 wounded.

On the following morning the *Néréide* and *Staunch* arrived, and Pym, giving charge of Ile de la Passe to Willoughby, sailed to rejoin the *Iphigenia* off Port Louis. Willoughby garrisoned the place with 50 of the grenadiers, under Captain Todd, and at once began preparations for further attacks.[2]

On August 17th, Willoughby landed at Canaille de Bois, near Grand Port, with about 170 seamen, Marines, and soldiers, for the purpose of distributing among the inhabitants of Mauritius a proclamation of Governor Farquhar, of Réunion. He moved twenty miles into the enemy's country, and, incidentally, attacked and carried a fort at Pointe du Diable, spiking eight guns and two mortars, blowing up the magazines, and carrying off a 13-in. mortar. The French made little resistance, and caused no loss to the British; and Willoughby returned to his frigate in the evening. On the 18th he again landed and destroyed the signal station, etc., at Grande Rivière, in face of a body of seven or eight hundred Frenchmen. Soon afterwards the *Staunch* left him, and proceeded to Port Louis. On the 19th and 20th further expeditions were made on shore, the inhabitants being tolerably friendly, and the enemy's troops not interfering. But on the 20th the entire situation, until then apparently so favourable for a speedy conquest of the island, was suddenly changed. A strange squadron, which proved to be the

---

[1] Norman was promoted before his death, but never received his commission.
[2] James, v. 273; *Gazette*, 1811, 261.

French *Bellone*, 40, Commodore V. G. Duperré, *Minerve*, 40, Commander P. F. H. E. Bouvet, and *Victor*, 16, Commander N. Morice,
with the prize Indiamen *Windham* and *Ceylon*,[1] was sighted in the
offing. Realising that if the three men-of-war should form a junction with the French vessels then in the harbour of Port Louis,
the British force on that part of the station would be hopelessly
overmatched, Willoughby hoisted French colours, and, by means
of a hostile signal-book which he had taken, induced the headmost
of the new comers to enter Grand Port. As they did so, he substituted British for French colours, and poured so heavy a broadside
into the *Victor*, the leading vessel, that she instantly struck, and
anchored on his starboard quarter. But when the *Minerve*, followed
by the *Ceylon*, entered soon afterwards, she ordered the *Victor* to
cut her cable; and this the corvette did, rejoining her consorts.
Both the *Néréide* and the fort on Ile de la Passe fired at the
advancing enemy; but an accidental explosion in the fort put a
number of the men there out of action, and six of the guns were
quickly dismounted by the French broadsides. At that time some
of the British frigate's boats, containing about 160 of her officers
and men, narrowly escaped being cut off by the *Minerve* and
Ceylon, which were between them and their ship; but, owing to
some inexplicable mistake on the part of the enemy, they were
suffered to rejoin without even being fired at.

When the *Minerve*, *Ceylon*, and *Victor* had passed in towards
Grand Port, it looked for a few moments as if the *Bellone* and
Windham were about to bear away for some other harbour.
Willoughby, gallantly determined that he would not retire before
the *Minerve* and *Victor*, was preparing to remove the remnant of the
troops from Ile de la Passe, preparatory to attacking the enemy,
when he perceived that the *Bellone* had left the *Windham* to proceed
alone to the westward, and was bearing up after her consorts. The
Néréide therefore made ready to receive her. The *Bellone* passed in
at 2.45 P.M., exchanging broadsides with the *Néréide*, and killing
2 men and wounding 1, but doing less damage than might have
been expected looking to the closeness of the range. At 4 o'clock
Willoughby sent away Lieutenant Henry Colins Deacon in the
launch, to inform Pym, off Port Louis, of the arrival of the French,
and to say that with one frigate besides the *Néréide*, he would go
in and attack them. As it happened, the *Néréide*, which was then

[1] *See* p. 456.

to seaward of her enemies, could have herself weighed and joined the *Sirius* ; but her Captain had been ordered to protect Ile de la Passe, and, perhaps quixotically, he decided to do so as long as possible. His subsequent defence of his charge was certainly one of the most remarkable on record.

Soon after the French had taken up their anchorage off Grand Port, Willoughby ordered his mortars on Ile de la Passe to try the range, the result being that the vessels presently shifted their billets to points somewhat further removed from the *Néréide*. Willoughby also sent in a flag of truce to demand the surrender of the *Victor*, on the ground that she had struck to him. He thus assumed from the first an undaunted attitude, while, at the same time, he did all that lay in his power, by means of works on the islet, and by rowing guard, to defend his position pending the arrival of reinforcements.

It has been mentioned that the prize Indiaman, *Windham*, proceeded to the westward, instead of entering Grand Port with her consorts. On the 21st, as she was about to make Rivière Noire, on the south-west of Mauritius, she was sighted by the *Sirius*, which chased, but failed, in consequence of the wind, in an attempt to cut her off from the protection of the batteries. Not knowing what she was, Lieutenant John Wyatt Watling volunteered to catch her and board her with the launch. He went off with five seamen, and was followed by Midshipman John Andrews, in the jolly-boat, with four men ; yet, strange to say, neither boat took in her a single weapon. Watling soon discovered the approximate force of his enemy ; but, having consulted with Andrews, pushed on with extraordinary pluck, and, arming the men with the stretchers, actually boarded and carried an Indiaman mounting 26 guns, and manned by at least 30 Frenchmen, without loss. Moreover he managed to bring her out from under the batteries.

Captain Pym had not then received the message sent him by the hands of Lieutenant Deacon, but, learning from his prisoners something of the situation off Grand Port, he despatched the *Windham* to Commodore Josias Rowley, who was at St. Paul's Bay, Réunion, and sent the *Magicienne*, 36, Captain Lucius Curtis, to pick up the *Iphigenia*, 36, Captain Henry Lambert (2), and *Staunch*, 14, off Port Louis, and to proceed with them to Ile de la Passe, while he himself went thither by the south of the island. General Decaen, at Port Louis, seems to have got wind of these movements, for, in consequence of his communications to Duperré, the latter, on the 21st, moored his ships, with springs, in the form of a crescent off Grand Port, in a position where the ends of his line were protected by reefs.

The *Sirius* met the launch containing Lieutenant Deacon, and, on the morning of the 22nd, arrived off Ile de la Passe, and exchanged numbers with the *Néréide*, Willoughby characteristically signalling, "Ready for action.   Enemy of inferior force."   Pym, with as little delay as possible, led in to the attack, the *Néréide* falling into station behind him ; but, having no competent pilot on board, the *Sirius* unhappily piled up on a shoal on the left hand of the channel.   Willoughby brought up, and went on board his consort to assist in floating her ; yet this could not be effected until 8.30 A.M. on August 23rd, when the *Sirius* anchored near the *Néréide*.   An hour and a half later, the *Iphigenia* and *Magicienne* were seen, and at 2.10 P.M. they also anchored in the channel.

At 4.40, all four frigates weighed, and stood for Grand Port, it being arranged that the *Néréide*[1] should anchor between the *Victor*, the rearmost ship, and the *Bellone* ; the *Sirius*,[2] abreast of the *Bellone* ; the *Magicienne*,[1] between the *Ceylon* and the *Minerve* ; and the *Iphigenia*[2] upon the broadside of the *Minerve*.   The order of approach was, *Néréide*, *Sirius*, *Magicienne*, and *Iphigenia*.   The *Néréide* passed in safely ; but, unfortunately, the *Sirius* ran upon a coral rock before she got within range, and the *Magicienne* grounded on a bank in such a position that only three of her foremost guns would bear on the enemy, then distant about two cables. The *Iphigenia* promptly dropped her stream anchor and came to by the stern, then letting go her best bower under foot, and so bringing her starboard broadside to bear upon the *Minerve*, and at once pouring a heavy fire into that frigate at pistol shot distance.   At the same time, Willoughby, seeing that the original plan of attack had failed, placed his frigate abeam of the *Bellone*, and not a cable's length from her, and opened a furious cannonade upon his very superior antagonist.   At 6.15 P.M., the *Ceylon*, thanks to the effect of the bow guns of the *Magicienne* and the quarter guns of the *Iphigenia*, was obliged to haul down her colours, though immediately afterwards she made sail in order to run ashore.   A quarter of an hour later the *Minerve*, having her cable shot away, made sail after the *Ceylon* ; and one or other of those ships, presently fouling the *Bellone*, compelled her also to cut and run aground, where, however,

[1] Carrying 12-prs.   [2] Carrying 18-prs.

she lay so that her broadside still bore upon the *Néréide*. The *Iphigenia* would have followed up the *Minerve*, had not an intervening shoal prevented her from doing so.

Shortly before 7 P.M. the *Néréide's* spring was shot away, and the frigate swung stern on to the *Bellone's* broadside, and was severely raked. To save herself, and to bring her starboard broadside to bear, she cut her small bower cable, and let go her best bower. The fire of the *Minerve* being then masked by that of the *Bellone*, and Duperré being wounded, Bouvet moved into the *Bellone* and took command. The following, from the *Néréide's* log, continues the story :—

". . . Captain Willoughby severely wounded on the head. At 10, most of the quarter-deck and forecastle guns being dismounted, most of the guns disabled on the main deck, the squadron on shore and unable to render us any assistance, hulled from shipping and batteries, *Néréide* aground astern, Captain Willoughby ordered a boat to be sent to inform Captain Pym of our situation. At 10.30 the boat returned with orders for Captain Willoughby to repair on board the *Sirius*, which he declined doing. A boat was then ordered to the *Bellone*, to say we had struck, being entirely silenced, and a dreadful carnage on board. An officer came from the *Iphigenia* to know why we had ceased firing. At midnight, moderate rain, wind S.E. At 12.30 A.M.[1] the main mast went by the board. At 1.30 several ropes on fire, which were luckily extinguished. Hoisted French colours in the fore rigging, the batteries and the *Bellone* still firing into us, although we hailed the latter to say we had struck. Perceiving the Union Jack, which had been nailed to the mizen mast-head, still flying, and no rigging or ropes to go aloft by, cut away the mizen mast, on which the enemy ceased firing. About 2 P.M., the *Bellone's* boat boarded, spiked the guns, and took possession of the keys of the magazine. At 5 we observed the *Magicienne's* quit her, she being on fire. At 11.30 she blew up. *Iphigenia* warping out. At 2[2] two French officers came on board, and committed the bodies of the slain to the deep. The *Iphigenia* trying to get the *Sirius* off. At 9, observed the boats to quit the *Sirius*, she being on fire. At 10 the boats came from the *Bellone* to land the prisoners. Wet the decks by order from the French officers, who were fearful the explosion from the *Sirius* should set fire to the *Néréide*, she being to leeward, and the wind strong."

When she began the action, the *Néréide* had on board 281 souls, including 69 men of the 33rd and 69th Regiments, and of the Madras Artillery. Of these she appears to have had 92 killed, including Lieutenant John Burns, and Midshipman George Timmins, and about 137 wounded, including Willoughby, who had his left eye torn out, Lieutenant Henry Colins Deacon, Lieutenant (R.M.) Thomas S. Cox, Master William Lesby, Boatswain John Strong, and Midshipman Samuel Costerton. In all, the whole of the ship's company, except 52 persons, was placed *hors de combat*. The *Iphigenia* lost 5 killed, and 13, including Lieutenant Robert Tom

---

[1] On Aug. 24th.   [2] A.M. of Aug. 25th.

Blackler, wounded.   The *Magicienne* lost 8 killed and 20 wounded.
The *Sirius*, being nearly out of range, sustained neither loss nor
damage ; but both she and the *Magicienne* had to be destroyed by
their people to save them from capture.   The loss in the French
ships was officially stated at 37 killed and 112 wounded, the *Bellone*
being the chief sufferer.

The *Sirius* blew up at 11 A.M.   Her people, and some of her
stores, as well as those of the *Magicienne*, had been removed to the
Iphigenia, which, during the afternoon of the 25th, continued to
warp out, but made little progress.   In the evening, Pym sent off
Lieutenant Watling, in the pinnace, with dispatches for the Commander-in-Chief.   Watling was chased by the *Entreprenante*, 14,
which had that morning arrived off Ile de la Passe ; but he escaped
by pulling among the breakers, and, early on the 27th, reached
St. Dénis, Réunion.

Continuously warping, the *Iphigenia*, on the 27th, reached a
position under Ile de la Passe, cleared for action, and sent to the
guns on the islet as many men as left her with between 400 and 500
people on board.   Lambert desired to do his best to maintain the
position, but, unfortunately, he was short of ammunition.   Moreover, new forces were gathering against him.

All the ships in Grand Port were by that time afloat, and, in
addition, three fresh ships, with which the *Entreprenante* exchanged
signals, were discovered outside.   These were the 40-gun frigates
Vénus, *Astrée*, and *Manche*, which, under Commodore Hamelin, had
quitted Port Louis, then no longer blockaded, on the night of the
21st–22nd, but which had been delayed by adverse winds.   At
5 P.M. on the 27th, Hamelin summoned Lambert to surrender.
Lambert refused, but offered to surrender Ile de la Passe if his ship
and people were allowed to retire to a British port.   That night he
sent Master John Jenkins, late of the *Sirius*, in the launch, to
Réunion.   On the following day, having been promised that the
ship's crew, and the garrison of the islet, should be sent to the
Cape or to England, not to serve again until regularly exchanged,
Lambert wisely surrendered to the fivefold superior force arrayed
against him.

There was some question of trying the gallant Willoughby for
having distributed subversive proclamations on the island ; but his
bravery, and his terribly injured condition, decided his late foes not
to proceed against him.   The other prisoners were not well treated,

nor were any of them, in accordance with the stipulations of August 28th, ever sent to the Cape or England. They were still in Mauritius at the time of its capture in the following December.[1] The four Captains, and their officers and men, were soon afterwards tried for the loss of their ships, and were most honourably acquitted. In Willoughby's case, the sentence ran :—

"The court is of opinion that the conduct of Captain Willoughby was injudicious in making the signal, 'Enemy of inferior force,' to the *Sirius*, she being the only ship in sight, and not justifiable, as the enemy evidently was superior. But the court is of opinion that his Majesty's late ship *Néréide* was carried into battle in a most judicious, officer-like, and gallant manner; and the court cannot do otherwise than express its high admiration of the noble conduct of the Captain, officers, and ship's company during the whole of the unequal contest, and is further of opinion that the *Néréide* was not surrendered to the enemy until she was disabled in every respect, so as to render all further resistance useless : and that no blame whatever attaches to them for the loss of the said ship." [2]

It has been said that Captain Pym despatched the *Windham* to Commodore Josias Rowley, with news of the state of affairs at Grand Port. The *Windham* reached St. Paul's Bay, Réunion, on August 22nd. The Commodore's ship, *Boadicea*, 38, at once took on board two companies of the 86th Regiment, and a detachment of artillery, and sailed the same evening, leaving the transport *Bombay* to follow as soon as possible with more troops, and with stores for Ile de la Passe. The *Boadicea* made slow progress. On the 27th, however, she learnt more of what had been going forward off Grand Port, for on that day she picked up the *Magicienne's* barge, which, under Lieutenant Robert Wauchope, had been detached with letters by Captain Lambert on the previous day. When, on the 29th, she made Ile de la Passe, she found there the *Vénus* and *Manche*, which chased her back to St. Dénis, Réunion, and, on September 1st, joined their consorts, the *Astrée* and *Entreprenante*, in the harbour of Port Louis. The *Boadicea* subsequently returned to Ile de la Passe, but, seeing that, single handed, she could effect nothing, went to St. Paul's Bay, and re-anchored there on September 11th.

Desiring to take full advantage of their success at Grand Port, the French formed a squadron, under Captain Bouvet, composed of the *Iphigénie* (late *Iphigenia*), *Astrée*, and *Entreprenante*, to

---

[1] *See* p. 294.

[2] James, v. 273–296; Brenton, ii. 363; Dupin, ii. 85; Disp. of Duperré; *Nav. Chron.*, xxv. 72–74, 158–160; Marshall, ii. 718; Supp. Pt. ii. 154–182; Mins. of C. Ms.

be subsequently joined by the *Victor*. The three first of these, on September 9th, began a cruise off Réunion.

On that same day, the *Africaine*, 38, Captain Robert Corbett, on her way from England to Madras, touched at Rodriguez, and heard of the misfortunes in Mauritius. Corbett, therefore, changed his route, and steered to join Rowley at Réunion. On the way thither, on the 11th, he sighted and drove ashore near Cape Malheureux, Mauritius, the French dispatch vessel *No. 23*. In an attempt to destroy her, the British unhappily lost 2 killed and 16 wounded, and had to retire.

Corbett made St. Dénis, Réunion, early on the 12th, and found in the offing the *Iphigénie* and *Astrée*. These were presently chased by the *Boadicea*, 38, the *Otter*, 16, Commander James Tomkinson, and the *Staunch*, 14, Lieutenant Benjamin Street, which had left St. Paul's Bay for the purpose, and which were at once recognised by the *Africaine*. Corbett hastily took on board a few men of the 86th Regiment, and made sail to support his friends ; but towards evening, while rapidly gaining on the chase, he lost sight of his consorts. During the night, however, he sent up rockets and burnt blue lights to indicate his position ; and, in the early morning of the 13th, when he found himself close on the weather quarter of the *Astrée*, the *Boadicea* was only four or five miles on his own lee quarter. As the enemy was nearing the shelter of Port Louis, Corbett pluckily attacked, without waiting for the Commodore to come up. He opened fire at 2.20 A.M., and, within a few seconds, was seriously wounded, the command devolving on Lieutenant Joseph Crew Tullidge, who fought the ship bravely until a few minutes before 5 A.M., when, having suffered terribly, and the *Boadicea* being still far off, the *Africaine* struck to her two opponents. Of 295 people on board, she had 49 killed, including Master Samuel Parker, and 114 wounded, including Corbett (mortally), Lieutenants Tullidge[1] and Robert Forder, Master's Mates John Theed and Jenkin Jones, and Midshipmen Charles Mercier and Robert Leech. The French lost 9 killed and 33 wounded in the *Iphigénie*, and 1 killed and 2 wounded in the *Astrée*. The *Africaine* was an utter wreck aloft.[2] There is, unfortunately, much reason to suppose that Captain Corbett's reputation for extreme severity had

---

[1] Com., Aug. 1st, 1811.

[2] James, v. 296–304 ; O'Byrne, 1211 ; *Gazette*, 1811, 263 ; Mins. of C. M., Apr. 23rd, 1811.

antagonised his crew, and that the men did not behave as loyally as they should have behaved.[1] Brenton unwarrantably suggests that this gallant but harsh officer committed suicide, rather than become a prisoner.[2]

Not long after the *Africaine* had struck, the *Boadicea* began to feel a strengthening breeze, and, coming up, passed within musket-shot of the enemy; but, instead of at once engaging, she tacked, and stood to windward to look for the *Otter* and *Staunch*. At 10 A.M. she was joined by them, and at 12.40 the three British vessels bore up with a fine breeze from S.S.E. As they approached the enemy, the *Astrée* and *Iphigénie* abandoned their prize and made sail to windward; and at 5 P.M., the *Africaine*, after having fired a couple of guns, hauled down her French colours, and was taken possession of. On September 15th, never having lost sight of the enemy for more than a few hours at a time, Rowley's squadron anchored in St. Paul's Bay, and, later in the day, the Commodore, with the *Otter* and *Staunch*, put to sea again to look for the French; but, though he saw them, no engagement resulted, and Rowley returned to St. Paul's Bay on the 18th at 5 A.M. In the interval, the *Astrée* and *Iphigénie* captured the East India Company's armed brig *Aurora*, 16. On September 22nd, they anchored with her at Port Louis. Seeing that the *Boadicea* was, so far as her Captain knew, the only British frigate on the station, and that, besides the *Astrée* and *Iphigénie*, the French had the *Vénus* and *Manche* in the immediate neighbourhood, Rowley's recapture of the *Africaine* must be regarded as a very creditable exploit.[3]

A few days earlier, the *Ceylon*, 32, Captain Charles Gordon (1), had been despatched from Madras to join Rowley. Looking in at Port Louis on September 17th, she saw what appeared to be a considerable French force in the harbour, and, bearing up, made all sail for Réunion. Commodore Hamelin, with the *Vénus* and *Victor*, promptly put to sea in chase of her. The *Ceylon* descried her enemies at 2 P.M., and, at a few minutes past midnight, observing that the *Vénus* was far ahead of her consort, shortened sail to begin action. Nominally a 32-gun frigate, she actually carried twenty-four long 18-prs., two long 9-prs., and fourteen 24-pr. carronades, or forty guns in all, while the *Vénus* mounted twenty-eight long 18-prs., four long 8-prs., and twelve 36-pr. carronades, or forty-four

---

[1] *See* note in Brenton, ii. 370.   [2] James, v. 307.

[3] Log of *Boadicea*; James, 304.

guns in all, so that the broadside weight of metal of the British ship
was only 343 lbs. against the *Vénus's* 484 lbs. Moreover, the *Ceylon*
had on board but about 295 people, including 100 men of the 69th
and 86th Regiments, and the Frenchman probably nearly her full
complement of 380. In spite of the disparity of force, Gordon
maintained a hot fight for an hour, at the expiration of which time
the *Vénus* dropped astern, and gave him an opportunity of repairing
damages, and of endeavouring to escape, ere the *Victor* should get
up. But at 12.15 A.M., the *Vénus* again overtook him, and the
battle was renewed, until both frigates became unmanageable. At
4.30 the *Victor* arrived, and, placing herself athwart the *Ceylon's*
bows, prepared to rake her, whereupon Gordon struck. At 5.10 his
ship was taken possession of. She had lost 10 killed, and 31,
including Gordon himself, and Master William Oliver, wounded.
The losses of the *Vénus* cannot be specified, but were no doubt
severe. Had the *Ceylon* realised in time that the *Victor*,[1] though a
three-masted vessel of imposing appearance, was only a mere shell
of a craft, less formidable than the ordinary 18-gun brig, she might
have sunk her with a broadside, and, perhaps, have kept her flag
flying for a few hours, when, as will be seen, she would have been
relieved.[2]

At 7.30 A.M. on the 18th, Rowley, who was then at anchor in
St. Paul's Bay, saw the French ships and their prize at a distance
of about nine miles from the shore. The *Boadicea*, reinforced with
50 volunteers from the *Africaine*, at once got under way with the
Otter and *Staunch*, and made sail in chase. The *Victor* took the
Ceylon in tow, and the three endeavoured to make the best of their
way to Mauritius; but they were delayed, first by the tow-rope
breaking, and then by the disproportion in size between the *Ceylon*
and the *Victor*. At 3.30 P.M., therefore, the prize was cast off, the
Vénus lay by to protect her, and the *Victor*, in accordance with
orders, stood away to the eastward. Scarcely was the corvette out
of range ere the *Ceylon* rehoisted her colours, Lieutenant Philip
Gibbon having temporarily taken command of her, in the absence
of his seniors, who had been removed to the *Vénus*. At 4.40 P.M.
the *Boadicea* ran alongside the *Vénus*, and, in ten minutes, obliged
her to strike, with a loss of 9 killed and 15 wounded. The *Boadicea*

---

[1] Ex *Jéna*, taken from the French in 1808; renamed *Victor*, and retaken by the
French in 1809. Morice reduced her armament to 16 guns.

[2] James, v. 307; *Gazette*, 1811, 264; *Moniteur*, Dec. 18th, 1810; Log of *Ceylon*.

had only 2 wounded. Rowley then put back to St. Paul's Bay. The *Vénus* was a fine frigate of 1105 tons, and, to commemorate Willoughby's splendid defence at Grand Port, she was added to the Navy as the *Néréide*.[1]

On August 29th, off Alderney, the hired armed cutter *Queen Charlotte*, of eight 4-prs., 27 men, and 76 tons, commanded by Master Joseph Thomas, while on her way to the blockading squadron off Cherbourg, fell in with a cutter of sixteen 6-prs., 120 men, and 200 tons, under British colours, but of so suspicious appearance that Thomas, as the two neared one another, made all suitable preparations. As soon as the stranger changed her colours to French, she received a broadside, and from 3.30 to 5 P.M. there followed a close action, which was ended by the Frenchman hauling off. The *Queen Charlotte*, which was too disabled to pursue, had 15 of her people wounded, one mortally. Her antagonist was the ex-British revenue cutter *Swan*. Thomas's action was most gallant throughout.[2]

On September 5th, the *Surveillante*, 38, Captain Sir George Ralph Collier, and *Constant*, 14, Lieutenant John Stokes, drove back part of a convoy which was attempting to escape from the Morbihan. A brig of the convoy took refuge between the batteries of St. Gildas and St. Jacques; but, covered by the fire of the *Constant*, the boats of the *Surveillante*, under Lieutenant the Hon. James Arbuthnot, and Master's Mate John Illingworth, pushed in, and brought out the vessel without loss. On the night of the 6th–7th, two of the frigate's boats, under Illingworth, accompanied by Midshipmen John Kingdom and Hector Rose, seized a battery and guardhouse at the mouth of the Crache, spiked a gun, blew up the works, and returned under fire without casualty.[3]

An unfortunate affair happened near Ushant on September 9th. It had been reported to Rear-Admiral Thomas Sotheby, who was cruising off the coast in the *Dreadnought*, 98, Captain Valentine Collard, that a vessel was among the rocks on the west side of the promontory. Early in the morning, seven boats, under Lieutenant Thomas Pettman, were sent in to bring her out. They were received with a heavy fire from troops and a couple of field-pieces on the beach; but they boarded and carried the craft, which proved

[1] James, v. 310; *Nav. Chron.*, xxv., 162; Mins. of C. M.

[2] James, v. 233; *Nav. Chron.*, xxiv. 332.

[3] *Nav. Chron.*, xxiv. 417, 418; James, v. 234.

to be the Spanish merchantman *Maria Antonia*, prize to a French privateer. Just then, about 600 troops, on a precipice almost immediately above the boats, began to pour in volleys of musketry, to which no adequate return could be made. In consequence, the attacking party had to retire, with a loss of two boats, and 6 killed, 31 wounded, and 6 missing.[1]

On the night of September 27th, three French brigs lay under a strong battery on Pointe du Ché, in Basque Road. They were further protected by four field-pieces on the beach, and by a considerable force of cavalry and infantry. It was determined to attack them, and, with that object, the boats of the *Caledonia*, 120, flagship of Rear-Admiral Sir Harry Burrard Neale, Bart., *Valiant*, 74, Captain Robert Dudley Oliver, and *Armide*, 38, Captain Richard Dalling Dunn, were sent in under Lieutenant Arthur Philip Hamilton.[2] In the small hours of the 28th, a body of Royal Marines, under Captains Thomas Sherman and Archibald M'Lachlan, R.M., Lieutenants John Coulter and John Couche, R.M., and Lieutenant Robert John Little, R.M.A., was landed by the boats. The battery was quickly carried; the guns were spiked; the French troops were charged and deprived of one of their field-pieces; and, in the meantime, the seamen took two of the brigs and destroyed the third. The entire force was then withdrawn, with a loss of but two (including Lieutenant Little) wounded. The French had 14 killed in the battery alone.[3]

On the night of September 28th, Commander Robert Hall (2), of the *Rambler*, 14, with 30 men from his own sloop and from other craft stationed at Gibraltar, pulled into the mouth of the river Barbate, westward of Cape Trafalgar, and, landing, found a French privateer at anchor, protected on shore by her crew, 30 French dragoons, and a couple of 6-prs. This party was driven off, losing 7 men and 7 horses, and the British then swam to the privateer and carried her, losing but 1 killed and 1 wounded in the whole operation. Among the officers engaged were Lieutenant James Seagrove (actg.),[4] and Lieutenant (R.M.) William Halsted.[5]

In the autumn of 1810, the Franco-Venetian force in the Adriatic consisted of the *Favorite*, 44, Commodore Bernard Dubourdieu, Captain A. F. Z. La Marre La Meillerie, *Uranie*, 40, Captain F. J.

[1] James, v. 236.
[2] Com., Oct. 21st, 1810.
[3] James, v. 235; *Nav. Chron.*, xxiv. 422.
[4] Confirmed Oct. 29th, 1810.
[5] James, v. 258.

B. Margollé Lanier, *Corona*, 44, Captain Nicola Pasqualigo, *Bellona*, 32, Captain Duodo, *Carolina*, 32, Captain Baratovich, and the brigs *Jéna* and *Mercurio*. The duty of watching these lay with Captain William Hoste, of the *Amphion*, 32, who still had with him the *Active*, 38, and *Cerberus*, 32. On September 29th, the enemy's squadron left Chioggia, and on October 6th it was found in the act of weighing, off Ancona, by Hoste, who then had with him only the *Amphion* and *Active*. Dubourdieu made sail in chase, but soon returned to Ancona. Hoste then went to Lissa, where, on the 9th, he found the *Cerberus*; and, on the 12th, having been joined by the *Acorn*, 18, Commander Robert Clephane, he set sail for Ancona in search of Dubourdieu. Not finding him there, Hoste, who believed that he had gone to Corfu, went in chase; but, having reached Cattaro, and getting no tidings there, the British captain headed again for Lissa. Dubourdieu had, in fact, proceeded directly thither, and had arrived off Port St. Giorgio on October 22nd, when the British were passing Pelagoso, steering S.E. The enemy, who had troops on board, disembarked them, and took possession of the port and some prizes, a British Midshipman, who was in charge, withdrawing to the mountains; and, upon learning in the evening that Hoste had been seen off Pelagoso, they precipitately put to sea again as soon as they had re-embarked the troops. When, in consequence, Hoste did reach Lissa, Dubourdieu was once more entering Ancona, whence he did not issue during the remainder of the year. Captain Richard Hussey Moubray had arrived in the *Montagu*, 74, to take command in the Adriatic, and the French Commodore was thus provided with an excellent excuse for not showing himself at sea.[1] It will be seen that, in 1811, he had an opportunity of proving whether, as he wrote to Murat in October, 1810, his crews *étaient dans les meilleures dispositions, et fort désireux de se battre*. It is curious that, had Hoste reached Lissa while Dubourdieu was still busy there, the conditions of the resulting action would have been almost exactly similar to those of the Austro-Italian battle which was fought off the island in 1866.

On October 14th, in the North Sea, the *Briseis*, 10, Lieutenant George Bentham [2] (actg. Commander), chased the Franco-Dutch privateer *Sans Souci*, 14, and, bringing her to action, fought her at close quarters for an hour, the enemy making three ineffectual

---

[1] James, v. 253; Randaccio, i. 170.
[2] Com., Oct. 14th, 1810, for this service.

attempts to board. When the *Sans Souci* struck, she had 8 killed
and 19 wounded. The British loss was 4 killed, including Master's
Mate Alexander Gunn, and 11 wounded.[1] A very similar affair
occurred, also in the North Sea, on October 25th, when the *Calliope*,
10, Commander John M'Kerlie, chased, fought, and subdued the
privateer schooner *Comtesse d'Hambourg*, 14. On that occasion,
however, the British loss was but 3 wounded. The enemy's loss is
unspecified.[2]

Another privateer action was fought on October 27th, at the
mouth of the Channel, between the *Orestes*, 16, Commander John
Richards La Penotière, and the French brig *Loup Garou*, 16. After
half-an-hour's close fighting the latter struck, with 4 men wounded.
No one in the *Orestes* was hurt.[3]

A gallant but somewhat costly affair took place on November
4th. The *Blossom*, 18, Commander William Stewart, cruising off
Cape Sicié, chased the privateer xebec *César*, until becalmed. Two
boats, one under Master's Mate Richard Hambly, and the other
under Lieutenant Samuel Davis and Midshipman John Marshall (4),
were then sent after the enemy, which mounted four guns, and had
a crew of 59 men. The *César* opened a deadly fire, which killed
Davis and three men, and wounded five others; but, with the
remaining 26 seamen and Marines, young Marshall pluckily leapt
on board and carried the privateer, losing, however, 5 more men
wounded. The enemy had 4 killed and 9 wounded. Mr. Marshall,
afterwards well known as the compiler of the 'Royal Naval
Biography,' richly deserved promotion for this affair, but did not
obtain a Lieutenant's commission until February 14th, 1815.[4]

A most successful and gallant cutting-out exploit was accomplished on the night of November 8th. The *Quebec*, 32, Captain
Charles Sibthorp John Hawtayne, had observed the privateer
schooner *Jeune Louise*, 14, at anchor in the Vlie. Lieutenant
Stephen Popham volunteered to lead an attack on her, and, with
three boats, under himself, Lieutenant Richard Augustus Yates, and
Master's Mate John M'Donald (2), pulled in against a strong tide.
When within pistol-shot of their quarry, the boats grounded on a
sand-bank, and received three broadsides from the enemy; but

---

[1] James, v. 236; *Nav. Chron.*, xxiv. 424.
[2] James, v. 237; *Nav. Chron.*, xxiv. 430.
[3] James, v. 237; *Nav. Chron.*, xxiv. 431.
[4] James, v. 258.

Popham extricated his party, and boarded and carried the privateer, Yates killing her commander. The British lost 1 killed, 1 wounded, and 1 drowned, and had a boat destroyed. The French had only 2 killed and 1 wounded. Great skill was shown by Popham in bringing out the prize from the sands and shoals.[1]

On the night of November 12th, the two 40-gun frigates *Amazone* and *Eliza* left Le Hâvre with a N.E. wind, steering N.W., with the object of joining the French squadron in Cherbourg, which, since the summer of 1809, had been blockaded with some closeness. At about 12.30 A.M. on the 13th, when the wind had shifted to N. by E., the frigates were sighted by the British 38-gun ships *Diana*, Captain Charles Grant, and *Niobe*, Captain John Wentworth Loring, which were to leeward, and inshore. At 4 A.M., the French, in order to weather the land, tacked off shore. The *Diana* followed, and exchanged broadsides with them, while the *Niobe* endeavoured to head them off; but the enemy, probably well acquainted with the local navigation, bore up, and managed to anchor between Marcouf and the mainland, under the protection of the works on shore. In the forenoon they shifted their berths to the road of La Hougue, where they re-anchored beneath a strong battery. On the following day, Captain Grant sent the *Niobe* with news of the situation to Captain Pulteney Malcolm, of the *Donegal*, 74, who was senior officer off Cherbourg. In the meantime, the *Eliza*, having been partially disabled by a southerly gale, the *Diana*, first in the road of La Hougue, and afterwards within the shoals of St. Vaast, whither the Frenchman had removed, made three separate attempts, but in vain, to get near enough to the *Amazone* to cause her serious damage. When, before noon on the 15th, the *Donegal* and *Niobe*, with the *Revenge*, 74, Captain the Hon. Charles Paget, arrived on the scene, the four ships stood in and renewed the attack; but after going about three times, each time delivering a broadside, they had to desist, and retire out of range of the frigate and batteries. The British vessels all suffered considerably aloft, and lost among them 11 wounded, 2 mortally. That night Malcolm tried the effect of some Congreve rockets upon the two frigates; but it is doubtful whether he did them any great injury. On the night of the 27th, the *Amazone* slipped out, and returned unmolested to Le Hâvre. The *Eliza* was carefully watched. On December 6th, the excellent practice of a British bomb drove her into a position where she

[1] James, v. 238; *Nav. Chron.*, xxiv. 496.

eventually bilged, and on the night of the 23rd, the *Diana's* boats, under Lieutenant Thomas Rowe, completed her destruction.[1]

On the night of November 15–16th, the *Phipps*, 14, Commander Christopher Bell, chased, and drove inshore near Calais, a lugger privateer. In the early morning of the 16th, she found and engaged another lugger, which, after a sharp action, she carried by boarding. The prize proved to be the *Barbier de Séville*, 16. Her capture was largely due to the gallantry with which Lieutenant Robert Tryon (1), who was dangerously wounded, leapt into her through the smoke, at the head of a small party. The enemy lost 6 killed and 11 wounded. On the British side, only one man, besides Tryon, was hit. Unfortunately, the prize was so injured, that she soon foundered.[2] Tryon died, unpromoted, on January 24th, 1811, from the effects of his wound.

On the evening of December 7th, the *Rinaldo*, 10, Commander James Anderson (1), being off Dover, chased two French lugger privateers, and, having gained on one, the *Maraudeur*, 14, engaged her, and ran her on board. The Frenchmen, 85 in number, tried to rush on to the *Rinaldo's* deck, but were repulsed, though the brig's crew did not exceed 65 all told. The latter, indeed, under Lieutenant Edward Gascoigne Palmer, who received a slight wound, boarded presently in return, and carried the enemy without any loss of life. The *Maraudeur* had 5 wounded. The other lugger escaped into Calais.

Ten days later, on the 17th, the same brig, while on her way from Dover to Spithead, induced four lugger privateers to chase her. It was nearly dark when the two foremost overtook her, and, with a volley from their small-arms, hailed her to strike. One being upon each of her quarters, she tacked, and poured a broadside into each; then, wearing, delivered a second broadside into the larger, which thereupon became unmanageable, and shouted that she was sinking. The second lugger, after endeavouring to run the *Rinaldo* down, was also reduced to call for quarter. While wearing round, and manning her boats, the brig fouled the Owers lightship, and could not for some time clear herself. This gave opportunity for three of the luggers to make off. The one which sank, unhappily with 77 out of a crew of 80, was the *Vieille Joséphine*, 16. No one in the *Rinaldo* was hurt.[3]

[1] James, v. 239; *Nav. Chron.*, xxiv. 498; xxv. 75.
[2] *Nav. Chron.*, xxiv. 500; xxv. 175; James, v. 241.   [3] James, v. 243.

In the evening of December 10th, the *Rosario*, 10, Commander Booty Harvey, being off Dungeness, fell in with two large lugger privateers. With remarkable gallantry and decision, Harvey ran his brig between the two, laid himself alongside one, and simultaneously engaged the other with his starboard broadside. A party, under Lieutenant Thomas Daws, boarded and carried the first, which proved to be the *Mamelouck*, 16, of whose crew of 45, seven were wounded. The other got away, chiefly in consequence of the *Rosario* losing her jib-boom. The brig had 5 people wounded.[1]

On the morning of December 12th, the cutter *Entreprenante*, 8 (4-prs.), Lieutenant Peter Williams, with a crew on board of 33, found four French privateers at anchor under the castle of Faro, midway between Malaga and Almeria. They mounted among them 15 guns, and carried 170 men. Presently they swept out and engaged. After about ninety minutes' action, the cutter was without her topmast, peak halliards and blocks, fore jeers, fore halliards, and jib-tie, all of which had been shot away; and she had two of her starboard guns disabled. Thereupon, one of the largest privateers tried twice to board, but in vain. Williams then manned his starboard sweeps, and got the cutter round so as to bring her port guns to bear. With two broadsides she drove off three of her assailants. Her ammunition was falling short, but she succeeded, in addition, in shooting away the fore mast and bowsprit of the fourth, which, nevertheless, tried again to board, but was beaten off. Having persisted for three and a half hours, the least injured of the privateers towed the others away. The cutter's loss was only 1 killed and 10 wounded. The gallant Williams was not made a Commander until August 27th, 1814.[2]

One of the most disastrous episodes of the year 1810 occurred on December 13th. Captain Thomas Rogers, of the *Kent*, 74, having under his orders the *Ajax*, 74, Captain Robert Waller Otway (1), *Cambrian*, 40, Captain Francis William Fane, *Sparrowhawk*, 18, Commander James Pringle, and *Minstrel*, 18, Commander Colin Campbell (1), sent in his boats, with 350 seamen, 250 Marines, and a couple of field-pieces, under Captain Fane, to destroy a convoy lying within the mole of Palamos, in Catalonia. This convoy consisted of eight merchantmen, two 3-gun xebecs, and a 14-gun ketch, covered by a 24-pr. over the mole, and by another 24-pr. and a 13-in.

---

[1] James, v. 242; *Nav. Chron.*, xxv. 74.
[2] James, v. 242; Marshall, iv. Pt. I. 325.

mortar in a battery on a height.   The French, who were in possession of the town, made no great resistance when the landing-party
seized the batteries and the convoy.   The mortar was spiked; the
guns were thrown into the sea; the magazine was blown up; and
all the vessels, except two, were carried out, burnt or destroyed,
with a loss of but 4 or 5 men.   In the meantime, however, the
French had been reinforced, and the British, who were so ill-advised
as to pass through the town on the way back to their boats, were
subjected to a very severe fire from men concealed in houses and
behind walls.   The result was that an enterprise which, at one time,
appeared to have been accomplished in a particularly facile manner,
terminated in a loss to the attacking force of no fewer than 33
killed, 89 wounded, and 87 missing.   Fane himself was among the
prisoners.   Lieutenants George Godfrey and Matthew Connolly (1)
greatly distinguished themselves in taking off the survivors.[1]

On February 4th, 1811, the *Cerberus*, 32, Captain Henry Whitby,
and *Active*, 38, Captain James Alexander Gordon (1), while cruising
off the coast of the Abruzzi, sent into the port of Pescara two boats
under Lieutenant George Haye.   These, in spite of a heavy musketry
fire, and with the loss of only 1 man wounded, captured three merchant vessels, and destroyed a fourth.   On the 12th of the same
month, the same frigates despatched their boats, under Lieutenants
James Dickinson (3), George Haye, and George Cumpston, to bring
out some vessels from the neighbouring harbour of Ortona.   As the
party rowed in, fire was opened upon it from an armed Venetian
vessel which had not previously been noticed, and from troops on
the beach.   The Venetian, which mounted 6 guns, was promptly
carried, a landing was effected, the troops were kept in check
while ten merchantmen were secured and two magazines were
burnt; and the retirement was effected with the loss of but 4 men
wounded.[2]

It has been seen how, in November, 1810, the *Amazone*, 40,
escaped from the road of St. Vaast to Le Hâvre.   In the course of
the following months she made several attempts to proceed thence
to Cherbourg; and, early on March 24th, 1811, she was observed
in the course of one of these by the *Berwick*, 74, Captain James
Macnamara (2).   The frigate was chased, and driven into a rocky
bay near Barfleur lighthouse, where, in anchoring, she lost her

---

[1] *Nav. Chron.*, xxv. 155; James, v. 259.
[2] James, v. 350; *Gazette*, 1811, 997.

rudder. Macnamara summoned to his aid, or was presently joined by, the *Amelia*, 38, Captain the Hon. Frederick Paul Iroy, *Goshawk*, 16, Commander James Lilburn, *Hawk*, 16, Commander Henry Bourchier, and *Niobe*, 38, Captain John Wentworth Loring; and the three largest ships of the squadron then stood in as close as possible to the Frenchman, firing at her as they wore, but doing her little damage, and themselves suffering a good deal aloft, besides having 1 killed and 1 wounded in the *Amelia*. Macnamara, however, was about to renew the attack on the 25th, when he discovered that Captain B. L. Rousseau had saved him the trouble by burning his frigate.[1]

A famous action, which, on some grounds, should, perhaps, have been described in the previous chapter, was fought in the Adriatic on March 13th. As, however, in spite of its brilliance and importance, no ship bigger than a frigate was concerned in it, it is chronicled here.

On March 11th, Commodore Dubourdieu sailed from Ancona with a squadron and 400 or 500 troops under Colonel A. Giflenga, in order to capture and garrison the island of Lissa. Early on the 13th, being then off the north point of the island, this squadron fell in with a British squadron under the orders of Dubourdieu's old enemy, Captain William Hoste.[2] The forces thus brought in face of one another were as follows :—

FRANCO-VENETIAN.			BRITISH.		
Ships.	Guns.	Commanders.	Ships.	Guns.	Commanders.
Favorite	44	Commod. Dubourdieu. Capt. La Marre La Meillerie.	*Amphion*	32	Capt. William Hoste.
Flore.	44	,, J. A. Péridier.	*Cerberus*	32	,, Henry Whitby.
Danaé	44	,, Villon.			
Corona (Venet.)	44	,, Pasqualigo.	*Active*	38	,, Jas. Alex. Gordon (1).
Bellona (Venet.)	32	,, Duodo.			
Carolina (Venet.).	32	,, Baratovich.	*Volage*	22	,, Phipps Hornby.
Principessa Augusta[1] (Venet.)	18	Com. Bolognini.			
Principessa di Bologna (Venet.)	10	,, Raggio.			
Lodola (Venet.)	2	,, Cotta.			
Eugenio (Venet.)	6	Lieut. Rosenquest (?).			

[1] James wrongly calls this craft the *Mercure*, 16.

At about 3 A.M., the *Active* made the signal for a strange fleet to windward, and at daylight, when the enemy's strength was visible,

[1] James, v. 332; *Nav. Chron.*, xxv. 342.
[2] Born, 1780; entered Navy, 1793; Com., 1798; Capt., 1802; Bart., 1814; K.C.B., 1815; died, Dec. 6th, 1828, being still a Capt.

Hoste made all sail in chase, with a fine breeze from N.N.W. At
about 6 A.M., the enemy, having formed in two divisions, bore down
to the attack with every possible sail set, the starboard or weather
division consisting of the *Favorite, Flore, Bellona,* and *Principessa
Augusta,* and the larboard, or lee one, of the *Danaé, Corona, Carolina,* and small craft. The British line, formed of the *Amphion,
Active, Volage,* and *Cerberus,* in the order named, was ranged in the
closest possible order on the starboard tack to receive the enemy.

CAPTAIN HENRY WHITBY, R.N.

At 9 A.M. the action began by the British firing on the headmost
ships as they came within range. The aim of Dubourdieu was
obviously to break the line in two places; but his effort was foiled
by the hotness of the British fire, and the compactness of the formation. The French commodore then endeavoured to round the British
van-ship, the *Amphion,* and to engage from leeward; but in attempting to accomplish this, he ran his frigate on the rocks of Lissa,
she having first been rendered well nigh unmanageable. Hoste
thereupon wore his ships, and the enemy's weather division passed
under the stern of the line and engaged it from leeward, while the

lee division tacked and remained to windward, hotly engaging the
Cerberus, Volage, and *Active.* Owing to the narrow waters in which
the battle was fought, and to the numbers of the assailants, the
British ships were frequently in positions which exposed them to
raking fire; but officers and men fought magnificently, and at
11.20 A.M. they were rewarded by seeing the *Flore* strike. At noon
her example was followed by the *Bellona.* The enemy to windward
then tried to make off, and was followed as closely as the disabled
state of the British ships would permit. At 3 P.M. the *Active* and
Cerberus succeeded in obliging the sternmost of the frigates, the
Corona, to surrender, and thus the battle ended with three frigates
taken and one on shore. The *Favorite* was set on fire by her crew,
and at 4 P.M. blew up.

" I must now," says Hoste, " account for the *Flore's* getting away after having
struck her colours. At the time I was engaged with that ship, the *Bellona* was
raking us; and when she struck, I had no boat that could possibly take possession of
her. I therefore preferred closing with the *Bellona* and taking her, to losing time
alongside the *Flore,* which I already considered belonging to us. I call on the officers
of my own squadron, as well as those of the enemy, to witness my assertion. The
correspondence I have had on this subject with the French Captain of the *Danaé* (now
their Commodore), and which I enclose herewith, is convincing; and even their own
officers (prisoners here) acknowledge the fact. Indeed, I might have sunk her, and so
might the *Active;* but as the colours were down, and all firing from her had long
ceased, both Captain Gordon and myself considered her as our own. The delay of
getting a boat on board the *Bellona,* and the anxious pursuit of Captain Gordon after
the beaten enemy, enabled him to steal off, till too late for our shattered ships to come
up with him; his rigging and sails apparently not much injured; but, by the laws of
war, I shall ever maintain he belongs to us."

The losses on board the British ships in this most admirably
managed action were:—

Ship.	Complement.[1]	Killed.	Wounded.	Total.
Amphion	251	15	47	62
Active	300	4	24	28
Volage	175	13	33	46
Cerberus	160	13	41	54
	886	45	145	190

[1] On going into action.

The officers killed included Midshipmen John Robert Spear-
man, Charles Hayes, Francis Surrage Davey, and John George,
and Purser Samuel Jeffery. Among the officers wounded were

Hoste, and Lieutenants David Dunn and George Cumpston. The enemy suffered much more severely. In the *Favorite*, upwards of 150 people were killed or wounded, and among the killed were Dubourdieu[1] and La Marre La Meillerie. The *Corona* is believed to have sustained a loss of upwards of 200 in killed and wounded. The *Bellona* lost 70, including Duodo, who was fatally hurt. Captain Péridier, of the *Flore*, was badly wounded; but it cannot be ascertained what were the total losses of his ship.

After the battle, the *Corona*, when in tow of the *Active*, caught fire. In extinguishing the flames, the victors increased their losses by 5 drowned and 4 injured.

Seeing that on this occasion 886 British seamen were opposed to at least 2500 French and Venetians, and that the allies had a gun superiority of more than 100 per cent., Hoste's victory off Lissa may be regarded as one of the most creditable in British annals. Each of the Captains present was given a gold medal, and the first Lieutenants of the ships engaged, David Dunn of the *Amphion*, James Dickinson (3), of the *Cerberus*, William Wilmot Henderson, of the *Active*, and William Wolrige, of the *Volage*, were promoted to the rank of Commander as from the day of the action.[2]

After the *Favorite* had been set on fire, about 200 of her crew retired to Lissa, which was held by two Midshipmen of the *Active*, James Lew and Robert Kingston, who also had charge of two prizes that lay in the port. These youngsters, assisted by a few privateersmen, summoned the French, who actually laid down their arms. Very different was the behaviour of the master of the Sicilian privateer *Vincitore*, 14, who lay in San Giorgio.. He was threatened by a small Venetian schooner, probably the *Lodola*, previous to the commencement of the action, and, in spite of the presence of the British squadron, hauled down his flag without resistance. Lew[3] and Kingston[4] presently drove off the schooner and retook the privateer.[5]

The capture, on May 18th, 1809, of the Danish island of Anholt, in the Kattegat, has been noticed in the previous chapter.[6] The place

---

[1] Bernard Dubourdieu, born 1773; entered navy as quartermaster, 1793; enseigne de vaisseau, 1797 : one of the best French cruiser captains of his day.

[2] James, v. 351; Randaccio, i. 171; *Nav. Chron.*, xxv. 429; *Moniteur*, Apr. 11th, 1811.

[3] Lieut., June 2nd, 1812.

[4] Lieut., Sept. 17th, 1811.

[5] *Nav. Chron.*, xxv. 436; James, v. 361.   [6] *See* p. 270.

was thenceforward garrisoned and held; and, in the early part of
1811, its garrison consisted of 350 Royal Marines and 31 Marine
Artillery, under Captain Robert Torrens, R.M., the whole being
under Captain James Wilkes Maurice, the defender of the Diamond
Rock. For some time the Danes had meditated the reconquest of the
island, but circumstances did not appear to be favourable until after
the break up of the ice in the spring of 1811. In March, a flotilla of
twelve gunboats, each mounting two long guns and four howitzers,
and carrying from 60 to 70 men, together with twelve transports
carrying about a thousand troops and seamen, was assembled in
a convenient bay, which it quitted on the 26th. Early on the
following morning, in darkness and a thick fog, the troops were
disembarked, unopposed and unseen, on the westward side of the
island, four miles from the headquarters at Fort York. When, at
about dawn, Maurice was warned of the presence of the enemy's
flotilla on the south side of the island, he found, on advancing, that
the Danes had already landed. To avoid being outflanked by them
he retreated; but he was pursued, until a battery opened fire and
drove back the foe. As daylight increased, it was perceived that the
Danish flotilla had taken up a position within point blank shot of the
British works on the south side of the island. Before the combined
assault was fairly begun, Maurice signalled to the *Tartar*, 32, Captain
Joseph Baker, and *Sheldrake*, 16, Commander James Pattison
Stewart, which had arrived on the previous day from England,
and which were on the north side, that the enemy had landed, and
that the gunboats were opening. The *Sheldrake* remained on the
north side, while the *Tartar*, the presence of which was quite un-
suspected by the Danes, worked round to the south by the shortest
route. In the meantime, a most determined assault was made, and
repeated, by the troops, assisted by the gunboats. The fire from the
works, however, mowed down the advance, and killed several of the
Danish leaders; and, to complete the discomfiture, a small armed
schooner, the *Anholt*, which was attached to the island, and which
was manned by volunteers under Lieutenant Henry Loraine Baker,
anchored at the critical moment on the flank of one body of the
besiegers; the result being that, after some parley, this, and another
detachment of the Danes, surrendered unconditionally. They had,
indeed, no alternative, for their gunboats, perceiving the approach of
the *Tartar*, had abandoned them, and made sail to the westward.
The prisoners thus taken numbered 540, besides 23 wounded men.

The rest of the assailants, having fled to the west end of the island, were there picked up by the gunboats and transports, Maurice and Torrens not being strong enough to prevent their escape. The Danish loss was between 30 and 40 killed, in addition to the wounded and prisoners already mentioned. The British had 2 killed and 30 wounded, including Torrens, slightly. Neither the *Sheldrake* nor the *Tartar* was able to molest the re-embarkation, but each pursued a division of the escaping boats. The *Sheldrake* eventually took *No.* 9, gunboat, and *No.* 1, lugger, and, it was believed, sank another gunboat; and the *Tartar* captured a couple of transports. Maurice was somewhat strangely rewarded for this service by the promotion of his brother, Lieutenant Ferdinand Moore Maurice,[1] to the rank of Commander. Lieutenant Henry Loraine Baker[2] was also promoted.[3]

On March 31st, the *Ajax*, 74, Captain Robert Waller Otway (1), and *Unité*, 36, Captain Edwin Henry Chamberlayne, having been detached by Sir Charles Cotton to intercept three French vessels which had left Toulon with stores for Corfu, overtook and captured the *Dromadaire*, 20, off Elba. The two other vessels, the 40-gun frigates *Amélie* and *Adrienne*, got into Porto Ferrajo.[4] They proceeded thence to Genoa, and, in July, returned to Toulon in circumstances which have been described in the previous chapter.[5]

At the end of April, the *flûtes*, *Girafe* and *Nourrice*, together with an armed merchantman, all three laden with ship timber for Toulon, lay at anchor in the Gulf of Sagone, Corsica, under a battery of four guns and a mortar, and with further protection from a martello tower mounting one gun.

On the evening of the 30th, the *Pomone*, 38, Captain Robert Barrie, *Unité*, 36, Captain Edwin Henry Chamberlayne, and *Scout*, 18, Commander Alexander Renton Sharpe, arrived off the coast to attack them. The French made all possible preparations, the *Nourrice* landing some of her guns, and troops being posted on the heights. The crews of the British ships volunteered either to land or to cut out the enemy's craft; but Barrie determined to employ the vessels, and, on May 1st, there being no wind, the two frigates and the brig were towed by their people into positions within grape range, in spite of a severe raking fire. The action began at

[1] Lost in the *Magnet*, 1812.
[2] Com., Apr. 8th, 1811.
James, v. 341; *Nav. Chron.*, xxv. 343, 302.
[4] *Nav. Chron.*, xxv. 428.
[5] *See* p. 295.

8 P.M., and, after about an hour and a half, the French ships burst into flames. The *Pomone* and consorts thereupon towed themselves out of danger, and, in a short time, the *Girafe* and *Nourrice* blew up, the battery and the tower sharing their fate. In this affair the British loss was 2 killed and 25, including Lieutenant William Neame, wounded.[1]

After the battle of Lissa, the French frigates *Danaé* and *Flore* took refuge in Ragusa, where, apparently, they soon began to lack supplies. The *Belle Poule*, 38, Captain James Brisbane, and *Al-*

H.M.S. " YORK," PRISON-SHIP IN PORTSMOUTH HARBOUR, 1828.
(A 74-gun ship, built in 1807.)
(*From an etching by E. W. Cooke, R.A.*)

ceste, 38, Captain Murray Maxwell, cruising off the coast of Istria on May 4th, sighted a French brig of war, which they suspected to be the bearer of the wished for stores, and drove her into Parenzo, where she anchored under a battery. Brisbane and Maxwell stood in as close as they dared, and cannonaded her, until she hauled on shore under the town, out of gunshot. In the mouth of the harbour is the island of San Nicolo, from which the town can be commanded. That night the boats, under Lieutenants John M'Curdy, Robert Ball Boardman, Edward A—— Chartres, Alexander Morrison, John

[1] *Nav. Chron.*, xxvi. 78.

Collman Hickman, and Rickard Lloyd, quietly took possession of it, and by the early morning of the 5th, mounted two howitzers, two 9 prs., and a field piece there. At dawn the French opened on the works, but, after a five hours' hot engagement, the brig having been sunk and the object accomplished, the British re-embarked with their guns and ammunition. Their loss was 4 killed and 4 wounded.[1]

On May 8th, the French gun-brig *Canonnier*, 11, was proceeding with a convoy of five small craft from Perros-Guirec for Brest, when, being off Ile de Batz, she was chased by the *Scylla*, 18, Commander Arthur Atchison. After a brief action, the British boarded, and, in three minutes, carried the enemy, losing only 2 killed and 2 wounded, but causing a loss of 6 killed and 11 wounded. One vessel of the convoy was also taken.[2]

On May 26th, Commander John Toup Nicolas, of the *Pilot*, 18, found four settees drawn up on the beach midway between Neto and Lipuda, in the gulf of Taranto, and sent in his boats, under Lieutenants Alexander Campbell (3), and Francis Charles Annesley (2), to bring them off. Although covered by the fire of about 150 troops, three of the craft were captured, and one was destroyed, only 1 person being wounded on the British side.[3]

On May 26th, off Corsica, the *Alacrity*, 18, Commander Nesbit Palmer, chased the *Abeille*, 20, Lieutenant A. R. A. de Mackau.[4] The British brig mounted sixteen 32-pr. carronades and two long 6-prs. ; the French, twenty 24-pr. carronades. The *Alacrity* had on board 100, and the *Abeille* 130, men and boys; so that the forces were almost equally matched.[5] The Frenchman shortened sail and awaited the attack ; and, after about three quarters of an hour's hot action, the *Alacrity* struck, having lost 5 killed, including Lieutenant Thomas Gwynne Rees, and 13 wounded. The *Abeille*, which lost 7 killed and 12 wounded, seems to have been much more ably handled than her antagonist; but that by no means wholly explains the result. Palmer, early in the fight, received a wound, not in itself serious, in the hand, and went below, leaving the command to Rees, who fought the ship most gallantly until he was severely wounded, and who, even then, sat

[1] James, v. 363; *Nav. Chron.*, xxvi. 166.
[2] James, v. 332; *Nav. Chron.*, xxv. 428.
[3] James, v. 372.
[4] Baron of the Empire, 1812; capt., 1819; died, 1855, an admiral.
[5] Broadside weight of metal, *Alacrity*, 262, *Abeille*, 260 lbs.

on a carronade slide, and encouraged his men until he was killed. There was no other Lieutenant on board; and when the Master, and the Master's Mate had been wounded, the command was assumed by Boatswain James Flaxman, who, though himself wounded, did his best, until Palmer sent up word from below that the colours were to be struck. No sooner, however, had he done this than, apparently repenting, he rushed on deck, and, pistol in hand, threatened to blow out the brains of any man who should attempt to execute the order. A little later, nevertheless, the colours were struck by the Gunner, while Flaxman's attention was otherwise engaged. Fortunately, perhaps, for himself, Commander Nesbit Palmer's slight wound induced lockjaw, from which he died ere any inquiry could be held concerning the manner in which he had lost his sloop.[1]

On the evening of May 26th, the *Sabine*, 16, Commander George Price, detached her five boats, under Lieutenants William Usherwood and Patrick Finucane, to attempt to cut out five 2-gun French privateers from the harbour of Sabiona, on the Cadiz station. Although the enemy lay under a battery, each boat boarded and carried a prize without loss; but, during a subsequent successful effort on the part of the French to drag two of the vessels ashore, a Marine was wounded. The three other privateers were brought off. Though Lieutenant Usherwood received high praise for this exploit, he was not made a Commander until July 22nd, 1830.[2]

On June 27th, the *Guadeloupe*, 16, Commander Joseph Swabey Tetley, being off Cape de Creus on the north-east coast of Spain, chased two strange sail, which proved to be the *Tactique*, 18, and *Guêpe*, 8. At about 12.40 P.M. a spirited action opened; and, fifty minutes later, the *Tactique* made an ineffectual and costly attempt to board. Soon afterwards, two batteries near the town of St. André began to annoy the *Guadeloupe*; but close action was continued until 2.15 P.M., when both Frenchmen, having had enough of it, bore up and stood in-shore for protection. The British sloop had 1 killed and 10 severely wounded, and was much cut about aloft.

---

[1] James, v. 364; C. M., May 30th, 1814; *Nav. Chron.*, xxv. 504. James (vi. 53) believes that at the time of the action Palmer had his post commission in his pocket, and may thus have lacked the hope of promotion as an incentive to do his best. I can find no corroboration of this.

[2] James, v. 380; *Gazette*, 1811, 1084.

It is alleged that the *Tactique* had no fewer than 11 killed and 48 wounded.[1]

On February 2nd, 1811, the three 40-gun frigates *Renommée*, Commodore François Roquebert, *Clorinde*, Captain Jacques St. Cricq, and *Néréide*, Captain François Lemaresquier, quitted Brest. Their destination was Mauritius. On May 6th they made Isle de la Passe, at the entrance to Grand Port; and on the following morning they not only found that the island was in British occupation, but also sighted and were chased by the *Phœbe*, 36, Captain James Hillyar, *Galatea*, 36, Captain Woodley Losack, and *Racehorse*, 18, Commander James de Rippe, which, with other vessels, had been specially detached to intercept them. Previous to going in chase, the *Galatea* sent her gig, with the intelligence of the presence of the French, to Captain Charles Marsh Schomberg, who, in the *Astræa*, 36, was lying at Port Louis; and, when their quarry temporarily escaped them, the British ships also went thither.

Commodore Roquebert eventually stood for Madagascar, in order to obtain provisions; and, on May 19th, he surprised the small British force at Tamatave, which post had been captured from the French, on the previous February 12th, by a little expedition sent from Mauritius in the *Eclipse*, 18, Commander William Jones Lye.

Schomberg, fearing for the safety of Tamatave, had left Port Louis on the 14th; and at dawn on the 20th he discovered Roquebert off Foul Point, and brought him to action. After the squadrons had nearly passed one another on opposite tacks at long range, and had exchanged fire, the breeze failed, and the leading ship, the *Astræa*, in endeavouring to wear and renew the fight, missed stays, the consequence being that the *Clorinde* and *Renommée*, which, owing to their weatherly position, kept the wind longest, were able to take up station nearly astern of the *Phœbe* and *Galatea*, and to inflict considerable damage. The *Néréide* also was able to annoy those frigates, while the *Astræa* was for the time practically out of the action. But at about 6.30 P.M. a light wind from S.E. altered the complexion of affairs. The *Galatea* had by that time been so terribly mauled that she was powerless to greatly help her consorts; but the *Phœbe* so disabled the *Néréide* as to oblige that ship to make for the land; and, when she had refitted, joined her

---

[1] James, v. 368; *Nav. Chron.*, xxiii. 166.

consorts for the final attack. At 9.50 the *Renommée* was brought
to close action, and, within half an hour, surrendered. The *Clorinde*,
which had disgracefully held aloof, managed to escape. Schomberg
and Hillyar returned to cover the captured ship and the disabled
Galatea; but, ere they got up, Losack had deemed it wise to make
for Port Louis. The little prize party in the *Renommée* had not
been permitted by its numerous prisoners to hoist the British over
the French ensign; and Losack, seeing other ships approaching in
the distance, feared to fall into the hands of enemies.

Not until Schomberg had removed the prisoners from the
Renommée did he learn of what had happened at Tamatave. He
then sent the *Racehorse* to that place. She returned on the 24th,
with news that the *Néréide* lay there prepared to defend herself.
On the following day the three British ships appeared off the
settlement, and summoned Lieutenant Ponée, who had succeeded
to the command on the death of Lemaresquier. Ponée obtained
advantageous terms, and, on the 26th, gave up his frigate and the
town.[1] The *Clorinde* managed to reach Brest on September 16th.
In March, 1812, St. Cricq was tried for his misconduct, and was
deservedly sentenced to be dismissed the service, degraded from the
Legion of Honour, and imprisoned for three years. The *Néréide*
was added to the Navy as the *Madagascar*, and the *Renommée* as
the *Java*.

In this action, the *Astræa* had 2 killed, and 16, including
Lieutenant John Baldwin, wounded. She received little material
damage. The *Phœbe*, which was very badly cut about, had 7 killed,
and 24, including Midshipman John Wilkie, wounded. The *Galatea*,
which was terribly battered, had 16 killed, including Lieutenant
Hugh Peregrine, R.M., and 46 wounded, including Lieutenant
Thomas Bevis, Lieutenant Henry Lewis, R.M., and Midshipmen
Henry Williams and Alexander Henning. The *Racehorse* had a
topmast carried away, but no one hurt. As for the French ships,
the *Renommée* had 145, and the *Néréide* 130 people put out of action.
Roquebert was among the killed. Lieutenants John Baldwin,[2] of
the *Astræa*, and George Scott (2),[3] of the *Phœbe*, were promoted
for their services; but, owing to the tone, wholly unmerited, of
Schomberg's dispatch, in so far as it concerned the *Galatea*,

---

[1] James, vi. 14; Chevalier, 384; Brenton, ii. 416; *Nav. Chron.* xxvi. 431, 435.

[2] Com. Nov. 18th, 1811; died a Capt., 1840.

[3] Com. March 24th, 1812; died a retired rear-admiral.

Lieutenant Thomas Bevis, of that frigate, remained a Lieutenant until the year 1829.

At daylight on July 4th, Captain Edwin Henry Chamberlayne, of the *Unité*, 36, sent in his boats, under Lieutenant Joseph William Crabb, to cut out an armed brig which lay in Porto Ercole, on the Tuscan coast. The brig, which was the *St. François de Paule*, mounted 8 guns, and was protected by a couple of 8-prs. on the beach : and, as the wind was so variable that Chamberlayne could not carry out his original intention of closing to co-operate, he finally sent his launch, under Lieutenant John M'Dougall (3), in support ; but ere she was able to assist, the other boats, which had suffered no loss, were bringing out the brig from under a brisk fire of grape. That evening the *Cephalus*, 18, Commander Augustus William James Clifford, joined ; and the two vessels stood along the coast to the south-east. Early next morning they discovered several vessels at anchor between Civita Vecchia and the mouth of the Tiber. The ships closed and drove the garrison out of a 4-gun battery ; and the boats, under Clifford and the officers already named, then went in and brought out, again without loss, three merchantmen.[1]

On July 21st, the *Thames*, 32, Captain Charles Napier (2), joined the *Cephalus*, off Porto del Infreschi, into which the latter had, on the previous day, driven a French convoy of 26 sail, of which 11 were gunboats, mounting among them 13 guns. The *Cephalus*, followed by the *Thames*, stood in, anchored, and opened fire, being replied to by the gunboats, a round tower on shore, and a body of troops. The opposition was, however, soon silenced ; and the boats, under Clifford, then took possession of the convoy, while the Marines, under Lieutenant David M'Adams, R.M., landed and stormed the tower, capturing 80 prisoners. The only loss was 4 wounded.[2]

On July 27th, the *Active*, 38, Captain James Alexander Gordon (1), anchored off Rogoznica, in the Adriatic, and sent in her boats under Lieutenants James Henderson (1), George Haye, and Robert Gibson (1),[3] to attack a grain convoy which

---

[1] James, v. 370; *Nav. Chron.*, xxvi. 345.

[2] James, v. 371; *Nav. Chron.*, xxvi. 344; 'Life of Napier,' i. 41.

[3] There were at the time two Lieuts. of the name, one of Aug. 6th, 1807, and the other of Aug. 28th, 1807. This last was then in the *Partridge ;* but it is sometimes extremely difficult to distinguish between them. *See* p. 396, where I have been unable to discriminate.

had run up a creek on the mainland behind the island, and which
was bound for Ragusa. At the mouth of the creek lay three gunboats ; and on each bank a force of armed men had been posted.
Part of the British detachment, therefore, was landed on the right,
to take possession of a commanding eminence ; and, this being
accomplished, the other part made for and boarded the gunboats,
while the first party descended and attacked the enemy in flank.
The convoy was then taken possession of, ten vessels being burnt,
and the rest brought out. The British lost only 4 wounded.[1]

On July 31st, off the coast of Norway, the *Algerine*, 10, Lieutenant John Aitken Blow, and *Brevdrageren*, 12, Lieutenant
Thomas Barker Devon, saw three Danish brigs standing towards
them. These were the *Langeland*, 20, *Lügum*,[2] 18, and *Kiel*, 16.
Blow, being thus vastly outmatched, was justified in retreating ;
and, as the breeze was light, the two British craft endeavoured
to escape by sweeping. Early on August 1st, however, the Danes
had gained considerably. The *Langeland* being then about two
miles ahead of her consorts, Blow proposed to Devon to bear down
with him and cut off that vessel. Devon cheerfully agreed ; but
as soon as the intention was manifest, the *Langeland* bore away to
close her friends. The British, therefore, resumed their efforts to
escape ; but they had lost ground. Once more, when the *Langeland*
had drawn ahead of her consorts, the British turned upon her. On
that occasion the Dane awaited the attack ; and, at about noon,
the engagement began. The *Brevdrageren* fought most gallantly,
both with the *Langeland* and also with the *Lügum*, when that craft
got up ; but in the thick of the action, Blow ceased firing, swept
out of range, and signalled to Devon to do likewise. Devon continued fighting, and hoisted the recall ; but Blow paid no heed.
The *Brevdrageren* was consequently faring very badly when, a
light air springing up, she was able to free herself. She was chased,
but receiving two additional sweeps and 10 men from the *Algerine*,
she steadily increased her distance for some time ; and, when at
length the *Lügum* began to gain, the *Algerine* hauled up and
hove to, thus inducing the Danes to abandon the pursuit. The
Brevdrageren had 1 killed and 3 wounded ; the *Algerine*, 1 killed.
Devon behaved most creditably. On October 30th, following, in
consequence of a dispute with a Marine officer whom he challenged,

---

[1] James, v. 371; *Nav. Chron.*, xxvi. 492.   [2] *See* note, p. 410.

Blow was sentenced by court-martial to be dismissed from the command of the *Algerine*. It is alleged by Brenton that this sentence saved the officer from a serious investigation which would have been otherwise inevitable.[1]

On August 1st, a British squadron, consisting of the *Quebec*, 32, Captain Charles Sibthorp John Hawtayne, *Raven*, 16, Commander George Gustavus Lennock, *Exertion*, 12, Lieutenant James

H.M.S. " PRINCE," 110, WITH STERN BALCONIES, AS FITTED BEFORE CLOSE STERNS
WERE INTRODUCED.

Jury-rigged, Portsmouth Harbour, 1828.

(*From an etching by E. W. Cooke, R.A.*)

Murray (2), *Redbreast*, 14, Lieutenant Sir George Mouat Keith, Bart., and hired armed cutters *Alert* and *Princess Augusta*, was cruising off the Elbe; and, it becoming known that a division of gunboats lay at anchor inside the island of Norderney, Samuel Blyth, first Lieutenant of the *Quebec*, volunteered, and was permitted,

[1] James, v. 345; Mins. of C. M.

to try to cut them out. He took command of 10 boats, containing
117 seamen and Marines, with, among others, Lieutenants John
O'Neale, Samuel Slout, and Charles Wolrige, Lieutenant (R.M.)
Humphrey Moore, Sub-Lieutenant Thomas Hare, Master's Mates
Robert Cook and John M'Donald (2), and Midshipman Richard
Millett. On the 2nd, the boats crossed the mouth of the Jade,
capturing a customs' vessel, and then passed within the islands of
Wangeroog and Spiekeroog, sighting in the afternoon the gunboats,
four in number, each mounting one long 12, and two long 6 or 8-prs.,
and carrying 25 men. One of the gunboats was quickly mastered
by Blyth ; but while he was employing the 12-pr. of the captured
craft against the other vessels of the enemy, the Gunner inad-
vertently brought about an explosion of cartridges, which killed
or wounded 19 persons, including Blyth himself, who had been
previously injured, but who was fortunately picked up. In spite
of this disaster, the remaining gunboats were soon taken. In
addition to the sufferers from the accident, the British lost 2 killed
and 9 wounded, the latter including Lieutenants Blyth and Slout,
Midshipman Millett and Mr. James Muggridge, who had piloted
the expedition, but who did not belong to the Navy. Several of
the wounded, including Lieutenant Slout, ultimately died.[1] Blyth,
for his gallantry, was promoted.[2]

On August 19th, the *Hawk*, 16, Commander Henry Bourchier,
being off St. Marcouf, chased a convoy which was steering for
Barfleur, and which was soon made out to be under the protection
of three gun-brigs and two large luggers. These hauled out to give
battle, and the *Hawk* hove to to receive them. After a hot action,
the *Hawk* had succeeded in driving ashore the two luggers, two of
the brigs, and 15 sail of the convoy, when, in wearing to prevent the
third brig from raking her, she ran aground. This gave opportunity
for that brig, and some of the merchantmen which had struck, to
escape. While she was getting afloat, the sloop was exposed to a
heavy fire from the shore. When she was again free, Bourchier
sent his boats, under Lieutenant David Price, to bring out or destroy
as many of the enemy as possible. Price brought out the gun-brig
Héron, 10, and three merchantmen, but could not, on account of
the strength of the tide, approach the remaining craft. This credit-

---

[1] James, v. 339; *Nav. Chron.*, xxvi. 257.
[2] Com., Sept. 5th, 1811; killed in action in the *Boxer*, Sept. 5th, 1813, aged 30.
Life: *Nav. Chron.*, xxxii. 441.

able affair, which gained Bourchier his promotion,[1] was conducted
with a loss of only 1 killed and 4 wounded. Mr. Henry Campling,
Purser of the *Hawk*, much distinguished himself by voluntarily
taking charge of the Marines and small-arm men.[2]

An interesting piece of work was done on August 24th, in the
mouth of the Gironde. On that day the *Diana*, 38, Captain William
Ferris, and *Semiramis*, 36, Captain Charles Richardson, were
standing towards Cordouan lighthouse, when they discovered six
sail within the shoals. Five of these were small merchantmen,
under convoy of the *Teazer* (ex British), 14 ; and the convoy had
come from Rochefort. As the enemy was well protected amid
shallows and batteries, Ferris determined to try to effect his object
by stratagem ; and, accordingly, he and his consort stood in under
French colours, flying the signal for a pilot. A suspicious battery
fired a few shot at them, but ceased on being informed by the
commander of the *Teazer* that they were the *Pallas* and *Elbe*,
from Rochefort. In time, a pilot came alongside the *Diana*, and
was, of course, taken care of, and his boat secured astern. It was
then nearly dark, and, shortly afterwards, the British frigates
calmly anchored off Pointe de Graves, under the batteries close to
which lay not only the *Teazer*, but also the *Pluvier*, 16. A little
later, Ferris despatched seven boats under Lieutenants Francis
Sparrow, George B—— Roper, Thomas Gardner, Percy Grace, and
Robert Nicholson, and Master's Mates William Holmes and
Timothy Renou, to cut out the convoy, which lay about four
miles further up the river. This business was duly accomplished ;
but, at daylight on the 25th, the boats and their prizes were still up
the river. As they could not well descend while the *Teazer* and
Pluvier remained uncaptured, Ferris ordered the *Semiramis* to stand
towards the latter, while he himself made for the former. The
Pluvier was laid on board, and quickly carried by a party under
Lieutenant Robert White Parsons and Lieutenant (R.M.) Lewis
Pryse Madden. The *Teazer* hurriedly cut, and ran ashore under
the Royan batteries, where she was engaged by the *Semiramis*, until
some of the returning boats, under Gardner, boarded her. As
she could not be removed, she was set on fire ; and eventually she
blew up. This most gallant service cost the loss, on the British
side, of only 1 drowned, and 3 wounded. The success of Ferris's

---

[1] Posted, Aug. 22nd, 1811.   [2] James, v. 335 ; *Nav. Chron.*, xxvi. 255.

ruse was so complete that in the early morning the captain of the *Pluvier* unsuspectingly visited the *Diana*, where he was detained.[1]

On September 2nd, off the coast of Norway, the *Chanticleer*, 10, Commander Richard Spear, and *Manly*, 10, Lieutenant Richard William Simmonds, fell in with and engaged the Danish *Laaland*, 18, *Alsen*, 18, and *Samsö*, 18, each of which would have been almost a match for both the British vessels. The three Danish craft ultimately concentrated on the *Manly*, which, after having been cut to pieces aloft, and deprived of the use of four of her guns, struck, although she had lost only 1 killed and 3 wounded. Lieutenant Simmonds, upon trial, was honourably acquitted. When the *Manly* was most pressed, the *Chanticleer*, to use Simmonds's words, " still kept her course, steering from the enemy;' and seemed to decline, on her part, to renew the action." Comment is unnecessary: but it may be added that Spear, who had originally been a banker's clerk in Dublin, though posted in 1813, appears to have never held another command.[2]

On September 3rd, some movement was observed among the vessels of the Boulogne flotilla; and, hoping to be able to take advantage of it if any of the craft ventured far from shore, the *Rinaldo*, 10, Commander James Anderson (1), and *Redpole*, 10, Commander Colin M'Donald, hovered about them to windward, and eventually followed a 12-gun prame and a 4-gun brig within the Basse Bank, where an action began between the British vessels and the rear of that part of the flotilla which lay there. No very great amount of harm seems to have been done on either side; but the behaviour of Anderson and M'Donald, in attacking a very superior force, was so spirited as to deserve notice.[3]

On September 6th, an armed ketch was burnt under the walls of Castella, in Calabria, by the boats of the *Pilot*, 18, Commander John Toup Nicolas, under Lieutenant Alexander Campbell (3), in spite of the opposition of a body of troops. The party also brought off without loss a quantity of corn and flax.[4]

Early in September, Captain Pulteney Malcolm, of the *Royal*

[1] James, v. 333; *Nav. Chron.*, xxvi. 258.
[2] James, v. 347; Simmonds to Sir H. E. Stanhope, Sept. 4th, 1811; Mins. of C. M., Jan. 6th, 1812; Holm, of *Laaland*, to R.-Ad. Lutkin, Sept. 16th, 1811.
[3] James, v. 337.
[4] James, v. 372; *Nav. Chron.*, xxvi. 493.

Oak, 74, senior officer off Cherbourg, obtained through deserters certain information, in consequence of which he detached the *Barbados*, 28, Captain Edward Rushworth, and *Goshawk*, 16, Commander James Lilburn, to the eastward of Barfleur. On the 7th those vessels fell in with seven French gun-brigs, each carrying three 24-prs. and a mortar, and, attacking them, chased them among the Calvados rocks, driving one ashore. On the 8th, the *Hotspur*, 36, Captain the Hon. Josceline Percy, arrived off Les Calvados, and, although she grounded under a heavy fire, managed to sink one of the brigs and to drive two more ashore. Unhappily, ere, assisted by the boats of the *Barbados* and *Goshawk*, she could get off again, she lost 5 killed, including Midshipmen William Smith (5a) and Alexander Hay, and 22 wounded, and was much cut up.[1]

On September 20th, Bonaparte having arrived at Boulogne, a grand marine fête took place there, the Emperor, in his barge, visiting several vessels of the flotilla. Off the road lay the *Naiad*, 38, Captain Philip Carteret (3); and Bonaparte presently ordered a division of seven 12-gun prames, under Rear-Admiral Baste, to stand out and attack her. Carteret waited with springs on his cable, and, for about half an hour, sustained a distant action with the foe. The French were then reinforced by ten 4-gun brigs, and a bomb; and the engagement continued for two hours more, the frigate weighing before the close of it with a view to repair slight damages and to improve her position. At 4.45 P.M. the flotilla retired under the batteries. The *Naiad* lost neither man nor spar. On the following day the seven prames, with fifteen smaller vessels, renewed the attack; but, in the interval, the *Naiad* had been joined by the *Rinaldo*, 10, Commander James Anderson (1), *Redpole*, 10, Commander Colin M'Donald, *Castilian*, 18, Commander David Braimer, and *Viper*, 8, Lieutenant Edward A—— d'Arcey. After some manœuvring, the enemy was thrown into confusion by the British fire; Rear-Admiral Baste's prame narrowly escaped capture; and the *Ville de Lyon*, 12, in endeavouring to succour her, was first badly mauled by the *Rinaldo* and *Redpole*, and then boarded and carried, after she had lost between 30 and 40 men, by the *Naiad*. The engagement lasted for some time longer, until, the French being close under the batteries, the British drew off. Their loss was 3 killed, including Lieutenant Charles Cobb (2), of the *Castilian*, and 16 wounded.[2]

---

[1] James, v. 336; *Nav. Chron.*, xxvi. 260.
[2] James, v. 337; *Nav. Chron.*, xxvi. 241, 242.

On October 11th, the *Impérieuse*, 38, Captain the Hon. Henry Duncan (3), discovered three gunboats, each mounting a long 18-pr., moored under the walls of a strong fort at Positano, in the gulf of Salerno. The frigate anchored within grape-shot range, and soon silenced the fort and sank one of the boats, but failed to dislodge the enemy from the work. The boats, under Lieutenant Eaton Stannard Travers and Lieutenant (R.M.) Philip Pipon, were therefore sent in ; and, in face of a very heavy fire, the seamen and Marines stormed the fort, took a number of prisoners, threw the guns over a cliff, destroyed the magazines, and brought away the two remaining gunboats, with a loss of only 1 killed and 2 wounded.[1]

On October 19th, the *Impérieuse*, 38, Captain the Hon. Henry Duncan (3), and *Thames*, 32, Captain Charles Napier (2), anchored near Point Palinuro, in Campania, and sent in boats, under Lieutenant Eaton Stannard Travers. These brought off without casualty ten armed polaccas, laden with oil, in spite of the fact that the craft had been banked up with sand, and were in charge of a body of Neapolitan troops.[2]

On October 21st, the same frigates came upon ten Neapolitan gunboats, with a number of merchantmen, in the harbour of Palinuro. The defences being strong, Duncan sent the *Thames* to Sicily with a request to Lieut.-General Maitland for the loan of a detachment of troops. The *Thames* returned on the 28th with 250 men of the 62nd Regt. under Major Darley. As soon as the weather proved favourable, *i.e.*, on the evening of November 1st, the troops, with the Marines of both frigates, under Lieutenant Eaton Stannard Travers, the whole commanded by Captain Napier, were landed at the rear of the port. A commanding height was gallantly carried under a heavy fire, while the *Impérieuse* occupied the attention of the gunboats and a battery, although she was able to engage them only at long range. On the morning of the 2nd, finding that little could be accomplished from the land side, Duncan recalled Napier from the shore, and, with both frigates, bore down and ran along the line of gunboats, pouring in a tremendous fire at close range, the result being that two were sunk, and the rest surrendered within a few minutes. The ships next silenced the fort, and obliged it to haul down its flag, whereupon Travers took possession of it. Its guns, 24-prs., were thrown into the sea ; and, in the course of that

---

[1] James, v. 373; *Nav. Chron.*, xxvii. 71.   [2] James, v. 373.

and the following day, two gunboats were destroyed, the six remaining gunboats, 22 feluccas, and a number of valuable spars were got off, and the troops and Marines were re-embarked, after all the defences had been blown up.   This important service was accomplished with a loss of 5 killed and 11 wounded.[1]   Travers, though warmly recommended by Vice-Admiral Sir Edward Pellew, was not made a Commander until June 15th, 1814.   He had then been upwards of 100 times engaged with the enemy, and had been in command at the capture of about 60 sail.

On November 27th, in the Adriatic, the *Eagle*, 74, Captain Charles Rowley, discovered and chased three vessels which proved to be the *Uranie*, 40, *Corcyre*, *flûte*, and a brig, bound from Triest for Corfu.   The brig soon parted company.   The other vessels were chased, and, after about ten hours' pursuit, the *Corcyre*, being crippled by the British fire, and by the carrying away of her fore top-mast, struck.   She was pierced for 40 guns, and had 28 mounted.   Owing to the disabled state of the prize, the *Eagle* had to stand by her, and could not therefore continue the chase of the *Uranie*.[2]

On the morning of November 28th, when the *Alceste*, 38, Captain Murray Maxwell, *Active*, 48, Captain James Alexander Gordon (1), *Unité*, 36, Captain Edwin Henry Chamberlayne, and *Acorn*, 20, Captain George Miller Bligh, were lying in Port St. Giorgio, Lissa, they were apprised, from the signal station on the heights, of the presence, to the southward, of three suspicious sail.   Maxwell, who believed the strangers to be the vessels which had escaped from the battle of Lissa in the preceding March, unmoored his squadron, in order to go in pursuit; but, as he dared not leave the island without any defence, seeing that a French force was at the time assembled at no great distance on purpose to attack it, he transferred from the *Alceste* and *Active* to three prize gunboats which lay in harbour, a Lieutenant, a Midshipman, and about 30 seamen, and, at the same time, landed the whole of the Marines of those frigates and of the *Unité* to garrison batteries on Hoste Island near the mouth of the harbour.   Then, leaving the *Acorn*, with Captain Bligh, in command of the place, he warped out, and by 7 P.M. was at sea.   On the morning of the 29th, the *Active* signalled three strange sail in the E.N.E.   These were presently made out to be, not the remnants of M. Dubourdieu's squadron, but the

---

[1] James, v. 373; 'Life of Napier,' i. 46; *Gazette*, 1812, 143.
[2] *Nav. Chron.*, xxvii. 169.

Pauline, 40, Commodore François Gilles Montfort (1), *Pomone*, 40, Captain C.C.M. Ducamp-Rosamel, and *Persanne*, 26, Captain J. A. Satie, bound from Corfu to Triest. The wind was fresh from E.S.E., and at first the enemy, formed in line on the port tack, stood towards the British; but soon M. Montfort bore up to N.W., and was chased, all the ships setting every possible stitch of canvas. At 11 A.M. the *Persanne*, being unable to keep up with her consorts, stood to the N.E. The *Unité* was sent after her, and the pursuit of the *Pauline* and *Pomone* was continued by the *Alceste* and *Active*.

The action began at 1.20 P.M., the *Alceste*, in the first fire, having her main top-gallant mast splintered. Twenty minutes later she had her main topmast carried away just above the cap by a shot from the *Pomone*, which was then abeam of her. This bred great enthusiasm in the French ships, and caused the *Alceste* to drop astern a little; but at about 2 P.M. the *Active* placed herself upon the *Pomone's* starboard or lee quarter, and brought her to close action. The *Pauline* tacked, and, taking in sail, stood back to assist her consort, and at about 2.30 was hotly engaged; but, about half an hour afterwards, perceiving that the *Pomone* was weakening, and that the *Kingfisher*, 18, Commander Ewell Tritton, was approaching, Montfort set all sail again, and stood to the westward. Some desultory firing ensued between the *Active* and the *Pomone*, owing to the former having accidentally shot ahead of her antagonist. The *Pomone*, however, was beaten, and when, at about 3.40 P.M. the *Alceste* got up, and opened her starboard broadside, the *Pomone* struck. Neither the *Alceste* nor the *Active* was in a condition to pursue, so that the *Pauline* escaped without difficulty; but the *Persanne* was overtaken at about noon by the *Unité*, and, after a running fight, which lasted till four, struck when Chamberlayne drew near enough to use his broadside. The loss of the *Alceste*, which had only 218 men and boys on board, was 7 killed, including Midshipman Charles Nourse, and 13 wounded. The *Active*, which also was short-handed, had 8 killed, including Midshipman George Osborne, and 27 wounded, including Captain Gordon, and Lieutenants William Bateman Dashwood and George Haye, each of whom displayed great gallantry. Out of a crew of 332, the *Pomone* had 50 killed and wounded. Two of her masts fell during the action, and the third followed them soon afterwards. Captain Rosamel, who was wounded, fought his ship bravely. As much cannot be said of Montfort, who certainly deserted his colleague too hastily. The *Unité*, in her conflict with the *Persanne*, had but 1 wounded ; the *Persanne* had 2 killed and 4 wounded.[1] Lieutenant Andrew Wilson, first of the *Alceste*, was made a Commander on September 17th, 1812. Dashwood and Haye, first and second of the *Active*, were similarly promoted on May 19th, 1812. But Lieutenant Joseph William Crabb, first of the *Unité*, remained in that rank until his retirement in 1851.

CAPTAIN JAMES NEWMAN NEWMAN, R.N.

(*From E. Scriven's engraving, after the painting by A. J. Oliver.*)

The year 1811 closed with a series of wrecks, such as, happily, had been unparalleled for a long period. In November, when part of the Baltic fleet was returning for the winter to England, the *St. George*, 98, Captain Daniel Oliver Guion, bearing the flag of Rear-Admiral Robert Carthew Reynolds (1), encountered, off Seeland, a violent storm which drove her ashore and dismasted her. The same storm also caused the destruction of about 30 vessels of a

---

[1] James, v. 375 ; *Nav. Chron.*, xxvii. 260, 342.

homeward-bound convoy. The *St. George* was got off, and fitted
with jury masts and a Pakenham's rudder. On December 17th, in
company with the fleet, she sailed again, and, in consideration of
her condition, the *Cressy*, 74, Captain Charles Dudley Pater, and
Defence, 74, Captain David Atkins, were ordered to attend her.
Upon clearing Cape Skagen, the ships met with terrible weather;
and, after five days of it, the *St. George* and *Defence* were driven
ashore near Ringkjöbing, and soon went to pieces. Of the *St. George's*
ship's company of about 850 officers and men, all but 6 perished.
Of the *Defence's* complement of about 530, only 12 survived. Among
the lost were the Rear-Admiral and both Captains, besides fourteen
Lieutenants. The *Defence* might have escaped, had not Atkins
chivalrously refused to part company without permission or order.
On December 25th the same storm was fatal to the *Hero*, 74, Captain
James Newman Newman, which was returning from Göteborg, and
which was wrecked on the Haak Sand, off the Texel. In her case,
all on board, save 12, were lost, among the number being the Captain
and five Lieutenants. The *Grasshopper*, 18, Commander Henry
Fanshawe (2), was in company, and also struck, but, driving over
the bank, got into a less dangerous position, and, being helpless,
was ultimately surrendered to the enemy, having, however, suffered
no loss.[1]

One of the most significant events of the year 1811 was the
unfortunate encounter between the United States' frigate *President*
and the British sloop *Little Belt*. It was the prologue to a struggle
which began in the following year, and which lasted till 1815. But
the new conflict into which Great Britain was precipitated, although
it arose indirectly out of her difficulties with Napoleon, was a conflict totally distinct from that which raged among the Powers of
Europe. It was altogether a separate quarrel. The fact that
America was for the time Great Britain's enemy, and that France
was also Britain's foe, did not bring about alliance or co-operation
of any sort between the United States and France. On the contrary,
America's grievances against France were in those days almost as
acute as her grievances against Britain ; and, if they did not lead
her into hostilities with France as well as with Britain, it was
mainly because Britain was an active and vigorous sea power and
France had ceased to be one. The nature and origin of America's
grievances against both countries will be found set forth in brief at

[1] James, v. 349; *Nav. Chron.*, xxvii. 43, etc., 113; Mins. of C. M.'s.

the close of Chapter XXXVIII. of the present volume, and, more
fully, by Governor Roosevelt, in the Chapter which follows this.
Governor Roosevelt also describes all the episodes of the conflict
during the three years of hostilities; and it is, therefore, needless
to make any further reference to them in the present Chapter.

So far as the events of the great Napoleonic struggle are concerned, the following were the most important minor naval actions
of the year 1812.

On January 9th, the French 40-gun frigates, *Ariane* and *Andromaque*, with the brig *Mamelouck*, 16, under Commodore Martin Le
Foretier, sailed from Nantes on a. cruise in the Atlantic. On the
15th, they were in vain chased by the *Endymion*, 40, Captain Sir
William Bolton (2), and by the *Leopard*, 50, Captain William
Henry Dillon. The enemy then began a series of semi-piratical
depredations upon commerce; and the Admiralty, receiving news
of this, directed that a force should be detached from the squadron
off Brest, to intercept the French on their return. In pursuance of
instructions, therefore, Rear-Admiral Sir Harry Burrard Neale
ordered the *Northumberland*, 74, Captain the Hon. Henry Hotham,
to part company from off Ushant on May 19th. Hotham was so
fortunate as to discover his quarry on the 22nd, the enemy then
crowding sail for Lorient, and he having the *Growler*, 12, Lieutenant
John Weeks, within signalling distance. By smart manœuvring he
was able to fetch to windward of Lorient ere the French could
reach it. He continued working into the Basse des Bretons,
occasionally exposed to the fire of the batteries on each side.
Foretier tried to push in between the *Northumberland* and Pointe
Talieu, but failed, owing to the magnificent way in which the line-
of-battle ship was handled. Indeed, her Master, Mr. Hugh Stewart,
betrayed greater familiarity with the charts than the French themselves, and, in spite of the smoke and the risky navigation, so
manœuvred the vessel that he forced all his opponents upon the
rocks between Le Graul and the mainland. As soon as he saw
them thus fast, Hotham hauled off to repair his own damages; and
the falling tide soon left the French on their beam ends, with their
masts towards the shore. In the meantime, the *Growler* annoyed
the unfortunate frigates. At 5.28 P.M., the *Northumberland*, having
refitted, anchored in a convenient position, and deliberately set to
work to blow the bottoms out of the enemy's ships. When it was
evident that they had been deserted by their crews, and when the

headmost frigate was in flames, Hotham, who had been much
interfered with by a strong battery, weighed, but left the *Growler*
under sail near the foe to prevent the people from returning to their
vessels.   At about 8 P.M., the burning frigate, the *Andromaque*, blew
up.   Two hours later the second frigate was seen to be on fire, and
at 11 she was clearly doomed.   The *Northumberland* and *Growler*
then stood to sea.   Ere they were out of sight, the second frigate,
and also the *Mamelouck*, blew up.   The *Northumberland* gained
this most creditable success at the cost of only 5 killed, and 28,
including Lieutenant William Fletcher, wounded.   The *Growler*
had no one hurt.[1]   There can be little doubt that, had the French
made a fight for it, and tried to board the 74, one at least of them,
aided by the numerous batteries, might have got into port.   For
this service Lieutenant John Weeks, of the *Growler*, and Lieutenant
John Banks, first of the *Northumberland*, were promoted.[2]

In February, 1812, a curious state of things prevailed in Hayti.
Two parties, one headed by Petion, and the other by Christophe,
held divided possession of the country; and Captain Sir James
Lucas Yeo, of the *Southampton*, 32, who was off the coast, had
instructions to respect the flags of both.   But a third party had
been formed from deserters from both the others; and this party
had managed to possess itself of a frigate, a corvette and a brig-of-
war, which, under a certain M. Gaspard, an old privateer's man,
tended to become little different from pirates.   On February 2nd,
Yeo, then at Port au Prince, learnt that Gaspard's squadron was
cruising outside.   Unwilling to take the risk of allowing such
dangerous vessels to leave the bight of Léogane, and undeterred
by the representations that were made to him concerning the overwhelming force of Gaspard's frigate, Yeo weighed at night, and
went in quest of the squadron.   The *Southampton*, it may be
explained, was the oldest frigate in the Navy, dating from 1757,
and mounted 38 guns, including ten 24-pr. carronades and two
long 6-prs., with 12-prs. as the chief part of her battery.   Gaspard's
frigate, the *Améthyste*, had been, until her capture by the *Latona*
in 1809, the French *Félicité*.   Not being considered fit for the
British service, she had been sold, and bought for Christophe.
Thence she passed, probably by treachery, into the hands of one
Borgellat, Gaspard's principal, who headed a rebellion in the south
of the island, and who called her *Heureuse Réunion*, though the

name of *Améthyste* still stuck to her. She carried 44 guns, made
up of twenty-two long 12's, eight long 18's, and fourteen 24-pr.
carronades. Early on the 3rd, Yeo fell in with the three vessels,
and, getting unsatisfactory answers when he hailed them, ordered
Gaspard to accompany him to the Commander-in-Chief at Port
Royal. Gaspard said that he would rather sink than obey; and,
after the *Southampton* had fired a warning gun ahead of the
Améthyste, she followed it with her entire broadside. Gaspard
replied, and made several fruitless efforts to board. After less than
half-an-hour's action, the enemy's main and mizen masts fell, and
she was terribly mauled ; but not until a further three-quarters of
an hour had elapsed was it ascertained that she had struck. Her
consorts had meanwhile made off. The *Southampton* had only
1 killed and 10 wounded, out of 212 people on board. On the
other hand, the *Améthyste*, out of a crew of nearly 700, had 105
killed, including Gaspard, and 120 wounded. She was taken under
jury masts to Jamaica, and eventually restored to Christophe.
Very naturally, Yeo's conduct was approved of.[1]

On February 13th, the *Apollo*, 38, Captain Bridges Watkinson
Taylor, while off Cape Corso, sighted and chased the French storeship *Mérinos* and a corvette. The *Mérinos,* which was pierced for
36 guns, but mounted only twenty long 8-prs., struck, after she
had lost 6 killed and 20 wounded. The corvette escaped. The
Apollo, although exposed for some time to the fire of works on
shore, had no one hurt.[2]

On February 16th, the *Victorious*, 74, Captain John Talbot, and
Weazel, 18, Commander John William Andrew, arrived off Venice
to watch the motions of the new 74, *Rivoli*, and of two or three
brigs which lay in the port ready for sea. It was foggy ; and when
the weather cleared on the 21st, the enemy's squadron, which had
come out, was seen, steering in line of battle for Pola. Talbot
chased, and soon began to gain on his foe. The hostile force
consisted of the *Rivoli*, Commodore J. B. Barré, *Jéna*, 18,
Mercure, 18, *Mamelouck*, 10, and two gunboats. Very early on
the 22nd, perceiving that the *Mercure* had dropped behind her
consorts, and that the *Rivoli* had shortened sail to allow the brig
to close, Talbot ordered Andrew to endeavour to pass the *Victorious*
and bring the laggard to action. This Andrew promptly did, en-

---

[1] James, vi. 76; *Nav. Chron.*, xxviii. 451; *Kingston Gazette*, Feb. 29th, 1812.
[2] *Nav. Chron.*, xxvii. 434; James, vi. 64.

gaging not only the *Mercure*, but also for a time, and distantly, the *Jéna*. After forty minutes' action the *Mercure* blew up, the *Weazel* succeeding in saving three men only. In the interval, the *Jéna* made off. At 4.30 A.M. the *Victorious* brought the *Rivoli* to action. A running engagement, interrupted at times by fog and smoke, ensued. Talbot, nearly blinded by a splinter, had to hand over much of his duties to Lieutenant Thomas Ladd Peake, who fought the ship admirably until, after three hours, the enemy became perfectly unmanageable, and both vessels were nearly aground close under the Istrian coast. Peake, therefore, recalled the *Weazel*, which, at 8 A.M., stood across the bows of the *Rivoli*, and poured in a couple of broadsides at short range, the *Victorious* also continuing the cannonade. At 9 o'clock the *Rivoli*, which had lost her mizen mast, struck. Out of about 810 men [1] on board, she had the huge number of 400 killed and wounded. Her hull was shot to pieces; and, a day or two after the action, her fore and main masts fell over the side. The *Victorious* had 27 killed, including Lieutenant (R.M.) Thomas H—— Griffiths; and 99 wounded, including Captain Talbot, Lieutenant (R.M.) Robert S—— Ashbridge (mortally), and Master's Mates William Henry Gibbons, and George Henry Ayton. The *Weazel* fortunately escaped with not a man hurt. The *Rivoli*, under Lieutenants Edward Whyte and John Townsend Coffin, was escorted to Port St. Giorgio, Lissa, and arrived there on March 1st. She was subsequently added to the Navy. Talbot was given the gold medal for his gallantry; Lieutenant Peake was made a Commander on May 8th; and Commander Andrew was posted on September 26th following.[2]

On March 27th, off Dieppe, the *Rosario*, 10, Commander Booty Harvey, observed a division of twelve brigs and a lugger, part of the Boulogne flotilla, standing along shore, and bound, as subsequently appeared, for Cherbourg. The *Rosario* gallantly tried to cut off the leewardmost of the brigs, each of which mounted three long 24-prs. and an 8-in. howitzer, and carried 50 men. Finding, however, that she was exposing herself to be boarded by the other brigs, which promptly bore down in support, the *Rosario* made for a brig which she descried in the offing, and flew the signal for an enemy. The new-comer was the *Griffon*, 16, Commander George Barne Trollope; and as soon as she had answered his signal, Harvey

---

[1] Talbot says 862.   [2] James, vi. 64; *Nav. Chron.*, xxvii. 502.

again hauled to the wind, and returned to his business of harassing the rear of the flotilla, which was then striving to get into Dieppe. After nearly an hour's desultory action, Harvey ran into the midst of the enemy, drove two of the brigs on board one another, engaged them and a third, which she partially dismasted, forced a fourth brig on shore, and boarded and carried a fifth, all before the *Griffon* could get within gunshot. When she did get up, the *Griffon* drove another brig on shore near St. Aubin, and carried yet another by boarding. The dismasted brig, which had been abandoned by her crew, was later taken possession of by the *Rosario* ; so that in all three were captured, and two driven ashore. The only British losses were Midshipman Jonathan Widdicombe Dyer and four men wounded, in the *Rosario*. Harvey was deservedly posted, and Dyer made a Lieutenant, on March 31st, for this service.[1]

On April 16th, being off the town of Policastro, in Campania, the *Pilot*, 18, Commander John Toup Nicolas, discovered nine coasting vessels hauled up on the beach. Having anchored close in, and opened fire in order to drive off any troops that might be in the immediate neighbourhood, she sent in her boats, under Lieutenant Alexander Campbell (3) ; and, in face of some slight resistance, brought off all the craft without casualty. On the 28th, the same sloop fell in with a large convoy protected by several gun-vessels ; but, as it was quite calm, she could not manœuvre, and they escaped.[2]

On April 29th, Captain Patrick Campbell (1), of the *Leviathan*, 74, sent his boats, under Lieutenant Alexander Dobbs, with those of the *Undaunted*, 38, Captain Richard Thomas (2), to attack a privateer and several merchantmen in the road of Agay, near Fréjus. The vessels were carried ; but the privateer could not be got afloat ; and, in the efforts to get her off, 2 men were killed and 4 wounded. Four of the merchantmen were, however, carried away.[3]

The end of April witnessed what was practically the conclusion of the European exploits of one of the most famous of the Genoese privateers, Giuseppe Bavastro, whose name to this day is a centre of wondrous traditions in Italy. On April 29th, 1812, Captain Thomas Ussher, of the *Hyacinth*, 20, with his own boats, and those of the *Goshawk*, 16, Commander James Lilburn, and *Resolute*, Lieu-

---

[1] *Nav. Chron.*, xxvii. 346; James, vi. 45.

[2] James, vi. 67; *Nav. Chron.*, xxviii. 162.

[3] James, vi. 68; *Nav. Chron.*, xxviii. 75.

tenant John Keenan, and with the gunboat *No.* 16, Lieutenant
Thomas Cull (2), attacked a flotilla of privateers commanded by
Bavastro, then lying within the mole of Malaga, under the protection of two batteries. In his gig, supported by Lieutenant
Thomas Hastings, Ussher dashed at the larger battery, which
mounted fifteen long 24-prs., and carried it in less than five
minutes, turning its guns on the opposite castle of Gibralfaro. In
the meantime, the other boats had pulled into the harbour, and
taken several prizes ; but, when Ussher joined them, he found them
much exposed to the fire from Gibralfaro and from the French
57th Regt., on the mole ; and, as the moon then shone brightly, the
position was so critical that he contented himself with bringing out
Bavastro's own vessel, the *Intrepido*, 10, and the *Napoleone*, of the
same force, and with leaving the rest as much damaged as possible.
In this most gallant affair the British, out of 149 people engaged,
had 15, including Commander James Lilburn, of the *Goshawk*,
killed, and 53 wounded.[1] Among the officers who specially distinguished themselves, other than those already mentioned, were
Lieutenants Francis Brockell Spilsbury (wounded) and Allen Otty.

On April 29th, the boats of the *Undaunted*, 38, Captain Richard
Thomas (2), *Volontaire*, 38, Captain Charles Bullen, and *Blossom*, 18,
Commander William Stewart, under Lieutenant John Eagar,
attacked a convoy of 26 French vessels at anchor near the mouth of
the Rhône, and, without loss, brought out 7, burnt 12, including a
4-gun man-of-war schooner, and left 2 stranded. The guns of the
Blossom covered the operations.[2]

On May 3rd, the *Apelles*, 14, Commander Frederick Hoffman,
and *Skylark*, 16, Commander James Boxer, went ashore to the
westward of Boulogne. The former was captured and floated by
the French. The latter was burnt by her people, who subsequently
escaped. News of the double misfortune was signalled from the
Castilian, 18, Commander David Braimer, off Dungeness, to the
Bermuda, 10, Commander Alexander ˙Cunningham (2), and the
Rinaldo, 10, Commander Sir William George Parker, Bart. ; and those

---

[1] O'Byrne, 1223; *Nav. Chron.*, xxvii. 515; Marshall, Supp., Pt. I. 345; Randaccio, i. 189; *Monitore delle Due Sicilie* (Bavastro's account), May 21st, 1812,
Ussher translates *Intrepido* as *Brave*, and calls his opponent Barbastro. Randaccio
confuses accounts. Bavastro, who is the hero of a novel published at Toulon in 1853.
was born in 1760. Bonaparte decorated him in 1804. After 1814 he fought for the
South American republics. In 1830 he served France in Algier. He died in 1833.

[2] James, vi. 68; *Nav. Chron.*, xxviii. 75.

two sloops at once got under way and made for the French coast, in
order, if possible, to render assistance. On the morning of the 4th,
they chased the *Apelles*, closed her, and drove her ashore under a
battery near Etaples. A little later, the *Castilian* and the *Phipps*,
14, Commander Thomas Wells (2), joined, and the four brig-sloops
stood in, and, with successive broadsides, drove the French out
of their prize. The British boats, under Lieutenant Thomas
Saunders (2), then went in, and, in spite of a hot fire from the
battery and from field pieces on the beach, floated the *Apelles* and
restored her to the service. Strange to say, not a man on the British
side was hit.[1]

On May 9th, the *America*, 74, Captain Josias Rowley, *Leviathan*, 74, Captain Patrick Campbell (1), and *Eclair*, 18, Commander John Bellamy, drove a French convoy of eighteen
vessels to take refuge under the batteries of Laigueglia, and, on
the 10th, early in the morning, landed the Marines, about 250
in number, from the two 74's, under Captains Henry Rea and
John Owen, R.M., to take possession of the works and bring
out or destroy the craft. Unfortunately, while the landing was
being effected, a chance shot from the shore sank the *America's*
yawl, and caused the drowning of 11 men. On land, however, all
went well. Captain Owen, R.M., carried a battery of five guns on
the right; and the main body of the attack took a battery of four
guns and a mortar near the town, and turned the weapons on the
enemy, while the fire of the *Eclair* drove the French from the
houses facing the beach. A large force of seamen, under Lieutenants
William Richardson (3), Bourchier Molesworth, Robert Moodie,
Alexander Dobbs, and Richard Hambly, was then despatched to
bring out the convoy. After considerable exertions, sixteen of the
vessels were towed off and one was burnt, the remaining one being
too much damaged to be floated. Thereupon, the Marines were
re-embarked under cover of the *Eclair*. Apart from the casualties
due to the sinking of the yawl, the losses on this occasion were only
5 killed and 20 wounded.[2]

In May, the boats of the *Alcmene*, 38, Captain Edwards Lloyd
Graham, under Lieutenant Edward Saurin, were despatched from
Lissa to intercept any of the enemy's convoys that might endeavour
to pass between Curzola and the mainland. A few prizes of no great

---

[1] *Nav. Chron.,* xxvii. 505; James, vi. 47.
[2] James, vi. 68; *Nav. Chron.,* xxviii. 160.

importance had been made when, on the 12th, two sail were discovered, and chased by four of the boats. In the darkness the enemy
was overhauled, and was then found to be much stronger than had
been anticipated. In fact, there were thirteen vessels instead of only
two. Saurin, however, ordered his boats to make for the largest.
A deadly fire was opened on them; but at length the British gained
a footing and carried the craft, though not until every one of her
crew had been killed or wounded. Her consorts then fired upon her
and did not desist until she had been towed out of gunshot. In this
bloody affair, the *Alcmene's* pinnace alone, Saurin's boat, lost 20 killed
or wounded. Saurin himself was shot through both arms, and had
to have the right one amputated.[1] Strangely enough, the dispatches
relating to the matter were never published, but Saurin obtained his
promotion in the following December.

On May 14th, the *Thames*, 32, Captain Charles Napier (2), accompanied by the *Pilot*, 18, Commander John Toup Nicolas, opened
a heavy fire upon a tower and battery at Sapri, in the Gulf of Policastro, and, after two hours, obliged the small garrison to surrender.
When a landing had been effected, twenty-eight vessels, laden with
oil, were found and brought off, and the battery was blown up. The
Marines of the *Pilot* rendered good service under acting Master
Roger Langlands, who, apparently in consequence of Napier's
recommendation, was promoted to a lieutenancy on July 24th
following.[2]

The cause of the patriots in the south of Spain, and especially on
the coast of Grenada, was materially assisted by the operations of
the *Hyacinth*, 20, Captain Thomas Ussher, *Termagant*, 20, Captain
Gawen William Hamilton, and *Basilisk*, 6, Lieutenant George
French. The *Hyacinth*, on May 20th, destroyed the castle of
Nerja, the result being that on the 25th, the patriots occupied the
town, and informed Ussher that the enemy had retired to Almuñecar,
a town about twelve miles to the eastward. Thither Ussher proceeded, and, on the 26th, silenced the castle in less than an hour.
As the guerillas did not advance to storm it, the French re-opened
fire on the 27th, but were again silenced and driven into the town.
Ussher was desirous of sparing the inhabitants, so, having destroyed
a 2-gun privateer in port, he ran back to Nerja to concert plans with
the guerilla chiefs there. At Nerja he embarked 200 patriots, and

---

[1] Marshall, Supp., Pt. III. 394; O'Byrne, 1031.
[2] James, vi. 67; *Nav. Chron.*, xxviii. 163; 'Life of Napier,' i. 59.

arranged for the guerilla cavalry to advance through the mountains ; but, ere he got back to Almuñecar, the French had retired on Grenada. All he could do was to demolish the works.[1]

Since April, 1811, the storeship *Dorade* had been lying at Arcachon, waiting for an opportunity to put to sea, when, on the night of June 4th, 1812, the *Medusa*, 32, Captain the Hon. Duncombe Pleydell Bouverie, sent in her boats under Lieutenant Josiah Thompson, to cut the vessel out. The *Dorade* had on board 14 guns and 86 men ; but, though perfectly prepared for resistance, she was carried after a desperate struggle, in which all her people except 23 were killed or driven overboard. While going down the harbour at dawn on the following morning, the prize grounded ; and, as the tide ran with great violence, Thompson had to destroy her. He lost only 5 men wounded. In spite of his gallantry, he was not promoted until twenty-six years had elapsed after the capture of the *Dorade*.[2]

On June 15th, a French convoy of fourteen vessels, laden with naval stores, and bound from Toulon for Genoa, under protection of the *Renard*, 16, Lieutenant Charles Baudin, *Goéland*, 14, and some gunboats, took refuge under Isle Ste. Marguerite from a British squadron consisting of the *America*, 74, Captain Josias Rowley, *Curaçoa*, 36, Captain John Tower, and *Swallow*, 18, Commander Edward Reynolds Sibly. The last-named was sent in to reconnoitre. Early on the 16th, the convoy was observed to be getting under way, and eventually the *Renard* and *Goéland*, which had a light breeze, went in chase of the *Swallow*, which was almost becalmed. When, however, the enemy discovered that the breeze was reaching the ships in the offing, they hauled their wind, tacked, rejoined their charges, and stood with them towards the Bay of Fréjus. The *Renard* and *Goéland* were reinforced with volunteers and soldiers, and again stood out ; and towards 1 P.M., the *Swallow*, approaching on the opposite tack, neared them rapidly. She passed them, indeed, within thirty yards to windward, and gave and received a broadside as she did so. Sibly then wore under the *Renard's* stern, and endeavoured to keep her head off shore, but, being damaged aloft, he could not effect his object. After a brisk fight of forty minutes' duration, and the repulse of several attempts to board, the *Swallow*, then not far from the shore and batteries, hauled off and rejoined the squadron, having lost 6 killed and 17 wounded, and having been

[1] James, vi. 63 ; *Nav. Chron.*, xxviii. 75.
[2] James, vi. 57 ; *Nav. Chron.*, xxvii. 512.

much cut up. The *Renard* lost 14 killed and 28 wounded. The *Goéland's* loss does not appear.[1] In this little action the *Swallow's* twelve 32-pr. carronades and two long 6-prs. were opposed to twelve 18-pr. and fourteen 24-pr. carronades, and four long 6-prs. The affair was, therefore, very creditable to Sibly, although French writers, ignoring that the *Goéland* assisted the *Renard*, and laying stress upon the presence of the *America* and *Curaçoa* in the offing, claim it as one of the glories of their navy. M. Charles Baudin, of the *Renard*, lived to become the hero of San Juan de Ulloa, and died an Admiral of France in 1854. It is noteworthy that among the *Swallow's* killed was a woman, the wife of one Phelan, a seaman on board. Purser Eugene Ryan, who volunteered to serve on deck, and Lieutenants Daniel O'Hea and John Theed (actg.) seem to have specially distinguished themselves.

During part of the year 1812, a squadron, under Captain Sir Home Riggs Popham, of the *Venerable*, 74, was stationed off the north coast of Spain to co-operate with the Spanish patriots against the French invaders of their country. In the middle of June, the French held the town of Lequeitio and a hill fort commanding it; and, as Popham did not wish to damage the town, and could make no impression on the fort with the *Venerable's* guns, he decided to erect a battery on a hill, supposed to be inaccessible, that dominated the whole place. On the 20th, therefore, Lieutenant James Groves assisting him, Captain the Hon. Duncombe Pleydell Bouverie, managed to land a gun through a breaking sea, and drag it, with enormous difficulty, to the top of the hill, from which it opened fire in the afternoon. By sunset, the wall of the fort was breached, and that evening some Spanish guerillas, after a preliminary repulse, stormed it. At night, the sea having gone down a little, the island of San Nicolas was occupied by seamen under Lieutenant Dowell O'Reilly, of the *Surveillante*, 38, Captain Sir George Ralph Collier, and by Marines from that frigate and from the *Medusa*, 32, Captain the Hon. D. P. Bouverie, and *Rhin*, 38, Captain Charles Malcolm, the last mentioned officer taking command of the island, and Captain Collier, of the *Venerable's* battery on the hill. Early on the 21st, the landing of other guns induced the French garrison, of about 290 survivors, to capitulate.[2]

The squadron subsequently moved along the coast to the west-

---

[1] James, vi. 70; Marshall, Supp., Pt. III. 240; *Nav. Chron.*, xxviii. 194.
[2] *Nav. Chron.*, xxviii. 74.

ward, destroying works at Bermeo, Plencia, Algorta, Bagona, Cam-
pillo las Queras, and Xebiles.[1] On July 6th, 7th, and 8th, Castro
Urdiales was reduced. On July 10th, a projected attack upon
Puerto Galletta had to be abandoned owing to the unexpected
strength of the enemy; but Commander Robert Bloye, of the
Lyra, 10, landed with Marines and destroyed some guns at Bagona.
Early on July 18th, guns and men were landed near Guetaria, under
Captains Malcolm and Bouverie, Lieutenant James Groves, and
Lieutenant (R.M.A.) Thomas Lewis Lawrence; and progress was
made towards the reduction of that place; but the approach of a
large body of French troops necessitated the destruction of two of
the landed guns, and the hurried re-embarkation of the party, 3
Midshipmen and 29 men being even then left behind.[2]

Another French convoy of 18 vessels, assembled in Laigueglia
and Alassio, was attacked on June 27th, by parties from the
Leviathan, 74, Captain Patrick Campbell (1), *Impérieuse*, 38, Captain
the Hon. Henry Duncan (3), *Curaçoa*, 36, Captain John Tower, and
Eclair, 18, Commander John Bellamy. The loss was heavy,
amounting to 9 killed and 31 wounded. As the vessels could not
be brought off, they were destroyed by the guns of the squadron.[3]

On July 3rd, Commander George Gustavus Lennock, of the
Raven, 16, saw fourteen brigs belonging to the Schelde division of
the invasion flotilla exercising to leeward of the Wielings. Lennock
stood in, to endeavour to cut out some of them. He eventually got
into action with the seven rearmost, three of which he drove on
shore. On the following morning they appeared to be bilged, and
the sea was breaking over them. The *Raven* suffered no loss,
although she performed the service within sight of a large French
squadron which lay off Flushing.[4]

Towards evening on July 4th, Lieutenant Richard William
Simmonds, in the *Attack*, 12, saw a transport-galliot, a sloop, and
a privateer leave Calais Harbour and begin to run along shore.
Anxious not to intimidate them either into putting back or into
beaching themselves, he made sail to windward, and when at some
distance from the enemy, detached his gig, containing six men
under the Second Master, Mr. — Couney. At midnight she found

---

[1] *Nav. Chron.*, xxviii. 78.
[2] *Ib.*, xxviii. 164.
[3] James, vi. 69; *Nav. Chron.*, xxviii. 167
[4] James, vi. 51; *Nav. Chron.*, xxviii. 78.

the galliot, in tow of the privateer, close under the French shore, and boarded the transport on one side while a party from the privateer did the same on the other. The French soon retreated, leaving the seven British in possession of the prize, yet under fire of the privateer and of the batteries on shore ; but Couney managed to rejoin the *Attack* with his capture ; nor was anyone of his little party hurt.[1]

On the evening of July 6th, the *Dictator*, 64, Captain James Pattison Stewart, *Calypso*, 18, Commander Henry Weir, *Podargus*, 14, Commander William Robilliard, and *Flamer*, 12, Lieutenant Thomas England, discovered a Danish squadron inside some rocks off Mardö, on the coast of Norway. This consisted of the *Nayaden*, 40, *Laaland*, 20, *Samsö*, 18, and *Kiel*, 18. Robilliard, who had on board a man who knew the locality, offered to lead in, but ran aground in doing so. Stewart left the *Flamer* to attend upon the *Podargus*, and stood on in the *Dictator*, with the *Calypso*. At about 8 P.M. an engagement began, the Danes being aided by several gunboats. At 9.30, after much difficult manœuvring in the narrowest waters, Stewart ran his ship, bows on, on shore in Lyngö creek, in a position where her broadside bore at short range upon the frigate and the three brigs. The *Calypso* was just astern of the 64, and the two British vessels opened so heavy a fire that in a very brief time the *Nayaden* was knocked to pieces, and the brigs were compelled to strike, while the gunboats were either sunk or driven off. But as soon as the *Dictator* had got afloat again, the gunboats rallied, until they were once more beaten off by the *Calypso*. In the meanwhile, the *Podargus* and *Flamer*, both of which were aground, were warmly engaged with other gunboats, and with some batteries on shore ; nor did they get off till they had been severely mauled. At 3 A.M. on the 7th, as the *Dictator* and *Calypso*, with their prizes, were working out, they were assailed by fresh gunboats, which were so posted among rocks that not a gun could be brought to bear upon them. In these circumstances the prizes had to be abandoned, and, as they had wounded men on board, they could not first be set on fire. The British loss was, naturally, heavy. The *Dictator* had 5 killed and 24 wounded ; the *Podargus*, 9 wounded ; the *Calypso*, 3 killed, 1 wounded, and 2 missing ; and the *Flamer*, 1 killed, and 1 wounded. The Danes, however, acknowledged a loss of 300 officers and men. For this

[1] James, vi. 56 ; *Nav. Chron.*, xxviii. 77.

gallant service Weir and Robilliard were posted, and Lieutenant William Buchannan, first of the *Dictator*, was made a Commander.[1]

On July 16th, being off Helgoland, the *Osprey*, 18, Commander Timothy Clinch, *Britomart*, 10, Commander William Buckley Hunt, and *Leveret*, 10, Commander George Wickens Willes, detached a boat from each, under Lieutenants William Henry Dixon, William Malone (2), and Francis Darby Romney, in chase of the French lugger privateer *Eole*, 14 (only 5 mounted), which, after a determined pursuit, and an obstinate final struggle, was boarded and carried by Dixon and Malone, Romney's boat having dropped astern in consequence of an accident. The British lost 2 killed and 12 wounded.[2]

On July 21st, the *Sealark*, 10, Lieutenant Thomas Warrand, while cruising off the Start, was apprised by signal from the shore of the presence of an enemy in the S.E. She chased in the direction indicated, and, after about three hours, came in sight of a privateer lugger, the *Ville de Caen*, 16, in hot pursuit of two merchantmen which were standing up Channel. The enemy, perceiving the *Sealark*, soon quitted her quarry, altered course, endeavoured to get away, and, finding that impossible, manœuvred to place herself to windward of the British schooner. Ere she could do so, Warrand ran her on board, began a close and furious engagement with her, and, when she set herself on fire by carelessness in the employment of hand-grenades, boarded and carried her, the boarders being bravely led by Master James Beaver (actg.). The privateer's crew numbered 75, and the schooner's only 60 men and boys. In this affair, which lasted for ninety minutes, the *Sealark* had 7 killed, and 22, including Warrand, wounded. The enemy suffered even more seriously, having 15 killed and 16 wounded. Warrand received well merited promotion.[3]

On June 28th, the *Briseis*, 10, Commander John Ross, stood into Pillau road to communicate with the British merchantman *Urania*, but found that she was in possession of French troops, who intended to destroy her, should the *Briseis* approach. Ross, there-

---

[1] James, vi. 53; *Nav. Chron.*, xxviii. 80. Weir's report mentions a '*Logan*,' 20 (? *Lügum*), as having been burnt, in addition to the *Nayaden*. Weir was posted, July 22nd, 1812; Robilliard, Dec. 14th, 1812.

[2] James, vi. 55; *Nav. Chron.*, xxviii. 164.

[3] James, vi. 52; *Nav. Chron.*, xxviii. 166. Warrand was made Com., Dec. 27th, 1812.

fore, tacked and stood off, and at midnight detached his pinnace, under Lieutenant Thomas Jones (2), with Midshipman William Palmer and 18 men, to try to recapture the vessel. The French on board had six guns and four swivels mounted, and fired as the boat approached ; but Jones succeeded in boarding, and in driving the enemy into their boats; and he then took the *Urania* out, having lost only 1 killed and 2 slightly wounded.[1]

On July 30th and August 1st an attack was made on Santander and the castle of Ano by the Marines of the squadron under Captain Willoughby Thomas Lake, of the *Magnificent*, 74, and Sir George Ralph Collier, in conjunction with Spanish guerillas. The castle was taken, but the garrison of the town, having been heavily re-inforced, repulsed all attempts against it ; and the naval brigade had to withdraw with loss, Lake and Collier being among the wounded. On August 3rd, however, the French evacuated the place, and a detachment of Marines from the British frigates took possession of it.[2]

On August 1st, while the *Horatio*, 38, Captain Lord George Stuart, was running down the coast of Norway, she saw an armed cutter disappearing among some rocks. Three boats, with about 80 people, under Lieutenants Abraham Mills Hawkins and Thomas James Poole Masters, were sent after her; and on the following day the Danish cutter *No.* 97, mounting six 4-prs., was found lying far up a creek, together with the schooner *No.* 114, mounting six 6-prs., and their prize, an American vessel. These craft were favourably disposed for resistance, and opened a warm fire as the boats approached ; but, after a bloody conflict, they were carried. The Danes, out of about 52 men engaged, had 10 killed and 13 wounded. The British lost 9 killed, including Lieutenant (R.M.) George Syder, and 16 wounded, including both Hawkins and Masters ; and two of the wounded never recovered. Hawkins, for his gallantry, was made a Commander on December 12th following.[3]

On August 11th, the *Menelaus*, 38, Captain Sir Peter Parker (2), Bart., saw several small craft and a large brig enter Port San Stefano, below Mt. Argentario, on the Tuscan coast. The harbour

---

[1] James, vi. 54; *Nav. Chron.*, xxviii. 83; 'Letters of B. Martin,' ii. 206, perhaps alludes to this, and a similar case.

[2] *Nav. Chron.*, xxviii. 171; James, vi. 61; Var. desps., etc., in Popham Papers (Auth.'s Coll.)

[3] James, vi. 56; *Nav. Chron.*, xxviii. 251.

was found to be defended by a 2-gun battery, a 4-gun battery, a
tower with one gun, and a citadel mounting 14 pieces, and the
enemy's craft lay close under the defences; yet Parker resolved
to cut them out, and to lead the attack in person. Having stood
to sea in order to put the Italians off their guard, he returned at
night, and took in his boats, which, however, missed their way
in the darkness, and had to return under a heavy fire. On the
night of the 13th, nevertheless, he renewed the attempt, stormed
the 4-gun battery by means of his Marines, brought out the brig,
and scuttled the other vessels. The only loss was Midshipman
Thomas Munro killed, and 5 men wounded.[1]

On August 10th, three small French privateers entered the port
of Benidorm, near Alicante, where they lay under the protection of
a fort mounting 24 guns. For further safety they were themselves
hauled on shore, and a battery was formed near them with six of
their guns. In these circumstances, the *Minstrel*, 20, Captain John
Strutt Peyton, and *Philomel*, 18, Commander Charles Shaw (2),
which had noted their entrance, could only blockade them, and
send in a boat nightly to row guard near them, and watch the
motions of their people. On August 12th it fell to Lieutenant
Michael Dwyer, with seven seamen, to go away in the boat. Dwyer
had made private inquiries, and had, as he thought, ascertained that
there were but thirty men in the battery and twenty in the fort;
and he courageously determined to attempt to carry the former by
surprise. At 9.30 P.M. he and his small party landed to the westward of the town, and were almost immediately challenged; but
Dwyer was able to reply in Spanish, and to divert suspicion. He
then advanced, seized the battery, in which were, not 30, but 80
Genoese; and, ere he could do more, found himself surrounded by
200 French soldiers. Against these the British defended themselves,
until one was killed, two, including Dwyer, were wounded, and no
ammunition remained. By a rush, in which all the rest of the
defenders, except one, were wounded, the French recaptured the
work. They were then unable to conceal their admiration for
Dwyer and his associates, whom General Goudin treated with
exceptional kindness. The General further invited Captain Peyton
to dine with him ashore, and to carry back the prisoners with him.
Peyton accepted the invitation; and thus closed an affair which was
equally to the honour of both sides.[2] Dwyer, though a Lieutenant

[1] James, vi. 73.   [2] James, vi. 71; Marshall, Supp., Pt. II. 441; O'Byrne, 320.

of March 21st, 1812, had not at the time received his commission, and was still doing duty as a Midshipman. He was wounded in no fewer than eighteen places, and permanently deprived of the use of his right arm. He was, it is true, given a pension for wounds, and was presented with a sword by the Patriotic Society; but, though he served with distinction on many subsequent occasions, he was not promoted to be Commander until 1842, when, having attended Queen Victoria to Scotland, he being then in the *Fearless*, he seems to have owed his tardy advancement to her Majesty's admiration for his gallantry of thirty years before.

On the night of August 18th, in the Kattegat, the *Attack*, 12, Lieutenant Richard William Simmonds, observed the approach of two craft which looked like gun-vessels. She cleared for action, and, at about 11.20 P.M., when nearly becalmed, was attacked by what were believed to be ten or twelve Danish gunboats. The engagement lasted till 1.40 A.M. on the 19th, when the Danes ceased firing. The *Attack* then set all sail and got out her sweeps, hoping to join the *Wrangler*, Lieutenant John Campbell Crawford, which had been attacked by other gunboats; but, owing to the current and lack of wind, Simmonds could not gain his object, and soon lost sight of the *Wrangler*. The *Attack* had already suffered severely, and had had two guns dismounted, so that when, while she was refitting, fourteen Danish gunboats (each carrying two long 24-prs. and two howitzers), and four large row-boats, enveloped her, she was obliged to strike at 3.20 A.M., after having fought gallantly for an hour and ten minutes. She was then in a sinking condition, and had lost 2 killed and 12 wounded, A court-martial most honourably acquitted Lieutenant Simmonds, his officers and men.[1]

On August 31st, Captain William Hoste, of the *Bacchante*, 38, being at anchor off Rovigno, in Istria, learnt that several vessels laden with timber were in the neighbouring Canale di Leme. That evening, therefore, he sent away five boats, containing 62 officers and men, under Lieutenants Donat Henchy O'Brien and Francis Gostling. Two merchantmen were captured near the mouth of the Canale, and from them O'Brien heard that the craft of which he was in search were protected by a 3-gun xebec and two gunboats. Leaving his prizes under Midshipman Thomas William Langton and 6 men, O'Brien pressed on with the rest of his party, and, without loss, took seven timber ships, besides the xebec *Tisi-*

---

[1] James, vi. 57; *Nav. Chron.*, xxviii. 433; Mins. of C. M., Sept. 19th, 1812.

phone, 3, and the two gunboats, one of which mounted 3 guns, and the other, 1.[1]

On September 2nd, off the mouth of the Mignone on the Roman coast, Captain Sir Peter Parker (2), Bart., of the *Menelaus*, 38, found a large letter of marque at anchor under two strong batteries. At night he despatched Lieutenant Rowland Mainwaring with two boats, which, without any loss, brought out the *St. Esprit*.[2] On the following day the *Menelaus* drove three sloops of war into Porto Ercole; and on the 4th, her boats cut out from under a heavy fire the *Fidèle*, a large French storeship, from the mouth of the lake of Orbetello, the only loss on that occasion being 1 killed and Sir Peter himself wounded.[3]

On September 8th, the schooner *Laura*, 12, Lieutenant Charles Newton Hunter, while taking possession of an American prize, off the mouth of the Delaware, saw a large French armed brig about three miles to leeward, and, having recalled her boat, bore up for the stranger. She was the privateer *Diligente*, Grassin master, then mounting 15 guns, 24-pr. carronades and long 12-prs., and having 97 men on board. The *Laura's* guns were but 18-pr. carronades and short 9-prs., and she had only 41 people on board. She began the attack at 3.55 P.M.; and the two vessels engaged with varying fortunes, until, after an hour's fighting, Hunter was seriously wounded. The officer on whom the command would have devolved, Midshipman John C—— Griffith, was also wounded, and no other was on board. The *Diligente's* crew then boarded and hauled down the schooner's colours. The *Laura* had 15 killed or severely wounded, the *Diligente* had 9 killed and 10 badly wounded. It is pretty obvious, therefore, that a most creditable defence had been made; and such was the view taken when Lieutenant Hunter was subsequently tried by court-martial at Halifax.[4]

In consequence of calms, the *Eagle*, 74, Captain Charles Rowley, lay at anchor off Punta della Maestra, at the mouth of the Po; and on the evening of September 16th, she detached her three barges, under Lieutenant Augustus Cannon, to intercept the enemy's coasting trade. Early on the 17th, Cannon saw a convoy of 23 sail, protected by a couple of gunboats, making for Goro road.

---

[1] James, vi. 74; *Nav. Chron.*, xxix. 82.
[2] James wrongly calls her *St. Juan*, and gives an incorrect date.
[3] James, vi. 74; *Nav. Chron.*, xxviii. 346.
[4] James, vi. 139; Mins. of C. M.

As the boats advanced, the convoy formed line, while the gunboats moved forward between them and the British, who, however, quickly carried the larger gunboat, turned her guns upon the second, and eventually captured the entire convoy except two craft. Lieutenant Thomas Colson Festing, who succeeded to the command when Cannon was mortally wounded, burnt six of his prizes, which he was utterly unable to man, and with the rest, including the gunboats, rejoined Rowley on the 17th. Besides Cannon, 1 man was killed, 1 was mortally wounded, and 3 were slightly hurt.[1] Cannon left two brothers, Midshipmen, in the *Eagle*. One of them, Roquier, who had passed his examination, was made a Lieutenant on January 26th following, but, apparently, died in 1815.

On September 18th, having chased a convoy in the passage between Vasto and the island of Tremiti, off the coast of Apulia, Captain William Hoste, of the *Bacchante*, 38, despatched his six boats, under Lieutenants Donat Henchy O'Brien and Silas Thomson Hood, to follow up the enemy, the wind having failed the frigate. The convoy, of eighteen merchantmen, anchored and hauled aground, having outside of it eight armed vessels, carrying among them eight long guns, six swivels, and 104 men. The attacking party numbered only 72, but it rowed in with such determination, and boarded with such dash, that the enemy fled incontinently, leaving the entire convoy to the victors. On this and other occasions Lieutenant William Haig (R.M.) greatly distinguished himself. Only two of the *Bacchante's* people were hurt.[2]

On the evening of September 29th, having learnt that six French vessels laden with shells for Peniscola lay in the harbour of Valencia, Captain John Strutt Peyton, of the *Minstrel*, 20, sent in his boats under Lieutenant George Thomas (2) and Midshipmen William Lewis (2), B—— S—— Oliver, and Charles Thomas Smith, to bring them out. Although the vessels were moored head and stern to the beach between two batteries, Thomas brought out four of them. He took a fifth, but a sudden squall drove her aground, and she was retaken with three of his men in her. His further loss amounted only to 1 man badly wounded.[3]

On December 18, 1812, the *Gloire*, 40, Captain A. R. Roussin, bound from Le Hâvre to the West Indies, was becalmed off the

---

[1] James, vi. 75; *Nav. Chron.*, xxix. 80.

[2] James, vi. 75; *Nav. Chron.*, xxix. 82.

[3] James, vi. 73; *Nav. Chron.*, xxviii. 431.

Lizard, and at daylight found herself in the midst of nine vessels, most of which were merchantmen, but which included the *Albacore*, 18, Commander Henry Thomas Davies, and the schooner *Pickle*, 14, Lieutenant William Figg. As soon as there was wind, the *Gloire*, in spite of her overwhelming force, made sail to escape. The *Albacore* chased and fired at her; but when, partially disabled in the unequal action, she ceased the pursuit, the Frenchman, instead of completing her discomfiture, wore, and proceeded westward. In this affair the *Albacore* had Lieutenant William Harman (3) killed, and 6 or 7 men wounded. When the *Pickle* closed and the *Albacore* had repaired damages, the *Borer*, 12, Lieutenant Richard Coote, and the cutter *Landrail*, 4, Lieutenant John Hill (3),[1] joined, and the chase was resumed. There was little firing, and, by midnight on December 19th, the frigate had run herself out of sight. On the 20th she captured the *Spy*, armed storeship, bound from Halifax. Having visited the West Indies, she returned to Europe, and, in the chops of the Channel, on February 25th, 1813, fell in with the *Linnet*, 14, Lieutenant John Treacy.[2] Treacy tried to out-manœuvre his huge opponent, and handled his little vessel with extraordinary skill, managing even to brush away the frigate's jib-boom; but after a little more than an hour's action, the brig was obliged to surrender. On May 31st, 1814, a court-martial honourably acquitted Treacy, and complimented him on his conduct, and, on June 11th following, the gallant Lieutenant was made a Commander.[3]

On December 21st, 1812, off the coast of Apulia, the *Apollo*, 38, Captain Bridges Watkinson Taylor, and *Weazel*, 18, Commander James Black, chased a trabacolo under the tower of St. Cataldo, a work containing three carriage guns, three swivels, and a telegraph. The boats were sent in, under Lieutenants George Bowen (4), and Michael Quin, and the tower was carried without loss. It was then blown up.[4]

At dawn on January 6th, 1813, when the *Bacchante*, 38, Captain William Hoste, and *Weazel*, 18, Commander James Black, lay becalmed to the S.E. of Cape d'Otranto, at the mouth of the Adriatic, five French gunboats [5] were discovered, three in the S.W. making for Otranto, and two in the S.E., heading eastward. Hoste signalled to

---

[1] Lieut., May 4th, 1810.
[2] In some lists spelt Tracey and Tracy.
[3] James, vi. 158; *Nav. Chron.*, xxxi. 487; Mins. of C. M.
[4] James, vi. 175; *Nav. Chron.*, xxix. 507.
[5] For names, *see* Appendix.

the *Weazel* to attend to the smaller division, and sent after the larger one his own boats, under Lieutenants Donat Henchy O'Brien, Silas Thomson Hood, and Francis Gostling, with Lieutenant (R.M.) William Haig, Master's Mates George Eyre Powell[1] and James M'Kean, and Midshipmen the Hon. Henry John Rous, the Hon. William Waldegrave (3), Thomas Edward Hoste, James Leonard Few, and Edward O—— Pocock. O'Brien, in the barge, overhauled and captured the sternmost gunboat, and left it to young Hoste, who secured his prisoners, and then worked the bow gun of his prize against her late friends, which also were presently taken, astonishing to say, without loss to the British. The *Weazel*, not being able to get up with the smaller division, sent in chase two boats under Lieutenant Thomas Whaley and Midshipman James Stewart (6), and a boat belonging to the *Bacchante*, under Master's Mate Edward Webb.[2] This last boat, ere her consorts could overtake her, captured the two gunboats successively, and had no one hurt.[3]

On January 6th, on the Adriatic coast of Italy, some boats of the *Havannah*, 36, Captain the Hon. George Cadogan, under Lieutenant William Hamley, attacked and carried the French gunboat, *No.* 8, in face of a heavy musketry fire from the shore to which she was made fast. Three merchantmen were taken at the same, the British loss amounting to Master's Mate Edward Percival killed, and 2 men wounded.[4]

On January 18th, Rear-Admiral Thomas Francis Fremantle, commanding in the Adriatic, sent the *Apollo*, 38, Captain Bridges Watkinson Taylor, accompanied by the privateer, *Esperanza*, and four gunboats, with 250 troops,[5] under Lieutenant-Colonel Robertson, to attack the island of Lagosta, which surrendered on the 29th. The conduct of Lieutenant George Bowen (4), Purser Thomas Ullock, and Midshipmen William Henry Brand, William Hutchison (2),[6] and William David Folkes, on the occasion, was much praised. Having garrisoned Lagosta, the *Apollo* and her consorts[7] sailed on February 1st for the neighbouring island of Curzola; and on the same night, a body of seamen, Marines, and soldiers, was

---

[1] Lieut., Jan. 22nd, 1813.

[2] Lieut., June 14th, 1813.

[3] James, vi. 170; *Nav. Chron.*, xxix. 336; Marshall, Supp., Pt. IV., 278; IV. Pt. II. 245.

[4] James, vi. 175; *Nav. Chron.*, xxx. 76.   [5] Of 35th Regt.

[6] Lieut., Feb. 8th, 1815.

[7] *Imogene*, 14, Lieut. Charles Taylor (actg. Com.), and g. b. *No.* 43.

landed near the principal town. Finding, when he had occupied
the suburbs, that the enemy still attempted to hold the place, Taylor
took off his seamen, and, on February 3rd, attacked and silenced the
sea batteries, whereupon the island capitulated. The conquest cost
the British 2 killed and 1 slightly wounded.[1]

On February 2nd, at daylight, Fano bearing S.S.E., the *Kingfisher*, 18, Commander Ewell Tritton, saw several vessels near
Merlera steering south. As there was but little wind, he detached
two boats, under Lieutenant George H—— Palmer (actg.) and
Gunner John Waller; and these, after a five hours' chase, captured
a trabacolo, and drove ashore on Corfu nine others, five of which
were totally destroyed. The boats had 2 killed and 7 badly
wounded.[2]

It is convenient here to trace the adventures of two French
frigates, which sailed from Nantes on a cruise on November 25th,
1812. These were the *Aréthuse*, 40, Commodore Pierre François
Henri Etienne Bouvet, and *Rubis*, 40, Captain Louis François
Ollivier. Having picked up a Portuguese prize, the *Serra*, they
made, in January, 1213, for the coast of Africa; and, on the 27th of
that month, when off the Los Islands,[3] the *Rubis*, being the leading
ship, discovered and chased the *Daring*, 12, Lieutenant William
R—— Pascoe. The latter, taking the Frenchman for a British
frigate, sent his Master in a boat to board her. The Master, on
discovering his error, tried to get away, but was captured. The
Daring, thus made aware of her peril, crowded sail for the Los
Islands, upon one of which she ran herself ashore, and was burnt by
her crew. That evening the frigates anchored in the road, and learnt
that a British frigate was at anchor in the river of Sierra Leone.
The French refitted in a leisurely manner, and did not weigh until
February 4th. That day the *Aréthuse* struck on a coral bank, and
lost her rudder; and on the 5th, being still among the islands, the
Rubis also struck, and, as she was unable to free herself, began to
transfer her crew to the *Serra*. The *Aréthuse*, in the interval,
repaired and reshipped her rudder. Such was the situation at dawn
on February 6th.

In the meantime, Lieutenant Pascoe, and some of his people, had
managed to reach Freetown, where lay the *Amelia*, 38, Captain the

[1] James, vi. 175; *Nav. Chron.*, xxx. 80.

[2] James, vi. 174.

[3] Properly Islas de los Idolos; still a British dependency of Sierra Leone.

Hon. Frederick Paul Irby, and had reported that he had left " three French frigates " off the Los Islands. The *Amelia* at once began to prepare for action. That evening she was joined by the merchant schooner *Hawk*, with some more of the *Daring's* men; and, on January 30th, the *Amelia's* launch carronade having been put on board the *Hawk*, Pascoe went away in that vessel to reconnoitre. He returned on February 2nd with the names of the enemy's frigates and their prize, and with news of Bouvet's intention to put to sea immediately in order to prey upon commerce. On the day following, a cartel, sent by Bouvet, with a few prisoners for exchange, arrived, and confirmed the intelligence; and, without further delay, the *Amelia* weighed, and proceeded in search of the French, although her crew was sickly, and she was obviously no match for the force which her Captain believed to be awaiting him. Very early on the 6th she spoke the colonial schooner *Princess Charlotte*, and, an hour or two later, she sighted the French vessels in the N.E., one being about 12 miles from the islands, and the other aground, transferring her people to the *Serra*. Irby thereupon sent the *Princess Charlotte* to Sierra Leone to direct any British man-of-war that might call there to join him instantly; and he himself bore away to reconnoitre. At 3.20 P.M. the *Aréthuse* was observed to weigh; but, unaware that the *Rubis* was aground, Irby did not invite an encounter, and kept on and off all night, and until the evening of the 7th, when, having drawn the *Aréthuse* to some distance from her consorts, he wore, and steered to cross his opponent's stern. It was then 7.20 P.M., with a smooth sea, moderate wind, and brilliant moon. Bouvet tacked to avoid being raked; but, a little later, the Frenchman was brought to close action. Owing to injuries aloft, the *Amelia* unintentionally fell on board the *Aréthuse*, which opened a heavy musketry fire, and threw hand grenades, with a view to preparing the way for an attempt to board. This aim was, however, frustrated by the fire of the *Amelia's* Marines; and the *Aréthuse*, throwing all aback, dropped clear. The unmanageable state of the *Amelia*, nevertheless, presently brought the two frigates again into contact, broadside to broadside; and, from about 9.15 P.M., the two crews fired, and slashed at one another through the ports, until the concussion of the guns drove the ships apart. They continued the engagement so long as they were within gunshot; but all firing ceased at about 11.20 P.M. Irby says that the *Aréthuse* bore up, the *Amelia* being ungovernable. Bouvet says

that the *Amelia* crowded sail, and abandoned the field to him.   It
seems likely enough that the frigates merely drifted out of range of
one another.   No matter what may have occurred to separate them,
the action was certainly well fought, as the following facts will
prove.

The *Amelia* appears to have had on board, including the people
of the *Daring*, 319 men and boys.   Of these she lost no fewer than
51 killed or mortally wounded, including Lieutenants John James
Bate, John Pope, George Wells, and William R—— Pascoe (of the
Daring), Lieutenant (R.M.) Robert G—— Grainger, Midshipman
Charles Kennicott, and Purser John Bogue.   She had, moreover,
90 wounded, including Captain Irby, Lieutenant William Reeve,
Master Anthony de Mayne, Lieutenant (R.M.) John Simpson,
Purser John Collman, Boatswain John Parkinson, Master's Mate
Edward Robinson, and Midshipmen George Albert Rix, Thomas
D—— Buckle, George Thomas Gooch, and Arthur Beever.   All her
masts and yards were badly wounded, and her hull was shattered.
As for the *Aréthuse*, she apparently had on board about 340 men, of
whom 31 were killed and 74 wounded.   She also was terribly cut
about aloft, and otherwise well mauled.   The relative force of the
combatants, as stated by James, was :—

			Amelia	*Aréthuse*
Broadside guns	{ No.	24	22
	{ lbs.	549	463
Crew		319	340
Size	tons.	1059	1073

At daylight on the 8th the frigates were about five miles apart.
When a breeze sprang up, the *Aréthuse* stood back to the Los
Islands, and the *Amelia* made sail for Madeira and England.   The
Aréthuse was joined on the 10th by the *Serra*, with the crew of
the *Rubis*; and, with the prize in tow, she steered for France.
On the way, however, Bouvet took the people out of the *Serra*
and destroyed her.   On April 19th, having made in all about 15
prizes, he reached St. Malo.   The *Amelia* had anchored at Spithead
on March 22nd.[1]

In the early morning of February 14th, the *Bacchante*, 38,
Captain William Hoste, sent her barge, armed and manned, under
Lieutenant Silas Thomson Hood, in pursuit of a vessel which was

---

[1] James, vi. 183; *Nav. Chron.*, xxix. 243, 256; Marshall, ii. 492.

seen to be making for Otranto. Hood poured in a fire of round shot and musketry, and then boarded and carried the French gunboat *Alcinoüs*, 2, the only person hurt on the British side being Hood himself. The French had 2 killed and 9 wounded. In this affair, Lieutenant (R.M.) William Haig, and Master's Mates William Lee Rees [1] and Charles Bruce distinguished themselves. The prize, owing to her damaged condition, had to be destroyed.[2]

Works having been thrown up by the enemy at Pietra Nera, on the coast of Calabria, and a convoy of about 50 armed vessels, including many Neapolitan gunboats, with stores for Naples, having been assembled there, Captain Robert Hall (2),[3] R.N., who commanded the Sicilian flotilla at Messina, volunteered to attack the position. With two divisions of gunboats, and four companies of the 75th Regt., supplied by Lieutenant-General Lord William C. Bentinck, at Palermo, he arrived off the port just before daylight on February 14th, and landed about 150 men under Major Stewart, and some seamen under Lieutenant Francis Le Hunte, who charged and carried a well-defended height above the beach. The flotilla cannonaded the batteries without much result, and Hall had to order them also to be stormed by Le Hunte and some seamen. By 8 A.M., everything was in possession of the assailants, and about 150 of the enemy had been killed or wounded, and 163 made prisoners. The best of the vessels were launched and brought off, and the rest were burnt. Hall praised the behaviour of Captain Imbert, Neapolitan Navy, and of Le Hunte, as well as that of Major Stewart (75th Regt.), who fell in the assault. The Navy's loss was 2 killed and 7 wounded.[4]

On February 26th, acting in pursuance of orders from Vice-Admiral Sir Edward Pellew, the *Thames*, 32, Captain Charles Napier (2), and *Furieuse*, 36, Captain William Mounsey, with the 2nd Batt. of the 10th Regt. on board, suddenly bore up for the narrow entrance of the harbour of Ponza, on the island of that name, off the coast of Naples, and, returning the fire of the batteries on both side, anchored across the mole-head. Lieut.-Colonel J. P. Coffin, with the troops, then landed. This demonstration, and the heavy fire from the ships, induced the governor to hoist a flag of

---

[1] Lieut., Sept. 15th, 1813.

[2] James, vi. 171.

[3] Com., June 27th, 1808; Capt., March 4th, 1811; C.B. 1815; Kt.; died, Feb. 7th, 1818.

[4] James, vi. 169; *Nav. Chron.*, xxix. 344.

truce, and eventually to surrender. In this dashing affair no British life was lost, although the batteries mounted ten 24- and 18-prs., and two 9-in. mortars.[1] It was in recollection of this exploit that Napier assumed the name of Don Carlos de Ponza when, in 1833, he accepted command of the Portuguese fleet.

On March 14th, Lieutenant Francis Banks (2), of the *Blazer*, 14, who was senior officer of the small force stationed off Helgoland, learnt that the French at Cuxhaven were in a distressed condition, and that the Russians had entered Hamburg. He therefore took the *Brevdrageren*, 14, Lieutenant Thomas Barker Devon, under his orders, and proceeded up the Elbe in order to annoy the enemy to the best of his ability. At Cuxhaven, 20 French gun-vessels were found in the act of being destroyed. On the 16th, by invitation from the shore, Banks landed with 32 soldiers, whom he had embarked at Helgoland, and took possession of the batteries there. On the 20th, while the brigs were still off Cuxhaven, Devon volunteered to go up the river, with a boat from each vessel, in search of a privateer which was believed to lie there. His offer being accepted, he departed, and off Brunsbüttel, at daylight on the 21st, found two large galliots at anchor. He at first believed them to be merchantmen, but, on approaching, found them to be gunboats,[2] and was fired at, the craft hoisting Danish colours. Devon, however, boarded the nearest galliot in the smoke of a second discharge, and, with his brother, Midshipman Frederick Devon, and 8 men only, captured without loss the Danish gunboat *Unge Troutman*, 5. The second boat, under Master William Dunbar, arriving, the prisoners were secured, and sail was made after the other galliot, which had cut and made for Brunsbüttel. The prize gained upon the chase, but, as the wind was light, Dunbar, with 11 men, was sent in a boat to cut off the fugitive, which, on being captured without opposition, proved to be the *Liebe*, 5. Devon was deservedly promoted on May 4th following.[3]

On March 18th, the *Undaunted*, 38, Captain Thomas Ussher, chased a tartan under a battery about fifteen miles to the westward of Marseilles. Lieutenant Aaron Tozer offering to destroy the work, a landing was effected under him, Lieutenant Thomas Salkeld (actg.), Master Robert Clennan, and Lieutenant (R.M.) Harry Hunt,

---

[1] James, vi. 169; *Nav. Chron.*, xxx. 71; 'Life of Napier,' i. 62.
[2] Each of two long 18-prs., and three 12-pr. carrs., with 25 men.
[3] James, vi. 156; *Nav. Chron.*, xxix. 335.

and the battery was carried in a few minutes, with a loss to the British of but 2 killed and 1 wounded.[1]

Between that date and March 30th, the *Undaunted* joined the *Volontaire*, 38, Captain the Hon. Granville George Waldegrave (senior officer), and the *Redwing*, 18, Commander Sir John Gordon Sinclair, Bart. On the day last named, the three vessels discovered fourteen merchantmen at anchor in the little harbour of Morgiou, between Marseilles and Toulon, and at night, Lieutenant Isaac Shaw, and Lieutenants (R.M.) William Burton and Harry Hunt, went in with the boats to cut out the convoy. Landing at Sour-miou, to the westward of the port, the party marched across the hills, and, on the morning of the 31st, carried two batteries in the rear of the place, destroying the guns and ammunition. Other boats, under Lieutenant Dey Richard Syer, in spite of the opposi-tion of two field-pieces, brought out eleven vessels laden with oil, and destroyed some more. The service was performed with a loss of 1 killed and 4 wounded. In addition to those already named, Midshipman Christopher Wyvill [2] is mentioned in terms of great praise.[3]

On March 22nd, the boats of the *Havannah*, 36, Captain the Hon. George Cadogan, under Lieutenant William Hamley, assisted by Lieutenant (R.M.) William Hockly, took a 3-gun trabacolo, and destroyed another, in front of the town of Vasto, on the coast of the Abruzzi. On the 26th of the same month, off the town of Fortore, Hamley and Hockly took five armed trabacolos, and five feluccas laden with salt, from under the protection of a strong body of troops and some guns, and lost but 2 men wounded in the affair. And on June 27th, Hamley led the *Havannah's* boats in an attack on ten merchantmen lying under an 8-gun battery at Vasto, and brought off all of them. On that occasion he had 3 men slightly hurt.[4]

On the night of April 11th, Captain Bridges Watkinson Taylor, of the *Apollo*, 38, sent three boats of that frigate, and two of the *Cerberus*, 32, Captain Thomas Garth, to take temporary possession of Devil's Island, near the north entrance to Corfu. A grain-laden brig and trabacolo were captured there. On the 14th of the same

[1] James, vi. 166 ; *Nav. Chron.*, xxx. 75.
[2] Lieut., July 5th, 1813.
[3] James, vi. 167 ; *Nav. Chron.*, xxx. 74.
[4] James, vi. 175 ; *Nav. Chron.*, xxx. 238, 436.

month the two frigates chased a vessel which escaped into Merlera.
The five boats above mentioned had already proceeded to attack her,
when Taylor, aware of the strength of the island, sent to order them
to wait until the *Apollo* should come up.   The message, however,
arrived too late ; and, in the fight which ensued, Lieutenant Edward
Hollingworth Delafosse and Purser Thomas Ullock were wounded.
On the arrival of the *Apollo* the Marines were landed, the island,
after a little skirmishing, was taken, and eight grain-laden vessels
were found to have been scuttled to save them from falling into
British hands.[1]

On April 17th, the *Mutine*, 16, Commander Nevinson de Courcy,
fell in with the privateer *Invincible*, 16, in the bay.   While chasing,
the *Mutine* was temporarily disabled, but, refitting, began a running
fight, which lasted for upwards of two hours.   She then closed, and,
after fifty minutes' further action, reduced her enemy.   The *Mutine*
had but 2 people wounded.[2]

A piece of gallant and excellently conducted work was done in
April by the *Weazel*, 18, Commander James Black.   On the 22nd
of that month, at dawn, she was cruising E.N.E. of the island of
Zirona [3] when she saw and chased a convoy which was making for
the ports of Trau and Spalato, in Dalmatia.   As the brig-sloop
approached, the enemy separated, the greater number, with ten
gunboats, bearing up for the Bay of Bassoglina.   The *Weazel* held
on after these, which ultimately anchored in line about a mile from
the shore, and hoisted French colours as they opened fire.   She was
considerably damaged as she entered the bay, but at 6 A.M. she
anchored with springs within pistol shot, and began a furious action.
In twenty minutes she forced her opponents to cut, and run further
in ; but they opened fire again from their new position, aided by
three guns and about 200 troops on the heights above the *Weazel*.
So the fight continued until 10 A.M., when three of the gunboats
had struck, two were ashore, and one had been sunk.   The remaining
four gunboats were then reinforced by four more, which came from
the eastward, and anchored outside the *Weazel*, thus obliging her to
engage on both sides for a time, though presently the outer gunboats ran in and joined their consorts.   The whole then retired

---

[1] James, vi. 176 ; *Nav. Chron.*, xxx. 239.

[2] James, vi. 160 ; *Nav. Chron.*, xxix, 436.

[3] James misspells many of these names, writing Zirana, Spalatro, Boscalina, etc.
The spelling given is after Andree.

behind a point of land, and, while their hulls were protected by it, fired at the sloop across it. This state of affairs lasted until 3 P.M., when the fire temporarily ceased; but it was renewed at 3.40, and carried on without further interruption until 6.30.

The *Weazel* was at that hour a wreck, a few yards from a lee shore, her anchors destroyed or rendered useless, her hold half full of water, and her pumps shot away. She had, moreover, already lost 25 killed or wounded. Nevertheless, Black, in the darkness, sent in his boats and destroyed such of the gunboats as had struck or were ashore, besides eight of the convoy. His people also brought off some anchors, by means of which the sloop was enabled to warp herself out. Yet her troubles were not over. At daybreak on the 23rd, ere she was well clear, she was again attacked by the gunboats, which raked her, and to which she could make no proper reply. All that day and the following night she continued to warp out slowly and laboriously, her people being half dead from fatigue. At noon on the 24th, the enemy opened on her from a battery on a point close to which she had to pass, and the gunboats pulled out astern of her; but at 5 P.M., after receiving a broadside, the boats sheered off, and did not again molest the *Weazel*. The plucky sloop's total loss was 5 killed, including Boatswain James Toby, and 25 wounded, including Black,[1] Lieutenant Thomas Whaley, Master's Mate William Simkin, and Midshipman James Steuart.[2]

At daylight, on April 24th, Captain Taylor, of the *Apollo*, landed thirty Marines at St. Cataldo, in southern Apulia, under Lieutenants (R.M.) John Tothill and Colin Campbell, dislodged some troops who had just before been disembarked there, made 26 prisoners, killed 1 and wounded several, and brought out the felucca which had disembarked them, all without loss.[3]

On April 29th, the boats of the *Elizabeth*, 74, Captain Edward Leveson Gower, and *Eagle*, 74, Captain Charles Rowley, under Lieutenants Mitchell Roberts, Richard Greenaway, and Thomas Holbrook, met with seven oil-laden merchantmen off Goro, near the mouth of the Po. Four were captured. The rest ran themselves ashore under the protection of a 2-gun battery, two schooners, and three gunboats, that opened a heavy fire; yet one of the

---

[1] Posted, July 29th, 1813; C.B., 1815; died 1835, still a Captain.
[2] James, vi. 173; *Nav. Chron.*, xxx. 169.
[3] James, vi. 176; *Nav. Chron.*, xxx. 239.

craft was brought off, and another was destroyed, without casualty.[1]

On May 2nd, the Marines of the *Repulse*, 74, Captain Richard Hussey Moubray, *Volontaire*, and *Undaunted*, under Captain (R.M.) Edward Michael Ennis, were landed to destroy some newly erected works near Morgiou, while the boats of the same ships, under Lieutenant Isaac Shaw, covered by the launches, and by the *Redwing*, brought out some craft from the port. A detachment of French troops was driven to the heights, the batteries were blown up, and nine small laden vessels were captured, all with a loss of only 2 killed, and 4, including Lieutenant Shaw,[2] wounded.[3]

On May 11th, Captain William Hoste, of the *Bacchante*, received information that an enemy's convoy was lying in the Canale di Carlopago, on the coast of Croatia; and he accordingly arrived off the port on the 15th. By that time the convoy had disappeared, but, since the works of Carlopago afforded excellent shelter, he brought up within pistol-shot of the batteries, and opened a heavy fire. Upon the surrender of the place, a party, under Lieutenant Silas Thomson Hood, landed, blew up the fort, destroyed the public buildings, and carried off eight guns. The *Bacchante*, on this occasion, had 4 men badly wounded.[4]

Between May 10th and May 15th, largely owing to the careful "shepherding" of the *Euryalus*, 36, Captain Charles Napier (2), about twenty French coasters were collected in Cavalaire road, between Hyères and Fréjus. Early on May 16th, Captain Edward Brace, of the *Berwick*, 74, detached the boats of his ship, and of the *Euryalus*, under Lieutenants Henry Johnston Sweedland and Alexander Albert Sandilands, with the Marines of both vessels, under Captain (R.M.) William T. J. Matthews, to take the convoy. The covering batteries were stormed, the national xebec *Fortune*, 10, was abandoned and captured, and all the craft in the road were either carried off or destroyed, the total British casualties being no more than 1 killed and 1 missing.[5]

On May 17th, in the absence of the *Apollo*, which was watering, the *Cerberus*, 32, Captain Thomas Garth, discovered an enemy under the land to the southward of Brindisi, and, chasing her,

[1] James, vi. 177; *Nav. Chron.*, xxx. 255.   [2] Com., August 9th, 1813.
[3] James, vi. 167; *Nav. Chron.*, xxx. 79.
[4] James, vi. 171; *Nav. Chron.*, xxx. 255.
[5] James, vi. 167; *Nav. Chron.*, xxx. 77; 'Life of Napier,' i. 65.

caused her to run ashore under a martello tower. Three boats from the *Cerberus* were at once sent in, under Lieutenant John William Montagu, with two belonging to the *Apollo*, under Lieutenant William Henry Nares; and the vessel, which mounted a 6-pounder and a swivel, was brought out without loss, the troops who had come down to protect her being driven up country. On the 18th, the boats carried off a gun from a martello tower somewhat to the southward.[1]

A BRITISH FRIGATE UNDER ALL SAIL.

(*From an etching by E. W. Cooke, R.A.*, 1828.)

On May 27th, observing in Otranto a convoy which, it was expected, would make for Corfu with the first favourable wind, Captain Thomas Garth, with the *Cerberus*, took up a station off Fano, having first sent in two boats from the *Cerberus*, and two belonging to the *Apollo*, under Lieutenants John William Montagu and William Henry Nares, to lie in wait under the Apulian shore. At 1 A.M. on the 28th, the convoy came out, protected by eight gunboats; yet, in spite of the inequality of force, the boats attacked them with great determination. Nares boarded and carried one;

[1] James, vi. 176; *Nav. Chron.*, xxx. 257.

Midshipman William Hutchison (2) mastered another. In attempting a third, Master's Mate Thomas Richard Suett was shot through the heart. He, and 1 seaman, were the only British killed, and but one other person was wounded. Each of the captured gunboats mounted three guns. Four of the convoy were taken also.[1]

The British squadron co-operating with the patriots on the north coast of Spain was under the orders of Sir George Ralph Collier, of the *Surveillante*, 38, who, in May, when Castro Urdiales was pressed by the French, detached the *Lyra*, 10, Commander Robert Bloye, *Royalist*, 18, Commander James John Gordon Bremer, and *Sparrow*, 16, Commander Joseph Needham Tayler, to assist in defending the place. The enemy, however, was in too great force, and the British officers were fortunate in being able to bring off the garrison of about 1150 men, and convey it safely to Bermeo. In performing this service the squadron had 10 people wounded, including Lieutenant Samuel Kentish, and Midshipman Charles Thomas Sutton. Castro Urdiales was then rigorously blockaded, until, on June 22nd, the French evacuated it, after committing horrible excesses, and retired to Santoña. Commander Joseph Needham Tayler[2] took possession of, and garrisoned the castle.

Collier's force also co-operated with General Graham in the reduction of San Sebastian, a detachment of seamen being landed on July 10th, under the orders of Lieutenant Dowell O'Reilly.[3] On August 31st, two divisions of boats, under Commanders James Galloway and Robert Bloye,[4] were sent to make a diversion, while some of the men-of-war stood into the harbour, and a general assault was made from the land side. These combined movements resulted in the occupation of the town, early in the afternoon, though the citadel still held out. That day Commander John Smith (5), of the *Beagle*, and three or four seamen, were wounded. On September 8th, the batteries opened on the citadel; and, in a very short time, terms of capitulation were proposed and agreed to. In these operations, in addition to the vessels above named, the *Ajax*, 74, Captain Robert Waller Otway (1), *Revolutionnaire*, 38, Captain John Charles Woollcombe, *Freja*, 36, Commander William Isaac Scott, *Andromache*, 36, Captain George Tobin, *President*, 38, Captain Francis Mason, *Dispatch*, 18, Commander James Galloway, *Challenger*, 18, Commander Frederick Edward Venables Vernon,

---

[1] James, vi. 177; *Nav. Chron.*, xxx. 257.
[2] Posted, August 16th, 1813.
[3] Com., Sept. 23rd, 1813.
[4] Posted, Sept. 23rd, 1813.

Magicienne, 36, Captain the Hon. William Gordon (2), *Constant*, 12, Lieutenant John Stokes, schooners *Holly*, and *Juniper*, Lieutenant Nathaniel Vassall, cutter *Nimble*, and two gunboats (*Nos.* 14 and 16) took part. Among the officers mentioned as having distinguished themselves were Lieutenants the Hon. James Arbuthnot and Robert Graham Dunlop, and Midshipmen Digby Marsh, George Harvey, Henry Bloye, and William Lawson.[1]

More than once in the course of 1812 and 1813 did Lieutenant George Canning, acting Commander of the *Kite*, 16, come into conflict in the Mediterranean with Turkish subjects, whom, rightly or wrongly, he believed to be pirates, but whom he failed to prove to be so. His proceedings, dictated no doubt by somewhat mis-directed zeal, ended on June 5th, 1813, in a serious catastrophe. He attacked some supposed pirates on the island of Chiliodromia, in the northern Sporades, and sent in his boats to destroy their vessels. The natives, who had taken up positions on commanding heights, attacked the party by rolling down huge boulders on it, the result being that, out of 40 officers and men employed, no fewer than 20 were killed and 18 wounded, among the former being Lieutenant C—— Williams. Canning was superseded on July 23rd, but pro-moted on June 15th, 1814.[2]

On the forenoon of the 11th, the *Eagle*, 74, Captain Charles Rowley, attacked Farasina, on the island of Cherso. The works, mounting five 18-prs., were cannonaded, and then stormed and carried by seamen and Marines under Lieutenants Richard Green-away and William Hotham (3), and Lieutenant (R.M.) Samuel Lloyd. The guns were disabled and the batteries ruined, with a loss to the party of only Midshipman John Hudson (3) wounded.[3]

On June 8th, the town of Umago, on the Istrian coast, was captured by a party from the *Elizabeth*, 74, Captain Edward Leveson Gower, and *Eagle*, 74, Captain Charles Rowley, under Captain (R.M.) John Hore Graham, and Lieutenants (R.M.) Thomas Price and Samuel Lloyd, while the boats, under Lieu-tenants Mitchell Roberts, Martin Bennet, Richard Greenaway, and William Hotham (3), destroyed a 2-gun battery, and brought off four vessels. Only 1 man was wounded.[4]

---

[1] James, vi. 165; *Nav. Chron.*, xxx. 77, 236, 240, 247, 259, 351.

[2] *Nav. Chron.*, xxxi. 26; Marshall, IV. Pt. I., 236.

[3] James, vi. 179.

[4] James, vi. 178; *Nav. Chron.*, xxx. 434.

At daylight on June 12th, the *Bacchante* discovered an enemy's convoy under the town of Giulianova, on the coast of the Abruzzi. The frigate being some miles to leeward, the wind light, and the currents adverse, Captain Hoste detached his boats, under Lieutenant Silas Thomson Hood, with discretionary orders, either to attack or to await the *Bacchante's* arrival. Hood found the enemy stronger than had been anticipated. There were seven large gunboats, each mounting a long 18-pr., three smaller gunboats, each with a 4-pr., and fourteen sail of merchantmen, four of which were armed; and in rear of the convoy were troops with two field pieces. In spite of this display of force, and although he himself was half crippled from the effects of his injury of February 14th, Hood dashed in under a withering fire, and drove the people from the vessels and the troops from the beach, taking and destroying the field pieces. The whole convoy was captured, only 3 men being killed and 6 wounded on the side of the attack. Among those mentioned as having distinguished themselves were Lieutenants Francis Gostling, and Edward Webb (acting), Lieutenants (R.M.) Charles Holmes and William Haig, Master's Mates William Lee Rees and James M'Kean, and Midshipmen James Rowe, Thomas Edward Hoste, Francis George Farewell, the Hon. William Waldegrave (3), and Thomas William Langton, and Mr. Samuel Richardson.[1]

On June 17th, Commander John Harper, of the *Saracen*, 18, with Lieutenant William Holmes (2)[2] and Lieutenant (R.M.) Edward Hancock, and boats containing 40 men, effected a landing on the island of Giuppana,[3] off the Dalmatian coast, and, after some skirmishing, made himself master of the place, capturing 36 prisoners, and the commandant of Giuppana and the neighbouring island of Mezzo. No one of the attacking party received more than trivial wounds.[4] Mezzo itself was taken by the *Saracen*, and *Weazel*, 18, Commander James Black, on July 22nd.[5]

At dawn on June 20th, Captain Edward Leveson Gower, of the *Elizabeth*, 74, landed a body of seamen and Marines, under Lieutenants Mitchell Roberts and Martin Bennet, and Captain

---

[1] James, vi. 172; *Nav. Chron.*, xxx. 258. Mr. Richardson was not promoted to be Lieut. till July 25th, 1828. James calls him a Mid.; but he was not one until after 1813.

[2] Com., August 19th, 1815; drowned in *Arab*, December 12th, 1823.

[3] The *Gazette* wrongly says Zapano, and James follows it.

[4] James, vi. 177; *Nav. Chron.*, xxx. 435.

[5] *Nav. Chron.*, xxx. 511.

(R.M.) John Hore Graham and Lieutenant (R.M.) Thomas Price. Assisted by armed boats, under Lieutenant Henry Richard Bernard, the party captured the town of Dignano, in Istria, and made prisoners of its small French garrison, without losing a man.[1]

In 1813 Fiume was not a place of as much strength as it is now. It was nevertheless of much local importance. On July 3rd, Rear-Admiral Thomas Francis Fremantle, in the *Milford*, 74, Captain John Duff Markland, with the *Elizabeth*, 74, Captain Edward Leveson Gower, *Eagle*, 74, Captain Charles Rowley, *Bacchante*, 38, Captain William Hoste, and *Haughty*, 12, Lieutenant James Harvey, weighed from an anchorage about four miles from the port. Dropping the *Haughty* and a division of boats to storm the mole-head battery, the other ships proceeded to attack the sea-face batteries, which mounted 15 heavy guns. Owing to a shift of wind, the arrangements could not be entirely carried out as intended; but, after the *Eagle* had silenced one battery, Fremantle made the signal to storm. Rowley, leading in his gig, took the fort, which he had silenced; Hoste, with Marines from the *Milford*, occupied another battery, which had been evacuated after a cannonade by the *Milford* and *Bacchante*. Having turned the guns of his battery against the other works, Rowley dashed through the town, regardless of the fire from the windows, and from a field piece in the main street, and chased the defenders into a large house in the chief square. By that time a party from the *Milford*, under Markland, had begun to open with carronades upon the building, whereupon the French gave way and fled. Hoste and Rowley joining, the remaining batteries, with the field piece, stores, and shipping, were taken possession of. In all this fighting, only 1 of the attackers was killed, and but 6 were wounded. Of the 90 vessels captured, about half were handed back to their owners, 13 sent to Lissa, and the rest destroyed. Ere the place was abandoned the guns in the batteries were rendered useless.[2]

On July 5th, the British squadron in the Adriatic moved to Porto Re, at the mouth of the Canale di Maltempo. When Captains Hoste and Markland landed, they found the forts abandoned, and 13 sail of vessels scuttled in a neighbouring creek. They rendered the guns, 10 in number, useless, and destroyed the carriages and works.[3]

---

[1] James, vi. 178; *Nav. Chron.*, xxx. 435.
[2] James, vi. 178; *Nav. Chron.*, xxx. 433.
[3] James, vi. 179; *Nav. Chron.*, xxx. 434.

On the evening of August 2nd, as the *Eagle*, 74, Captain Charles
Rowley, and *Bacchante*, 38, Captain William Hoste, were standing
along the Istrian coast, they discovered a convoy of 21 sail in the
harbour of Rovigno. The *Bacchante* leading, both ships went in
and opened a brisk fire on the batteries, which, after some reply,
were abandoned; whereupon Hoste landed with seamen and Marines,
cleared the town, disabled the guns, and brought out or destroyed
the vessels, suffering no greater loss than 1 Marine wounded.[1]

H.M. BRIG WOLF, 18, SIGNALLING FOR A PILOT.

(*From an etching by E. W. Cooke, R.A.*)

On the evening of August 4th, the boats of the *Milford*, 74, and
Weazel, 18, under Captain James Black, of the latter, assisted by
Lieutenant John Grant, and Lieutenant (R.M.) Kenyon Stevens
Parker, landed unperceived at the back of the island of Rogoznica,
off the Dalmatian coast; and at daylight on the 5th, British cheers
from the top of the highest point of the island saluted the French
garrison, which was easily driven out of its works, where six 24-prs.
and two 7·5 in. mortars were found and disabled. The party

[1] James, vi. 179; *Nav. Chron.*, xxx. 510.

returned without loss to the ships.[1] On the 24th, off Otranto, the
Weazel captured the French gunboats *Auguste*, 2, and *Tonnante*, 2.[2]

On August 18th, an attack was made upon the batteries of Cassis,
between Marseilles and Toulon, by the *Undaunted*, 38, Captain
Thomas Ussher, *Redwing*, 18, Commander Sir John Gordon Sinclair, Bart., and *Kite*, 16, Commander the Hon. Robert Cavendish
Spencer, with the boats of those vessels, and some from the *Caledonia*, 110, flagship of Vice-Admiral Sir Edward Pellew, Captain
Jeremiah Coghlan, *Hibernia*, 110, flagship of Vice-Admiral Sir
William Sidney Smith, Captain Charles Thurlow Smith, *Barfleur*,
98, Captain Sir Edward Berry, Bart., and *Prince of Wales*, 98,
Captain John Erskine Douglas. The *Undaunted* was unable to
reach her designed position, but the *Redwing* and *Kite* took up an
excellent covering station. The Marines, led by Captain Coghlan,
stormed the citadel battery, and drove the French to the heights
behind the town, whereupon a division of boats, under Sir John
Sinclair, pulled within the mole, and captured or destroyed three
gunboats and twenty-five sail of merchantmen. The cost was somewhat serious, amounting, as it did, to 4 killed and 16, including
Lieutenant Aaron Tozer, wounded. Among those specially mentioned in Ussher's despatch were Lieutenants Joseph Robert
Hownam and Joseph Grimshaw, Captains (R.M.) Thomas Sherman
and Thomas Hussey, and Lieutenants (R.M) Harry Hunt, first in
the battery, Robert Turtliff Dyer, William Blucke, John Maule,
Thomas Reeves, Alexander Jervis, Edward Mallard, and Samuel
Burdon Ellis.[3]

On September 9th, off the Start, the *Alphea*, 8 (18-pr. carronades),
Lieutenant Thomas William Jones,[4] chased the privateer schooner
Renard, 14, and, having overhauled her, fought her most gallantly at
close quarters for three hours and a half, at the expiration of which
time, it being 3.30 A.M. on the 10th, the unfortunate *Alphea* blew up,
all on board her perishing. The *Renard* admitted a loss of 5 killed
and 31 wounded; and, as the entire crew of the *Alphea* numbered at
most only 41, the British must have fought magnificently.[5]

Early on September 16th, the *Swallow*, 18, Commander Edward
Reynolds Sibly, being well in-shore between the mouth of the Tiber

[1] James, vi. 179; *Nav. Chron.*, xxx. 509.

[2] *Nav. Chron.*, xxx. 511.

[3] James vi. 168; *Nav. Chron.*, xxx. 436.

[4] Born 1783, Plympton; Lieut. 1801.

[5] James, vi. 160; *Moniteur*, Sept. 21st, 1813; *Nav. Chron.*, xxxi. 262.

and Anzio, discovered a brig and xebec between herself and the latter. Three of the brig's boats, under Lieutenant Samuel Edward Cook, Master's Mate Thomas Cole (2), and Midshipman Henry Thomas, were despatched in chase, and, after a two hours' row, they overhauled the French brig *Guerrier*, 4,[1] which was then in tow of two gun-vessels and numerous other boats that had been sent out from Anzio to her succour. These held on until the British were actually alongside. Cook and his party gallantly carried the enemy, losing, however, 2 killed and 4 wounded.[2]

On the morning of October 5th, the *Edinburgh*, 74, Captain George Heneage Lawrence Dundas, *Impérieuse*, 38, Captain the Hon. Henry Duncan (3), *Resistance*, 38, Captain Fleetwood Broughton Reynolds Pellew, *Swallow*, 16, Commander Edward Reynolds Sibly, *Eclair*, 16, Commander John Bellamy, and *Pylades*, 16, Commander James Erskine Wemyss, assembled off Anzio, where lay a convoy of 29 sail, which had previously been watched for some days by Captain Duncan. The place was defended by two batteries, each mounting three heavy guns, on the mole, by a tower to the northward, with one gun, and by a two-gun battery covering the mole. At 1.30 P.M. the ships bore up and took station, the *Impérieuse* and *Resistance* opposite the mole, the *Swallow* against the tower, and the *Eclair* and *Pylades* against the covering battery, supported by the *Edinburgh*. They opened fire simultaneously by signal; and, soon afterwards, a detachment of seamen, under Lieutenant Stannard Eaton Travers, and Marines under Captain (R.M.) Thomas Mitchell,[3] landed under the south, or covering battery, which Travers immediately carried. Another party, under Lieutenant David Mapleton, having taken possession of the mole head, the entire convoy was brought out, and the works were then blown up. The ships were but little injured, and there was no loss of life on the British side. Duncan had been provided with very valuable information concerning the strength of Anzio by Lieutenant Travers, who, a few nights earlier, had landed with a boat's crew, stormed a tower, and brought off the garrison as prisoners.[4]

On October 9th, the *Thunder*, bomb, Commander Watkin Owen Pell, being off the Owers, induced the privateer *Neptune*, 16, to hail

---

[1] Apparently a privateer.

[2] James, vi. 181 ; *Nav. Chron.*, xxxi. 77.

[3] There were then two captains (R.M.) of that name, one of July 1st, 1803, and the other of May 19th, 1812.

[4] James, vi. 181 ; *Nav. Chron.*, xxxi. 77 ; O'Byrne, 1196.

her as a merchantman, and then to lay her on board. A party
then rushed on to the privateer's deck, and, after a hot struggle,
carried her, losing only 2 wounded. The *Neptune* had 4 killed and
10 wounded.[1]

On October 11th, the *Bacchante*, 38, Captain William Hoste,
arrived off Ragusa, and was joined by the *Saracen*, 18, Commander
John Harper, and by three gunboats, with a detachment of troops
from the garrison of the island of Curzola. Learning from Harper
that the inhabitants were in revolt to the southward, Hoste proceeded at once for Castelnuovo, in the Bocche di Cattaro. On the
12th, the *Bacchante* and *Saracen* forced the passage, and, after some
firing, secured a capital anchorage about three miles above the town.
At 10 P.M. that day, Hoste detached Harper with two gunboats
(Sicilian), the launch and barge of the *Bacchante*, and the boats of
the *Saracen*, to seize such naval force as was lying off the town of
Cattaro. The expedition was heavily fired at as it passed the island
of San Giorgio ; but at midnight, when the enemy's four gunboats
were encountered, they were found to be in a state of revolt, and
were easily taken possession of. Harper landed near Cattaro, and
summoned the inhabitants to rise against the French. They did
so gladly, and armed themselves, whereupon Harper, having manned
his prizes, moved down to attack San Giorgio. Early on the 13th,
Lieutenant Francis Gostling, commanding the gunboats, opened
fire upon the island batteries, which replied ; but, in a quarter of
an hour, the French deserted their guns, and eventually they
surrendered.[2]

On October 5th, Rear-Admiral Thomas Francis Fremantle arrived
off Triest to co-operate with the Austrians who, under General Count
Nugent, invested the place on the land side. On the 10th, the
French opened a masked battery of two guns upon the stern of the
flagship *Milford*, which happened to lie towards the shore ; but, in a
few minutes, Captain John Duff Markland got a spring upon' the
cable, and, in another quarter of an hour, put both guns out of
action, killing or wounding 9 of the men serving them. Later in the
day he landed with his Marines and a couple of field pieces. A
systematic siege was then laid to the castle, and by the 16th, the
British had twelve guns in battery. The besiegers made steady

---

[1] James, vi. 164 ; *Gazette*, 1813, 2011.

[2] James, vi. 180 ; *Nav. Chron.*, xxxi. 72. The disps. of Hoste and Harper confuse
dates, but those given in the text seem to be correct. *See* Logs.

progress, and on the 29th, the French capitulated. In these operations Captains Charles Rowley, of the *Eagle*, and John Duff Markland, of the *Milford*, Commanders Fairfax Moresby, of the *Wizard*,
and David Dunn, of the *Mermaid, flûte*, Lieutenants William
Hotham (3), and Charles Moore, Acting Master William Watt
(wounded), and Midshipmen Edward Hibbert and Edward Young
(wounded), appear to have much distinguished themselves. The
total loss on the British side was 10 killed and 35 wounded.[1]

In October, the *Flibustier*, 16, with stores and a few troops on
board, lay in St. Jean de Luz, awaiting an opportunity to put to sea.
The near approach of Wellington's army obliged her to move ; and,
on the night of the 12th, she weighed and stood to the S.W. At
dawn on the 13th, being then becalmed near the mouth of the
Bayonne river, she was seen by the *Telegraph*, 12, Commander
Timothy Scriven, *Challenger*, 18, Commander Frederick Edward
Venables Vernon, and *Constant*, 12, Lieutenant John Stokes.
Before the *Telegraph* could close, the *Flibustier* had anchored
under some batteries, but at 6.45 P.M. the British vessel began to
rake the Frenchman. At about 7, seeing that the other British
vessels were approaching, the *Flibustier* set herself on fire, and, in
spite of efforts made to save her, blew up at 8.10. The *Telegraph*
had no casualties. Scriven was made a Commander, not, as James
says, in consequence of the action, but six days prior to it. For this
and other services he received a C.B. in 1815 ; but although he was
posted on August 12th, 1819, his commission in that rank was can-
celled on the 20th, in consequence of his having been wrecked in the
Erne, 20, on the previous June 1st. He was never again employed,
and died in 1824.[2]

On October 14th, the *Furieuse*, 36, Captain William Mounsey,
while running along the coast towards the Ponza Islands, discovered
in the harbour of Sta. Marinella, a little to the eastward of Civita
Vecchia, a convoy of 19 sail, under the protection of two gunboats,
a fort mounting two 24-prs., and a fortified tower and castle. Lieutenants Walter Croker and William Lester, and Lieutenants (R.M.)
James Whylock and William Davis, volunteered to storm the fort
on the land side, while the frigate engaged it from seaward ; and this
service was gallantly and promptly performed. The French, however, retreated to the strong position afforded by the castle and

[1] James, vi. 180 ; *Nav. Chron.*, xxx. 514.
[2] James, vi. 161 ; Marshall, iv., Pt. i. 122 ; *Nav. Chron.*, xxx. 506.

tower, whence they kept up an annoying fire of musketry, and could not be dislodged, even by the entire broadsides of the *Furieuse*. Nevertheless, the landing party boarded and cut the cables of sixteen vessels of the convoy, sank two, and brought out the remaining fourteen, suffering a loss of no more than 2 killed and 10 wounded in the three hours during which the affair lasted.[1]

On September 30th, the Franco-Batavian frigates *Trave*, 40, and *Weser*, 40, put to sea from the Texel for a cruise to the Azores. On October 16th, they were separated by a gale which dismasted both of them. On the 18th, the *Weser*, then off Ushant, making for Brest, was found by the *Scylla*, 18, Commander Colin M'Donald, which repeatedly hailed, received a broadside, and then made sail ahead.

On the 20th, the *Scylla* fell in with the *Royalist*, 18, Commander James John Gordon Bremer; and the two sloops together went in search of the enemy. They discovered her in a few hours, and, at 3.30 P.M. brought her to action. In an hour and a half they were so cut up that they had to haul off to refit; but on the following morning they renewed the action, and the *Ripon*, 74, Captain Sir Christopher Cole, then nearing, the *Weser* struck, and was taken possession of by the *Royalist*. The *Scylla* had 2 men wounded, and the *Royalist*, 2 killed and 9 wounded, including Lieutenant James Waring, and Master William Wilson. The *Weser* had 4 killed and 15 wounded.

On the same day, October 21st, the *Achates*, 16, Commander Isaac Hawkins Morrison, fell in with the *Trave*, and made sail in chase. The brig pluckily engaged the frigate, but finally lost her in a squall at night. On the afternoon of the 23rd the *Trave* encountered the *Andromache*, 36, Captain George Tobin, and sustained a running fight with her for about an hour, hauling down her colours as the *Eurotas*, 38, Captain John Phillimore, approached from the N.E. The *Andromache* lost only 2 wounded, including Lieutenant Thomas Dickinson. The *Trave* had 1 killed and 25 wounded, besides 2 wounded in the fight with the *Achates*, which had no one hurt. Both the *Trave* and the *Weser* were added to the Navy.[2]

On November 1st, off St. Valery en Caux, the *Snap*, 16, Commander William Bateman Dashwood, sighted five armed luggers, and stood for the three weathermost ones, which first separated,

[1] James, vi. 182; *Nav. Chron.*, xxxi. 78.
[2] James, vi. 162; *Nav. Chron.*, xxx. 441, 443.

and then escaped by superior sailing. Dashwood next bore up after
the two leewardmost craft, and, by deception, enticed one of them
alongside, whereupon he opened fire, and in ten minutes was
master of the *Lion*, 16, of Boulogne. The capture did not cost him
a man, but the prize had 5 killed and 6 badly wounded.[1]

On the night of November 8th, the boats of the *Revenge*, 74,
Captain Sir John Gore (2), under Lieutenants William Richards
and Thomas Blakiston, went into the harbour of Palamos, on the
coast of Catalonia, and cut out a French felucca privateer, without
having a man hurt.[2]

On November 9th, Captain Thomas Ussher, of the *Undaunted*,
38, sent his boats, under Lieutenants Joseph Robert Hownam and
Thomas Hastings, into La Nouvelle, on the south coast of France.
The batteries were stormed and carried, and, of the craft in harbour,
two were captured and five destroyed. The force suffered no
casualties.[3]

On November 26th, off Ile Rousse, on the north-west coast of
Corsica, the boats of the *Swiftsure*, 74, Captain Edward Stirling
Dickson, under Lieutenant William Smith (4 b.), were detached in
chase of the privateer schooner *Charlemagne*, 8, which tried to make
off by using her sweeps. She reserved her fire till the boats were
close upon her and had themselves opened; but she was boarded
with the utmost determination and carried. Unhappily, 5 people,
including Midshipman Joseph Douglas, were killed, and 15, including Lieutenants Rose Henry Fuller and John Harvey (2 a.),
(mortally), wounded.[4]

In October, Captain Arthur Farquhar (1), of the *Desirée*, 36,
arrived at Helgoland to take duty as senior officer. By that time
the French had regained possession of Cuxhaven; and, on November
30th, Farquhar, with a small squadron, co-operated with a Russian
force in an attack upon the batteries defending the place. After
this had succeeded, he crossed the Elbe and pushed up to Glück-
stadt, in the reduction of which he assisted the Crown Prince of
Sweden. The fortress capitulated on January 5th, 1814, after six
days' bombardment. In these operations there were engaged, in
addition to the *Desirée*, the *Shamrock*, 10, Commander John
Marshall (2), *Hearty*, 14, Commander James Rose, *Blazer*, 14,

---

[1] James, vi. 165; *Gazette*, 1813, 2167.
[2] James, vi. 183; *Nav. Chron.*, xxxi. 79.
[3] James, vi. 183, *Nav. Chron.*, xxxi. 79.
[4] James, vi. 183; *Nav. Chron.*, xxxi. 75.

Lieutenant Francis Banks (2), *Piercer*, 14, Lieutenant Joshua Kneeshaw, *Redbreast*, 14, Lieutenant Sir George Mouat Keith, Bart., and gunboats, *No.* 1, Lieutenant Job Hanmer, *No.* 2, Master's Mate Thomas Riches, *No.* 3, Lieutenant Charles Henry Seale, *No.* 4, Lieutenant John Tulloh, *No.* 5, Midshipman John Hallowes, *No.* 8, Lieutenant Richard Roper, *No.* 10, Lieutenant Francis Darby Romney, and *No.* 12, Lieutenant John Henderson (2). Among others employed and favourably mentioned were Commander Andrew Pellet Green,[1] Lieutenants Charles Haultain, and John Archer (2), and Midshipman George Richardson.   The loss sustained was 3 killed and 16 wounded, including Commander James

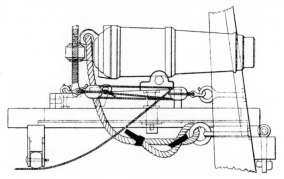

A 24-PR. CARRONADE, *ca.* 1820.

(From Ch. Dupin.)

Rose, Midshipman Richard Hunt, and Captain's Clerk John Riches.[2]

On January 5th, the *Niger*, 38, Captain Peter Rainier (2), and *Tagus*, 36, Captain Philip Pipon (1), with a convoy bound to the westward, were off São Antonio, one of the Cape de Verde Islands, when, at 10 A.M., they discovered nearly ahead of them the *Cérès*, 40, Captain Baron de Bougainville (2), which, in company with the *Clorinde*, 40, Captain R. J. M. D. Lagarde, had quitted Brest in the early part of December.   The British chased, with a light E.S.E. breeze, the *Niger* leading.   By 11 P.M. she was near enough to open from her bow-chasers; but only distant and desultory shots were fired until the morning of the 6th, by which time the wind had drawn to the N.E., and had enabled the *Tagus* to pass her consort

---

[1] Who commanded the *Shamrock* before Com. John Marshall (2).
[2] James, vi. 157; *Nav. Chron.*, xxx. 513; xxxi. 72, 80.

and to begin a running fight with the Frenchman. This continued
until 9.30 A.M., when, having lost her main topmast, the *Cérès*
struck. The *Niger* had just previously repassed her consort, and
was pouring in a heavy fire. No one was killed on either side,
neither did either party sustain a loss of more than one man
wounded. Both the *Tagus* and the *Cérès*, however, were somewhat
cut about aloft. The prize was added to the Navy as the *Seine*,
there being a *Cérès* already in the service.

After having parted company with the *Cérès*, the *Clorinde* cruised

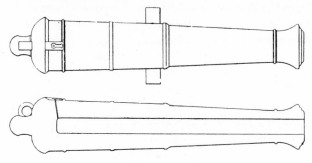

A LONG 24-PR., *ca.* 1818.

(*From Ch. Dupin.*)

with some success until February 25th, when, being nearly due west
of Ushant, heading for Brest, she was sighted by the *Eurotas*, 38,
Captain John Phillimore. The latter at once went in chase. The
Eurotas, it should be explained, was one of certain frigates which
had been fitted with medium 24-prs., in order to prepare them to
meet the heavy American frigates on fairly equal terms. She
carried, it would seem, twenty-eight Congreve 24-prs., sixteen 32-pr.
carronades, two long 9's, an 18-pr. launch carronade, and a Blomefield 24-pr.: in all, 48 guns. The *Clorinde* carried twenty-eight long
18-prs., fourteen 24-pr. carronades, and two long 8-prs., or 44 guns
in all.

Although the wind shifted to N.W., and fell considerably, the
Eurotas gained; and her advantage in this respect was increased by
the apparent indecision of the French captain. At 4.45 P.M. fire
was opened, and at 5, having bore up, the *Eurotas* passed under the
Clorinde's stern and discharged her starboard broadside. As she
luffed up under her opponent's quarter she received a close fire, and,
ere she forged forward on to her enemy's port bow, she lost her
mizen mast by the board. At about the same time the *Clorinde* lost

her fore topmast. The Frenchman shot ahead and tried to cross the British frigate's bows; but the *Eurotas* evaded this by luffing up; and although she could not, as she desired, lay her enemy on board, she passed close under her stern and gave her the port broadside. Thenceforward, until the vessels separated at 7.10 P.M., the action was a very furious muzzle-to-muzzle engagement, the *Eurotas* losing in succession her main and fore masts, and the *Clorinde* her mizen and main masts. When the *Clorinde* stood out of gunshot, her antagonist was temporarily unmanageable. Not till then did Phillimore,[1] who had been dangerously wounded early in the affair, consent to go below, and to hand over the command to Lieutenant Robert Smith (2),[2] who, by immense exertions throughout the night, got up jury masts of sorts, and was able, by the following noon, to go at a speed of 6·5 knots through the water, and to gain on the *Clorinde*. It was, therefore, most mortifying when the *Dryad*, 36, Captain Edward Galwey, and *Achates*, 16, Commander Isaac Hawkins Morrison, appeared on the scene. Their presence, after some parley, and a single shot from the *Dryad*, caused the *Clorinde* to surrender. She had had 20 killed and 40 wounded. The *Eurotas's* losses had been almost exactly the same. She had had 21 killed, including Midshipmen Jeremiah Spurking and Charles Greenway, and first-class Volunteer John T—— Vaughan, and 39 wounded, including Captain Phillimore, Lieutenant (R.M.) Henry Foord, and Midshipman Thomas Robert Brigstocke. The comparative force of the combatants at the outset had been as follows (omitting, in the *Eurotas's* case, the Blomefield gun, which may possibly not have been on board at the time, and the launch carronade):—

		Eurotas	*Clorinde*
Broadside guns {	No.	23	22
	lbs.	601	463
Crew	No.	329	344
Size	tons.	1084	1083

The mettle of the *Eurotas's* crew was shown not less in the celerity with which the crippled ship was refitted than in the spirit with which the action was fought. The British gunnery, however, left much to be desired, or the slaughter in the *Clorinde* would have been greater. The French, on the other hand, though they fought well against a superior antagonist, evinced little resource, and no

---

[1] A Capt. of 1807; C.B., 1815; Kt., 1820; died still a Capt., 1840.
[2] Com., March 4th, 1814, for this service. Died in the same rank, 1849.

power of recuperation. Eighteen hours after the fight, the *Clorinde* was still as dismantled as she had been at its close. She was towed to Portsmouth, and added to the Navy as the *Aurora*, a *Clorinde* already flying the pennant.[1]

On October 20th, 1813, the French 40-gun frigates *Iphigénie*, Captain Jacques Léon Emeric, and *Alcmène*, Captain Alexandre Ducrest de Villeneuve, had left Cherbourg for a six months' cruise. They had subsequently made several prizes on the west coast of Africa and off the Canary Islands. They were still cruizing off those islands when, on January 16th, 1814, they fell in with the *Venerable*, 74, Captain James Andrew Worth, *Cyane*, 22, Captain Thomas Forrest, and *Jason*, 2, a privateer prize,[2] Lieutenant Thomas Moffat. The *Venerable* carried the flag of Rear-Admiral Philip Charles Calderwood Durham, who was on his way to take charge of the Leeward Islands station. When the *Cyane* had reconnoitred and reported, the *Venerable* went in chase, and, towards evening, got within hail of the *Alcmène*, which was the leewardmost of the two frigates. As the French ship would not answer him, Worth opened with such guns as would bear, whereupon Villeneuve pluckily put his helm up, and, under all sail, laid the 74 on board. Villeneuve, no doubt, expected to be supported by Emeric, but the latter lost no time in hauling sharp up, and so left his colleague at Worth's mercy. After a brief struggle, in which, nevertheless, the *Alcmène* lost 32 killed, and 50, including Villeneuve, wounded, the Frenchman's colours were struck by a boarding party headed by the *Venerable's* Captain. The British had but 2 killed and 4 wounded.

In the interval the *Cyane* and *Jason* had gone in chase of the *Iphigénie*.

The *Jason* outsailed her consort, and at 10 P.M. had the temerity to begin firing into the frigate with the only two guns which were on board. It was nearly three hours later when the *Cyane* drew close enough to co-operate; and, by about 4.30 A.M. on the 17th, she began to realise that her opponent was too big for her, and to drop astern. Forrest soon afterwards despatched the *Jason* in search of the flagship, and himself continued after the frigate, which, though she did her best with guns as well as with sails,

---

[1] James, vi. 267; Logs of *Eurotas* and *Dryad*; *Nav. Chron.*, xxxi. 183, 256; Marshall, Supp., Pt. I. 247.

[2] Taken Dec. 31st, 1813; *Nav. Chron.*, xxxi. 254.

failed to shake him off. The chase was, in fact, persisted in until
the evening of the 19th, when the *Venerable* was fast coming up.
In vain did Emeric cut away his boats and anchors. The 74 overhauled him at 8 A.M. on the 20th, and having once fired her starboard
broadside for form's sake, the *Iphigénie* struck, before she had lost
a man. The *Venerable* and the *Cyane* also escaped casualties, and
even the bold little *Jason* had no one hurt. Both prizes were
added to the Navy.[1]

Another pair of 40-gun French frigates had set out on a cruise
at about the same time as the *Iphigénie* and *Alcmène*. These were
the *Etoile*, Captain Pierre Henri Philibert, and *Sultane*, Captain
Abel Dupetit Thouars,[2] which sailed from Nantes at the end of
October, 1813. On January 18th, 1814, they were in nearly mid-
Atlantic, when they sighted the *Severn*, 40, Captain Joseph Nourse,
which was in charge of a convoy from England to Bermuda. After
ascertaining that the strangers were enemies, Nourse made all
possible sail from them, and signalled to the vessels in his company
to take care of themselves. At 10.30 A.M. the *Severn* began firing
her stern chasers at the *Etoile*, which was the leading Frenchman ;
but not till 4.5 P.M. did the *Etoile* reply. From that time until 5.30
there ensued a running fight ; but the *Severn* gradually drew ahead,
and, though the chase continued for some time, it was abandoned
at 8 A.M. on the 19th. The convoy got away in safety to the
westward.

The *Etoile* and *Sultane* proceeded to the Cape de Verde Islands,
and anchored in English Harbour, Maïo. On January 23rd, they
were found there by the *Creole*, 36, Captain George Charles Mackenzie, and *Astræa*, 36, Captain John Eveleigh (1), which, making
them out to be enemies, wore, and made sail for the anchorage.
When the British vessels were about a mile distant, the Frenchmen
cut or slipped, and made sail free on the port tack, with a strong
N.E. wind. Thereupon the *Creole* and *Astræa* set their topgallant
sails and chased. At about 12.45 the *Creole*, then leading, fired a
shot ahead of the *Sultane*, which was on her starboard bow, and
somewhat astern of the *Etoile* ; and she continued firing occasionally
until, at 1 P.M., she ranged up on the *Sultane's* starboard beam, and

---

[1] James vi. 259; *Nav. Chron.*, xxxi. 254.

[2] Son of Capt. A. A. Dupetit Thouars, who fell at the Nile. Born 1793; comd.
Vénus in voyage round the world, 1837–39 ; R.-Ad., 1841 ; estabd. protect. over Tahiti,
1842; died Adm., 1864. His son, Abel (2), born 1832, died a V.-Ad., 1890.

exchanged broadsides.   Soon afterwards the *Astræa* crossed the
Sultane's stern, passed between the latter ship and the *Creole*,
poured in and received two broadsides at close quarters, and stood
on to engage the *Etoile*, which was half a mile ahead, with her
mizen topsail aback.

Twice was the *Creole* set on fire in the two hours during which
her action with the *Sultane* lasted.   At the expiration of that time,
being cut to pieces aloft, and having 10 people killed and 26
wounded, Mackenzie abandoned the contest, put his helm a-lee,
and steered for São Thiago.

The *Astræa* had quitted the *Sultane* at 2.15.   She got alongside
of the *Etoile* a quarter of an hour later, exchanging broadsides,
ranging ahead, luffing up, and raking her enemy; but, losing her
wheel, she fell round off; and the *Etoile*, wearing, raked her very
destructively.   The *Astræa*, however, backed round, and got her
starboard guns to bear; and a yard-arm to yard-arm action began.
In a few minutes Eveleigh was mortally wounded, and the
command devolved on Lieutenant John Bulford.   In spite of the
discouragement caused by the retirement of the *Creole*, by a fire in
the *Astræa's* mizen top, and by the approach of the *Sultane*,
Bulford fought on gallantly, and tried, though without success, to
board his immediate opponent.   The *Sultane*, passing to leeward,
raked him, but then, fortunately, stood away before the wind.   At
3.45 the *Etoile* had had enough of it, and wore round, subsequently
standing after her consort, while the *Astræa's* mizen mast, in flames,
went by the board.   Bulford, of course, could not follow.   When
he had partially refitted, he made after the *Creole*, which he joined
at about 5.15 P.M. in Porto Praya Bay.   The *Astræa* had lost 9
killed, including Eveleigh, and 37 wounded; so that the total loss
in the two British frigates was 19 killed and 63 wounded.   The
enemy had about 40 killed and 60 wounded between them.[1]   It was,
all things considered, a tolerably well matched struggle, ending in
a draw.

On March 26th, the two French frigates, the *Sultane* having
jury topmasts and mizen mast, were about 35 miles N.W. of Ile
Batz, making for St. Malo, in thick weather, with a S.W. breeze,
when they fell in with the *Hebrus*, 36, Captain Edmund Palmer,
and *Sparrow*, 16, Commander Francis Erskine Loch.   The latter
was so close to the enemy ere she discovered them that she received

---

[1] James, vi. 261; *Nav. Chron.*, xxxi. 495.

several shots from each, sustained considerable damage aloft, lost
her Master, killed, and had a seaman wounded. The *Hannibal*, 74,
Captain Sir Michael Seymour (1), Bart., was in the immediate
neighbourhood; and the *Hebrus*, as she distantly engaged the
Frenchmen with her starboard battery, fired her port guns in hopes
of attracting the attention of her consort. At 9.40 A.M., as the fog
cleared, the *Hannibal* was seen coming down under a cloud of
canvas; and soon afterwards the *Hebrus* crowded sail in chase. In
an hour, on the wind suddenly shifting to N.N.W., the French
separated, the *Sultane* changing course to E. by N., and the *Etoile*
hauling up to the S.E. Seymour signalled the *Hebrus* and *Sparrow*
to chase the latter, and himself followed the *Sultane*.

The *Hebrus* soon lost sight of the *Hannibal*, and, later, of the
Sparrow also, and, steadily gaining on the *Etoile*, overhauled her
soon after midnight in the Race of Alderney. At 1.45 A.M. on the
27th, as the *Etoile* was wearing round the Nez de Jobourg, close to
the breakers, she opened fire upon the *Hebrus*, which was nearing
her on the port quarter. The *Hebrus*, being within pistol-shot,
replied, and then ran athwart the enemy's stern, to get between her
and the shore. The British frigate thus placed herself in very shoal
water; yet at 2.20 the *Etoile* crossed her bows to get inside her
again, and, while doing so, crippled her very seriously aloft. During
all this time it was nearly calm; but, at 3 o'clock, a light breeze
sprang up from the land, and, taking full advantage of it, Palmer
was able to rake his antagonist several times, finally knocking away
her mizen mast close to the deck. At 4 A.M. the *Etoile* ceased
firing, and hailed to say that she had struck; and, the heads of both
ships having been got off shore, and a battery which, in the semi-
darkness, had impartially annoyed both, having been placed out of
range, the *Hebrus* and her prize, not without difficulty, anchored in
Vauville Bay at 7 A.M., about five miles from the shore. The victor
sustained her principal damages aloft, but also lost 13 killed, including Midshipman P—— A—— Crawley, and 25 wounded. The
Etoile's main injuries were in her hull; and she had, in consequence,
as many as 40 killed and 73 wounded. The comparative force of
the ships was :—

		Hebrus	*Etoile*
Broadside guns . . . . . {	No.	21	22
	lbs.	467	463
Crew	No.	284	315
Size	tons.	939	1060

Captain Palmer mentions with great approval the conduct in the action of Commander William Sargent, a volunteer on board, and of Lieutenants Robert Milborne Jackson,[1] and George Addis, as well as of other officers.[2]

The *Hannibal* soon overtook the disabled *Sultane*, which, after very little firing, surrendered at 3.15 P.M. on the 26th. Both prizes were added to the Navy.[3]

On the morning of February 2nd, nearly midway between the Azores and Madeira, the *Majestic*, 56, Captain John Hayes (1), which was on the look-out for the American frigate *Constitution*, chased the American privateer *Wasp*, 20, and continued doing so until daylight on the 3rd, when she sighted three suspicious ships and a brig in the south-south-east. Having made the private signal, and getting no answer, she shortened sail to reconnoitre the strangers, which proved to be the French *Atalante*, 40, Captain Mallet, and *Terpsichore*, 40, Captain F. D. Breton, with their prizes, the *San Juan Baptista*, 20, and an unarmed brig. Giving up his chase of the *Wasp*, Hayes made after the hostile squadron. Although apprised by Breton that the British ship was of force inferior to the two French frigates, Mallet ordered his subordinate to "make more sail"; and both fled under a press of canvas. Towards noon the *Majestic* gained on the *Terpsichore*, opened fire from her bow guns at 3 P.M., and continued a running fight with the rearmost Frenchman until 4.56, when the *Terpsichore* struck and brought to, the *Atalante* not offering to aid her in the slightest. As the prize was in a state of confusion, and the wind was increasing, Hayes did not pursue the remaining vessels. In the action, the *Terpsichore* had 3 killed and 6 wounded. The *Majestic* escaped scot free. As for the *Atalante*, she was subsequently chased into Concarneau Bay, on March 25th, by the *Menelaus*, 38, Captain Sir Peter Parker (2), Bart. Parker sent in Lieutenant James Seagrove and Midshipman Frederic Chamier[4] with a challenge to Mallet to come out with his ship, and not to allow her to be blockaded by a vessel of equal force; but the French captain, still not over-anxious for an encounter, replied that his frigate could not leave a French port without an order from his chiefs, adding, "Je le réclamerai, mais je

---

[1] Com., March 31st, 1814.   [2] James, vi. 265; *Nav. Chron.*, xxxi. 417, 424.

[3] James, vi. 267; *Nav. Chron.* xxxi. 422.

[4] Frederic Chamier, the novelist; born 1796; Lieut., 1815; Com., 1826; retired as a captain, 1856: died 1870.

ne peux pas assurer que je l'obtiendrai." It is hardly necessary to say that he did not secure permission. The prize, *San Juan Baptista*, had already fallen into the hands of the *Menelaus*, on February 14th, off Lorient.[1]

An exceedingly painful incident occurred in March. On the 12th, near the mouth of the Bay of Biscay, the *Primrose*, 18, Commander Charles George Rodney Phillott, and the Falmouth packet, *Duke of Marlborough*, John Bull, master, bound for Lisbon, mistook one another for enemies. The error was facilitated by the smallness of the flags supplied to the packet, by the end-on position of the two vessels when the *Duke of Marlborough* hoisted the private signal, and by the rather slovenly manner in which the packet was sailed when first sighted. The *Primrose* fired the first shot at 6.50 P.M.; but nothing approaching to an engagement began until 7.55, ere which time the packet had attempted to make the private night signal, though it is probable that she did not make it correctly. At 8.15, a close action commenced, the *Primrose's* repeated hails not having been answered. Not until Phillott had hailed an obviously beaten ship, did the unfortunate truth come out. The packet had 2 passengers killed and 9 or 10 men wounded, and was in an almost sinking state. The *Primrose* had 1 man killed and 14 people (2 fatally) wounded, including Master Andrew Leech, and Master's Mate Peter Belches.[2]

The brief revival of the war with France in 1815 witnessed no naval events of any importance other than those which have been described in the previous chapter.

---

[1] James, vi. 279; *Nav. Chron.*, xxxi. 423.
[2] James, vi. 278; Mins. of C. of Inq. Mr. Belches, born 1796, retired with the rank of com. in 1877, and survived until 1890.

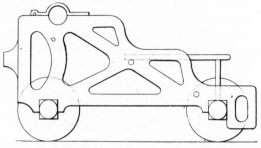

IRON CARRIAGE FOR A 24-pr., *ca.* 1820.
The first iron gun-carriage used in the Navy. (*From Ch. Dupin.*)

APPENDIX TO CHAPTERS XXXIX., XL., AND XLI.

LOSSES OF THE BELLIGERENT POWERS, 1803–15.

NOTE.—As most of the events referred to in the following tables occurred in the course of the campaigns which have been described in the present volume, the tables are inserted here. It should be noted, however, that they include the captures and losses during the American War of 1812–15, a campaign which still remains to be dealt with.

A.—LIST OF H.M. SHIPS TAKEN, DESTROYED, BURNT, FOUNDERED OR WRECKED DURING THE YEARS 1803–1815.

Year.	Date.	H.M. Ship.	Guns.	Commander. [* Lost his life on the occasion.]	Remarks.
1803	Mar. 26	*Déterminée*	22	Capt. Alexander Becher.	Wrecked near Jersey.
	May 31	*Resistance*	36	„ Hon. Philip Wode-house.	Wrecked on Cape St. Vincent.
	July 2	*Minerve*	38	„ Jahleel Brenton (2).	Grounded and taken near Cherbourg.
	„ 21	*Seine*	38	„ David Milne.	Wrecked off the Texel.
		Surinam	18	Lieut. Robert Tucker (actg. Com.).	Detained by the Dutch at Curaçoa.
	Aug.	*Calypso*	16	Com. William Venour.*	Run down in the Atlantic.
	„	*Redbridge*, sch.	12	Lieut. George Lempriere.	Taken by French off Toulon.
	„ 17	*Porpoise*, storeship		„ Robert Merrick Fowler.	Wrecked in the S. Pacific.
	Nov. 16	*Circe*	28	Capt. Charles Feilding (2).	Wrecked on the Lemon and Ower.
	„	*Garland*	22	„ Frederick Cottrell.	Wrecked off Cape François.
	Dec. 10	*Shannon*	36	„ Edward Leveson Gower.	Wrecked and burnt near La Hougue.
	„	*Avenger*	14	Com. Francis Jackson Snell.	Foundered off the Weser.
	„ 15	*Suffisante*	16	„ Gilbert Heathcote.	Wrecked in Cork Harbour.
	„ 31	*Grappler*, g. v.	12	Lieut. Abel Wantner Thomas.	Grounded and burnt by French at Chausey.
1804	Jan. 2	*Créole*	38	Com. Austin Bissell (actg. Capt.)	Foundered in the Atlantic.
	„ 6	*Raven*	18	„ Spelman Swaine.	Wrecked near Mazari, Sicily.
	„	*York*	64	Capt. Henry Mitford.*	Supposed foundered in N. Sea. All lost.
	Feb.	*Fearless*	12	Lieut. George Williams (1).	Wrecked in Cawsand Bay.
	„	*Hussar*	38	Capt. Philip Wilkinson.	Wrecked on the Saintes, B. of Biscay.
	„ 19	*Cerbère*	10	Lieut. Joseph Patey.	Wrecked on Berry Head.
	Mar. 1	*Weazel*	14	„ William Layman (actg. Com.)	Wrecked near Gibraltar.
	„ 24	*Wolverine*	14	Com. Henry Gordon.	Taken by French privateer *Blonde*, Atlantic.
	„ 25	*Magnificent*	74	Capt. William Henry Ricketts Jervis.	Wrecked near the Pierres Noires, Brest.
	April 2	*Apollo*	36	„ John William Taylor Dixon.*	Wrecked on coast of Portugal.
	„ „	*Hindostan*, storeship		Com. John Le Gros.	Accidentally burnt, Rosas Bay.
	„ 3	*Swift*, hired cutter.	8	Lieut. William Thomas Martin Leake.*	Taken by a French privateer, Medit.
	May 8	*Vencejo*	16	Com. John Wesley Wright.	Taken by French gunboats, Quiberon Bay.
	July 14	*Demerara*	6	Lieut. Thomas Dutton.	Taken by priv. *Grand Décidé*, 22, W. Indies.
	„ 15	*Lily*	16	Com. William Compton.*	Taken by priv. *Dame Ambert*, 16, off Georgia.

Year.	Date.	H.M. Ship.	Guns.	Commander. [* Lost his life on the occasion.]	Remarks.
1804	Aug. 26	Constitution, hired cutter	10	Lieut. James Samuel Aked Dennis (1).	Sunk in action, off Ambleteuse.
	Sept. 3	De Ruyter, storeship	64	„ Joseph Beckett.	Wrecked at Antigua.
	„	Drake	14	Capt. William Ferris.	Wrecked off Nevis.
	„ 25	Georgiana, hired cutter		Lieut. Joshua Kneeshaw.	Burnt to avoid capture, mouth of the Seine.
	Oct. 24	Conflict	12	„ Charles Cutts Ormsby.	Wrecked off Newport, I. W.
	Nov. 12	Lord Eldon, hired A. S.	16	Com. Francis Newcombe.	Taken by Spanish gunboats. Retaken later.
	„ 19	Romney	50	Capt. Hon. John Colville.	Wrecked near the Texel.
	„ 24	Venerable	74	„ John Hunter.	Wrecked off Roundham Head, Torbay.
	„	Hannibal, hired A.S.	16	Com. Richard James Lawrence O'Connor.	Wrecked near Sandown Castle.
	Dec.	Duke of Clarence, hired cutter	10	Lieut. Nicholas Brent Clements.	Wrecked on coast of Portugal.
	„ 6	Morne Fortunée, sch.	6	Lieut. John L—— Dale.	Wrecked on Atwood Key, W. Indies.
	„	Constance, hired cutter	6	„ Duncan Menzies.	Lost off the Irish coast.
	„ 15	Gertrude, hired sch.	16	„ —— Broad.	Run down by the *Aigle*, Channel.
	„ 18	Starling	12	„ George Skottowe.	Wrecked near Calais.
	„ 20	Tartarus, bomb	12	Com. Thomas Withers.	Wrecked on Margate Sands.
	„	Mignonne	18		Driven ashore in the W. Indies.
	„ 21	Severn, flûte	44	Capt. Philip d'Auvergne, P. de Bouillon.	Wrecked in Grouville Bay, Jersey.
1805	„ 25	Mallard	12	Lieut. John William Miles.	Grounded and taken near Calais.
	Jan. 7	Sheerness	44	Capt. Lord George Stuart.	Wrecked near Trincomale.
	„ 21	Doris	36	„ Patrick Campbell (1).	Wrecked in Quiberon Bay.
	„ 29	Raven	18	Lieut. William Layman (actg. Com.).	Wrecked in Cadiz Bay.
	Feb. 4	Arrow	30	Com. Richard Budd Vincent.	Taken by the *Hortense* and *Incorruptible*, Mediterranean.
	„ „	Acheron, bomb.	8	„ Arthur Farquhar (1).	Taken by the *Hortense* and *Incorruptible*, Mediterranean.
	„	Arthur, hired cutter	6	Lieut. R—— Cooban.	Taken by a French squadron, Mediterranean.
	„ 17	Cleopatra	32	Capt. Sir Robert Laurie, Bart.	Taken by the *Ville de Milan*, North America.
	„	Bouncer	12	Lieut. Samuel Bassan.	Wrecked off Dieppe.
	Mar. 1	Imogene	18	Com. Henry Vaughan.	Foundered in the Atlantic.
	„	Redbridge, sch.	10	Lieut. (actg.) Francis Blower Gibbes.	Foundered near Jamaica.
	(?) May	Hawk	18	Com. James Tippet.*	Foundered in the Channel. All lost.
	(?)	Seagull	18	„ Henry Burke.*	Foundered, date unknown. All lost.
	(?)	Mary, hired.	16	Lieut. T— S— Pacy.*	Foundered, date unknown. All lost.
	May	Fly	16	Com. Pownoll Bastard Pellew.	Wrecked in the Gulf of Florida.
	„ 12	Cyane	18	„ Hon. George Cadogan.	Taken by the *Hortense* and *Hermione*. Retaken, 5 Oct., 1805.
	July 12	Orestes	14	„ Thomas Brown.	Wrecked off Dunquerque.
	„ 16	Plumper	12	Lieut. James Henry Garrety.	Taken by five gun-brigs, off St. Malo.
	„ „	Teazer	12	„ George Lewis Ker.	Taken by five gun-brigs, off St. Malo.
	„ 17	Ranger	16	Com. Charles Coote.	Taken and burnt by the Rochefort squadron.
	„ 19	Blanche	36	Capt. Zachary Mudge.	Taken and burnt by a French squadron, W. Indies.
	Aug. 5	Dove, cutter.	6	Lieut. Alexander Boyack.	Taken by the Rochefort squadron.
	„	Pigmy, sch.	14	„ William Smith (4).	Wrecked in St. Aubin's Bay, Jersey.
	..	Althorpe, hired cutter	16	„ William Scott (2).*	Foundered in the Channel.
	Sept. 26	Calcutta.	54	Capt. Daniel Woodriff.	Taken by Allemand's squadron, off Scilly.
	Oct. 2	Barracouta, sch.	4	Lieut. Joel Orchard.	Wrecked on Jordan Key, Cuba.
	„	Orquijo	18	„ Charles Balderson (actg. Com.).	Foundered near Jamaica.
	„ 11	Squib, hired.	4		Driven ashore and bilged, off Deal.
	Nov. 10	Biter.	12	„ George Thomas Wingate.	Wrecked near Calais.
	„ 18	Woodlark	12	„ Thomas Innes (3).	Wrecked near St. Valery.
		Pigeon, sch.	4	„ John Luckraft.	Wrecked off the Texel.
1806	Jan.	Manly	12	„ Martin White.	Seized by the Dutch in the Ems.
	„ 6	Favourite	18	Com. John Davie.	Taken by a French squadron, Atlantic.
	..	Papillon	10	„ William Woolsey.*	Foundered in the Atlantic. All lost.
	..	Berbice	4	Lieut. James Glassford Gooding.	Foundered at Demerara. Date unknown.
	Feb.	Seaforth.	14	„ George Steele.*	Capsized, W. Indies. All lost save two.
	„ 23	Unique	10	„ George Rowley Brand.*	Taken by a large French privateer, W. Indies.
	Mar.	Agnes, hired lugger	6		Lost off the Texel.
	Apr. 12	Brave	74	Com. Edmund Boger (actg. Capt.).	Foundered off the Azores.

Year.	Date.	H.M. Ship.	Guns.	Commander. [* Lost his life on the occasion.]	Remarks.
1806	..	*Dominica* . . .	6	Lieut. Robert Peter.	Seized by mutinèers. Retaken by *Wasp*, May 24.
	Aug.	*Dover*, prison .ship (in ord.) . . .	44		Accidentally burnt off Woolwich.
	..	*Heureux* . . .	22	Capt. John Morrison (1).*	Foundered in the Atlantic. All lost.
	,, 12	*Belem*, sch. . . .	6	Lieut. James Groves.	Taken at the recapture of Buenos Aires.
	Sept. 5	*Wolf*	16	Com. George Charles Mackenzie.	Wrecked among the Bahamas.
	..	*Serpent*	16	,, John Waller (1).*	Foundered on the Jamaica station. All lost.
	..	*Martin*	16	,, Thomas Prowse.*	Foundered in the Atlantic. All lost.
	Oct. 12	*Constance* . .	22	Capt. Alexander Saunderson Burrowes.*	Grounded and taken, near C. Fréhel.
	,, 18	*Tobago*, sch. . .	10	..	Taken by priv. *Général Ernouf;* W. Indies.
	,, 25	*Hannah*, gunboat .	..	Lieut. John Foote (1).	Taken by Spanish privateer, off Algeciras.
	,, 27	*Athénien* . . .	64	Capt. Robert Raynsford.*	Wrecked near Sicily; many lost.
	..	*Zenobia*, sch. . .	10		Wrecked off Florida; date unknown.
	Nov. 4	*Redbridge*, sch. .	12	Lieut. Edward Burt.	Wrecked near Providence.
	Dec. 9	*Adder*	12	,, Molyneux Shuldham (2).	Driven ashore and taken near Abreval.
	,, 17	*Netley*, sch. . . .	14	,, William Carr.	Taken by two French cruisers, W. Ind.
	,,	*Clinker*	12	,, John Salmon.*	Foundered off Le Hávre; all lost.
1807	Jan. 4	*Nautilus* . . .	22	Com. Edward Palmer (1).*	Wrecked on Cerigotto, Mediterranean.
	,, 6	*United Brothers*, hired tender . .	6	Lieut. W— M'Kenzie.	Taken by a 12-gun priv., off the Lizard.
	,,	*Jackdaw* . . .	4	,, Nathaniel Brice.	Taken by a Spanish row-boat. Retaken 15 Feb., 1807.
	,, 22	*Felix*	12	,, Robert Clarke (2).	Wrecked near Santander; all lost save three.
	,, 23	*Orpheus*	32	Capt. Thomas Briggs.	Wrecked on a coral reef, W. Indies.
	..	*St. Lucia* . . .	14	Lieut. Hon. Michael de Courcy (2).	Taken by the French; W. Indies.
	(?) Feb. 2	*Blenheim* . . .	74	Rear-Adm. Sir Thomas Troubridge, Bart.* Capt. Austin Bissell.*	Foundered in Indian Ocean; all lost.
	(?) ,, 2	*Java*	32	Capt. George Pigot (1).*	Foundered in Indian Ocean; all lost.
	Feb. 13	*Woodcock* . . .	4	Lieut. Isaac Charles Smith Collett.	Wrecked at St. Michael's, Azores.
	,, 13	*Wagtail*. . . .	4	,, William Cullis.	Wrecked at St. Michael's, Azores.
	,, 14	*Ajax*	74	Capt. Hon. Henry Blackwood.	Accidentally burnt, Mediterranean.
	,, 18	*Prospero*, bomb .	8	Com. William King (1).*	Foundered off Dieppe.
	,, 18	*Inveterate* . . .	12	Lieut. George Norton.	Wrecked off St. Valery en Caux.
	,, 18	*Griper*	12	,, Edward Morris.*	Foundered off Ostend; all lost.
	,, 18	*Speedwell* . . .	14	,, William Robertson (1).	Foundered off Dieppe.
	,, 19	*Ignition*, fire vessel	8	,, Philip Griffin.*	Wrecked off Dieppe.
	,, 19	*Magpie*	4	,, Edward Johnson.	Driven into and taken at Perros.
	..	*Busy*	18	Com. Richard Keilly.*	Foundered, Halifax station; all lost.
	,,	*Atalante* . . .	16	Lieut. John Bowker (actg. Com.).	Wrecked off Rochefort.
	Mar. 2	*Pigmy*	14	,, George Montagu Higginson.	Wrecked off Rochefort.
	,, 4	*Blanche*	38	Capt. Sir Thomas Lavie.	Wrecked off Ushant.
	,, 9	*Crafty*	10	Lieut. Richard Spencer.	Taken by three privateers, south of Gibraltar.
	,,	*César*	16	..	Wrecked off the Gironde.
	,, 31	*Ferreter*	12	Lieut. Henry Weir.	Taken by seven Dutch gunboats, River Ems.
	April 20	*Pike*	4	,, John Ottley.	Taken by a French priv. W. Indies.
	May 26	*Dauntless* . . .	18	Com. Christopher Strachey.	Taken at the surrender of Danzig.
	,, 29	*Jackal*	12	Lieut. Charles Stewart.	Wrecked near Calais.
	..	*Cassandra* . . .	10	,, George Le Blanc.	Foundered off Bordeaux.
	Sept. 10	*Explosion* . . .	12	Com. Edward Ellicott.	Wrecked near Helgoland.
	,, 17	*Barbara* . . .	10	Lieut. Edward d'Arcy.	Taken by priv. *Général Ernouf*, 14, W. Indies. As *Pératy*, retaken, 17 July, 1808.
	..	*Moucheron* . . .	16	Com. James Hawes.*	Wrecked in the Mediterranean.
	Oct. 16	*Pert*	14	,, Donald Campbell (2).	Wrecked off Sta. Margarita.
	,, 26	*Subtle*	8	Lieut. William Dowers.	Wrecked off Bermuda.
	Nov. 10	*Leveret*	18	Com. Richard James Lawrence O'Connor.	Wrecked on the Galloper.
	,, 11	*William*, storeship	12	Master John Foxton.	Wrecked in the Gut of Canso.
	,, 17	*Firefly*	12	Lieut. Thomas Price.*	Foundered off Curaçoa; nearly all lost.
	Dec. 5	*Boreas*	22	Capt. Robert Scott.*	Wrecked near Guernsey; many lost.
	,, 29	*Anson*	44	,, Charles Lydiard.*	Wrecked off Mount's Bay.
	..	*Elizabeth* . . .	12	Lieut. John Sedley.*	Foundered in the W. Indies; all lost.
	..	*Maria*	10	,, John Henderson (1).*	Foundered in the W. Indies; all lost.

Year.	Date.	H.M. Ship.	Guns.	Commander. [* Lost his life on the occasion.]	Remarks.
1808	Jan. 12	*Sparkler* . . .	12	Lieut. J a m e s S a m u e l Aked Dennis (1).	Wrecked on the Dutch coast.
	,, 15	{*Lord Keith*, hired} cutter . . . . }	10	,,　Mitchell Roberts.	Driven into, and seized at Cuxhaven.
	..	*Kingfish*, sch. . .	6	,,　Charles Hunter.	{Taken by a French priv., W. Indies. Retaken by *Pheasant.*
	..	*Bacchus*, cutter. .	10	,,　Henry Murray.	Taken by the French, Leeward Islands.
	,, 19	*Flora*	36	Capt. Loftus Otway Hand.	Wrecked and destroyed on Dutch coast.
	,, 31	*Delight*	16	{Com. Philip Cosby Hand-} field.* }	Wrecked and burnt on Calabrian coast.
	,, 31	*Leda*	33	Capt. Robert Honyman.	Wrecked at mouth of Milford Haven.
	Feb. 15	*Raposa*	10	Lieut. James Violett.	{Destroyed to prevent capture, near Cartagena.
	Mar.	*Hirondelle* . . .	14	,,　Joseph Kidd.*	Wrecked near Tunis ; nearly all lost.
	,, 24	*Muros*	20	Capt. Archibald Duff.	Wrecked in Honda Bay, Cuba.
	,, 25	*Electra*	16	{Com. George Barne Trol-} lope. }	Wrecked on coast of Sicily.
	,, 26	*Milbrook*. . . .	12	Lieut. James Leach.	Wrecked on the Burlings.
	April 20	*Widgeon*. . . .	8	,,　George Elliot (2).	Wrecked on Scots coast.
	,, 22	*Bermuda* . . .	18	{Com. W i l l i a m H e n r y} Byam. }	{Wrecked on Memory Rock, Little Bermuda.
	May 18	*Rapid*	12	Lieut. Henry Baugh.	Sunk by batteries in the Tagus.
	,, 24	*Astræa*	32	Capt. Edmund Heywood.	Wrecked off Anegada, W. Indies.
	June 4	*Tickler*	12	Lieut. John W— Skinner.*	{Taken by four Danish gunboats, Great Belt.
	,, 9	*Turbulent* . . .	12	,,　George Wood.	Taken by a Danish flotilla, Malmö Bay.
	,, 19	*Seagull*	16	Com. Robert Cathcart.	Taken by a Danish flotilla, off the Naze.
	,, 30	*Capelin*	8	Lieut. Josias Bray.	Wrecked off Brest Harbour.
	July 10	*Netley*	12	,,　Charles Burman.	Wrecked on Leeward Islands station.
	,, 27	*Pickle*	10	,,　Moses Cannadey.	Wrecked off Cadiz.
	,, 30	*Meleager*. . . .	36	Capt. Frederick Warren.	Wrecked on Barebush Key, Jamaica.
	Aug. 2	*Tigress*	12	{Lieut. Edward Nathaniel} Greensword. }	{Taken by sixteen Danish gunboats, Great Belt.
	,, 4	*Delphinen* . . .	16	Com. Richard Harward.	Wrecked on the Dutch coast.
	,, 18	*Rook*	4	Lieut. James Lawrence.*	{Taken by two French privs., off San Domingo.
	Sept. 15	*Laurel*	22	{Capt. John Charles Wooll-} combe. }	{Taken by the *Canonnière*, 40, Indian Ocean.
	,, 29	*Maria*	14	Lieut. James Bennett.*	{Taken by *Dépt. des Landes*, 22, off Guadeloupe.
	Oct. 3	*Carnation* . . .	18	{Com. C h a r l e s M a r s} Gregory.* }	{Taken by *Palinure*, 16, off Martinique.
	,, 4	*Greyhound* . . .	32	{Capt. Hon. W i l l i a m} Pakenham. }	Wrecked on coast of Luconia.
	,, 24	*Volador*	16	{Com. Francis George} Dickins. }	Wrecked in Gulf of Čoro, W. Indies.
	,, 26	*Crane*	8	Lieut. Joseph Tindale.	Wrecked off West Hoe.
	Dec. 4	*Banterer*	22	Capt. Alexander Shippard.	Wrecked in the St. Lawrence.
	,, 6	*Crescent.* . . .	36	,,　John Temple (2).*	Wrecked on the coast of Jutland.
	,, 10	*Jupiter*	50	{ Henry E d w a r d} Reginald Baker. }	Wrecked in Vigo Bay.
	,, 15	*Flying Fish*, sch. .	4	{Lieut. James Glassford} Gooding. }	Wrecked off San Domingo.
	,, 23	*Fama*	16	,,　Charles Tapping.	Wrecked in the Baltic.
	,, 26	*Bustler*	12	,,　Richard Welch.	Wrecked on coast of France.
	..	*Tang.*	8	..	Foundered in the Atlantic.
1809	Jan. 9	*Morne Fortunée* .	12	Lieut. John Brown (2).*	Wrecked off Martinique.
	,, 11	*Magnet*	18	Com. George Morris.	Wrecked in the ice, Baltic.
	,, 15	*Pigeon*	4	Lieut. Richard Cox.	Wrecked near Margate.
	,, 20	*Claudia*	10	{ ,,　Anthony Bliss Wil-} liam Lord. }	Wrecked off Norway.
	,, 22	*Primrose* . . .	18	Com. James Mein.*	{Wrecked on the Manacle, near Falmouth.
	,,	*Proselyte*, bomb .	4	,,　Henry James Lyford.	Wrecked in the Baltic.
	,, 30	*Haddock*. . . .	4	{Lieut. Charles W i l l i a m} Selwyn. }	Taken by the *Génie*, 16, Channel.
	Feb. 5	*Carrier*	4	,,　William Milner.	Wrecked on the French coast.
	,,	*Viper*, sch. . . .	8	..	Supposed foundered off Gibraltar.
	,, 28	*Proserpine* . . .	32	Capt. Charles Otter.	{Taken by *Pénélope* and *Pauline*, off Toulon.
	Mar.	*Harrier*	18	Com. John James Ridge.*	Supposed foundered, Indian Ocean.
	April 11	{*Mediator*, t.s. as.f.} ship . . . . }	36	,,　James Wooldridge.	Expended in Basque Road.
	,, 29	*Alcmene*	32	{Capt. William Henry} Brown Tremlett. }	Wrecked off Nantes.
	May 31	*Unique*	12	Lieut. Thomas Fellowes.	Burnt at Basseterre, Guadeloupe.
	June 18	*Sealark*	4	,,　James Proctor.	Wrecked in the North Sea.
	,, 20	*Agamemnon* . .	64	Capt. Jonas Rose.	Wrecked in the River Plate.
	July 11	*Solebay*	32	{ Edward H e n r y} Columbine. }	Wrecked on the coast of Africa.
	Aug. 8	*Lark*	18	Com. Robert Nicholas.*	Foundered off San Domingo.

Year.	Date.	H.M. Ship.	Guns.	Commander. [* Lost his life on the occasion.]	Remarks.
1809	Aug. 16	*Alaart*	16	Com. James Tillard.	Taken by a Danish flotilla.
	,,	*Lord Nelson*, cutter	8	..	Wrecked near Flushing.
	,,	*Hurd*, cutter . .	8	..	Wrecked near Flushing.
	,,	*Dominica* . . .	14	Lieut. Charles Welsh.*	Capsized off Tortola.
	,, 31	*Foxhound* . . .	18	{Com. James M'Kenzie (2).*	Foundered in the Atlantic; all lost.
	Sept. 2	*Minx*	12	Lieut. George Le Blanc.	Taken by six Danish gunboats.
	Nov. 2	*Victor*	18	Com. Edward Stopford (1).	Taken by the *Bellone*, 40, B. of Bengal.
	,, 3	*Curieux*	16	{Lieut. Henry George Moysey.	Wrecked in the W. Indies.
	,,	*Glommen* . . .	16	Com. Charles Pickford.	Wrecked in Carlisle Bay, Barbados.
	Dec. 7	*Harlequin* . . .	16	Lieut. P— C— Anstruther.	Wrecked near Seaford.
	,, 13	*Junon*	38	Capt. John Shortland.*	Taken by the *Renommée* and *Clorinde*.
	,, 14	*Defender* . . .	12	Lieut. John George Nops.	Wrecked near Folkestone.
	,, 22	*Salorman* . . .	10	,, Andrew Duncan.	Wrecked in the Baltic.
	..	*Contest*	12	Lieut. John Gregory (1a).*	Supposed foundered in the Atlantic.
	..<	*Shamrock*, sch.. .	8	,, Abram Bowen.	Lost in the Atlantic.
	Dec.	*Pelter*	12	,, William Evelyn.*	Lost in the Atlantic.
1810	Feb.	*Achates*	10	Com. Thomas Pinto.	Wrecked in the W. Indies.
	,,	*Wild Boar* . .	10	,, Thomas Burton.	Wrecked within the Scilly Isles.
	Apr. 4	*Cuckoo*	4	{Lieut. Silas Hiscutt Paddon.	Wrecked off the Dutch coast.
	May 24	*Flèche*	16	Com. George Hewson.	Wrecked off the mouth of the Elbe.
	,, ,,	*Alban*	10	Lieut. Samuel Thomas.*	Taken by a flotilla of Danish gunboats.
	,, ,,	*Racer*, cutter . .	12	,, Daniel Miller.	Wrecked on the coast of France.
	Aug. 24	*Néréide*	36	{Com. Nisbet Josiah Willoughby (actg. Capt.).	{Taken by a French squadron, off Grand Port.
	,, 25	*Magicienne* . . .	36	Capt. Lucius Curtis.	{Destroyed to avoid capture, off Grand Port.
	,, ,,	*Sirius*	36	,, Samuel Pym.	{Destroyed to avoid capture, off Grand Port.
	,, 26	*Lively*	38	Capt. George M'Kinley.	Wrecked near Malta.
	,, 28	*Iphigenia* . . .	36	,, Henry Lambert (2).	{Taken by a French squadron, near Grand Port.
	Nov. 9	*Conflict*	12	Lieut. Joseph B— Batt.*	Foundered in the B. of Biscay.
	..	*Mandarin* . . .	12		{Wrecked on Red Island, Strait of Singapore.
	,,	*Plumper* . . .	12	,, W— Frissel.	Foundered in the St. Lawrence.
	Dec. 18	*Pallas*	32	Capt. George Paris Monke.	Wrecked off the Firth of Forth.
	,, 18	*Nymphe*	36	,, Edward Sneyd Clay.	Wrecked off the Firth of Forth.
	,, 22	*Minotaur* . . .	74	,, John Barrett.	Wrecked on the Haak Sand, Texel.
	,, 25	*Monkey* . . .	12	Lieut. Thomas Fitzgerald.	Wrecked near Belle Isle.
1811	Jan. 8	*Fleur de la Mer* .	10	,, John Alexander (3).	Foundered in the Atlantic.
	,, 19	*Satellite*	16	{Com. Hon. Willoughby Bertie.*	Foundered in the Channel.
	Feb. 13	*Pandora* . . .	18	{,, John Macpherson Ferguson.	Wrecked in the Kattegat.
	,, 16	*Amethyst* . . .	36	Capt. Jacob Walton.	Wrecked in Plymouth Sound.
	,, 25	*Shamrock* . . .	10	{Lieut. Wentworth Parsons Croke.	Wrecked on C. St. Mary.
	Mar. 6	*Thistle*	10	,, George M'Pherson.	Wrecked near New York.
	,, 12	*Challenger* . . .	16	{Com. Goddard Blennerhassett.	{Taken by a French frigate, etc., off Ile Ratz.
	May 2	*Dover*	38	{Lieut. Charles Jeneris (actg. Capt.).	Wrecked in Madras Road.
	,, ,,	*Chichester*, storeship	32	Master William Kirby.	Wrecked in Madras Road.
	,, 26	*Alacrity* . . .	18	Com. Nesbit Palmer.	Taken by the *Abeille*, 20, off Corsica.
	Mar. 2	*Olympia* . . .	10	Lieut. Henry Taylor.	Taken by French privs., off Dieppe.
	..	{*Black Joke*, hired cutter . . .	4	,, Moses Cannadey.	Taken by the French in the Channel.
	June 28	*Firm*.	12	,, John Little (2).	Wrecked on the French coast.
	,, 29	*Safeguard* . . .	12	,, Thomas England.	Taken by the Danes in the Baltic.
	..	*Staunch* . . .	14	,, Hector Craig.*	Wrecked off Madagascar; all lost.
	July 15	*Snapper*. . . .	4	,, Henry Thrackston.	Taken by the *Rapace*, off Brest.
	,, 29	{*Guet-apens* ("Guachapin"). . .	10	,, Michael Jenkins.	Wrecked off Antigua.
	Aug. 18	*Tartar*	32	Capt. Joseph Baker.	Wrecked in the Baltic.
	Sept. 2	*Manly*	12	{Lieut. Richard William Simmonds.	Taken by three Danish brigs.
	..	*Swan*, cutter . .	..	..	Taken by Danish gunboats.
	Oct. 14	*Pomone*	38	Capt. Robert Barrie.	Wrecked on the Needles.
	,, 21	*Grouper*. . . .	4	Lieut. James Atkins (2).	Wrecked off Guadeloupe.
	Dec. 4	*Saldanha* . . .	36	{Capt. Hon. William Pakenham.*	{Wrecked off Lough Swilly; nearly all lost.
	..	*Bloodhound*. . .	12	Lieut. Thomas Warrand.	Wrecked near Trevose Head.
	,, 24	*Fancy*	12	,, Alexander Sinclair.*	Foundered in the Baltic; all lost.
	,, ,,	*St. George* . . .	98	{Rear-Adm. Robert Carthew Reynolds (1).* Capt. Daniel Oliver Guion.*	{Wrecked on the coast of Jutland; nearly all lost.
	,, ,,	*Defence*	74	,, David Atkins.*	{Wrecked on the coast of Jutland; nearly all lost.

Year.	Date.	H.M. Ship.	Guns.	Commander. [* Lost his life on the occasion.]	Remarks.
1811	Dec. 25	Hero	74	Capt. James Newman Newman.*	Wrecked on the Haak Sand; all lost.
	,, ,,	Grasshopper . .	18	Com. Henry Fanshawe (2).	Taken in Nieuwe Diep, Texel.
	,, 26	Ephira . . .	10	Lieut. Thomas Everard.	Wrecked near Cadiz.
1812	Jan. 28	Manilla	36	Capt. John Joyce.	Wrecked on the Haak Sand, Texel.
	,, 31	Laurel	38	,, Samuel Campbell Rowley.	Wrecked on the Govivas Rock, Teigneux Passage.
	Feb. 29	Fly	16	Com. Henry Higman.	Wrecked off Anholt.
	May 3	Skylark	16	,, James Boxer.	Grounded and was destroyed, near Boulogne.
	,, ,,	Apelles	14	,, Frederick Hoffman.	Grounded and was taken, near Boulogne. Retaken, 4 Mar., 1812.
	July 8	Exertion . . .	12	Lieut. James Murray (2).	Grounded and was destroyed in the Elbe.
	,, 11	Encounter . . .	12	,, James Hugh Talbot.	Wrecked off San Lucar, Spain.
	Aug. 3	Emulous . . .	18	Com. William Howe Mulcaster.	Wrecked on Sable Island.
	,, 13	Alert	16	Com. Thomas Lamb Polden Laugharne.	Taken by the U. S. S. Essex, 32.
	,, 14	Chubb	4	Lieut. Samuel Nisbett.*	Capsized off Halifax; all lost.
	,, 19	Attack . . .	12	Lieut. Richard William Simmonds.	Taken by fourteen Danish gunboats, off Anholt.
	,, ,,	Guerrière . . .	38	Capt. James Richard Dacres (2).	Taken by U. S. S. Constitution, 44.
	,, 22	Whiting . . .	4	Lieut. Lewis Maxey.	Taken by the French priv. Diligente.
	Sept. 8	Laura	12	,, Charles Newton Hunter.	Taken by the French priv. Diligente.
	,, 28	Barbados . . .	28	Capt. Thomas Huskisson.	Wrecked on Sable Island.
	Oct. 8	Avenger	16	Com. Urry Johnson.	Wrecked off St. John's, Newfoundland.
	?	Magnet . . .	16	,, Ferdinand Moore Maurice.	Supposed foundered in the Atlantic; all lost.
	,, 10	Sentinel	12	Lieut. William Elleston King.	Wrecked off Rügen.
	,, 18	Frolic	18	Capt. Thomas Whinyates.	Taken by U. S. S. Wasp, 20.
	,, 25	Macedonian . .	38	,, John Surman Carden.	Taken by U. S. S. United States, 44.
	Nov. 6	Nimble . . .	10	Lieut. John Reynolds (3).	Foundered in the Kattegat.
	,, 24	Bellette	18	Com. David Sloane.*	Wrecked in the Kattegat; nearly all lost.
	,, 27	Southampton . .	32	Capt. Sir James Lucas Yeo.	Wrecked off Conception Island, Bahamas.
	,, 30	Subtle, sch.	10	Lieut. Charles Brown (2).*	Foundered in the W. Indies; all lost.
	Dec. 5	Plumper . . .	12	,, James Bray.	Wrecked in the B. of Fundy.
	,, 8	Fearless	12	,, Harry Lord Richards.	Wrecked off the coast of Spain.
	,, 13	Alban, cutter . .	10	,, William Sturges Key.*	Wrecked off Aldborough; nearly all lost.
	,, 29	Java	38	Capt. Henry Lambert (2).*	Taken by U. S. S. Constitution, 44.
	?	Porgey	4	. .	Foundered in the W. Indies.
1813	? Jan. 1	Sarpedon . . .	10	Com. Thomas Parker.*	Supposed foundered; all lost.
	,, 7	Ferret	18	,, Francis Alexander Halliday.	Wrecked near Leith.
	,, 27	Daring	12	Lieut. William R— Pascoe.*	Destroyed to prevent capture by Rubis.
	,, 21	Rhodian. . . .	10	Com. John George Boss.	Foundered in the Atlantic.
	,, 24	Peacock . . .	18	,, William Peake.*	Taken by U. S. S. Hornet. Sank.
	,, 25	Linnet	14	,, John Treacy.	Taken by the Gloire, 40, off Madeira.
	Mar. 22	Captain	74	(in ordinary).	Accidentally burnt in Hamoaze.
	May 20	Algerine. . . .	10	Lieut. Daniel Carpenter.	Wrecked in the W. Indies.
	June 16	Persian	18	Com. Charles Bertram.	Wrecked on Silver Keys, W. Indies.
	July 2	Dædalus. . . .	38	Capt. Murray Maxwell.	Wrecked off Ceylon.
	Aug. 5	Dominica . . .	14	Lieut. George Wilmot Barreté.*	Taken by U. S. priv. Decatur.
	,, 22	Colibri	18	Com. John Thomson.	Wrecked at Port Royal, Jamaica.
	Sept. 5	Boxer . . .	12	,, Samuel Blyth.*	Taken by U. S. S. Enterprise, 16.
	,, 9	Highflyer . . .	8	Lieut. William Hutchinson (1).	Taken by U. S. S. President.
	,, 10	Alphea, sch.. . .	10	,, Thomas William Jones.*	Blew up in action with priv. Renard; all lost.
	,, 21	Goshawk . . .	16	Com. Hon. William John Napier.	Wrecked in the Mediterranean.
	,, 27	Bold	12	,, John Skekel.	Wrecked on P. Edward's Island.
	Oct. 22	Laurestinus . .	22	,, Alexander Gordon (2).	Wrecked on the Silver Keys.
	Nov. 5	Tweed	18	,, William Mather.	Wrecked in Shoal Bay, Newfoundland.
	,, 6	Woolwich, en flûte.	40	,, Thomas Ball Sulivan.	Wrecked off Barbuda.
	,, 10	Atalante. . . .	18	,, Frederick Hickey.	Wrecked off Halifax.
	? Dec.	Dart	10	Lieut. Thomas Allen (3).*	Foundered in the Atlantic.
1814	Jan. 29	Holly, sch.. . .	10	,, Samuel Sharpe Treacher.*	Wrecked off San Sebastian.
	Feb. 14	Pictou	16	,, Edward Stephens.	Taken by the U. S. S. Constitution.

Year.	Date.	H.M. Ship.	Guns.	Commander. [* Lost his life on the occasion.]	Remarks.
1814	Feb. 28	*Anacreon* . . .	18	Com. John Davies (2).	Foundered in the Channel.
	Mar. 22	*Decoy*	10	Lieut. John Pearse.	Taken by French in the Channel.
	..	*Rapide,* tender . .	6	..	Wrecked on the Saintes.
	..	*Vautour*	16	Com. Paul Lawless.*	Supposed foundered; all lost.
	Apr. 29	*Epervier* . . .	18	Com. Richard Walter Wales.	Taken by U. S. S. *Peacock.*
	,, ,,	*Ballahou* . . .	4	Lieut. Norfolk King.	Taken by U. S. priv. *Perry.*
	May 19	*Halcyon*	18	Com. John Houlton Marshall.	Wrecked on a reef, W. Indies.
	June 28	*Reindeer* . . .	18	,, William Manners.*	Taken by U. S. S. *Wasp,* Channel.
	,, ,,	*Leopard,* troopship.	50	Capt. Edward Lowther Crofton.	Wrecked off Anticosti.
	July 12	*Landrail,* cutter .	4	Lieut. Robert Daniell Lancaster.	Taken by U. S. priv. *Siren,* Channel.
	Aug.	*Peacock*	18	Capt. Richard Coote.	Foundered off S. Carolina; all lost.
	Sept. 1	*Avon*	18	Com. Hon. James Arbuthnot.	Sank after action with U. S. S. *Wasp.*
	,, 15	*Hermes*	20	Capt. Hon. William Henry Percy.	Destroyed in attacking batteries at Mobile.
	,, 30	*Crane*	18	Com. Robert Standly.*	Foundered in the W. Indies.
	Oct.	*Elizabeth* . . .	10	Lieut. Jonathan Widdicombe Dyer.	Foundered in the W. Indies.
	Oct. 10	*Racer*	14	Lieut. Henry Freeman Young Pogson.	Wrecked in the Gulf of Florida.
	Nov. 24	*Fantôme*	18	Com. Thomas Sykes.	Wrecked on the Halifax station.
	..	*Cuttle*	4	..	Foundered on the Halifax station.
	..	*Herring*	4	Lieut. John Murray (3).	Foundered on the Halifax station.
1815	Jan. 17	*Sylph*	18	Com. George Dickins.*	Wrecked on Southampton Bar, North America.
	Feb. 26	*Statira*	38	Capt. Spelman Swaine.	Wrecked off Cuba.
	,, 26	*St. Lawrence* . .	12	Lieut. James Edward Gordon.	Taken by U. S. priv. *Chasseur,* 24.
	Mar. 20	*Levant*	22	Capt. Hon. George Douglas	Taken by U. S. S. *Constitution.* Retaken.
	,, 20	*Cyane*	20	,, Gordon Thomas Falcon.	Taken by U. S. S. *Constitution.* Retaken.
	,, 23	*Penguin* . . .	18	Com. James Dickinson (3).*	Taken by U. S. S. *Hornet,* off Tristan d'Acunha.
	May 1	*Penelope,* troopship	36	,, James Galloway.	Wrecked off Newfoundland.
	Aug. 15	*Dominica* . . .	14	Lieut. Richard Crawford.	Wrecked off Bermuda.
	?	*Cygnet*	16	Com. Robert Russell (1).	Wrecked off the R. Courantyn.

LISTS OF ENEMY'S MEN-OF-WAR TAKEN, DESTROYED, OR BURNT, AND, SO FAR AS CAN BE ASCERTAINED, WRECKED OR FOUNDERED DURING THE YEARS 1803–15.

FRENCH LOSSES.

Year.	Date.	Name. [* Added to the Royal Navy.]	Guns.	Fate. M Medals granted in 1849, in pursuance of *Gazette* notice of June 1st, 1847. M Flag-officers' and Captains' gold medals.
1803	May 18	*Affronteur* (* as *Caroline,* hired)	14	Taken by *Doris,* 36, Capt. R. H. Pearson, off Ushant.
	,, 28	*Franchise**.	40	Taken by *Minotaur, Thunderer,* and *Albion,* Channel.
	,, ,,	*Embuscade* (* as *Ambuscade*).	32	Retaken by *Victory,* 100, Capt. Sam. Sutton, Atlantic.
	,, 29	*Impatiente*	10	Taken by *Naiad,* 36, Capt. Jas. Wallis (1).
	June 3	*Betsy*	4	Taken and destroyed by *Russell,* 74.
	,, 7	*Vertu,* sch.	2	Taken by *Racoon,* 18, Com. Austin Bissell, San Domingo.
	,, ,,	*Ami de Colonnot* . . .	2	,, ,, ,, ,,
	,, 14	*Inabordable,* sch. . , . .	4	Taken by boats of *Immortalité,* 36, etc., Cape Gris Nez.
	,, ,,	*Commode*	4	,, ,, ,, ,,
	,, ,,	*Arabe*	8	Taken by *Maidstone,* 36, Capt. Rich. H. Moubray, Med.
	,, 18	*Colombe**.	16	Taken by *Dragon,* 74, and *Endymion,* 44, off Ushant.
	,, 24	*Enfant Prodigue* (* as *Sta. Lucia*).	16	Taken by *Emerald,* 36, Capt. Jas. O'Bryen, off St. Lucia.
	,, 25	*Bacchante**	18	Taken by *Endymion,* 44, Capt. Hon. Chas. Paget.
	,, 27	*Venteux*	10	Cut out by two boats of *Loire,* 36, Capt. Fred. L. Maitland (2), Ile Batz.
	,, 23	*Légère*	2	Taken by priv. *Alarm,* Channel.
	,, ,,	*Mignonne**	16	Taken by *Goliath,* 74, off San Domingo.
	,, 29	*Dart*	4	Taken by *Apollo,* 36, Bay of Biscay.

Year	Date.	Name. [* Added to the Royal Navy.]	Guns.	Fate. M Medals granted in 1849, in pursuance of *Gazette* notice of June 1st, 1847. M Flag-officers' and Captains' gold medals.
1803	June 30	*Aiguille*	..	Taken by squadron of Capt. Hy. Wm. Bayntun, off San
	,, ,,	*Vigilante* (* as *Suffisante*)	..	,, ,, ,, ,, [Domingo.
	,, ,,	*Supérieure*	,,	,, ,, ,, ,, ,,
	,, ,,	{ *Poisson Volant* (* as *Flying* *Fish*) . . . . . }	..	,, ,, ,, ,, ,,
	,, ,,	*Créole*	40	,, ,, ,, ,, ,,
	July 4	*Providence*, sch. . . .	2	{ Taken by boats of *Naiad*, 36, under Lieut. Wm. Dean, off Ile de Seins.
	,, 8	*Alcion* (* as *Halcyon*) . .	16	{ Taken by *Narcissus*, 36, Capt. Ross Donnelly, off Sardinia.
	,, 11	*Lodi*	10	{ Taken by *Racoon*, 18, Com. Austin Bissell, Léogane Road.
	,, 16	*Adour*	20	{ Taken by *Endymion*, 44, Capt. Hon. Chas. Paget, Atlantic.
	,, 25	*Duquesne*	74	{ Taken by *Bellerophon*, 74, *Vanguard*, 74, *Tartar*, 32, etc., San Domingo.
	,, ,,	*Oiseau*, sch.	16	
	,, 27	*Epervier*	16	{ Taken by *Egyptienne*, 40, Capt. Hon. Chas. E. Fleeming, Atlantic.
	Aug.	*Deux Amis*, sch. . . .	3	Taken by *Racoon*, 16, Com. Austin Bissell, off Cuba.
	,,	*Trois Frères*, sch. . . .	3	
	,,	A schooner	2	Destroyed ,, ,, ,, ,,
	,, 17	*Mutine*	18	,, ,, ,, ,, ,,
	Sept. 4	*Papillon*	6	Taken by *Vanguard*, 74, St. Marc, San Domingo.
	,, 5	*Courier de Nantes*, sch. . .	2	,, ,, ,, off San Domingo.
	,, 8	*Sagesse*	28	Taken by *Theseus*, 74, Port Dauphin, San Domingo.
	,, 9	Two *chasse-marées* . . .	..	{ Taken by boats of *Sheerness*, 8, Lieut. Henry Rowed, near Brest.
	,, 27	A schooner	4	Taken by *Jackal*, sch., Lieut. C.P. Leaver, off Nieuport.
	Oct.	*Goéland* (* as *Goelan*) . .	18	{ Taken by *Pique*, 36, and *Pelican*, 18, at Aux Cayes, San Domingo.
	,,	A cutter	12	
	,, 14	*Petite Fille*, gun-brig . .	..	Taken by *Racoon*, 16, Com. Austin Bissell, off Cuba.
	,, ,,	*Jeune Adèle*	6	,, ,, ,, ,, ,,
	,, ,,	*Amélie*	4	,, ,, ,, ,, ,,
	Nov. 8	No. 86 (gunboat) . . .	2	Taken by *Conflict*, 14, Lieut. Dav. Chambers, off Calais.
	,, 10	*Messager*, lugger . . .	6	{ Taken by boats of *Ville de Paris*, 110, under Lieut. — Watts, off Ushant.
	,, 16	*Renard*	12	Taken by Lord Nelson's squadron, Mediterranean.
	,, 25	*Vautour* . .* . . .	12	{ Taken by *Boadicea*, 38, Capt. Jno. Maitland (2), off Finisterre.
	,, 28	*Bayonnaise*	28	{ Destroyed to prevent capture by *Ardent*, 64, Capt. Robt. Winthrop.
	,, 30	*Surveillante*	40	Surrendered to Commod. John Loring at Cape François.
	,, ,,	*Clorinde*	40	,, ,, ,, ,, ,,
	,, ,,	*Vertu*	40	,, ,, ,, ,, ,,
	,, ,,	*Cerf*	12	,, ,, ,, ,, ,,
	,, ,,	*Découverte*	6	,, ,, ,, ,, ,,
	Dec. 18	No. 436 (gunboat) . . .	2	{ Taken by *Basilisk*, 14, Lieut. Wm. Shepheard, Home station.
1804	Jan. 3	No. 432 (lugger) . . .	2	Taken by *Archer*, 14, Lieut. Jno. Sherriff.
	,, 14	*Passe-Partout*, chasse marée .	2	Taken by boats of *St. Fiorenzo*, 40, E. Indies.
	,, 21	*Chameau*	4	Taken by *Cerberus*, 32, off La Hougue.
	,, 30	No. 43 (g.-brig) . . .	3	Taken by *Tribune*, 36.
	,, ,,	No. 47 (g.-brig) . . .	3	
	,, ,,	No. 51 g.-brig) . . .	3	Taken by *Hydra*, 38.
	,, ,,	No. 411 (lugger) . . .	1	
	Feb. 4	*Curieux*	16	{ Cut out by boats of *Centaur*, 74, under Lieut. Robt. Carthew Reynolds (2), Martinique. M
	,, 24	*Coquette*, sch.	2	Taken by *Stork*, 18, Com. Geo. Le Geyt, Jamaica station.
	Mar. 8	*Colombe*, cutter	4	{ Cut out of Sluys by boats of *Cruiser* and *Rattler* and burnt.
	,, 12	*Penriche*	2	Taken by *Harpy*, 18, Com. Edm. Heywood, near Calais.
	,, 18	*Terreur*, cutter	10	Taken by *Pique*, 40, Jamaica station.
	Apr. 28	*Hirondelle*	14	Taken by *Bittern*, 18, Com. Robt. Corbett, Med.
	,, 29	No. 360 (gunboat) . . .	..	Taken by boats of *Doris*, 36, Audierne Bay.
	July 12	*Charente*	20	{ Driven ashore and burnt off the Gironde by *Aigle*, 36, Capt. Geo. Wolfe.
	,, ,,	*Joie*	8	
	Aug. 23	*Laurette*, sch.	5	{ Taken by *Pelican*, 18, Com. Jno. Marshall (1), Jamaica station.
	Oct. 1	*Hasard*	16	Taken by *Echo*, 16, Com. Edm. Boger, off Curaçoa.
	,, 21	*Gracieuse*	14	Taken by *Blanche*, 36, off Curaçoa.
1805	Feb. 14	*Psyché* (* as *Psyche*) . .	32	{ Taken by *St. Fiorenzo*, 36, Com. Hy. Lambert (2) (actg. Capt.), E. Indies. M [station.
	,, 23	*Ville de Milan*	40	Taken by *Leander*, 50, Capt. John Talbot, Halifax
	,, ,,	*Cleopatra* (* formerly British)	32	Retaken ,, ,, ,, ,,
	Apr. 9	A schooner	7	{ Sunk by *Gracieuse*, 12, Mids. Johne Bernhard Smith, Jamaica station.
	June 10	*Amitié*, sch.	14	Taken by *Blanche*, 36, Jamaica station.
	,, 18	*Colombe*	16	Taken by *Endymion*, 44, Capt. Hon. Chas. Paget.

Year.	Date.	Name. [* Added to the Royal Navy.]	Guns.	Fate. M Medals granted in 1849, in pursuance of *Gazette* notice of June 1st, 1847. M Flag-officers' and Captains' gold medals.
1805	Aug. 10	*Didon**	40	Taken by *Phœnix,* 36, Capt. Thomas Baker (1), off C. Finisterre. **M**
	,, 15	*Faune.*	16	Taken by *Goliath,* 74, and *Camilla,* 20, Channel.
	,, 16	*Torche**	18	,, ,, ,, Channel.
	Sept.	*Hypolite*	4	Driven ashore and destroyed by *Duncan,* 38, Lieut. Clem. Sneyd (actg. Capt.).
	Oct. 2	*Actéon**	16	Taken by *Egyptienne,* 40, off Rochefort.
	,, 5	*Cyane* (* formerly British). .	34	Taken by *Princess Charlotte,* 38, Capt. Geo. Tobin, off Tobago.
	,, 13	*Naïade* (* as *Melville*) . . .	22	Taken by *Jason,* 32, Capt. Wm. Champain, Leeward Islands.
	,, 21	*Swiftsure**	74	Taken by the fleet of Lord Nelson at Trafalgar (formerly British).
	,, ,,	*Achille*	74	Taken by the fleet of Lord Nelson at Trafalgar, but blew up. } **M M**
	,, ,,	*Fougueux*	74	Taken by the fleet of Lord Nelson at Trafalgar, but wrecked.
	,, ,,	*Aigle* . . . . . .' .	74	Taken by the fleet of Lord Nelson at Trafalgar, but wrecked.
	,, ,,	*Intrépide*	74	Taken by the fleet of Lord Nelson at Trafalgar, and burnt.
	,, ,,	*Redoutable*	74	Taken by the fleet of Lord Nelson at Trafalgar, but sank.
	,, ,,	*Berwick*	74	Taken by the fleet of Lord Nelson at Trafalgar, but wrecked. } **M M**
	,, ,,	*Bucentaure*	80	Taken by the fleet of Lord Nelson at Trafalgar, retaken, and wrecked.
	,, ,,	*Algésiras*	74	Taken by the fleet of Lord Nelson at Trafalgar, but retaken.
	,, 25	*Indomptable*	80	Wrecked off Rota, Cadiz.
	Nov. 3	*Formidable* (* as *Brave*) . .	80	Taken by the squadron of Sir Richard John Strachan.
	,, ,,	*Duguay Trouin* (* as *Implacable*)	74	,, ,, ,, ,, } **M**
	,, ,,	*Mont Blanc**	74	,, ,, ,, ,,
	,, ,,	*Scipion**	74	,, ,, ,, ,,
	Dec. 24	*Libre*	38	Taken by the *Loire,* 40, and *Egyptienne,* 40, off Rochefort.
	,,	*Atalante*	40	Wrecked off the Cape of Good Hope.
1806	Feb. 6	*Alexandre** (ex *Indivisible*) .	80	Taken by squadron of V.-Ad. Sir Jno. Thos. Duckworth, off San Domingo.
	,, ,,	*Jupiter** (* as *Maida*) . .	74	,, ,, ,, ,,
	,, ,,	*Brave**	74	,, ,, ,, ,, } **M M**
	,, ,,	*Imperial* (ex *Vengeur*) . .	120	Destroyed ,, ,, ,,
	,, ,,	*Diomède*	72	,, ,, ,, ,,
	,, 21	*Rolla**	16	Taken by squadron of Sir Home R. Popham, C. of Good Hope.
	,, 27	*Furet*	20	Taken by *Hydra,* 38, Capt. Geo. Mundy, off Cadiz.
	Mar. 4	*Volontaire**	40	Surrendered to squadron of Sir Home R. Popham, C. of Good Hope.
	,, 12	*Tremeuse,* sch.	3	Taken by *Wolverine,* 18, Com. Fras. Aug. Collier, W. Indies.
	,, 13	*Marengo**	74	Taken by squadron of V.-Ad. Sir Jno. B. Warren, Atlantic. } **M** (*London* and *Amazon*).
	,, ,,	*Belle Poule**	40	,, ,, ,,
	,, 24	*Lutine* (* as *Hawk*). . . .	18	Taken by *Carysfort,* 28, and *Agamemnon,* 64, Leeward Islands.
	,, 26	*Phaëton* (* as *Mignonne*) . .	16	Taken by the *Pique,* 36, Capt. Chas. B. H. Ross, Jamaica station. } **M**
	,, ,,	*Voltigeur* (* as *Pelican*) . .	16	,, ,, ,, ,,
	,, 28	*Néarque*	16	Taken by *Niobe,* 38, Capt. Jno. Wentworth Loring, off Lorient.
	Apr. 5	*Tapageuse*	14	Cut out of R. Garonne by boats of *Pallas,* Capt. Lord Cochrane.
	,, 6	*Malicieuse*	18	Driven ashore in the Garonne by *Pallas,* 32, Capt. Lord Cochrane.
	,, ,,	*Garonne*	24	,, ,, ,, ,,
	,, ,,	*Gloire*	24	,, ,, ,, ,,
	,, 17	*Bergère**	18	Taken by *Sirius,* 36, Capt. Wm. Prowse (1), Medit.
	,, 19	Two *chasse-marees*	..	Cut out by boats of *Colpoys* and *Attack,* Doälan.
	May 1	*Pandour*	18	Taken by squadron of R.-Ad. Chas. Stirling (1), Irish station.
	,, 28	*Diligent* (* as *Wolf*) . . .	16	Taken by *Renard,* 18, Com. Jer. Coghlan, Jamaica station.
	,, 24	*Impériale,* sch.	3	Taken by *Cygnet,* 18, Com. Robt. Bell Campbell, off Dominica.
	June 9	*Observateur**	18	Taken by *Tartar,* 32, Capt. Edw. Hawker, W. Indies.
	July 15	*César*	18	Taken by boats of squadron of Sir Sam. Hood (2), under Lieut. Ed. Reynolds Sibly. } **M**
	,, ,,	*Charles,* ketch	3	Taken by *Seaflower,* 14, off Rodriguez.

Year.	Date.	Name. [* Added to the Royal Navy.]	Guns.	Fate. M Medals granted in 1849, in pursuance of *Gazette* notice of June 1st, 1847. M Flag-officers' and Captains' gold medals.
1806	July 19	*Guerrière**	40	Taken by *Blanche*, 38, Capt. Thos. Lavie, off Färöe Isles. } M
	,, 27	*Rhin**.	40	Surrendered to *Mars*, 74, Capt. Robt. Dudley Oliver, off Rochefort.
	Sept. 14	*Impétueux*	74	Taken and burnt by *Belleisle*, 74, *Bellona*, 74, and *Melampus*, 36, off C. Henry.
	,, 25	*Gloire**	40	Taken by squadron of Commod. Sir Sam. Hood (2) off Rochefort.
	,, ,,	*Infatigable*	40	,, ,, ,, ,, ,,
	,, ,,	*Minerve* (* as *Alceste*) . . .	40	,, ,, ,, ,, ,,
	,, ,,	*Armide**	40	,, ,, ,, ,, ,,
	,, ,,	*Emilien* (ex Br. *Trincomale*) .	18	Taken by *Culloden*, Capt. Christ. Cole, E. Indies.
		Napoléon, sch.	1	Taken by *Diligente*, 16, Jamaica station.
	,, 27	*Présidente* (* as *Piémontaise*, 1815) . .	40	Struck to *Dispatch*, 18, Capt. Edw. Hawkins, with squadron of Sir Thos. Louis.
	Oct. 2	*Manette*, slp.	..	Cut out by boats of *Dominica*, 14, Lieut. Wm. Dean, St. Pierre, Martinique.
	,, ,,	*Dauphin*, slp.	..	,, ,, ,, ,,
	,, 4	*Chiffonne*, sch.	..	Taken by *Dominica*, Lieut. Wm. Dean.
	,, 12	*Salamandre*, flûte . . .	26	Taken and burnt at St. Malo by *Constance*, *Sheldrake*, *Strenuous*, and *Britannia*.
	Nov. 12	*Réunion*, sch.	10	Taken by boats of *Galatea*, 32, Capt. Geo. Sayer (1), off Guadeloupe.
1807	Jan. 2	*Créole*.	1	Taken by a boat of the *Circe*, 32, under Lieut. — Thomas, Leeward Islands.
	,, 21	*Lynx* (* as *Heureux*) . . .	16	Taken by boats of *Galatea*, 32, under Lieut. Wm. Coombe, off Caracas. M
	,, 28	*Favourite* (ex British) . .	18	Taken by *Jason*, 32, Capt. Thos. Jno. Cochrane, off Guiana.
	Feb. 14	*Dauphin*, sch.	3	Taken by *Bacchante*, 20, Capt. Jas. Rich. Dacres (2), Jamaica station.
	July 10	*Jaseur*	12	Taken by *Bombay*, 38, Capt. Wm. Jones Lye, E. Indies.
	Aug. 23	*Mosquito*	8	Taken by *Lark*, 18, and *Ferret*, 18, Jamaica station.
	Oct. 7	*Safo* (Venetian). . . .	1	Cut out by boats of *Porcupine*, 22, Giuppana.
	Nov. 6	*Succès*, cutter.	10	Taken by *Volage*, 22, Capt. Phil. Lew. J. Rosenhagen, Medit.
1808	Feb. 13	*Gunboat No. 1*	3	Cut out by boats of *Confiance*, 20, mouth of the Tagus. M
	Mar. 8	*Piémontaise*	40	Taken by *St. Fiorenzo*, 36, Capt. Geo. Nicholas Hardinge, E. Indies. M
	,, 13	*Apropos*	8	Driven ashore and burnt by *Emerald*, 36, Capt. Fredk. Lewis Maitland (2), Vivero. M
	,, 26	*Friedland* (Italian). . . .	16	Taken by *Standard*, 64, and *Active*, 38, off C. Blanco.
	May 2	*Ronco* (Italian) (* as *Tuscan*).	16	Taken by *Unité*, 40, Capt. Pat. Campbell (1), off C. Promontoro.
	,, 11	*Griffon**.	16	Taken by *Bacchante*, 20, Capt. Sam. Hood Inglefield, off C. Antonio.
	June 1	*Nettuno* (Italian) (* as *Cretan*)	16	Taken by *Unité*, 40, Capt. Pat. Campbell (1), Medit.
	,, ,,	*Teulie* (* as *Roman*) . . .	16	,, ,, ,, ,, ,,
	,, 14	*Neptune*	80	Surrendered to the Spanish patriots, Cadiz harbour.
	,, ,,	*Algésiras*.	74	,, ,, ,, ,, ,,
	,, ,,	*Pluton*	74	,, ,, ,, ,, ,,
	,, ,,	*Héros*	74	,, ,, ,, ,, ,,
	,, ,,	*Argonaute*	74	,, ,, ,, ,, ,,
	,, ,,	*Cornélie*	40	,, ,, ,, ,, ,,
	,, ,,	*Atlas*	74	Surrendered to the Spanish patriots, Vigo.
	,, 26	*Volpe* (Neapolitan)	1	Taken by boats of *Standard*, 64, off Corfu.
	,, ,,	*Léger*	..	,, ,, ,, ,, ,,
	July 16	*Ortenzia* (Venetian) . . .	10	Taken by *Minstrel*, 18, Com. Jno. Hollinworth, Medit.
	,, 17	*Serpent* (* as *Pert*) . . .	18	Taken by *Acasta*, 40, Capt. Ph. Beaver, off La Guaira.
	,, 28	*Requin*	16	Taken by *Volage*, 22, Capt. Ph. Lew. J. Rosenhagen, Medit.
	Aug. 1	*Vigilante*.	2	Taken by boats of *Kent*, 74, and *Wizard*, 16, Noli.
	,, 11	*Sylphe* (* as *Seagull*) . .	16	Taken by *Comet*, 18, Com. Cuthbert Featherstone Daly, Channel. M
		Artémise	40	Driven ashore near Brest and burnt by blockading squadron.
		Mouche, sch.	..	Taken by *Cossack*, 22, Capt. Chas. Geo. Digby, Channel.
	,, 16	*Espiègle* (* as *Electra*) . .	16	Taken by *Sibylle*, 38, Capt. Clotworthy Upton, Channel.
	Oct. 8	*Jéna* (*as *Victor*) . . .	18	Taken by *Modeste*, 36, B. of Bengal.
	,, 20	*Pilade*	16	Taken by *Pompée*, 74, off Barbados.
	,, 31	*Palinure*.	16	Taken by *Circe*, 32, off Diamond Rock.
	Nov. 11	*Thétis* (* as *Lrune*). . .	40	Taken by *Amethyst*, 36, Capt. Mich. Seymour (1), off Lorient. M M
	,, 14	*Colibri*	3	Taken by boats of *Polyphemus*, 64, San Domingo.
	Dec. 13	*Cygne*	16	Destroyed at St. Pierre by *Amaranthe*, 18. etc.
1809	Jan. 1	*Gauloise*, cutter	7	Taken by *Imperieuse*, 38, Capt. Lord Cochrane, Medit.
	,, ,,	*Julie*, lugger	5	,, ,, ,, ,, ,,
	,, 2	*Iris* (* as *Rainbow*). . .	24	Taken by *Aimable*, 32, Capt. Lord Geo. Stuart, N. Sea.
	,, 5	*Hébé* (* as *Ganymede*). . .	20	Taken by *Loire*, 38, Capt. Alex. Wilmot Schomberg.
	,, 16	*Colibri*	16	Taken by *Melampus*, 36, Capt. Edw. Hawker, Halifax station.

Year.	Date.	Name. [* Added to the Royal Navy.]	Guns.	Fate. M Medals granted in 1849, in pursuance of *Gazette* notice of June 1st, 1847. M Flag-officers' and Captains' gold medals.
'809	Jan. 22	*Topaze* (* as *Jewel*) . . .	40	Taken by *Cleopatra*, 32, *Jason*, 32, and *Hazard*, 18, off Guadeloupe.
	Feb. 4	*Amphitrite*	40	Destroyed at the attack on Martinique.
	,, 10	*Junon* *	40	Taken by *Horatio*, 38, *Supérieure*, 14, *Latona*, 38, and *Driver*, 18, Halifax station. M (*Horatio* and *Supérieure*.)
	,, 15	*Var* (* as *Chichester*) . . .	26	Taken by *Belle Poule*, 38, Capt. Jas. Brisbane, off Valona.
	,, 24	*Italienne*	40	Driven ashore by squadron of R.-Ad. Hon. Robt. Stopford, Sables d'Olonne.
	,, ,,	*Calypso*	40	,, ,, ,, ,, ,,
	,, ,,	*Cybèle*	40	,, ,, ,, ,, ,,
	,, ,,	*Rossollis*	18	Burnt to avoid capture at the taking of Martinique. } M
	,, ,,	*Carnation*	18	,, ,, ,, ,, ,,
	,, ,,	*Diligente* (* as *St. Pierre*). .	18	Taken at the capture of Martinique.
	Mar. 10	*Joseph*, felucca	3	Cut out by boats of *Argo*, 44, under Lieut. Chas. Fraser, San Domingo.
	Apr. 1	*Léda*	1	Cut out by boats of *Mercury*, 28, Rovigno.
	,, 6	*Niémen* *	40	Taken by *Amethyst*, 36, Capt. Mich. Seymour (1), coast of France. M
	,, 12	*Ville de Varsovie* . . .	80	Destroyed by fleet of Ad. Lord Gambier, Basque Road.
	,, ,,	*Tonnerre*	74	,, ,, ,, ,, ,,
	,, ,,	*Aquilon*	74	,, ,, ,, ,, ,, } M
	,, ,,	*Calcutta*, en flûte . . .	50	,, ,, ,, ,, ,,
	,, ,,	*Indienne*	40	,, ,, ,, ,, ,,
	,, 17	*d'Hautpoult* (* as *Abercrombie*)	74	Taken by *Pompée*, 74, *Castor*, 32, and *Recruit*, 18, off Puerto Rico. M
	May 4	*Champenoite*	12	Taken by *Renown*, 74, Capt. Phil. Chas. Durham, off Toulon.
	,, 28	*Beau Narcisse*	8	Taken by *Moselle*, 18, Com. Henry Boys (1), W. Indies.
	June 10	*Mouche*	16	Taken by the *Amelia*, 38, and *Statira*, 38, off Santander.
	,, 18	*Félicité*, * en flûte . . .	36	Taken by *Latona*, 38, Capt. Hugh Pigot (3), W. Indies.
	,,	*Réjouie*	14	Taken by the *Amelia*, 38, and *Statira*, 38, off Santander.
	,,	No. 7, sch.	4	,, ,, ,, ,, ,,
	,,	*Légère*	2	,, ,, ,, ,, ,,
	,,	*Notre Dame*	2	,, ,, ,, ,, ,,
	July 6	*Furieuse* (* as 36)	20	Taken by *Bonne Citoyenne*, 20, Com. Wm. Mounsey, Atlantic. M
	,, 28	Six Italian gunboats (2 guns each)	..	Cut out by boats of squadron, Duino.
	Aug. 16	*Fidèle* (* as *Bourbonnaise*) .	40	Taken at the surrender of Flushing.
	,, 27	Four gunboats (Venetian, each 1 gun)	..	Cut out by boats of *Amphion*, 32, Cortellazzo.
	,, ,,	Two gunboats (Venetian, each 2 guns).	..	,, ,, ,, ,,
	Sept. 1	*Jason*	10	Taken by *Helena*, 18, Com. Jas. And. Worth, coast of Ireland.
	,, ,,	*Jean Bart*	4	Taken by *Nassau*, 64, off the Start.
	,, 7	*Pugliese*	7	Cut out by boats of *Mercury*, 28, Barletta.
	,, 18	*Aurore*	16	Taken by *Plover*, 18, Com. Philip Browne (2), off Beachy Head.
	,, 21	*Caroline*	40	Taken by a military and naval force, Réunion.
	Oct.	*Zéphyr*	18	Taken by *Seine*, 36, Capt. Dav. Atkins, Channel.
	,,	*Améthyste*	14	Taken by *Minerva*, 32, Capt. Rich. Hawkins.
	,,	*Incomparable*, brig	8	Taken by *Emerald*, 36, Capt. Fredk. Lewis Maitland (2), off Ireland.
	,, 22	*Hirondelle*, sch.	16	Taken by *Plover*, 18, Com. Philip Browne (2), off Falmouth.
	,, 26	*Robuste*	80	Destroyed to avoid capture by Brit. fleet, off Frontignan.
	,, ,,	*Lion*	74	,, ,, ,, ,,
	,, 30	*Milan*	18	Taken by *Surveillante*, 38, Capt. Sir Geo. Ralph Collier, off Ushant.
	Nov.	*Etoile*	14	Taken by *Euryalus*, 36, Capt. Hon. Geo. H. L. Dundas, off Cherbourg.
	,, 6	*Fanfaron*	16	Taken by *Emerald*, 36, Capt. Fredk. Lewis Maitland, off Guadeloupe.
	,, 13	*Basque*	16	Taken by *Druid*, 32, Capt. Sir Wm. Bolton (2).
	,, ,,	*Revanche*	16	Taken by *Helena*, 18, Com. Jas. And. Worth.
	,, 17	*Grand Napoléon*	18	Taken by *Royalist*, 18, Com. Jno. Maxwell, off Dungeness.
	,, 19	*Intrépide*	20	Taken by *Vestal*, 28, Capt. Edwards Lloyd Graham, off Newfoundland.
	Dec. 3	*Comtesse Laure*	16	Taken by *Surveillante*, 38, Capt. Sir Geo. Ralph Collier.
	,, 6	*Heureuse Etoile*	2	Taken by *Royalist*, 18, Com. Jno. Maxwell.
	,, 10	*Grand Rodeur*	16	Taken by *Redpole*, 16, Com. Colin M'Donald.
	,, ,,	*Beau Marseille*	14	Taken by *Royalist*, 18, Com. Jno. Maxwell, Downs station.
	,, 12	*Nisus* (* as *Guadaloupe*) .	16	Taken by boats of *Thetis*, 38, Capt. Geo. Miller, etc., at Guadeloupe. M
	,, 14	*Béarnais* (* as *Curieux*) . .	16	Taken by *Melampus*, 36, Capt. Edw. Hawker, W. Indies.
	,, ,,	*Aigle*	14	Taken by *Pylades*, 18, Com. Geo. Ferguson.

Year.	Date.	Name. [* Added to the Royal Navy.]	Guns.	Fate. M Medals granted in 1849, in pursuance of *Gazette* notice of June 1st, 1847. M Flag-officers' and Captains' gold medals.
1809	Dec. 18	*Loire*, en flûte	40	Destroyed by a squadron at Anse La Barque, Guadeloupe.
	„ „	*Seine*, en flûte	40	
	„ 19	*Papillon* *	16	{Taken by *Rosamond*, 18, Com. Benj. Walker, off Guadeloupe.
	„ 31	*François*	14	Taken by *Royalist*, 18, Com. Jno. Maxwell.
		Joubert	8	Taken by *Topaze*, 36, Capt. Hy. Hope, Mediterranean.
		Mentor	6	„ „ „ „ „
		Espérance	3	„ „ „ „ „
1810	Jan. 12	*Oreste* (* as *Wellington*) . .	14	{Taken by *Scorpion*, 18, Com. Francis Stanfell, off Guadeloupe. M
	Feb. 3	{*Confiance* (ex *Canonnière*), en flûte}	40	Taken by *Valiant*, 74, off Belle Isle.
	Mar. 21	*Nécessité*	28	Taken by *Horatio*, 38, Capt. Geo. Scott (1), Atlantic.
	Apr. 12	{*Espérance* (ex Brit. *Laurel*) (* as *Laurestinus*)}	22	Retaken by *Unicorn*, 32, Capt. Alex. Robt. Kerr.
	May 1	*Estafette*	4	Taken at Jacolet by *Néréide*, 36.
	3	*Sparviero* (Neapolitan) . .	8	{Taken by *Spartan*, 38, Capt. Jahleel Brenton (2), G. of Naples. M
	„ 10	*Canonnière*	3	{Taken by *Nonpareil*, 14, Lieut. Jas. Dickinson (3) off the Vilaine.
	„ 17	*Minerve*	18	Taken by *Bustard*, 16, Com. Jno. Duff Markland.
	July 25	Six gunboats (Neapolitan) . .	··	{Taken by squad. of Capt. Hon. G. G. Waldegrave, Amantea.
	Sept. 18	*Vénus* (* as *Néréide*) . . .	40	{Taken by *Boadicea*, 38, Capt.} M (*Boadicea*, Josias Rowley, off Réunion. } *Otter*, and *Staunch*.)
	Dec. 6	*Astrée* (* as *Pomone*) . . .	40	{Taken by squadron of V.-Ad. Albemarle Bertie at capture of Mauritius.
	„ „	*Bellone* (* as *Junon*) . . .	40	„ „ „ „ „
	„ „	*Minerve*	40	„ „ „ „ „
	„ „	*Manche*	40	„ „ „ „ „
	„ „	*Iphigénie* * (ex British) . .	36	„ „ „ „ „
	„ „	*Néréide* (ex British) . . .	36	„ „ „ „ „
	„ „	*Victor*	14	„ „ „ „ „
	„ „	*Entreprenante*	14	„ „ „ „ „
	„ „	A brig.	14	·· „ „ „ „
	„ „	5 gunboats	··	·· „ „ „ „
	„ „	*Ceylon*, pris. ship . . .	30	„ „ „ „ „
	„ „	*Charlton*, pris. ship . . .	30	„ „ „ „ „
	„ „	*United Kingdom*, pris. ship .	30	„ „ „ „ „
	„ 23	*Eliza*	8	{Destroyed by boats of *Diana*, 38, Capt. Chas. Grant, near La Hougue.
1811	Feb. 12	A trabacolo (Venetian) . .	6	Taken by boats of *Cerberus* and *Active*, Ortona.
	Mar. 13	*Favorite*	40	{Destroyed by squadron (*Amphion*, *Active*, *Cerberus*, and *Volage*) of Capt. Wm. Hoste, off Lissa.
	„ „	{*Corona* (Venetian) (* as *Dædalus*).}	40	Taken „ „ „ „ } M M
	„ „	*Bellona* (Venetian) (* as *Dover*)	32	„ „ „ „ „
	„ 14	*Etourdie*	18	{Burnt to avoid capture by *Pomone*, 38, Capt. Robt. Barrie, Monte Cristo.
	„ 25	*Amazone*	40	{Burnt to avoid capture by *Berwick*, 74, Capt. Jas. Macnamara (2), near Barfleur.
	„ 31	*Dromadaire*, en flûte . . .	··	Taken by *Ajax*, 74, and *Unité*, 36, off Elba.
	May 1	*Girafe*, en flûte	20	{Blew up in action with boats of *Pomone*, *Unité* and *Scout*, off Corsica.
	„ „	*Nourrice*, en flûte	20	„ „ „ „ „
	„ 5	A gun-brig	18	Destroyed by *Belle Poule* and *Alceste*, Parenzo.
	„ 8	*Canonnier*	11	{Taken by *Scylla*, 18, Com. Arthur Atchison, off Isle Batz.
	„ 20	*Renommée*	40	{Taken by squadron of Capt. Chas. Marsh Schomberg, off Madagascar. } M (*Astræa*, *Phœbe*, *Galatea* and *Racehorse*.)
	„ 26	*Néréide*	40	{Taken by squadron of Capt. Chas. Marsh Schomberg, at Tamatave.
	July 21	Eleven gunboats	··	Taken by *Thames* and *Cephalus*, Porto del Infreschi.
	„ 27	Three gunboats	··	{Taken by boats of *Active*, 38, Capt. Jas. Alex. Gordon (1), Ragoznica.
	Aug. 2	{Gunboats 22, 28, 31 and 71 (each) . . . . . . }	3	Taken off Norderney by boats under Lieut. Sam. Blyth.
	„ 19	*Héron*	10	Taken by *Hawk*, 16, Com. Henry Bourchier, Channel. M
	„ 25	*Teazer* (ex British) . . .	14	{Re-taken by *Diana*, 38, and *Semiramis*, 36, mouth of Gironde.
	„ „	*Pluvier*	16	{Burnt by *Diana*, 38, and *Semiramis*, 36, mouth of Gironde.
	Sept. 21	*Ville de Lyon*, praam . . .	12	Taken by squadron of Capt. Phil. Carteret (3).
	Oct. 11	Two gunboats (each of) . .	1	Taken by boats of *Impérieuse*, 38, Positano.
	„ „	One gunboat	1	Sunk by *Impérieuse*, 38, Capt. Hon. Hy. Duncan (3).
	Nov. 2	Four gunboats (Neapolitan) . .	··	Destroyed by *Impérieuse* and *Thames*, Palinuro.
	„ „	Six gunboats (Neapolitan) . .	··	Taken by *Impérieuse* and *Thames*, Palinuro.
	Nov. 27	*Corcyre*	28	Taken by *Eagle*, 74, Capt. Chas. Rowley, Adriatic.
	„ 29	*Pomone*	40	Taken by *Alceste*, *Unité*, and *Active*, Adriatic. M

Year.	Date.	Name. [* Added to the Royal Navy.]	Guns.	Fate. M Medals granted in 1849, in pursuance of *Gazette* notice of June 1st, 1847. M Flag-officers' and Captains' gold medals.
1811	Nov. 29	*Persanne,* storeship. . . .	29	Taken by *Alceste, Unité,* and *Active,* { M { *Alceste, Active,* Adriatic. { an t *Unité.*
	Dec. 4	A settee	8	Taken off Bastia by boats of *Sultan,* 74, Capt. } M Jno. West.
	,, ,,	A brig.	6	
		Victoire	16	Taken by *Zephyr,* 16, Com. Fras. Geo. Dickins, off Dieppe.
		Flore	40	Wrecked in the Adriatic, date unknown.
1812	Feb. 13	*Mérinos,* en flûte	20	Taken by *Apollo,* 38, Capt. Bridges W. Taylor, off Corsica.
	,, 22	*Rivoli* *	74	Taken by *Victorious,* 74, Capt. Jno. Talbot, and *Weazel* 18, Com. Jno. Wm. Andrew. M M
	,, ,,	*Mercure*	18	Blown up by ,, ,, ,, ,, ,,
	,, 29	*St. Joseph* (pierced for 16). .	..	Taken by boats of *Menelaus,* 38, under Lieut. Rowland Mainwaring, off Fréjus.
	Mar. 27	Three brigs (each)	4	Taken by *Rosario,* 10, and *Griffin,* 16, off Dieppe. M
	Apr. 29	A schooner	4	Burnt by boats of *Undaunted,* etc., mouth of the Rhône.
	May 22	*Ariane*	40	Destroyed by *Northumberland,* 74, Capt. Hon. Hy. Hotham, and *Growler,* 12, Lieut. Jno. Weeks } M
	,, ,,	*Andromaque.*	40	,, ,, ,, ,, ,,
	,, ,,	*Mamelouck*	16	,, ,, ,, ,, ,,
	June 4	*Dorade,* storeship	14	Taken by boats of *Medusa,* 32, under Lieut. Josiah Thompson, at Arcachon. Burnt.
	Aug. 31	*Tisiphone,* xebec	3	Cut out by boats of *Bacchante,* 38, under Lieut. Donat Henchy O'Brien, Canale di Leme. } M
	,, ,,	A gunboat	3	,, ,, ,, ,, ,,
	,, ,,	A gunboat	1	,, ,, ,, ,, ,,
	Sept. 9	*Danaé.*	40	Accidentally burnt at Venice.
	,, 17	Two gunboats (each of) . . .	1	Taken by boats of *Eagle,* 74, under Lieut. Aug. Cannon.
	,, 20	*Ulysse,* xebec	6	Taken by *Apollo,* 38, Capt. Bridges W. Taylor, off Corfu.
	Dec. 23	A brig	22	Driven ashore by *Dryad,* 36, Capt. Edw. Galwey, Isle d'Yeu.
1813	Jan. 6	*Indomptable*	2	Taken by boats of *Bacchante,* 38, and *Weazel,* 18, off C. Otranto.
	,, ,,	*Diligente*	2	,, ,, ,, ,,
	,, ,,	*Arrogante*	2	,, ,, ,, ,, } M (*Bacchante.*)
	,, ,,	*Salamine*	2	,, ,, ,, ,,
	,, ,,	*Calypso*	1	,, ,, ,, ,,
	,, 6	No. 8 (gunboat)	1	Cut out by boats of *Havannah,* 36, under Lt. Wm. Hamley.
	,, 29	*Véloce.*	1	Taken by *Cerberus,* 32, Capt. Thos. Garth.
	Feb. 5	*Rubis.*	40	Wrecked off Los Islands.
	,, 7	Four gunboats	..	Destroyed by boats of *Havannah,* 36, under Lieut. Wm. Hamley, off Manfredonia.
	,, 14	*Alcinoüs*	2	Taken by barge of *Bacchante,* 38, under Lieut. Silas Thos. Hood, off Otranto.
	,, ,,	*Vigilante,* desp. boat . . .	..	Taken by *Bacchante,* 38, Capt. Wm. Hoste.
	Apr. 22	Six gunboats	..	Destroyed by *Weazel,* 18, Com. Jas. Black, Bassoglina bay.
	May 16	*Fortune,* xebec	10	Taken by boats of *Berwick,* 74, and *Euryalus,* 36.
	,, 27	Two gunboats (each) . . .	3	Taken by boats of *Apollo,* 38, and *Cerberus,* 32.
	June 8	*Agile*	8	Taken by *Alcmene,* 38, Capt. Edwards Ll. Graham.
	,, 12	Ten gunboats (Neapolitan), (each) .	1	Taken by boats of *Bacchante,* 38, under Lieut. Silas Thomson Hood, Giulianova.
	July 18	Two gunboats (each) . . .	1	Taken by *Havannah,* 36, and *Partridge,* 16.
	Aug. 18	Three gunboats	..	Taken or destroyed at Cassis by boats of squadron.
	,, 24	*Tonnante.*	2	Taken by *Weazel,* 18, Capt. Jas. Black.
	,, ,,	*Auguste.*	2	
	Oct. 7	No. 961 (lugger).	6	Taken by *Wolverine,* 16, Com. Charles Julius Kerr.
	,, 13	*Flibustier*	22	Destroyed by *Telegraph,* 12, Com. Tim. Scriven.
	,, ,,	A gunboat	2	Taken by boats of *Bacchante,* 38, etc., under Com. Jno. Harper, of *Saracen,* 18.
	,, ,,	A gunboat	2	,, ,, ,, ,, ,,
	,, ,,	A gunboat	1	,, ,, ,, ,, ,,
	,, ,,	A gunboat	1	,, ,, ,, ,, ,,
	,, 21	*Weser* *	40	Taken by *Scylla,* 18, Com. Colin M'Donald, and *Royalist,* 18, Com. Jas. Jno. Gordon Bremer.
	,, 23	*Trave* *	40	Taken by *Andromache,* 36, Capt. Geo. Tobin.
	,, 31	Two corvettes, building . .	..	Taken by boats, etc., under Com. Jno. M'Kerlie, in the Weser.
	,, ,,	Two gun brigs	..	,, ,, ,, ,, ,,
	Dec. 20	*Prospère,* sch.	2	Taken by *Andromache,* 36, Capt. Geo. Tobin, coast of France.
	,, 23	*Baleine,* storeship	22	Driven ashore near Calvi by *Euryalus,* 36, Capt. Chas. Napier (2).
	,, ,,	*Flèche,* sch.	12	Taken by *Alcmene,* 38, Capt. Jerem. Coghlan.
1814	Jan. 6	*Cérès* (* as *Seine*)	40	Taken by *Niger,* 38, and *Tagus,* 36, off Cape Verde.
	,, 16	*Iphigénie* (* as *Gloire*). . .	40	Taken by the *Venerable,* 74, and *Cyane,* 22, off } M Madeira.

Year.	Date.	Name. [* Added to the Royal Navy.]	Guns.	Fate. M Medals granted in 1849, in pursuance of *Gazette* notice of June 1st, 1847. M̲ Flag-officers' and Captains' gold medals.
1814	Jan. 20	*Alcmène* (* as (a) *Dunira*, (b) *Immortalité*).	40	Taken by the *Venerable*, 74, and *Cyane*, 22, off Madeira. M
	Feb. 3	*Uranie*	40	Destroyed to avoid capture at Brindisi.
	,, ,,	*Terpsichore*	40	Taken by *Majestic*, 56, Capt. Jno. Hayes (1).
	,, 26	*Clorinde* (* as *Aurora*)	40	Taken by *Eurotas*, 38, Capt. Jno. Phillimore, and *Dryad*, 36, Capt. Edw. Galwey. M (*Eurotas*.)
	Mar. 17	*Alcion*	16	Taken by *Ajax*, 74, Capt. Robt. Waller Otway (1).
	,, 26	*Sultane* *	40	Taken by *Hannibal*, 74, Capt. Sir Mich. Seymour (1), off Cherbourg.
	,, 27	*Etoile* (* as *Topaze*).	40	Taken by *Hebrus*, 36, Capt. Edm. Palmer, off La Hougue.
	Apr. 2	A gun brig	..	Taken by boats under Lieut. Robt. Graham Dunlop, in the Gironde.
	,, ,,	A schooner	..	,, ,, ,, ,, ,,
	,, ,,	Six gunboats.	..	,, ,, ,, ,, ,,
	,, ,,	Three chasse-marées	..	,, ,, ,, ,, ,,
	,, ,,	An imperial barge	..	,, ,, ,, ,, ,,
	,, ,,	A gun brig	.	Burnt by ,, ,, ,, ,,
	,, ,,	Two gunboats	.	,, ,, ,, ,, ,,
	,, ,,	A chasse-marée	.	,, ,, ,, ,, ,,
	,, 6	*Regulus* (and other vessels)	74	Burnt to avoid capture in the Gironde.
	,, 18	*Brillant* (* as *Genoa*)	74	Taken at the surrender of Genoa.
	,, ,,	Four brigs		
	May 25	*Aigle*, xebec	6	Taken by boats of *Elizabeth*, 74, under Lieut. Mitchell Roberts, off Corfu. M
1815	Apr. 30	*Melpomène*	40	Taken by *Rivoli*, 74, Capt. Edw. Stirling Dickson, off Ischia.

SPANISH LOSSES.

Year.	Date.	Name. [* Added to the Royal Navy.]	Guns.	Fate. M Medals granted in 1849, in pursuance of *Gazette* notice of June 1st, 1847. M̲ Flag-officers' and Captains' gold medals.
1804	Oct. 5	*Medea* (* as *Impérieuse*)	40	Taken by *Indefatigable*, 40, Capt. Graham Moore, *Medusa*, 38, Capt. Jno. Gore (2), *Lively*, 38, Capt. Graham Eden Hamond, and *Amphion*, 32, Capt. Sam. Sutton.
	,, ,,	*Fama* *	34	
	,, ,,	*Clara* (* as *Leocadia*)	34	
	,, ,,	*Mercedes*	34	Blown up in action with *Amphion*, 32, Capt. Sam. Sutton.
	Nov. 25	*Matilda* (* as *Hamadryad*)	34	Taken by *Medusa*, 38, Capt. Jno. Gore (2), and *Donegal*, 80.
	,, ,,	*Amfitrite* (* as *Blanche*)	40	Taken by *Donegal*, 80, Capt. Sir Rich. Jno. Strachan.
	Dec. 7	*Sta. Gertrudis*	36	Taken by *Polyphemus*, 64, and *Lively*, 38, off C. St. Mary.
	,,	*Infanta Don Carlos* *	16	Taken by *Diamond*, 38, Capt. Thos. Elphinstone.
	,,	*Diligencia* (* as *Ligœra*)	28	Taken by *Diana*, 38, and *Pique*, 40, off Altavela.
1805	Feb. 4	*Fuerte de Gibraltar*	4	Taken by *Mercury*, 28, Capt. Duncombe Pleydell Bouverie.
	,, 8	*Orquijo* *	18	Taken by *Pique*, 40, Capt. Chas. Bayne Hodgson Ross.
	Apr. 3	*Elizabeth*	10	Taken by *Bacchante*, 20, Capt. Chas. Dashwood, off Havana.
	May	*Asunción*	36	Wrecked in the River Plate.
	July 22	*San Rafael* *	80	Taken by squadron of V.-Ad. Sir Robt. Calder.
	,, ,,	*Firme* *	74	
	Aug. 13	*Caridad Perfecta*, sch.	12	Taken by *Mariamne*, sch., Lieut. Jas. Smith (3), at Truxillo.
	Sept. 30	*Galgo* (pierced for)	14	Taken by Port Mahon, 18, Com. Sam. Chambers.
	Oct. 11	No. 4 (gunboat)	1	Taken by *Dexterous*, 14, Lieut. Robt. Tomlinson, (2) off Gibraltar.
	,, 21	*Bahama* *	74	Taken by the fleet of Lord Nelson, at Trafalgar.
	,, ,,	*San Juan Nepomuceno* (* as *Berwick*)	74	,, ,, ,, ,,
	,, ,,	*San Ildefonso* *	74	,, ,, ,, ,,
	,, ,,	*Santisima Trinidad*	130	,, ,, ,, ,, and destroyed.
	,, ,,	*San Agustin.*	74	,, ,, ,, ,, and burnt.
	,, ,,	*Argonauta*	74	,, ,, ,, ,, but sank.
	,, ,,	*Monarca*	74	,, ,, ,, ,, but was wrecked.
	,, ,,	*Neptuno*	74	,, ,, ,, ,, but was retaken.
	,, ,,	*Santa Ana*	112	
	,, 24	*Rayo*	100	Taken by the fleet after Trafalgar, but was wrecked.
	Nov. 29	*San Cristovil Pano*	7	Taken by boats of *Serpent*, 16, Com. Jno. Waler (1), Jamaica station.
1806	Jan. 7	*Raposa* * (pierced for)	16	Taken by boats of *Franchise*, 36, Capt. Chas. Dashwood, off Campeche.

(M M)

Year.	Date.	Name. [* Added to the Royal Navy.]	Guns.	Fate. M Medals granted in 1849, in pursuance of *Gazette* notice of June 1st, 1847. M Flag-officers' and Captains' gold medals.
1806	Jan. 29	Carmen (pierced for) . . .	14	Taken by *Magicienne*, 32, Capt. Adam Mackenzie, Mona Passage.
	Feb.	Two gunboats, each of . . .	2	Taken by priv. *Felicity*, M. Novella, Medit.
	,, 11	No. 4 (gun-brig)	5	Taken by priv. *Envy*, off Cape de Gata.
	Apr. 4	Vigilante (* as Spider). . .	18	Taken by *Renommée*, 38, Capt. Sir Thos. Livingstone, Medit.
	,, 12	Argonauta	12	Taken by *Hydra*, 38, Capt. Geo. Mundy, coast of Spain.
	May 2	Virgen del Carmen, sch. . .	4	Taken by *Niger*, 32, Capt. Jas. Hillyar, coast of Spain.
	,, 4	Giganta	9	Cut out by boats of *Renommée*, 38, and *Nautilus*, 18, under Lieut. Sir Wm. Geo. Parker.
	June 27	Belem *	4	Taken by Commod. Sir Home Riggs Popham, at Buenos Aires.
	,, ,,	Dolores	4	,, ,, ,, ,, ,,
	,, ,,	Six gunboats.	..	,, ,, ,, ,, ,,
	July 30	Arrogante	2	Taken by *Diadem*, 64, off Montevideo.
	Aug. 23	Pomona (* as Cuba) . . .	34	Taken by *Arethusa*, 38, Capt. Chas. Brisbane, and *Anson*, 44, Capt. Chas. Lydiard, off Cuba. M
	,, ,,	Twelve gunboats	..	Destroyed by *Arethusa*, 38, Capt. Chas. Brisbane, and *Anson*, 44, Capt. Chas. Lydiard, off Cuba.
	,, 30	A schooner	10	Taken by *Pike*, 4, Lieut. Chas. Spence, Jamaica station.
	Sept. 3	A felucca	14	Taken by *Supérieure*, 14, *Flying Fish*, 12, and *Pike*, 4, off Batabano.
	,, ,,	A schooner	10	,, ,, ,, ,, ,,
	,, ,,	Three vessels, each of . . .	1	,, ,, ,, ,, ,,
	Oct. 3	No. 2 (gunboat).	3	Taken by barge of *Minerva*, 32, Capt. Geo. Ralph Collier, Arosa Bay.
	,, 9	A schooner	4	Cut out by boats of *Galatea*, 32, under Lieut. Rich. Gittins, Barcelona.
	,, 21	A tartan	4	Taken by boats of *Renommée*, 33, under Lieut. Sir Wm. Geo. Parker, Port Colon.
	,, ,,	Two settees, each of . . .	3	,, ,, ,, ,, off ,, ,,
	,, 22	A settee	2	,, ,, ,, ,, off tower of Falconara.
	Nov. 20	Velox	10	Taken by *Néréïde*, 36, Capt. Robt. Corbett, Atlantic.
	,, ,,	Dolores	3	Taken by boats of *Orpheus*, 32, Capt. Thos. Briggs, off Campeche.
1807	Jan. 1	A schooner	..	Capsized while chased by *Lark*, 18, Com. Robt. Nicholas.
	,, 27	Postillón	3	Taken by *Lark*, 18, Com. Robt. Nicholas, W. Ind. Subsequently destroyed.
	,, ,,	Carmen	5	,, ,, ,, ,, ,,
	Feb. 1	A schooner	3	Cut out by *Lark*, 18, Com. Robt. Nicholas, Cispata Bay.
	,, 3	Paula	22	Taken in Rattones Harbour by R.-Ad. Chas. Stirling (1), and Brig.-Genl. Auchmuty.
	,, ,,	Fuerte *	22	,, ,, ,, ,, ,,
	,, ,,	Héroe	20	,, ,, ,, ,, ,,
	,, ,,	Dolores	10	,, ,, ,, ,, ,,
	,, ,,	Paz *	10	,, ,, ,, ,, ,,
	,, ,,	Reina Luisa.	26	,, ,, ,, ,, ,,
	,, ,,	A frigate	28	Destroyed to prevent capture by ,, ,,
	,, ,,	Three gunboats	..	
	Aug. 7	Principe Eugenio	16	Taken by *Hydra*, 38, Capt. Geo. Mundy, from under forts of Bagur, Catalonia.
	,, ,,	Bella Carolina	10	,, ,, ,, ,, ,, } M
	,, ,,	Carmen del Rosario . . .	4	,, ,, ,, ,, ,,
	,, 14	No. 5, No. 9 (gunboats) . .	..	Taken off Majorca.
	,, 18	Cautela (pierced for 12) . .	6	Taken by *Narcissus*, 32, Capt. Chas. Malcolm, Atlantic.
	Dec. 11	San Josef	12	Taken by *Grasshopper*, 18, Com. Thos. Searle, off Cape Palos.
1808	Feb. 19	Two gunboats	..	Sunk by *Impérieuse*, 38, Capt. Lord Cochrane, near Cartagena.
	,, ,,	One gunboat	4	Taken by *Impérieuse*, 38, Capt. Lord Cochrane, near Cartagena.
	Apr. 4	Two gunboats	..	Destroyed by squadron of Capt. Murray Maxwell, off Cadiz.
	,, 23	Two gunboats	..	Taken by *Grasshopper*, 18, Com. Thos. Searle, and *Rapid*, 14, Lieut. Hy. Baugh.
	,, ,,	Two gunboats	..	Driven ashore by *Grasshopper*, 18, Com. Thomas Searle, and *Rapid*, 14, Lieut. Hy. Baugh.
	May 7	A mistico.	4	Taken by the *Redwing*, 18, Com. Thos. Ussher, near Trafalgar.
	,, ,,	Four gunboats	..	Destroyed by the *Redwing*, 18, Com. Thos. Ussher, near Trafalgar.

DUTCH LOSSES.

Year.	Date.	Name. [* Added to the Royal Navy.]	Guns.	Fate. M Medals granted in 1849, in pursuance of *Gazette* notice of June 1st, 1847. M Flag-officers' and Captains' gold medals.
1803	Aug. 2	*Haasje*	6	Taken by *Caroline*, 36, Capt. Benj. Wm. Page, off C. of Good Hope.
	Sept. 20	*Hippomenes* *	18	Taken by Commod. Sam. Hood (2) at surrender of Demerara.
	,, 26	*Serpent*, sch..	..	Taken by *Heureux*, 24, Capt. Loftus Otway Bland, at surrender of Berbice.
1804	Mar. 1	*Draak*, sch.	5	Taken by *Lily*, 18, Lieut. Wm. Lyall, off Bermuda.
	,, 23	*Antilope*	5	Taken by boats of *Stork*, 18, Com. Geo. Le Geyt, W. Indies.
	,, 31	*Athalante*	16	Taken in the Vlie by *Scorpion*, 18, and *Beaver*, 18. M
	May 4	*Proserpine* (* as *Amsterdam*)	32	Taken by Commod. Sam. Hood (2), at surrender of Surinam.
	,, ,,	*Pylades* (* as *Surinam*) . .	18	,,　　　,,　　　,,　　　,,　　　,,
	,, ,,	*George*, sch.	..	,,　　　,,　　　,,　　　,,　　　,,
	,, ,,	Seven gunboats	..	,,　　　,,　　　,,　　　,,　　　,,
	,, 16	No. 98 (a schuit)	..	Taken by squadron of Commod. Sir Wm. Sidney Smith, N. Sea.
	,, ,,	Five schuits	..	Sunk　　　,,　　　,,　　　,,　　　,,
1805	Apr. 24	Seven schuits	..	Taken by squadron of Capt. Robt. Honyman, off C. Gris Nez.
	,, 25	Two gunboats	..	Taken by *Archer*, 14, Lieut. Wm. Price, off C. Gris Nez.
1806	Jan. 9	*Bato*	68	Destroyed by Dutch at surrender of C. of Good Hope to Commod. Sir Home Riggs Popham.
	May 28	*Schrikverwekker*	68	Wrecked in the E. Indies.
	July 6	*Belgica*	12	Taken by *Greyhound*, 32. Capt. Chas. Elphinstone, and *Harrier*, 16, Com. Edw. Thos. Troubridge.
	,, 26	*Pallas* (* as *Celebes*) . . .	36	,,　　　,,　　　,,　　　,,　　　,,
	Oct. 18	*Zeerob*.	14	Taken by *Caroline*, 36, Capt. Pet. Rainier (2), E. Indies.
	,, ,,	*Maria Reijgersbergen* (* as *Java*)	36	Taken by *Caroline*, 36, Capt. Pet. Rainier (2), off Batavia.
	Nov. 27	*Phoenix*	36	Taken or destroyed at Batavia by squadron of R.-Ad. Sir Edw. Pellew.
	,, ,,	*Avonturier*	18	,,　　　,,　　　,,　　　,,　　　,,
	,, ,,	*Zeeploeg*	14	,,　　　,,　　　,,　　　,,　　　,,
	,, ,,	*William*	14	,,　　　,,　　　,,　　　,,　　　,,
	,, ,,	*Maria Wilhelmina*. . . .	14	,,　　　,,　　　,,　　　,,　　　,,
1807	Jan. 1	*Kenau Hasselaar* (* as *Halstaar*)	36	Taken at capture of Curaçoa by squadron of Capt. Chas. Brisbane.
	,, ,,	*Suriname* (* as *Surinam*). .	22	,,　　　,,　　　,,　　　,,
	,, ,,	*Vliegende Visch*	14	,,　　　,,　　　,,　　　,, M M
	,, ,,	A schooner	..	,,　　　,,　　　,,　　　,,
	Feb. 25	*Utrecht*	32	Wrecked among the Orkneys.
	Aug. 31	A schooner	8	Taken by *Psyche*, 36, Lieut. Wm. Fleetwood B. R. Pellew (actg. Capt.), at Samarang.
	Sept. 1	*Scipio*	24	Taken by *Psyche*, 36, Lieut. F. B. R. Pellew (actg. Capt.), off Java.
	Dec.	*Revolutie*.	68	Burnt by squadron of R.-Ad. Sir Edw. Pellew, at Griessee.
	,,	*Pluto*	68	,,　　　,,　　　,,　　　,,　　　,,
	,,	*Kortenaar*	68	,,　　　,,　　　,,　　　,,　　　,,
1808	May 19	*Gelderland* (* as *Helder*) . .	36	Taken by *Virginie*, 38, Capt. Edw. Brace, N. Sea. M
	Aug. 6	*Vlieg*	6	Taken by *Diana*, 14, Lieut. Wm. Kempthorne, off Java.
	Oct. 8	*Hoop*, armed transport . .	..	Taken by *Lightning*, 16, Com. Bentinck Cavendish Doyle.
1809	Jan. 1	*Manly* * (ex-British) . .	16	Retaken by *Onyx*, 10, Com. Chas. Gill, N. Sea. M
	May 20	*Piet Hein*, sch.	7	Taken in the Vlie by boats of *Princess Caroline*, 74.
	June	*Calais*, g.-boat	..	Taken in the Jade.
	July 15	*Tuijncelaar*	8	Cut out by boats of *Modeste* and *Barracouta*, under Lieut. Wm. Payne, St. of Sunda.
	Sept. 11	*Zefir*	14	Taken by *Diana*, 10, Lieut. Wm. Kempthorne, off Celebes. M
1810	Jan.	*Mandarin*	12	Sunk by Dutch at capture of Amboyna (*Mandarin* later weighed).
	,,	*San Pan*, cutter.	10	Sunk by Dutch at capture of Amboyna.
	,,	A cutter	12	,,　　　,,　　　,,　　　,,
	Feb. 6	*Rembang*.	18	Taken by *Dover*, 38, Capt. Edw. Tucker, E. Indies.
	,, ,,	*Hoop*	10	,,　　　,,　　　,,　　　,,
	,, 10	*Havik* . . . . :	10	Taken by *Thistle*, 10, Lieut. Pet. Proctor. M
	Mar. 1	*Margaretta* (pierced for 14) .	8	Taken at Amblaw by boats of *Cornwallis* under Lieut. Hy. Jno. Peachey.
	Apr. 26	*Echo*	8	Taken by *Sylvia*, 10, Lieut. Aug. Vere Drury, off Batavia. M
	Aug.	*Claudius Seurlis*	16	Taken at the reduction of Java by R.-Ad. Hon. Robt. Stopford.
	,,	Twelve gunboats	..	,,　　　,,　　　,,　　　,,　　　,,

DANISH LOSSES.

Year.	Date.	Name. [* Added to the Royal Navy.]	Guns.	Fate. M Medals granted in 1849, in pursuance of *Gazette* notice of June 1st, 1847. M Flag-officers' and Captains' gold medals.
1807	Aug. 16	*Frederikscoarn* *	32	Taken by *Comus*, 22, Capt. Edm. Heywood, off Marstrand. M
	Sept. 7	*Christian VII.* *.	84	Taken by British Navy (Lord Gambier) and Army at surrender of Copenhagen.
		Neptunos	84	,, ,, ,, ,,
		Waldemaar *	84	,, ,, ,, ,,
		Prindsesse Sophie Frederike (* as *Princess Sophia*) . .	74	,, ,, ,, ,,
		Justitia *	74	,, ,, ,, ,,
		Arveprinds Frederik (* as *Heir Apparent*) . . .	74	,, ,, ,, ,,
		Kronprindsesse Marie (* as *Kron Princessen*) . . .	74	,, ,, ,, ,,
		Fyen *	74	,, ,, ,, ,,
		Odin *	74	,, ,, ,, ,,
		Trekroner (* as *Tre Kronen*)	74	,, ,, ,, ,,
		Skjold (* as *Skiold*) . . .	74	,, ,, ,, ,,
		Kronprinds Frederik (* as *Kron Princen*)	74	,, ,, ,, ,,
		Danmark (* as *Dannemark*).	74	,, ,, ,, ,,
		Norge *	74	,, ,, ,, ,,
		Prindsesse Caroline (* as *Princess Caroline*) . . .	74	,, ,, ,, ,,
		Dithmarschen	64	,, ,, ,, ,, and destroyed.
		Mars	64	,, ,, ,, ,, ,,
		Seierherre (* as *Syeren*) . .	64	,, ,, ,, ,,
		Perlen (* as *Pearlen*) . . .	38	,, ,, ,, ,,
		Havfrue (* as *Har-Fruen*) .	36	,, ,, ,, ,,
		Freija (* as *Freya*). . . .	36	,, ,, ,, ,,
		Iris *	36	,, ,, ,, ,,
		Rota *	38	,, ,, ,, ,,
		Venus *	36	,, ,, ,, ,,
		Nayaden (* as *Nyaden*) . .	36	,, ,, ,, ,,
		Nympfen (* as *Nymphen*). .	36	,, ,, ,, ,,
		Triton	28	,, ,, ,, ,, ,,
		Frederiksteen (* as *Frederickstein*)	28	,, ,, ,, ,,
		Lille Belt (* *Little Belt*) . .	24	,, ,, ,, ,,
		St. Thomas	24	,, ,, ,, ,, ,,
		Pylla *	24	,, ,, ,, ,,
		Elven *	20	,, ,, ,, ,,
		Eyderen *	20	,, ,, ,, ,,
		Gluckstad (* as *Gluckstadt*) .	20	,, ,, ,, ,,
		Sarpen *	18	,, ,, ,, ,,
		Glommen	18	,, ,, ,, ,,
		Nid Elven *	18	,, ,, ,, ,,
		Delphinen	18	,, ,, ,, ,,
		Flyvendefiske (* as *Flewende Fisk*)	14	,, ,, ,, ,,
		Allart.	18	,, ,, ,, ,,
		Mercurius *	18	,, ,, ,, ,,
		Coureer (* as *Q. Mab.* and *Courier*)	18	,, ,, ,, ,,
		Ornen, sch.*	12	,, ,, ,, ,,
		Brevdrageren	14	,, ,, ,, ,,
		Three gunboats, each of . .	2	,, ,, ,, ,,
		Twenty-two gunboats, each of	2	,, ,, ,, and destroyed.
1808	Mar. 2	*Admiral Jawl*	28	Taken by *Sappho*, 18, Com. Geo. Langford, off Flamborough Head. M
	,, 23	*Prinds Christian Frederik* .	74	Burnt by *Stately*, 64, Capt. Geo. Parker, and *Nassau*, 64, Capt. Robt. Campbell (1). M
	May 15	A gunboat	2	Sunk off Bergen by *Tartar*, 32, Capt. G. E. B. Bettesworth.
	,, 24	A cutter	8	Blown up in action with *Swan*, 10, Lieut. M. R. Lucas.
	June 16	A gun-vessel	2	Taken by boats of *Euryalus*, 36, and *Cruiser*, 18, under Lieut. Michael Head, Great Belt.
	Aug. 11	*Fama*	18	Taken off Nyborg by boats under Capt. Jas. Macnamara (2). } M
	,, ,,	*Salorman* *	12	,, ,, ,, ,,
	,,	*Acertif* (pierced for 12) . .	8	Taken by *Daphne*, 22, Capt. Fras. Mason, Baltic.
	Oct. 1	A schuyt	10	Taken by *Cruiser*, 18, Lieut. Thos. Wells (2), off Göteborg.
1809	Mar. 2	*Aalborg*	6	Taken by *Egeria*, 18, Com. Lewis Hole.
	May	*Coureer*	1	Taken by boats of *Briseis*, 10, and *Bruiser*, 14, N. Sea.
	,,	*Edderkop*.	2	Taken by boats of *Majestic*, 74, Baltic.
	,, 29	*Snap*	3	Taken by *Patriot*, 10, Lieut. E— W— Mansell, N. Sea.

Year.	Date.	Name. [* Added to the Royal Navy.]	Guns.	Fate. M Medals granted in 1849, in pursuance of *Gazette* notice of June 1st, 1847. M Flag-officers' and Captains' gold medals.
1809	May 31	*Christianborg*	6	Taken by *Cruiser*, 18, Com. Thos. Rich. Toker, off Bornholm.
		A cutter	6	Destroyed by boats of *Melpomene*, 38, Capt. Pet. Parker (2), off Jutland.
	„	*Fire Bredre* (? priv.) . . .	4	Taken by *Earnest*, 14, Lieut. Rich. Templar, Wingö Sound.
	„	*Makrel*	2	„ „ „ „ „
	June 13	*Loven* (? priv.)	2	Taken by *Talbot*, 18, Com. Hon. Alex. Jones, N. Sea.
	Sept.	*Dorothea Catherine* (? priv.) .	6	Taken by *Strenuous*, 14, Lieut. Jno. Nugent, off the Naze.
	Oct.	*Christiania*	8	Taken by *Snake*, 18, Com. Thos. Young. off Bergen.
	Nov. 6	*Réciprocité* (? priv.) . . .	4	Taken by *Briseis*, 18, Com. Jno. Miller Adye, off Helgoland.
1810	July 23	*Balder*	8	Taken by boats of *Belvidera* and *Nemesis*, Studtland.
	„ „	*Thor*	8	„ „ „ „ „
	„ „	A gunboat (No. 5)	7	Burnt „ „ „ „ „
1811	Mar. 27	Two gunboats	..	Taken by *Sheldrake*, 16, Com. Jas. Pattison Stewart.
	May 11	*Alban*, cutter	..	Taken by *Rifleman*, 18, Com. Jos. Pearce. Retaken.
	July 5	Four gun-vessels, each of . .	5	Taken by *Sheldrake*, 16, Com. Jas. Pattison Stewart, and consorts.
	Aug. 2	Three gun-brigs.	..	Taken by boats under Lieut. Sam. Blyth, Jade. M
	Sept. 20	Two gun-vessels	..	Taken by boats of *Victory*, 100, under Lieut. Edw. Purcell, Wingö Sound. M
1812	July 6	*Nayaden*	40	Destroyed by a squadron on coast of Norway. M (*Dictator*,
	„ „	*Laaland*	20	Taken by a squadron on coast of Nor- *Podargus*, way, but abandoned. *Calypso*, and
	„ „	*Samsö*	18	„ „ „ „ *Flamer*.)
	„ „	*Kiel*	18	„ „ „ „
	Aug. 2	No. 114 (schooner)	6	Taken by boats of *Horatio*, 38, under Lieut. Abr. Mills Hawkins.
	„ „	No. 97 (cutter)	4	„ „ „ „
		No. 28 (lugger)	..	Taken by a boat of the *Dictator*, 74, under Lieut. Thos. Duell.
	Dec. 12	*Abigail*	3	Taken by *Hamadryad*, 36, Capt. Edw. Chetham.
1813	Mar. 21	*Unge Troutman*	5	Taken by two boats of *Blazer*, 14, and *Brevdrageren*, 14, under Lieut. Thos. Barker Devon.
	„ „	*Liebe*	5	„ „ „ „ „

RUSSIAN LOSSES.

Year.	Date.	Name. [* Added to the Royal Navy.]	Guns.	Fate. M Medals granted in 1849, in pursuance of *Gazette* notice of June 1st, 1847. M Flag-officers' and Captains' gold medals.
1808	June 24	*Apith*	14	Taken by *Salsette*, 38, Capt. Walt. Bathurst, off Nargen.
	Aug. 26	*Sewolod*	74	Taken and burnt by *Centaur*, 74, and *Implacable*, 74. M
1809		*Speshnoi*	44	Detained at Plymouth, but not proceeded against.
		Wilhemia	30	„ „ „ „ „
	July 7	Six gunboats (2 guns each) .	..	Taken by boats of squadron, Barö Sound.
	„ „	One gunboat	2	Sunk „ „ „
	„ 25	Gunboats No. 62, 65 and 66 (2 guns each)	..	Taken by boats of squadron, Frederikshamn.

TURKISH LOSSES.

Year.	Date.	Name. [* Added to the Royal Navy.]	Guns.	Fate. M Medals granted in 1849, in pursuance of *Gazette* notice of June 1st, 1847. M Flag-officers' and Captains' gold medals.
1807	Feb. 19	A corvette	18	{Taken off Point Pesquies by fleet of V.-Ad. Sir Jno. Thos. Duckworth.
	,, ,,	A gunboat	2	,, ,, ,, ,, ,,
	,, ,,	A ship of the line	64	Destroyed ,, ,, ,, ,,
	,, ,,	A frigate	40	,, ,, ,, ,, ,,
	,, ,,	A frigate	36	,, ,, ,, ,, ,,
	,, ,,	A frigate	36	,, ,, ,, ,, ,,
	,, ,,	A frigate	30	,, ,, ,, ,, ,,
	,, ,,	Three corvettes, in all . . .	42	,, ,, ,, ,, ,,
	,, ,,	A brig	10	,, ,, ,, ,, ,,
	,, ,,	Two gunboats, each . . .	2	,, ,, ,, ,, ,,
	Feb. 27	A gunboat	2	{Taken off Prota by fleet of V.-Ad. Sir Jno. Thos. Duckworth.
	Mar. 1	A brig	10	{Taken by boats of *Glatton*, 50, and *Hirondelle*, under Lieut. Edward Watson, at Sigri.
	,, 21	A frigate	40	{Taken by squadron of Capt. Benj. Hallowell, at surrender of Alexandria.
	,, ,,	A frigate	34	,, ,, ,, ,, ,,
	,, ,,	A corvette	16	,, ,, ,, ,, ,,
1808	July 6	*Badere-i-Zaffer*	44	{Taken by *Seahorse*, 38, Capt. Jno. Stewart, Archipelago. M

UNITED STATES' LOSSES.

Year.	Date.	Name. [* Added to the Royal Navy.]	Guns.	Commander. [* Lost his life on the occasion.]	Fate. M Medals granted in 1849, in pursuance of *Gazette* notice of June 1st, 1847. M Flag-officers' and Captains' gold medals.
1812	July 16	{*Nautilus* (* as *Emulous*) .}	14	Lieut. Crane.	Taken by squadron of Capt. Phil. Bowes Vere Broke.
	Aug. 22	{*James Madison* (rev. sch.) .}	10		Taken by *Barbados*, 28, Capt. Thos. Huskisson.
	Oct. 18	{*Wasp*(* as *Peacock*) . .}	18	Capt. Jacob Jones.	Taken by *Poictiers*, 74, Capt. Sir Jno. Poo Beresford.
	Nov. 22	*Vixen* . . .	14	Lt. Geo. U. Read.	Taken by *Southampton*, 32, but lost off the Bahamas.
1813	Jan. 17	*Viper* . . .	12	,, J. D. Henly.	Taken by *Narcissus*, 32, Capt. Jno. Rich. Lumley.
	June 1	*Chesapeake* * .	38	Capt. Jas. Lawrence.*	{Taken by *Shannon*, 38, Capt. Phil. Bowes Vere Broke. M
	July 14	*Asp*	3	Mr. Sigourney.*	Taken by boats of *Contest* and *Mohawk*.
	,, 29	{*No.* 121 (gunboat). . .}	1	Sailg.-Mast. Shead.	{Taken by boats of *Junon*, 38, under Lieut. Phil. Westphal.
	Aug. 14	*Argus* * . .	16	Lieut.Wm. Hy. Allen.*	{Taken by *Pelican*, 18, Com. Jno. Fordyce Maples. M
1814	Mar. 28	*Essex* * . . .	32	Capt. David Porter.	{Taken by *Phœbe*, 36, Capt. Jas. Hillyar, and *Cherub*, 20, Capt. Thos. Tudor Tucker. M
	Apr. 20	*Frolic* . . .	22	{Mast. Com. Jos. Bainbridge.}	Taken by *Orpheus*, 36, Capt. Hugh Pigot (3).
	June 22	*Rattlesnake* .	16	Lieut. Renshaw.	Taken by *Leander*, 50, Capt. Sir Geo. Ralph Collier.
	July 12	*Siren* . . .	16	,, N. J. Nicholson.	Taken by *Medway*, 74, Capt. Aug. Brine.
1815	Jan. 15	*President* * .	44	{Commod. Steph. Decatur.}	{Taken by *Endymion*, 40, Capt. Hy. Hope, and consorts.} M (*Endymion*.)

PUBLISHER'S NOTE

In the original edition the four photogravure plates and twelve full-page illustrations faced the text pages as listed on pages xvii–xviii. In this edition these illustrations are collected on the following pages in the order in which they appeared in the first edition. The original position indicators have been retained.

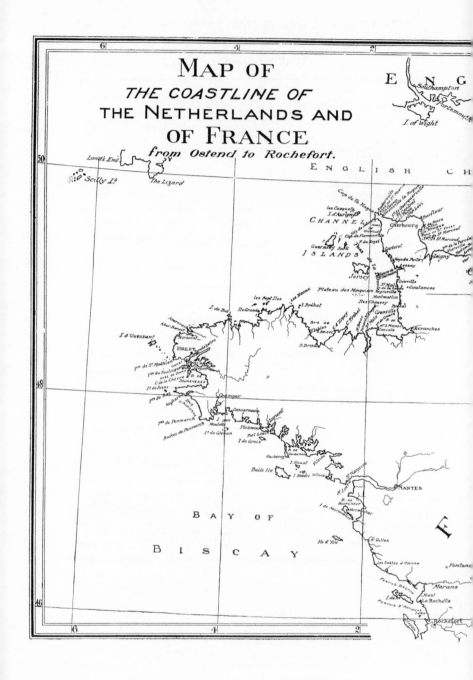

Map of
The Coastline of
The Netherlands and
of France
from Ostend to Rochefort.

THE NETHERLANDS

ENGLAND

Dover
STRAIT OF DOVER
Calais
St Sangatte
Wissant
Gris Nez
Amblateuse
BOULOGNE

Ostend
Dunkerque
Gravelines
Nieuport
BRUGES

St Omer

Lille

FRANCE

THE CHANNEL

Etaples

B. D'AUTHIE

B. DE SOMME
Crotoy
St Valery
Cayeux
Ault
Mers
Treport
Criel
St André
Veulettes
Arques
DIEPPE
St Pierre en Port
Fecamp
Etretat
Goteville
Tancarville
Caudebec
Villerville
Jumièges
Duclair
Quilleville
Honfleur

Bolbec
Lillebonne
ROUEN
Sotteville

50

49

48

Scale of Miles
0 10 20 30 40 50 60 70 80 90 100

2   4   6

SIR ROBERT CALDER'S ACTION, JULY 22ND, 1805.

(*From T. Sutherland's engraving, after T. Whitcombe's painting, which was based upon a plan drawn by Calder.*)

VICE-ADMIRAL VISCOUNT NELSON, K.B.　　　[*To face page* 144.

(*From an unpublished pencil sketch by Edridge, in the possession of Mrs. Nelson Ward.*)

POSITION OF THE *TÉMÉRAIRE* AT ABOUT 3 P.M., OCT. 21ST, 1805.   [*To face page* 146.

(*From J. Baily's engraving after the painting by T. Whitcombe, sometime in the possession of the Téméraire's captain, Sir Eliab Harvey.*)

Walter L. Colls. Ph. Sc.

Admiral Sir Edward Codrington. G.C.B. G.C.M.G. F.R.S.

From a Lithograph by R.J.Lane, R.A. after the picture by H.P.Briggs, R.A.

by kind permission of Major A.E.Codrington.

[To face page 162.

SITUATION OF H.M.S. *DEFENCE*, AND HER PRIZE THE *SAN ILDEFONSO*, ON THE MORNING OF OCT, 22ND, 1805.
CADIZ, ROTA, AND WRECKED PRIZES IN THE DISTANCE.

(*From Hall's engraving after a sketch by Mr. John Theophilus Lee.*)

SIR J. T. DUCKWORTH'S SQUADRON FORCING THE DARDANELLES, FEB. 19TH, 1807.   [To face page 224.

(From T. Sutherland's engraving after T. Whitcombe's painting, based on a drawing by Duckworth's Flag-Lieutenant, Sir Wm. Geo. Parker, Bart.)

THE CAPTURE OF CURAÇOA, 1807.

(From J. Bailey's engraving after T. Whitcombe's painting, based on a drawing by Capt. Sir Chas. Brisbane.)

[To face page 238.

Walter L. Colls, Ph. Sc.

The Rt. Hon. Thomas Cochrane,
10th Earl of Dundonald, G.C.B.
Admiral of the Red, Rear Admiral of the United Kingdom.

From the picture painted by Stroeling in 1809, of his Lordship,
then Captain Lord Cochrane, K.B.

CAPTURE OF BANDA NEIRA, AUG. 9TH, 1810.

(From T. Sutherland's engraving after T. Whitcombe's painting, based upon a plan by Capt. Sir Christopher Cole, R.N.)

[*To face page* 292.

Walter L. Colls, Ph. Sc.

Admiral Sir Edward Pellew, 1ˢᵗ Viscount Exmouth,
Bart., G.C.B.

From a Mezzotint by G. C. Turner, (in the possession of his Lordship's granddaughter
Mᵗˢ Crawford) after the picture by Sir Thomas Lawrence.

CAPTURE OF THE *GUERRIÈRE*, JULY 19TH, 1806.

(*From T. Sutherland's engraving after the painting by T. Whitcombe, based upon a plan by Captain Sir Thomas Lavie, R.N.*)

[*To face page* 386.

CAPTURE OF THE NIÉMEN BY H.M.S. AMETHYST, APRIL 6TH, 1809.

(From T. Sutherland's engraving after T. Whitcombe's painting, based upon a sketch by Lieut. Wm. Hill, first of the "Amethyst.")

[To face page 434.

Walter L. Colls. Ph. Sc.

Sir William Hoste, Bart, G.C.B.
Captain, R.N.

From a water-colour portrait by Charles Taylor,
in the possession of Lady Hoste.

THE ACTION OFF LISSA, MARCH 13TH, 1811.

(From the engraving by W. J. Bennett after a sketch by the Hon. Wm. Waldegrave (3), Midshipman in the "Amphion" in the action.)

[To face page 480.

CAPTURE OF THE *RIVOLI*, FEB. 22ND, 1812.

(*From T. Sutherland's engraving after a drawing by Com. John Wm. Andrew, R.N., of H.M.S. "Weazel."*)

INDEX.

VOLUME V.

NOTE.—*The names of executive officers of the Royal Navy are, so far as possible, entered with the rank and style attaching to their owners at the time when, by death or retirement, they ceased to belong to the Active List. Rank attained only on or after final retirement is not noticed in this Index.*

AALBERS, Capt. N. S., 386
Aalborg, 215, 565
Abdy, Capt. Anthony, 254, 255 n.
Abeille, 379, 485, 553
Abercrombie, 290, 436, 559
Abercromby, Maj.-Genl. Hon. John, 294
Aberdour, Capt. James, 213
Abigail, 566
Aboukir, 231
Abreval, 551
Abruzzi, The, 477, 524, 531
Abuses in the Navy, 2
Abydos, 218, 222
Acasta, 186 n., 187, 189, 192, 283 n., 424, 435 n., 558
Acertíf, 565
Achates, 446, 538, 542, 552
Acheron, 76, 352–355, 550
Achille, 75, 85 n., 107, 112, 120 n., 121 n., 131 (2), 150, 151, 154, 155, 156, 157, 160, 242, 390, 453, 454, 557
Achilles (see also *Achille*), 154 n.
Acklom, Capt. George, 158
Acorn, 442, 472, 495
A'Court (*later* Repington), R.-Ad. Edward Henry, 81, 330 and n., 331
Actæon, 294 n.
Actéon, 93, 182, 557
Actions, Principal: Defence of the *Vincejo*, 63, 64; attack on Ver Huell's flotilla, 65–67; Owen off Boulogne, 67–68; catamarans at Boulogne, 70–71; attempt on Curaçoa, 80–82; capture of Surinam, 82–84; defence of the Diamond Rock, 106; Calder's action, 111–120; battle of Trafalgar, 129–168; Strachan's action, 170–174; Honyman off Boulogne, 176; Adam off Fécamp, 177; capture of the *Plumper* and *Teazer*, 177; with Ver

Huell off Gravelines, 178, 179; Bromley with Hamelin, 179, 180; Duckworth's off San Domingo, 188–192; capture of Capri, 199; capture of the Cape of Good Hope, 201–204; capture of Buenos Aires, 205; defence of Danzig, 207, 208; capture of the *Frederikscoarn*, 211, 212; Gambier's attack on Copenhagen, 209–217; capture of Helgoland, 217; Duckworth in the Dardanelles, 219–230; capture of Alexandria, 230–231; taking of Montevideo, 234, 235; capture of Curaçoa, 236–239; capture of Rosily's squadron, 246; capture of the *Sewolod*, 248–250; capture of Marie Galante and Désirade, 251; Stopford at Sables d'Olonne, 253, 254; destruction of shipping in Aix Road (Cochrane), 255–270; expedition to the Schelde, 271–278; destruction of the *Robuste* and *Lion*, 278, 279; Hallowell in Rosas Bay, 280, 281; capture of Sénégal, 282; capture of Martinique, 283, 284; capture of Cayenne, 285–287; capture of Guadeloupe, etc., 290; capture of Amboyna, etc., 290–292; capture of Banda Neira, 292, 293; reduction of Mauritius, 293–295; conquest of Java, 297–302; defence and loss of the *Minerve*, 318–320; Lieut. Rowed near Audierne, 326, 327; cutting-out of the *Harmonie*, 331; seizure of the Diamond Rock, 332, 333; cutting-out of the *Curieux*, 334, 335; Dance and Linois, 336–339; defence of the *Wolverine*, 341, 342; cutting-out of the *Athalante*, 342, 343; the *Wilhelmina* and the *Psyché*, 343, 344; boat attack at Lavandou, 345, 346; loss of the *Lily*, 346; futile attack on the *Général Ernouf*, 347, 348; de-

Agay, 503
Agile, 561
Agincourt, 54, 282
Agincourt Sound, 54 and n., 55, 72, 73, 79, 86, 88, 91
Aglaé, 405
Agnes, 550
Aigle, 49, 77, 99, 112, 120 n., 122, 131, 132, 150, 151, 152, 153, 155, 156, 163, 255 n., 260, 265, 266, 268, 275, 346, 413, 550, 556, 557, 559, 562
Aiguille, 556
Aikenhead, Mids. John, 158
Aimable, 65, 66 and n., 430, 442, 558
Aimable Nelly, 449
Aix, Island and Road, 93, 183, 241, 252, 254, 255, 256, 257 n., 260–270, 304, 377, 378
Ajaccio, 91, 244
Ajax, 112, 114, 115, 116, 125, 131, 149, 158, 168, 219, 220, 221, 241, 289 (2), 290, 433, 476, 483, 529, 551, 560, 562
Akbar, 13, 298 n., 301
Alaart, 553
Alacrity, 485, 553
Alarm, 555
Alassio, 509
Alava, V.-Ad. Don I. M. de, 121, 130, 131, 136, 137, 150
Albacore, 71, 517
Alban, 553, 554, 566
Albanais, 271 n.
Albania, 432
Albatross, 31
Albion, 316, 329, 330, 338, 555
Alcedo, Capt. Don J., 131
Alceste, 234 n., 278, 414, 455, 484, 495, 496, 558, 560, 561
Alcide, 373, 452
Alcinoüs, 522, 561
Alcion, 320, 556, 562
Alcmene, 505, 506, 552, 561
Alcmène, 543, 562
Aldborough, 554
Alderney, 470, 546
Alert, 489, 554
Alexander, Com. John (3), 421, 553
Alexander, Admiral Thomas (1), 303
Alexander, Capt. Thomas (2), 242, 262 and n.
Alexandre, 122, 123, 184, 189, 190, 191, 192, 557
Alexandria, 91, 92, 98 n., 230, 231, 320, 567
Alexandria, 388
Alfred, 210, 233, 336, 337
Algeciras, 128, 551
Algerine, 488, 489, 554
Algésiras, 107, 112, 120 n., 131, 152, 162, 246 n., 557, 558
Algier, 72, 88, 353
Algorta, 509
Alicante, 513

Alis Fezzan, 421–423
Allart, 215, 565
Allemand, V.-Ad., 95, 118, 120, 121, 124, 169, 170, 186, 241, 242, 259–270, 288, 303, 304, 367, 368, 371, 377, 550
Allen, Lieut. Samuel, 293 and n.
Allen, Lieut. Thomas (3), 554
Allen (U.S.N.), Lieut. William Henry, 567
Allen, Purser William, 159
Alliance, 122
Alligator, 83
Almeria, 405, 476
Alms, V.-Ad. James (2), 39
Almuñecar, 506, 507
Aloft, Cause of accidents to men, 30
Alphea, 534, 554
Alsen, 492
Altavela, 562
Althorpe, 550
Amager Island, 214, 420
Amantea, 458, 560
Amaranthe, 283 n., 429, 430, 558
Amazon, 72, 73, 74, 102, 104, 195 n., 373, 374, 557
Amazone, 474, 477, 560
Ambassador in Paris, Recall of the British, 315
Amblaw, 292, 564
Ambleteuse, 62, 68, 176, 177, 179, 180, 550
Amboyna, 290, 291, 292, 564
Ambuscade, 53 n., 76, 94, 555
Amelia, 254, 255 n., 258 and n., 438, 478, 519–520, 559
Amélie, 289, 295, 296, 328, 483, 556
America, 84, 120, 208, 233
America, 505, 507, 508
América, 99, 112, 114, 120 n.
American cruisers, 13, 14, 15
American War, 1812–15, 3, 18
Amethyst, 186 n., 187, 253, 254, 275, 427, 428, 433–435, 553, 558, 559
Améthyste, 500, 501, 559
Amfitrite, 102, 562
Ami de Colonnot, 555
Amitié, 556
Amity, 70
Ammunition, Shortness of, 409, 465, 476, 513
Amphion, 53, 54, 102, 200, 350–352, 419, 432, 437, 443, 455, 456, 472, 478–481, 559, 560, 562
Amphitrite, 283, 284, 559
Amsterdam, 303
Amsterdam, 564
Amurang, 443
Anacreon, 555
Anchoring, after Trafalgar, 135, 145, 146, 161
Ancona, 472, 478
Andaman Islands, 400
Andero, 433
Anderson, Lieut. ——, 345
Anderson, Capt. James (1), 475, 492, 493

2 s 2

YACHTS, 307
Yarmouth, 209, 216
Yates, Capt. Richard Augustus, 473, 474
Yelland, Capt. John, 176
Yellow fever, 318
Yeo, Mids. George, 286
Yeo, Capt. Sir James Lucas, 232 and n., 285–287 and n., 362, 363, 401, 407, 500, 501, 554
Yeu, Isle d', 242, 253 and n., 561
York, 234, 283 n., 435, 549
Yorke, Rt. Hon. Charles, 3
Yorke, Admiral Sir Joseph Sydney, 41, 448
Young, Mids. Edward, 537
Young, V.-Ad. James (2), 43, 210
Young, Mids. John (2), 159
Young, Com. Robert Benjamin, 131
Young, Capt. Thomas, 566

Young, Admiral Sir William (1), 269, 295
Younghusband, Com. George, 329, 341
Yule, Com. John, 168 and n.

ZANTE, 281, 288
Zealous, 126
Zebra, 213
Zeeploeg, 392, 564
Zeerob, 392, 564
Zefir, 443, 444, 564
Zenobia, 551
Zéphyr, 559
Zephyr, 561
Zierikzee, 272
Zirona, 525
Zuid Beveland, 272, 273, 274, 277
Zwellendam, 202
Zwickau, 442